CADENCE BOOKS GRAPHIC NOVEL

ADOLF™
1945 and All That Remains

WITHDRAWN

YOLO COUNTY LIBRARY
226 BUCKEYE STREET
WOODLAND, CA 95695

CADENCE BOOKS GRAPHIC NOVEL

ADOLF™

1945 and All That Remains

YA
TEZUKA

STORY & ART BY

OSAMU TEZUKA

STORY & ART BY
OSAMU TEZUKA

Translation / Yuji Oniki
Touch-Up Art & Lettering / Viz Graphics
Cover Design / Viz Graphics
Editor / Annette Roman

Senior Editor / Trish Ledoux
Managing Editor / Satoru Fujii
Executive Editor / Seiji Horibuchi
Publisher / Keizo Inoue

Originally published as *Adolf ni Tsugu* by Bungei Shunju, Inc. in Japan in 1985.

© 1996 Tezuka Productions. *ADOLF: 1945 and All That Remains* is a trademark of Viz
Communications, Inc. All rights reserved. No unauthorized reproduction allowed. The
stories, characters and incidents mentioned in this publication are entirely fictional. For
the purposes of publication in English, the artwork in this publication is in reverse from
the original Japanese version.

Printed in Canada

Published by Cadence Books, Inc.
P.O. Box 77010 • San Francisco, CA 94107

10 9 8 7 6 5 4 3 2 𝑋
First printing, November 1996

❖

Osamu Tezuka's *ADOLF* Series:
A Tale of the Twentieth Century
An Exile in Japan
The Half-Aryan
Days of Infamy
1945 and All That Remains

CONTENTS

INTRODUCTION

THE BIG AND THE SMALL

By Gerard Jones

The art of comics is the art of reduction. Its principal tools are simplification, miniaturization, elimination, and compression. Yet in the hands of a great practitioner, that art of reduction can encompass the biggest dreams of our imaginations, the biggest conflicts of our lives, and the biggest events of our history. It's precisely this minimalist quality of comics—their freedom from cinema's obligation to replicate reality and movement, their ability to create a suspension of disbelief without the nuances and detail required of text—that makes comics the narrative medium best suited to the grandiose.

Flip through these small pages, view these thousands of small drawings by Tezuka, these compositions of a few black lines in small squares of white, and consider what he contains in them. Tezuka's manga captures half the world—Japan, Germany, Palestine, and lands between—and its history over a span of forty years. He captures the central cataclysm of the twentieth century, World War II, its build-up and its aftermath, from its leaders to its humblest victims. In so doing, he captures the century itself, not only its big events but its big forces and its big lies.

One of the big lies that made the war possible, Race—the preposterous idea that our constantly interbreeding and wholly intermingled species can be divided into discrete groups based on genetic origins—is still with us, although it is disparaged more widely now than before. One of the other lies, Nation— the deadly sentiment that an arbitrary and invisible political definition has some bearing on human relationships and is worth killing and dying for—is still deeply imbedded in our minds, and has even been enjoying a resurgence among Americans lately. Tezuka attacks both these lies not with reasoned arguments but with the powerful, emotional, and deceptively simple medium of fictional comic books.

Against the big lies and the big bloodshed Tezuka pits a little cartoon man. Sohei Toge is wonderfully, dramatically designed. His eyebrows, no more than two sweeps of ink, convey all his depression, curiosity, and anger. The addition of three dots below each eye tells us all we need to know of the weight of the years on him since the story began. Toge's elongated skull and angular cheekbones contrast with the finer features of Adolf Kaufmann and the smooth circular lines of Acetylene Lampe, marking Toge as a man of the earth, a block of stone, a simple man among schemers and ideologues. His flat nose and prominent chin give him a battered but indestructible look, and his bullet-shaped head suggests a lack of intellectual complexity to aid him in his journey, affording a streamlining to keep him moving through a world of hot air. His eyes—open at the sides and revealing complete irises—are the eyes of innocence through which we view horrors. Contrast them with the tormented eyes of Kaufmann on page 20, panel 6, and feel how different these characters are, what a vast emotional and cultural gap separates these two symbols of humanity. Then note how few lines Tezuka uses to make us feel so much.

Reductionism doesn't necessarily mean the elimination of visual devices and "tricks." Tezuka was nearly sixty when he finished *Adolf,* and he spent over forty of those years absorbing every cartooning influence he could find, synthesizing them into a style that was all his own and yet infinitely varied. For every new genre and subject he attacked (and he seems to have attacked all of them) he developed a new "Tezuka" to execute it. In *Adolf* we see a whole spectrum of Asian influences, along with echoes of pre- and postwar European cartooning (the *ligne claire* school of Hergé and Edgar Jacobs, for example), prewar American animation, and "classic Hollywood" storytelling. Here and there I think I even see a glimpse of Will Eisner and other American comic book artists. Tezuka's style spans nations and decades, making it ideal for *Adolf.* A sequence like the one in which Kaufmann entraps Elisa (pages 59 to 64), looks less like an eighties' vision of the forties than a creation *of* the forties. Then come the horrors of the next two pages, conceived with an intensity and daring and symbolism that forties' comics artists couldn't have imagined.

One of the oldest tools of the cartoonist's trade is "flop sweat." Obviously, those simple, teardrop-shaped ovals represent not physical perspiration but inner torment; part of the magical reductionism of comics is the diminution of the line between the physical and the symbolic, the inner and the outer. We become accustomed to seeing those beads of sweat marring Adolf Kaufmann's simple, empty face, a reminder of the agonies that churn constantly beneath his mask of youth and Aryan identity. We're less accustomed to associating them with Toge, and so when Tezuka tosses just two next to his head with a couple of quick twitches of his pen (page 21, panel 4), they come as a shock, a revelation of just how much emotion is flowing through the three stiff figures grouped around the table.

Tezuka unabashedly uses the cartoonist's bag of timeworn tricks to tell the biggest of stories. On pages 22 and 23 he pulls everything out: the silent pause (page 22, panel 1), a two-step cinematic close-up of the gun (6 and 7), action lines and sound effects (9), flop sweat galore, the black thought-cloud (page 23, panel 3), the old close-up-with-clock bit (5), the mental image (6), and a white nimbus of emotion and crosshatching behind the character's head to represent his inner torment (7). Tezuka's layout is pure comics: on the latter page, the "camera" keeps moving in closer from panels 3 to 4 to 5 to 7, trapping us in the same psychic claustrophobia that suffocates Adolf. Our view of Adolf twists slightly from one-quarter view (5) to full face (7); after having watched Adolf's agony discreetly, we suddenly find ourselves staring directly into the eyes of his horrible resolution. The movement of the panels is straight down, into the abyss of Adolf's pain, and in panel 7 his head is slightly off-center, so that the weight of the upper three panels rests right on it.

Amidst this sequence, panel 6, representing Adolf's mental image, floats as a reality unto itself. We are "supposed to" read it after panel 5—the clock is our visual bridge—but in fact we are aware of it throughout our descent. It tickles our minds below panel 2, then becomes increasingly clear as we pass through panels 3, 4, and 5, until we're forced to look directly at it. We find ourselves nearly as disturbed by the image as Adolf, although our own experience of the story has given us no reason to think of Toge making love with his wife as anything but sweet. Then our eye is dragged down to the lower right of the image, to the toned background beneath Adolf's mother's head, which proceeds to fragment into the tortured background behind her son's head in the next panel; the dark crosshatching of her hair is perfectly echoed in his pistol. In two pages, Tezuka has taken us through a critical turn in his character's life and given flesh to the lies of Race and Nation.

Contrast *Adolf* with its American contemporary, Art Spiegelman's *Maus*, another comic book about World War II and the Holocaust. Spiegelman is of the postwar generation, an academic artist who mastered cartoon tricks in order to make ironic sport of them in *Raw* and other esoteric comics. When he turned to the subject of his father's experiences in Auschwitz, he deliberately jettisoned nearly all those techniques, telling a sincere and human story through simplification and the steady repetition of narrative devices. Spiegelman too uses flop sweat and sound effects, but the general feeling of *Maus* is one of reductionism, not only in terms of reality being reduced to the iconography of cartoons but in terms of the cartoons themselves being reduced to their most basic elements. Partly as a result of this, *Maus* has room for more quotidian detail and character nuance than *Adolf*. Tezuka is not writing biography with *Adolf*, but telling a suspense story with some grand themes. His reductionism manifests itself in a simplification of character and world view, leaving room for every technique of cartoon storytelling.

That simplification has its price. Comics are made up of black lines on white paper, generally with little blocks of words beside big blocks of pictures. It's a hard format in which to convey ambiguities or complex information. Most of the great practitioners, including Tezuka, make their points by going for the heart and gut, not the head. The result is that big issues are often oversimplified to a point that makes our heads uneasy. I'm uncomfortable with Tezuka's identification of the PLO with the

Nazis. Yet it's through that identification that Tezuka makes us feel—in our guts and our hearts—that the real enemy isn't this or that bad nation, bad leader, or even bad ideology, but the concepts of Nation and Race themselves. When one of Tezuka's Palestinian characters describes his struggle with Israel as "a holy war between races," it's bad political science, a bad paraphrase of the PLO's position, yet it's the right stroke dramatically for Tezuka's story. With a single image and a single line it makes us see—and rightly—that lies about Nation and Race continue to drive us to kill each other, that the death of one Adolf, the fall of another, and the "homecoming" of a third haven't ended the deceptions and injustices.

Against the big lies and big bloodshed Tezuka pits a little cartoon man, and against the big words and big insanities he pits one little Japanese word: 正義 , or *seigi*. Toge uses the word many times, but most potently on the third-to-last page of this final volume of the series. *Seigi* is usually translated into English as "justice," although it carries few of the English implications of law, retribution, and reparation. *Seigi* suggests a broader sort of rightness, a Buddhist sense of peace and calm, a Confucian concept of things being in their proper places. With that simple ideogram, contained in a word balloon and placed behind a cartoon head, Tezuka suggests what mankind might become, what the world might be, if we leave behind the lies that have animated the hundreds of pages of violence and drama that have gone before. It is Tezuka's final and most powerful act of reduction.

Gerard Jones has written comic books for over a dozen publishers during the past nine years. His history of modern American comics, The Comic Book Heroes, *written with Will Jacobs, has just been released by Prima Publishing. Jones currently cotranslates manga for Viz Comics, particularly the work of Rumiko Takahashi, including* Ranma 1/2 *and* Maison Ikkoku. *In addition, he is working on several books and screenplays.*

CHAPTER ONE

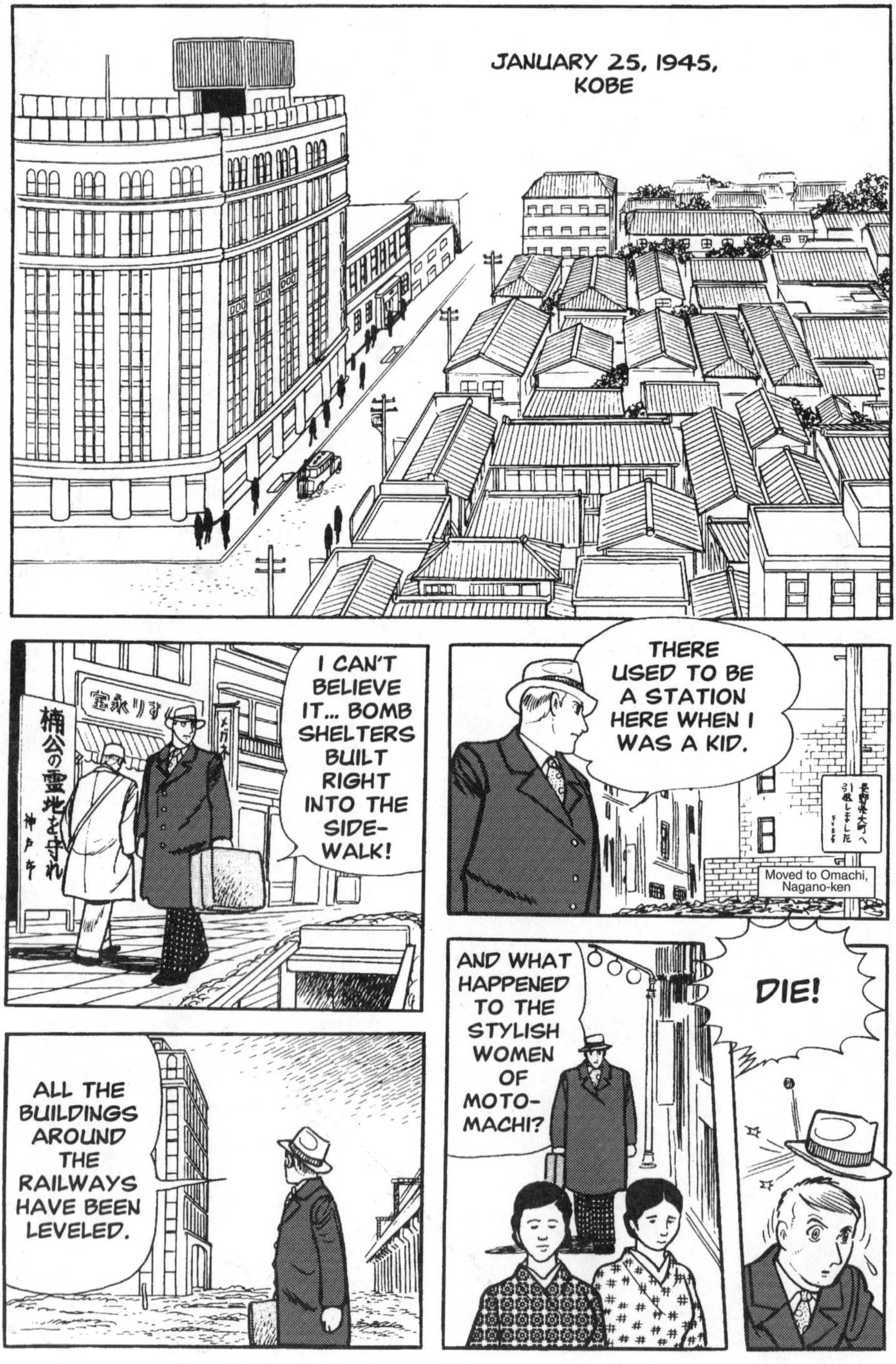
JANUARY 25, 1945, KOBE
楠公の霊地を守れ
神戸市
I CAN'T BELIEVE IT... BOMB SHELTERS BUILT RIGHT INTO THE SIDE-WALK!
THERE USED TO BE A STATION HERE WHEN I WAS A KID.
長野県大町へ引越しました
Moved to Omachi, Nagano-ken
ALL THE BUILDINGS AROUND THE RAILWAYS HAVE BEEN LEVELED.
AND WHAT HAPPENED TO THE STYLISH WOMEN OF MOTO-MACHI?
DIE!

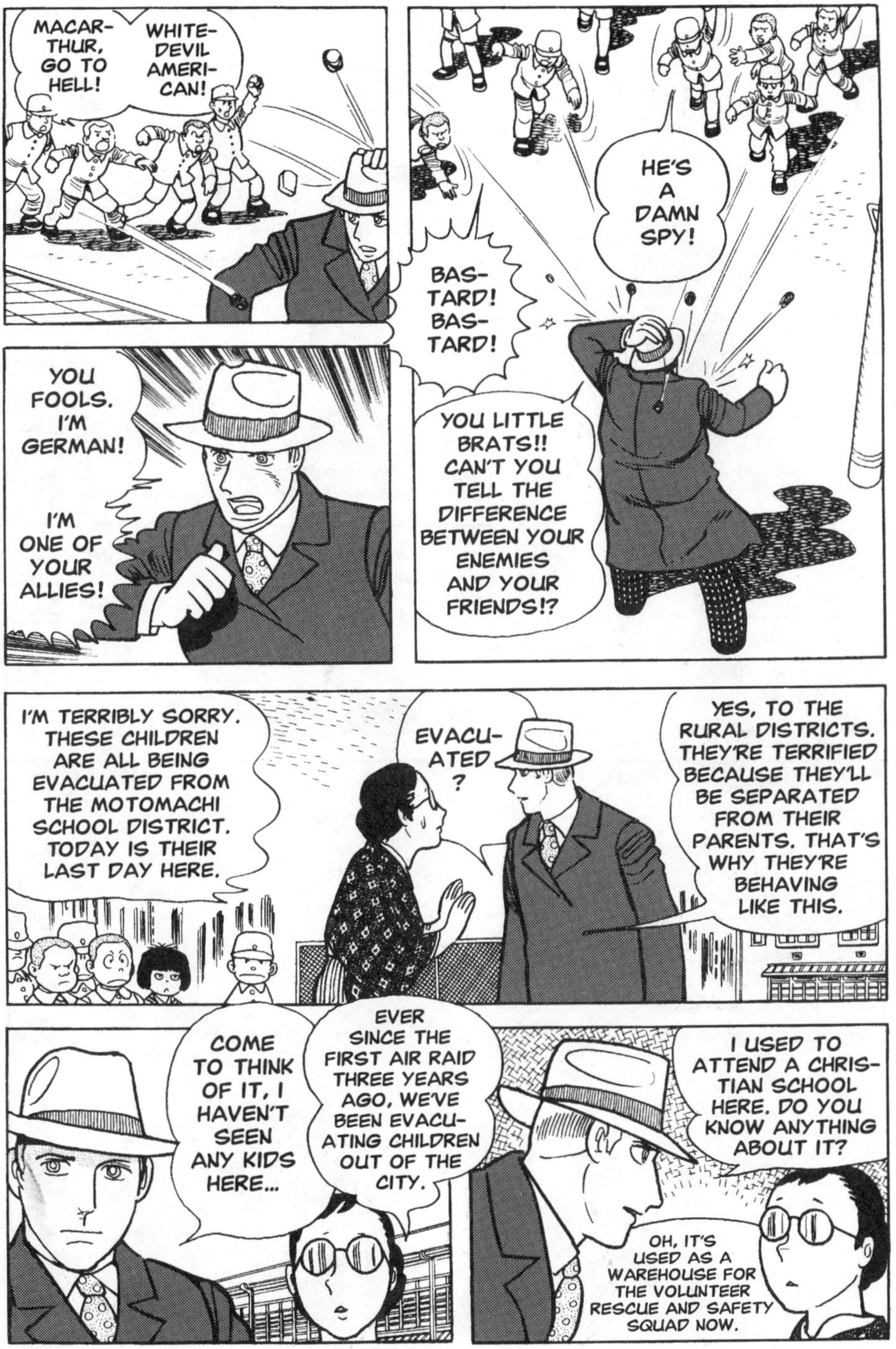
MACAR-THUR, GO TO HELL!
WHITE-DEVIL AMERI-CAN!
YOU FOOLS. I'M GERMAN!
I'M ONE OF YOUR ALLIES!
HE'S A DAMN SPY!
BAS-TARD! BAS-TARD!
YOU LITTLE BRATS!! CAN'T YOU TELL THE DIFFERENCE BETWEEN YOUR ENEMIES AND YOUR FRIENDS!?
I'M TERRIBLY SORRY. THESE CHILDREN ARE ALL BEING EVACUATED FROM THE MOTOMACHI SCHOOL DISTRICT. TODAY IS THEIR LAST DAY HERE.
EVACU-ATED?
YES, TO THE RURAL DISTRICTS. THEY'RE TERRIFIED BECAUSE THEY'LL BE SEPARATED FROM THEIR PARENTS. THAT'S WHY THEY'RE BEHAVING LIKE THIS.
COME TO THINK OF IT, I HAVEN'T SEEN ANY KIDS HERE...
EVER SINCE THE FIRST AIR RAID THREE YEARS AGO, WE'VE BEEN EVACU-ATING CHILDREN OUT OF THE CITY.
I USED TO ATTEND A CHRIS-TIAN SCHOOL HERE. DO YOU KNOW ANYTHING ABOUT IT?
OH, IT'S USED AS A WAREHOUSE FOR THE VOLUNTEER RESCUE AND SAFETY SQUAD NOW.

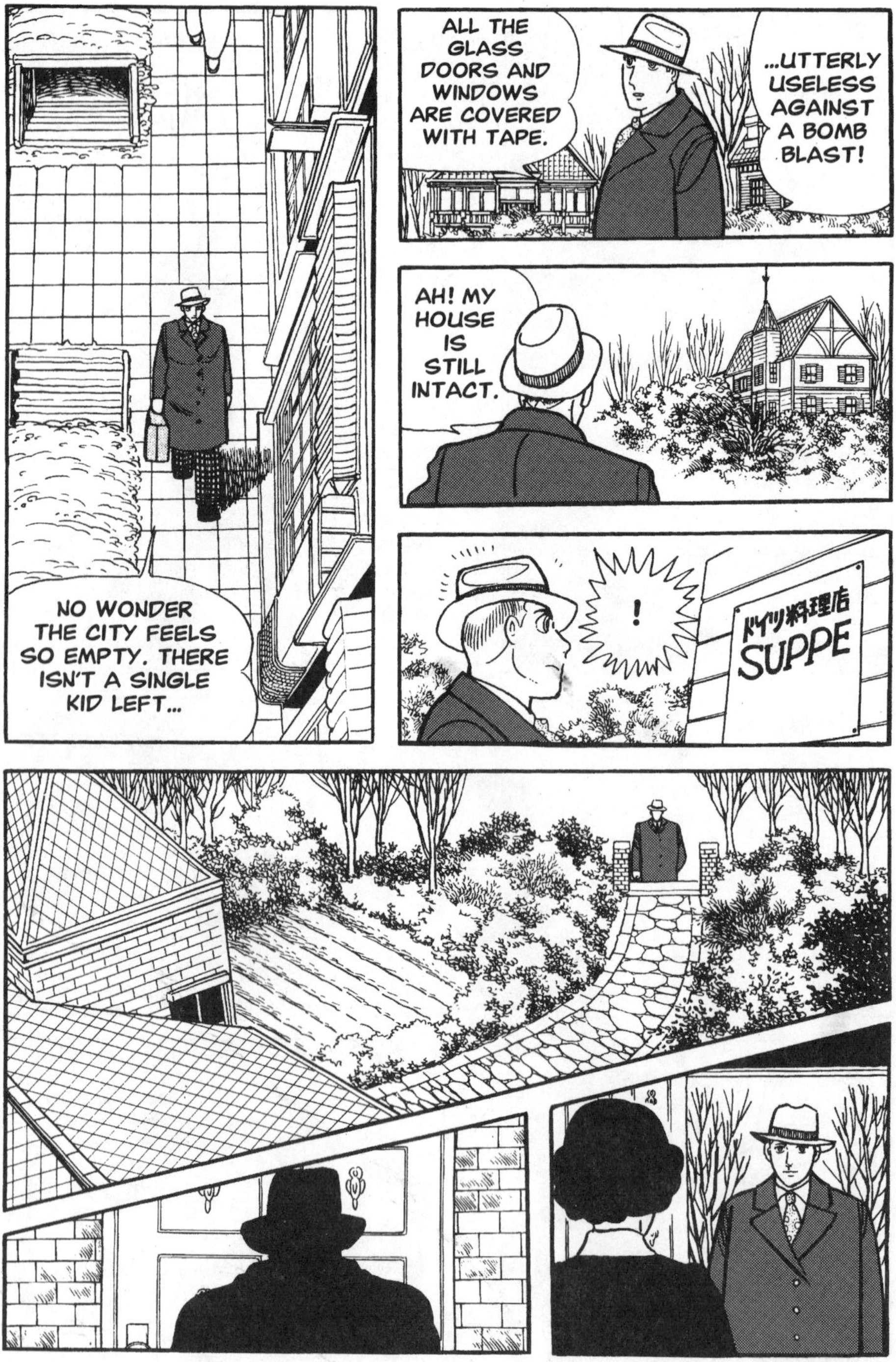
NO WONDER THE CITY FEELS SO EMPTY. THERE ISN'T A SINGLE KID LEFT...
ALL THE GLASS DOORS AND WINDOWS ARE COVERED WITH TAPE.
...UTTERLY USELESS AGAINST A BOMB BLAST!
AH! MY HOUSE IS STILL INTACT.
!
ドイツ料理店
SUPPE

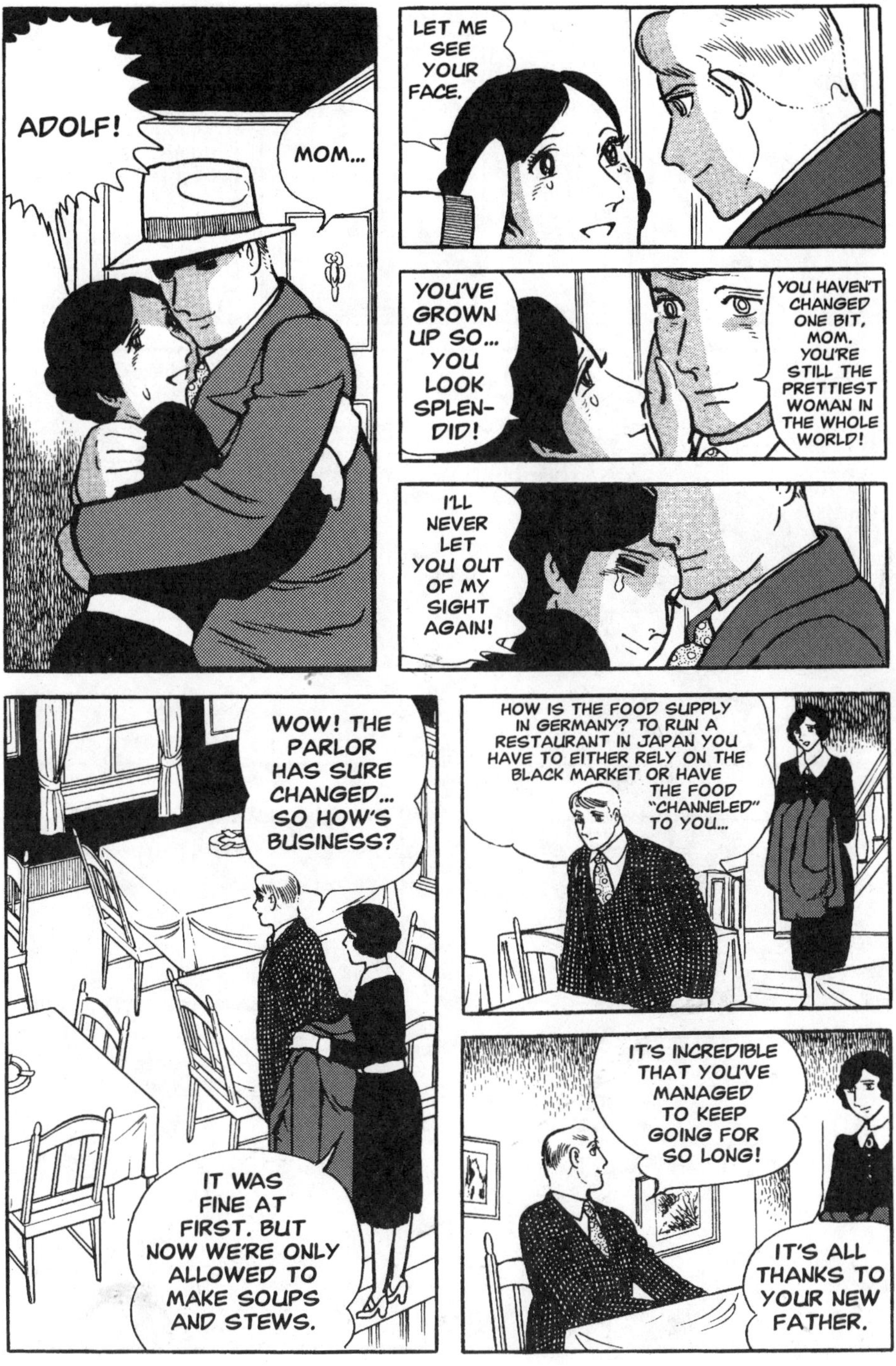
ADOLF!
MOM...
LET ME SEE YOUR FACE.
YOU'VE GROWN UP SO... YOU LOOK SPLEN-DID!
YOU HAVEN'T CHANGED ONE BIT, MOM. YOU'RE STILL THE PRETTIEST WOMAN IN THE WHOLE WORLD!
I'LL NEVER LET YOU OUT OF MY SIGHT AGAIN!
WOW! THE PARLOR HAS SURE CHANGED... SO HOW'S BUSINESS?
IT WAS FINE AT FIRST. BUT NOW WE'RE ONLY ALLOWED TO MAKE SOUPS AND STEWS.
HOW IS THE FOOD SUPPLY IN GERMANY? TO RUN A RESTAURANT IN JAPAN YOU HAVE TO EITHER RELY ON THE BLACK MARKET OR HAVE THE FOOD "CHANNELED" TO YOU...
IT'S INCREDIBLE THAT YOU'VE MANAGED TO KEEP GOING FOR SO LONG!
IT'S ALL THANKS TO YOUR NEW FATHER.

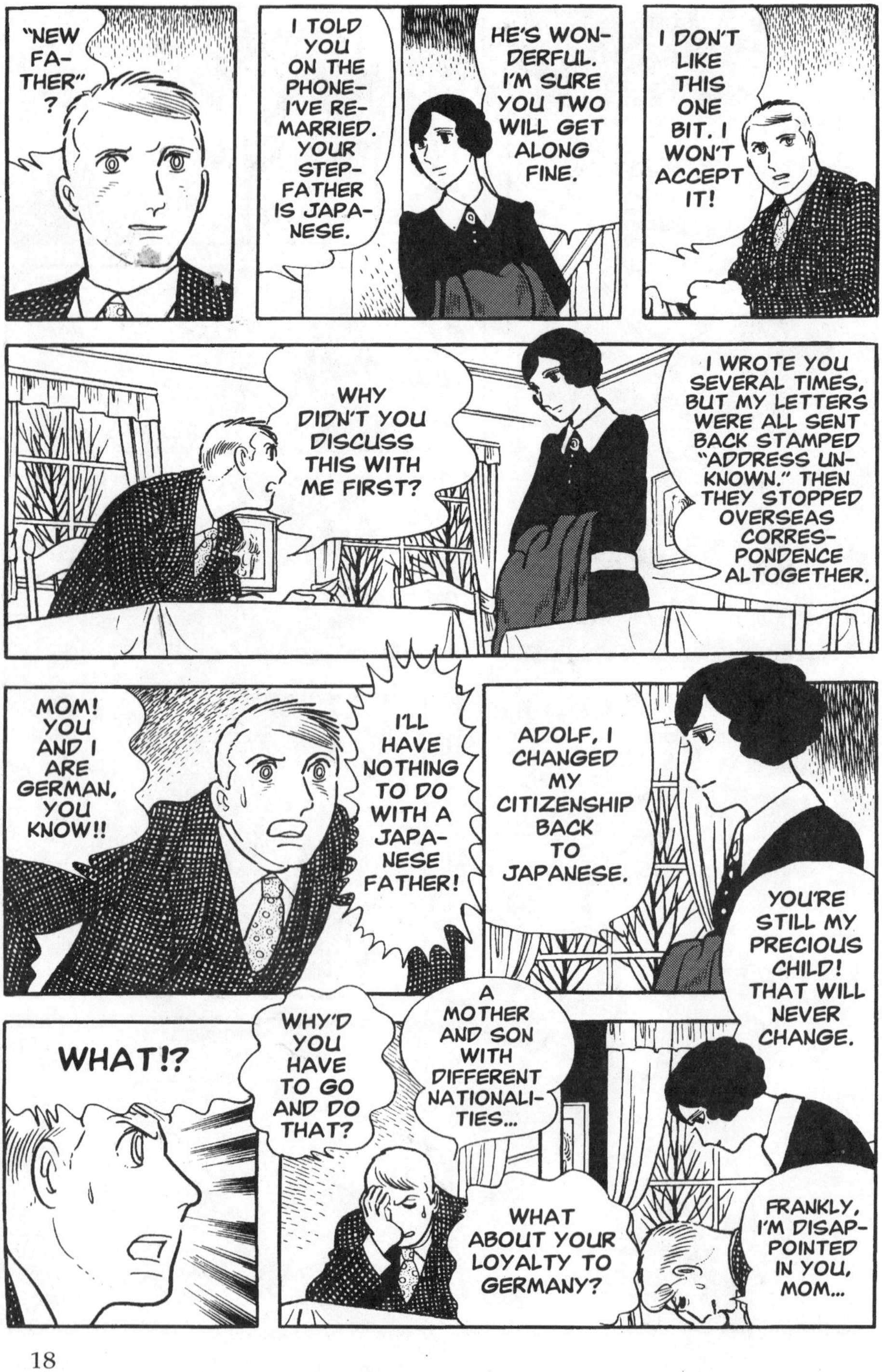
"NEW FATHER"?
I TOLD YOU ON THE PHONE— I'VE REMARRIED. YOUR STEPFATHER IS JAPANESE.
HE'S WONDERFUL. I'M SURE YOU TWO WILL GET ALONG FINE.
I DON'T LIKE THIS ONE BIT. I WON'T ACCEPT IT!
WHY DIDN'T YOU DISCUSS THIS WITH ME FIRST?
I WROTE YOU SEVERAL TIMES, BUT MY LETTERS WERE ALL SENT BACK STAMPED "ADDRESS UNKNOWN." THEN THEY STOPPED OVERSEAS CORRESPONDENCE ALTOGETHER.
MOM! YOU AND I ARE GERMAN, YOU KNOW!!
I'LL HAVE NOTHING TO DO WITH A JAPANESE FATHER!
ADOLF, I CHANGED MY CITIZENSHIP BACK TO JAPANESE.
YOU'RE STILL MY PRECIOUS CHILD! THAT WILL NEVER CHANGE.
WHAT!?
WHY'D YOU HAVE TO GO AND DO THAT?
A MOTHER AND SON WITH DIFFERENT NATIONALITIES...
WHAT ABOUT YOUR LOYALTY TO GERMANY?
FRANKLY, I'M DISAPPOINTED IN YOU, MOM...

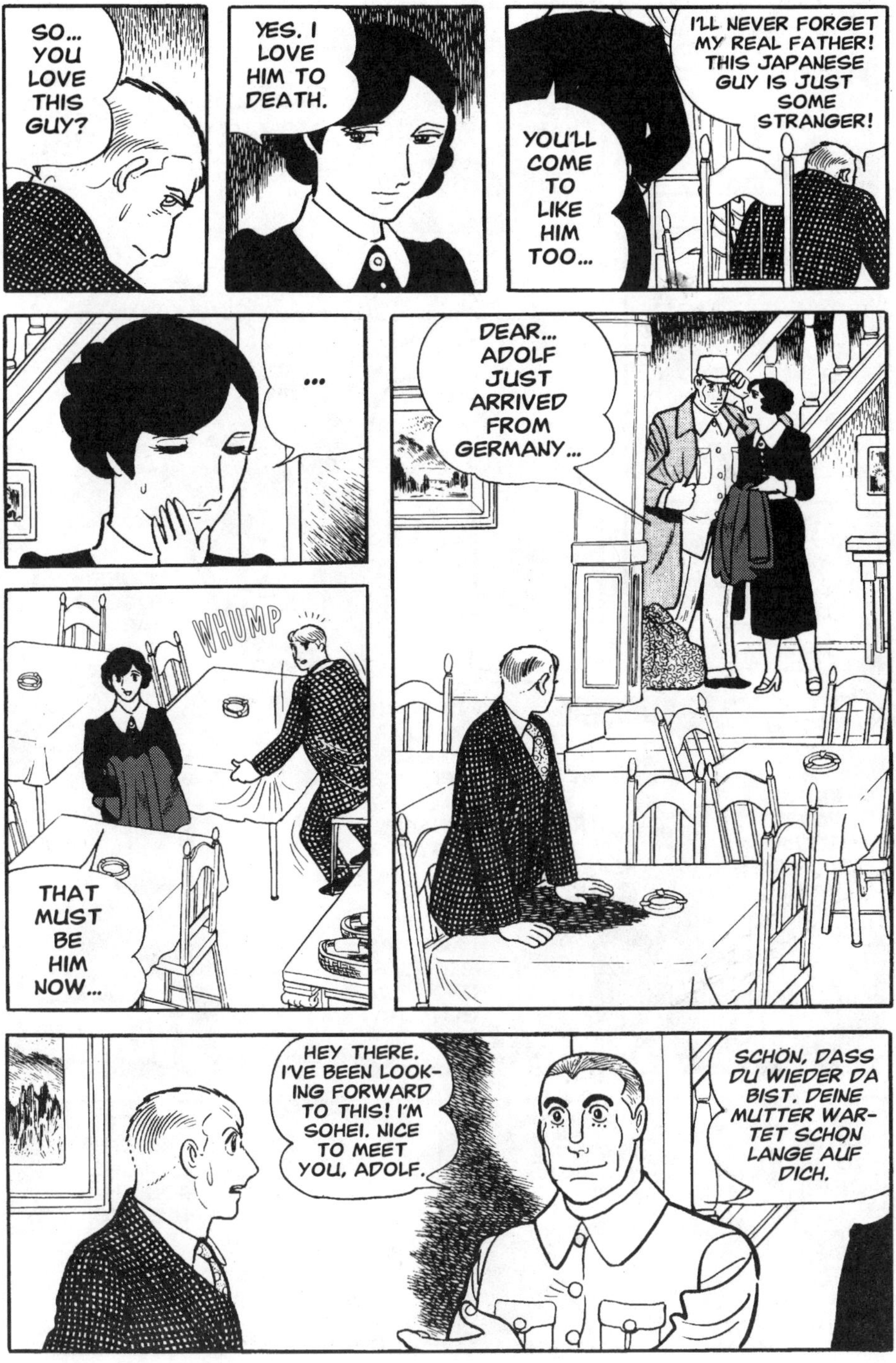
SO... YOU LOVE THIS GUY?
YES. I LOVE HIM TO DEATH.
I'LL NEVER FORGET MY REAL FATHER! THIS JAPANESE GUY IS JUST SOME STRANGER!
YOU'LL COME TO LIKE HIM TOO...
...
WHUMP
THAT MUST BE HIM NOW...
DEAR... ADOLF JUST ARRIVED FROM GERMANY...
HEY THERE. I'VE BEEN LOOKING FORWARD TO THIS! I'M SOHEI. NICE TO MEET YOU, ADOLF.
SCHÖN, DASS DU WIEDER DA BIST. DEINE MUTTER WARTET SCHON LANGE AUF DICH.

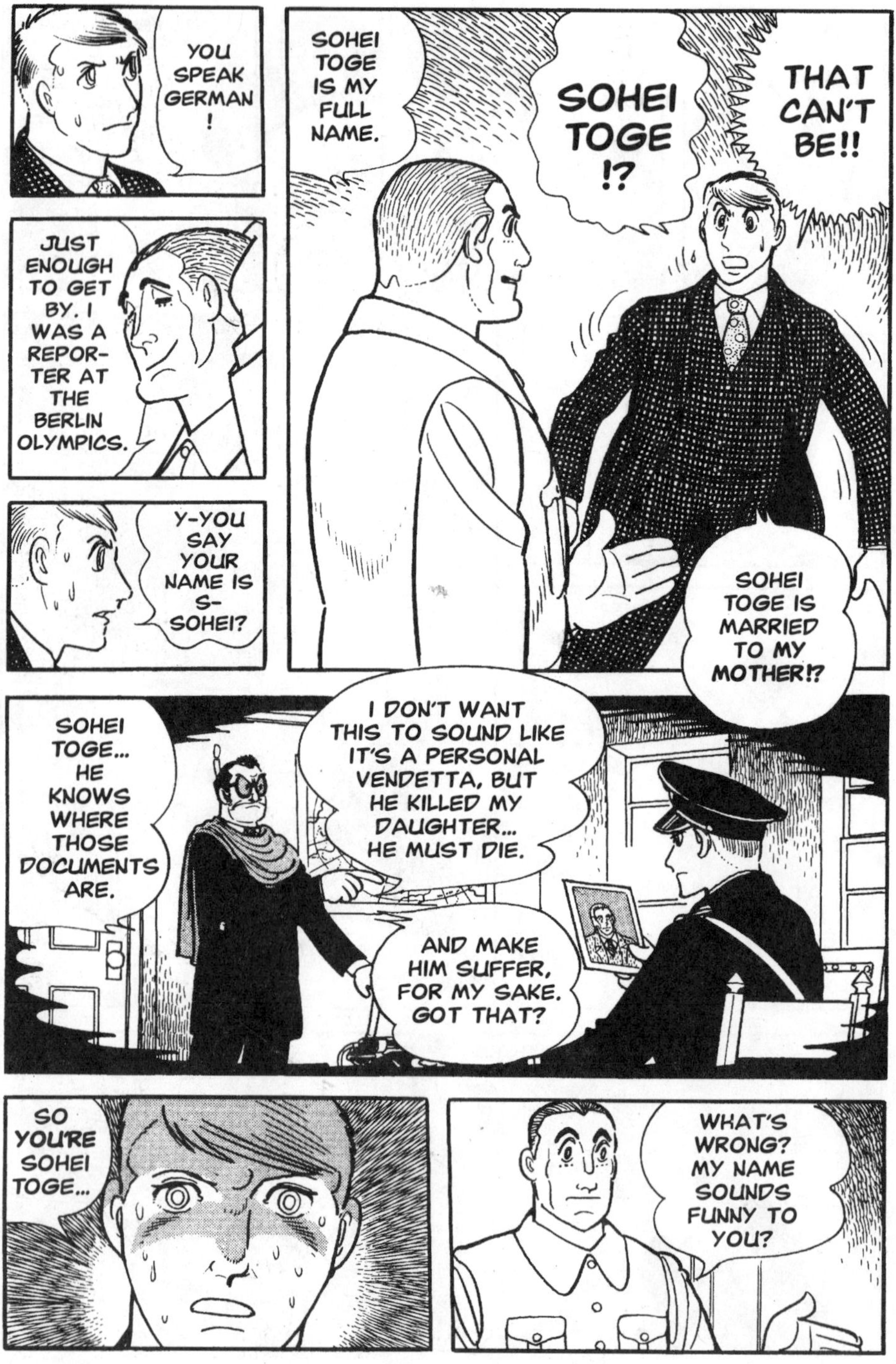
YOU SPEAK GERMAN!
JUST ENOUGH TO GET BY. I WAS A REPORTER AT THE BERLIN OLYMPICS.
Y-YOU SAY YOUR NAME IS S-SOHEI?
SOHEI TOGE IS MY FULL NAME.
SOHEI TOGE!?
THAT CAN'T BE!!
SOHEI TOGE IS MARRIED TO MY MOTHER!?
SOHEI TOGE... HE KNOWS WHERE THOSE DOCUMENTS ARE.
I DON'T WANT THIS TO SOUND LIKE IT'S A PERSONAL VENDETTA, BUT HE KILLED MY DAUGHTER... HE MUST DIE.
AND MAKE HIM SUFFER, FOR MY SAKE. GOT THAT?
SO YOU'RE SOHEI TOGE...
WHAT'S WRONG? MY NAME SOUNDS FUNNY TO YOU?

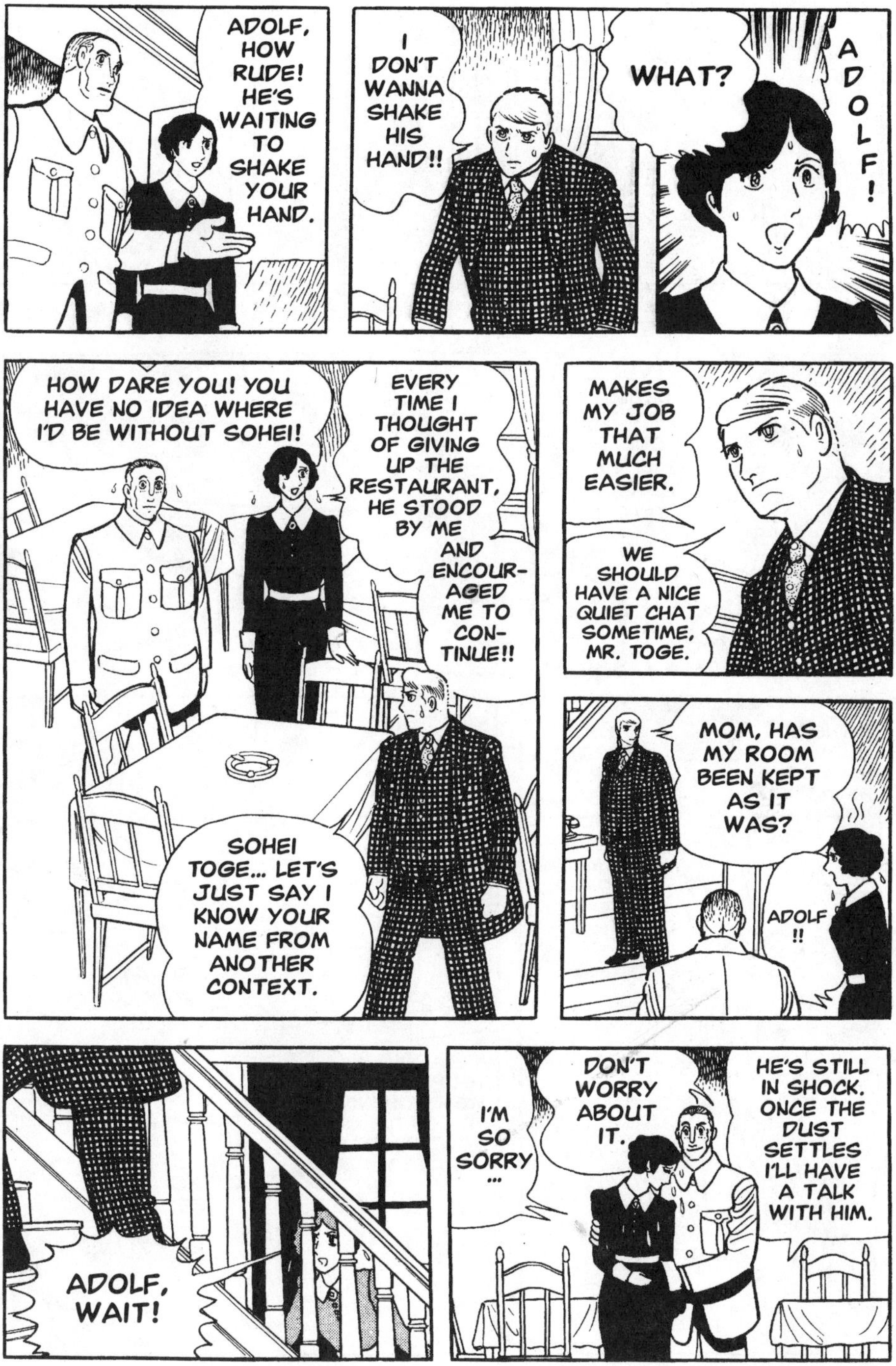
ADOLF, HOW RUDE! HE'S WAITING TO SHAKE YOUR HAND.
I DON'T WANNA SHAKE HIS HAND!!
WHAT?
ADOLF!
HOW DARE YOU! YOU HAVE NO IDEA WHERE I'D BE WITHOUT SOHEI!
EVERY TIME I THOUGHT OF GIVING UP THE RESTAURANT, HE STOOD BY ME AND ENCOURAGED ME TO CONTINUE!!
SOHEI TOGE... LET'S JUST SAY I KNOW YOUR NAME FROM ANOTHER CONTEXT.
MAKES MY JOB THAT MUCH EASIER.
WE SHOULD HAVE A NICE QUIET CHAT SOMETIME, MR. TOGE.
MOM, HAS MY ROOM BEEN KEPT AS IT WAS?
ADOLF!!
ADOLF, WAIT!
I'M SO SORRY...
DON'T WORRY ABOUT IT.
HE'S STILL IN SHOCK. ONCE THE DUST SETTLES I'LL HAVE A TALK WITH HIM.

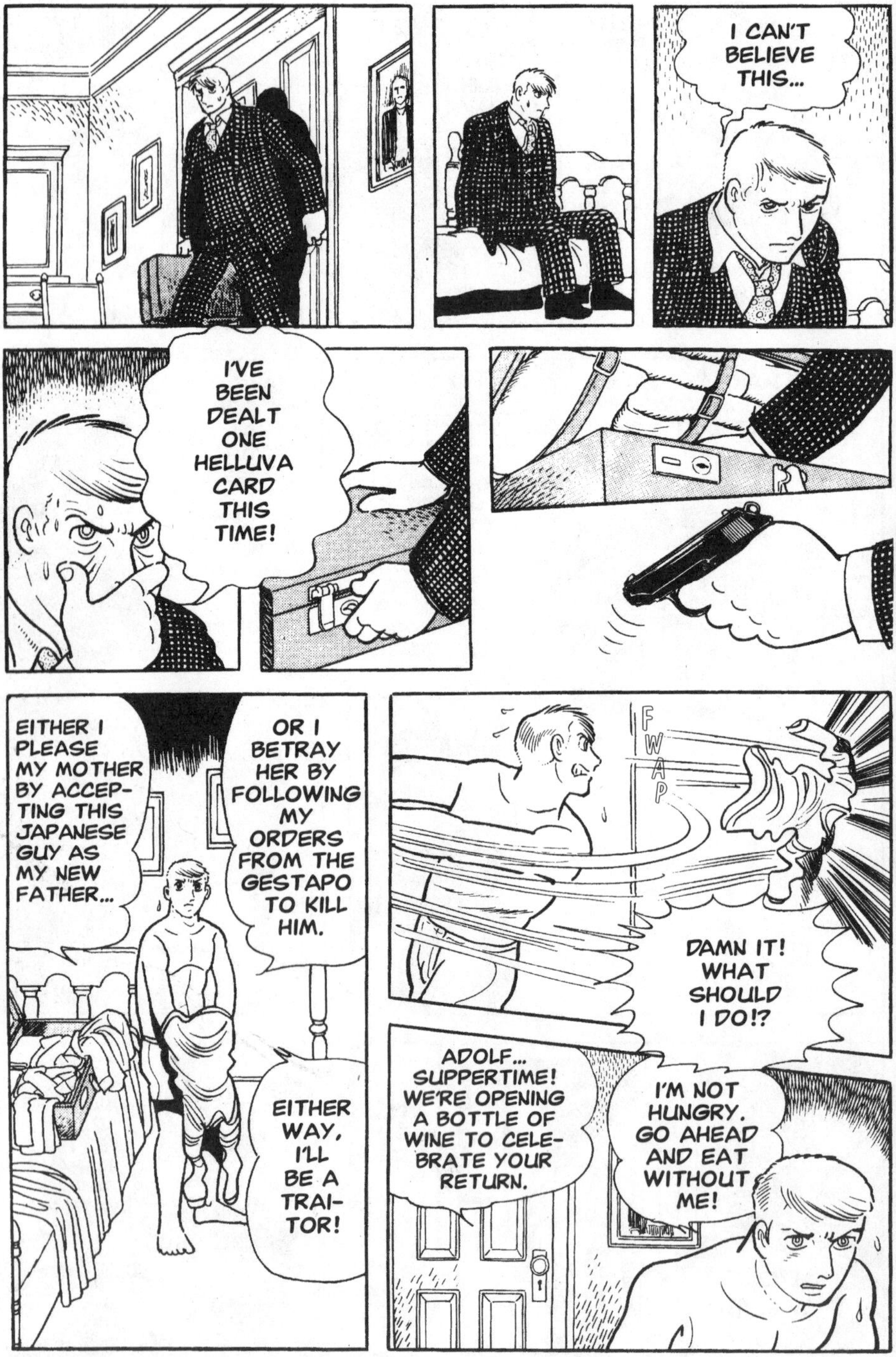
I CAN'T BELIEVE THIS...
I'VE BEEN DEALT ONE HELLUVA CARD THIS TIME!
EITHER I PLEASE MY MOTHER BY ACCEPTING THIS JAPANESE GUY AS MY NEW FATHER...
OR I BETRAY HER BY FOLLOWING MY ORDERS FROM THE GESTAPO TO KILL HIM.
EITHER WAY, I'LL BE A TRAITOR!
FWAP
DAMN IT! WHAT SHOULD I DO!?
ADOLF... SUPPERTIME! WE'RE OPENING A BOTTLE OF WINE TO CELEBRATE YOUR RETURN.
I'M NOT HUNGRY. GO AHEAD AND EAT WITHOUT ME!

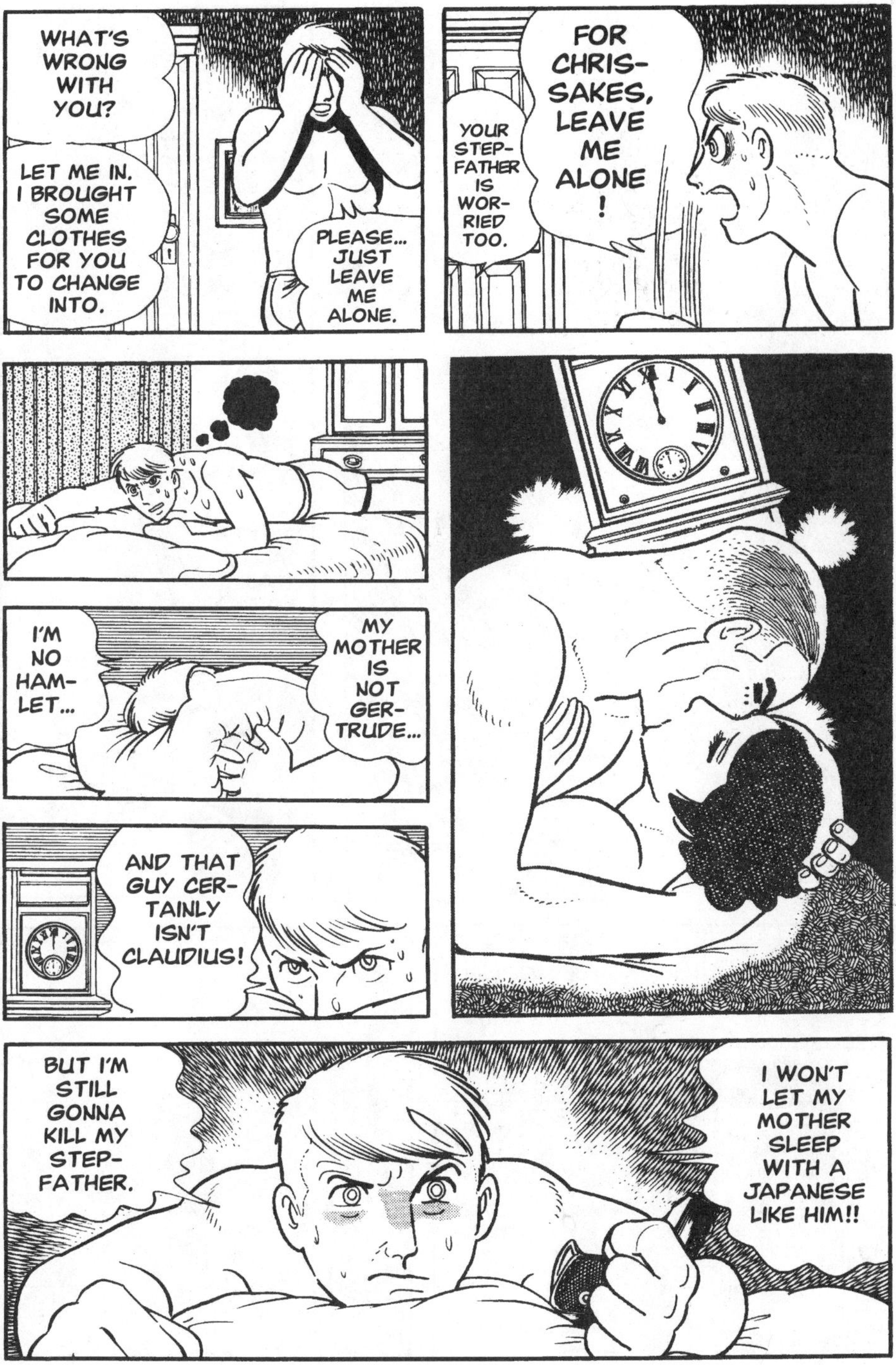
WHAT'S WRONG WITH YOU?
LET ME IN. I BROUGHT SOME CLOTHES FOR YOU TO CHANGE INTO.
PLEASE... JUST LEAVE ME ALONE.
YOUR STEP-FATHER IS WOR-RIED TOO.
FOR CHRIS-SAKES, LEAVE ME ALONE!
I'M NO HAM-LET...
MY MOTHER IS NOT GER-TRUDE...
AND THAT GUY CER-TAINLY ISN'T CLAUDIUS!
BUT I'M STILL GONNA KILL MY STEP-FATHER.
I WON'T LET MY MOTHER SLEEP WITH A JAPANESE LIKE HIM!!

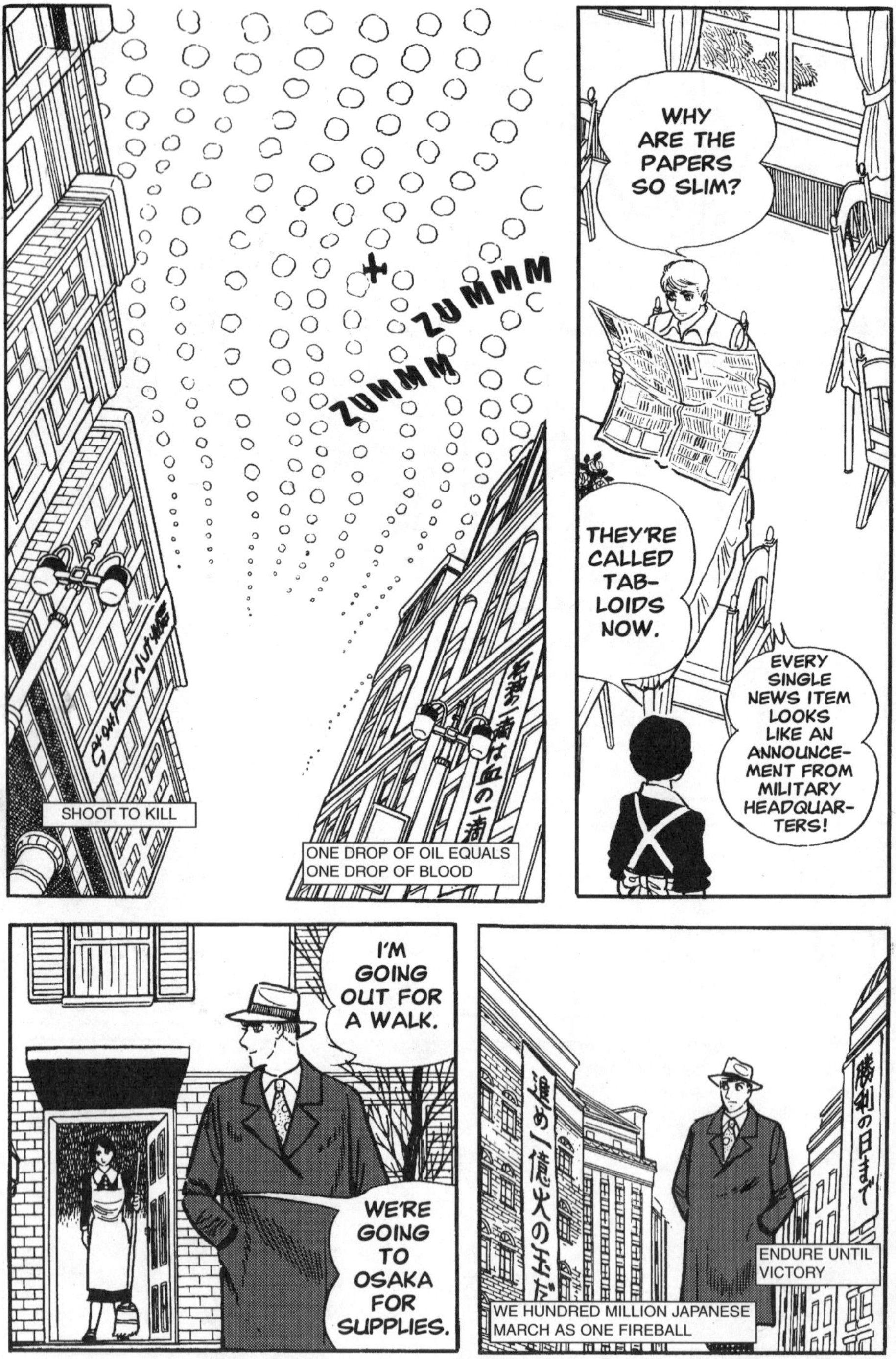
ZUMMM ZUMMM
SHOOT TO KILL
ONE DROP OF OIL EQUALS ONE DROP OF BLOOD
WHY ARE THE PAPERS SO SLIM?
THEY'RE CALLED TAB-LOIDS NOW.
EVERY SINGLE NEWS ITEM LOOKS LIKE AN ANNOUNCE-MENT FROM MILITARY HEADQUAR-TERS!
I'M GOING OUT FOR A WALK.
WE'RE GOING TO OSAKA FOR SUPPLIES.
進め一億火の玉だ
勝利の日まで
ENDURE UNTIL VICTORY
WE HUNDRED MILLION JAPANESE MARCH AS ONE FIREBALL

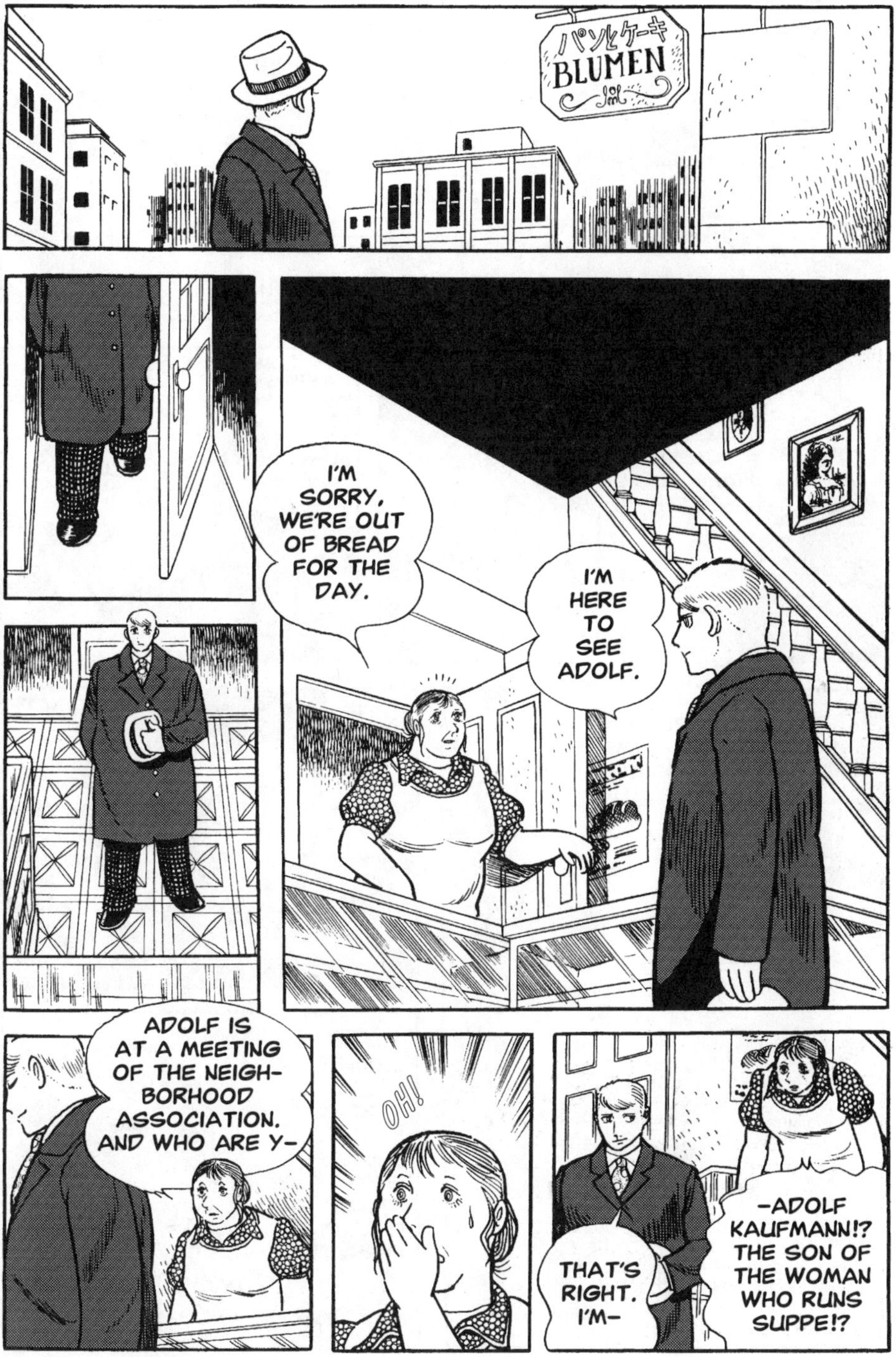
パンとケーキ
BLUMEN
I'M SORRY, WE'RE OUT OF BREAD FOR THE DAY.
I'M HERE TO SEE ADOLF.
ADOLF IS AT A MEETING OF THE NEIGH-BORHOOD ASSOCIATION. AND WHO ARE Y-
OH!
THAT'S RIGHT. I'M-
-ADOLF KAUFMANN!? THE SON OF THE WOMAN WHO RUNS SUPPE!?

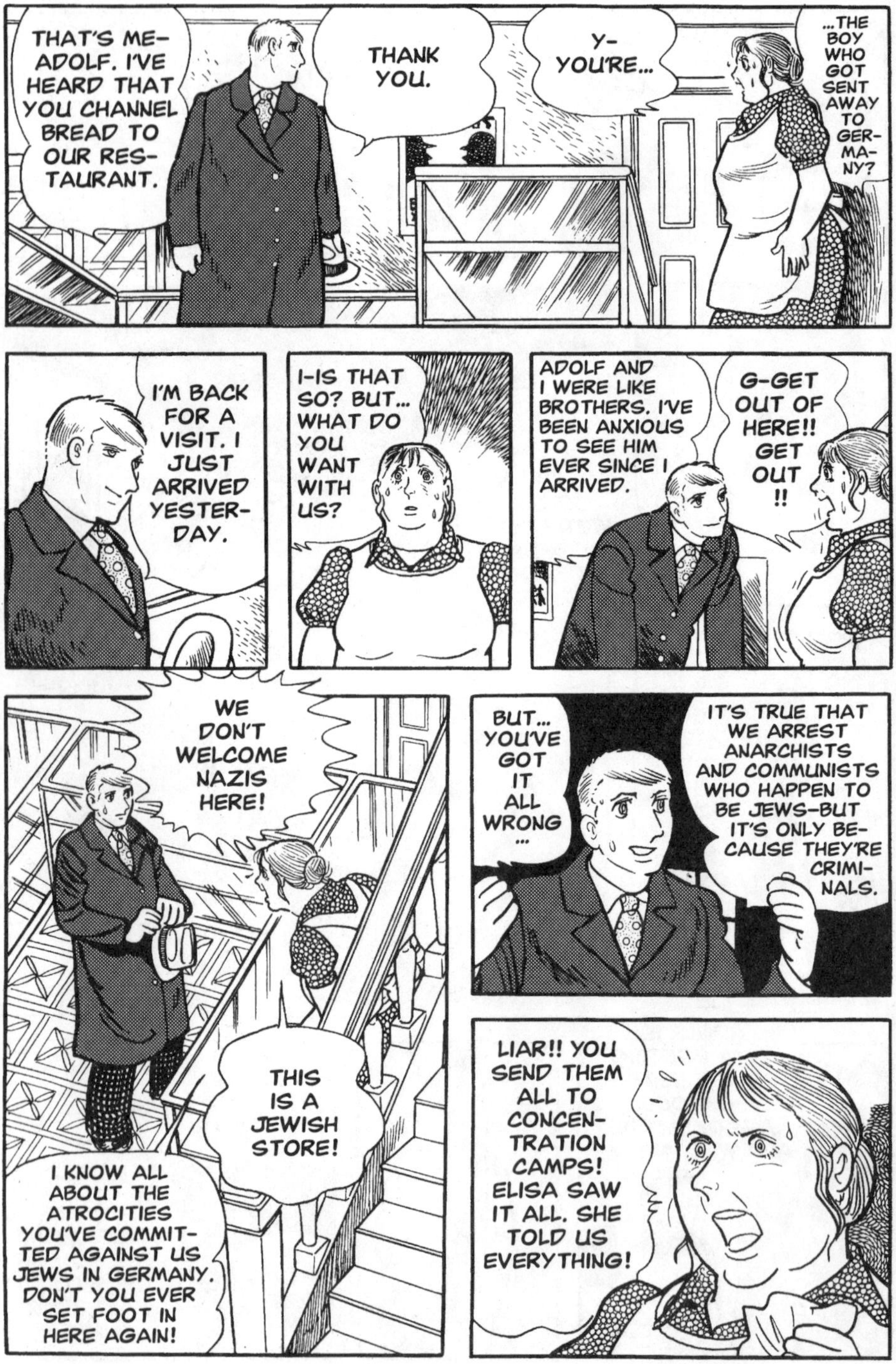
THAT'S ME–ADOLF. I'VE HEARD THAT YOU CHANNEL BREAD TO OUR RESTAURANT.
THANK YOU.
Y-YOU'RE...
...THE BOY WHO GOT SENT AWAY TO GERMANY?
I'M BACK FOR A VISIT. I JUST ARRIVED YESTERDAY.
I-IS THAT SO? BUT... WHAT DO YOU WANT WITH US?
ADOLF AND I WERE LIKE BROTHERS. I'VE BEEN ANXIOUS TO SEE HIM EVER SINCE I ARRIVED.
G-GET OUT OF HERE!! GET OUT !!
WE DON'T WELCOME NAZIS HERE!
THIS IS A JEWISH STORE!
I KNOW ALL ABOUT THE ATROCITIES YOU'VE COMMITTED AGAINST US JEWS IN GERMANY. DON'T YOU EVER SET FOOT IN HERE AGAIN!
BUT... YOU'VE GOT IT ALL WRONG ...
IT'S TRUE THAT WE ARREST ANARCHISTS AND COMMUNISTS WHO HAPPEN TO BE JEWS–BUT IT'S ONLY BECAUSE THEY'RE CRIMINALS.
LIAR!! YOU SEND THEM ALL TO CONCENTRATION CAMPS! ELISA SAW IT ALL. SHE TOLD US EVERYTHING!

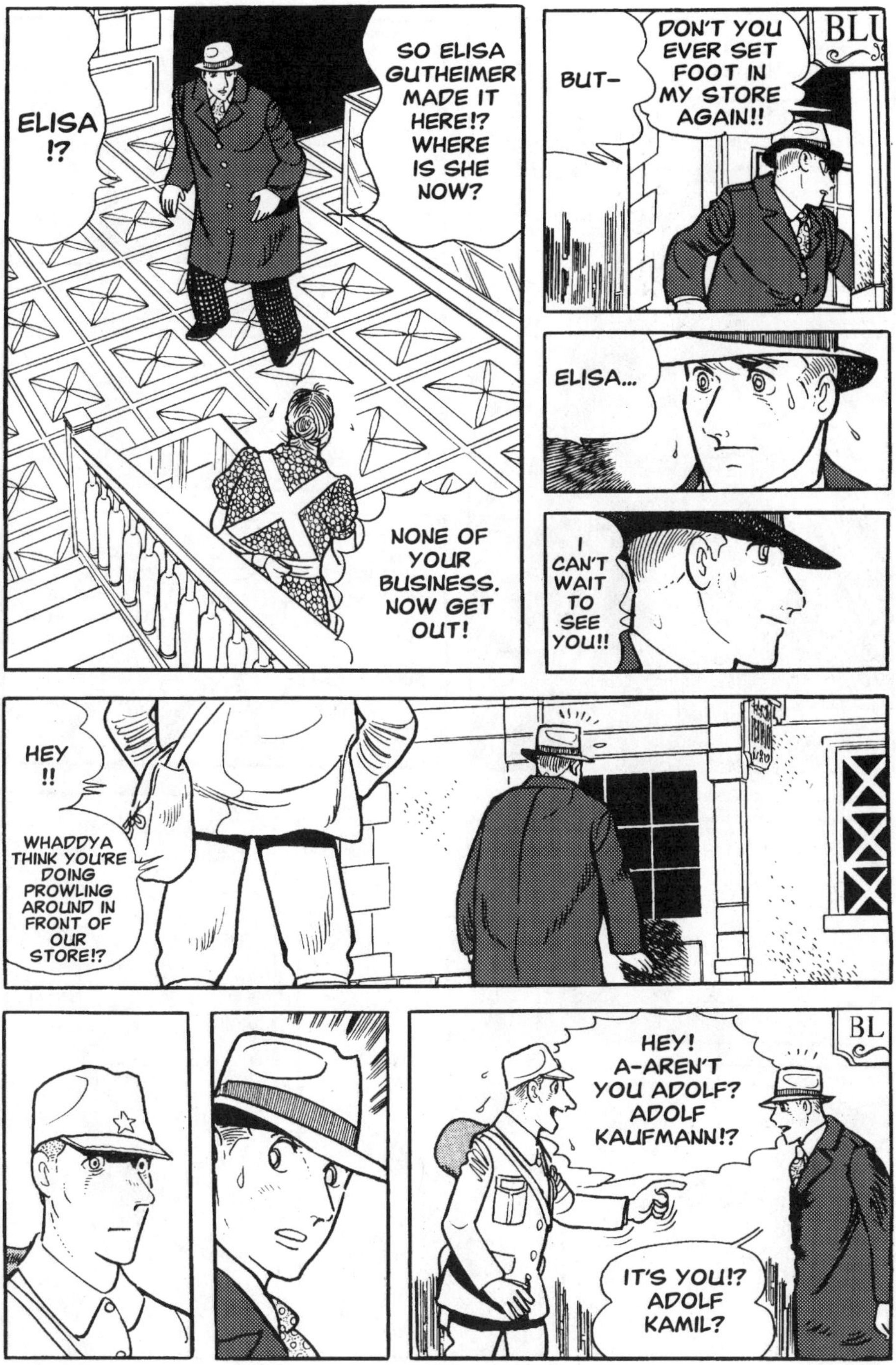
ELISA !?
SO ELISA GUTHEIMER MADE IT HERE!? WHERE IS SHE NOW?
NONE OF YOUR BUSINESS. NOW GET OUT!
BUT-
DON'T YOU EVER SET FOOT IN MY STORE AGAIN!!
ELISA...
I CAN'T WAIT TO SEE YOU!!
HEY !!
WHADDYA THINK YOU'RE DOING PROWLING AROUND IN FRONT OF OUR STORE!?
HEY! A-AREN'T YOU ADOLF? ADOLF KAUFMANN!?
IT'S YOU!? ADOLF KAMIL?

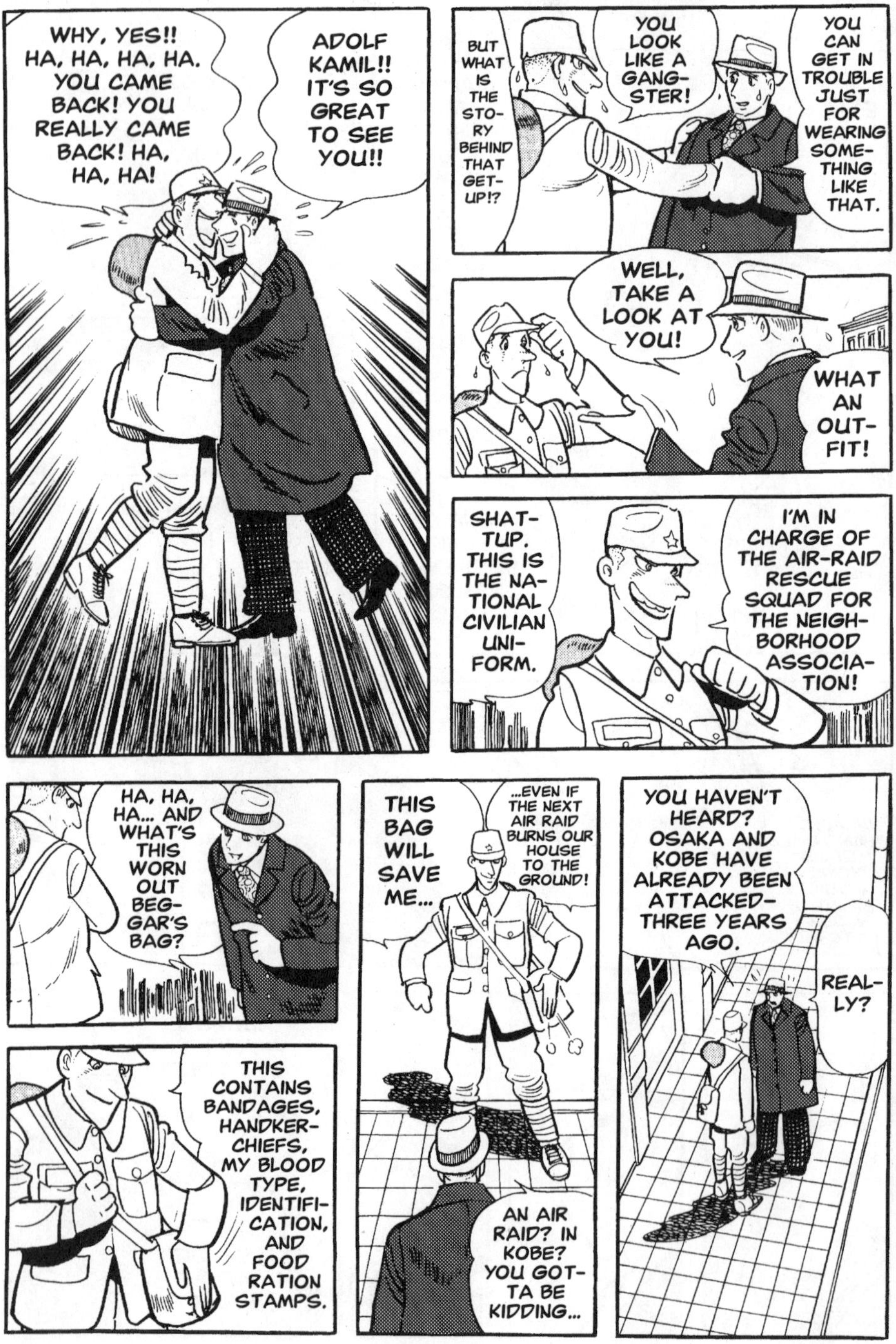
WHY, YES!! HA, HA, HA, HA. YOU CAME BACK! YOU REALLY CAME BACK! HA, HA, HA!
ADOLF KAMIL!! IT'S SO GREAT TO SEE YOU!!
BUT WHAT IS THE STORY BEHIND THAT GET-UP!?
YOU LOOK LIKE A GANGSTER!
YOU CAN GET IN TROUBLE JUST FOR WEARING SOMETHING LIKE THAT.
WELL, TAKE A LOOK AT YOU!
WHAT AN OUTFIT!
SHATTUP. THIS IS THE NATIONAL CIVILIAN UNIFORM.
I'M IN CHARGE OF THE AIR-RAID RESCUE SQUAD FOR THE NEIGHBORHOOD ASSOCIATION!
HA, HA, HA... AND WHAT'S THIS WORN OUT BEGGAR'S BAG?
THIS CONTAINS BANDAGES, HANDKERCHIEFS, MY BLOOD TYPE, IDENTIFICATION, AND FOOD RATION STAMPS.
THIS BAG WILL SAVE ME...
...EVEN IF THE NEXT AIR RAID BURNS OUR HOUSE TO THE GROUND!
AN AIR RAID? IN KOBE? YOU GOTTA BE KIDDING...
YOU HAVEN'T HEARD? OSAKA AND KOBE HAVE ALREADY BEEN ATTACKED—THREE YEARS AGO.
REALLY?

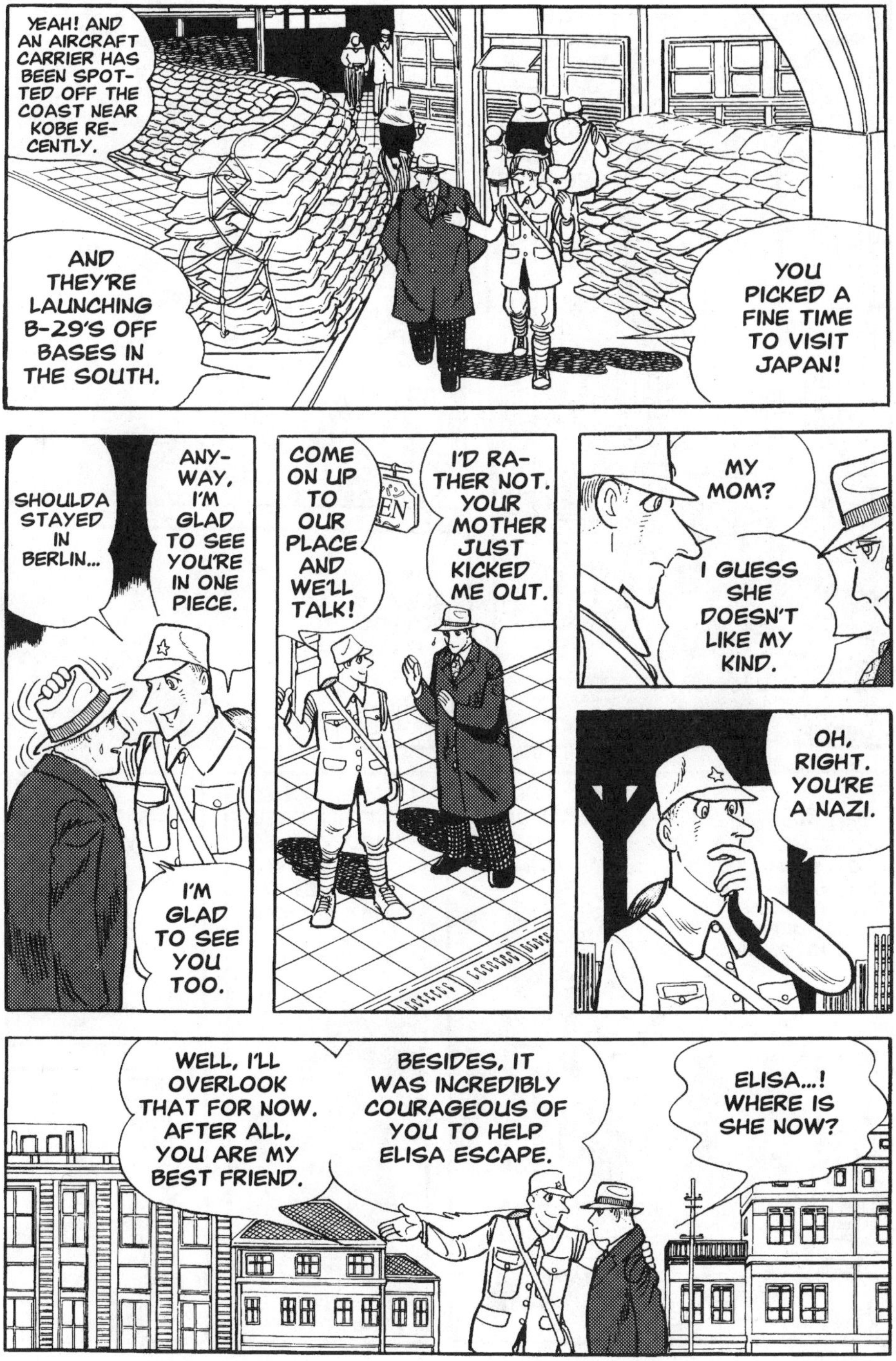
YEAH! AND AN AIRCRAFT CARRIER HAS BEEN SPOTTED OFF THE COAST NEAR KOBE RECENTLY.
AND THEY'RE LAUNCHING B-29'S OFF BASES IN THE SOUTH.
YOU PICKED A FINE TIME TO VISIT JAPAN!
SHOULDA STAYED IN BERLIN...
ANYWAY, I'M GLAD TO SEE YOU'RE IN ONE PIECE.
I'M GLAD TO SEE YOU TOO.
COME ON UP TO OUR PLACE AND WE'LL TALK!
I'D RATHER NOT. YOUR MOTHER JUST KICKED ME OUT.
MY MOM?
I GUESS SHE DOESN'T LIKE MY KIND.
OH, RIGHT. YOU'RE A NAZI.
WELL, I'LL OVERLOOK THAT FOR NOW. AFTER ALL, YOU ARE MY BEST FRIEND.
BESIDES, IT WAS INCREDIBLY COURAGEOUS OF YOU TO HELP ELISA ESCAPE.
ELISA...! WHERE IS SHE NOW?

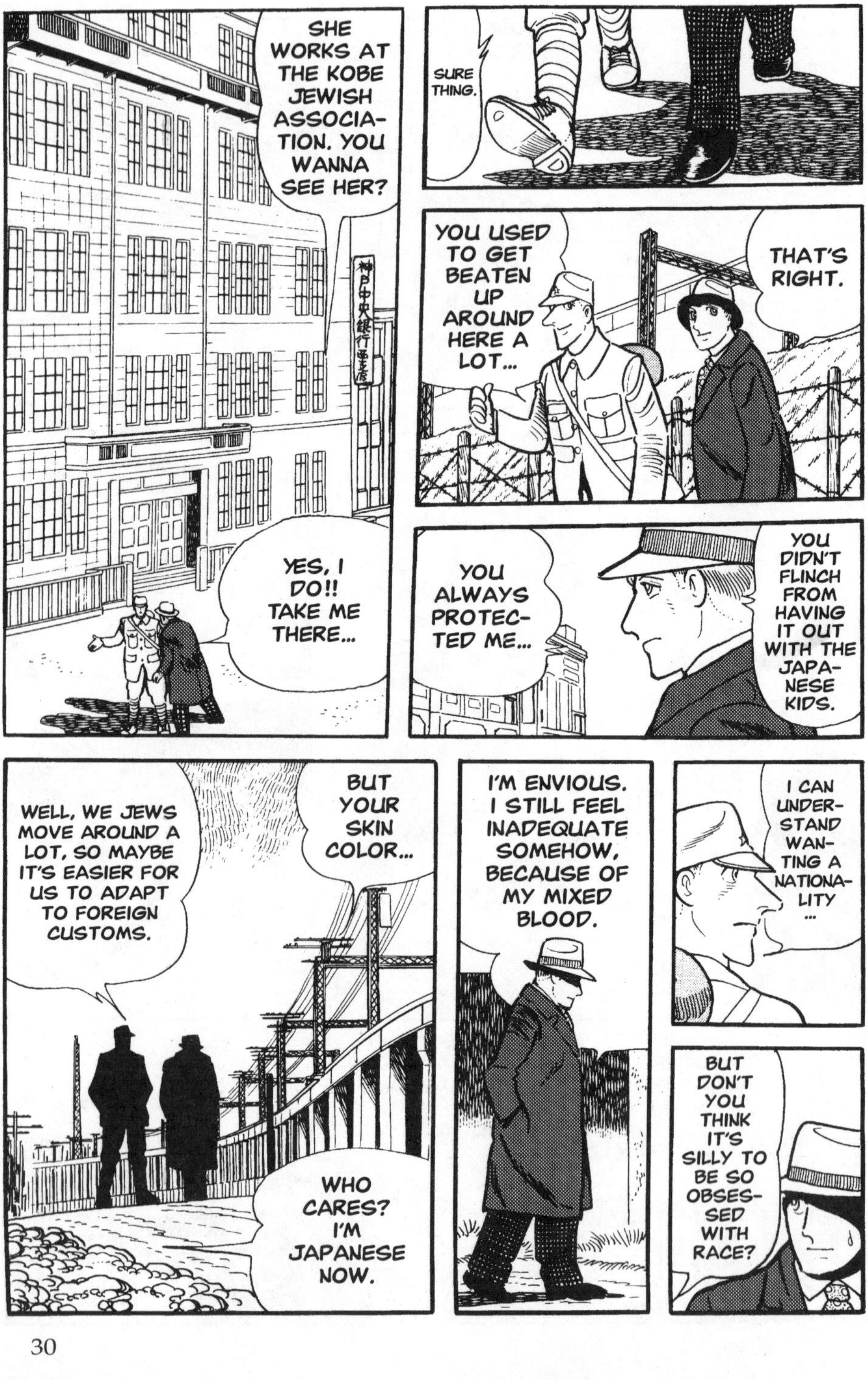
SHE WORKS AT THE KOBE JEWISH ASSOCIATION. YOU WANNA SEE HER?
YES, I DO!! TAKE ME THERE...
SURE THING.
YOU USED TO GET BEATEN UP AROUND HERE A LOT...
THAT'S RIGHT.
YOU ALWAYS PROTECTED ME...
YOU DIDN'T FLINCH FROM HAVING IT OUT WITH THE JAPANESE KIDS.
WELL, WE JEWS MOVE AROUND A LOT, SO MAYBE IT'S EASIER FOR US TO ADAPT TO FOREIGN CUSTOMS.
BUT YOUR SKIN COLOR...
WHO CARES? I'M JAPANESE NOW.
I'M ENVIOUS. I STILL FEEL INADEQUATE SOMEHOW, BECAUSE OF MY MIXED BLOOD.
I CAN UNDERSTAND WANTING A NATIONALITY...
BUT DON'T YOU THINK IT'S SILLY TO BE SO OBSESSED WITH RACE?

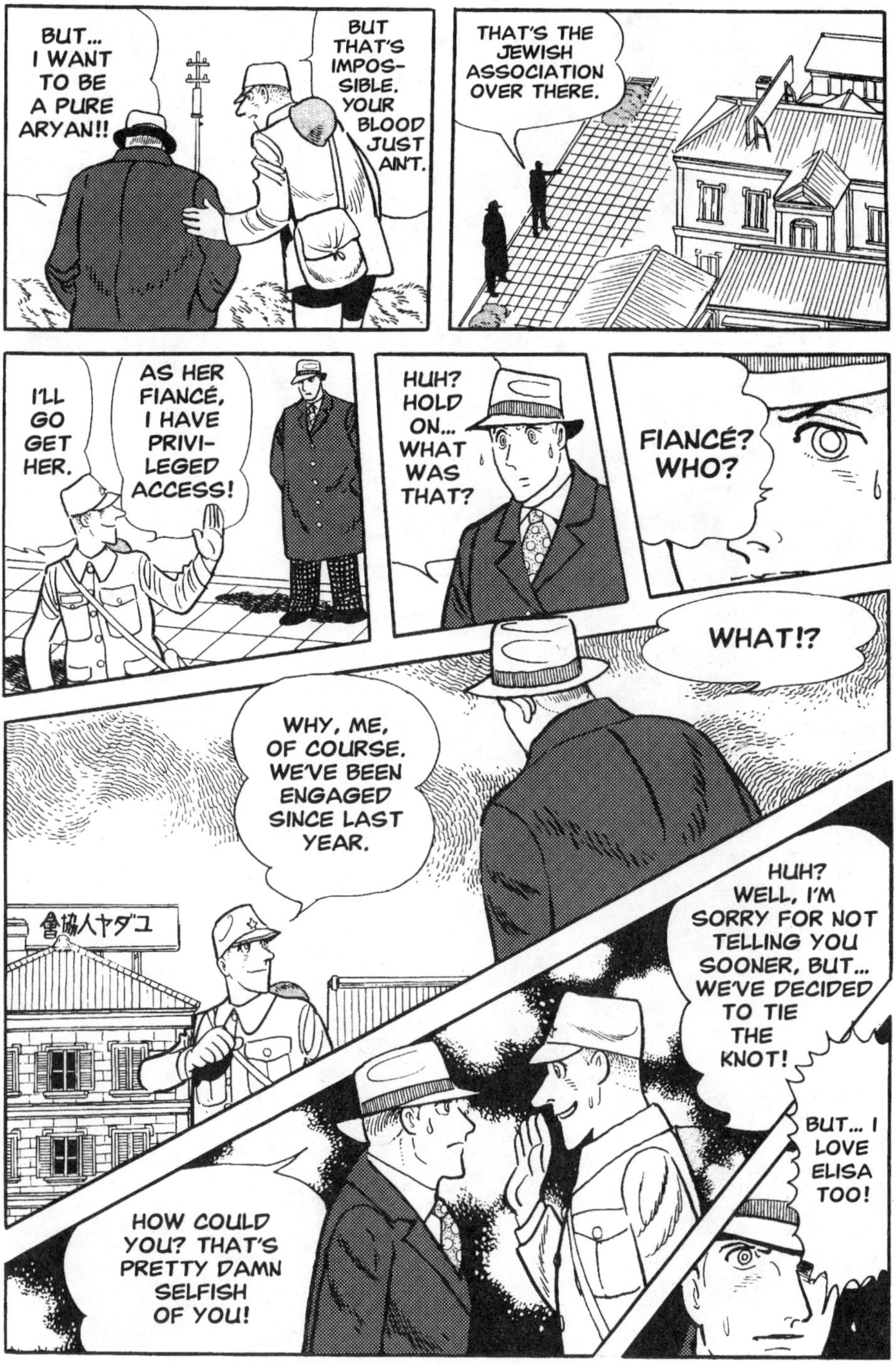
BUT... I WANT TO BE A PURE ARYAN!!
BUT THAT'S IMPOSSIBLE. YOUR BLOOD JUST AIN'T.
THAT'S THE JEWISH ASSOCIATION OVER THERE.
I'LL GO GET HER.
AS HER FIANCÉ, I HAVE PRIVILEGED ACCESS!
HUH? HOLD ON... WHAT WAS THAT?
FIANCÉ? WHO?
WHAT!?
WHY, ME, OF COURSE. WE'VE BEEN ENGAGED SINCE LAST YEAR.
ユダヤ人協會
HUH? WELL, I'M SORRY FOR NOT TELLING YOU SOONER, BUT... WE'VE DECIDED TO TIE THE KNOT!
HOW COULD YOU? THAT'S PRETTY DAMN SELFISH OF YOU!
BUT... I LOVE ELISA TOO!

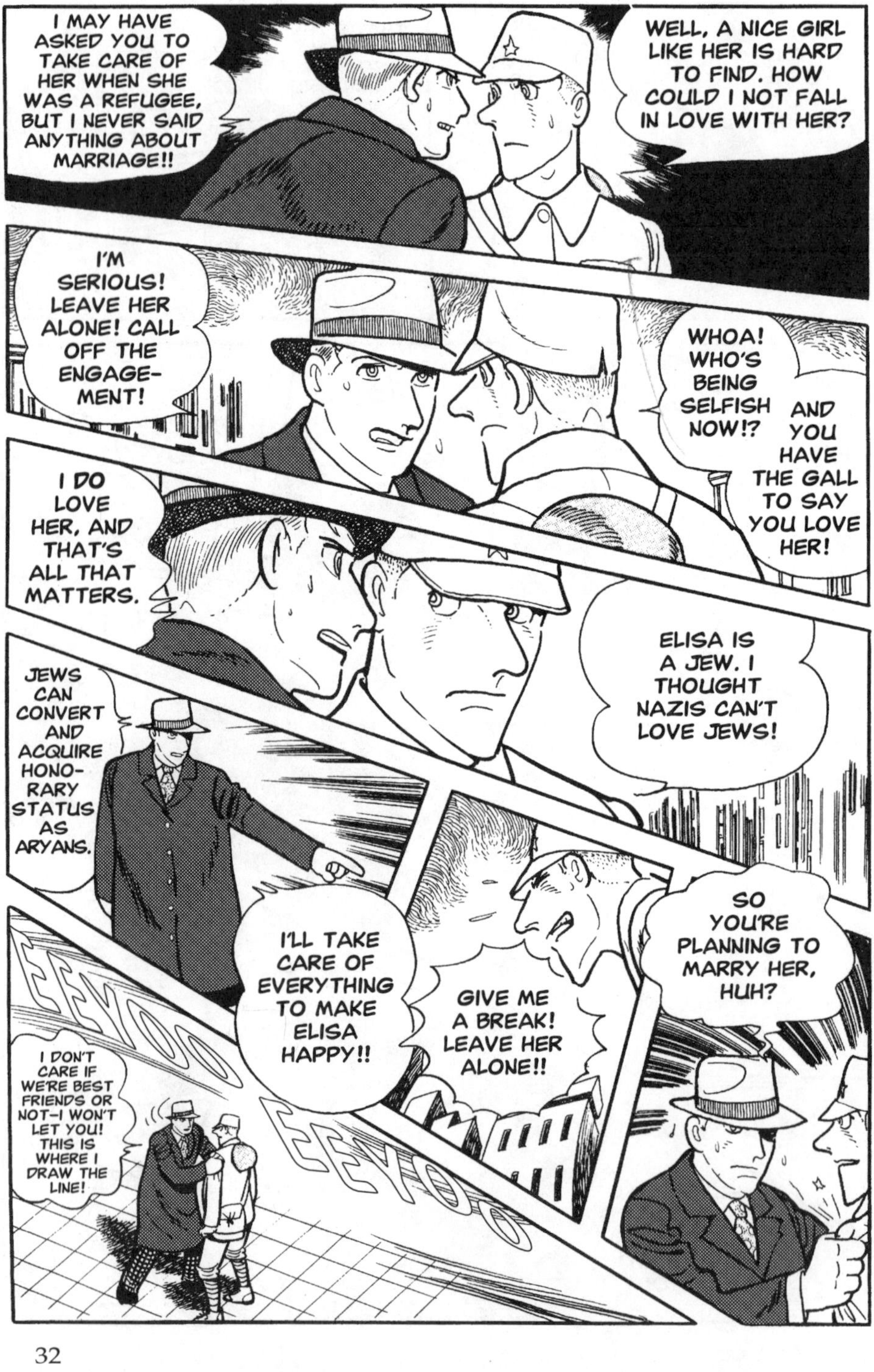
I MAY HAVE ASKED YOU TO TAKE CARE OF HER WHEN SHE WAS A REFUGEE, BUT I NEVER SAID ANYTHING ABOUT MARRIAGE!!
WELL, A NICE GIRL LIKE HER IS HARD TO FIND. HOW COULD I NOT FALL IN LOVE WITH HER?
I'M SERIOUS! LEAVE HER ALONE! CALL OFF THE ENGAGE-MENT!
WHOA! WHO'S BEING SELFISH NOW!?
AND YOU HAVE THE GALL TO SAY YOU LOVE HER!
I DO LOVE HER, AND THAT'S ALL THAT MATTERS.
ELISA IS A JEW. I THOUGHT NAZIS CAN'T LOVE JEWS!
JEWS CAN CONVERT AND ACQUIRE HONO-RARY STATUS AS ARYANS.
SO YOU'RE PLANNING TO MARRY HER, HUH?
I'LL TAKE CARE OF EVERYTHING TO MAKE ELISA HAPPY!!
GIVE ME A BREAK! LEAVE HER ALONE!!
EEYOOO
EEYOO O
I DON'T CARE IF WE'RE BEST FRIENDS OR NOT–I WON'T LET YOU! THIS IS WHERE I DRAW THE LINE!

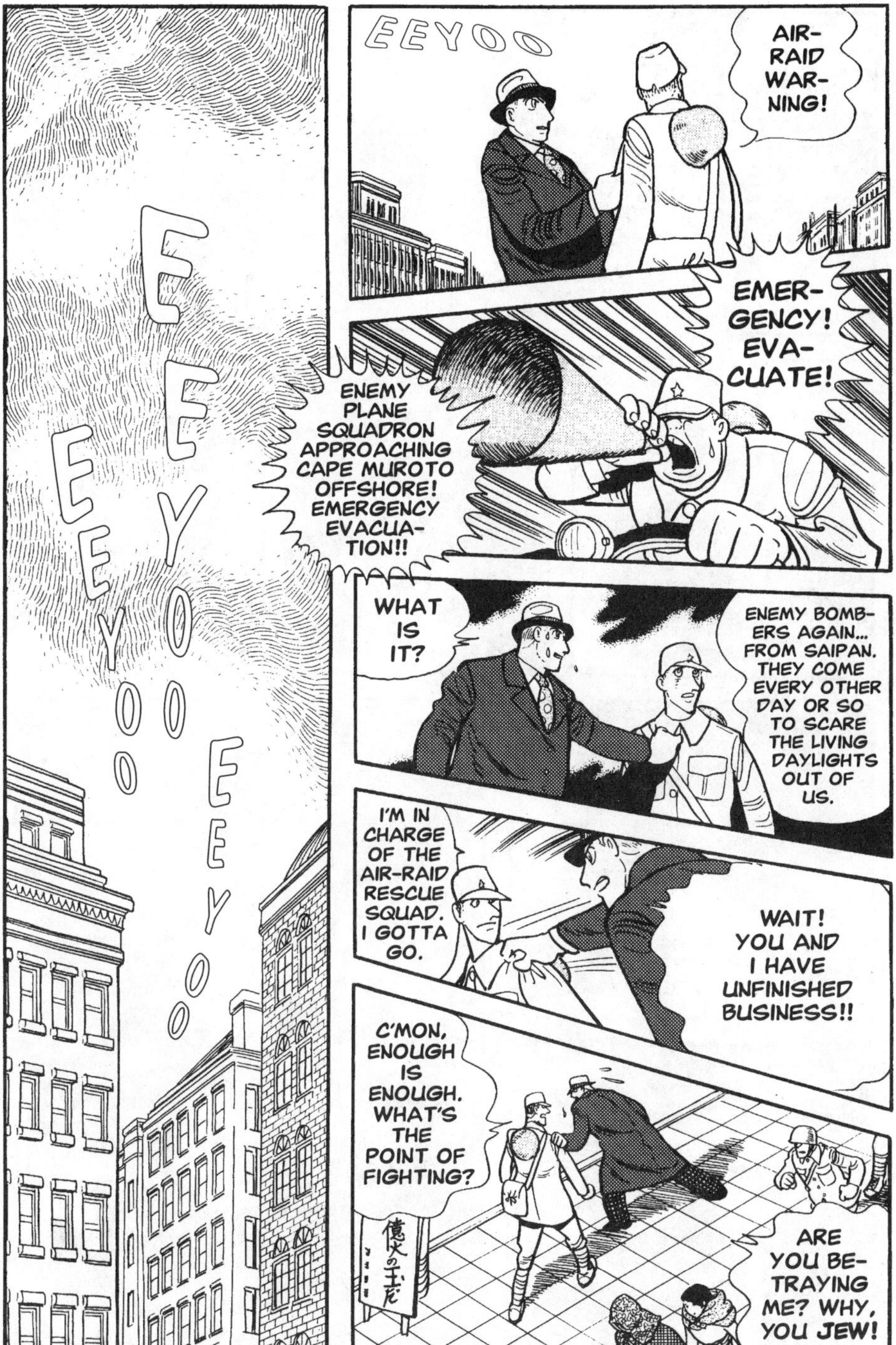
EEYOOO
EEYOO
EEYOO
EEYOO
AIR-RAID WAR-NING!
EMER-GENCY! EVA-CUATE!
ENEMY PLANE SQUADRON APPROACHING CAPE MUROTO OFFSHORE! EMERGENCY EVACUA-TION!!
WHAT IS IT?
ENEMY BOMB-ERS AGAIN... FROM SAIPAN. THEY COME EVERY OTHER DAY OR SO TO SCARE THE LIVING DAYLIGHTS OUT OF US.
I'M IN CHARGE OF THE AIR-RAID RESCUE SQUAD. I GOTTA GO.
WAIT! YOU AND I HAVE UNFINISHED BUSINESS!!
C'MON, ENOUGH IS ENOUGH. WHAT'S THE POINT OF FIGHTING?
億火の玉だ
ARE YOU BE-TRAYING ME? WHY, YOU JEW!

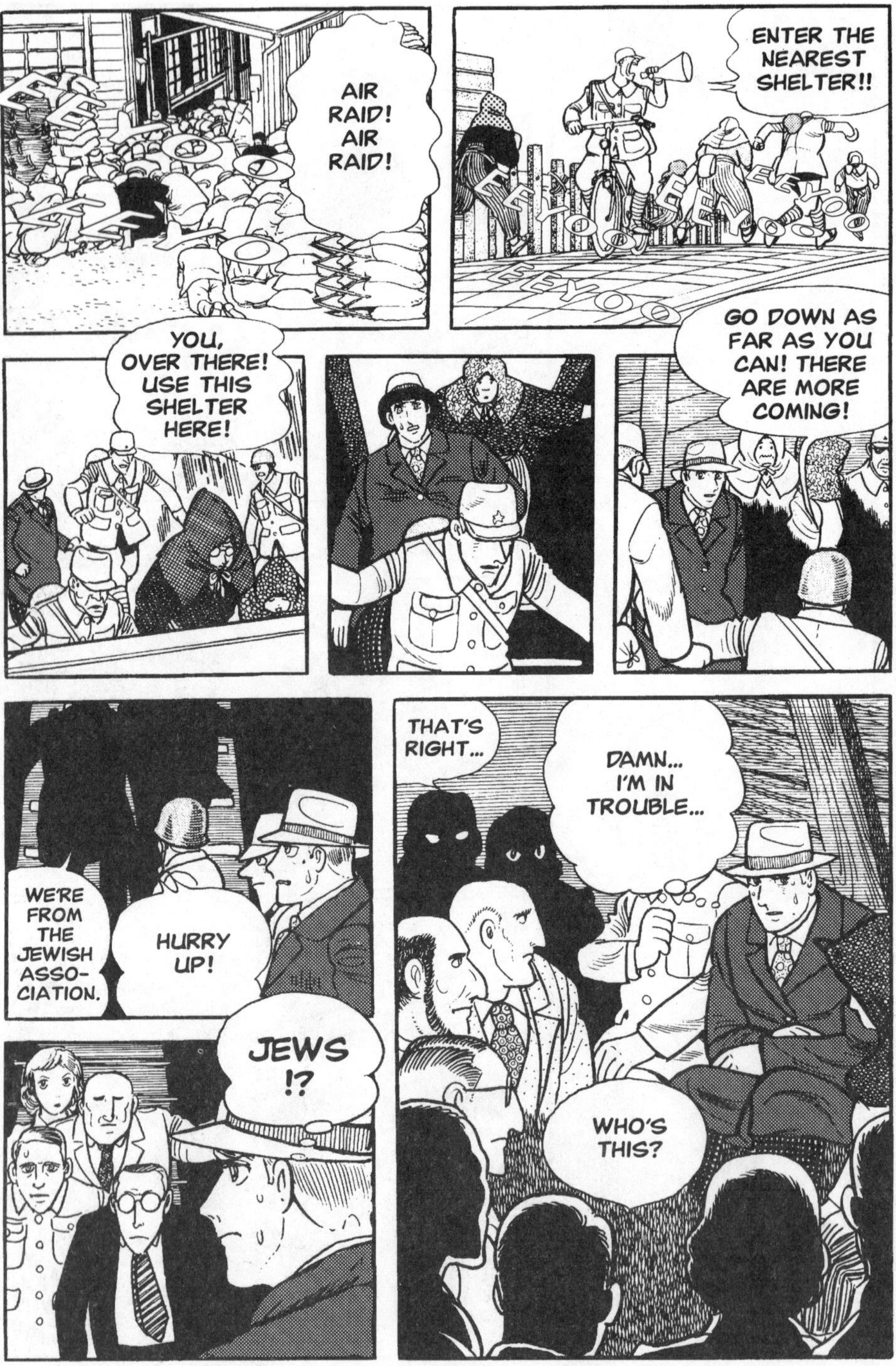
EEYOO
EEYOO
AIR RAID! AIR RAID!
ENTER THE NEAREST SHELTER!!
EEYOO
EEYOO
EEYOO
YOU, OVER THERE! USE THIS SHELTER HERE!
GO DOWN AS FAR AS YOU CAN! THERE ARE MORE COMING!
WE'RE FROM THE JEWISH ASSO-CIATION.
HURRY UP!
JEWS !?
THAT'S RIGHT...
DAMN... I'M IN TROUBLE...
WHO'S THIS?

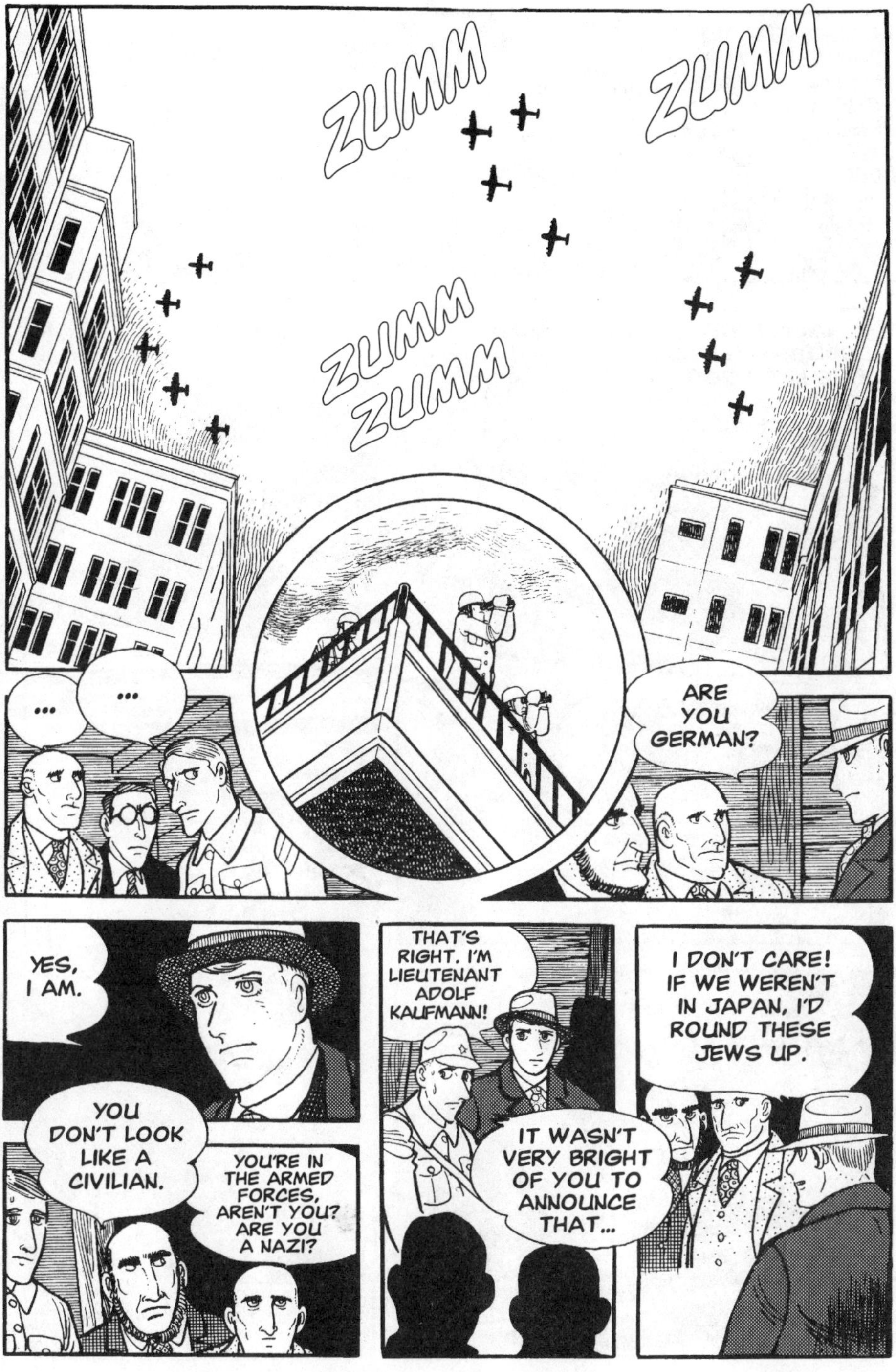
ZUMM
ZUMM
ZUMM
ZUMM
...
...
ARE YOU GERMAN?
YES, I AM.
YOU DON'T LOOK LIKE A CIVILIAN.
YOU'RE IN THE ARMED FORCES, AREN'T YOU? ARE YOU A NAZI?
THAT'S RIGHT. I'M LIEUTENANT ADOLF KAUFMANN!
IT WASN'T VERY BRIGHT OF YOU TO ANNOUNCE THAT...
I DON'T CARE! IF WE WEREN'T IN JAPAN, I'D ROUND THESE JEWS UP.

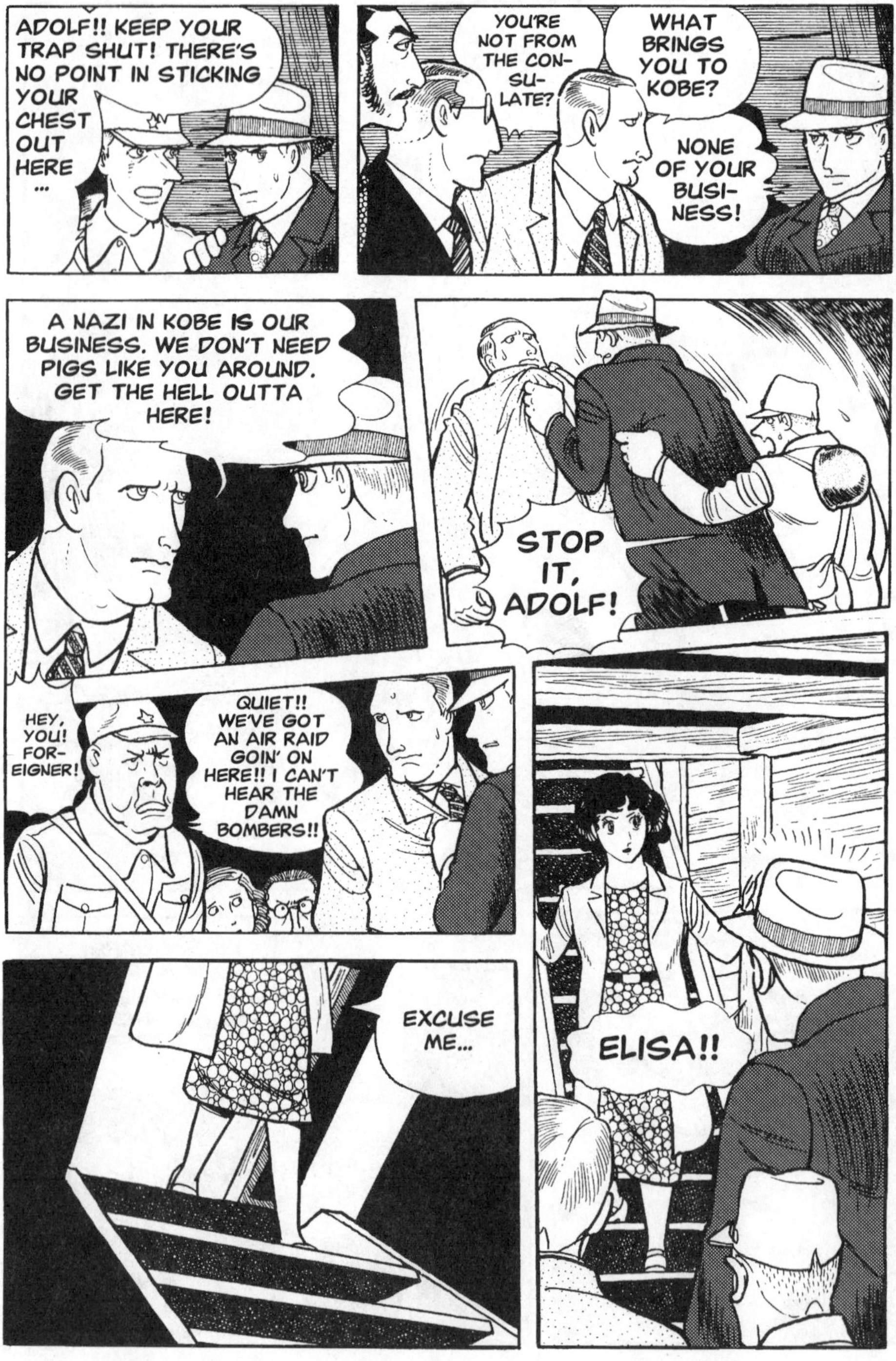
ADOLF!! KEEP YOUR TRAP SHUT! THERE'S NO POINT IN STICKING YOUR CHEST OUT HERE ...
YOU'RE NOT FROM THE CON-SU-LATE?
WHAT BRINGS YOU TO KOBE?
NONE OF YOUR BUSI-NESS!
A NAZI IN KOBE IS OUR BUSINESS. WE DON'T NEED PIGS LIKE YOU AROUND. GET THE HELL OUTTA HERE!
STOP IT, ADOLF!
HEY, YOU! FOR-EIGNER!
QUIET!! WE'VE GOT AN AIR RAID GOIN' ON HERE!! I CAN'T HEAR THE DAMN BOMBERS!!
EXCUSE ME...
ELISA!!

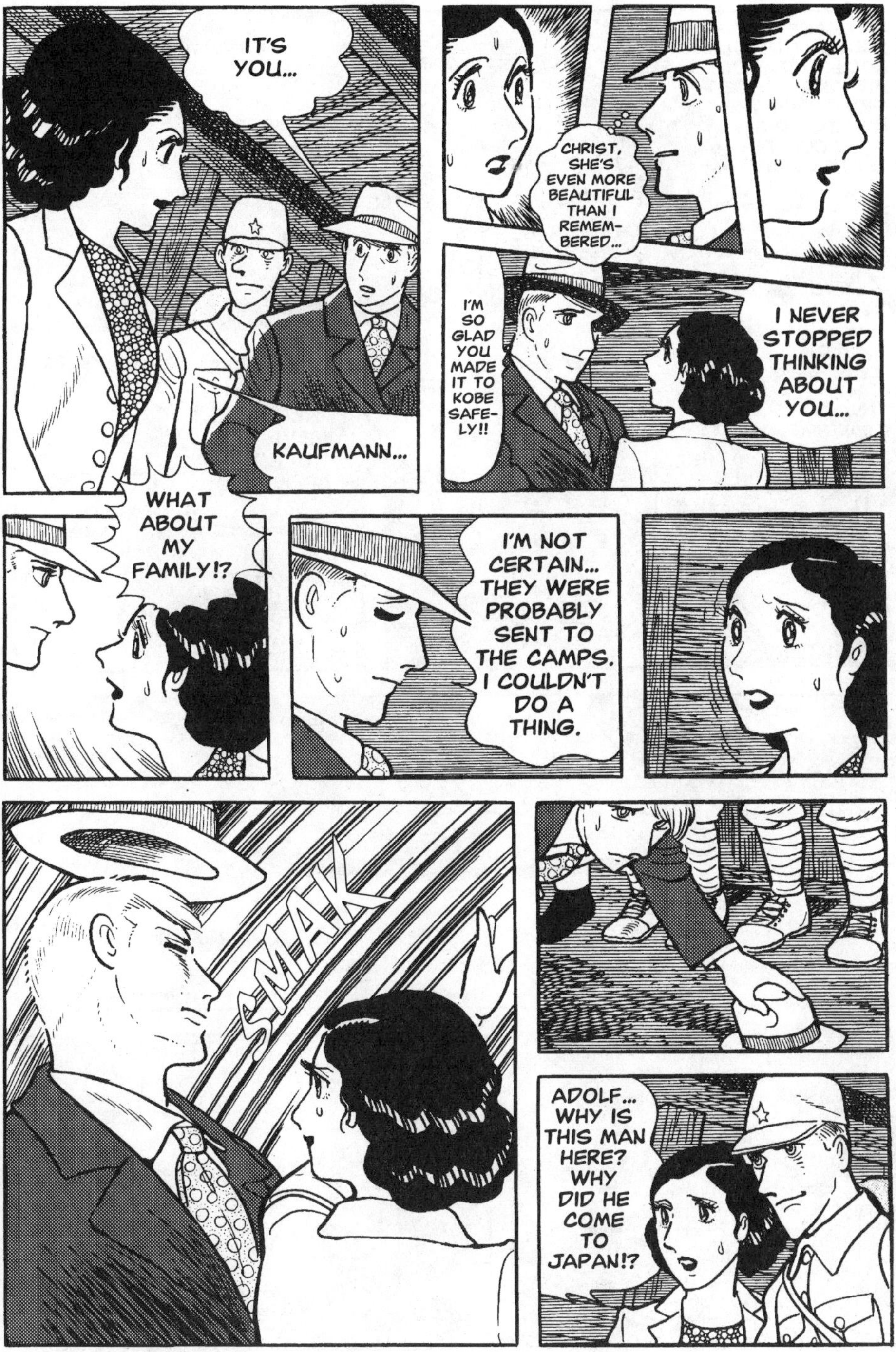
IT'S YOU...
KAUFMANN...
CHRIST, SHE'S EVEN MORE BEAUTIFUL THAN I REMEMBERED...
I'M SO GLAD YOU MADE IT TO KOBE SAFELY!!
I NEVER STOPPED THINKING ABOUT YOU...
WHAT ABOUT MY FAMILY!?
I'M NOT CERTAIN... THEY WERE PROBABLY SENT TO THE CAMPS. I COULDN'T DO A THING.
SMAK
ADOLF... WHY IS THIS MAN HERE? WHY DID HE COME TO JAPAN!?

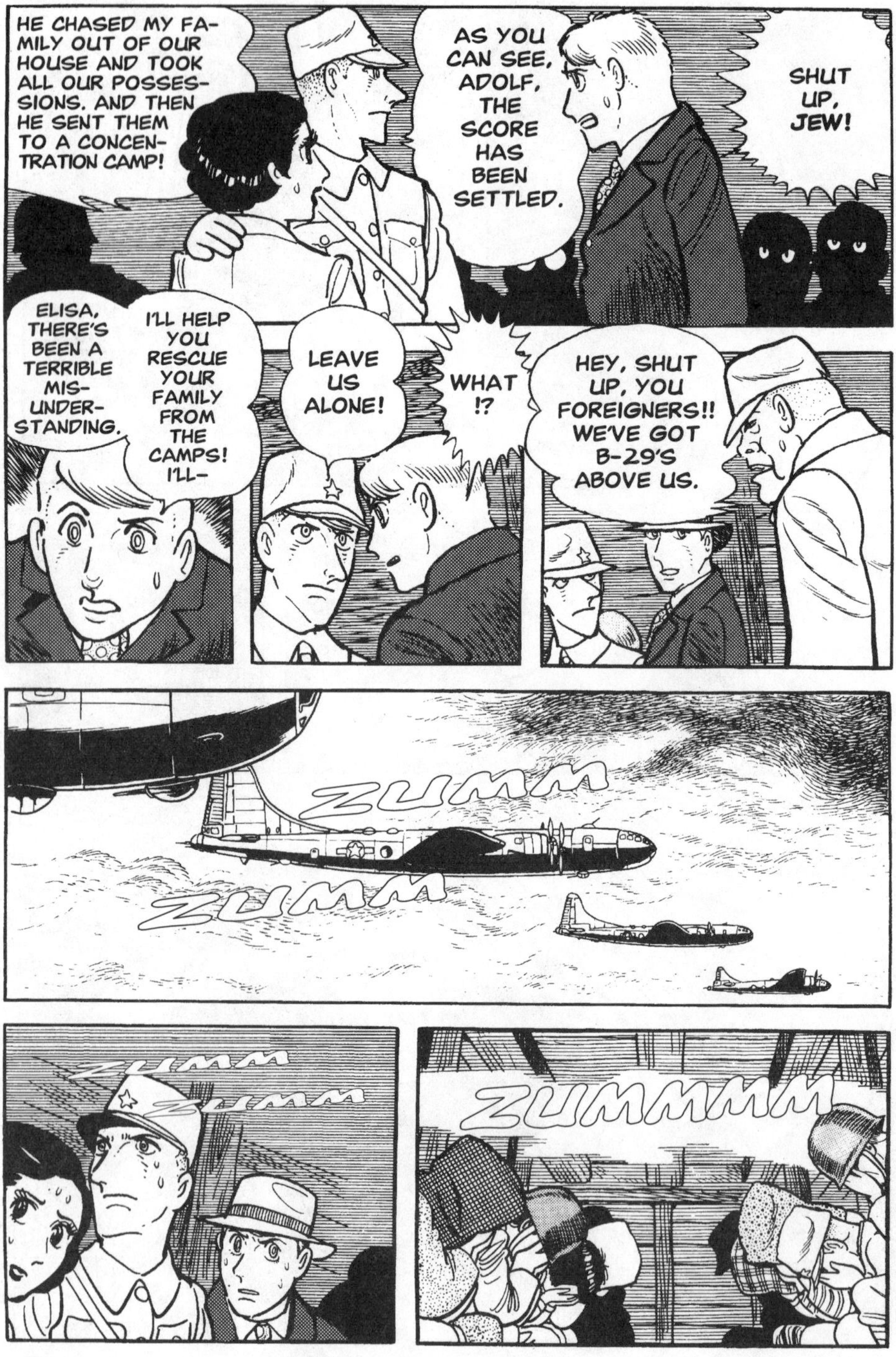
HE CHASED MY FAMILY OUT OF OUR HOUSE AND TOOK ALL OUR POSSESSIONS. AND THEN HE SENT THEM TO A CONCENTRATION CAMP!
AS YOU CAN SEE, ADOLF, THE SCORE HAS BEEN SETTLED.
SHUT UP, JEW!
ELISA, THERE'S BEEN A TERRIBLE MISUNDERSTANDING.
I'LL HELP YOU RESCUE YOUR FAMILY FROM THE CAMPS! I'LL-
LEAVE US ALONE!
WHAT!?
HEY, SHUT UP, YOU FOREIGNERS!! WE'VE GOT B-29'S ABOVE US.
ZUMM
ZUMM
ZUMM
ZUMM
ZUMMMMM

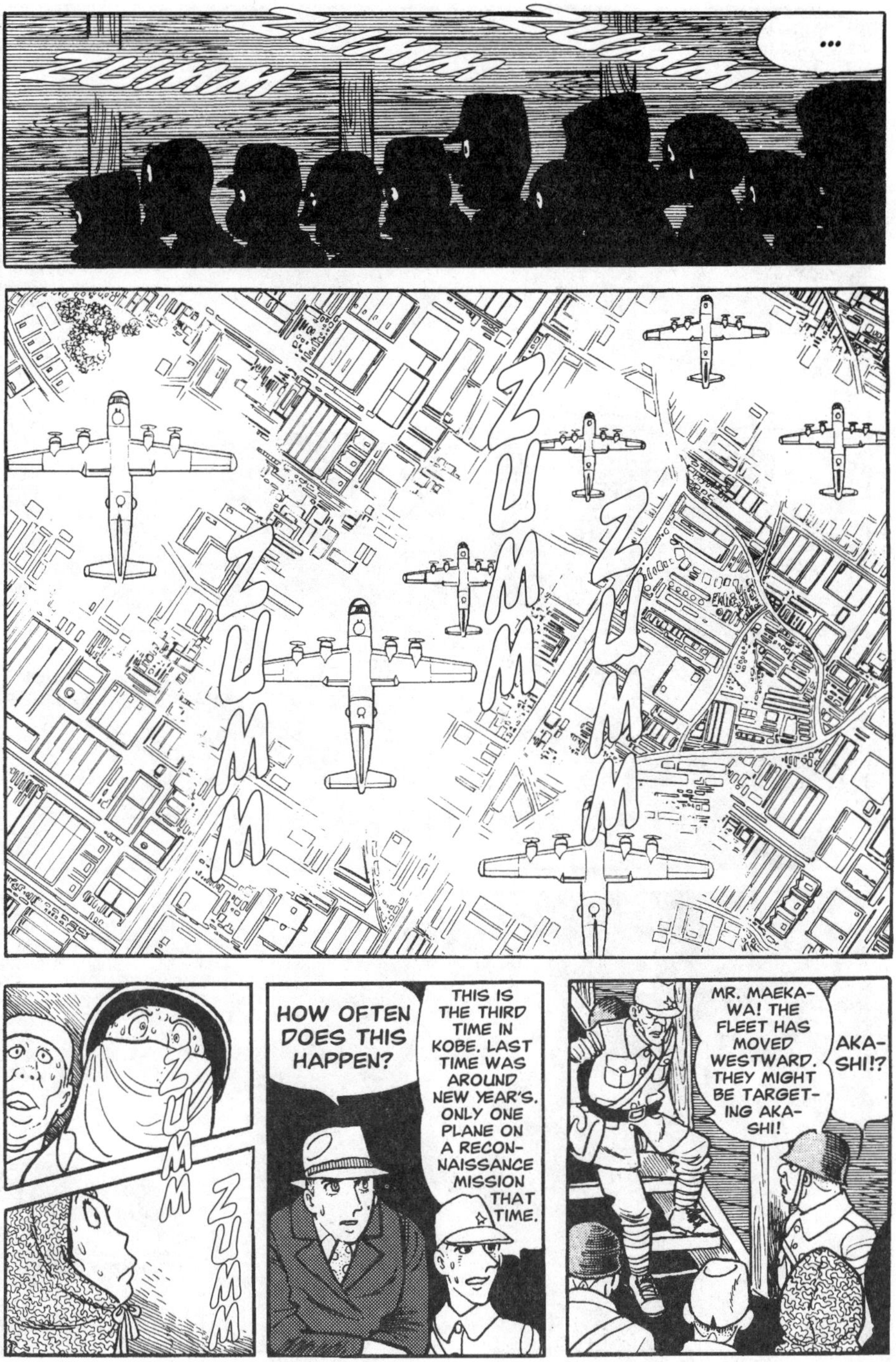
ZUMM
ZUMM
ZUMM
...
ZUMM
ZUMM
ZUMM
ZUMM
ZUMM
HOW OFTEN DOES THIS HAPPEN?
THIS IS THE THIRD TIME IN KOBE. LAST TIME WAS AROUND NEW YEAR'S. ONLY ONE PLANE ON A RECONNAISSANCE MISSION THAT TIME.
MR. MAEKAWA! THE FLEET HAS MOVED WESTWARD. THEY MIGHT BE TARGETING AKASHI!
AKASHI!?

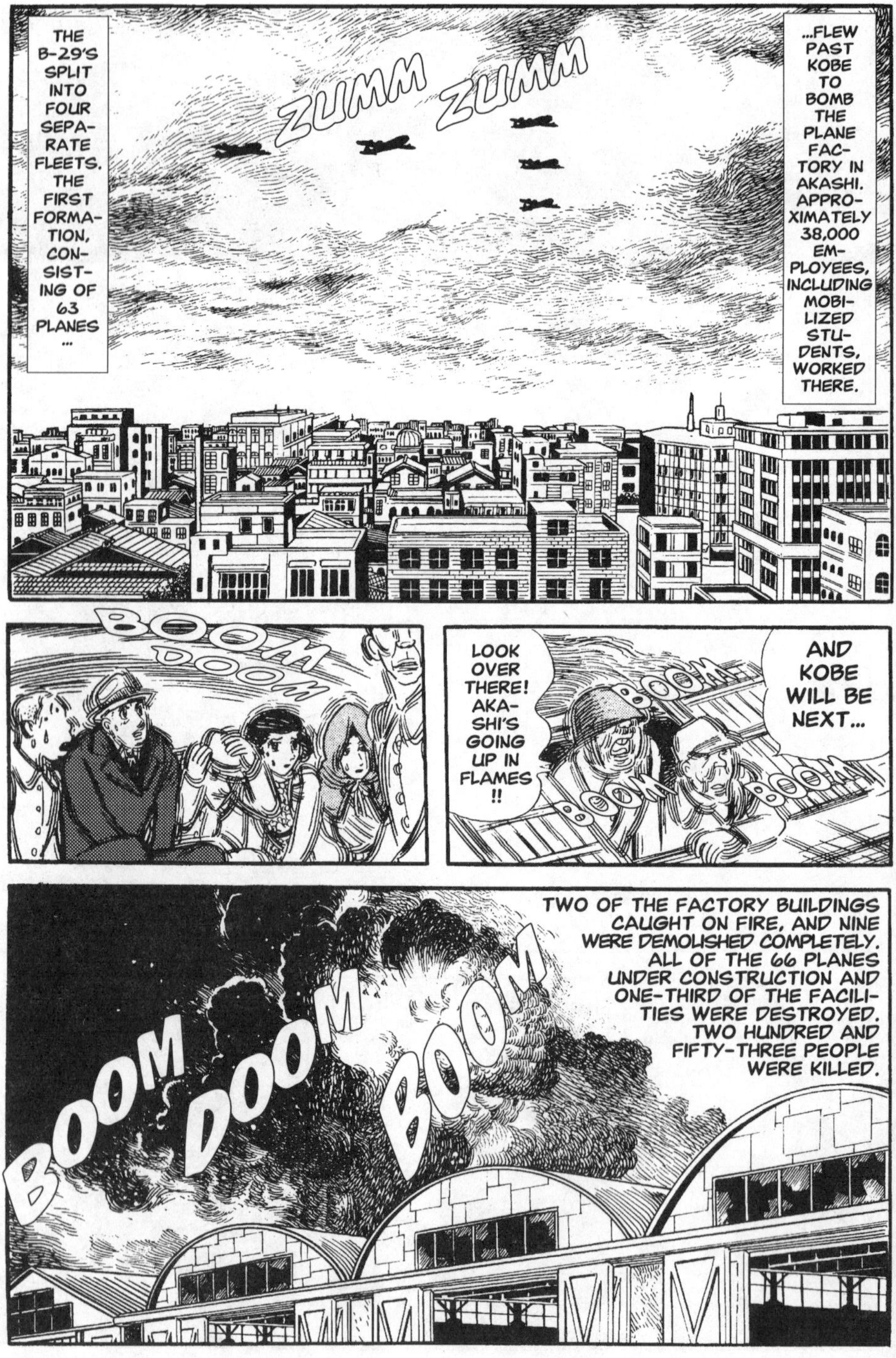
THE B-29'S SPLIT INTO FOUR SEPARATE FLEETS. THE FIRST FORMATION, CONSISTING OF 63 PLANES ...
ZUMM ZUMM
...FLEW PAST KOBE TO BOMB THE PLANE FACTORY IN AKASHI. APPROXIMATELY 38,000 EMPLOYEES, INCLUDING MOBILIZED STUDENTS, WORKED THERE.
BOOM DOOM
LOOK OVER THERE! AKASHI'S GOING UP IN FLAMES !!
BOOM
AND KOBE WILL BE NEXT...
BOOM BOOM
BOOM DOOM BOOM
TWO OF THE FACTORY BUILDINGS CAUGHT ON FIRE, AND NINE WERE DEMOLISHED COMPLETELY. ALL OF THE 66 PLANES UNDER CONSTRUCTION AND ONE-THIRD OF THE FACILITIES WERE DESTROYED. TWO HUNDRED AND FIFTY-THREE PEOPLE WERE KILLED.

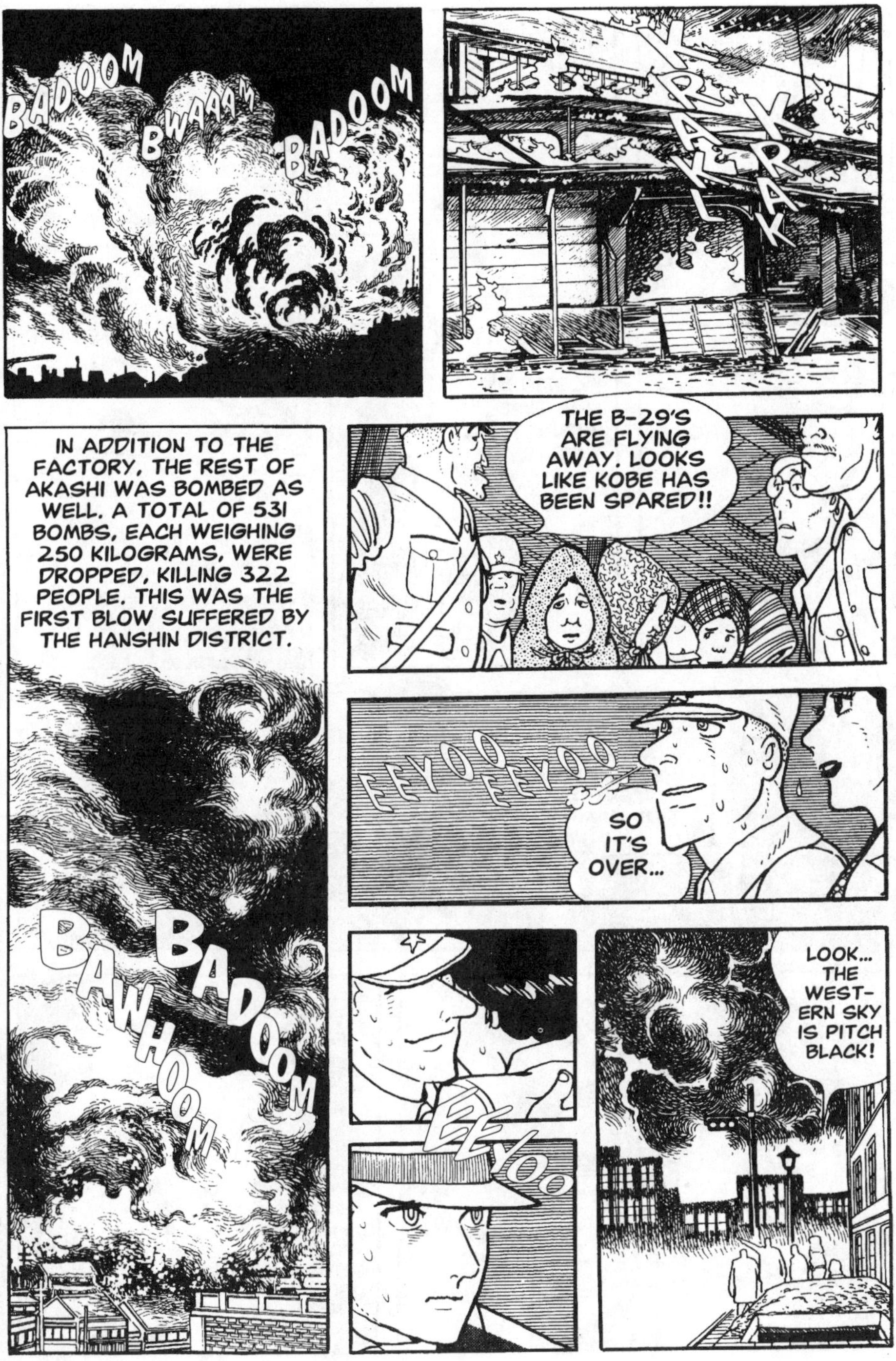
BADOOM
BWAAAM
BADOOM
KRAKLK
KRAK
IN ADDITION TO THE FACTORY, THE REST OF AKASHI WAS BOMBED AS WELL. A TOTAL OF 531 BOMBS, EACH WEIGHING 250 KILOGRAMS, WERE DROPPED, KILLING 322 PEOPLE. THIS WAS THE FIRST BLOW SUFFERED BY THE HANSHIN DISTRICT.
BADOOM
BAWHOOM
THE B-29'S ARE FLYING AWAY. LOOKS LIKE KOBE HAS BEEN SPARED!!
EEYOO EEYOO
SO IT'S OVER...
EEYOO
LOOK... THE WEST-ERN SKY IS PITCH BLACK!

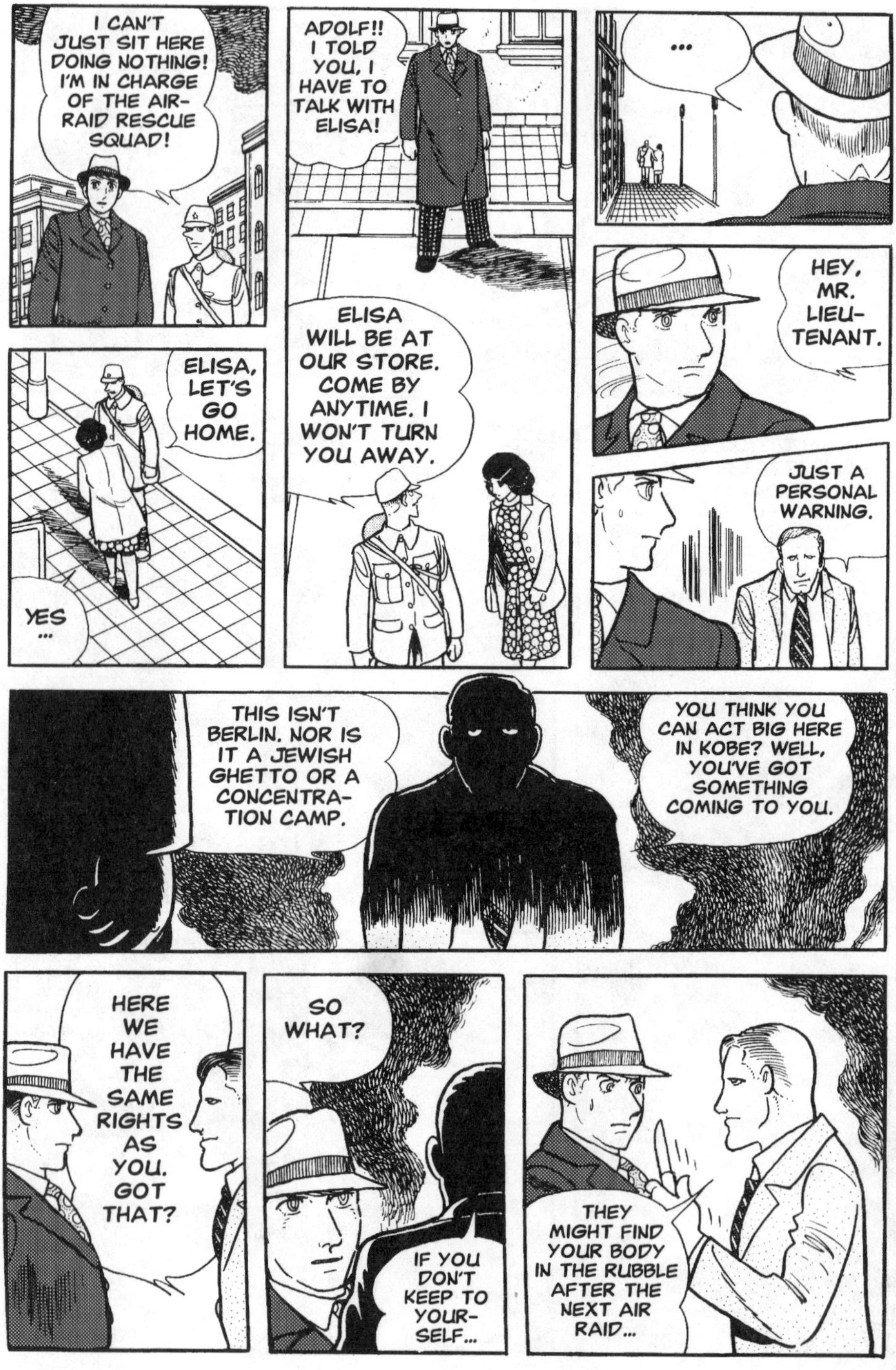
I CAN'T JUST SIT HERE DOING NOTHING! I'M IN CHARGE OF THE AIR-RAID RESCUE SQUAD!
ELISA, LET'S GO HOME.
YES ...
ADOLF!! I TOLD YOU, I HAVE TO TALK WITH ELISA!
ELISA WILL BE AT OUR STORE. COME BY ANYTIME. I WON'T TURN YOU AWAY.
...
HEY, MR. LIEU-TENANT.
JUST A PERSONAL WARNING.
THIS ISN'T BERLIN. NOR IS IT A JEWISH GHETTO OR A CONCENTRA-TION CAMP.
YOU THINK YOU CAN ACT BIG HERE IN KOBE? WELL, YOU'VE GOT SOMETHING COMING TO YOU.
HERE WE HAVE THE SAME RIGHTS AS YOU. GOT THAT?
SO WHAT?
IF YOU DON'T KEEP TO YOUR-SELF...
THEY MIGHT FIND YOUR BODY IN THE RUBBLE AFTER THE NEXT AIR RAID...

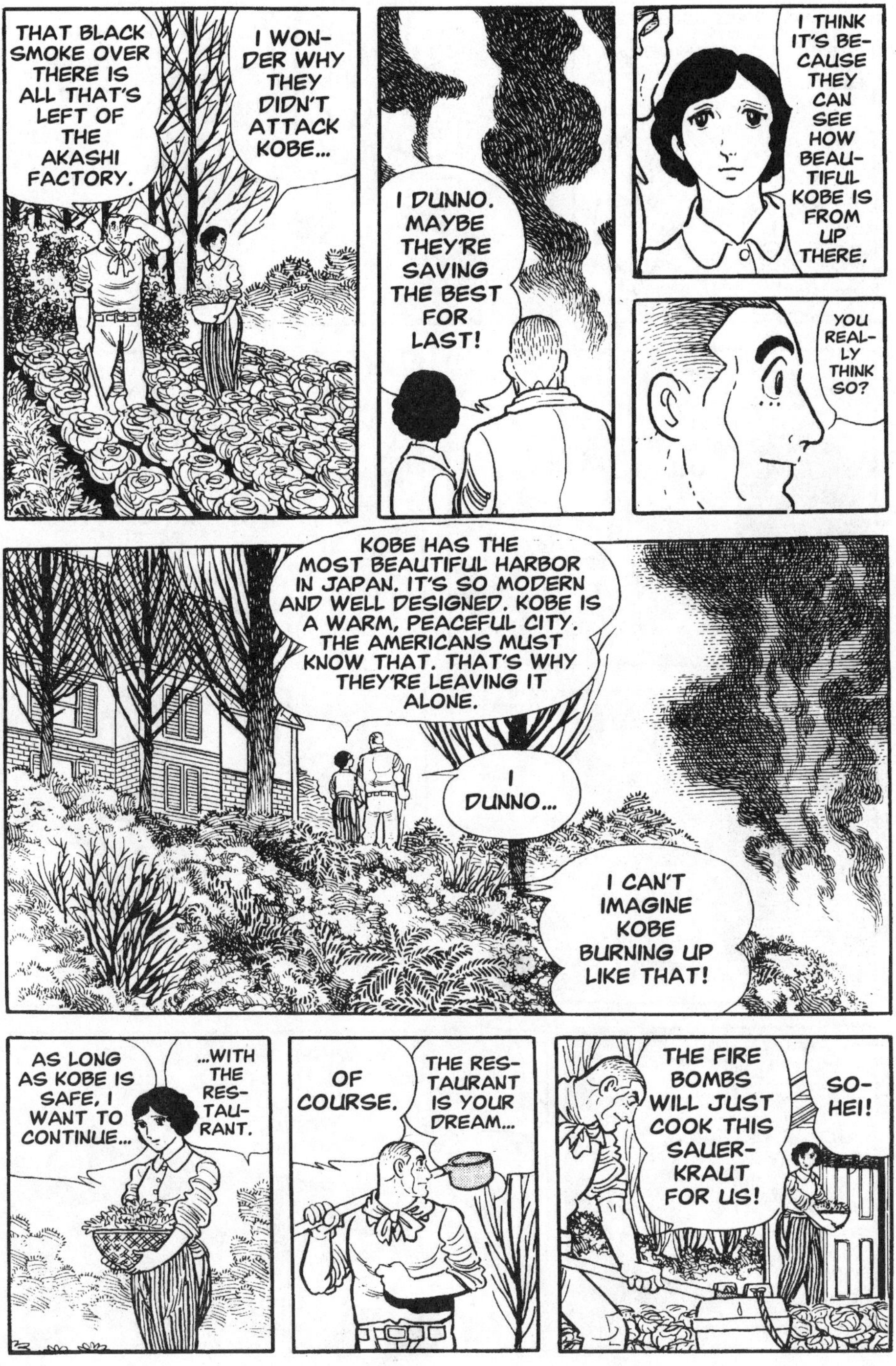
THAT BLACK SMOKE OVER THERE IS ALL THAT'S LEFT OF THE AKASHI FACTORY.
I WONDER WHY THEY DIDN'T ATTACK KOBE...
I DUNNO. MAYBE THEY'RE SAVING THE BEST FOR LAST!
I THINK IT'S BECAUSE THEY CAN SEE HOW BEAUTIFUL KOBE IS FROM UP THERE.
YOU REALLY THINK SO?
KOBE HAS THE MOST BEAUTIFUL HARBOR IN JAPAN. IT'S SO MODERN AND WELL DESIGNED. KOBE IS A WARM, PEACEFUL CITY. THE AMERICANS MUST KNOW THAT. THAT'S WHY THEY'RE LEAVING IT ALONE.
I DUNNO...
I CAN'T IMAGINE KOBE BURNING UP LIKE THAT!
AS LONG AS KOBE IS SAFE, I WANT TO CONTINUE...
...WITH THE RESTAURANT.
OF COURSE.
THE RESTAURANT IS YOUR DREAM...
THE FIRE BOMBS WILL JUST COOK THIS SAUERKRAUT FOR US!
SO-HEI!

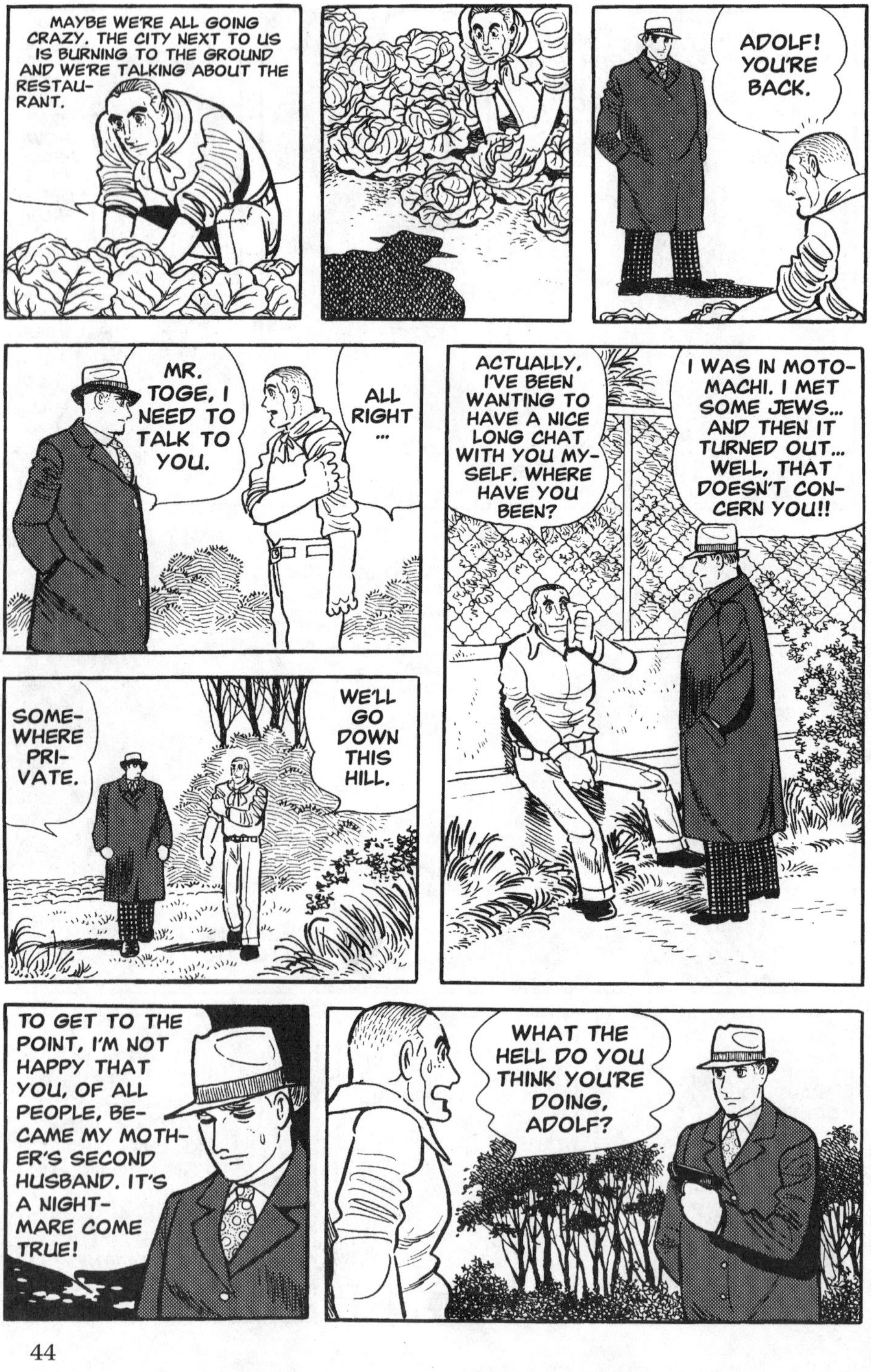
MAYBE WE'RE ALL GOING CRAZY. THE CITY NEXT TO US IS BURNING TO THE GROUND AND WE'RE TALKING ABOUT THE RESTAU-RANT.
ADOLF! YOU'RE BACK.
MR. TOGE, I NEED TO TALK TO YOU.
ALL RIGHT ...
SOME-WHERE PRI-VATE.
WE'LL GO DOWN THIS HILL.
ACTUALLY, I'VE BEEN WANTING TO HAVE A NICE LONG CHAT WITH YOU MY-SELF. WHERE HAVE YOU BEEN?
I WAS IN MOTO-MACHI. I MET SOME JEWS... AND THEN IT TURNED OUT... WELL, THAT DOESN'T CON-CERN YOU!!
TO GET TO THE POINT, I'M NOT HAPPY THAT YOU, OF ALL PEOPLE, BE-CAME MY MOTH-ER'S SECOND HUSBAND. IT'S A NIGHT-MARE COME TRUE!
WHAT THE HELL DO YOU THINK YOU'RE DOING, ADOLF?

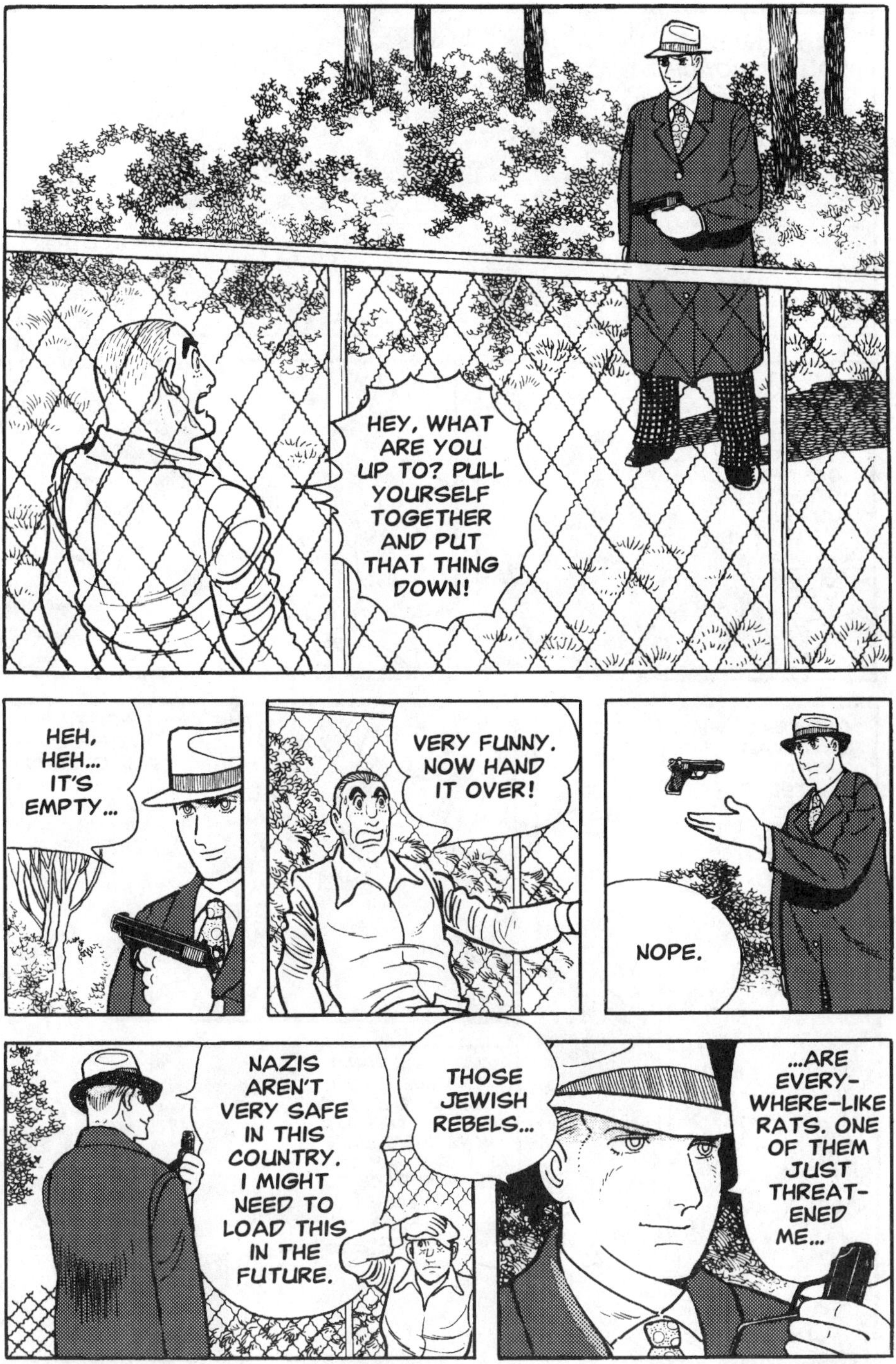
HEY, WHAT ARE YOU UP TO? PULL YOURSELF TOGETHER AND PUT THAT THING DOWN!
HEH, HEH... IT'S EMPTY...
VERY FUNNY. NOW HAND IT OVER!
NOPE.
NAZIS AREN'T VERY SAFE IN THIS COUNTRY. I MIGHT NEED TO LOAD THIS IN THE FUTURE.
THOSE JEWISH REBELS...
...ARE EVERY-WHERE—LIKE RATS. ONE OF THEM JUST THREAT-ENED ME...

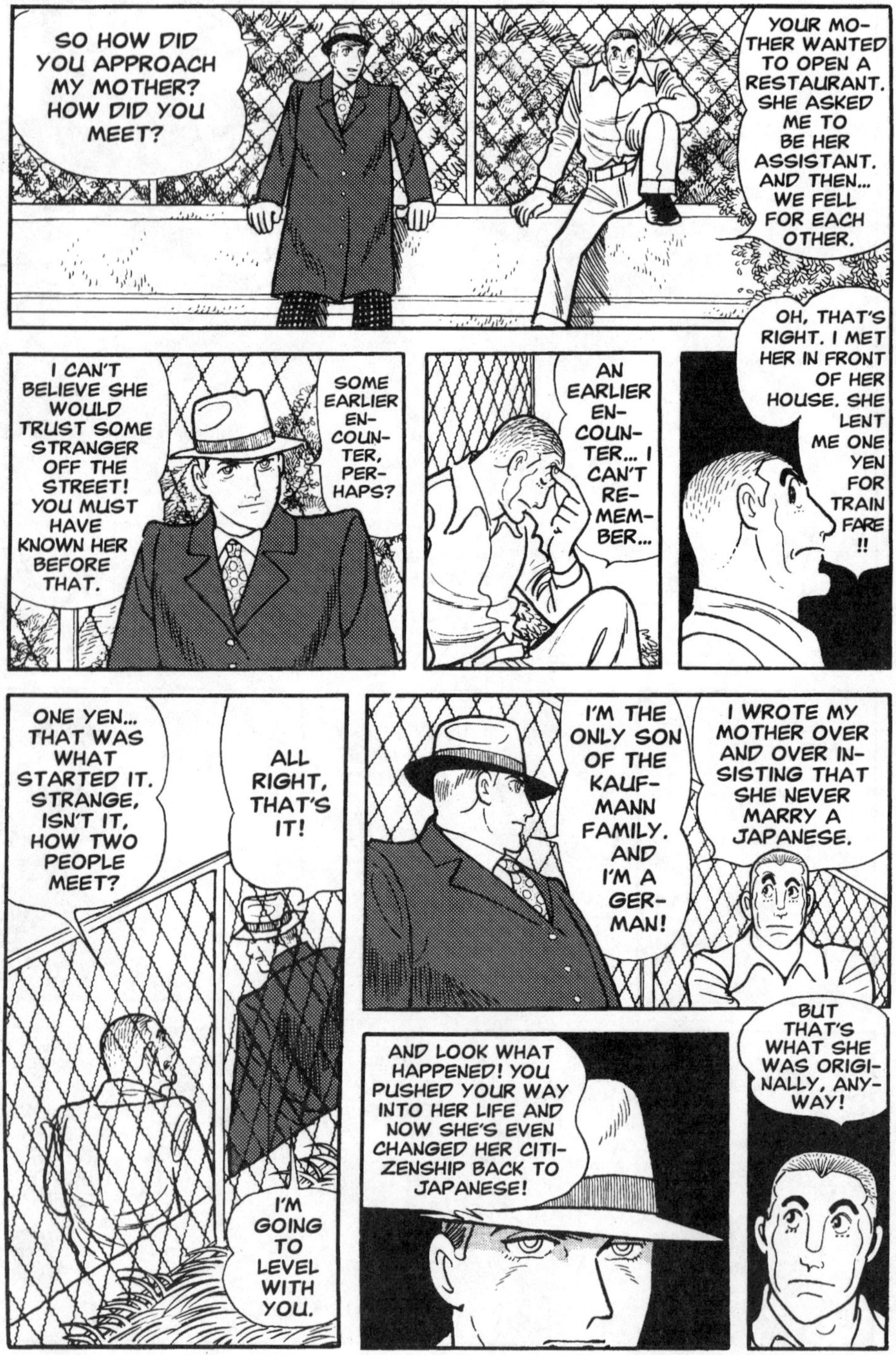
SO HOW DID YOU APPROACH MY MOTHER? HOW DID YOU MEET?
YOUR MOTHER WANTED TO OPEN A RESTAURANT. SHE ASKED ME TO BE HER ASSISTANT. AND THEN... WE FELL FOR EACH OTHER.
I CAN'T BELIEVE SHE WOULD TRUST SOME STRANGER OFF THE STREET! YOU MUST HAVE KNOWN HER BEFORE THAT.
SOME EARLIER ENCOUNTER, PERHAPS?
AN EARLIER ENCOUNTER... I CAN'T REMEMBER...
OH, THAT'S RIGHT. I MET HER IN FRONT OF HER HOUSE. SHE LENT ME ONE YEN FOR TRAIN FARE!!
ONE YEN... THAT WAS WHAT STARTED IT. STRANGE, ISN'T IT, HOW TWO PEOPLE MEET?
ALL RIGHT, THAT'S IT!
I'M GOING TO LEVEL WITH YOU.
I'M THE ONLY SON OF THE KAUFMANN FAMILY. AND I'M A GERMAN!
I WROTE MY MOTHER OVER AND OVER INSISTING THAT SHE NEVER MARRY A JAPANESE.
AND LOOK WHAT HAPPENED! YOU PUSHED YOUR WAY INTO HER LIFE AND NOW SHE'S EVEN CHANGED HER CITIZENSHIP BACK TO JAPANESE!
BUT THAT'S WHAT SHE WAS ORIGINALLY, ANYWAY!

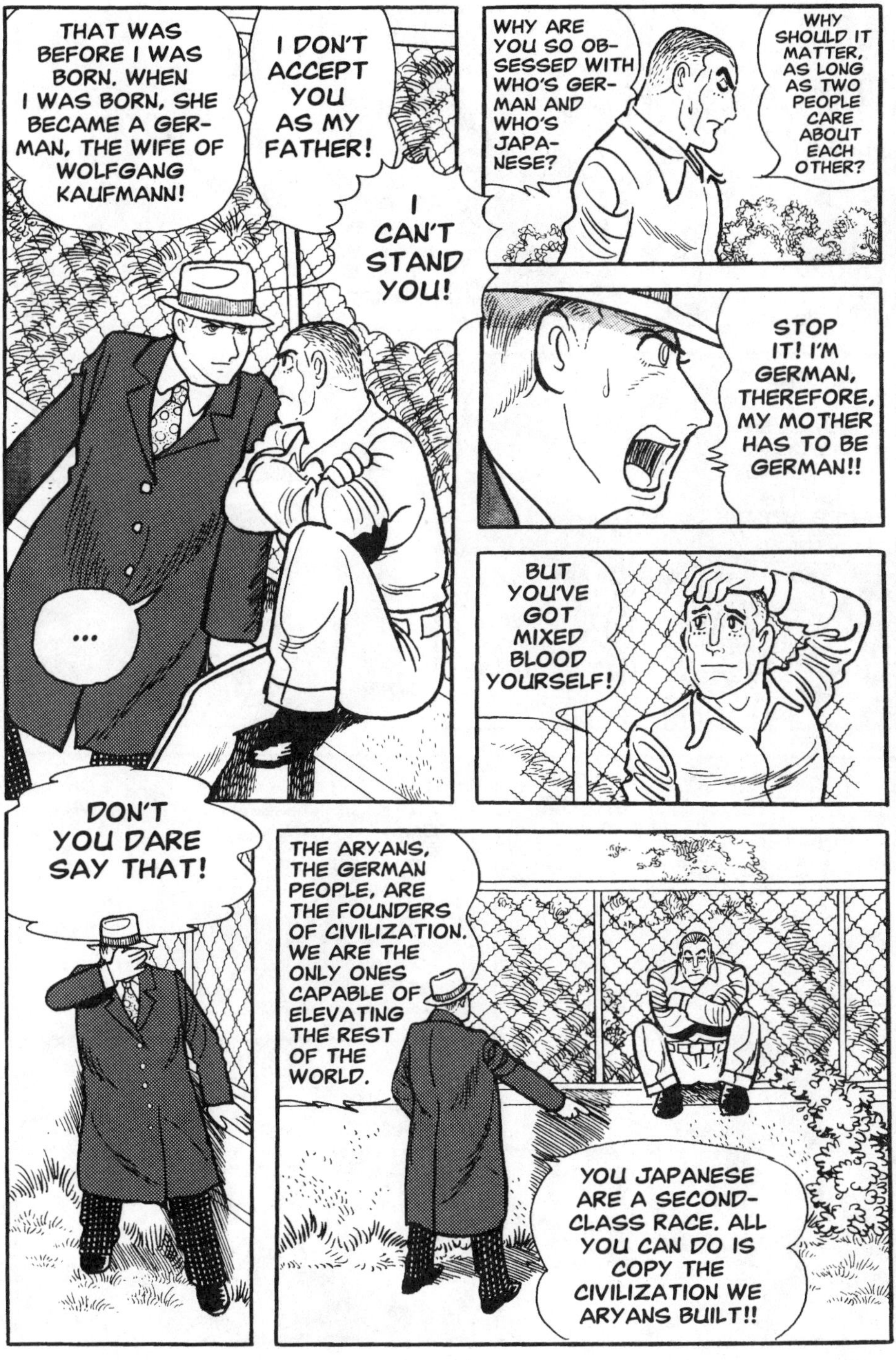
THAT WAS BEFORE I WAS BORN. WHEN I WAS BORN, SHE BECAME A GERMAN, THE WIFE OF WOLFGANG KAUFMANN!
I DON'T ACCEPT YOU AS MY FATHER!
I CAN'T STAND YOU!
...
WHY ARE YOU SO OBSESSED WITH WHO'S GERMAN AND WHO'S JAPANESE?
WHY SHOULD IT MATTER, AS LONG AS TWO PEOPLE CARE ABOUT EACH OTHER?
STOP IT! I'M GERMAN, THEREFORE, MY MOTHER HAS TO BE GERMAN!!
BUT YOU'VE GOT MIXED BLOOD YOURSELF!
DON'T YOU DARE SAY THAT!
THE ARYANS, THE GERMAN PEOPLE, ARE THE FOUNDERS OF CIVILIZATION. WE ARE THE ONLY ONES CAPABLE OF ELEVATING THE REST OF THE WORLD.
YOU JAPANESE ARE A SECOND-CLASS RACE. ALL YOU CAN DO IS COPY THE CIVILIZATION WE ARYANS BUILT!!

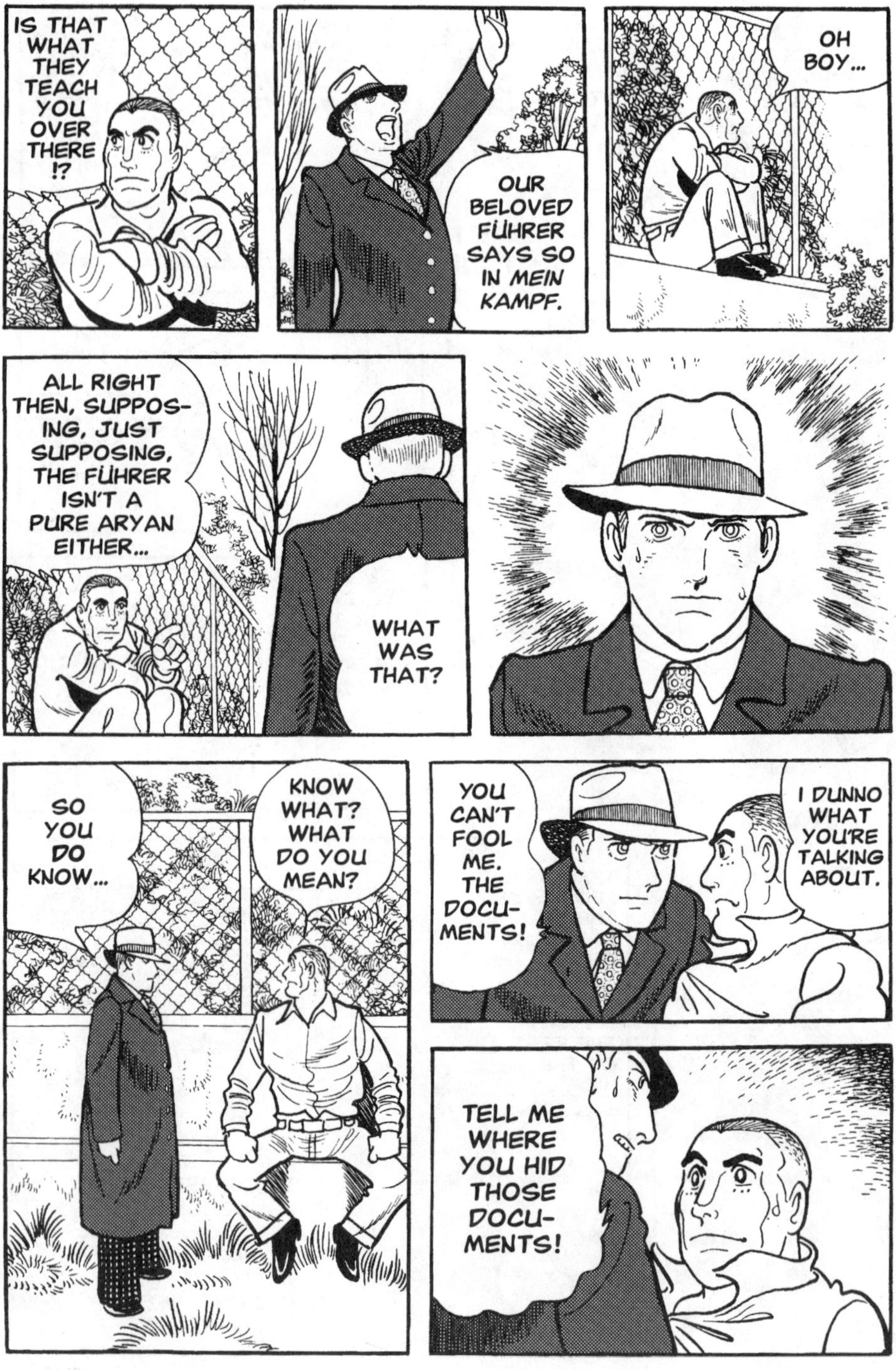
IS THAT WHAT THEY TEACH YOU OVER THERE!?
OUR BELOVED FÜHRER SAYS SO IN *MEIN KAMPF*.
OH BOY...
ALL RIGHT THEN, SUPPOSING, JUST SUPPOSING, THE FÜHRER ISN'T A PURE ARYAN EITHER...
WHAT WAS THAT?
SO YOU DO KNOW...
KNOW WHAT? WHAT DO YOU MEAN?
YOU CAN'T FOOL ME. THE DOCUMENTS!
I DUNNO WHAT YOU'RE TALKING ABOUT.
TELL ME WHERE YOU HID THOSE DOCUMENTS!

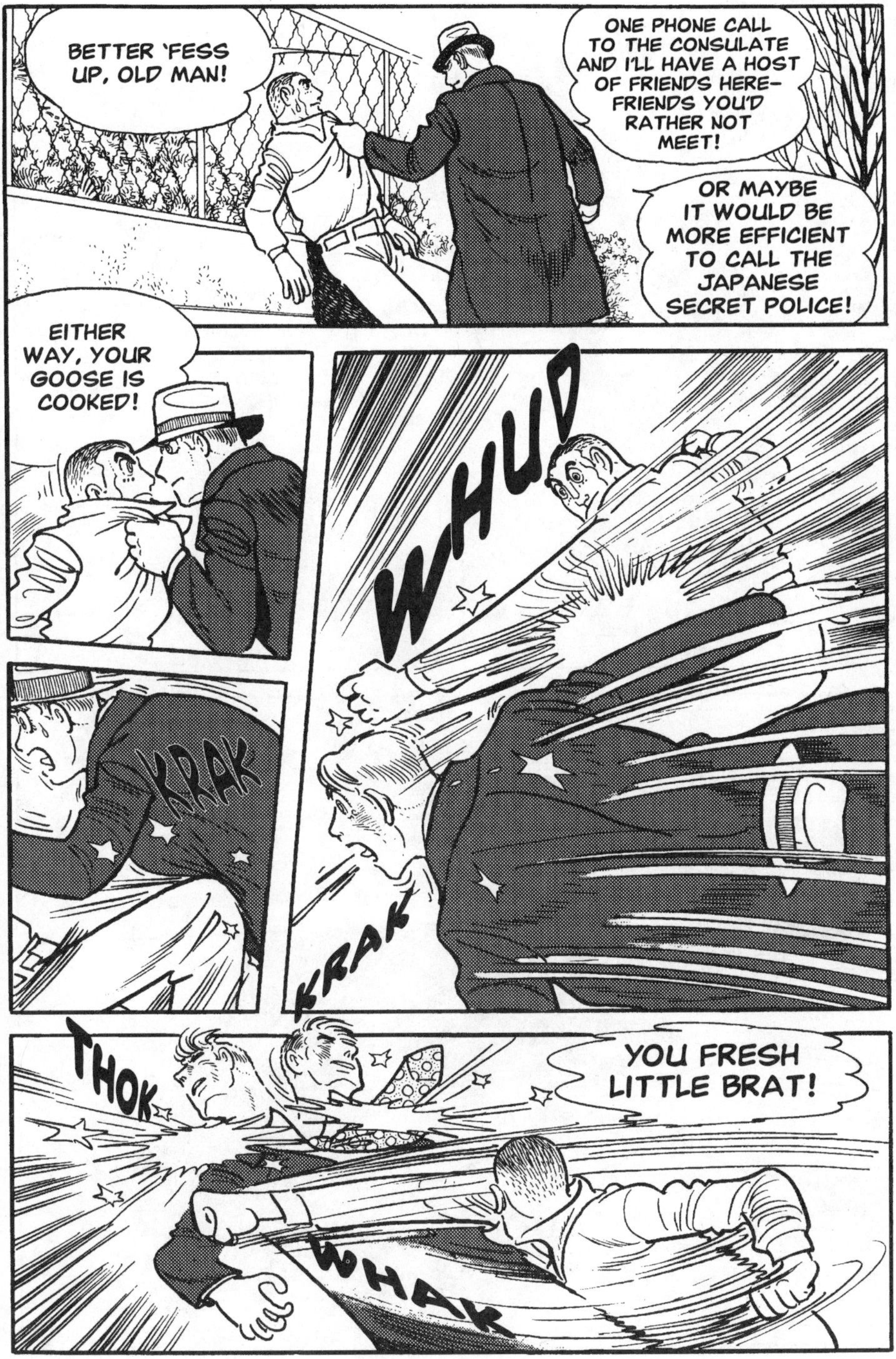
BETTER 'FESS UP, OLD MAN!
ONE PHONE CALL TO THE CONSULATE AND I'LL HAVE A HOST OF FRIENDS HERE– FRIENDS YOU'D RATHER NOT MEET!
OR MAYBE IT WOULD BE MORE EFFICIENT TO CALL THE JAPANESE SECRET POLICE!
EITHER WAY, YOUR GOOSE IS COOKED!
WHUD
KRAK
KRAK
THOK
YOU FRESH LITTLE BRAT!
WHAK

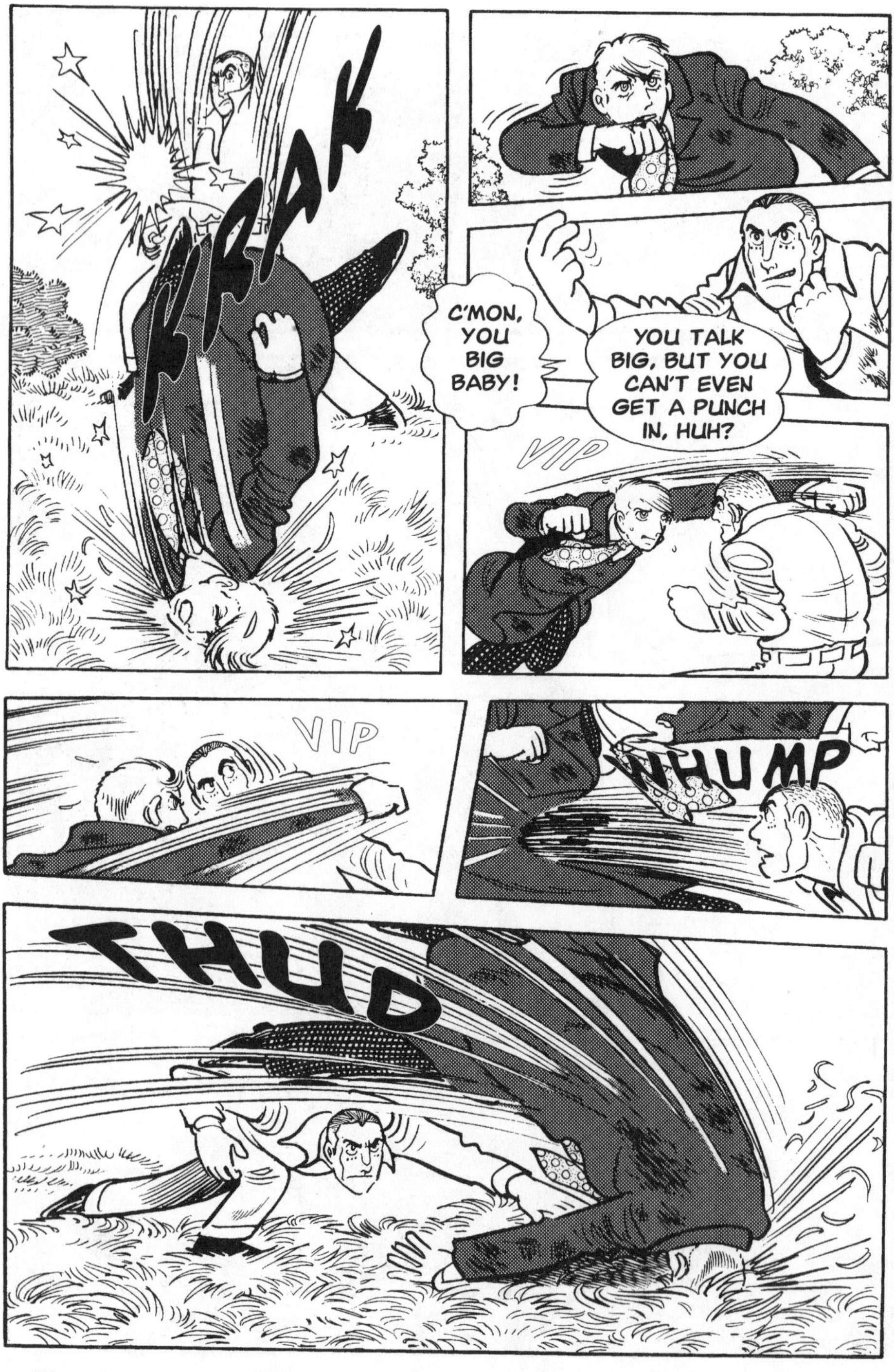
KRAK
C'MON, YOU BIG BABY!
YOU TALK BIG, BUT YOU CAN'T EVEN GET A PUNCH IN, HUH?
VIP
VIP
WHUMP
THUD

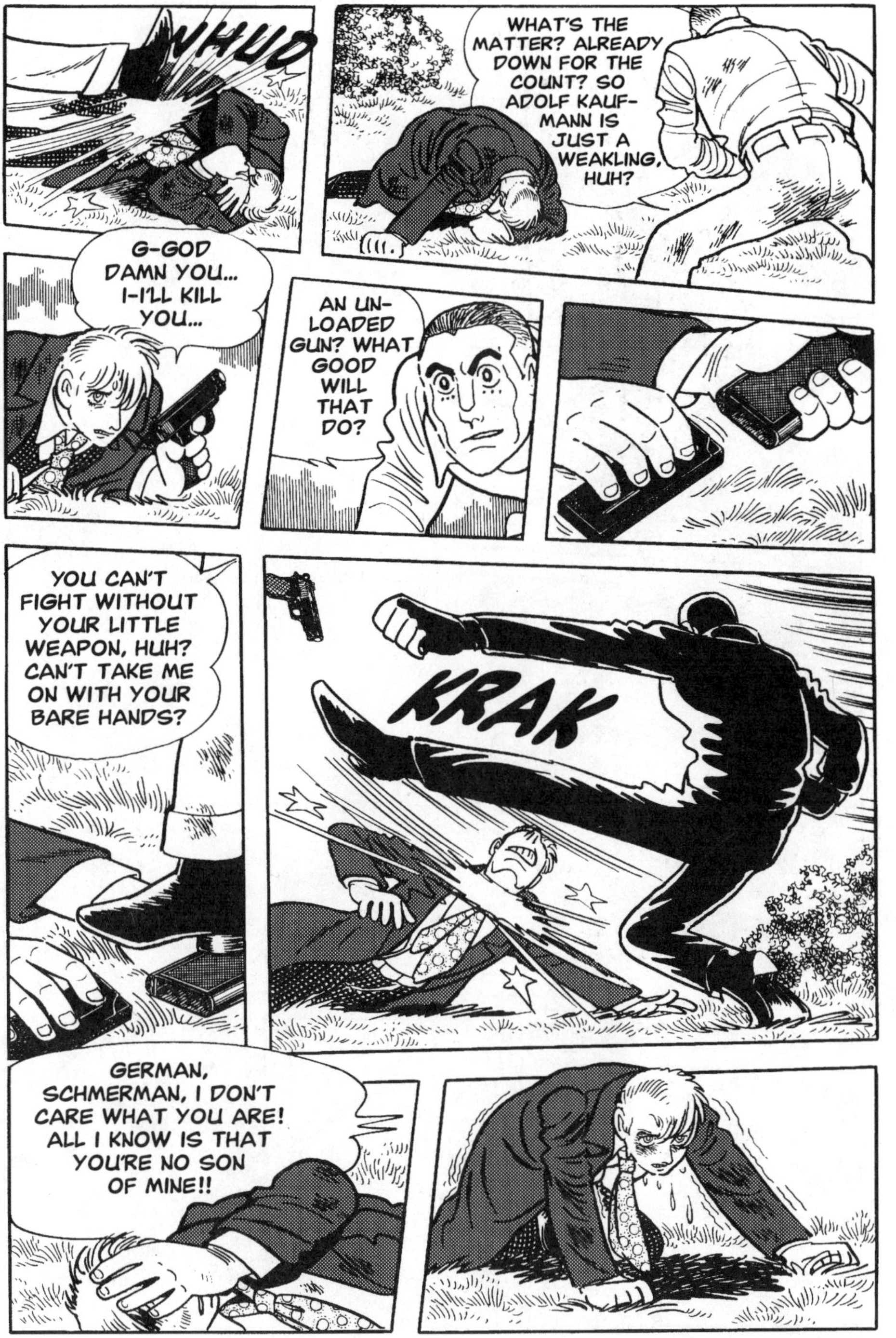
WHUD
WHAT'S THE MATTER? ALREADY DOWN FOR THE COUNT? SO ADOLF KAUFMANN IS JUST A WEAKLING, HUH?
G-GOD DAMN YOU... I-I'LL KILL YOU...
AN UNLOADED GUN? WHAT GOOD WILL THAT DO?
YOU CAN'T FIGHT WITHOUT YOUR LITTLE WEAPON, HUH? CAN'T TAKE ME ON WITH YOUR BARE HANDS?
KRAK
GERMAN, SCHMERMAN, I DON'T CARE WHAT YOU ARE! ALL I KNOW IS THAT YOU'RE NO SON OF MINE!!

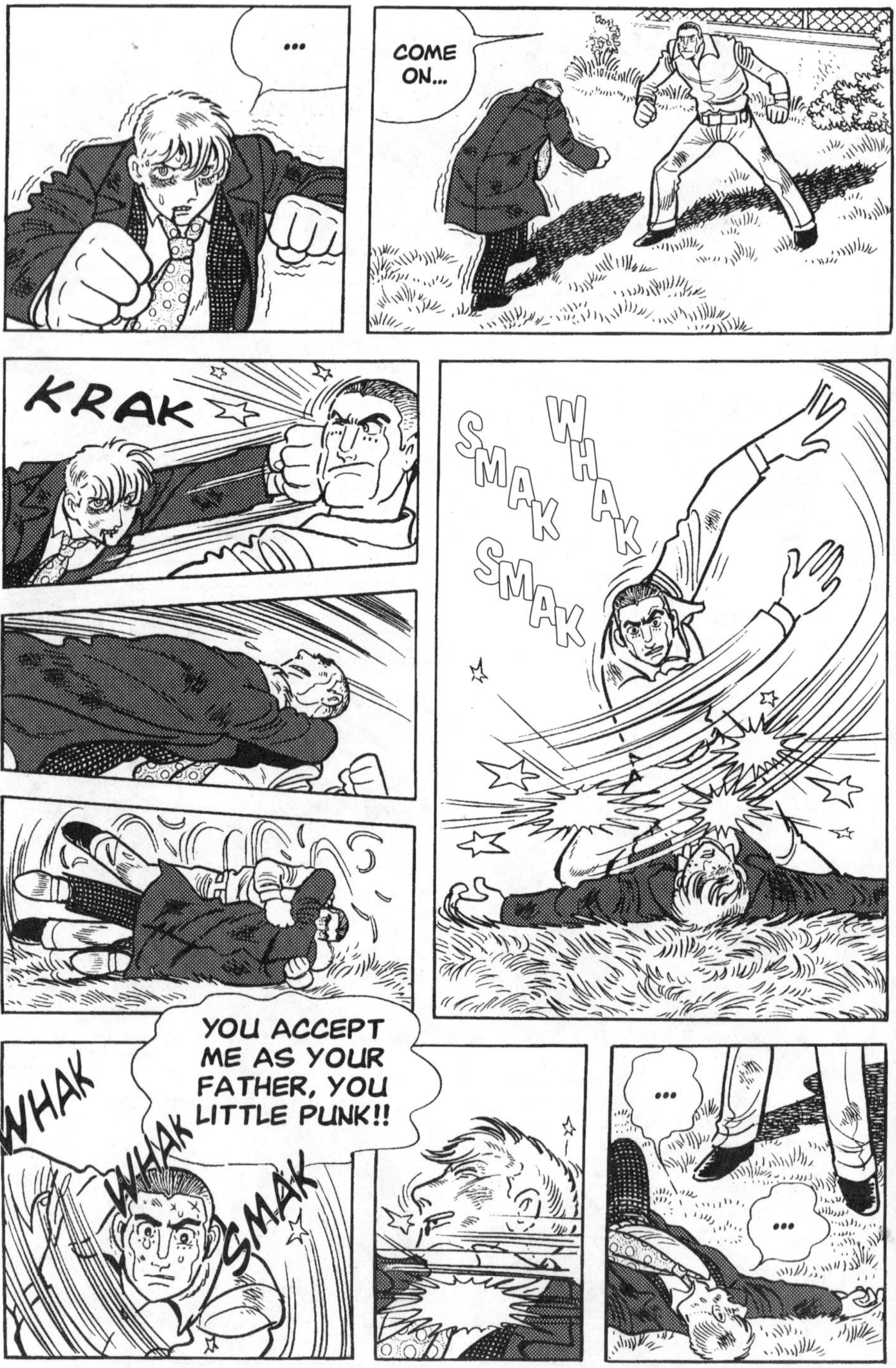
...
COME ON...
KRAK
WHAK
SMAK
SMAK
WHAK
WHAK
SMAK
YOU ACCEPT ME AS YOUR FATHER, YOU LITTLE PUNK!!
...
...

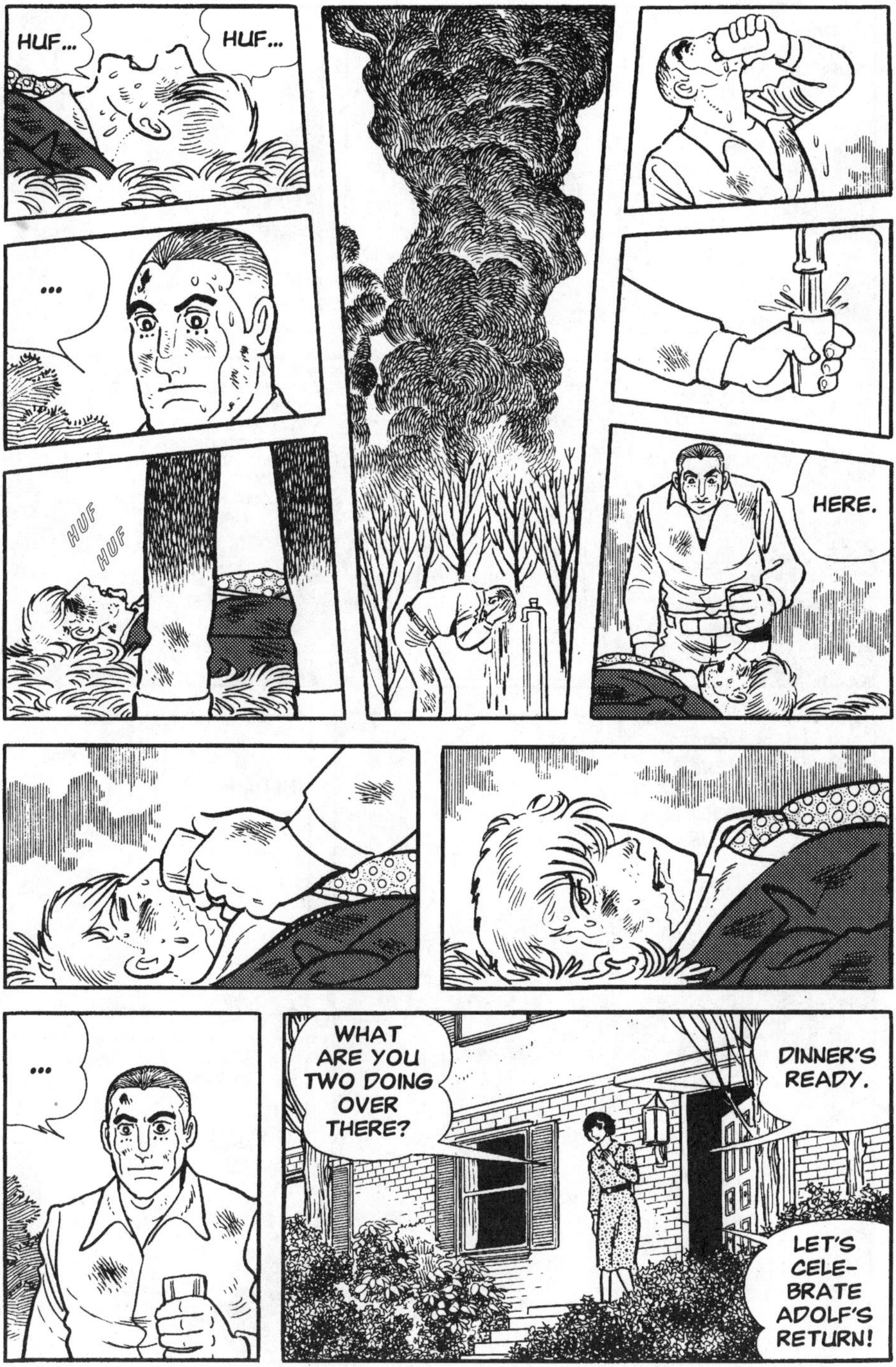
HUF...
HUF...
...
HUF
HUF
HERE.
...
WHAT ARE YOU TWO DOING OVER THERE?
DINNER'S READY.
LET'S CELE-BRATE ADOLF'S RETURN!

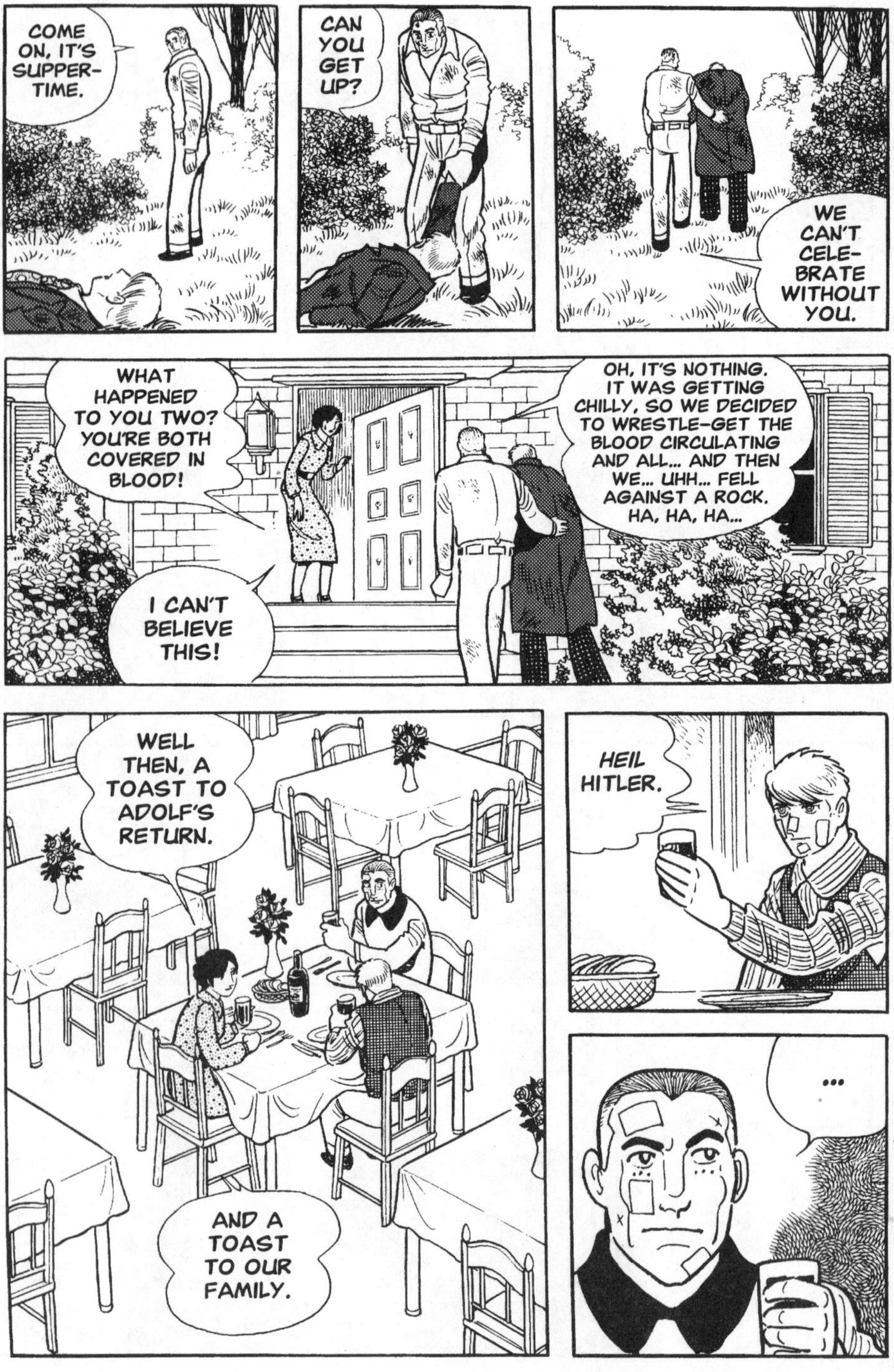
COME ON, IT'S SUPPER-TIME.
CAN YOU GET UP?
WE CAN'T CELE-BRATE WITHOUT YOU.
WHAT HAPPENED TO YOU TWO? YOU'RE BOTH COVERED IN BLOOD!
OH, IT'S NOTHING. IT WAS GETTING CHILLY, SO WE DECIDED TO WRESTLE–GET THE BLOOD CIRCULATING AND ALL... AND THEN WE... UHH... FELL AGAINST A ROCK. HA, HA, HA...
I CAN'T BELIEVE THIS!
WELL THEN, A TOAST TO ADOLF'S RETURN.
AND A TOAST TO OUR FAMILY.
HEIL HITLER.
...

CHAPTER
TWO

Adolf

3:30 PM, JANUARY 27, 1945, THE CONCORDIA CLUB

THE CITY OF AKASHI HAS SUFFERED SEVERE CASUALTIES.

NO DOUBT...

...KOBE WILL BE NEXT.

THIS BUILDING MAY BE LEVELED AS WELL.

WE'LL HAVE TO EVACUATE SOON.

YOU'RE GOING TO RUN AWAY, CONSULATE GENERAL?

YOU TRAITOR!

HERR KAUF-MANN...

WATCH YOUR TONGUE!

YOU'LL BE THE LAUGHING STOCK OF THE JEWS OF KOBE!

THEY'LL SAY THE NAZIS "PUT SAILS ON THEIR TAILS"!

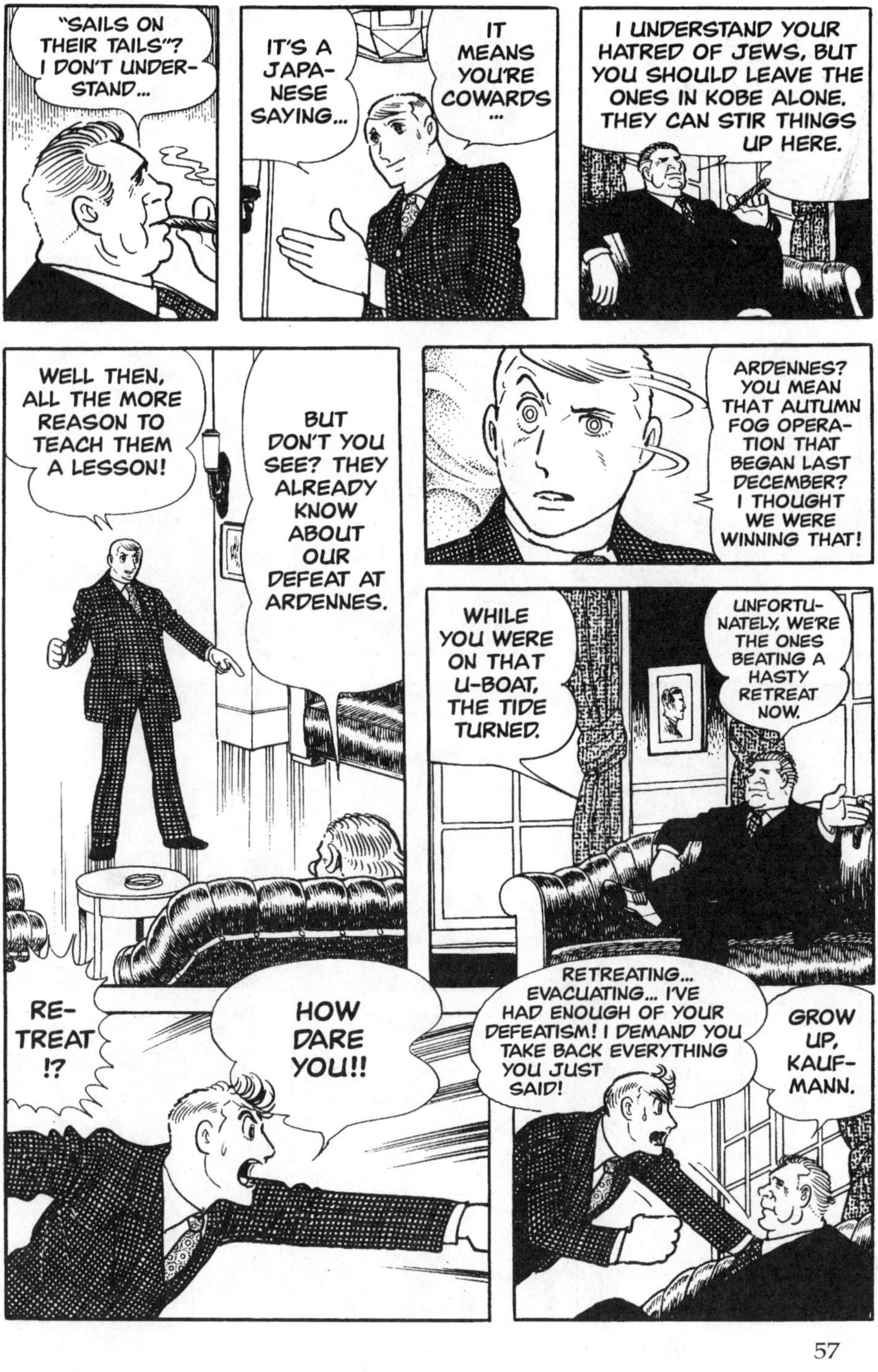
"SAILS ON THEIR TAILS"? I DON'T UNDERSTAND...
IT'S A JAPANESE SAYING...
IT MEANS YOU'RE COWARDS ...
I UNDERSTAND YOUR HATRED OF JEWS, BUT YOU SHOULD LEAVE THE ONES IN KOBE ALONE. THEY CAN STIR THINGS UP HERE.
WELL THEN, ALL THE MORE REASON TO TEACH THEM A LESSON!
BUT DON'T YOU SEE? THEY ALREADY KNOW ABOUT OUR DEFEAT AT ARDENNES.
ARDENNES? YOU MEAN THAT AUTUMN FOG OPERATION THAT BEGAN LAST DECEMBER? I THOUGHT WE WERE WINNING THAT!
WHILE YOU WERE ON THAT U-BOAT, THE TIDE TURNED.
UNFORTUNATELY, WE'RE THE ONES BEATING A HASTY RETREAT NOW.
RETREAT!?
HOW DARE YOU!!
RETREATING... EVACUATING... I'VE HAD ENOUGH OF YOUR DEFEATISM! I DEMAND YOU TAKE BACK EVERYTHING YOU JUST SAID!
GROW UP, KAUFMANN.

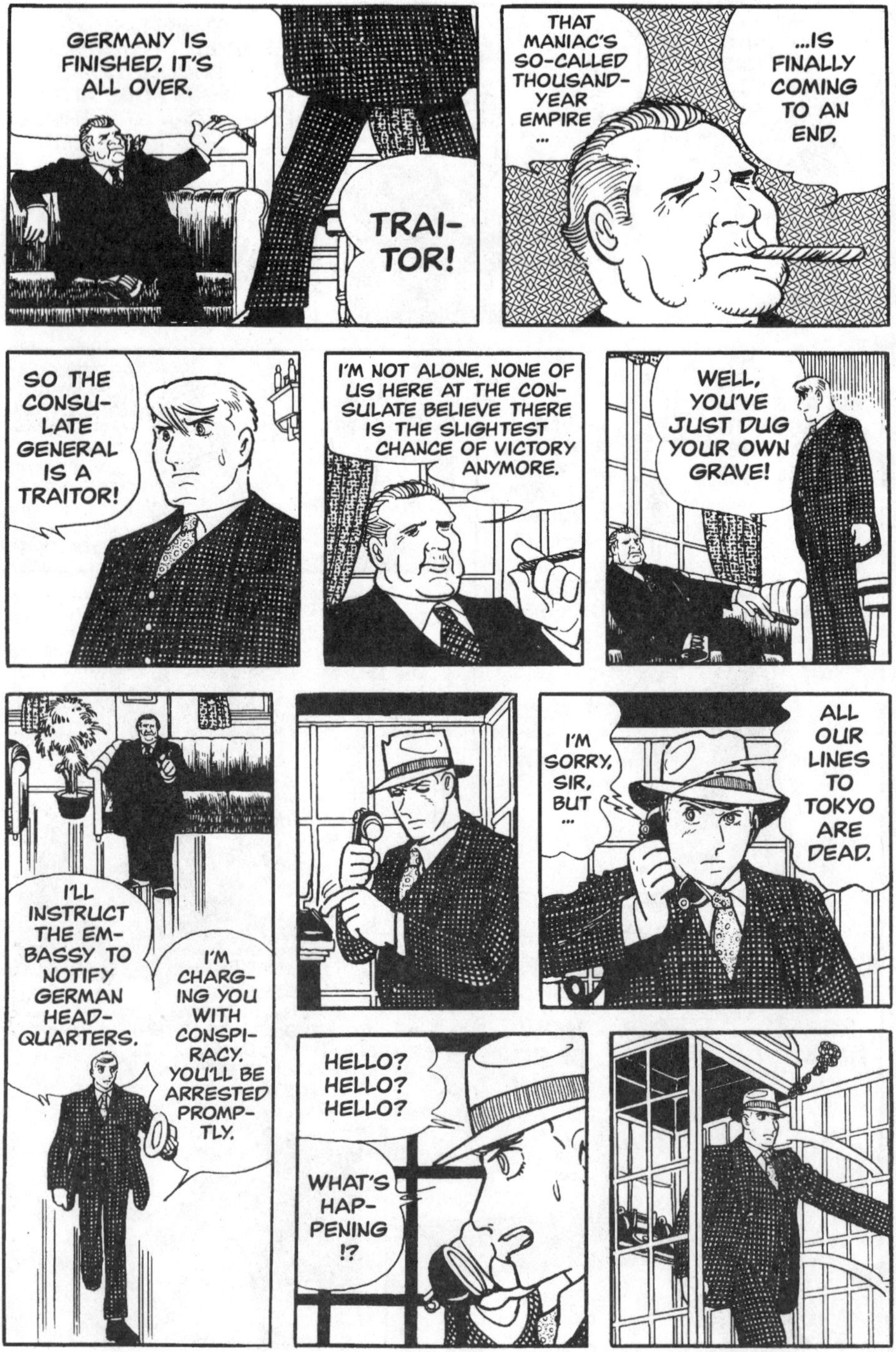
GERMANY IS FINISHED. IT'S ALL OVER.
TRAITOR!
THAT MANIAC'S SO-CALLED THOUSAND-YEAR EMPIRE ...
...IS FINALLY COMING TO AN END.
SO THE CONSULATE GENERAL IS A TRAITOR!
I'M NOT ALONE. NONE OF US HERE AT THE CONSULATE BELIEVE THERE IS THE SLIGHTEST CHANCE OF VICTORY ANYMORE.
WELL, YOU'VE JUST DUG YOUR OWN GRAVE!
I'LL INSTRUCT THE EMBASSY TO NOTIFY GERMAN HEADQUARTERS.
I'M CHARGING YOU WITH CONSPIRACY. YOU'LL BE ARRESTED PROMPTLY.
I'M SORRY, SIR, BUT ...
ALL OUR LINES TO TOKYO ARE DEAD.
HELLO? HELLO? HELLO?
WHAT'S HAPPENING!?

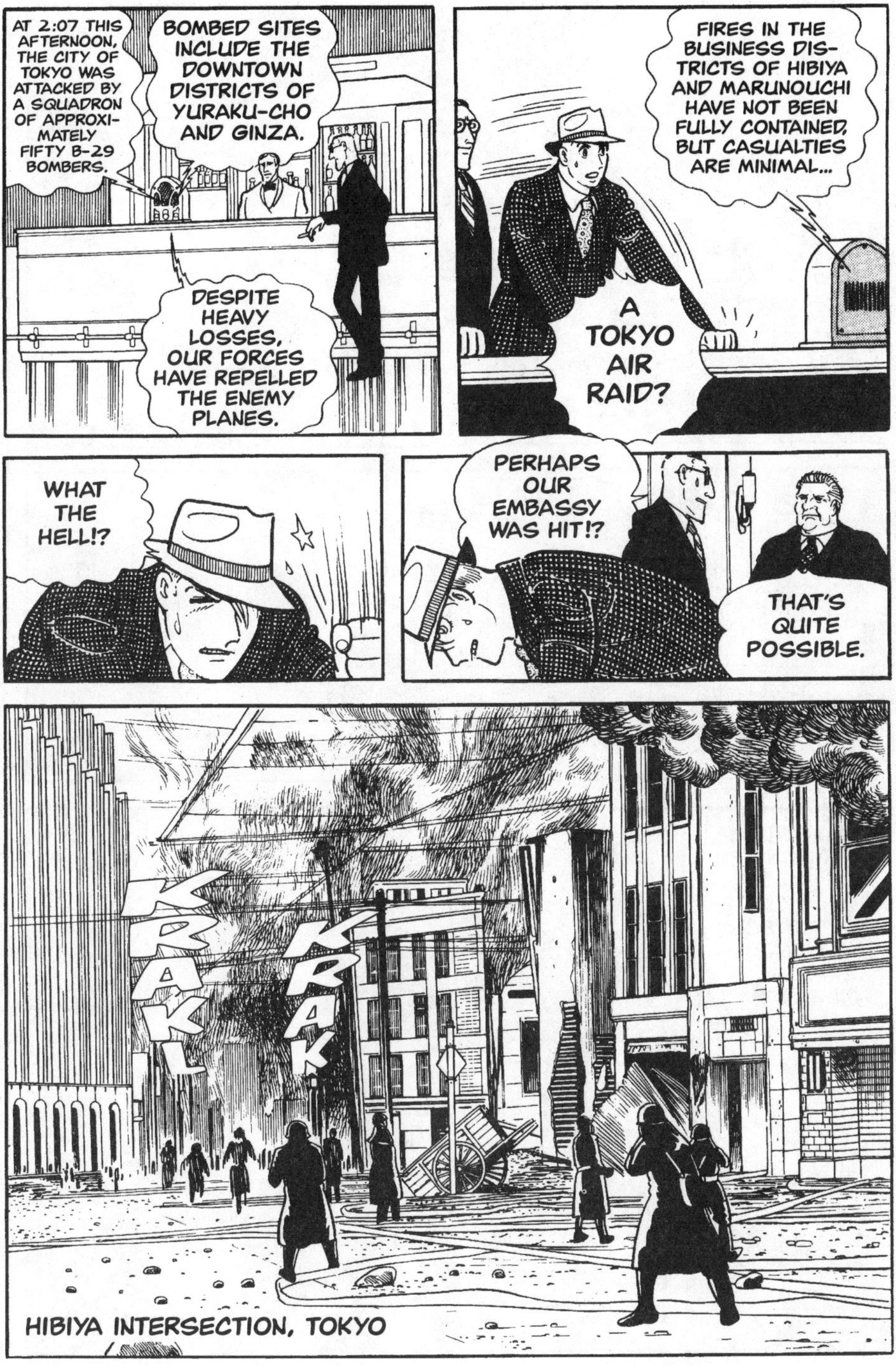
AT 2:07 THIS AFTERNOON, THE CITY OF TOKYO WAS ATTACKED BY A SQUADRON OF APPROXIMATELY FIFTY B-29 BOMBERS.
BOMBED SITES INCLUDE THE DOWNTOWN DISTRICTS OF YURAKU-CHO AND GINZA.
DESPITE HEAVY LOSSES, OUR FORCES HAVE REPELLED THE ENEMY PLANES.
FIRES IN THE BUSINESS DISTRICTS OF HIBIYA AND MARUNOUCHI HAVE NOT BEEN FULLY CONTAINED, BUT CASUALTIES ARE MINIMAL...
A TOKYO AIR RAID?
WHAT THE HELL!?
PERHAPS OUR EMBASSY WAS HIT!?
THAT'S QUITE POSSIBLE.
KRAKL
KRAK
HIBIYA INTERSECTION, TOKYO

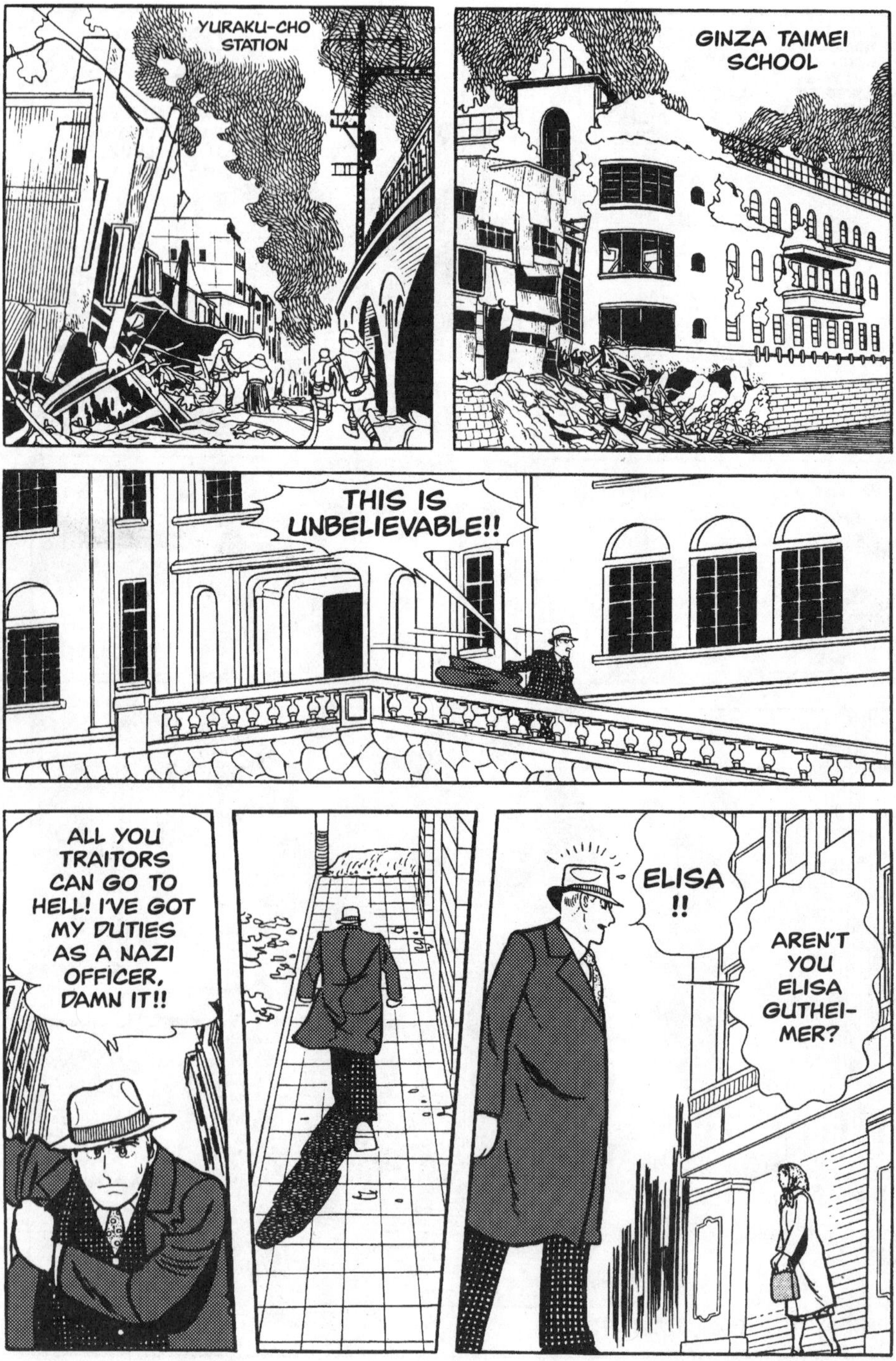
YURAKU-CHO STATION
GINZA TAIMEI SCHOOL
THIS IS UNBELIEVABLE!!
ALL YOU TRAITORS CAN GO TO HELL! I'VE GOT MY DUTIES AS A NAZI OFFICER, DAMN IT!!
ELISA !!
AREN'T YOU ELISA GUTHEI- MER?

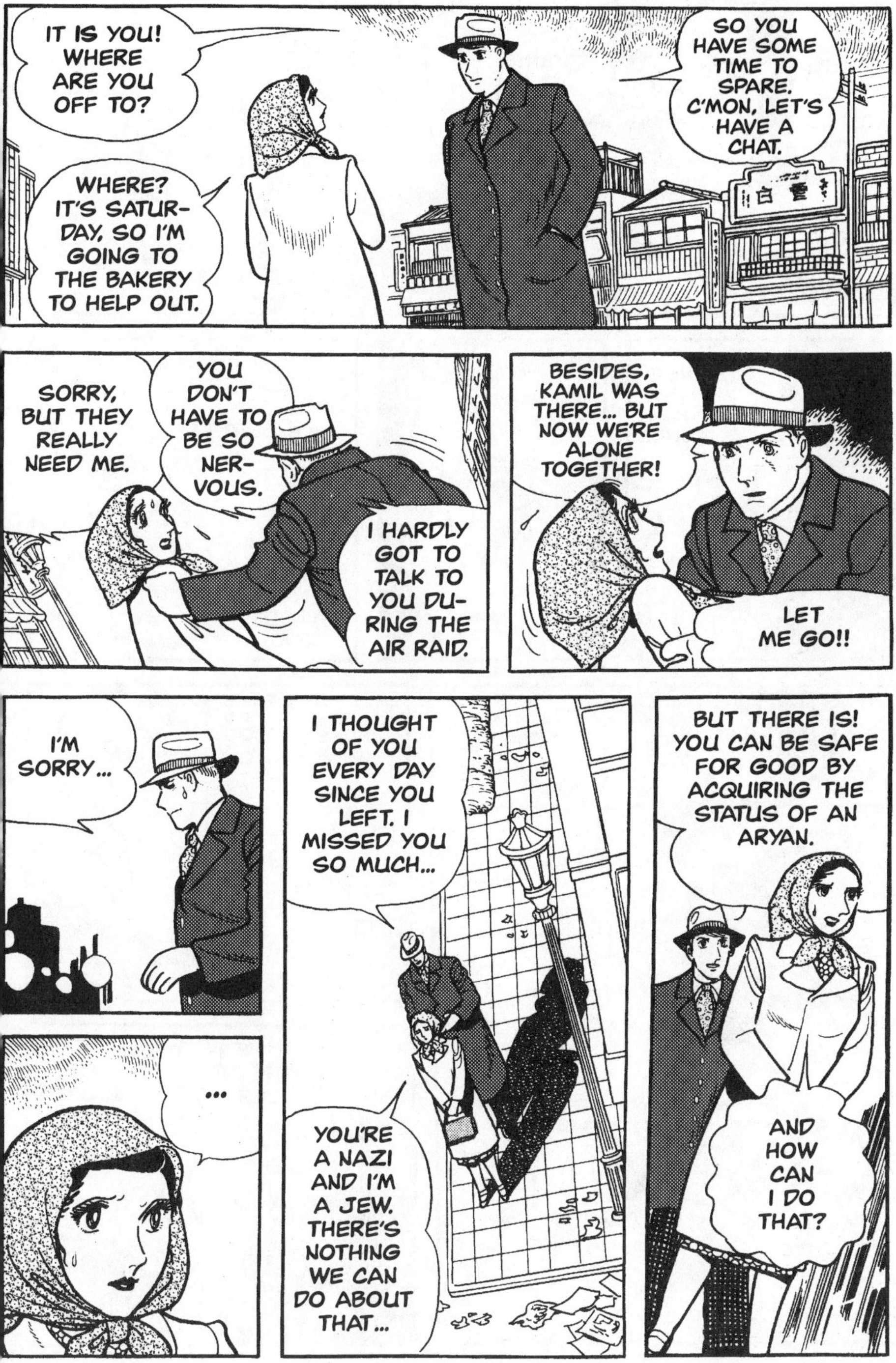
IT IS YOU! WHERE ARE YOU OFF TO?
WHERE? IT'S SATUR-DAY, SO I'M GOING TO THE BAKERY TO HELP OUT.
SO YOU HAVE SOME TIME TO SPARE. C'MON, LET'S HAVE A CHAT.
SORRY, BUT THEY REALLY NEED ME.
YOU DON'T HAVE TO BE SO NER-VOUS.
I HARDLY GOT TO TALK TO YOU DU-RING THE AIR RAID.
BESIDES, KAMIL WAS THERE... BUT NOW WE'RE ALONE TOGETHER!
LET ME GO!!
I'M SORRY...
...
I THOUGHT OF YOU EVERY DAY SINCE YOU LEFT. I MISSED YOU SO MUCH...
YOU'RE A NAZI AND I'M A JEW. THERE'S NOTHING WE CAN DO ABOUT THAT...
BUT THERE IS! YOU CAN BE SAFE FOR GOOD BY ACQUIRING THE STATUS OF AN ARYAN.
AND HOW CAN I DO THAT?

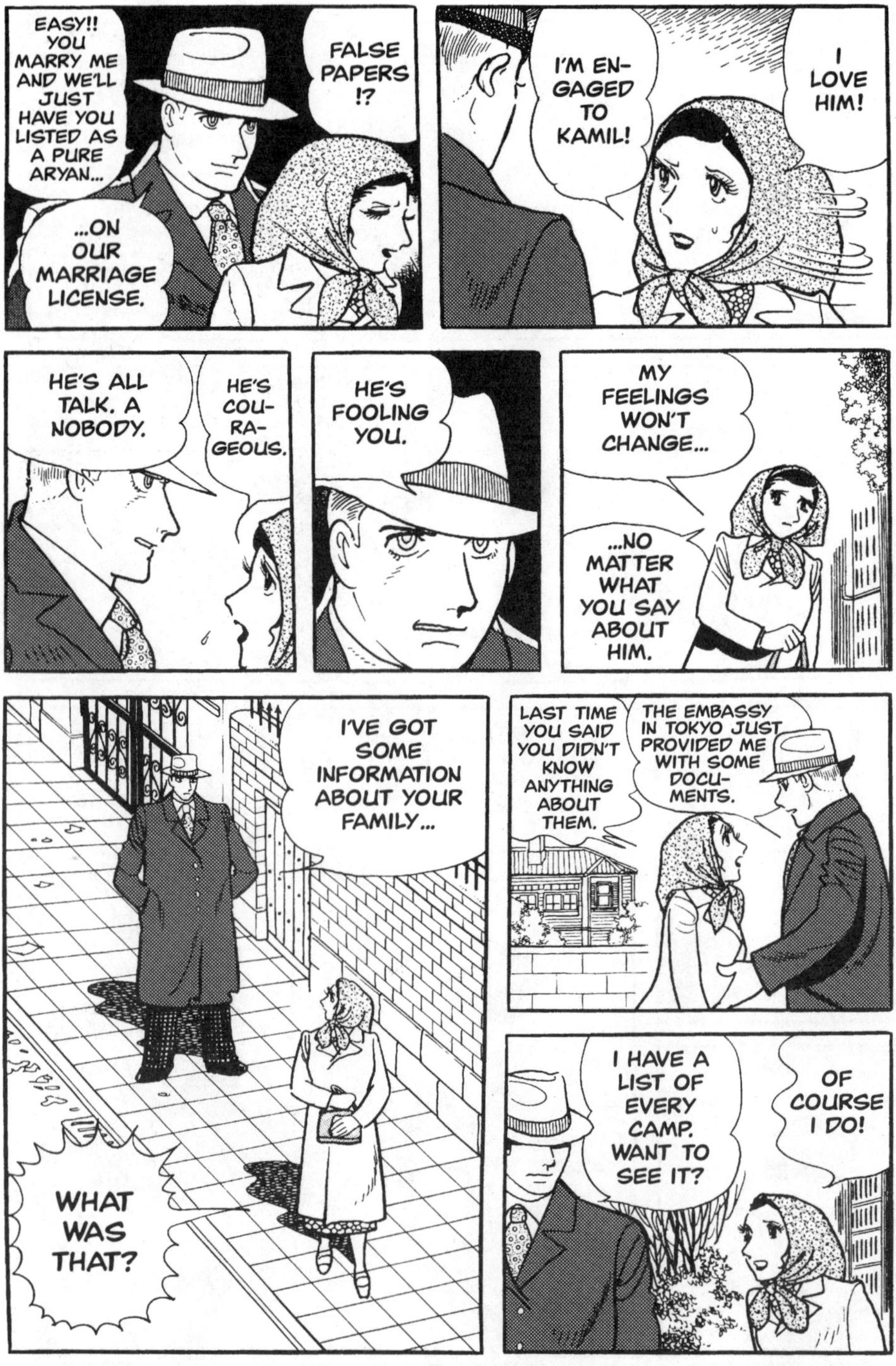
EASY!! YOU MARRY ME AND WE'LL JUST HAVE YOU LISTED AS A PURE ARYAN...
FALSE PAPERS !?
...ON OUR MARRIAGE LICENSE.
I'M ENGAGED TO KAMIL!
I LOVE HIM!
HE'S ALL TALK. A NOBODY.
HE'S COURAGEOUS.
HE'S FOOLING YOU.
MY FEELINGS WON'T CHANGE...
...NO MATTER WHAT YOU SAY ABOUT HIM.
I'VE GOT SOME INFORMATION ABOUT YOUR FAMILY...
WHAT WAS THAT?
LAST TIME YOU SAID YOU DIDN'T KNOW ANYTHING ABOUT THEM.
THE EMBASSY IN TOKYO JUST PROVIDED ME WITH SOME DOCUMENTS.
I HAVE A LIST OF EVERY CAMP. WANT TO SEE IT?
OF COURSE I DO!

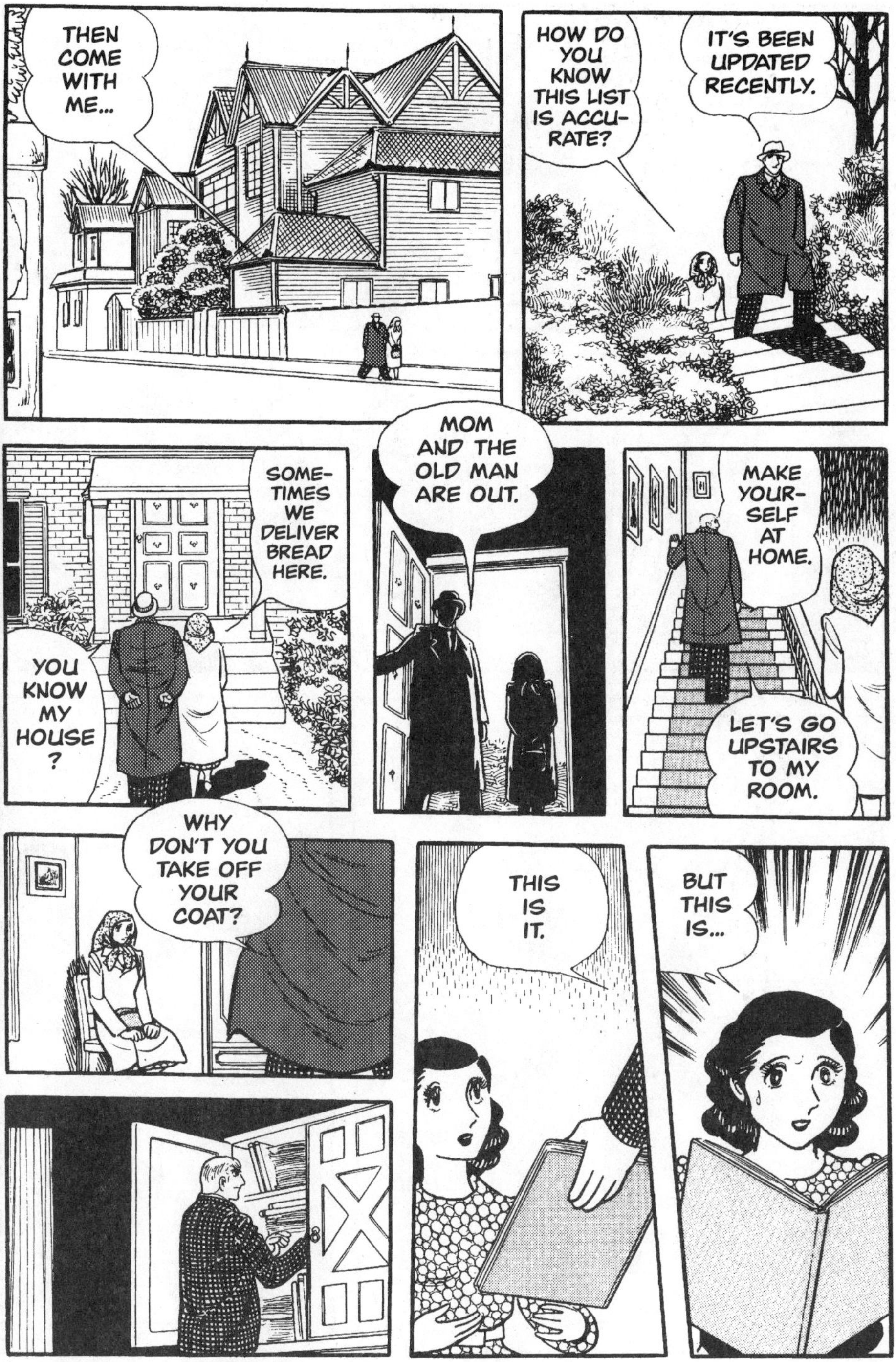
THEN COME WITH ME...
HOW DO YOU KNOW THIS LIST IS ACCU- RATE?
IT'S BEEN UPDATED RECENTLY.
SOME- TIMES WE DELIVER BREAD HERE.
YOU KNOW MY HOUSE ?
MOM AND THE OLD MAN ARE OUT.
MAKE YOUR- SELF AT HOME.
LET'S GO UPSTAIRS TO MY ROOM.
WHY DON'T YOU TAKE OFF YOUR COAT?
THIS IS IT.
BUT THIS IS...

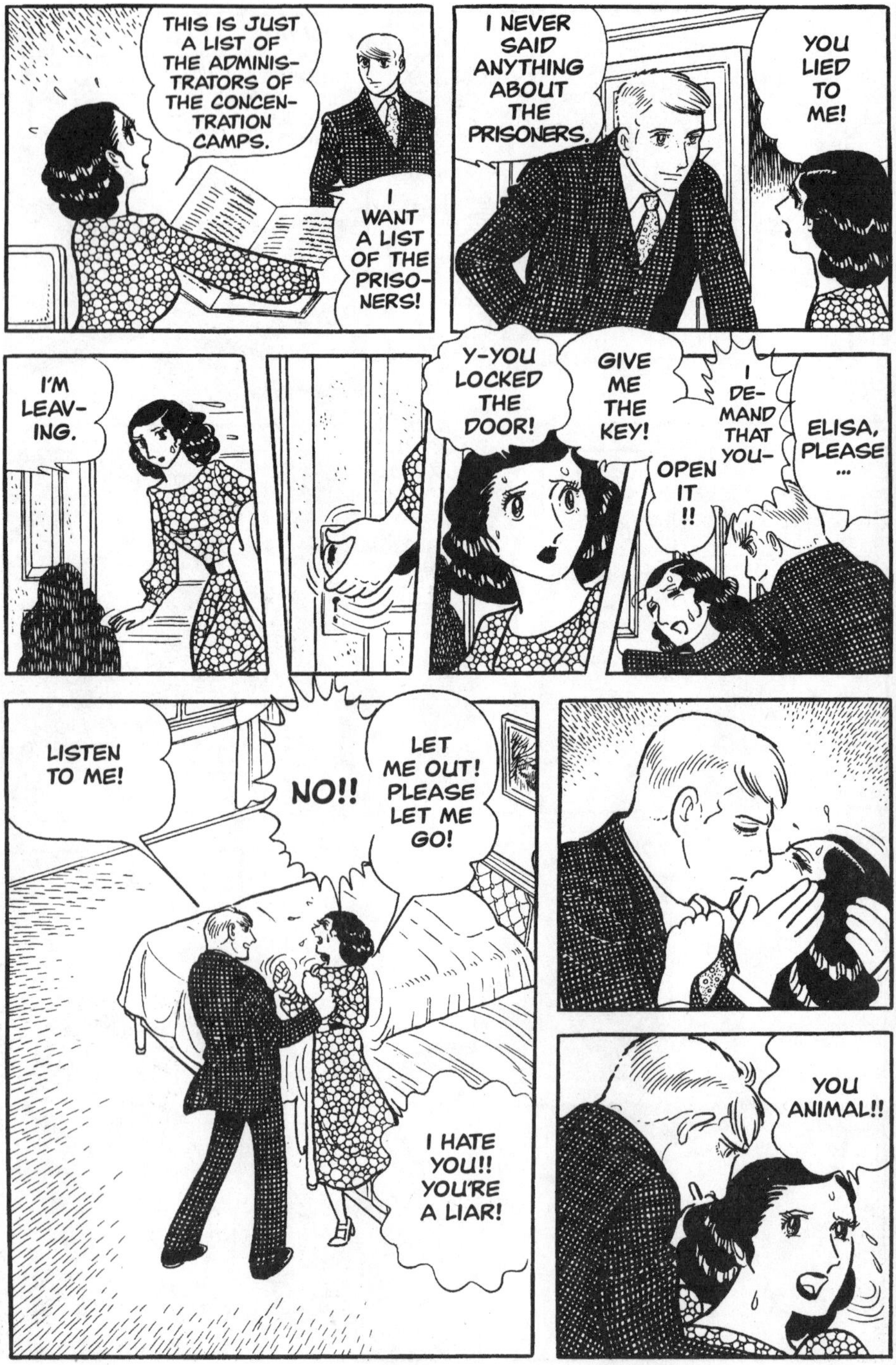
THIS IS JUST A LIST OF THE ADMINISTRATORS OF THE CONCENTRATION CAMPS.
I WANT A LIST OF THE PRISONERS!
I NEVER SAID ANYTHING ABOUT THE PRISONERS.
YOU LIED TO ME!
I'M LEAVING.
Y-YOU LOCKED THE DOOR!
GIVE ME THE KEY!
I DEMAND THAT YOU—
OPEN IT!!
ELISA, PLEASE ...
LISTEN TO ME!
NO!!
LET ME OUT! PLEASE LET ME GO!
I HATE YOU!! YOU'RE A LIAR!
YOU ANIMAL!!

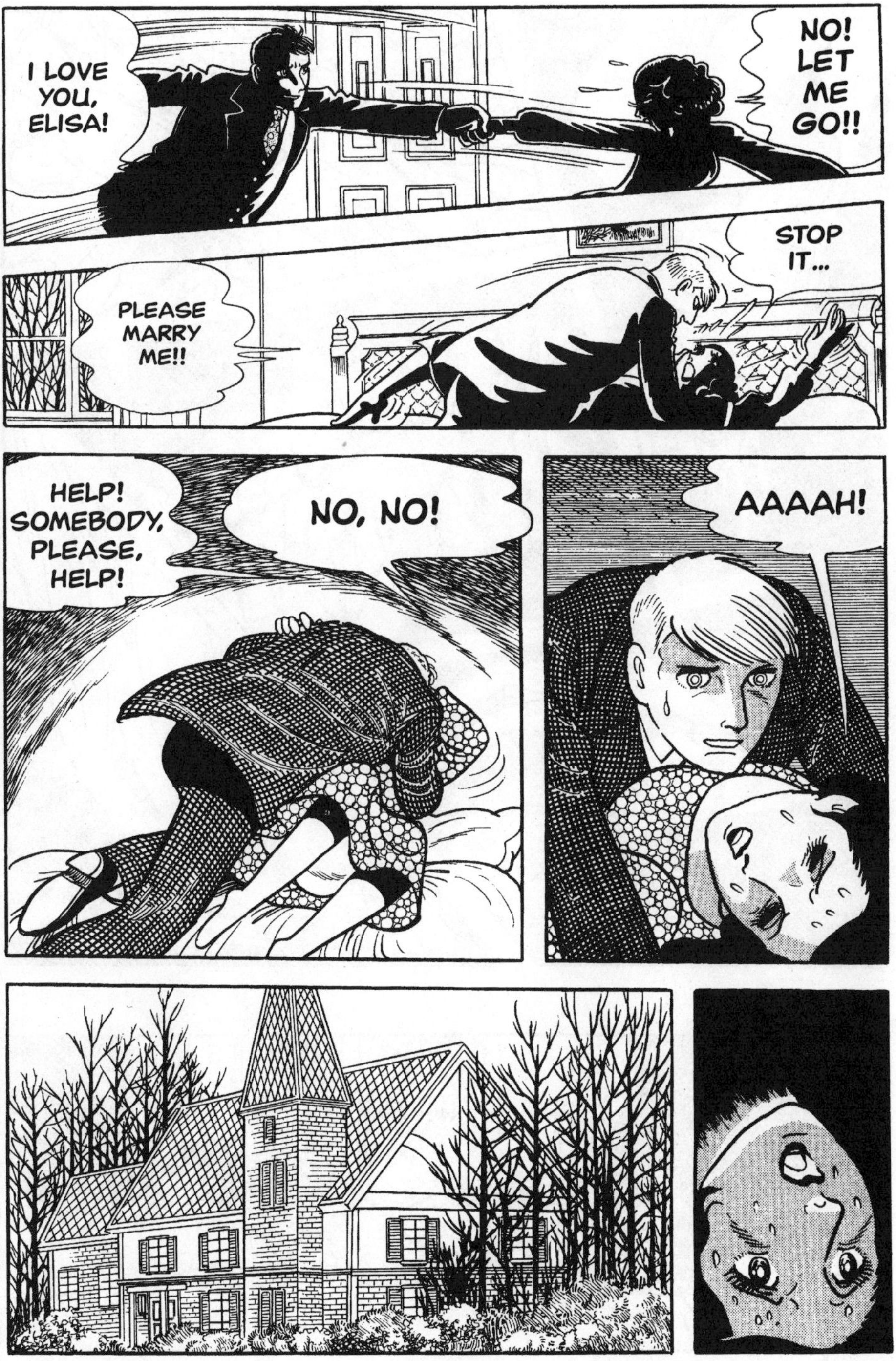
I LOVE YOU, ELISA!
NO! LET ME GO!!
PLEASE MARRY ME!!
STOP IT...
HELP! SOMEBODY, PLEASE, HELP!
NO, NO!
AAAAH!

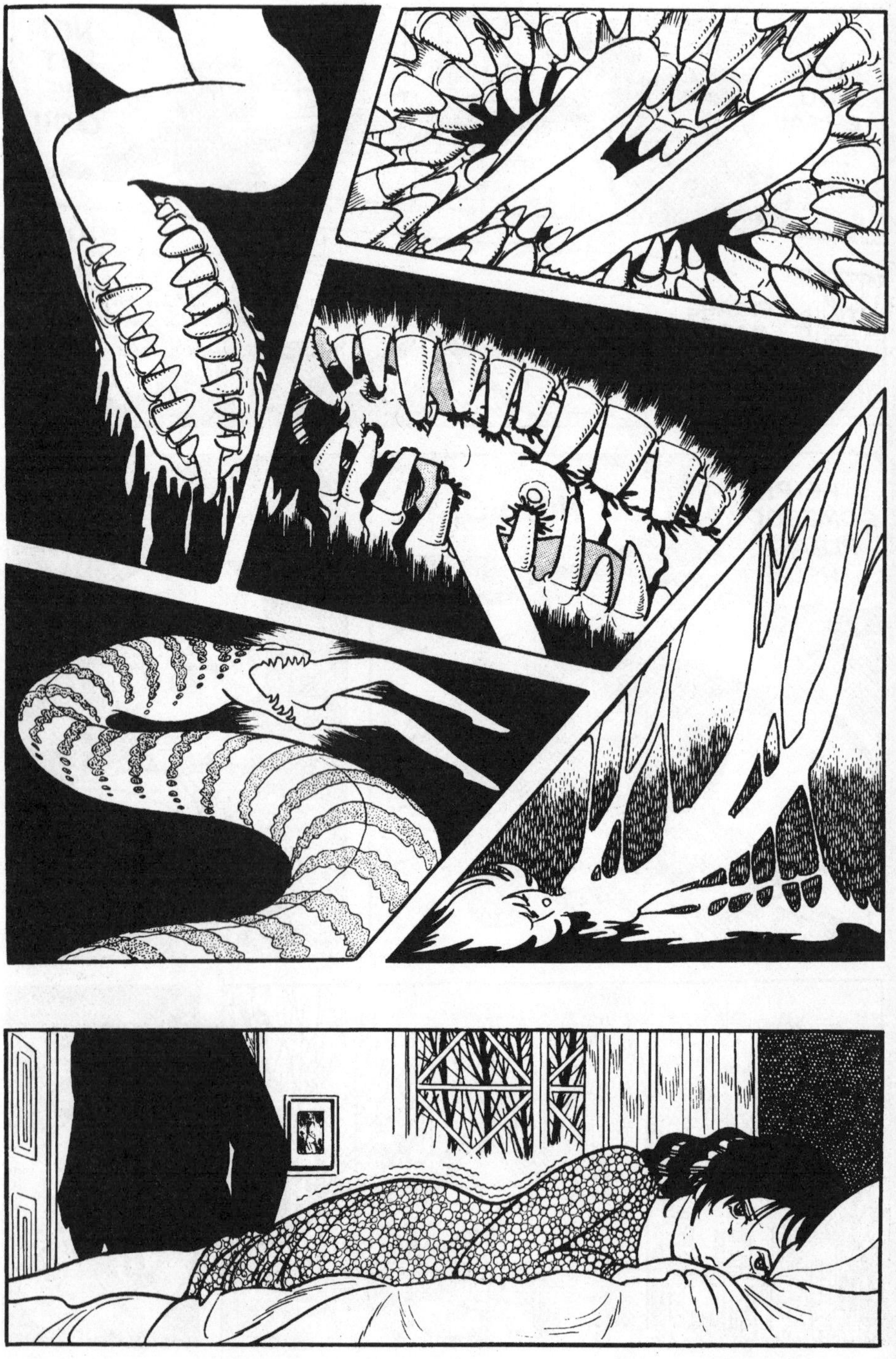

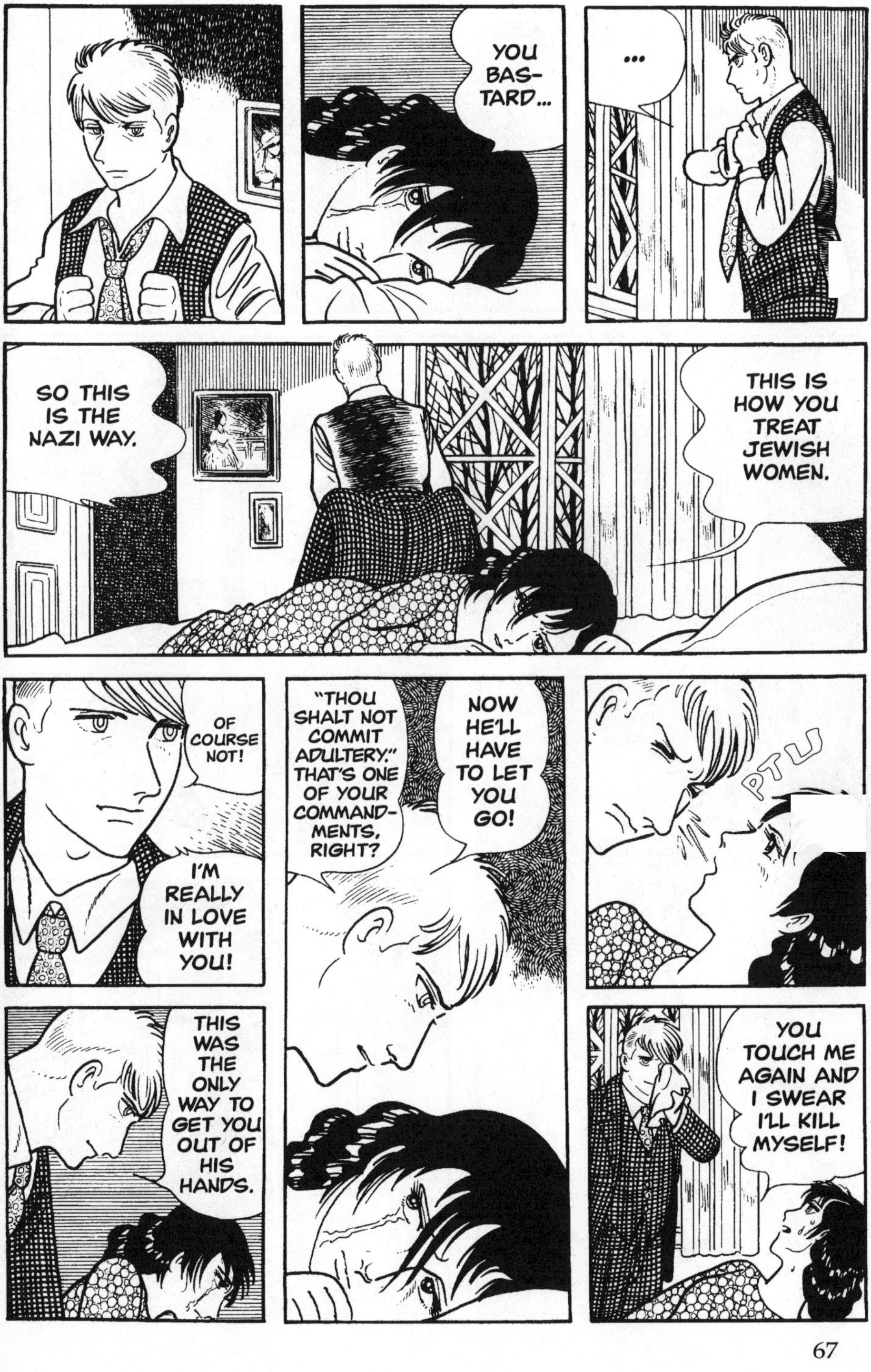
YOU BAS- TARD...
...
SO THIS IS THE NAZI WAY.
THIS IS HOW YOU TREAT JEWISH WOMEN.
OF COURSE NOT!
I'M REALLY IN LOVE WITH YOU!
"THOU SHALT NOT COMMIT ADULTERY." THAT'S ONE OF YOUR COMMAND- MENTS, RIGHT?
NOW HE'LL HAVE TO LET YOU GO!
PTU
THIS WAS THE ONLY WAY TO GET YOU OUT OF HIS HANDS.
YOU TOUCH ME AGAIN AND I SWEAR I'LL KILL MYSELF!

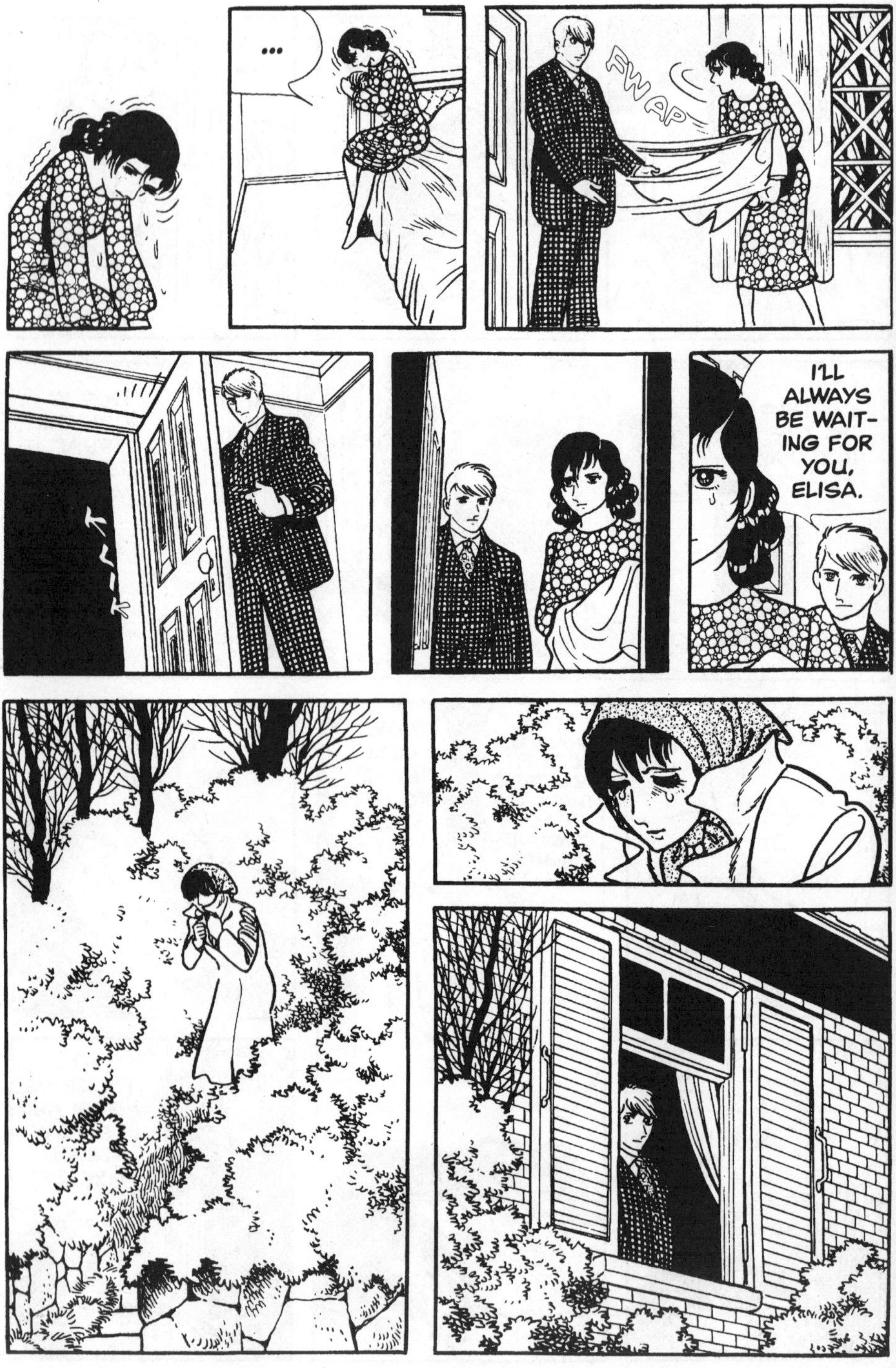
...
FWAP
KLIK
I'LL ALWAYS BE WAITING FOR YOU, ELISA.

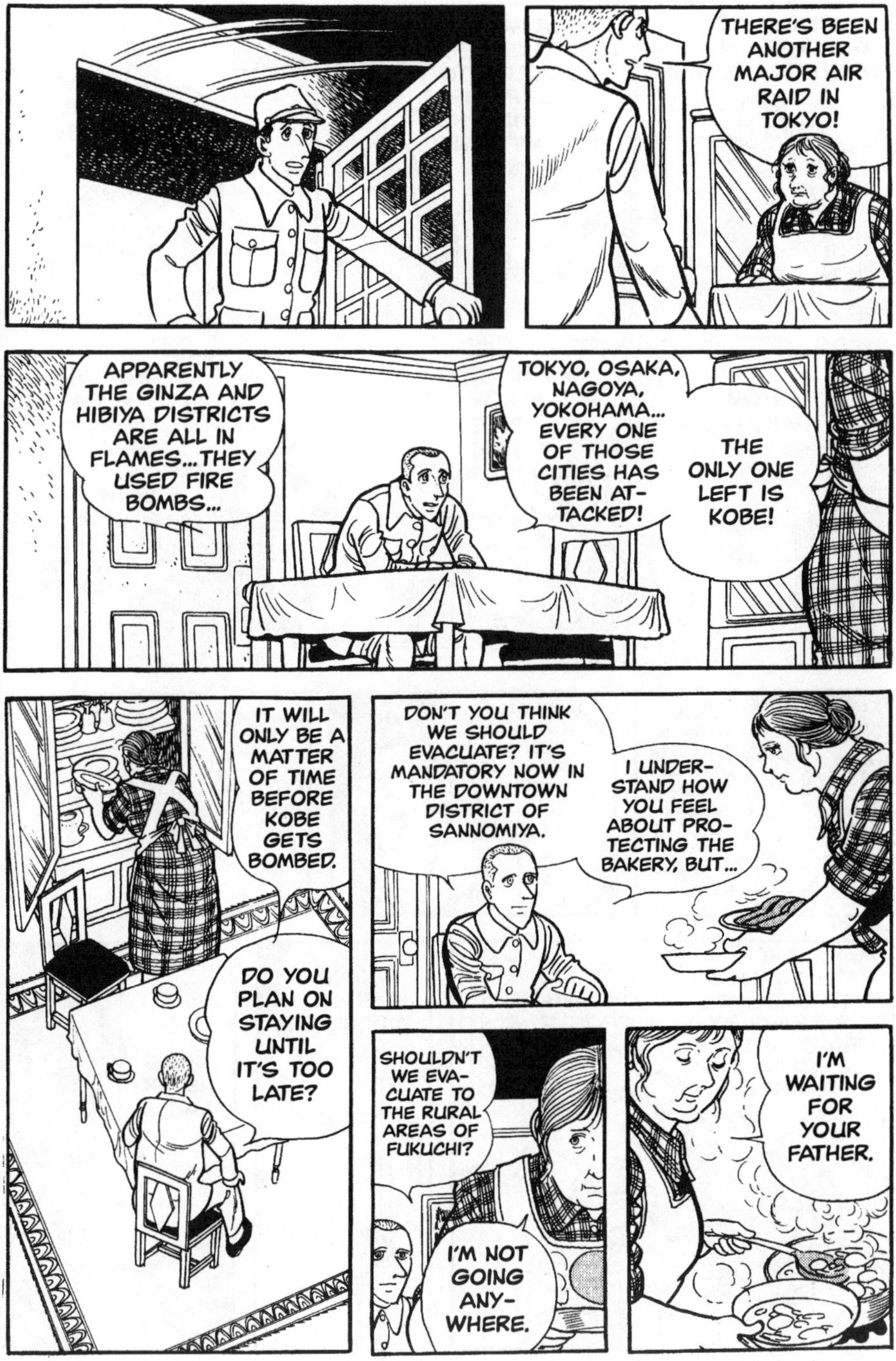
THERE'S BEEN ANOTHER MAJOR AIR RAID IN TOKYO!
APPARENTLY THE GINZA AND HIBIYA DISTRICTS ARE ALL IN FLAMES...THEY USED FIRE BOMBS...
TOKYO, OSAKA, NAGOYA, YOKOHAMA... EVERY ONE OF THOSE CITIES HAS BEEN AT-TACKED!
THE ONLY ONE LEFT IS KOBE!
IT WILL ONLY BE A MATTER OF TIME BEFORE KOBE GETS BOMBED.
DO YOU PLAN ON STAYING UNTIL IT'S TOO LATE?
DON'T YOU THINK WE SHOULD EVACUATE? IT'S MANDATORY NOW IN THE DOWNTOWN DISTRICT OF SANNOMIYA.
I UNDER-STAND HOW YOU FEEL ABOUT PRO-TECTING THE BAKERY, BUT...
SHOULDN'T WE EVA-CUATE TO THE RURAL AREAS OF FUKUCHI?
I'M NOT GOING ANY-WHERE.
I'M WAITING FOR YOUR FATHER.

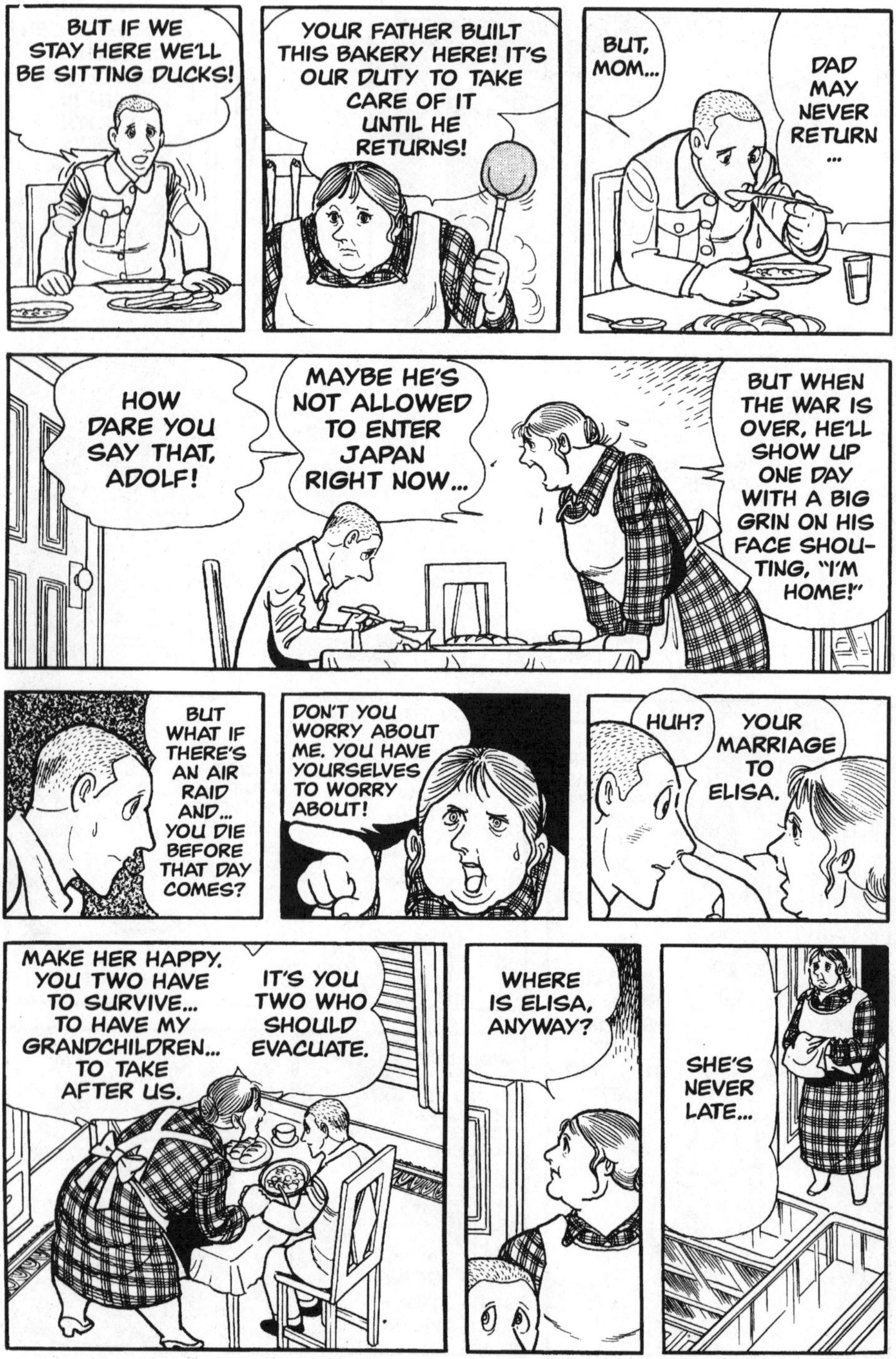
BUT IF WE STAY HERE WE'LL BE SITTING DUCKS!
YOUR FATHER BUILT THIS BAKERY HERE! IT'S OUR DUTY TO TAKE CARE OF IT UNTIL HE RETURNS!
BUT, MOM...
DAD MAY NEVER RETURN ...
HOW DARE YOU SAY THAT, ADOLF!
MAYBE HE'S NOT ALLOWED TO ENTER JAPAN RIGHT NOW...
BUT WHEN THE WAR IS OVER, HE'LL SHOW UP ONE DAY WITH A BIG GRIN ON HIS FACE SHOUTING, "I'M HOME!"
BUT WHAT IF THERE'S AN AIR RAID AND... YOU DIE BEFORE THAT DAY COMES?
DON'T YOU WORRY ABOUT ME. YOU HAVE YOURSELVES TO WORRY ABOUT!
HUH?
YOUR MARRIAGE TO ELISA.
MAKE HER HAPPY. YOU TWO HAVE TO SURVIVE... TO HAVE MY GRANDCHILDREN... TO TAKE AFTER US.
IT'S YOU TWO WHO SHOULD EVACUATE.
WHERE IS ELISA, ANYWAY?
SHE'S NEVER LATE...

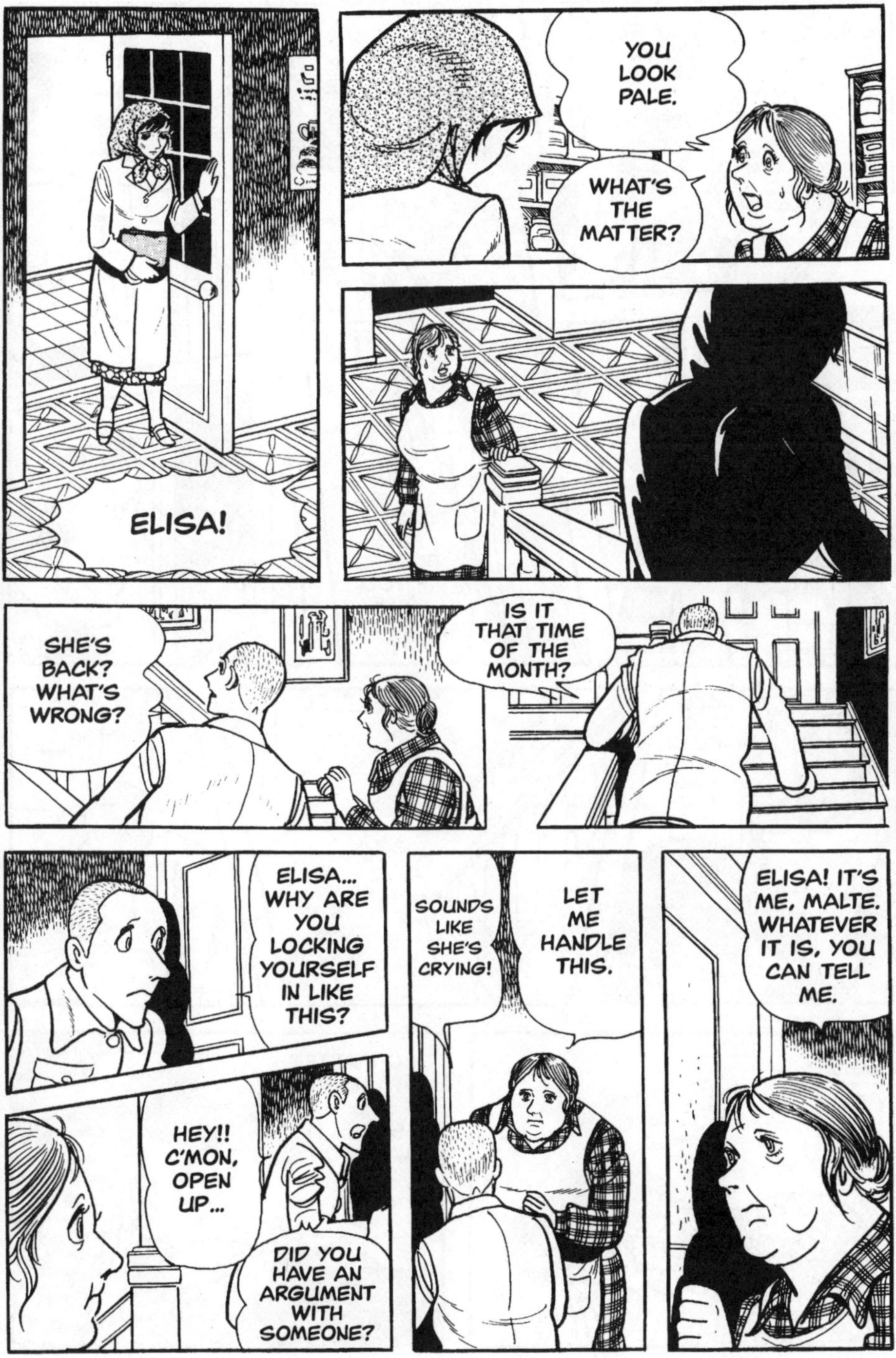
ELISA!
YOU LOOK PALE.
WHAT'S THE MATTER?
SHE'S BACK? WHAT'S WRONG?
IS IT THAT TIME OF THE MONTH?
ELISA... WHY ARE YOU LOCKING YOURSELF IN LIKE THIS?
HEY!! C'MON, OPEN UP...
DID YOU HAVE AN ARGUMENT WITH SOMEONE?
SOUNDS LIKE SHE'S CRYING!
LET ME HANDLE THIS.
ELISA! IT'S ME, MALTE. WHATEVER IT IS, YOU CAN TELL ME.

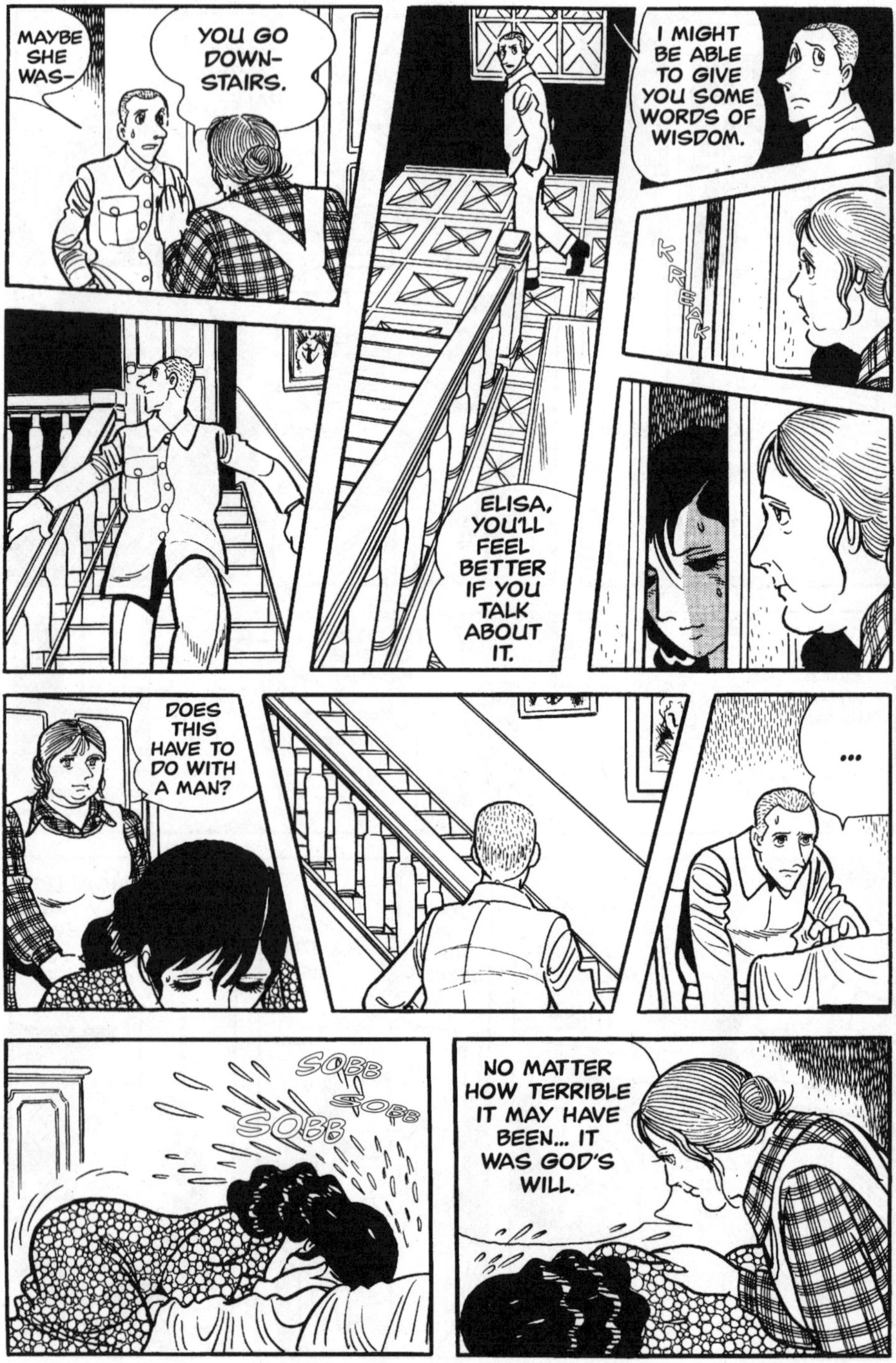
MAYBE SHE WAS-
YOU GO DOWN-STAIRS.
I MIGHT BE ABLE TO GIVE YOU SOME WORDS OF WISDOM.
KREAK
ELISA, YOU'LL FEEL BETTER IF YOU TALK ABOUT IT.
DOES THIS HAVE TO DO WITH A MAN?
...
SOBB
SOBB
SOBB
NO MATTER HOW TERRIBLE IT MAY HAVE BEEN... IT WAS GOD'S WILL.

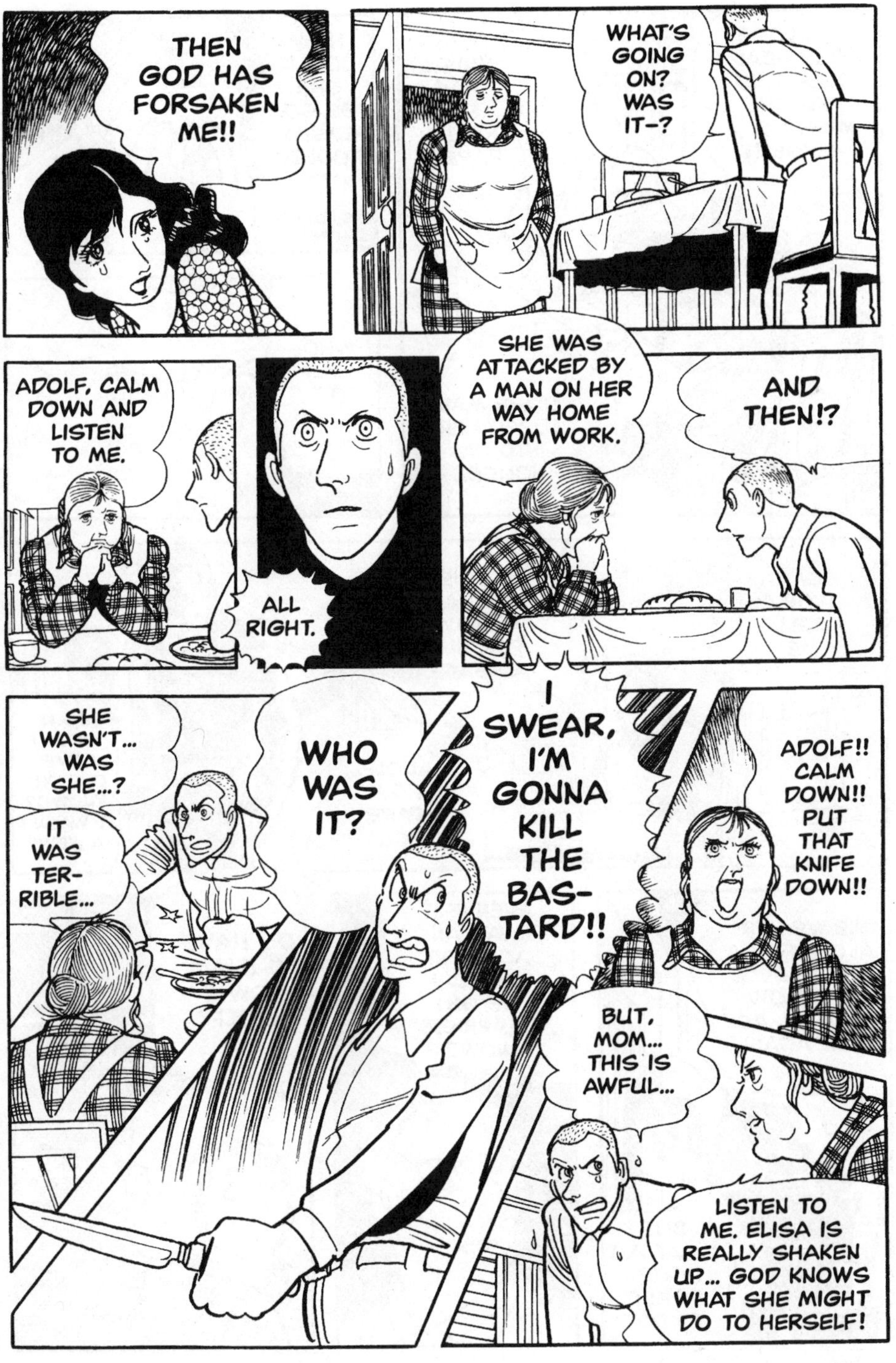
THEN GOD HAS FORSAKEN ME!!
WHAT'S GOING ON? WAS IT–?
ADOLF, CALM DOWN AND LISTEN TO ME.
ALL RIGHT.
SHE WAS ATTACKED BY A MAN ON HER WAY HOME FROM WORK.
AND THEN!?
SHE WASN'T... WAS SHE...?
IT WAS TERRIBLE...
WHO WAS IT?
I SWEAR, I'M GONNA KILL THE BASTARD!!
ADOLF!! CALM DOWN!! PUT THAT KNIFE DOWN!!
BUT, MOM... THIS IS AWFUL...
LISTEN TO ME. ELISA IS REALLY SHAKEN UP... GOD KNOWS WHAT SHE MIGHT DO TO HERSELF!

Adolf

YOU LOSE YOUR HEAD OVER THIS AND SHE MIGHT KILL HERSELF.

WAS... WAS SHE REALLY RAPED?

SOME MAN LURED HER INTO HIS HOUSE...

HOW COULD SHE BE SO EASILY FOOLED!?

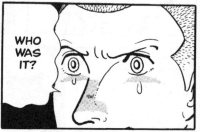

WHO WAS IT?

SHE WON'T TELL ME.

MAYBE SHE HAD A THING FOR HIM ALREADY.

ADOLF, HOW DARE YOU!

SO IT WASN'T SOMEONE SHE KNOWS? IT WASN'T A JEW?

LEAVE HER ALONE FOR A WHILE. ONCE THIS BLOWS OVER I'LL ASK HER AGAIN.

BUT WHAT AM I SUPPOSED TO DO?

EVEN IF IT WAS AN ACCIDENT, HOW CAN WE GET MARRIED NOW?

YOU HAVE TO CALM DOWN, ADOLF!

GOOD MORNING, ELISA.

I KNOW IT'S STILL EARLY, BUT I NEED YOU TO DELIVER THIS BREAD TO THE KAUFMANN RESTAURANT.

NOOOO!!

WHY NOT?

NO!!

NO!! NO!!

WHY, WHAT'S THE MATTER? YOU ALWAYS ENJOY DOING DELIVERIES.

NO !!

I DON'T WANT TO GO TO THAT HOUSE!!

IT WAS CLEAR NOW WHO HAD ATTACKED ELISA.

1944 TIMELINE

January 15	Soviet forces launch a massive offensive against the German forces occupying the Baltic states.
January 27	Soviet troops liberate Leningrad.
March 5	All restaurants, cafes, and other entertainment facilities are shut down in Japan.
April 14	The first Jews from Greece are transported to Auschwitz.
April 17	Japan launches its last major offensive in China.
May 15-July 9	438,000 Hungarian Jews are deported to Auschwitz. Only 10 percent are selected for slave labor. The rest are sent directly to the crematoriums.
June 4	Allied forces enter Rome.
June 6	D-Day. Allied forces launch a massive, successful offensive in Normandy, France.
June 13	Germany begins launching V-1 rocket bombs against English cities. American B-29's launch their first air strikes on Japan, from China.
June 19-20	After incurring heavy losses fighting the U.S. in the Battle of the Philippine Sea, the Japanese High Command abandons any hope of winning the war.
June 22	The GI Bill of Rights is signed into law, granting U.S. veterans educational and other special benefits.
June 30	Children are evacuated from major Japanese cities.
July 1	At the Bretton Woods International Monetary Conference, forty-four Allied nations establish the International Monetary Fund to provide aid to underdeveloped countries.

July 18	Due to Japan's military setbacks in the Pacific, Tojo is removed as Japanese premier, war minister, and army chief of staff, positions he had held concurrently since the beginning of the year. A new cabinet is formed.
July 20	The attempt to assassinate Hitler at his Wolf's Lair Headquarters fails.
August 19	French resistance fighters rise up in Paris.
August 25	Allied forces liberate Paris.
October 2	An uprising in Warsaw is crushed by the Germans. Russia encouraged the uprising, but reneged on its offer to provide military support, apparently in hopes that the conflict would eliminate Polish opponents to Communism.
October 10	The U.S. Navy attacks Okinawa and the Ryuku Islands.
October 18	The Japanese minimum age for military conscription is lowered to seventeen.
October 23-26	The U.S. Navy inflicts staggering losses on the Japanese in the Battle of Leyte Gulf. It is during this conflict that the Japanese fly their first *kamikaze* suicide missions.
November 7	Roosevelt is reelected for a fourth term. Master Soviet spy Richard Sorge is executed in Tokyo.
December 18	The U.S. flies its first air raid on Osaka.

CHAPTER THREE

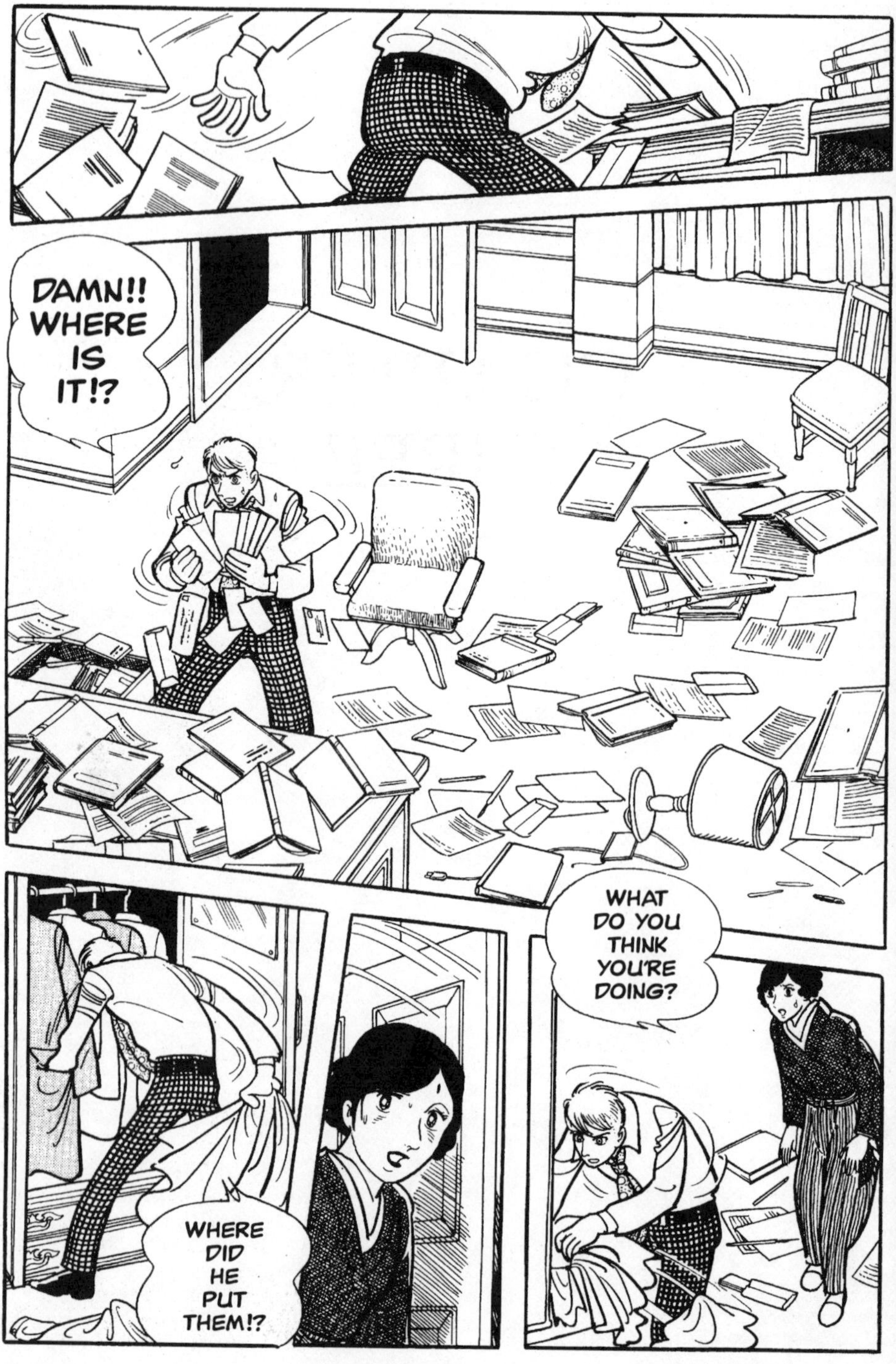
DAMN!! WHERE IS IT!?
WHERE DID HE PUT THEM!?
WHAT DO YOU THINK YOU'RE DOING?

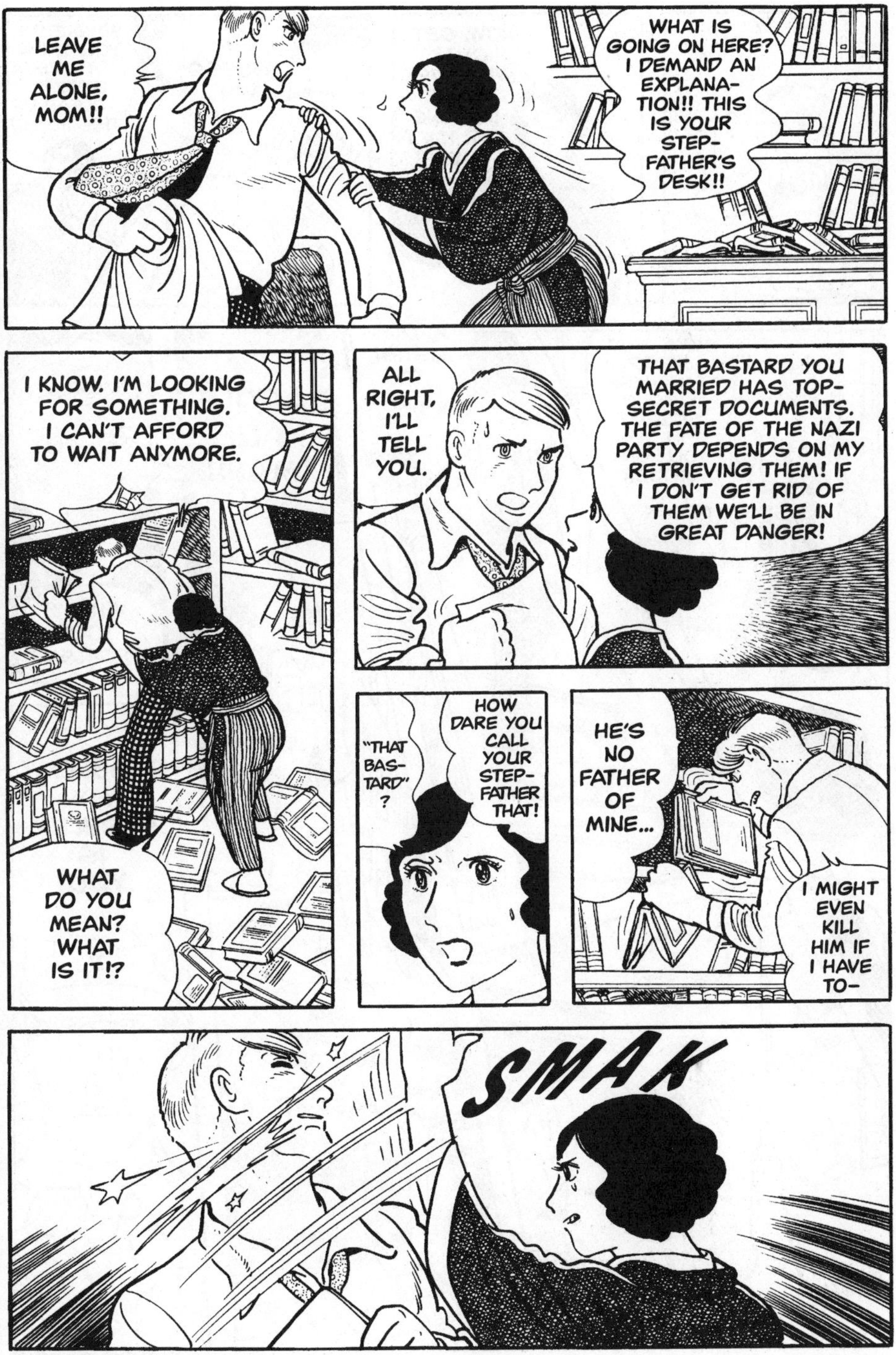
LEAVE ME ALONE, MOM!!
WHAT IS GOING ON HERE? I DEMAND AN EXPLANATION!! THIS IS YOUR STEP-FATHER'S DESK!!
I KNOW. I'M LOOKING FOR SOMETHING. I CAN'T AFFORD TO WAIT ANYMORE.
WHAT DO YOU MEAN? WHAT IS IT!?
ALL RIGHT, I'LL TELL YOU.
THAT BASTARD YOU MARRIED HAS TOP-SECRET DOCUMENTS. THE FATE OF THE NAZI PARTY DEPENDS ON MY RETRIEVING THEM! IF I DON'T GET RID OF THEM WE'LL BE IN GREAT DANGER!
"THAT BASTARD"?
HOW DARE YOU CALL YOUR STEP-FATHER THAT!
HE'S NO FATHER OF MINE...
I MIGHT EVEN KILL HIM IF I HAVE TO—
SMAK

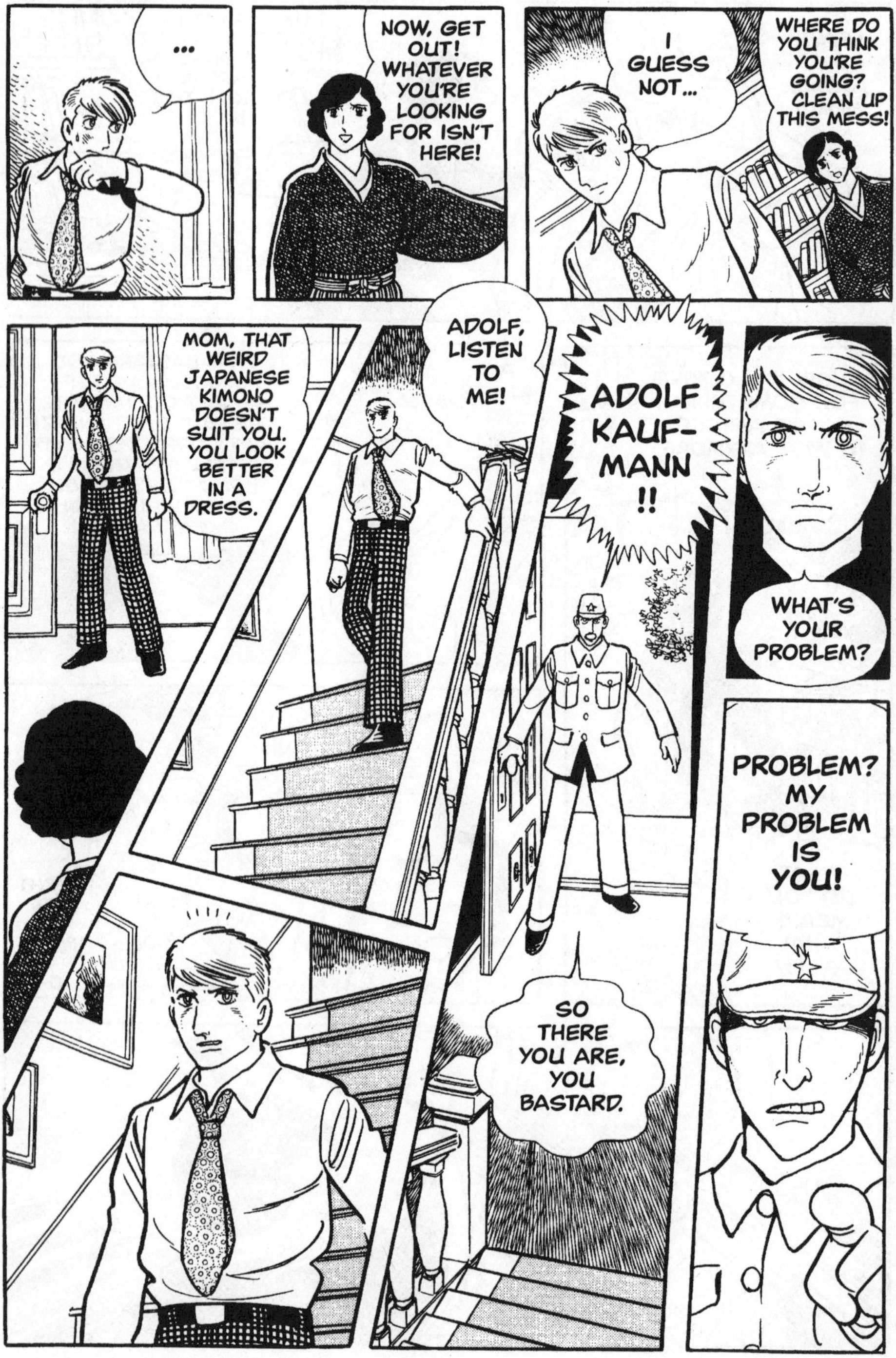
...
NOW, GET OUT! WHATEVER YOU'RE LOOKING FOR ISN'T HERE!
I GUESS NOT...
WHERE DO YOU THINK YOU'RE GOING? CLEAN UP THIS MESS!
MOM, THAT WEIRD JAPANESE KIMONO DOESN'T SUIT YOU. YOU LOOK BETTER IN A DRESS.
ADOLF, LISTEN TO ME!
ADOLF KAUF-MANN !!
SO THERE YOU ARE, YOU BASTARD.
WHAT'S YOUR PROBLEM?
PROBLEM? MY PROBLEM IS YOU!

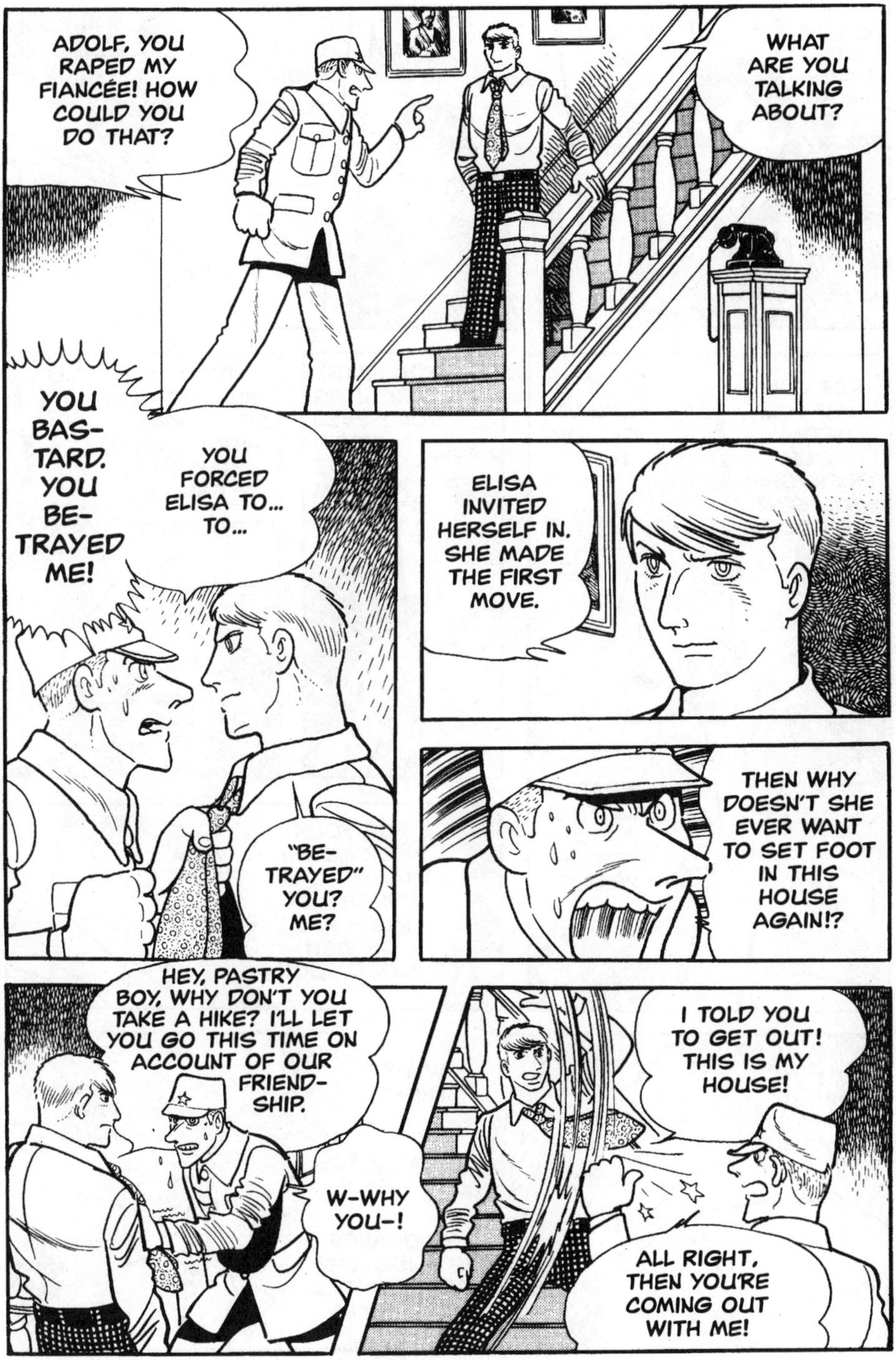
ADOLF, YOU RAPED MY FIANCÉE! HOW COULD YOU DO THAT?
WHAT ARE YOU TALKING ABOUT?
YOU BASTARD. YOU BETRAYED ME!
YOU FORCED ELISA TO... TO...
"BETRAYED" YOU? ME?
ELISA INVITED HERSELF IN. SHE MADE THE FIRST MOVE.
THEN WHY DOESN'T SHE EVER WANT TO SET FOOT IN THIS HOUSE AGAIN!?
HEY, PASTRY BOY, WHY DON'T YOU TAKE A HIKE? I'LL LET YOU GO THIS TIME ON ACCOUNT OF OUR FRIENDSHIP.
W-WHY YOU-!
I TOLD YOU TO GET OUT! THIS IS MY HOUSE!
ALL RIGHT, THEN YOU'RE COMING OUT WITH ME!

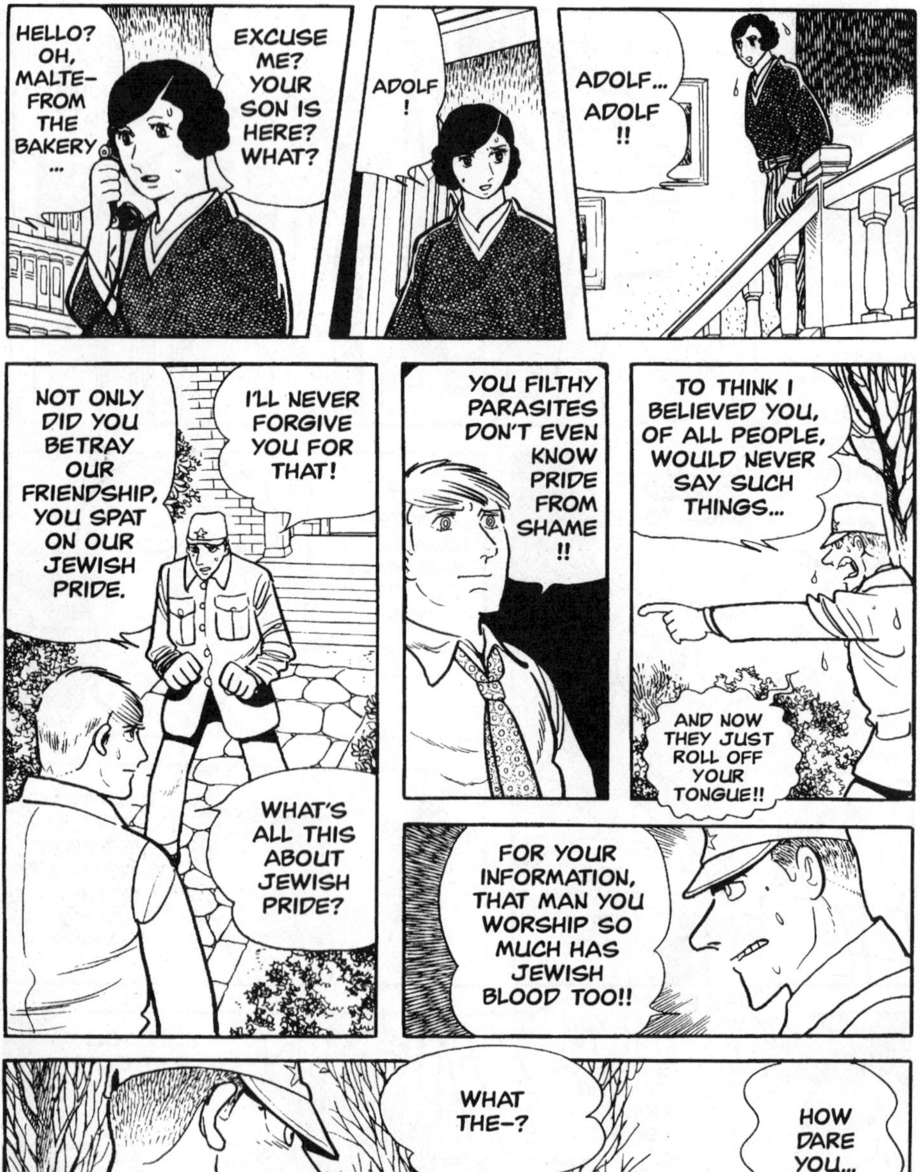
HELLO? OH, MALTE– FROM THE BAKERY ...
EXCUSE ME? YOUR SON IS HERE? WHAT?
ADOLF !
ADOLF... ADOLF !!
NOT ONLY DID YOU BETRAY OUR FRIENDSHIP, YOU SPAT ON OUR JEWISH PRIDE.
I'LL NEVER FORGIVE YOU FOR THAT!
WHAT'S ALL THIS ABOUT JEWISH PRIDE?
YOU FILTHY PARASITES DON'T EVEN KNOW PRIDE FROM SHAME !!
TO THINK I BELIEVED YOU, OF ALL PEOPLE, WOULD NEVER SAY SUCH THINGS...
AND NOW THEY JUST ROLL OFF YOUR TONGUE!!
FOR YOUR INFORMATION, THAT MAN YOU WORSHIP SO MUCH HAS JEWISH BLOOD TOO!!
WHAT THE–?
IGNORANCE IS BLISS, EH? I'VE SEEN THE EVIDENCE!
HOW DARE YOU...

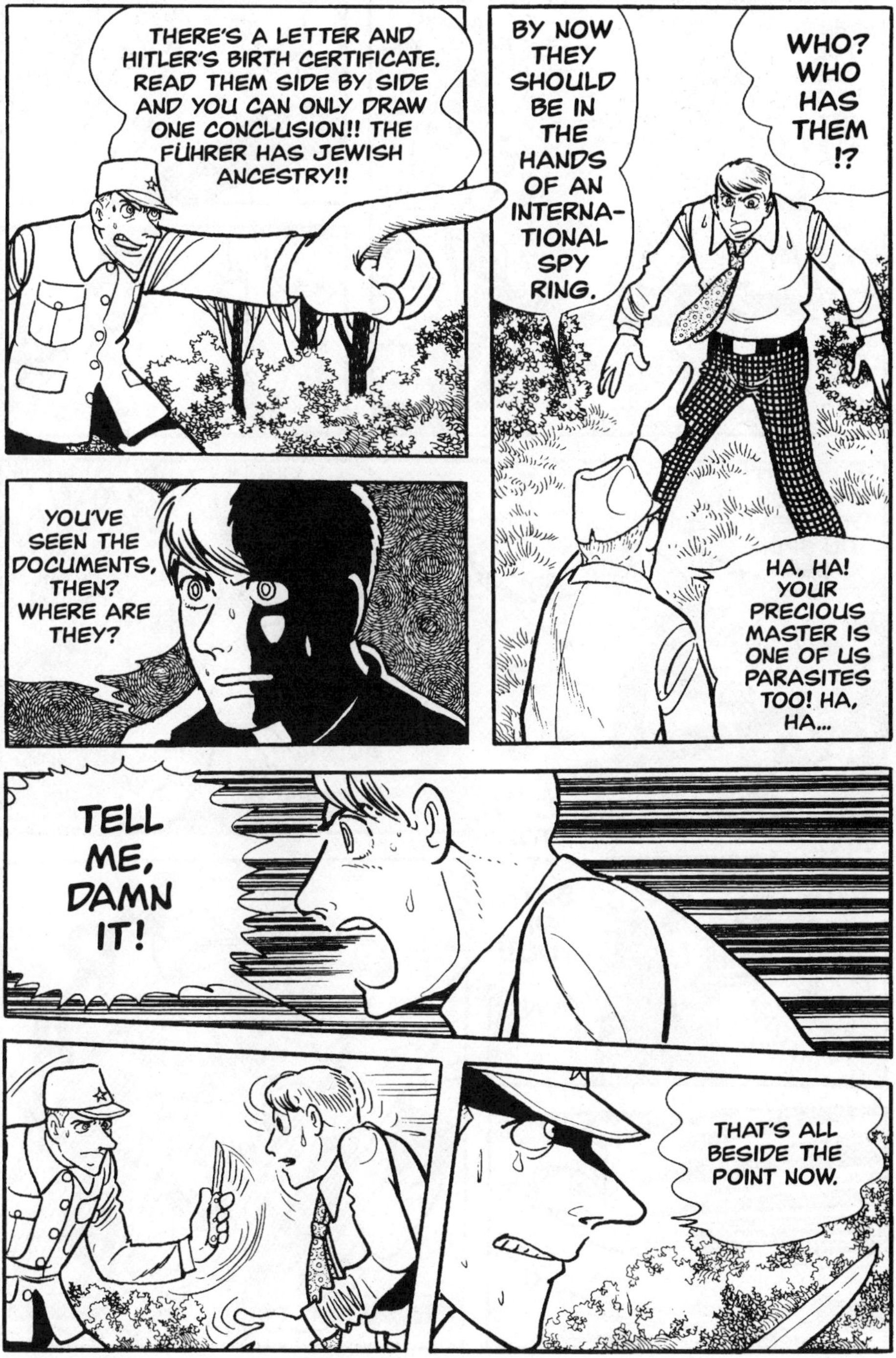
THERE'S A LETTER AND HITLER'S BIRTH CERTIFICATE. READ THEM SIDE BY SIDE AND YOU CAN ONLY DRAW ONE CONCLUSION!! THE FÜHRER HAS JEWISH ANCESTRY!!
YOU'VE SEEN THE DOCUMENTS, THEN? WHERE ARE THEY?
BY NOW THEY SHOULD BE IN THE HANDS OF AN INTERNA-TIONAL SPY RING.
WHO? WHO HAS THEM !?
HA, HA! YOUR PRECIOUS MASTER IS ONE OF US PARASITES TOO! HA, HA...
TELL ME, DAMN IT!
THAT'S ALL BESIDE THE POINT NOW.

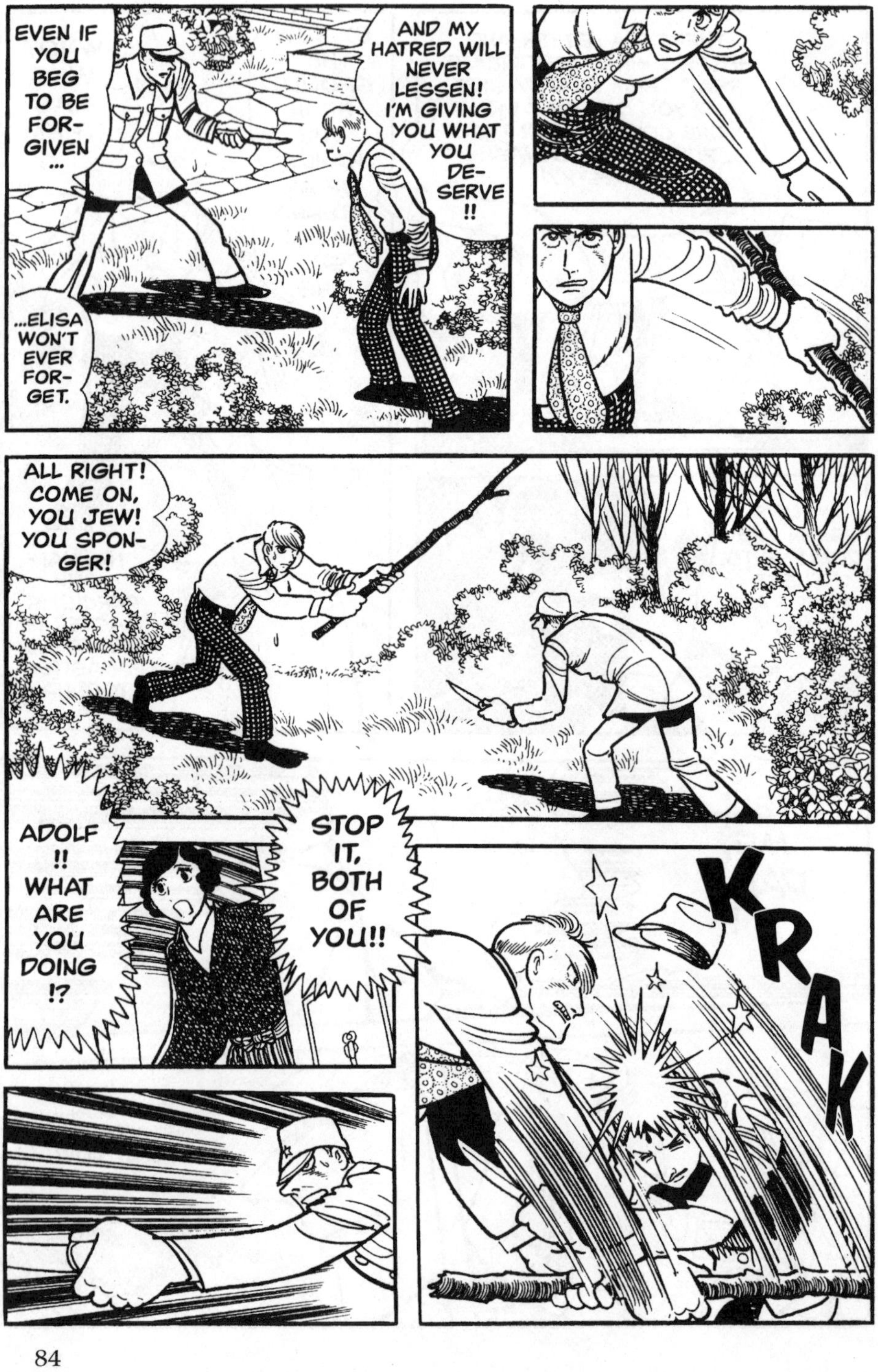
EVEN IF YOU BEG TO BE FOR-GIVEN ...
...ELISA WON'T EVER FOR-GET.
AND MY HATRED WILL NEVER LESSEN! I'M GIVING YOU WHAT YOU DE-SERVE !!
ALL RIGHT! COME ON, YOU JEW! YOU SPON-GER!
ADOLF !! WHAT ARE YOU DOING !?
STOP IT, BOTH OF YOU!!
KRAK

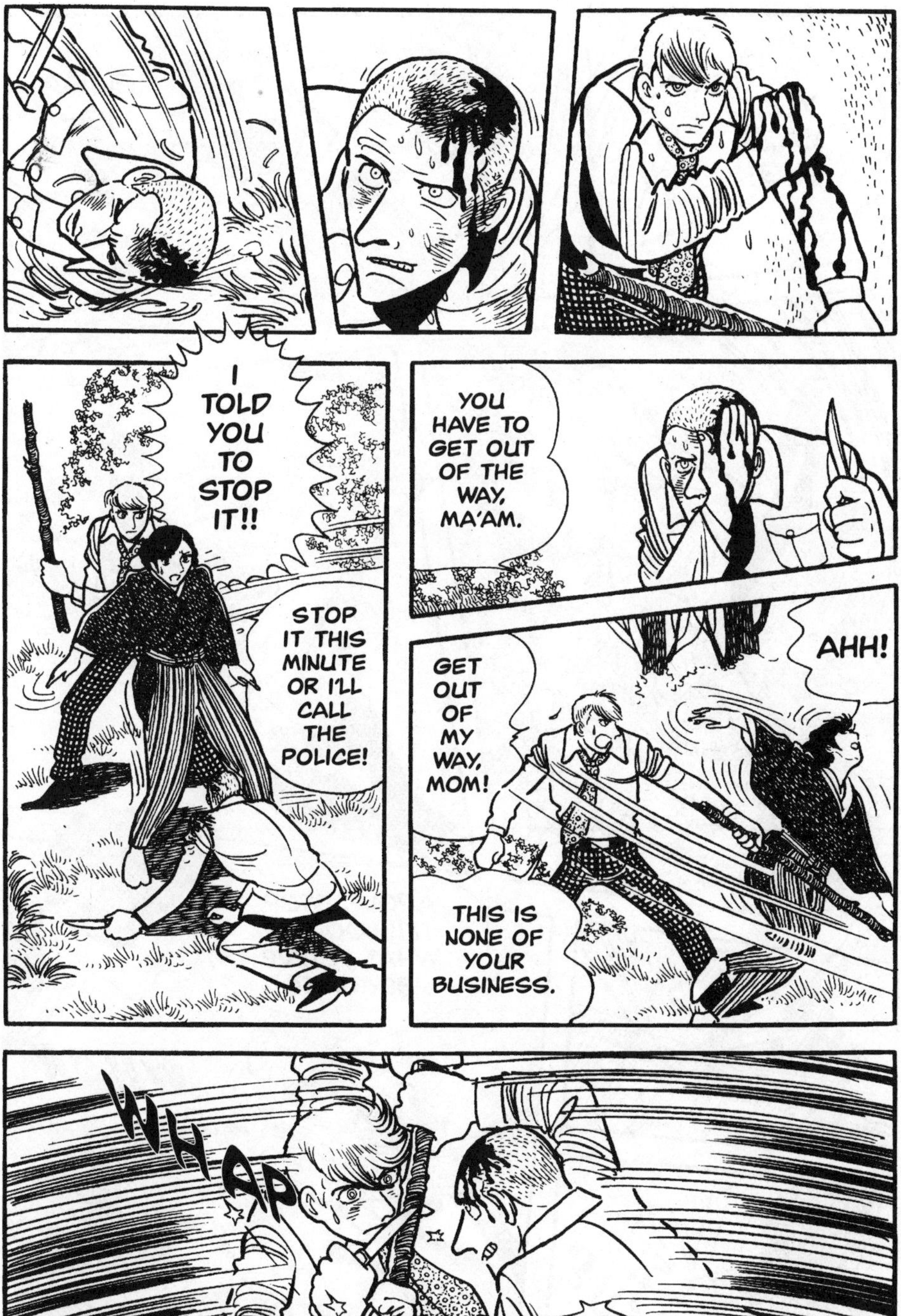
I TOLD YOU TO STOP IT!!
STOP IT THIS MINUTE OR I'LL CALL THE POLICE!
YOU HAVE TO GET OUT OF THE WAY, MA'AM.
GET OUT OF MY WAY, MOM!
AHH!
THIS IS NONE OF YOUR BUSINESS.
WHAP

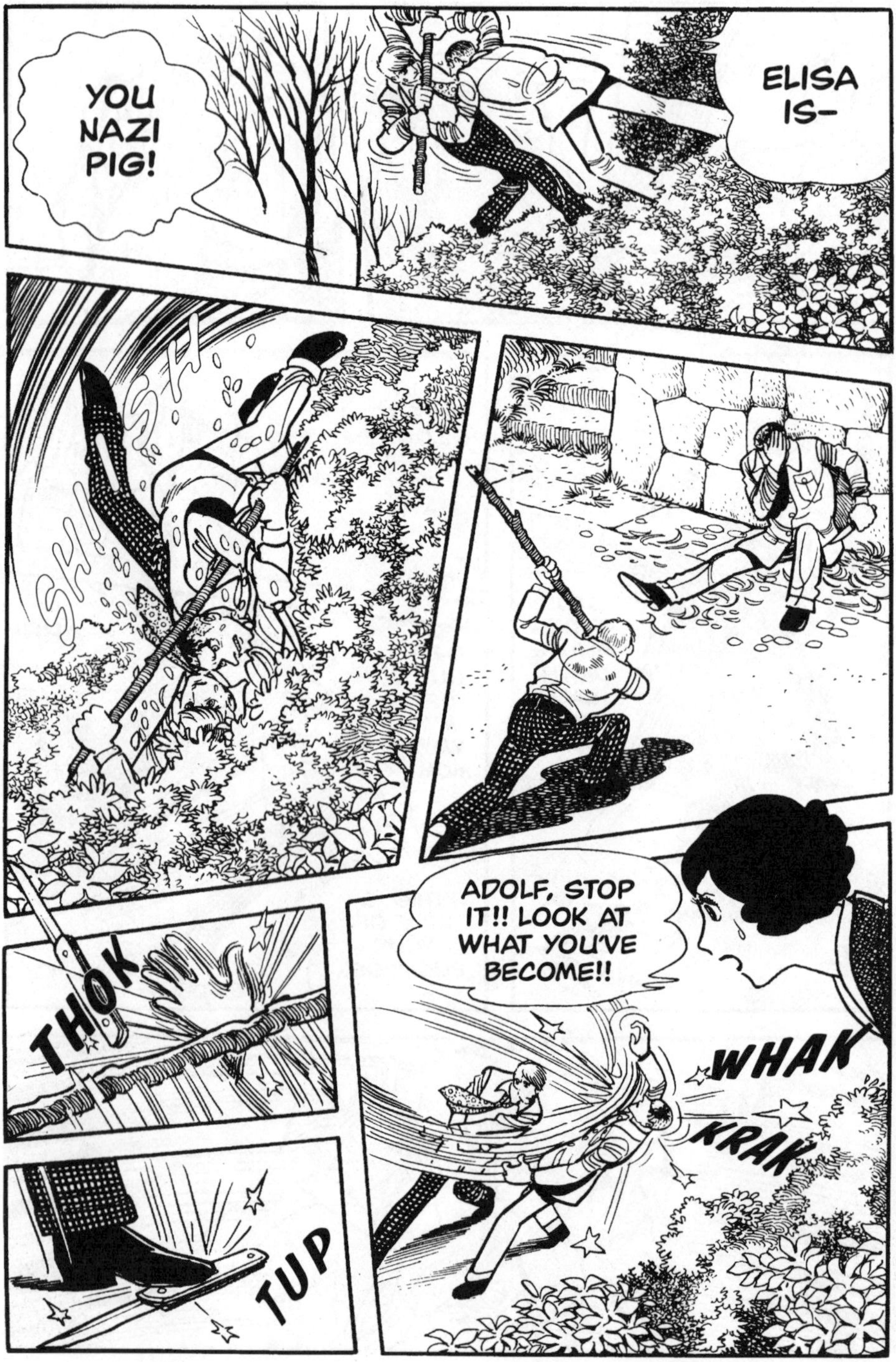
YOU NAZI PIG!
ELISA IS-
SHH SHH
THOK
TUP
ADOLF, STOP IT!! LOOK AT WHAT YOU'VE BECOME!!
WHAK
KRAK

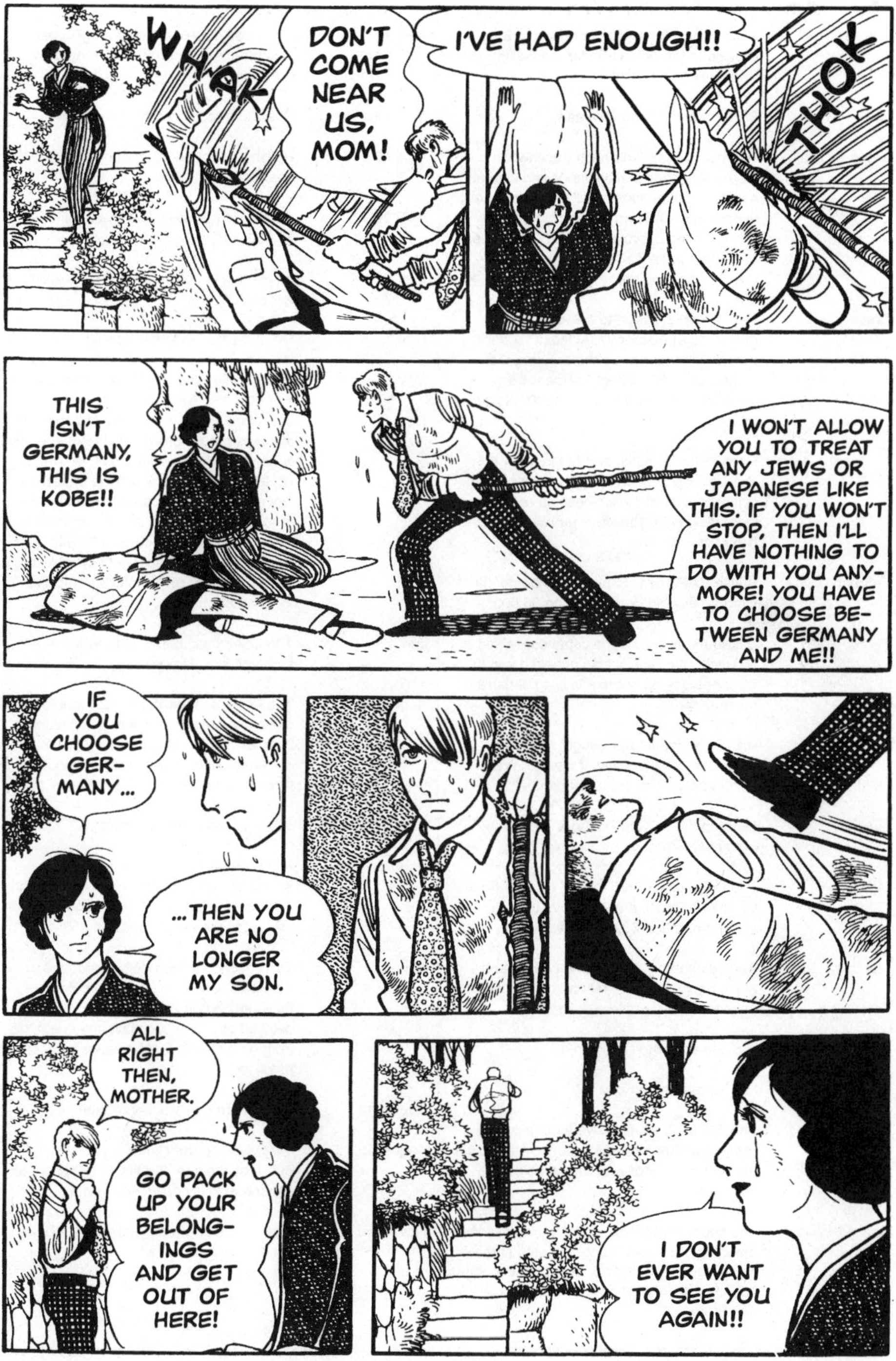
WHAK
DON'T COME NEAR US, MOM!
I'VE HAD ENOUGH!!
THOK
THIS ISN'T GERMANY, THIS IS KOBE!!
I WON'T ALLOW YOU TO TREAT ANY JEWS OR JAPANESE LIKE THIS. IF YOU WON'T STOP, THEN I'LL HAVE NOTHING TO DO WITH YOU ANY-MORE! YOU HAVE TO CHOOSE BE-TWEEN GERMANY AND ME!!
IF YOU CHOOSE GER-MANY...
...THEN YOU ARE NO LONGER MY SON.
ALL RIGHT THEN, MOTHER.
GO PACK UP YOUR BELONG-INGS AND GET OUT OF HERE!
I DON'T EVER WANT TO SEE YOU AGAIN!!

1945 TIMELINE

January 15	Hitler moves his headquarters from East Prussia to the bunker under the Reich Chancellery in Berlin.
January 17	Soviet troops occupy Warsaw.
January 18	As Soviet troops approach Auschwitz, Germany's largest slave labor and extermination camp, prisoners are forced to march deeper into the Third Reich. By early spring, of the approximately 62,000 that set out, one quarter had died of hunger, disease, and exposure.
January 26	Russian troops liberate 2,819 inmates remaining at Auschwitz. At least 1.1 million people were murdered there during the camp's operation. Ninety percent were Jews, 22,000 Gypsies, and 12,000 Soviet prisoners of war.
February 4-9	Roosevelt, Churchill, and Stalin meet at Yalta to plan their campaign against Japan. Unbeknownst to the Chinese, in return for its participation, Russia is promised a portion of Manchuria.
February 13-14	British RAF and U.S. planes firebomb the German city of Dresden, killing 35,000.
February 19	U.S. Marines invade the Japanese island of Iwo Jima, the "unsinkable airfield" used to intercept U.S. bombers attacking Japan's home islands.
February 25	U.S. B-29's begin flying night raids on Japanese cities instead of daylight precision raids against industrial centers.
March 3	German fifteen-year-old boys are ordered to front-line duty.
March 9	The U.S. drops 1,665 tons of napalm-filled bombs on Tokyo, the Japanese capital, killing more than 83,000 within 30 minutes.
March 13	Adolf Eichmann declares he can go to his grave happy knowing he has contributed to the deaths of six million Jews.
March 14-15	U.S. forces bomb Osaka.
March 16-17	U.S. forces bomb Kobe.
March 18	The Allies launch massive air attacks on Berlin and Frankfurt. All Japanese schools are ordered to close for one year, beginning April 1.
April 11	The concentration camp Buchenwald is liberated by American troops. Deaths at the camp numbered 56,000, but prisoners continued to die after liberation, from starvation and disease.
April 12	Roosevelt dies of a stroke and Truman becomes the United States' thirty-third president.
April 13	Russian troops capture Vienna.
April 15	British troops liberate Bergen-Belsen. The death toll is 50,000.
April 28	Dachau is liberated. The death toll is 50,000.
May 2	All fighting in Italy ceases and Russian forces control Berlin.
May 7	Germany surrenders unconditionally.
May 8	V-E Day. The war in Europe officially ends.
June 22	U.S. planes drop 3,000 tons of bombs on Japanese munitions plants in Kobe, Osaka, Nagoya, and Okayama, and Okinawa is captured by U.S forces. In the eighty-one day campaign to secure the island, considered essential for the invasion of Japan, 12,520 U.S troops died, and 36,631 were wounded. 110,000 Japanese were killed, fully 90 percent of the forces participating in the conflict.
July 16	The first atomic bomb is exploded at a test facility in New Mexico.
August 2	The leaders of the Big Three meet for the final conference of the war in Potsdam, Germany, to draw up the terms for Japan's surrender. This marks the end of World War II, and the onset of the Cold War.
August 3	Japan is completely blockaded.
August 6	A U.S. B-29, the *Enola Gay*, drops an atomic bomb on Hiroshima. The U.S. highest estimate of immediate deaths is 78,000; the Japanese estimate is 240,000.
August 9	The second atomic bomb is dropped on Nagasaki. Casualties are estimated between 35,000 and 74,000. Due to the delayed effects of radiation, the death toll from both atomic bombs grows for decades to follow.
August 14	Japan surrenders unconditionally.
August 15	V-J Day. Emperor Hirohito, addressing the public by radio for the first time, orders all Japanese to lay down their arms.
November 20	The Nuremberg trials, prosecuting Nazi war criminals, commence.

CHAPTER
FOUR

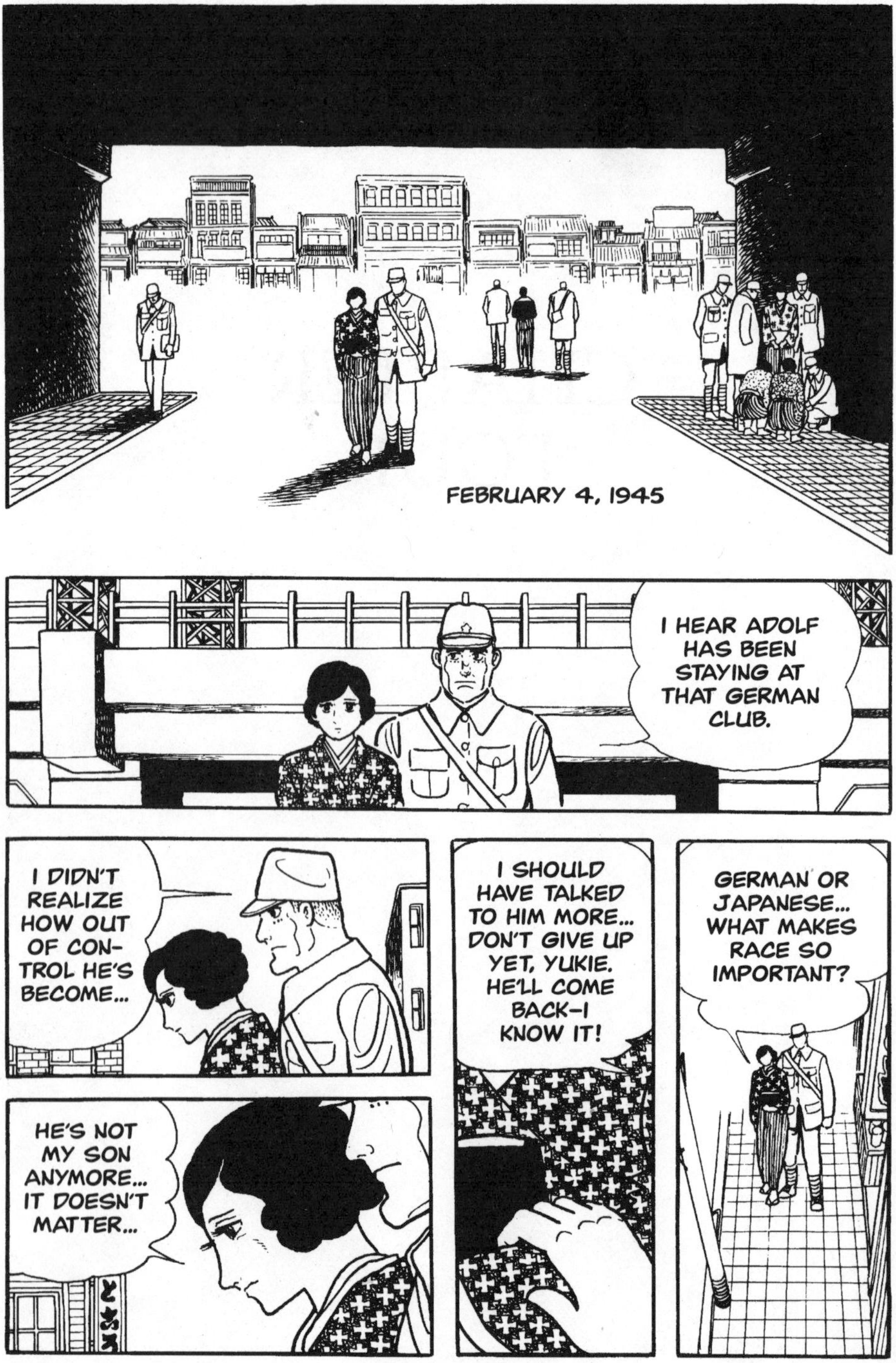
FEBRUARY 4, 1945
I HEAR ADOLF HAS BEEN STAYING AT THAT GERMAN CLUB.
I DIDN'T REALIZE HOW OUT OF CON-TROL HE'S BECOME...
HE'S NOT MY SON ANYMORE... IT DOESN'T MATTER...
I SHOULD HAVE TALKED TO HIM MORE... DON'T GIVE UP YET, YUKIE. HE'LL COME BACK—I KNOW IT!
GERMAN OR JAPANESE... WHAT MAKES RACE SO IMPORTANT?

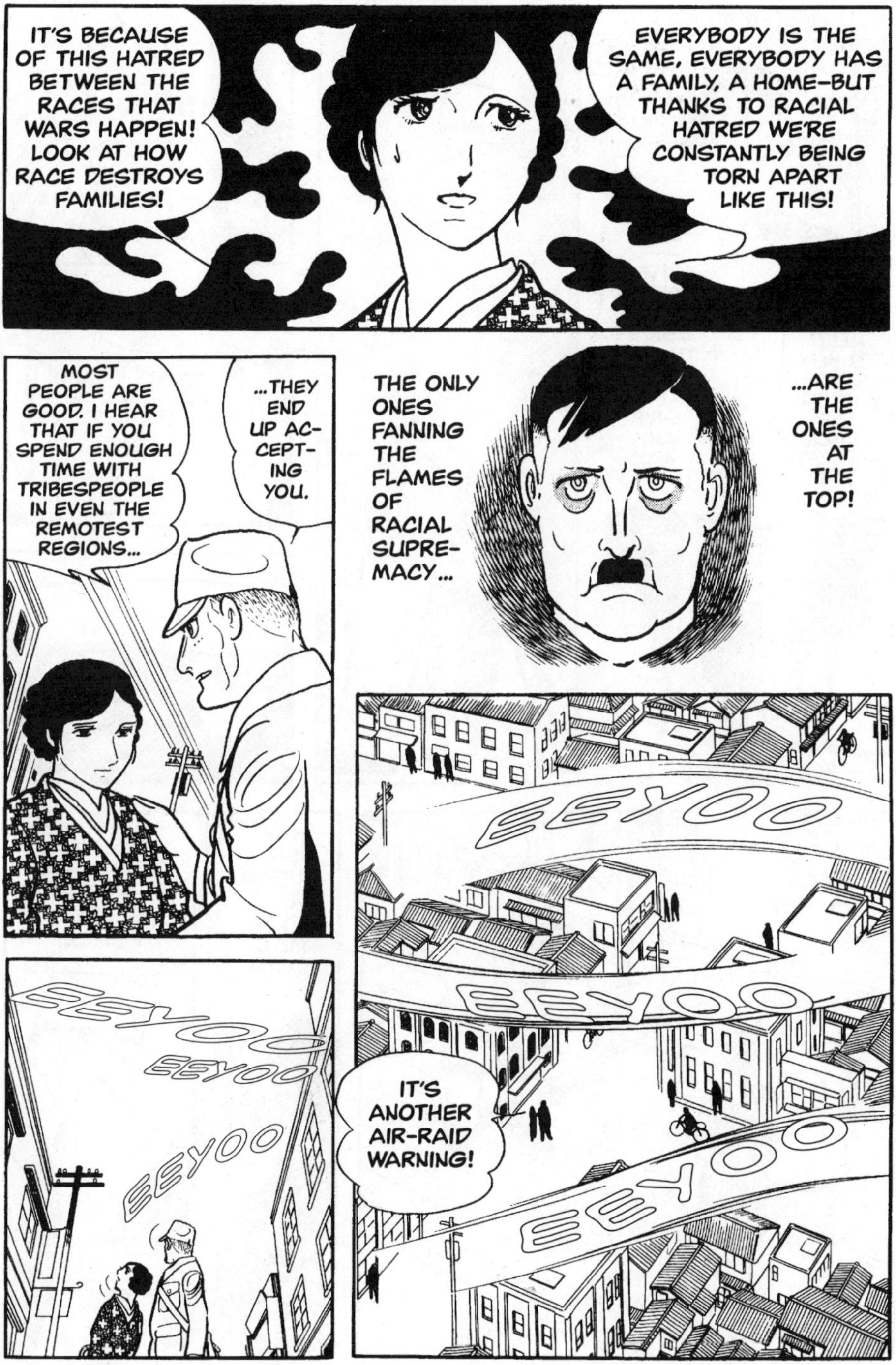
IT'S BECAUSE OF THIS HATRED BETWEEN THE RACES THAT WARS HAPPEN! LOOK AT HOW RACE DESTROYS FAMILIES!
EVERYBODY IS THE SAME, EVERYBODY HAS A FAMILY, A HOME—BUT THANKS TO RACIAL HATRED WE'RE CONSTANTLY BEING TORN APART LIKE THIS!
MOST PEOPLE ARE GOOD. I HEAR THAT IF YOU SPEND ENOUGH TIME WITH TRIBESPEOPLE IN EVEN THE REMOTEST REGIONS...
...THEY END UP AC-CEPT-ING YOU.
THE ONLY ONES FANNING THE FLAMES OF RACIAL SUPRE-MACY...
...ARE THE ONES AT THE TOP!
EEYOO
EEYOO
EEYOO
EEYOO
EEYOO
EEYOO
IT'S ANOTHER AIR-RAID WARNING!

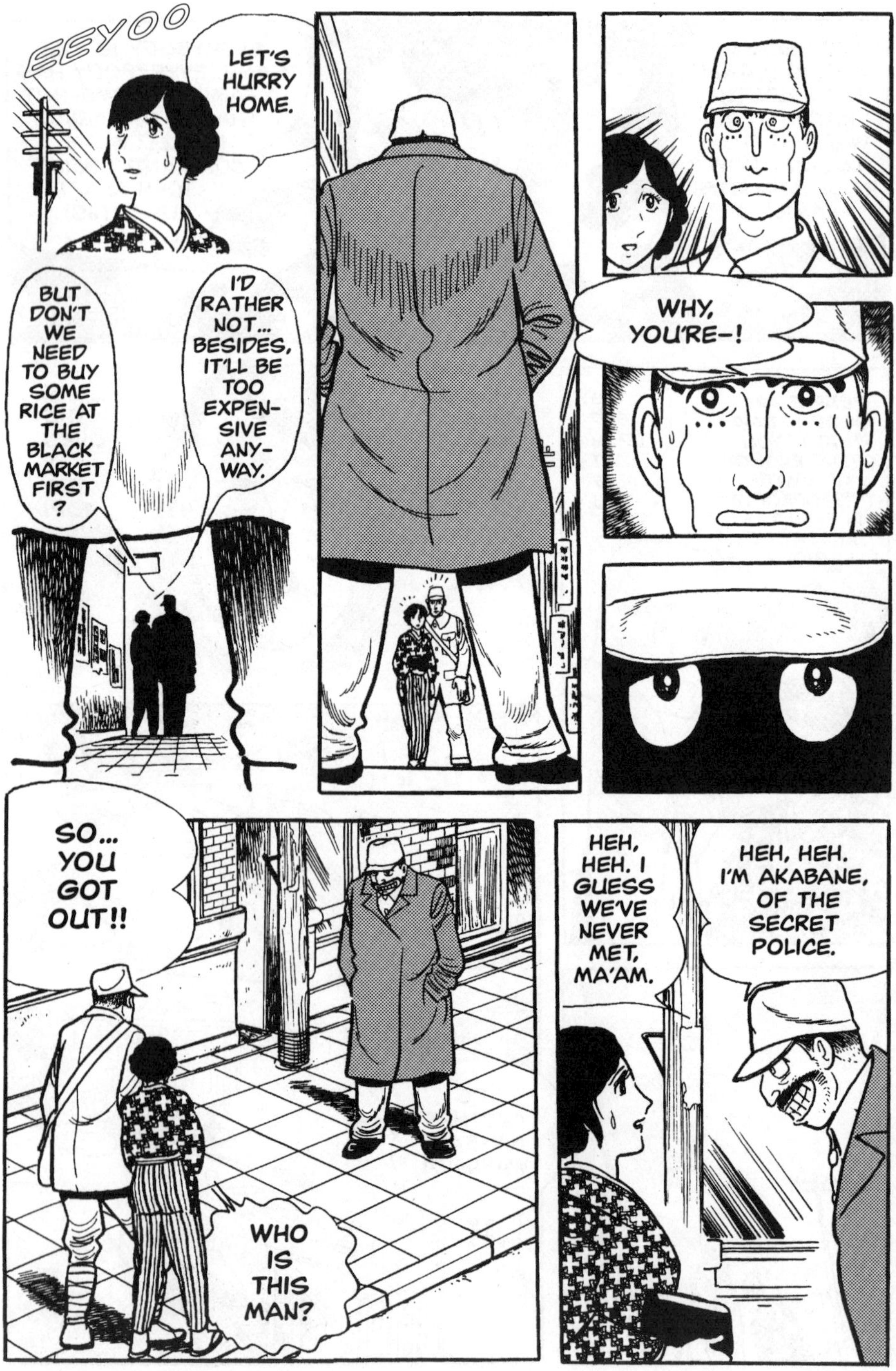
EEYOO
LET'S HURRY HOME.
BUT DON'T WE NEED TO BUY SOME RICE AT THE BLACK MARKET FIRST?
I'D RATHER NOT... BESIDES, IT'LL BE TOO EXPENSIVE ANYWAY.
WHY, YOU'RE–!
SO... YOU GOT OUT!!
WHO IS THIS MAN?
HEH, HEH. I GUESS WE'VE NEVER MET, MA'AM.
HEH, HEH. I'M AKABANE, OF THE SECRET POLICE.

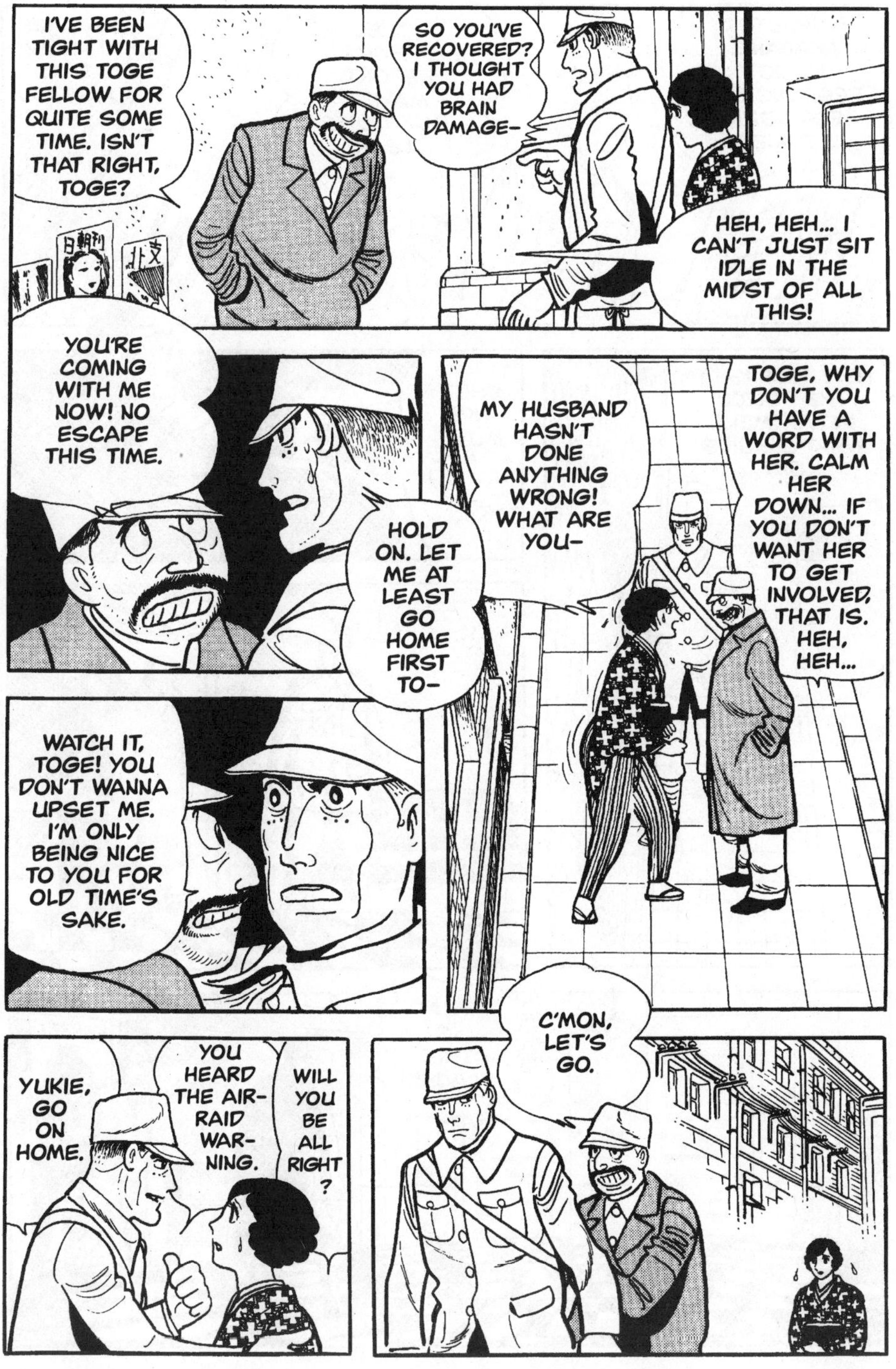
I'VE BEEN TIGHT WITH THIS TOGE FELLOW FOR QUITE SOME TIME. ISN'T THAT RIGHT, TOGE?
SO YOU'VE RECOVERED? I THOUGHT YOU HAD BRAIN DAMAGE-
HEH, HEH... I CAN'T JUST SIT IDLE IN THE MIDST OF ALL THIS!
YOU'RE COMING WITH ME NOW! NO ESCAPE THIS TIME.
HOLD ON. LET ME AT LEAST GO HOME FIRST TO-
WATCH IT, TOGE! YOU DON'T WANNA UPSET ME. I'M ONLY BEING NICE TO YOU FOR OLD TIME'S SAKE.
MY HUSBAND HASN'T DONE ANYTHING WRONG! WHAT ARE YOU-
TOGE, WHY DON'T YOU HAVE A WORD WITH HER. CALM HER DOWN... IF YOU DON'T WANT HER TO GET INVOLVED, THAT IS. HEH, HEH...
YUKIE, GO ON HOME.
YOU HEARD THE AIR-RAID WAR-NING.
WILL YOU BE ALL RIGHT?
C'MON, LET'S GO.

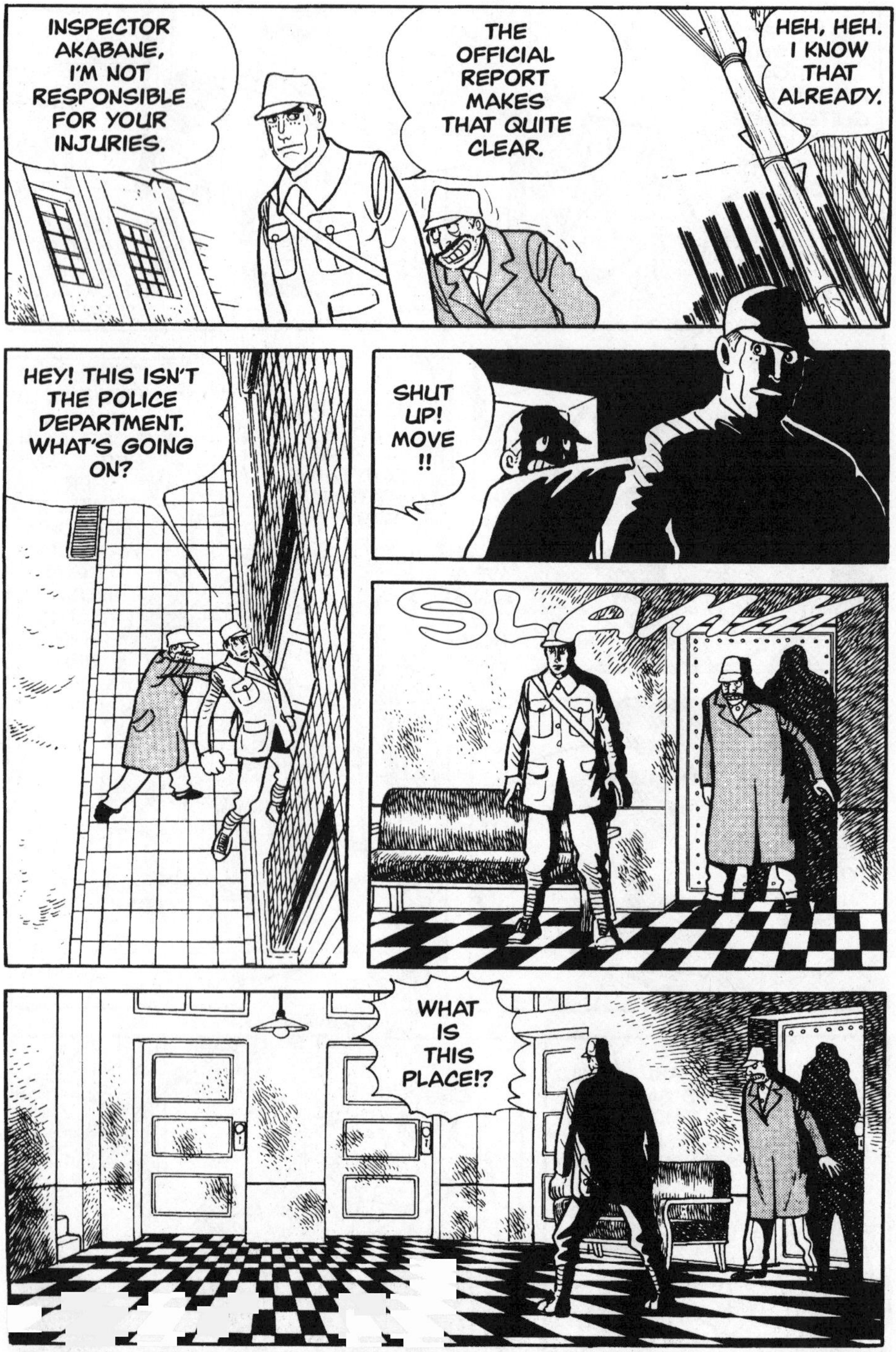
INSPECTOR AKABANE, I'M NOT RESPONSIBLE FOR YOUR INJURIES.
THE OFFICIAL REPORT MAKES THAT QUITE CLEAR.
HEH, HEH. I KNOW THAT ALREADY.
HEY! THIS ISN'T THE POLICE DEPARTMENT. WHAT'S GOING ON?
SHUT UP! MOVE !!
SLAMM
WHAT IS THIS PLACE!?

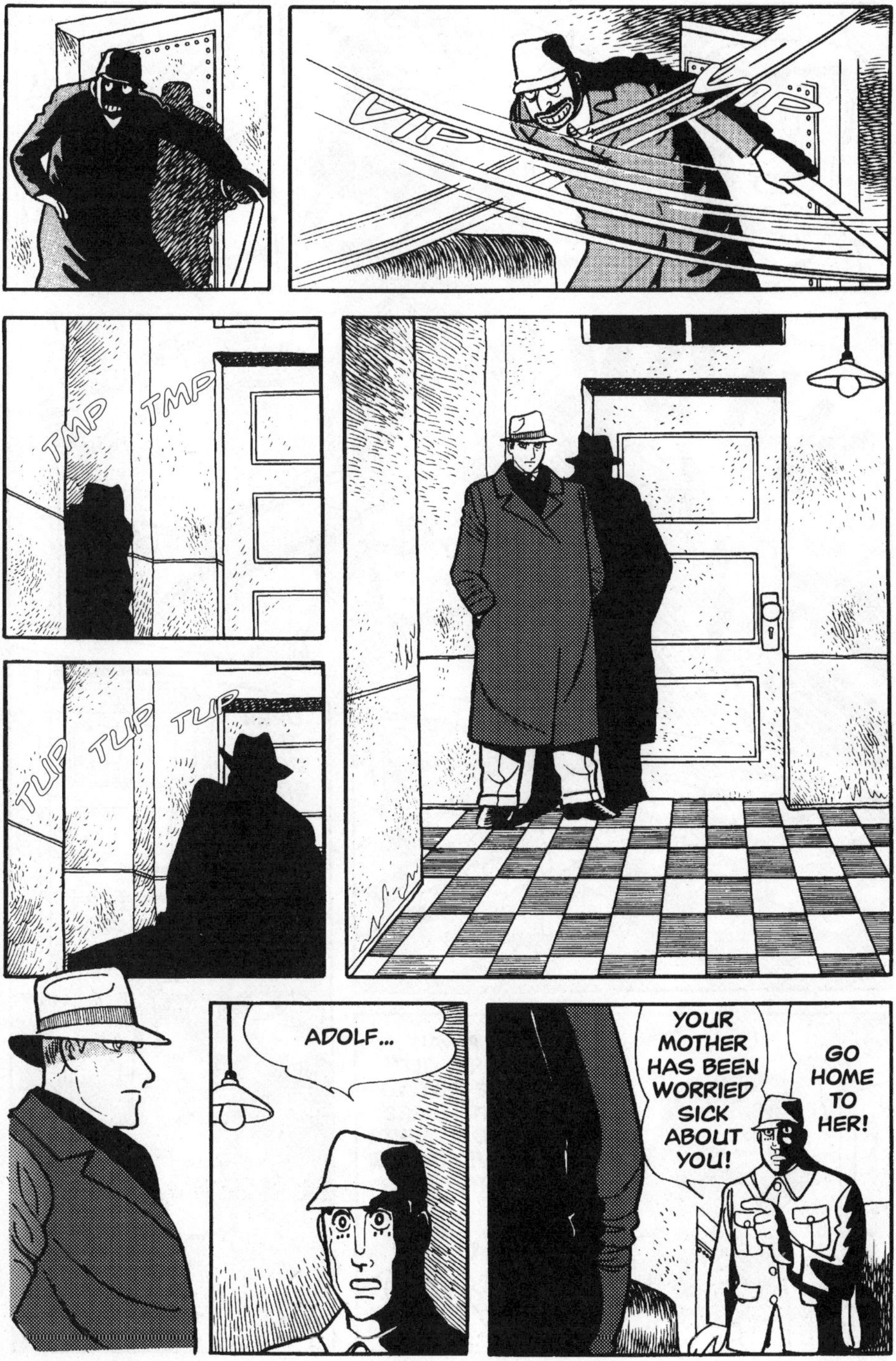
VIP
VIP
TMP TMP
TUP TUP TUP
ADOLF...
YOUR MOTHER HAS BEEN WORRIED SICK ABOUT YOU!
GO HOME TO HER!

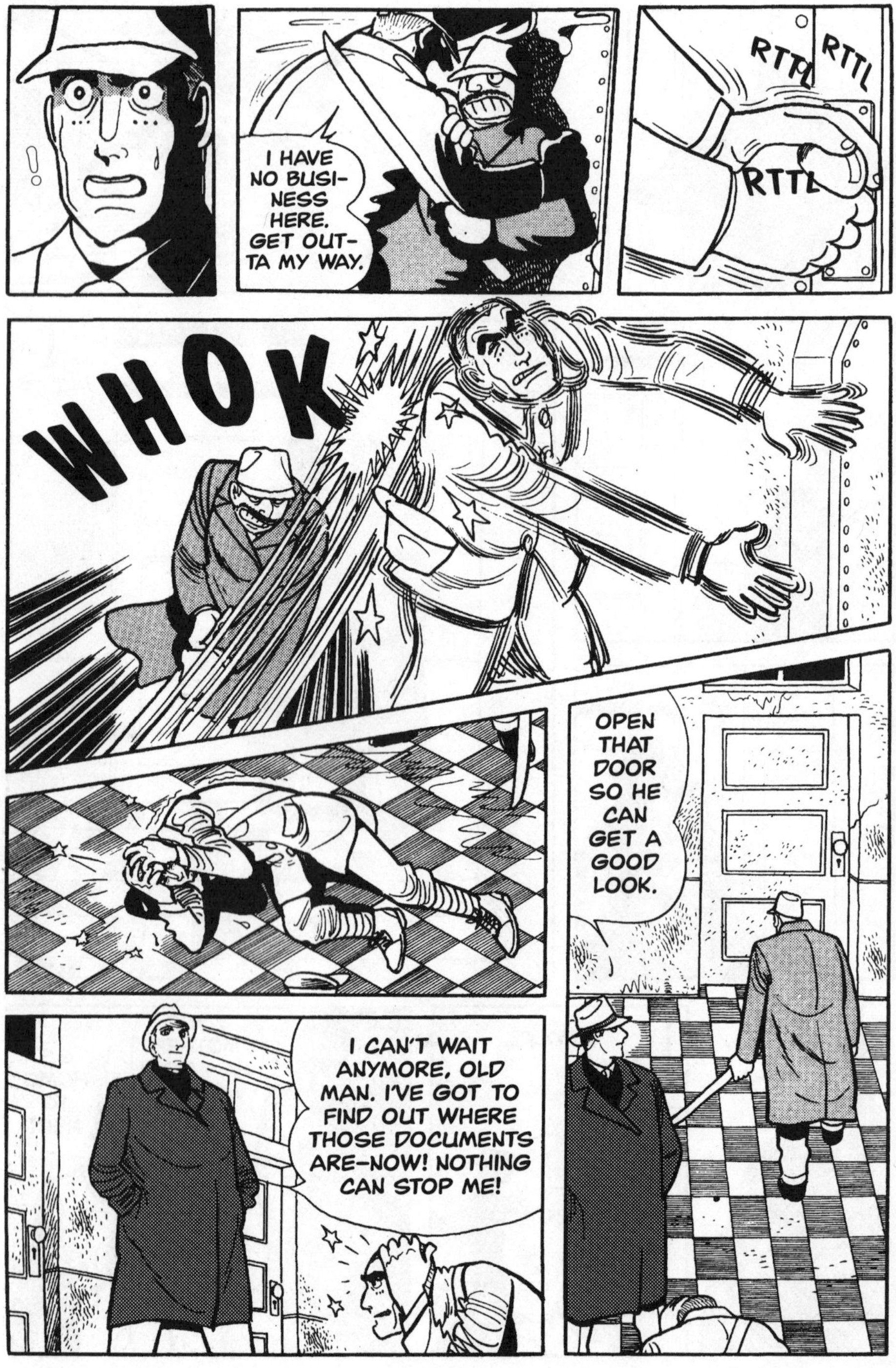
!
I HAVE NO BUSINESS HERE. GET OUTTA MY WAY.
RTTL RTTL RTTL
WHOK
OPEN THAT DOOR SO HE CAN GET A GOOD LOOK.
I CAN'T WAIT ANYMORE, OLD MAN. I'VE GOT TO FIND OUT WHERE THOSE DOCUMENTS ARE—NOW! NOTHING CAN STOP ME!

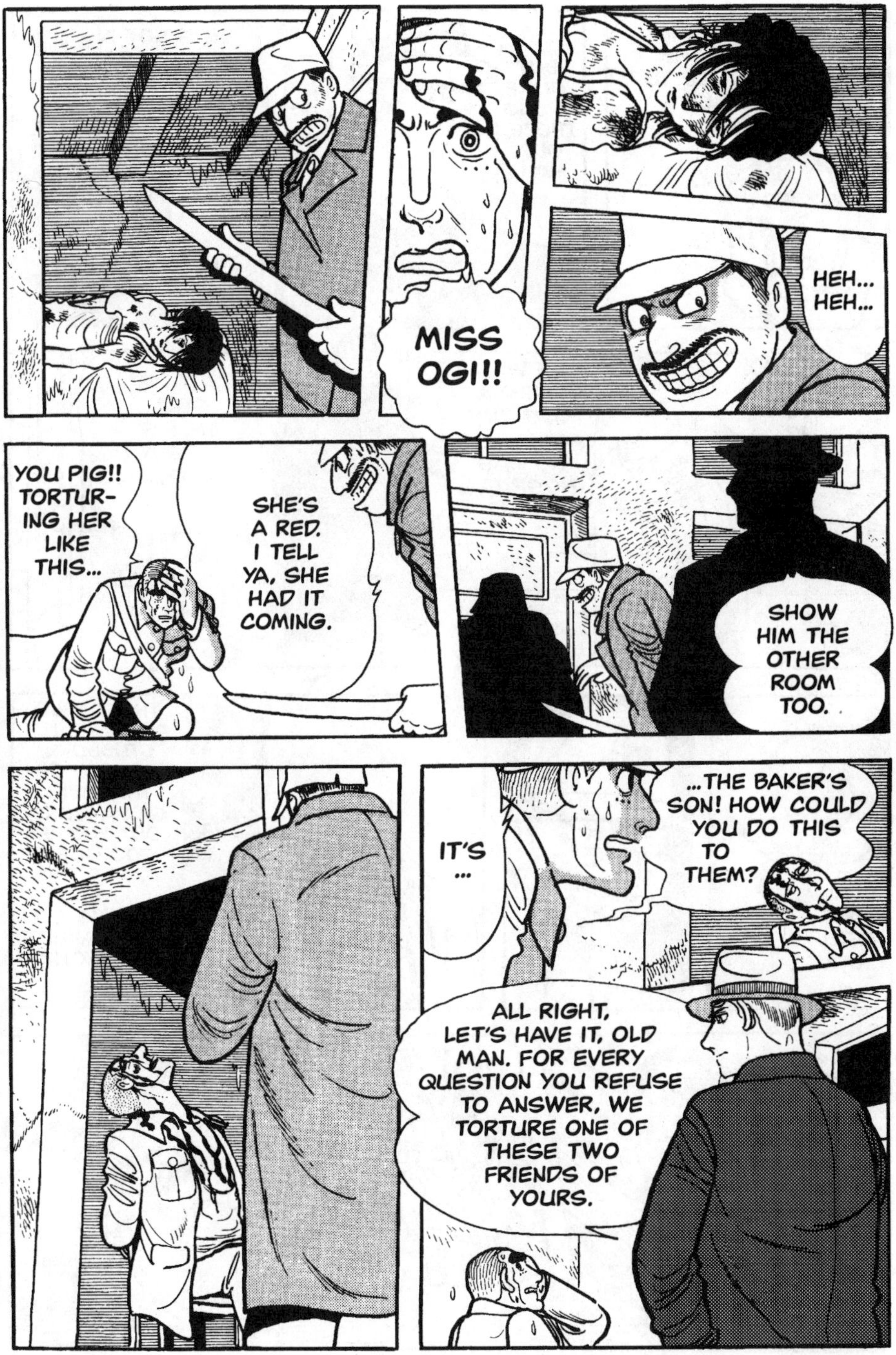
MISS OGI!!
HEH... HEH...
YOU PIG!! TORTURING HER LIKE THIS...
SHE'S A RED. I TELL YA, SHE HAD IT COMING.
SHOW HIM THE OTHER ROOM TOO.
IT'S ...
...THE BAKER'S SON! HOW COULD YOU DO THIS TO THEM?
ALL RIGHT, LET'S HAVE IT, OLD MAN. FOR EVERY QUESTION YOU REFUSE TO ANSWER, WE TORTURE ONE OF THESE TWO FRIENDS OF YOURS.

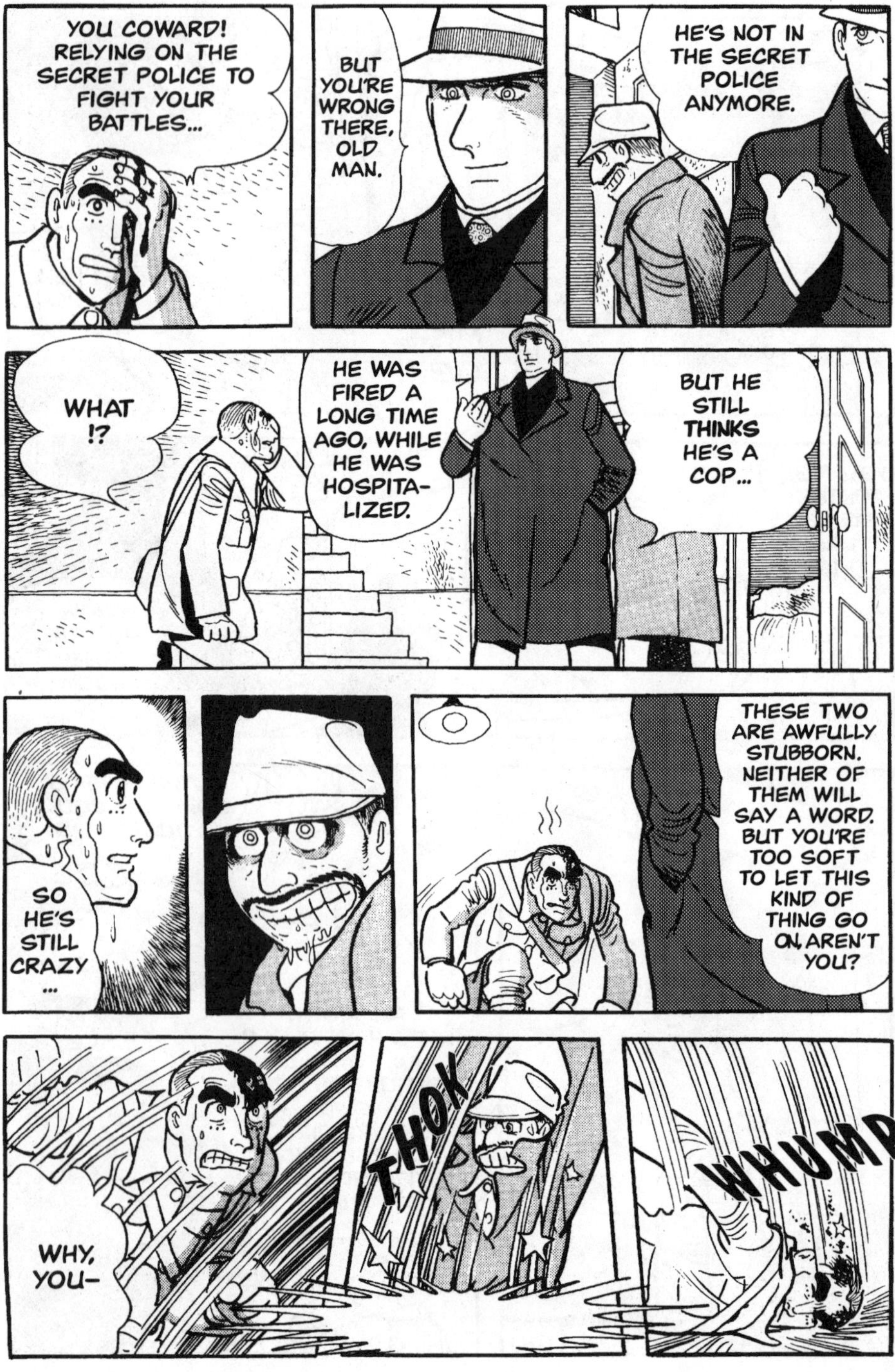
YOU COWARD! RELYING ON THE SECRET POLICE TO FIGHT YOUR BATTLES...
BUT YOU'RE WRONG THERE, OLD MAN.
HE'S NOT IN THE SECRET POLICE ANYMORE.
WHAT !?
HE WAS FIRED A LONG TIME AGO, WHILE HE WAS HOSPITALIZED.
BUT HE STILL **THINKS** HE'S A COP...
SO HE'S STILL CRAZY ...
THESE TWO ARE AWFULLY STUBBORN. NEITHER OF THEM WILL SAY A WORD. BUT YOU'RE TOO SOFT TO LET THIS KIND OF THING GO ON, AREN'T YOU?
WHY, YOU-
THOK
WHUMP

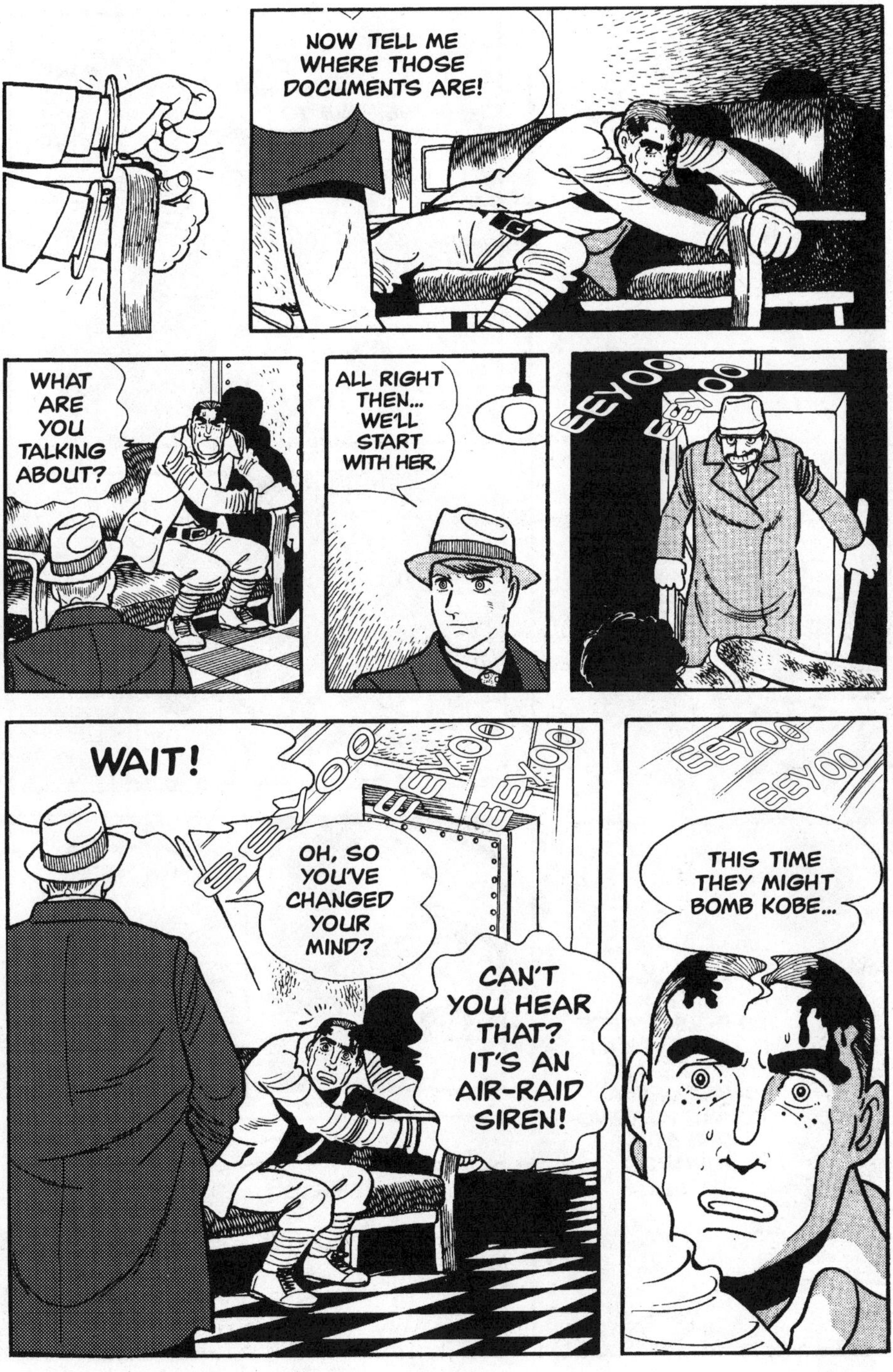
NOW TELL ME WHERE THOSE DOCUMENTS ARE!
WHAT ARE YOU TALKING ABOUT?
ALL RIGHT THEN... WE'LL START WITH HER.
EEYOO
EEYOO
WAIT!
EEYOO
EEYOO
EEYOO
OH, SO YOU'VE CHANGED YOUR MIND?
CAN'T YOU HEAR THAT? IT'S AN AIR-RAID SIREN!
EEYOO
EEYOO
THIS TIME THEY MIGHT BOMB KOBE...

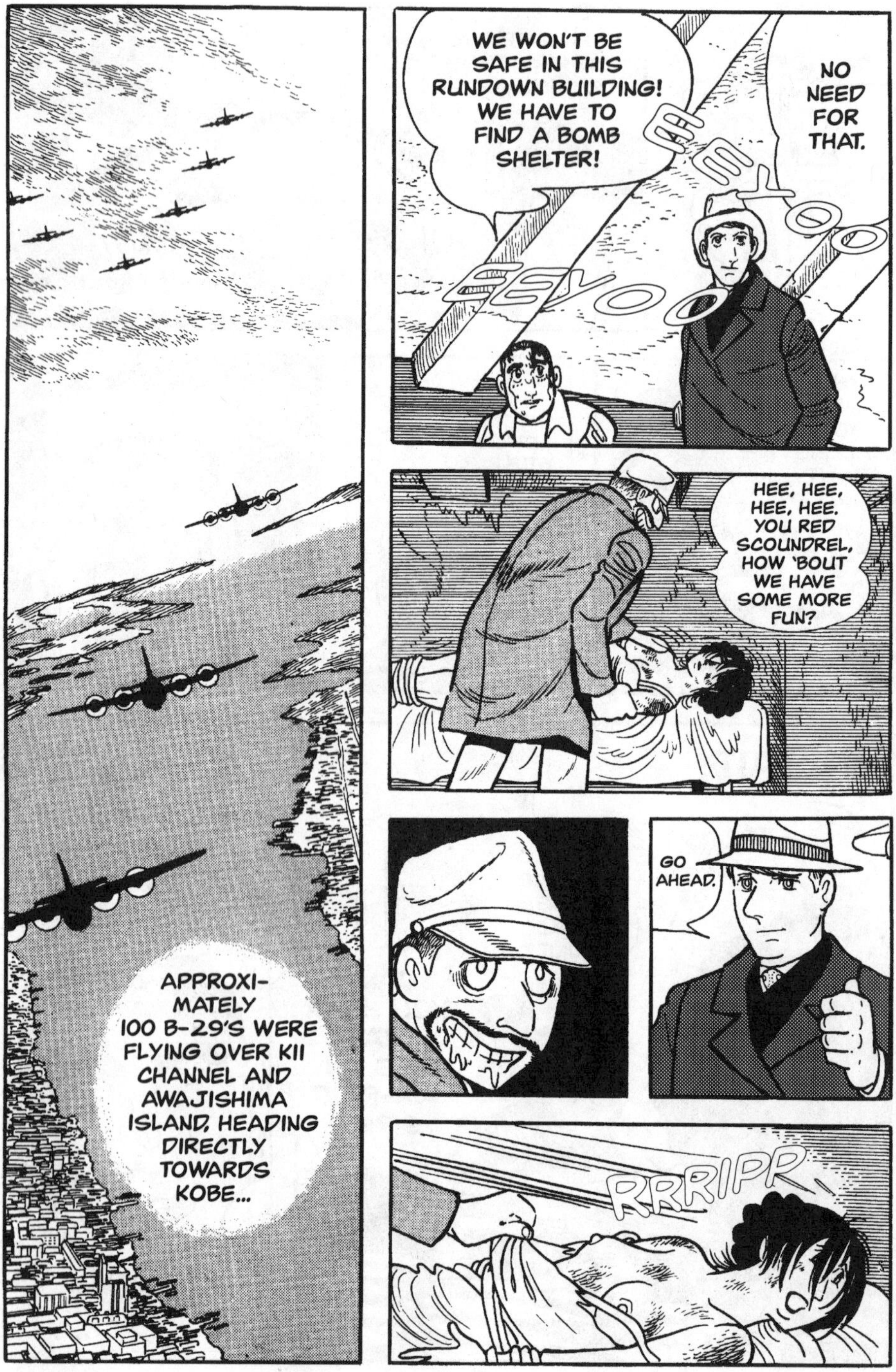
APPROXIMATELY 100 B-29'S WERE FLYING OVER KII CHANNEL AND AWAJISHIMA ISLAND, HEADING DIRECTLY TOWARDS KOBE...
WE WON'T BE SAFE IN THIS RUNDOWN BUILDING! WE HAVE TO FIND A BOMB SHELTER!
NO NEED FOR THAT.
EEYOO
EEYOO
HEE, HEE, HEE, HEE. YOU RED SCOUNDREL, HOW 'BOUT WE HAVE SOME MORE FUN?
GO AHEAD.
RRRIPP

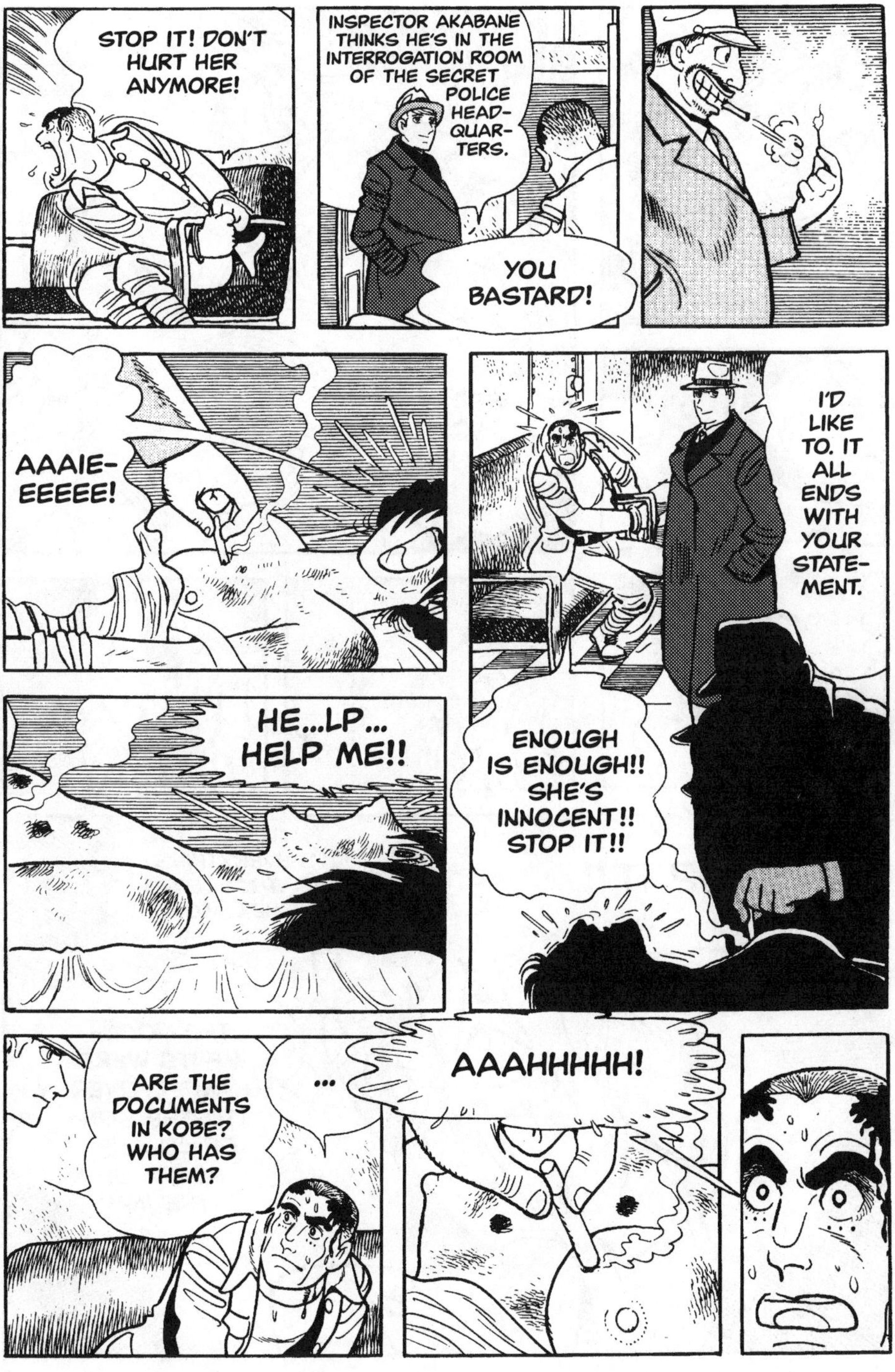
STOP IT! DON'T HURT HER ANYMORE!
INSPECTOR AKABANE THINKS HE'S IN THE INTERROGATION ROOM OF THE SECRET POLICE HEAD-QUAR-TERS.
YOU BASTARD!
AAAIE-EEEEE!
HE...LP... HELP ME!!
I'D LIKE TO. IT ALL ENDS WITH YOUR STATE-MENT.
ENOUGH IS ENOUGH!! SHE'S INNOCENT!! STOP IT!!
ARE THE DOCUMENTS IN KOBE? WHO HAS THEM?
...
AAAHHHHH!

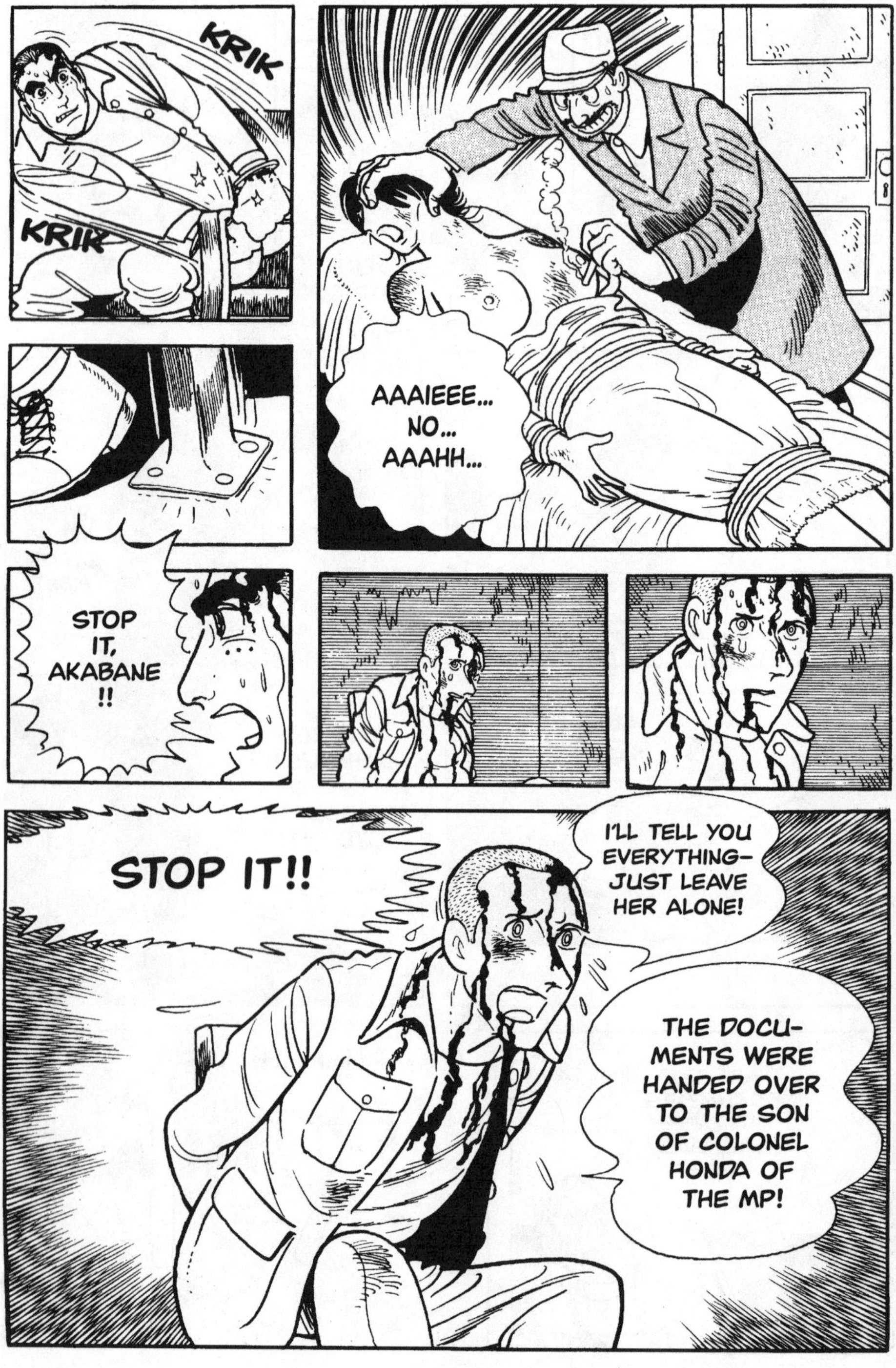
KRIK
KRIK
AAAIEEE... NO... AAAHH...
STOP IT, AKABANE !!
STOP IT!!
I'LL TELL YOU EVERYTHING– JUST LEAVE HER ALONE!
THE DOCU- MENTS WERE HANDED OVER TO THE SON OF COLONEL HONDA OF THE MP!

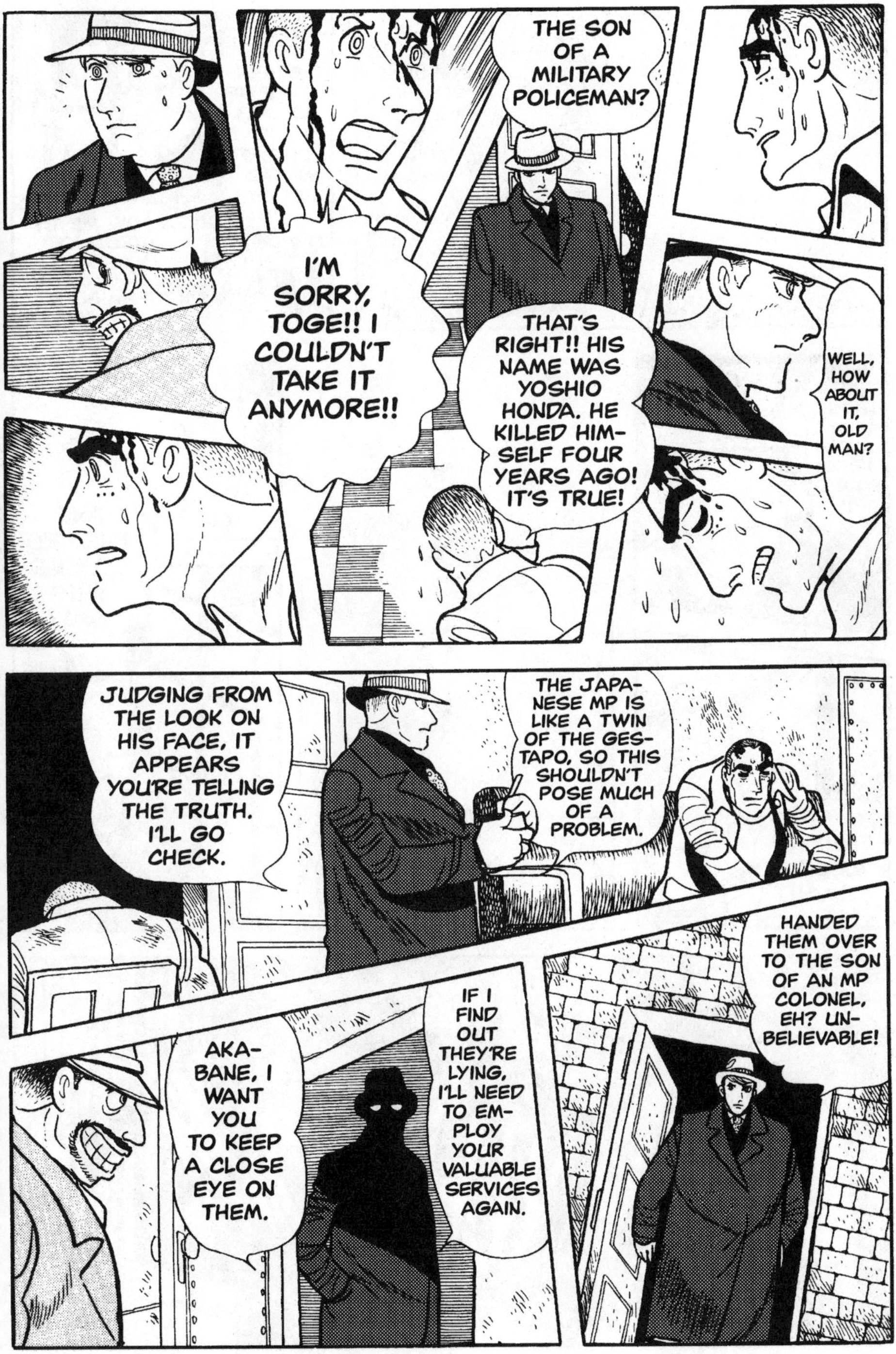
THE SON OF A MILITARY POLICEMAN?
I'M SORRY, TOGE!! I COULDN'T TAKE IT ANYMORE!!
THAT'S RIGHT!! HIS NAME WAS YOSHIO HONDA. HE KILLED HIM-SELF FOUR YEARS AGO! IT'S TRUE!
WELL, HOW ABOUT IT, OLD MAN?
JUDGING FROM THE LOOK ON HIS FACE, IT APPEARS YOU'RE TELLING THE TRUTH. I'LL GO CHECK.
THE JAPA-NESE MP IS LIKE A TWIN OF THE GES-TAPO, SO THIS SHOULDN'T POSE MUCH OF A PROBLEM.
AKA-BANE, I WANT YOU TO KEEP A CLOSE EYE ON THEM.
IF I FIND OUT THEY'RE LYING, I'LL NEED TO EM-PLOY YOUR VALUABLE SERVICES AGAIN.
HANDED THEM OVER TO THE SON OF AN MP COLONEL, EH? UN-BELIEVABLE!

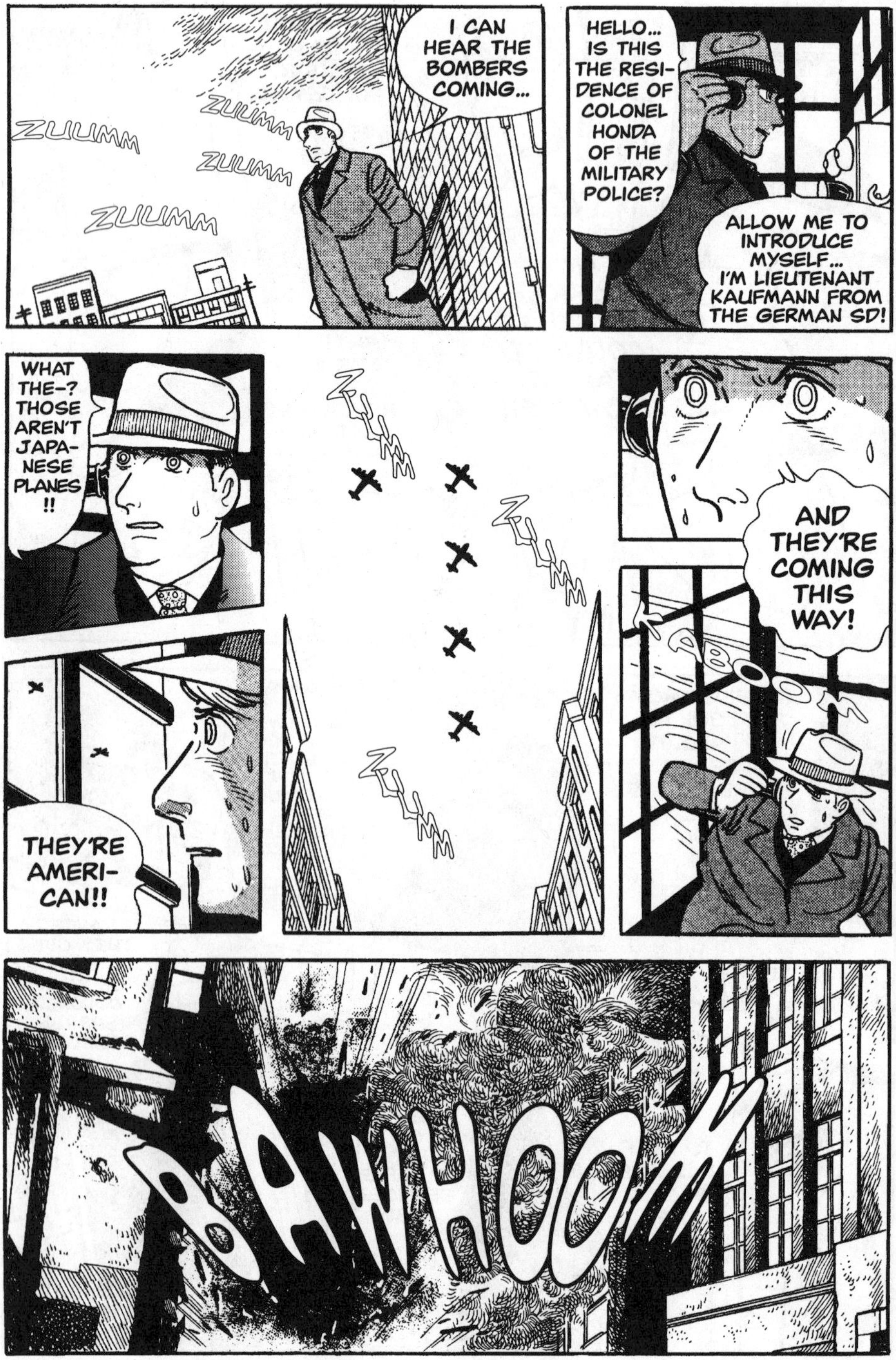
ZULUMM
ZULUMM
ZULUMM
ZULUMM
I CAN HEAR THE BOMBERS COMING...
HELLO... IS THIS THE RESIDENCE OF COLONEL HONDA OF THE MILITARY POLICE?
ALLOW ME TO INTRODUCE MYSELF... I'M LIEUTENANT KAUFMANN FROM THE GERMAN SD!
WHAT THE-? THOSE AREN'T JAPANESE PLANES!!
THEY'RE AMERICAN!!
ZULUMM
ZULUMM
ZULUMM
AND THEY'RE COMING THIS WAY!
ABOOM
BAWHOOM

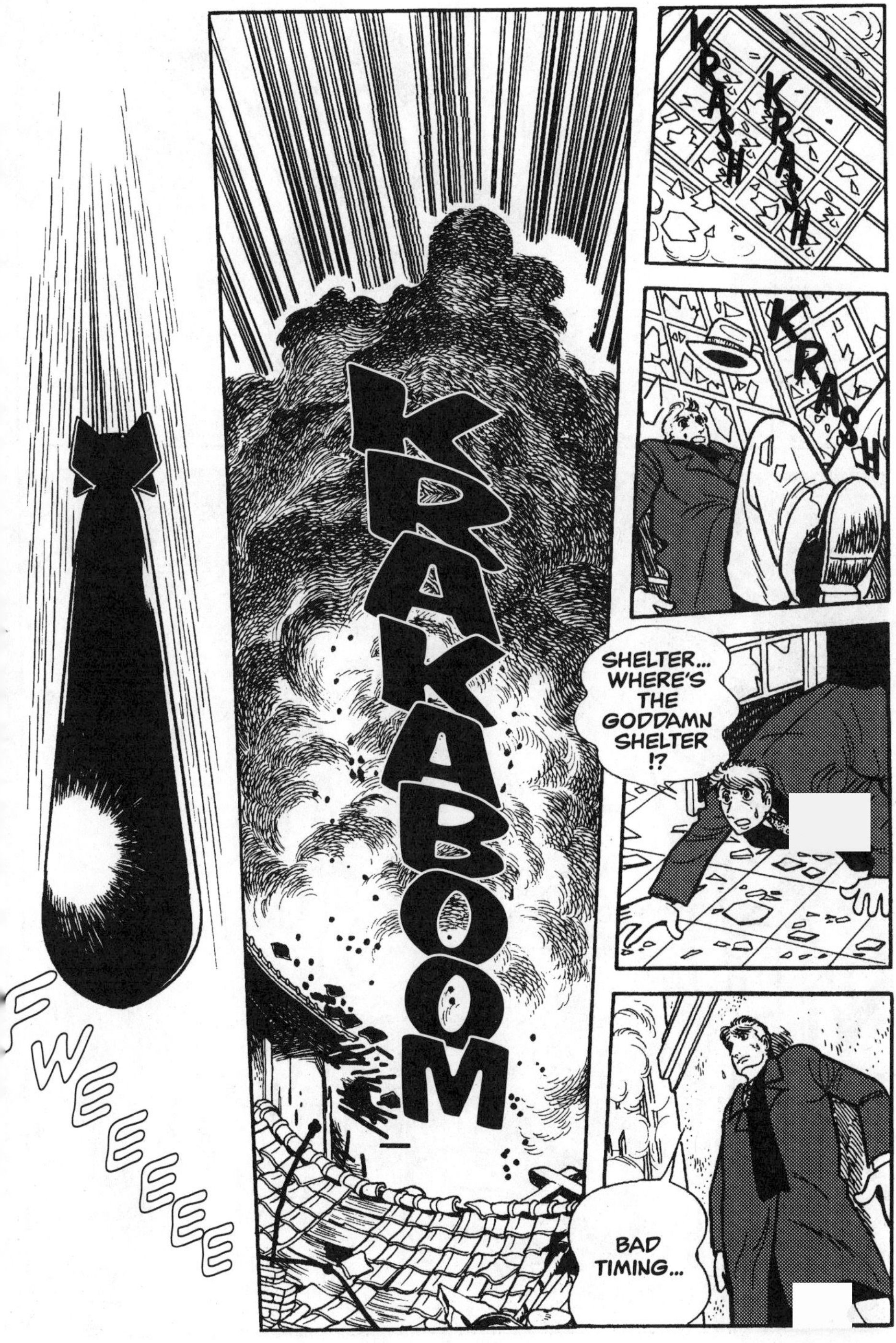
FWEEEEEE
KRAKABOOM
KRASH KRASH
KRASH
SHELTER... WHERE'S THE GODDAMN SHELTER !?
BAD TIMING...

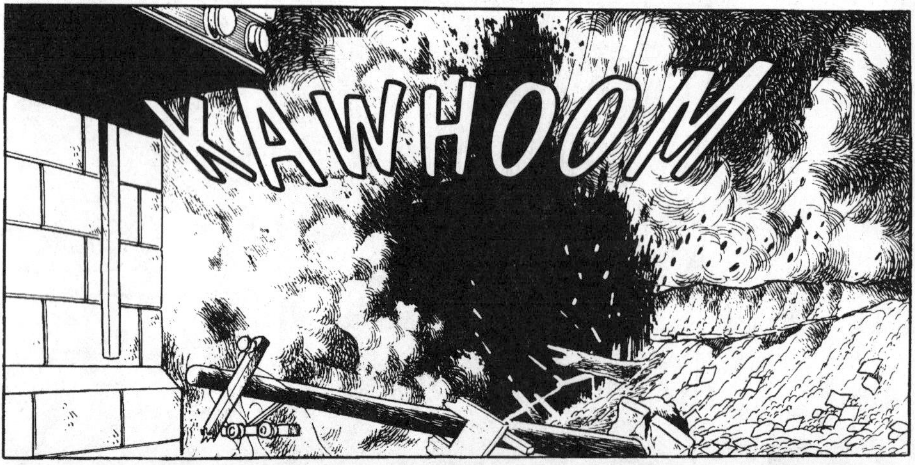
KAWHOOM

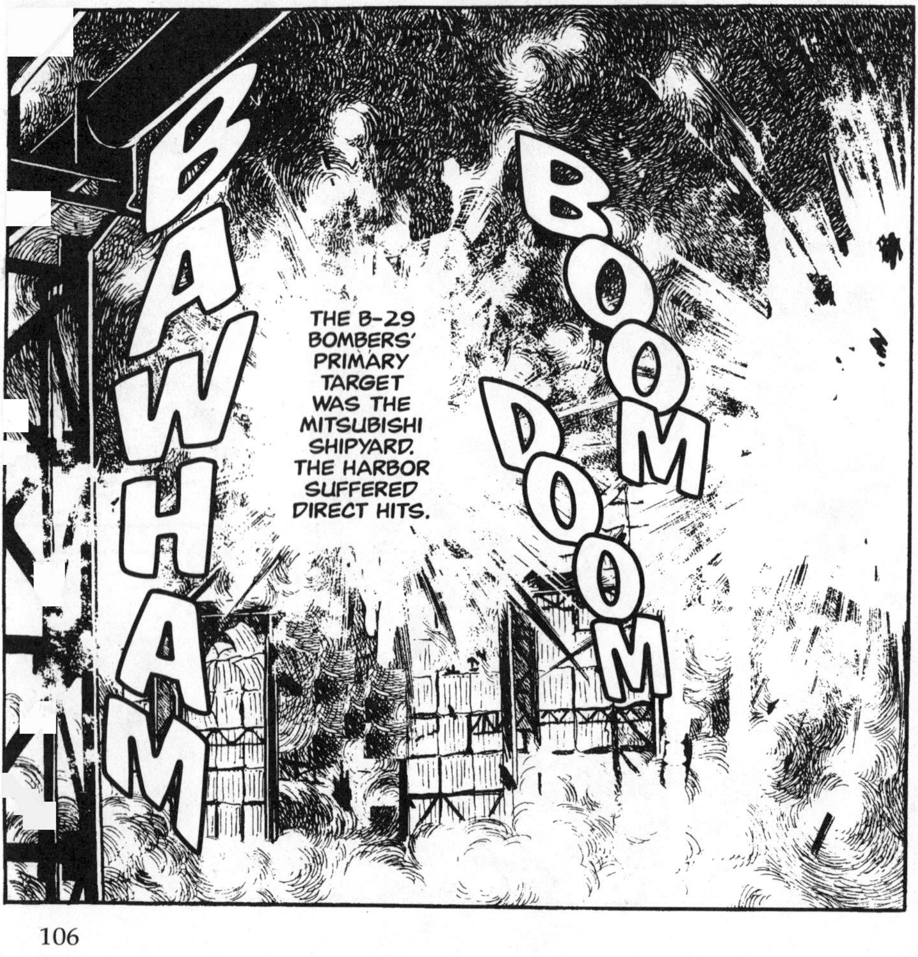
BAWHAM
THE B-29 BOMBERS' PRIMARY TARGET WAS THE MITSUBISHI SHIPYARD. THE HARBOR SUFFERED DIRECT HITS.
BOOOM
DOOOOM

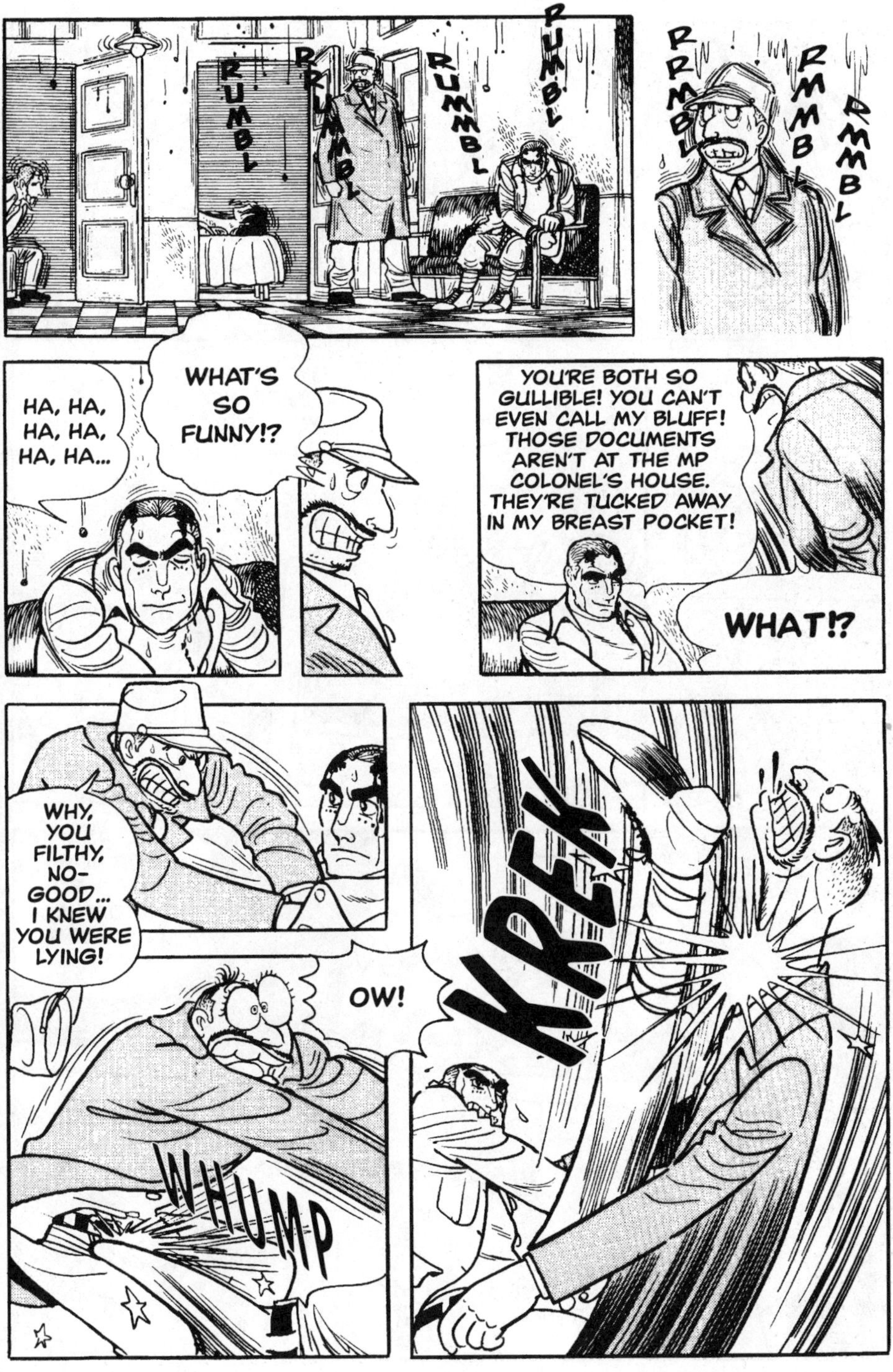
RUMMBL
RRUMMBL
RUMMBL
RUMMBL
RRMMBL
RMMBL
RMMBL
HA, HA, HA, HA, HA, HA...
WHAT'S SO FUNNY!?
YOU'RE BOTH SO GULLIBLE! YOU CAN'T EVEN CALL MY BLUFF! THOSE DOCUMENTS AREN'T AT THE MP COLONEL'S HOUSE. THEY'RE TUCKED AWAY IN MY BREAST POCKET!
WHAT!?
WHY, YOU FILTHY, NO-GOOD... I KNEW YOU WERE LYING!
OW!
WHUMP
KREK

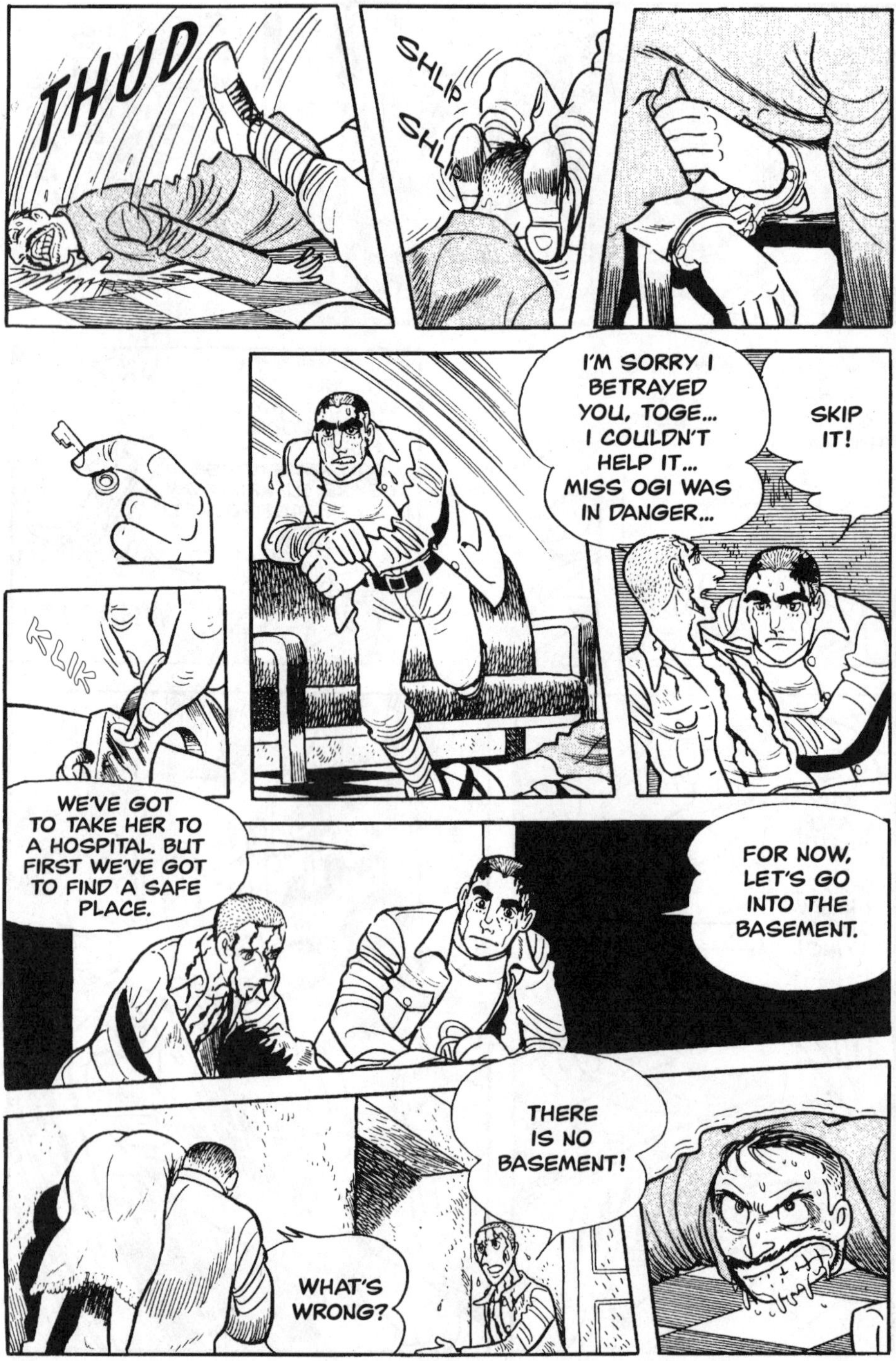
THUD
SHLIP
SHLIP
KLIK
I'M SORRY I BETRAYED YOU, TOGE... I COULDN'T HELP IT... MISS OGI WAS IN DANGER...
SKIP IT!
WE'VE GOT TO TAKE HER TO A HOSPITAL. BUT FIRST WE'VE GOT TO FIND A SAFE PLACE.
FOR NOW, LET'S GO INTO THE BASEMENT.
WHAT'S WRONG?
THERE IS NO BASEMENT!

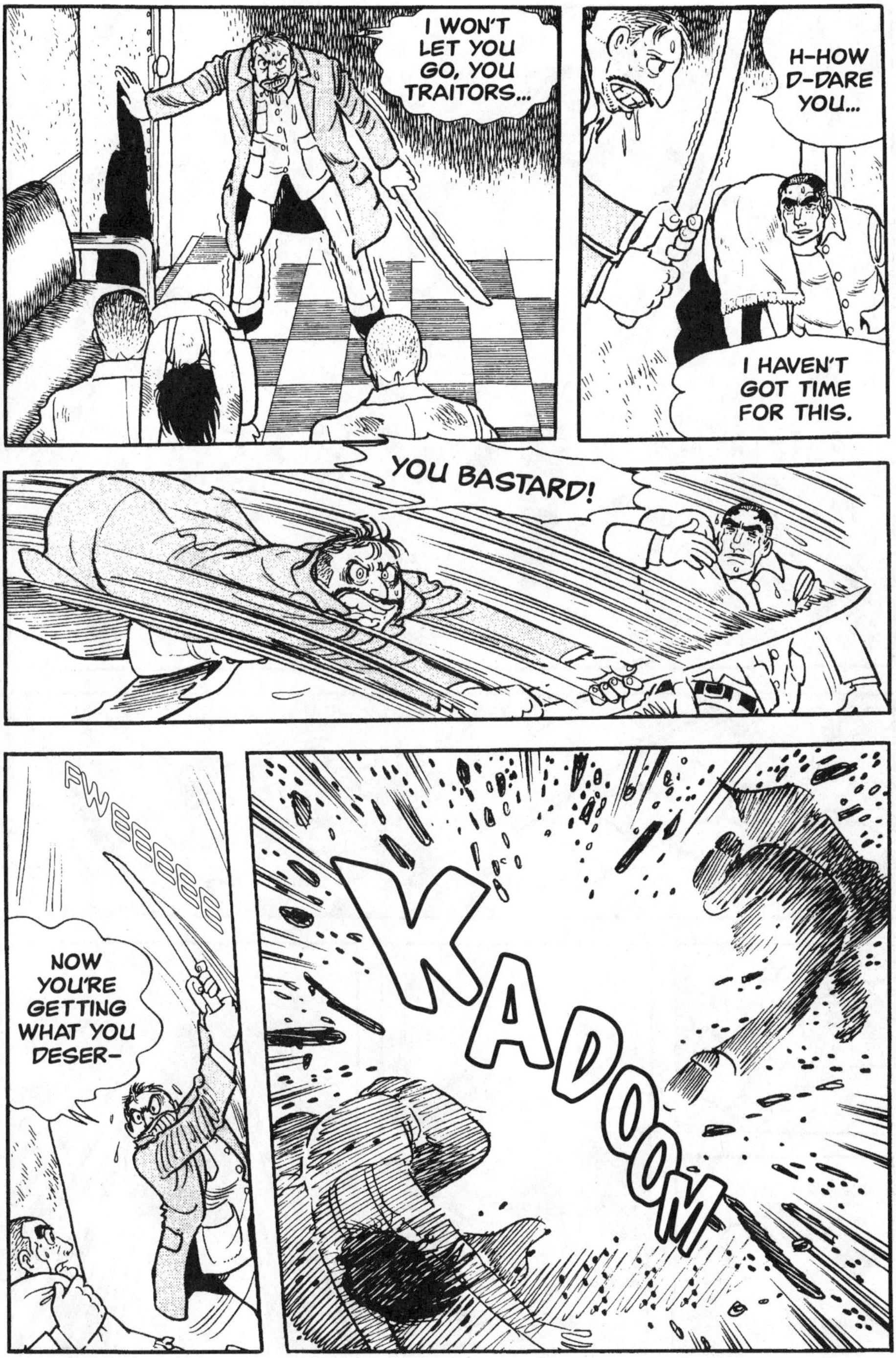
I WON'T LET YOU GO, YOU TRAITORS...
H-HOW D-DARE YOU...
I HAVEN'T GOT TIME FOR THIS.
YOU BASTARD!
FWEEEEEE
NOW YOU'RE GETTING WHAT YOU DESER-
KADOOM

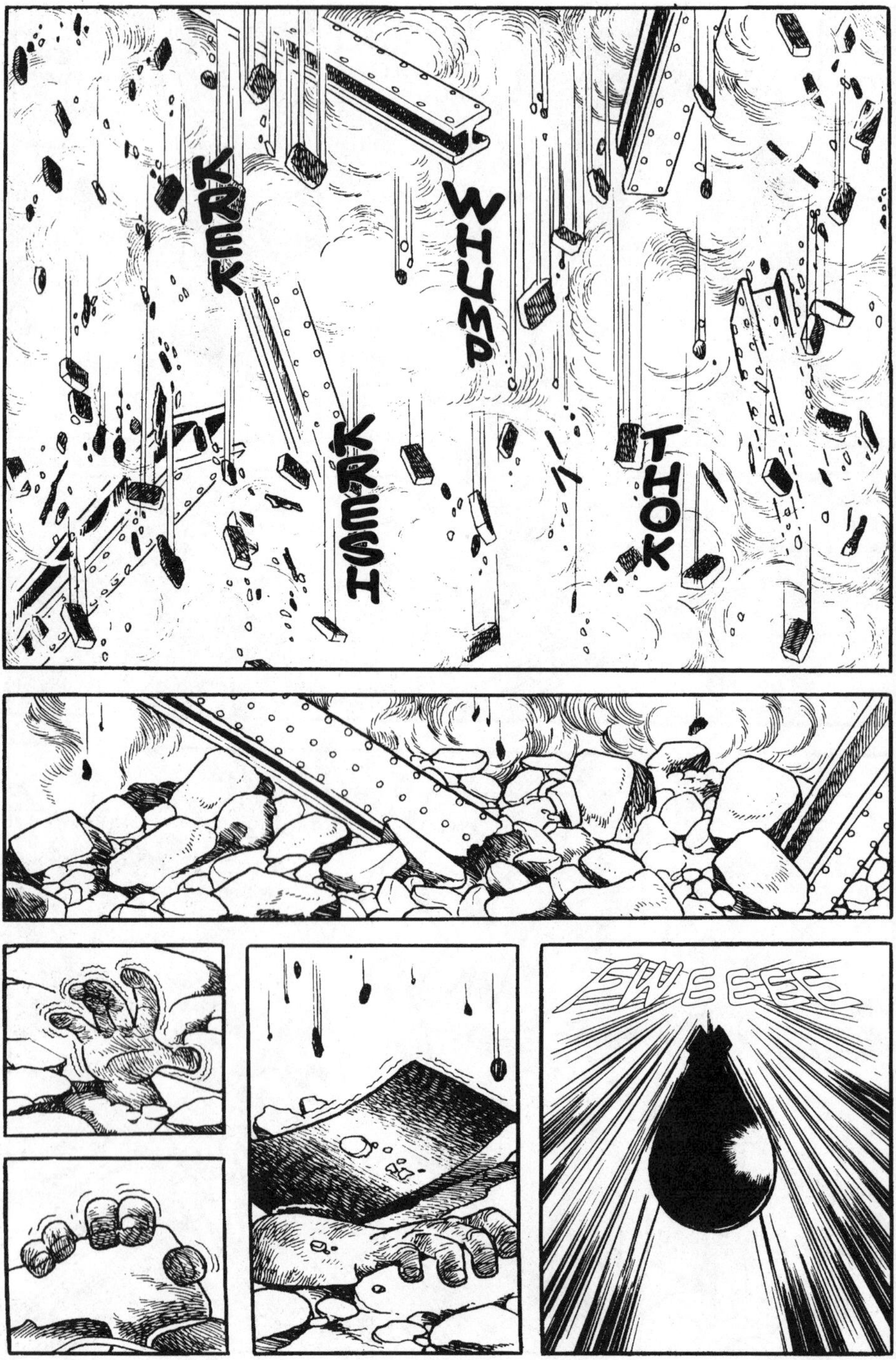
KREK
WHUMP
KRESH
THOK
SWEEEE

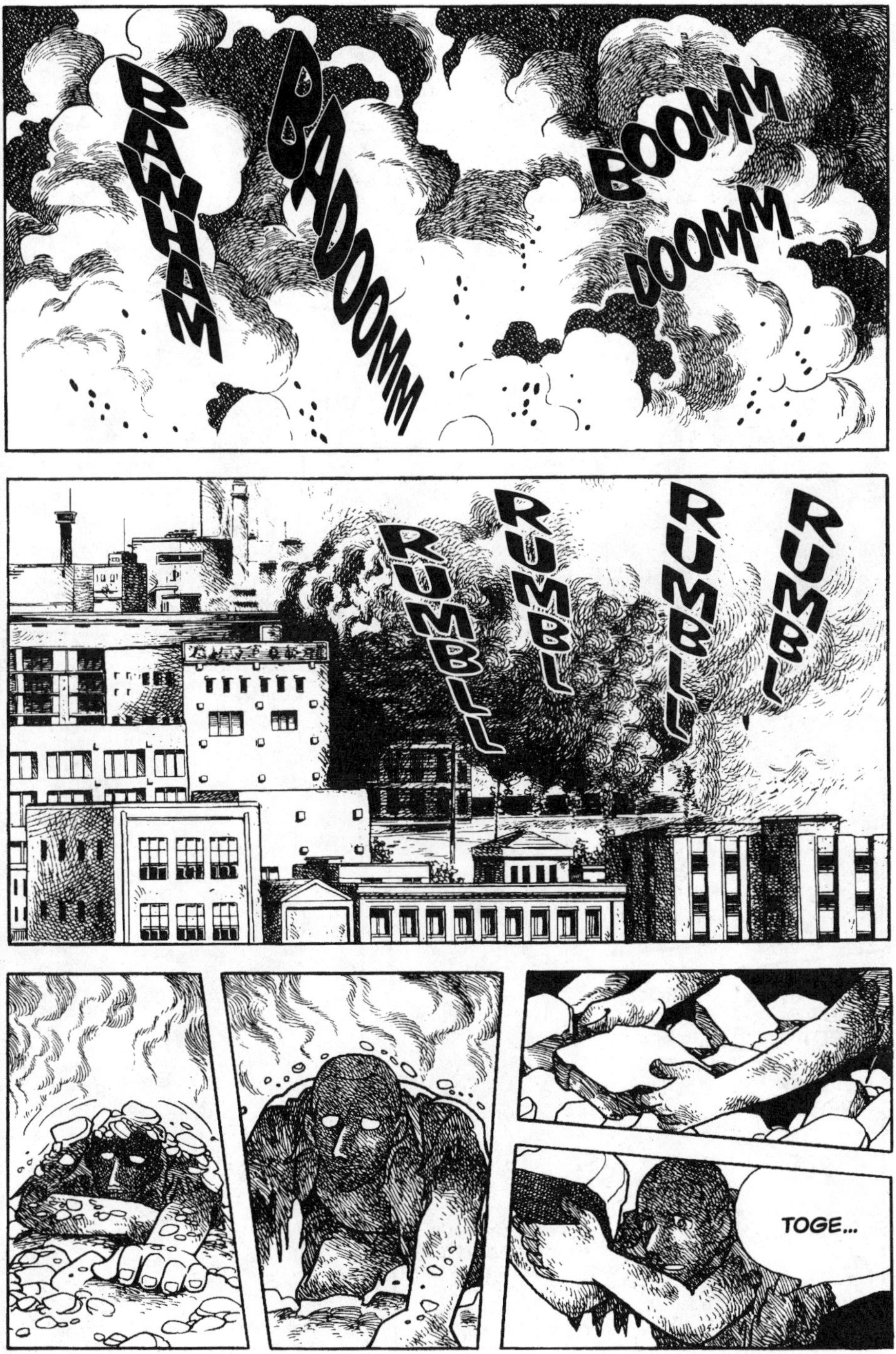
BAWHAM
BADOOMM
BOOMM
DOOMM
RUMBLL
RUMBL
RUMBLL
RUMBL
TOGE...

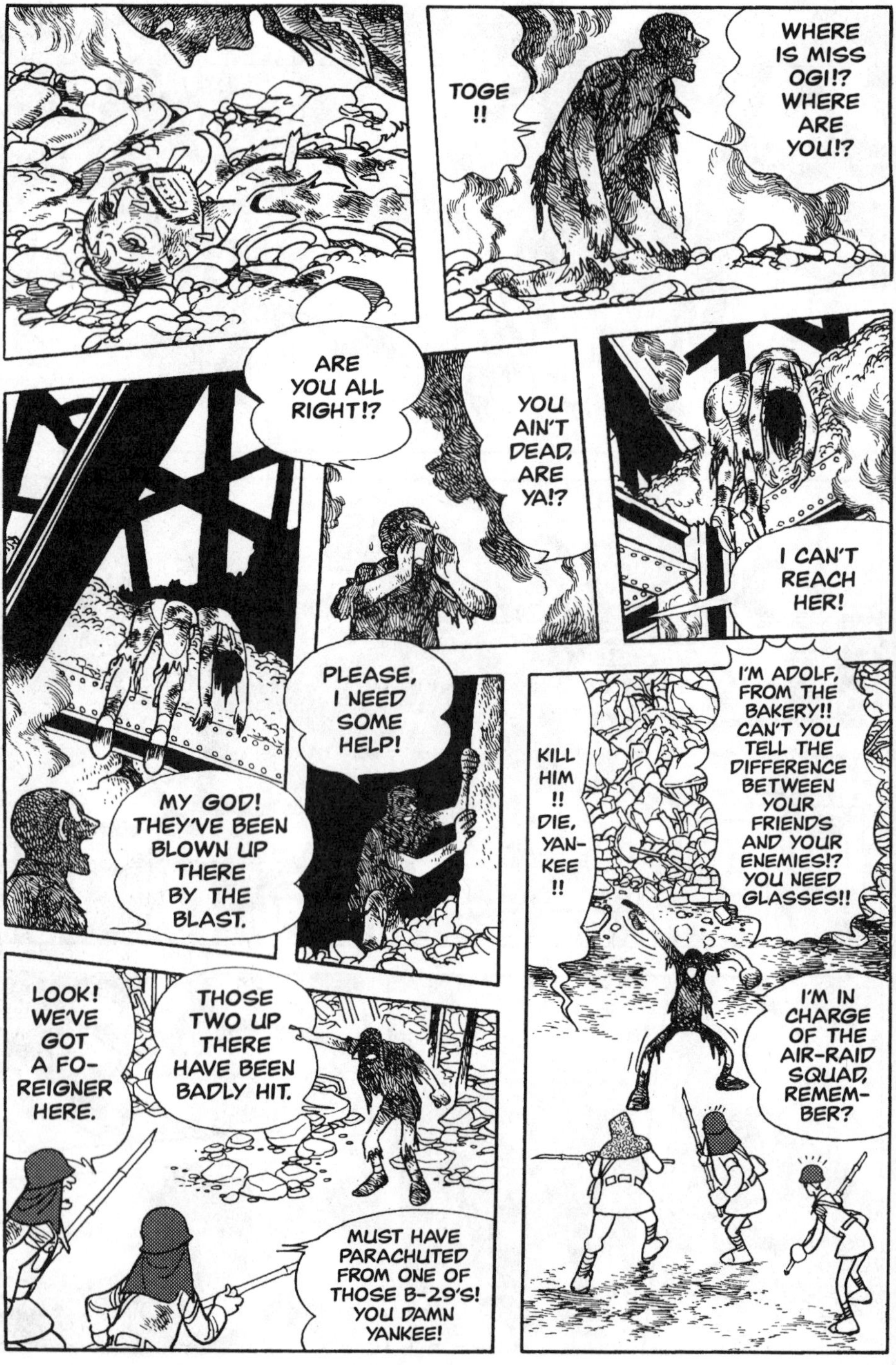
TOGE !!
WHERE IS MISS OGI!? WHERE ARE YOU!?
MY GOD! THEY'VE BEEN BLOWN UP THERE BY THE BLAST.
ARE YOU ALL RIGHT!?
YOU AIN'T DEAD, ARE YA!?
I CAN'T REACH HER!
PLEASE, I NEED SOME HELP!
LOOK! WE'VE GOT A FO-REIGNER HERE.
THOSE TWO UP THERE HAVE BEEN BADLY HIT.
MUST HAVE PARACHUTED FROM ONE OF THOSE B-29'S! YOU DAMN YANKEE!
KILL HIM !! DIE, YAN-KEE !!
I'M ADOLF, FROM THE BAKERY!! CAN'T YOU TELL THE DIFFERENCE BETWEEN YOUR FRIENDS AND YOUR ENEMIES!? YOU NEED GLASSES!!
I'M IN CHARGE OF THE AIR-RAID SQUAD, REMEMBER?

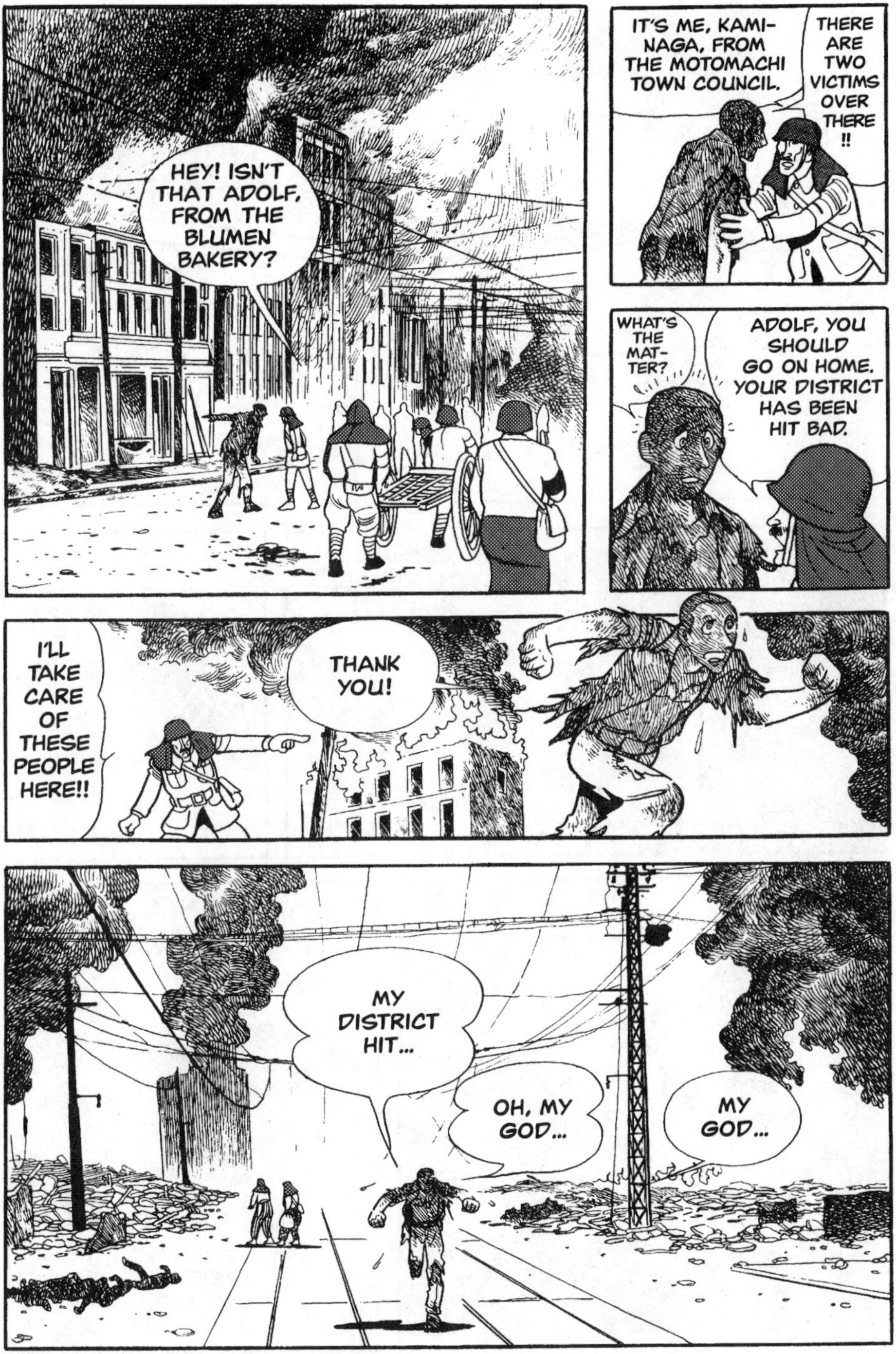
HEY! ISN'T THAT ADOLF, FROM THE BLUMEN BAKERY?
IT'S ME, KAMI-NAGA, FROM THE MOTOMACHI TOWN COUNCIL.
THERE ARE TWO VICTIMS OVER THERE!!
WHAT'S THE MAT-TER?
ADOLF, YOU SHOULD GO ON HOME. YOUR DISTRICT HAS BEEN HIT BAD.
I'LL TAKE CARE OF THESE PEOPLE HERE!!
THANK YOU!
MY DISTRICT HIT...
OH, MY GOD...
MY GOD...

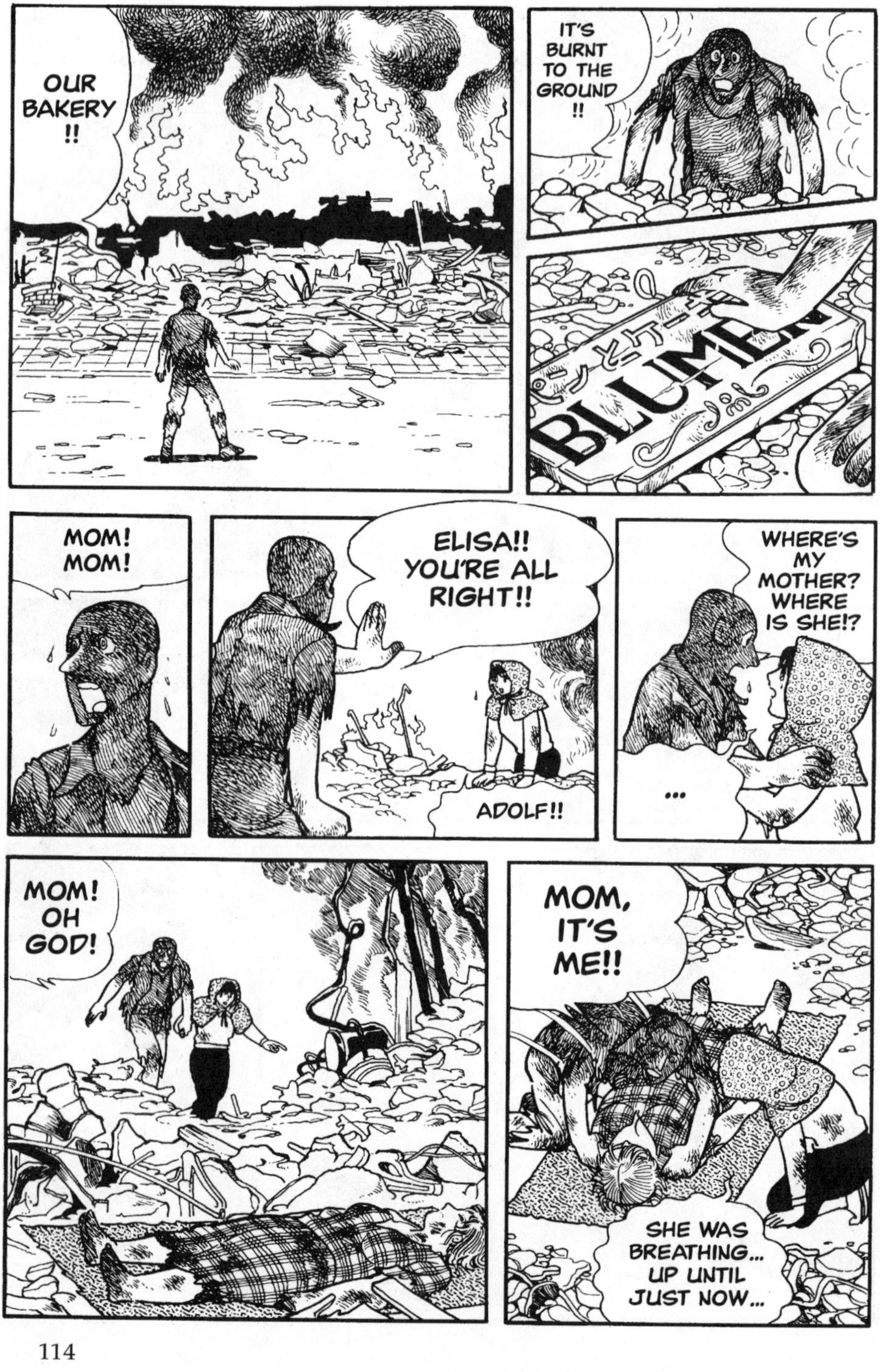
OUR BAKERY !!
IT'S BURNT TO THE GROUND !!
BLUMEN
MOM! MOM!
ELISA!! YOU'RE ALL RIGHT!!
ADOLF!!
WHERE'S MY MOTHER? WHERE IS SHE!?
...
MOM! OH GOD!
MOM, IT'S ME!!
SHE WAS BREATHING... UP UNTIL JUST NOW...

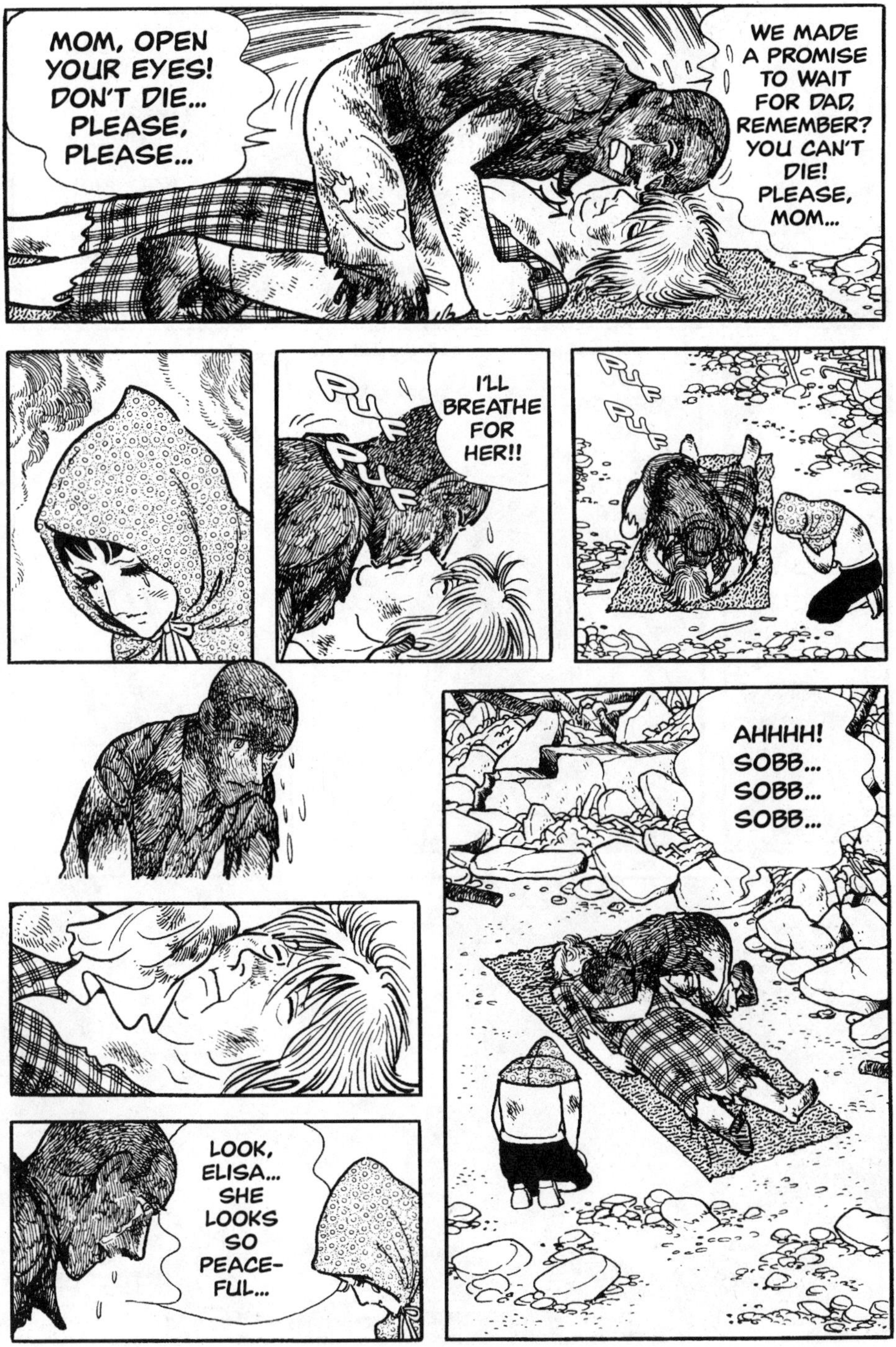
MOM, OPEN YOUR EYES! DON'T DIE... PLEASE, PLEASE...
WE MADE A PROMISE TO WAIT FOR DAD, REMEMBER? YOU CAN'T DIE! PLEASE, MOM...
PUF PUF
I'LL BREATHE FOR HER!!
PUF PUF
LOOK, ELISA... SHE LOOKS SO PEACE-FUL...
AHHHH! SOBB... SOBB... SOBB...

Adolf

LET'S TAKE HER SOMEPLACE SAFE...

I SWEAR I'LL START UP THE BLUMEN BAKERY AGAIN! I SWEAR IT ON THE HOLY BIBLE! YOU CAN REST IN HEAVEN...

YOU AMERICAN BAS-TARDS!! YOU'VE GOT JEWS TOO!

HOW DARE YOU KILL YOUR FELLOW JEWS! YOU'LL ALL BURN IN HELL!

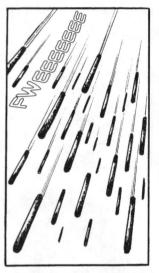

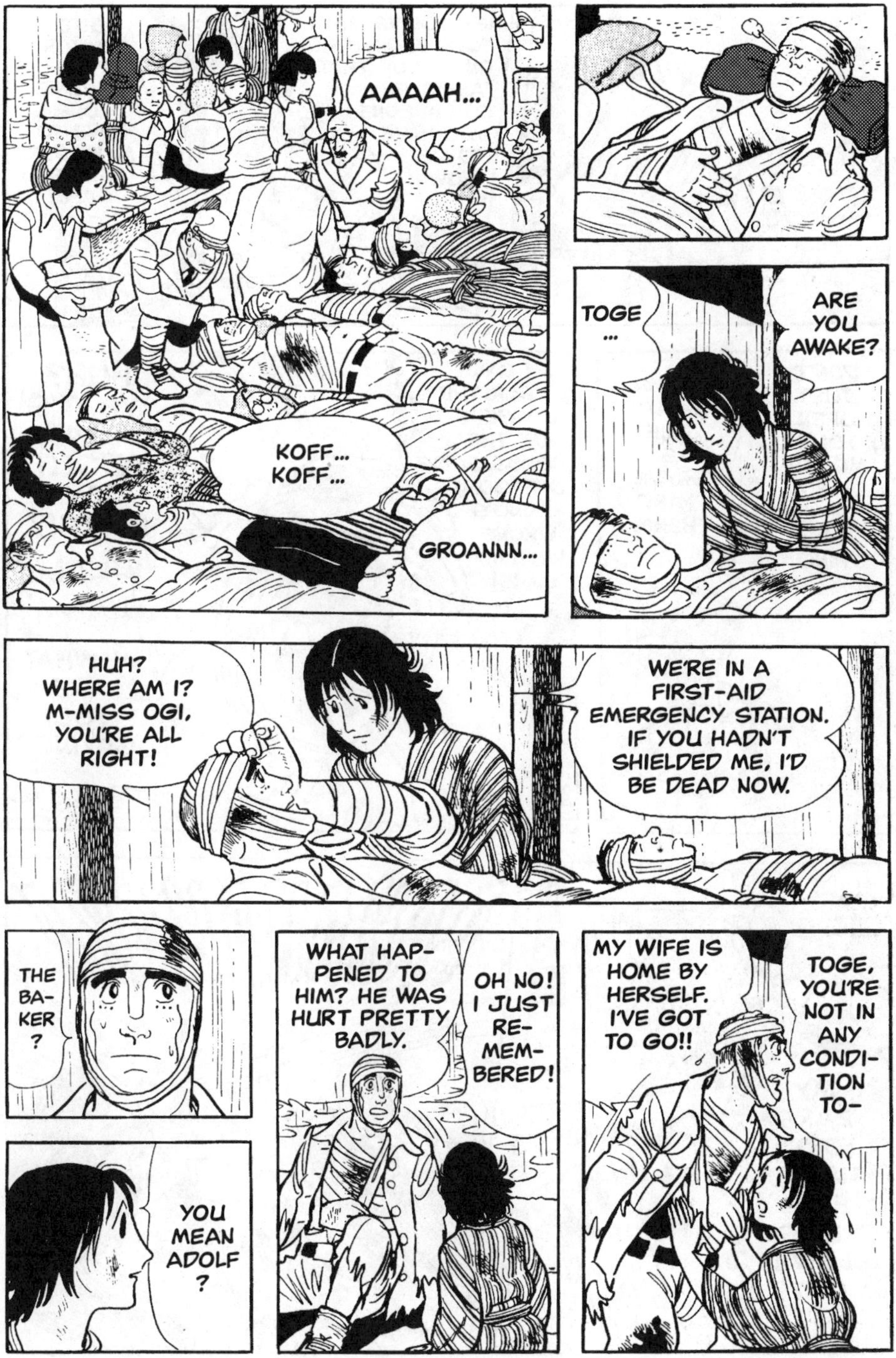
AAAAH...
KOFF... KOFF...
GROANNN...
TOGE ...
ARE YOU AWAKE?
HUH? WHERE AM I? M-MISS OGI, YOU'RE ALL RIGHT!
WE'RE IN A FIRST-AID EMERGENCY STATION. IF YOU HADN'T SHIELDED ME, I'D BE DEAD NOW.
THE BA-KER?
YOU MEAN ADOLF?
WHAT HAP-PENED TO HIM? HE WAS HURT PRETTY BADLY.
OH NO! I JUST RE-MEM-BERED!
MY WIFE IS HOME BY HERSELF. I'VE GOT TO GO!!
TOGE, YOU'RE NOT IN ANY CONDI-TION TO-

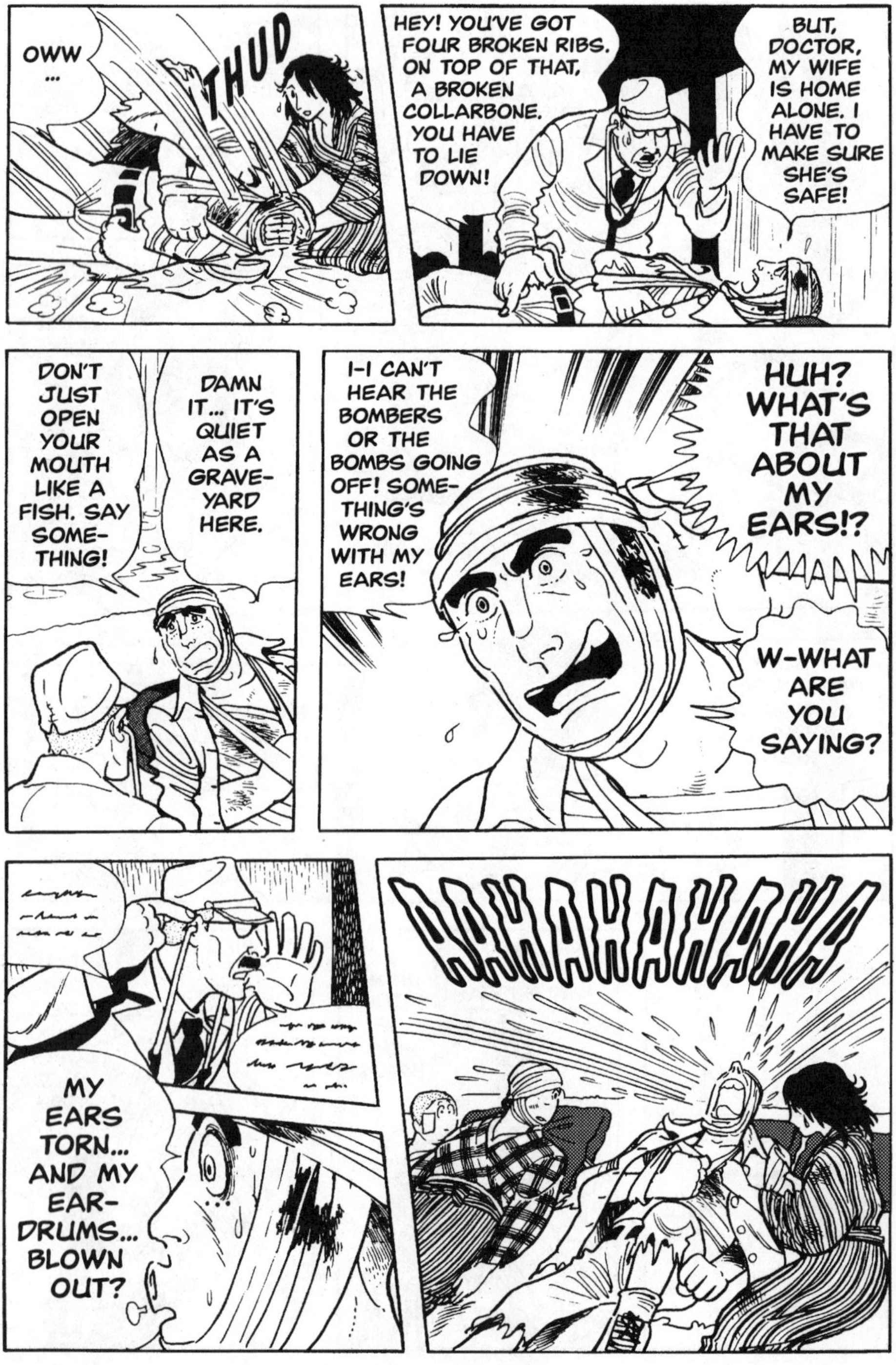
OWW ...
THUD
HEY! YOU'VE GOT FOUR BROKEN RIBS. ON TOP OF THAT, A BROKEN COLLARBONE. YOU HAVE TO LIE DOWN!
BUT, DOCTOR, MY WIFE IS HOME ALONE. I HAVE TO MAKE SURE SHE'S SAFE!
DON'T JUST OPEN YOUR MOUTH LIKE A FISH. SAY SOME-THING!
DAMN IT... IT'S QUIET AS A GRAVE-YARD HERE.
I-I CAN'T HEAR THE BOMBERS OR THE BOMBS GOING OFF! SOME-THING'S WRONG WITH MY EARS!
HUH? WHAT'S THAT ABOUT MY EARS!?
W-WHAT ARE YOU SAYING?
MY EARS TORN... AND MY EAR-DRUMS... BLOWN OUT?
AAHAHAHAHA

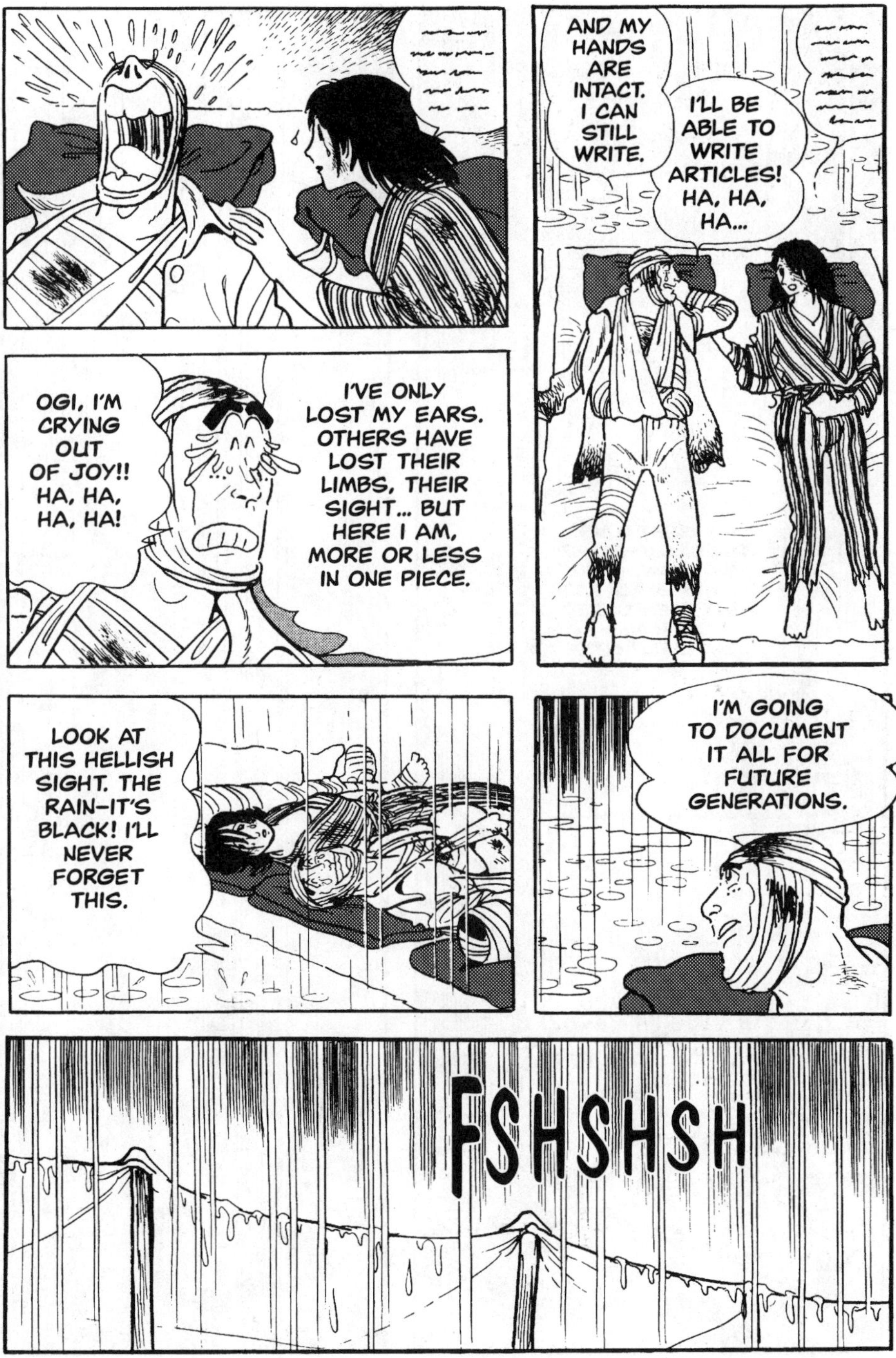
OGI, I'M CRYING OUT OF JOY!! HA, HA, HA, HA!
I'VE ONLY LOST MY EARS. OTHERS HAVE LOST THEIR LIMBS, THEIR SIGHT... BUT HERE I AM, MORE OR LESS IN ONE PIECE.
AND MY HANDS ARE INTACT. I CAN STILL WRITE.
I'LL BE ABLE TO WRITE ARTICLES! HA, HA, HA...
LOOK AT THIS HELLISH SIGHT. THE RAIN–IT'S BLACK! I'LL NEVER FORGET THIS.
I'M GOING TO DOCUMENT IT ALL FOR FUTURE GENERATIONS.
FSHSHSH

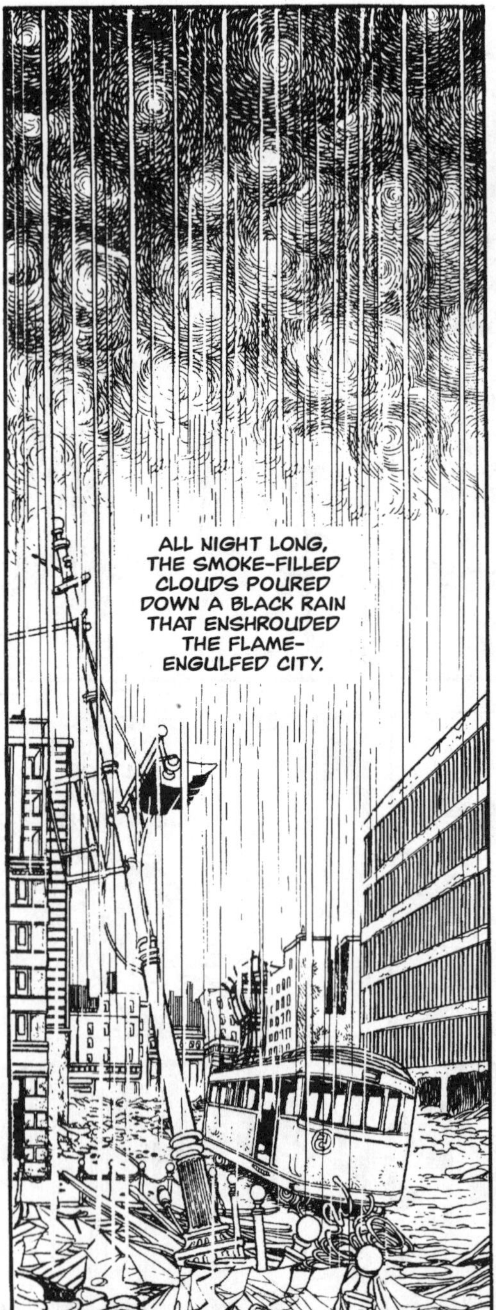
ALL NIGHT LONG, THE SMOKE-FILLED CLOUDS POURED DOWN A BLACK RAIN THAT ENSHROUDED THE FLAME-ENGULFED CITY.

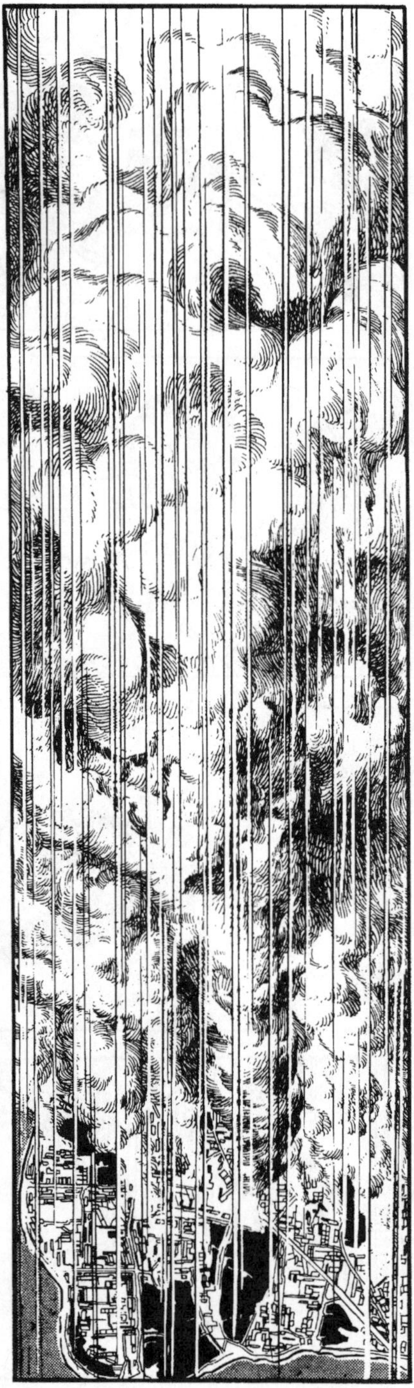

CHAPTER
FIVE

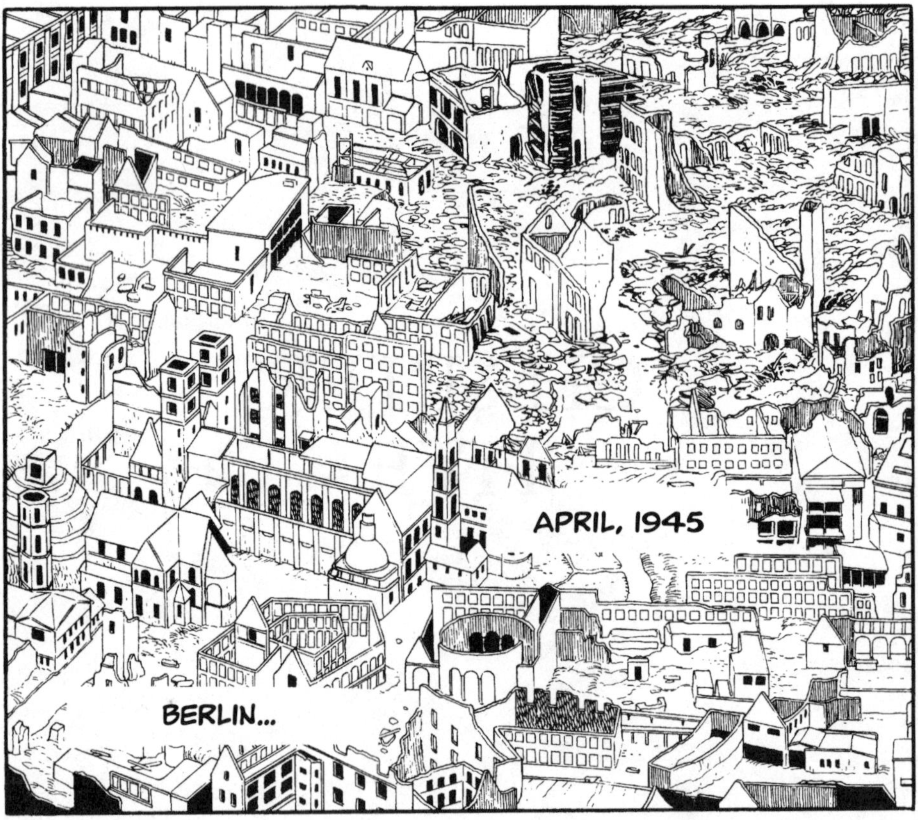
APRIL, 1945
BERLIN...

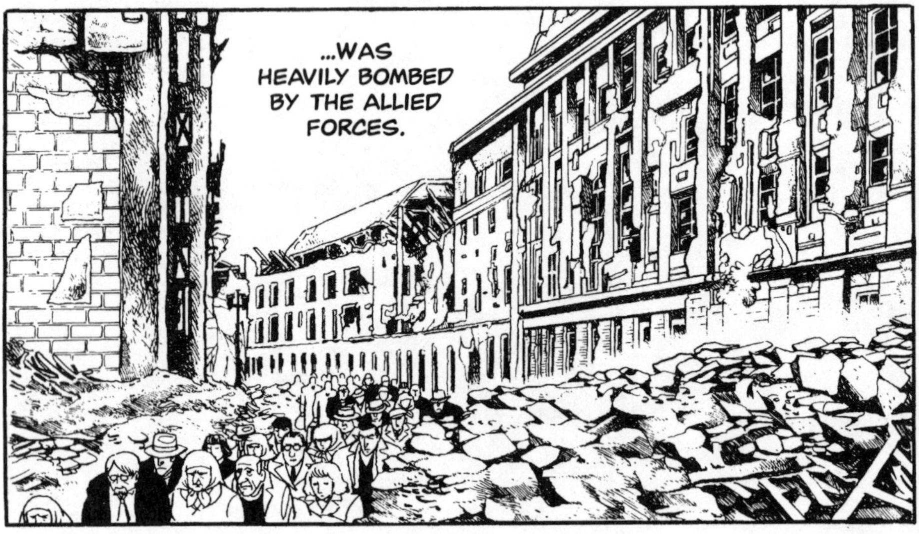
...WAS HEAVILY BOMBED BY THE ALLIED FORCES.

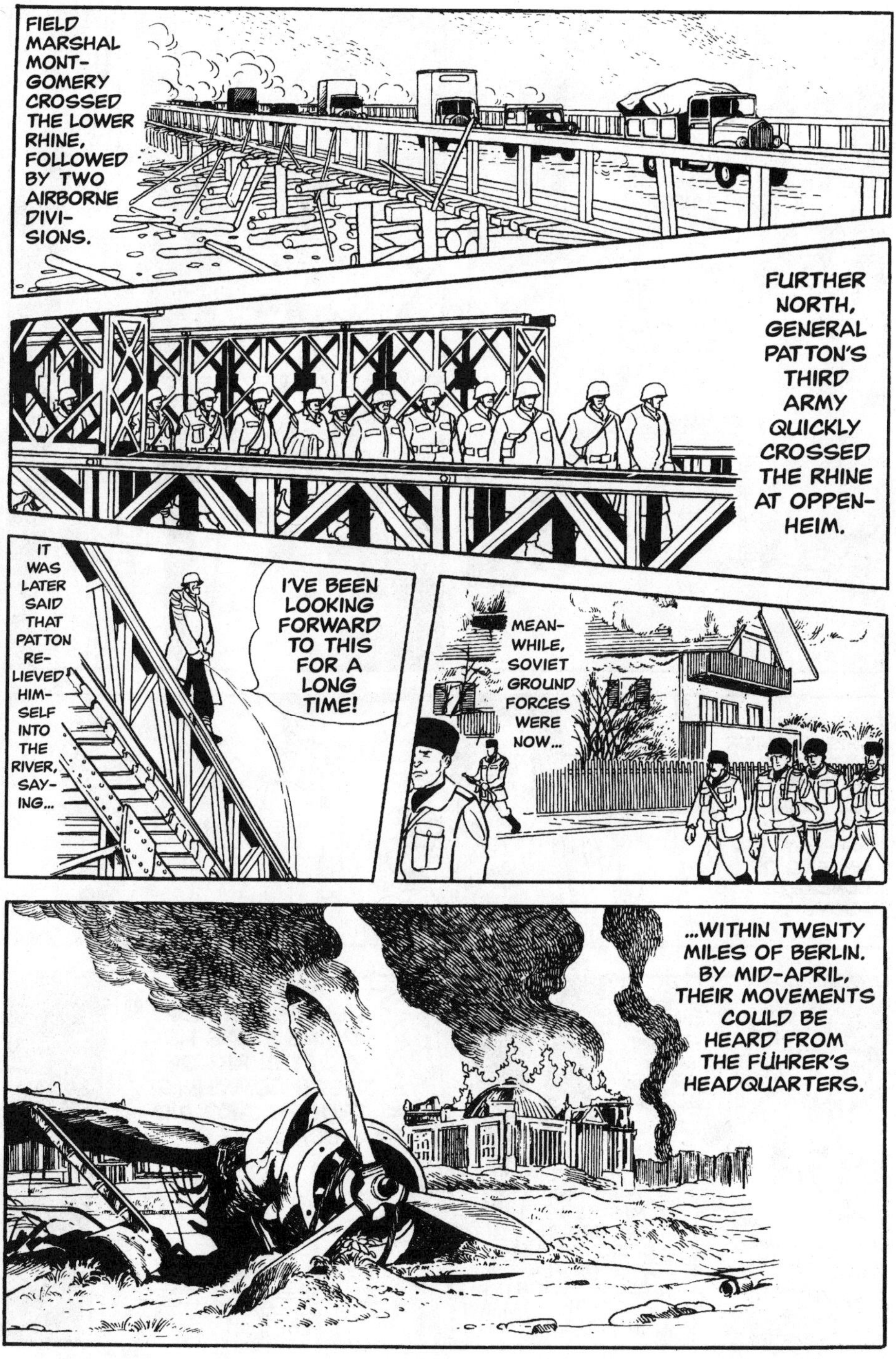
FIELD MARSHAL MONT-GOMERY CROSSED THE LOWER RHINE, FOLLOWED BY TWO AIRBORNE DIVI-SIONS.
FURTHER NORTH, GENERAL PATTON'S THIRD ARMY QUICKLY CROSSED THE RHINE AT OPPEN-HEIM.
IT WAS LATER SAID THAT PATTON RE-LIEVED HIM-SELF INTO THE RIVER, SAY-ING...
I'VE BEEN LOOKING FORWARD TO THIS FOR A LONG TIME!
MEAN-WHILE, SOVIET GROUND FORCES WERE NOW...
...WITHIN TWENTY MILES OF BERLIN. BY MID-APRIL, THEIR MOVEMENTS COULD BE HEARD FROM THE FÜHRER'S HEADQUARTERS.

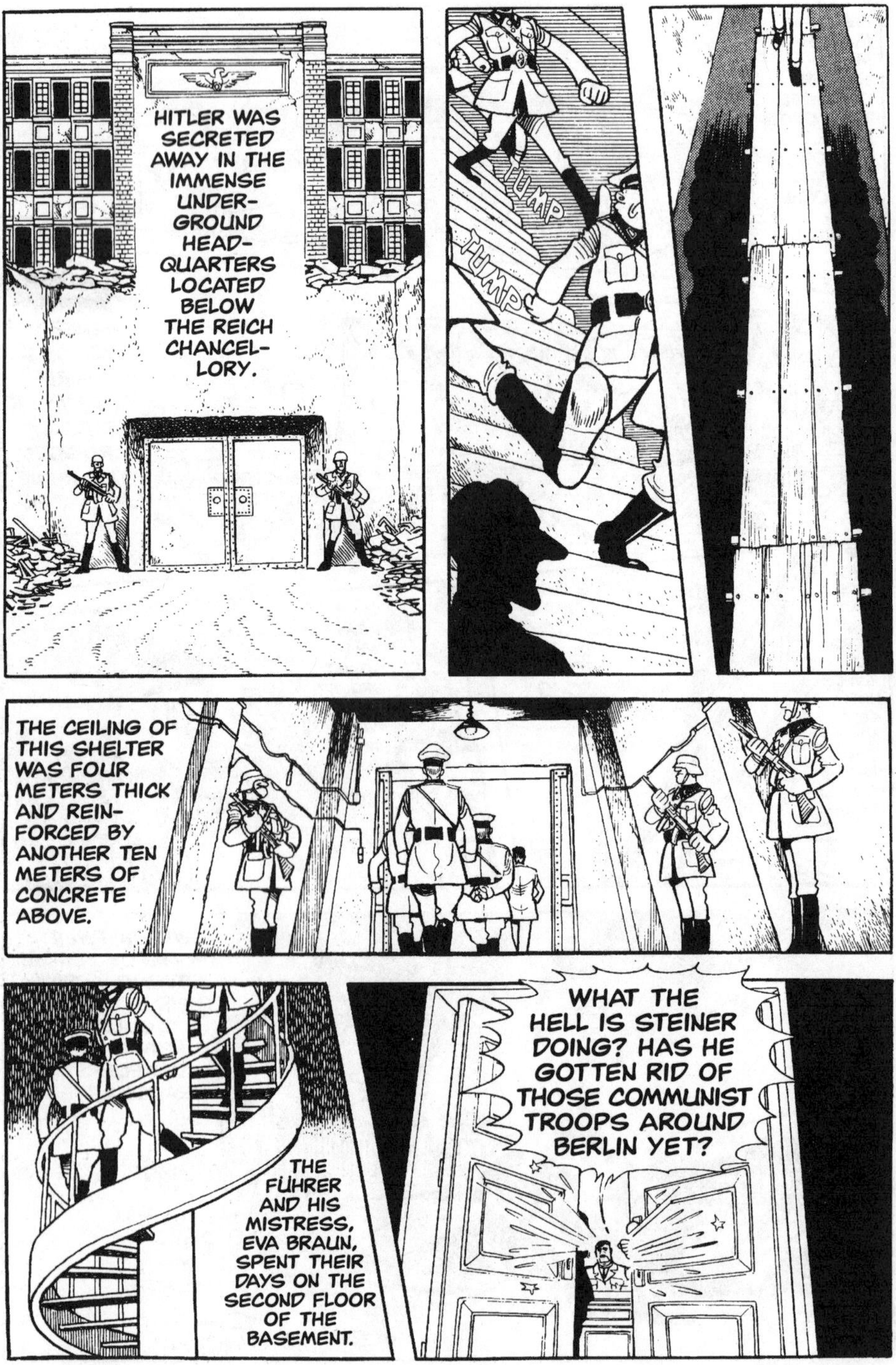
HITLER WAS SECRETED AWAY IN THE IMMENSE UNDER-GROUND HEAD-QUARTERS LOCATED BELOW THE REICH CHANCEL-LORY.
TUMP
TUMP
TUMP
THE CEILING OF THIS SHELTER WAS FOUR METERS THICK AND REIN-FORCED BY ANOTHER TEN METERS OF CONCRETE ABOVE.
THE FÜHRER AND HIS MISTRESS, EVA BRAUN, SPENT THEIR DAYS ON THE SECOND FLOOR OF THE BASEMENT.
WHAT THE HELL IS STEINER DOING? HAS HE GOTTEN RID OF THOSE COMMUNIST TROOPS AROUND BERLIN YET?

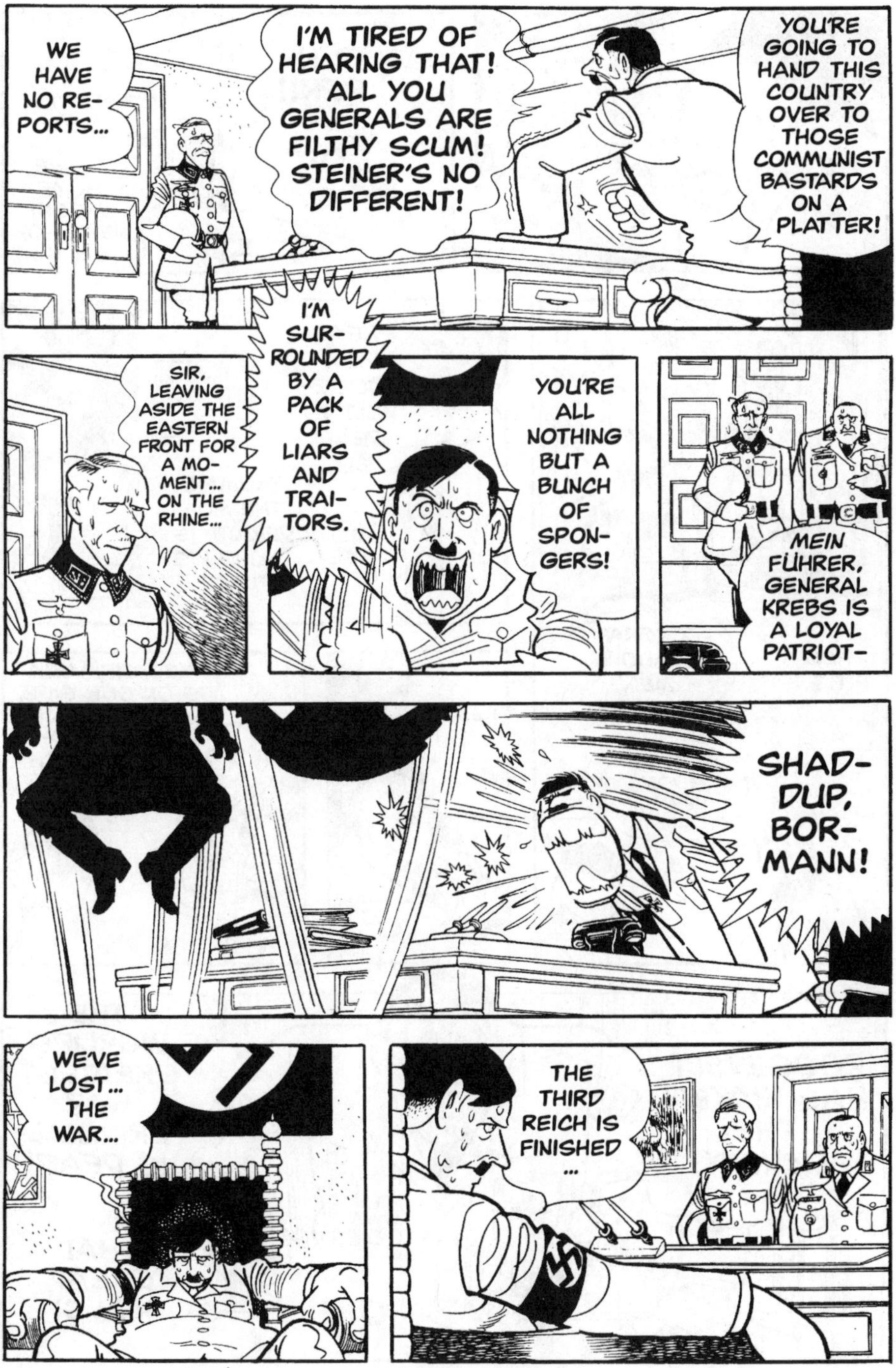
WE HAVE NO RE- PORTS...
I'M TIRED OF HEARING THAT! ALL YOU GENERALS ARE FILTHY SCUM! STEINER'S NO DIFFERENT!
YOU'RE GOING TO HAND THIS COUNTRY OVER TO THOSE COMMUNIST BASTARDS ON A PLATTER!
SIR, LEAVING ASIDE THE EASTERN FRONT FOR A MO- MENT... ON THE RHINE...
I'M SUR- ROUNDED BY A PACK OF LIARS AND TRAI- TORS.
YOU'RE ALL NOTHING BUT A BUNCH OF SPON- GERS!
MEIN FÜHRER, GENERAL KREBS IS A LOYAL PATRIOT-
SHAD- DUP, BOR- MANN!
WE'VE LOST... THE WAR...
THE THIRD REICH IS FINISHED ...

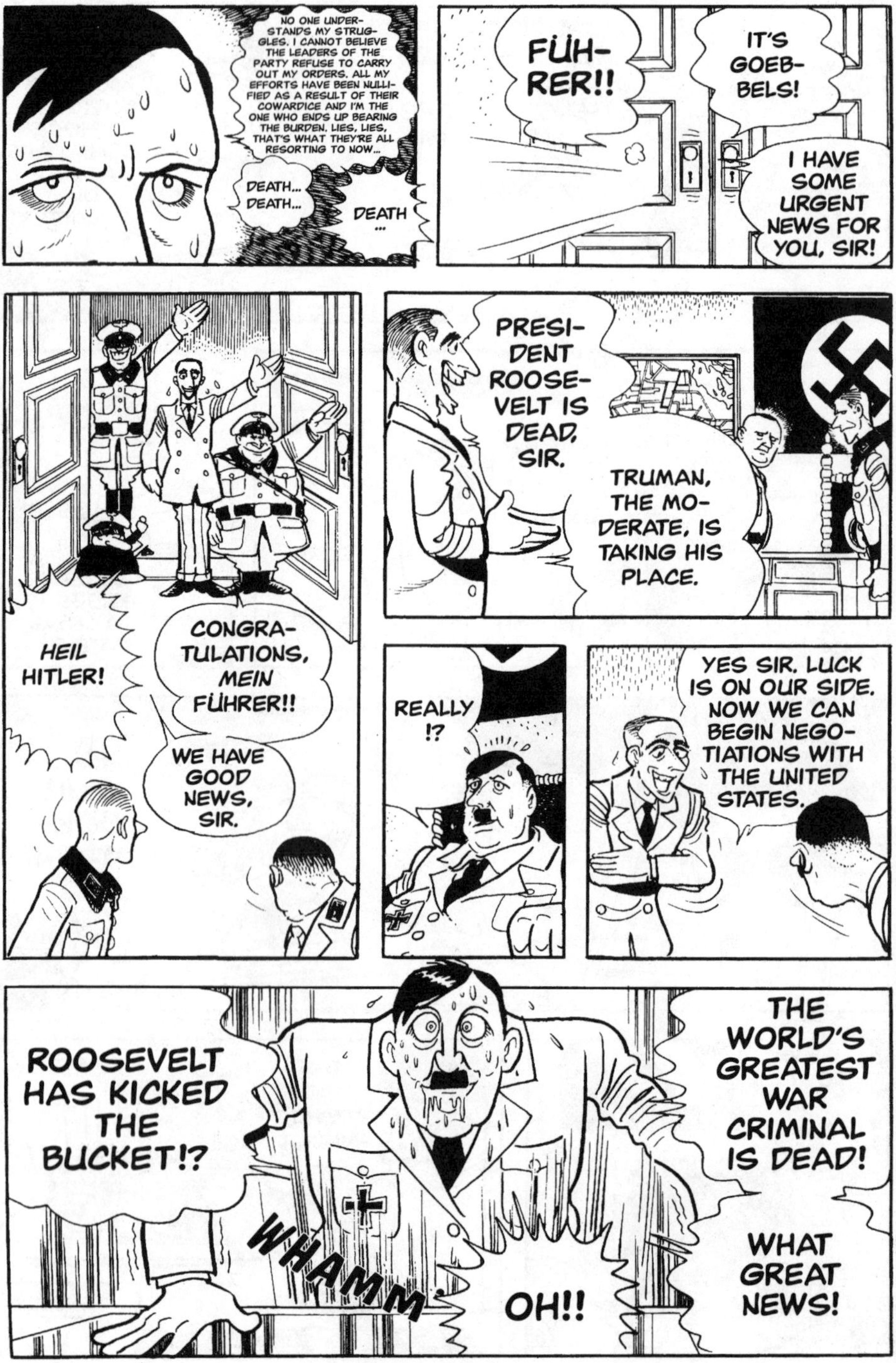
NO ONE UNDERSTANDS MY STRUGGLES. I CANNOT BELIEVE THE LEADERS OF THE PARTY REFUSE TO CARRY OUT MY ORDERS. ALL MY EFFORTS HAVE BEEN NULLIFIED AS A RESULT OF THEIR COWARDICE AND I'M THE ONE WHO ENDS UP BEARING THE BURDEN. LIES, LIES, THAT'S WHAT THEY'RE ALL RESORTING TO NOW...
DEATH... DEATH...
DEATH ...
FÜHRER!!
IT'S GOEBBELS!
I HAVE SOME URGENT NEWS FOR YOU, SIR!
HEIL HITLER!
CONGRATULATIONS, MEIN FÜHRER!!
WE HAVE GOOD NEWS, SIR.
PRESIDENT ROOSEVELT IS DEAD, SIR.
TRUMAN, THE MODERATE, IS TAKING HIS PLACE.
REALLY !?
YES SIR. LUCK IS ON OUR SIDE. NOW WE CAN BEGIN NEGOTIATIONS WITH THE UNITED STATES.
ROOSEVELT HAS KICKED THE BUCKET!?
WHAMM
OH!!
THE WORLD'S GREATEST WAR CRIMINAL IS DEAD!
WHAT GREAT NEWS!

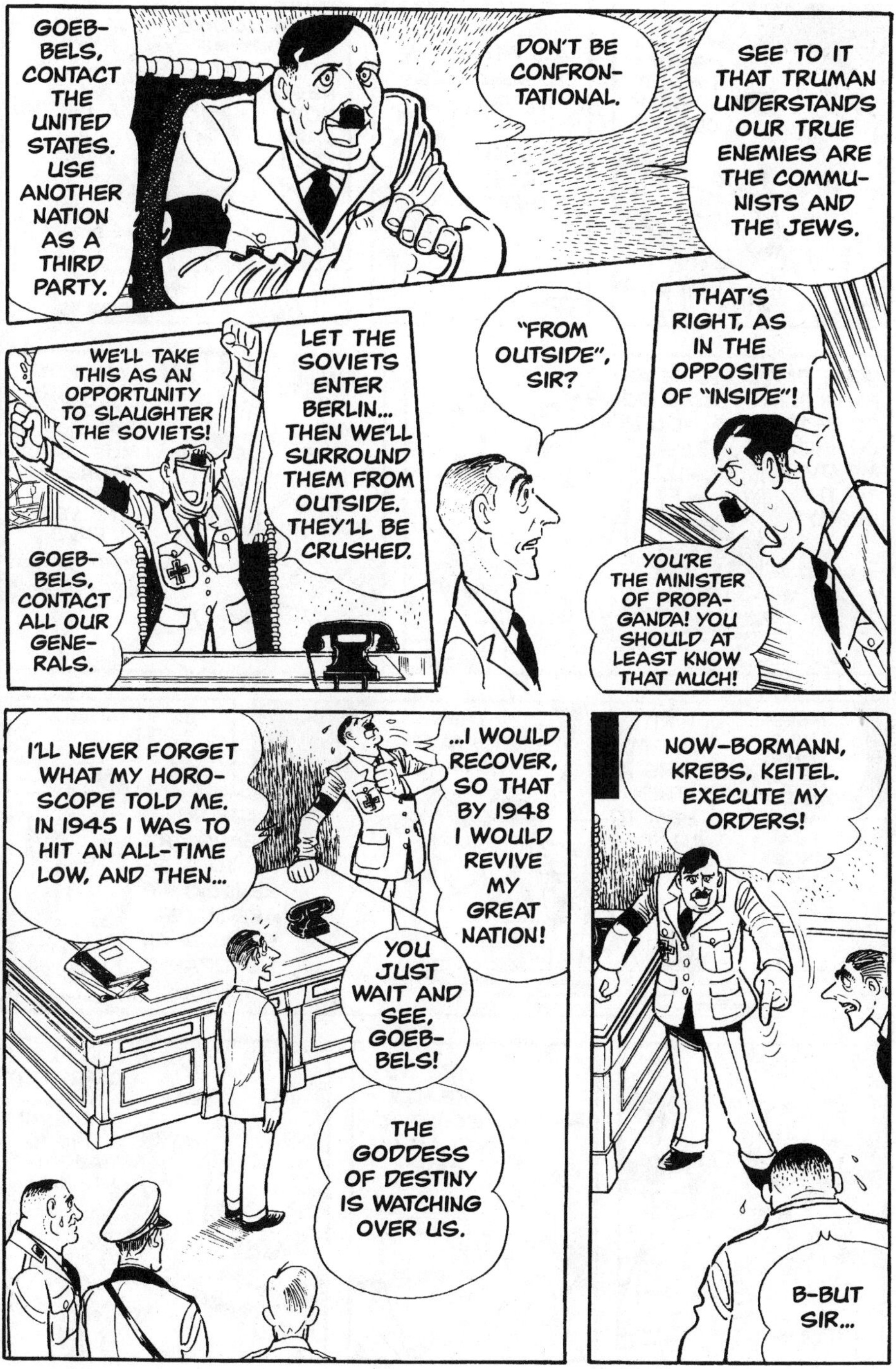
GOEB-BELS, CONTACT THE UNITED STATES. USE ANOTHER NATION AS A THIRD PARTY.
DON'T BE CONFRON-TATIONAL.
SEE TO IT THAT TRUMAN UNDERSTANDS OUR TRUE ENEMIES ARE THE COMMUNISTS AND THE JEWS.
WE'LL TAKE THIS AS AN OPPORTUNITY TO SLAUGHTER THE SOVIETS!
LET THE SOVIETS ENTER BERLIN... THEN WE'LL SURROUND THEM FROM OUTSIDE. THEY'LL BE CRUSHED.
GOEB-BELS, CONTACT ALL OUR GENE-RALS.
"FROM OUTSIDE", SIR?
THAT'S RIGHT, AS IN THE OPPOSITE OF "INSIDE"!
YOU'RE THE MINISTER OF PROPA-GANDA! YOU SHOULD AT LEAST KNOW THAT MUCH!
I'LL NEVER FORGET WHAT MY HORO-SCOPE TOLD ME. IN 1945 I WAS TO HIT AN ALL-TIME LOW, AND THEN...
...I WOULD RECOVER, SO THAT BY 1948 I WOULD REVIVE MY GREAT NATION!
YOU JUST WAIT AND SEE, GOEB-BELS!
THE GODDESS OF DESTINY IS WATCHING OVER US.
NOW—BORMANN, KREBS, KEITEL. EXECUTE MY ORDERS!
B-BUT SIR...

Adolf

 WHAT'S WRONG? HAVEN'T I MADE MYSELF CLEAR?

 SIR... WE MUST ALL WITHDRAW TO BERCHTES-GADEN. WE CAN REORGANIZE THERE...

 YOU'RE GOING TO LOCK ME UP IN THAT RESORT!? HOW DARE YOU!

 NONE OF YOU HAVE ANY FAITH IN ME. YOU'RE GOING TO BETRAY ME! YOU PLAN ON HANDING ME OVER TO THE ENEMY!

OF COURSE NOT, SIR.

 I WILL NOT MOVE ONE INCH FROM BERLIN!!

EVEN IF YOU COWARDS TRY TO ESCAPE, EVEN IF I MUST STAND ALONE, I'LL FIGHT TO THE VERY END!!

 GOEBBELS, YOU'RE THE ONLY ONE LEFT WHO I CAN TRUST.

WRITE OUT MY ORDERS AND DISTRIBUTE THEM TO ALL THE GENERALS.

THEN CONTACT TRUMAN.

BY NO MEANS ARE WE TO SURRENDER! WE ARE MERELY SEEKING AN HONORABLE PEACE.

 ARE WE REALLY GOING TO DO AS HE SAYS?

 I CAN'T CARRY OUT THESE ORDERS! THIS IS ABOMINABLE!

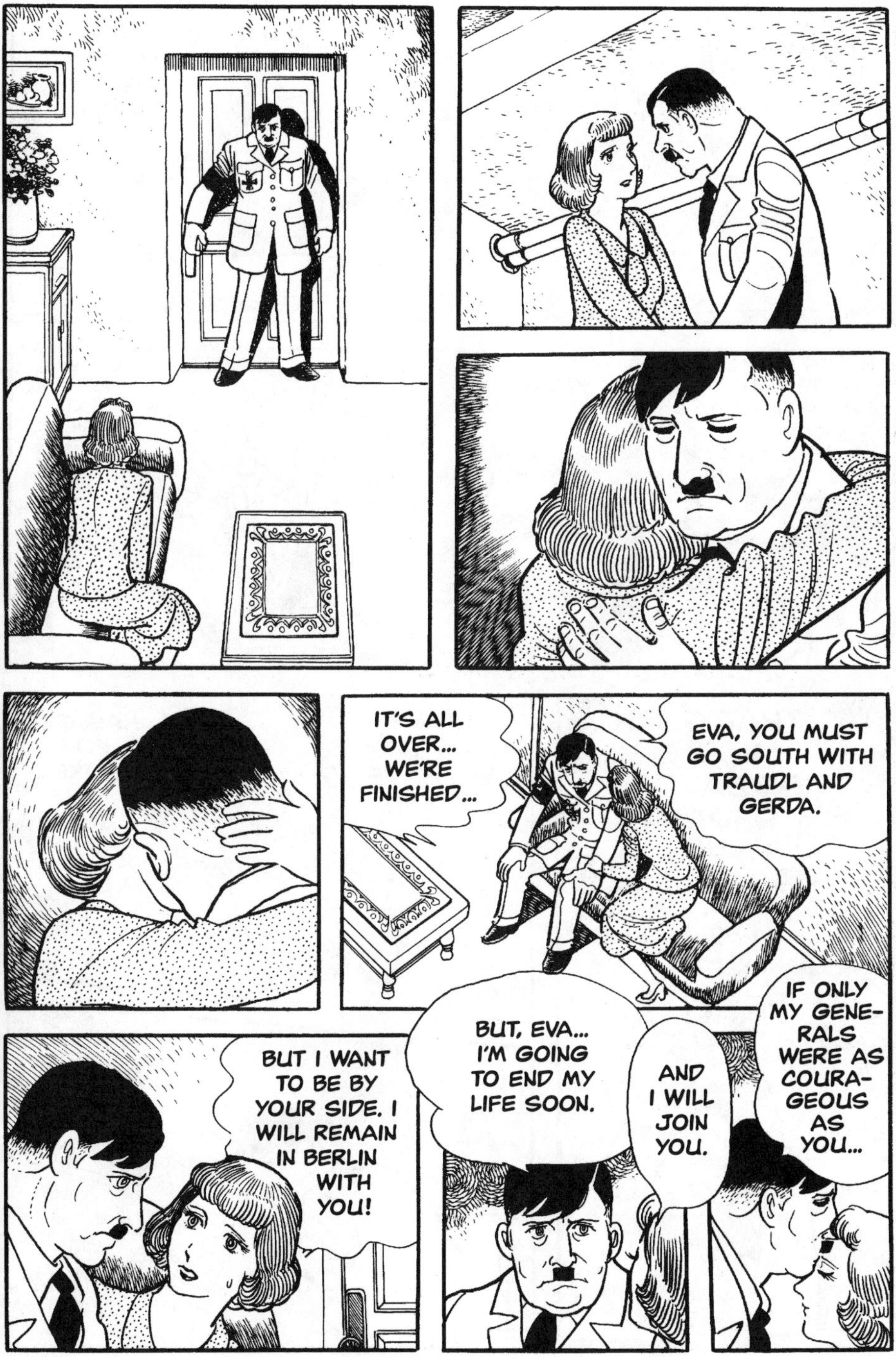
IT'S ALL OVER... WE'RE FINISHED...
EVA, YOU MUST GO SOUTH WITH TRAUDL AND GERDA.
BUT I WANT TO BE BY YOUR SIDE. I WILL REMAIN IN BERLIN WITH YOU!
BUT, EVA... I'M GOING TO END MY LIFE SOON.
AND I WILL JOIN YOU.
IF ONLY MY GENE-RALS WERE AS COURA-GEOUS AS YOU...

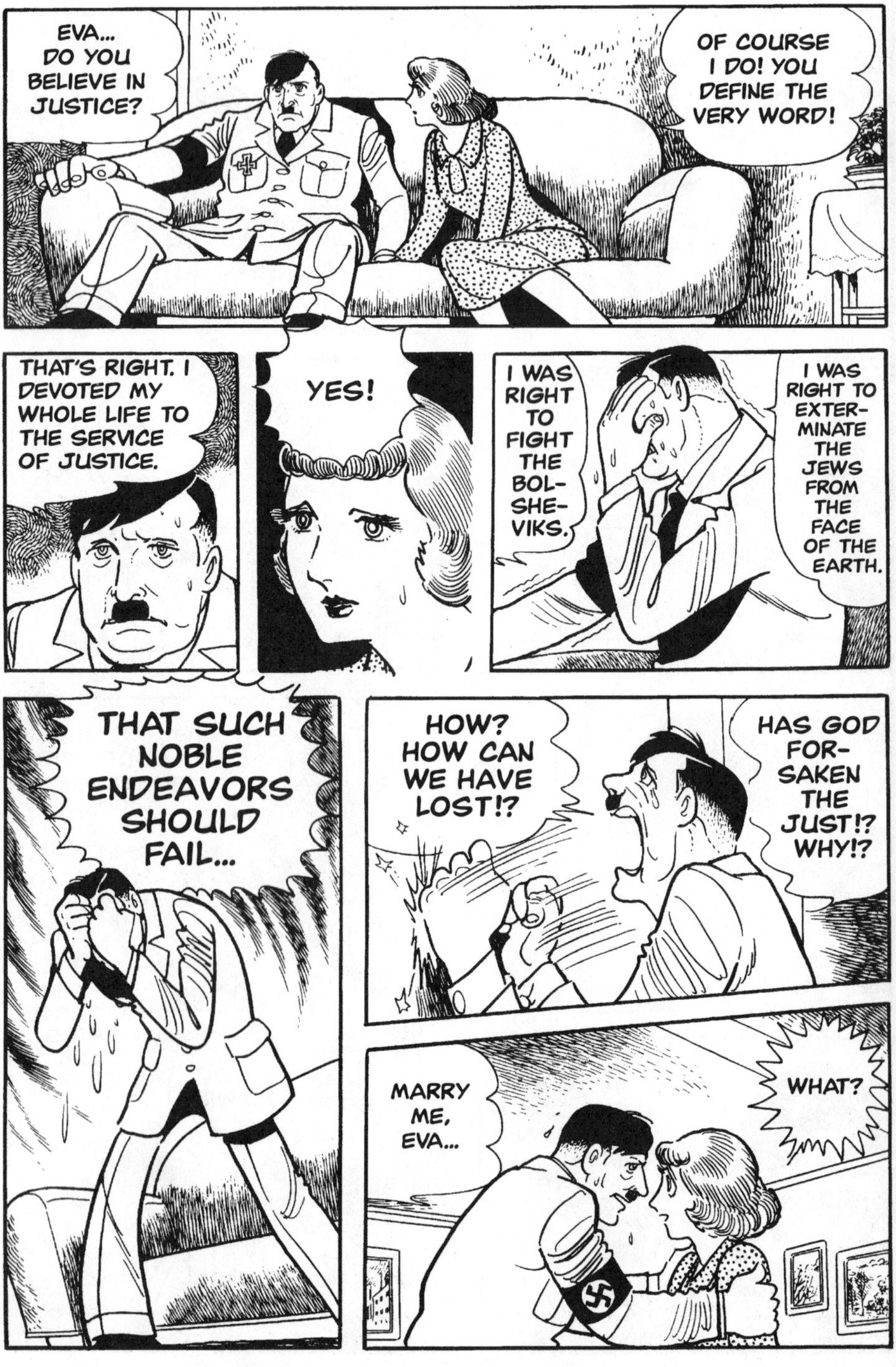
EVA... DO YOU BELIEVE IN JUSTICE?
OF COURSE I DO! YOU DEFINE THE VERY WORD!
THAT'S RIGHT. I DEVOTED MY WHOLE LIFE TO THE SERVICE OF JUSTICE.
YES!
I WAS RIGHT TO FIGHT THE BOL-SHE-VIKS.
I WAS RIGHT TO EXTER-MINATE THE JEWS FROM THE FACE OF THE EARTH.
THAT SUCH NOBLE ENDEAVORS SHOULD FAIL...
HOW? HOW CAN WE HAVE LOST!?
HAS GOD FOR-SAKEN THE JUST!? WHY!?
MARRY ME, EVA...
WHAT?

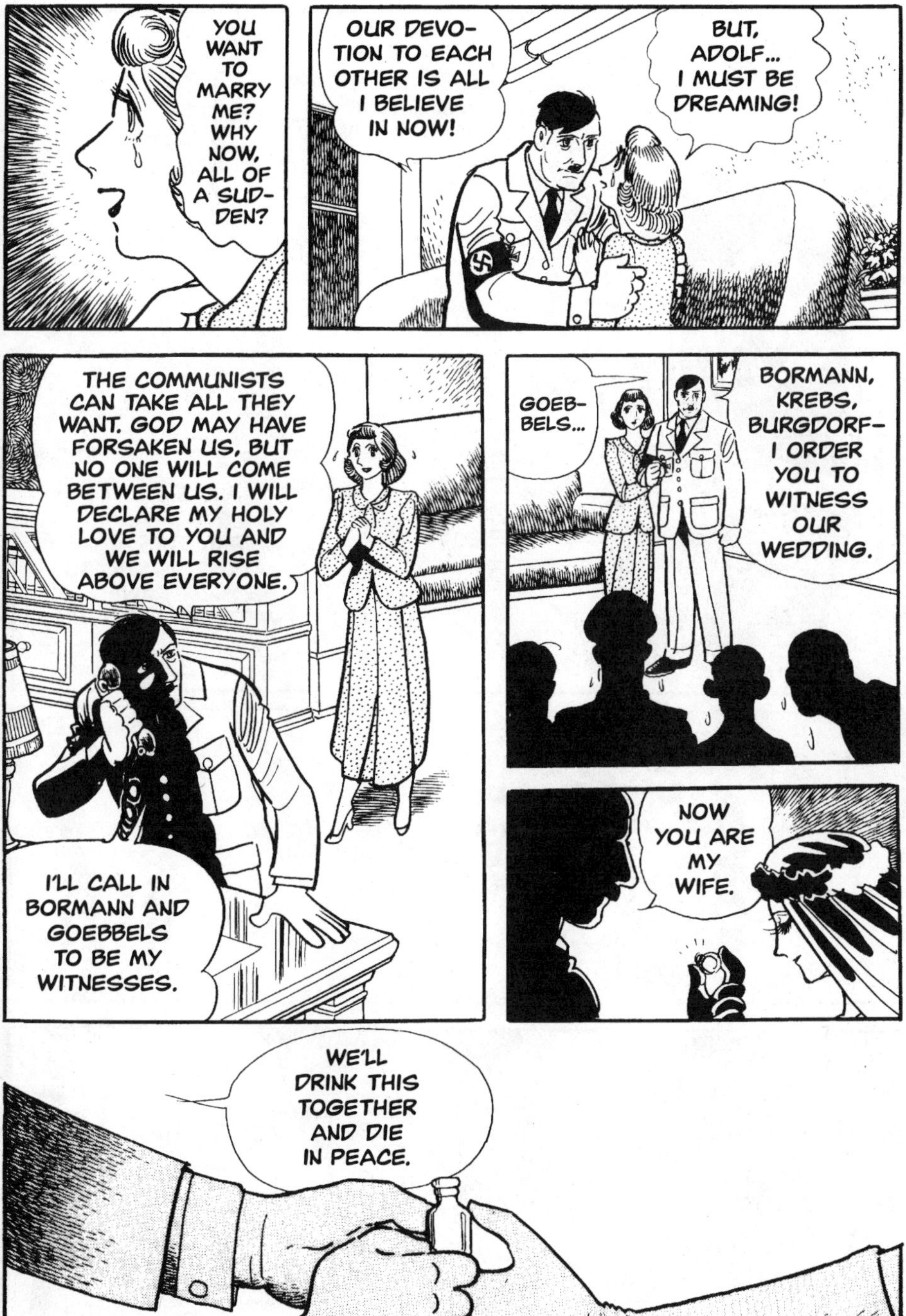
YOU WANT TO MARRY ME? WHY NOW, ALL OF A SUDDEN?
OUR DEVOTION TO EACH OTHER IS ALL I BELIEVE IN NOW!
BUT, ADOLF... I MUST BE DREAMING!
THE COMMUNISTS CAN TAKE ALL THEY WANT. GOD MAY HAVE FORSAKEN US, BUT NO ONE WILL COME BETWEEN US. I WILL DECLARE MY HOLY LOVE TO YOU AND WE WILL RISE ABOVE EVERYONE.
I'LL CALL IN BORMANN AND GOEBBELS TO BE MY WITNESSES.
GOEBBELS...
BORMANN, KREBS, BURGDORF- I ORDER YOU TO WITNESS OUR WEDDING.
NOW YOU ARE MY WIFE.
WE'LL DRINK THIS TOGETHER AND DIE IN PEACE.

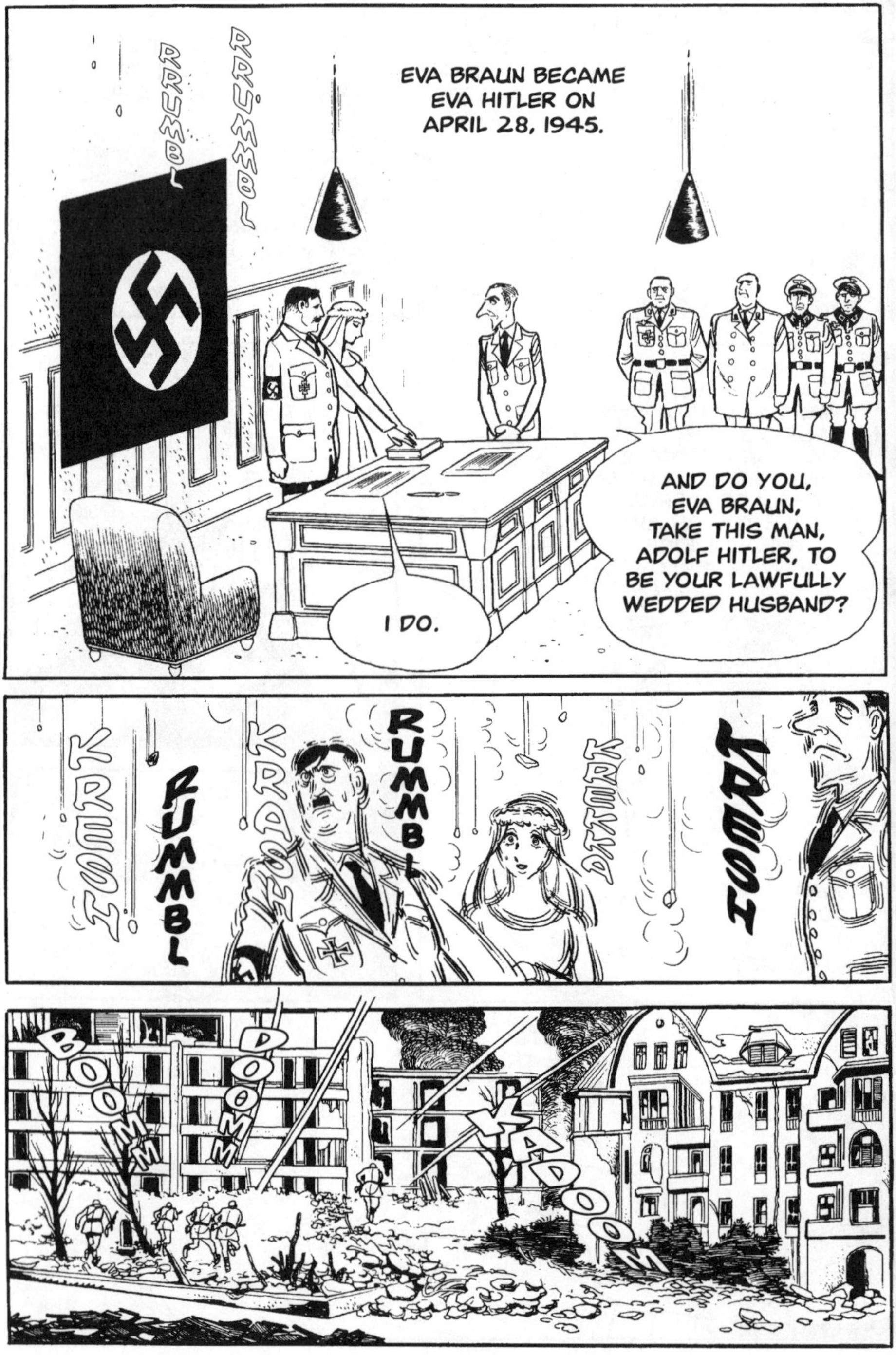
RRUMMBL
RRUMMBL
EVA BRAUN BECAME EVA HITLER ON APRIL 28, 1945.
AND DO YOU, EVA BRAUN, TAKE THIS MAN, ADOLF HITLER, TO BE YOUR LAWFULLY WEDDED HUSBAND?
I DO.
KREEOI
RUMMBL
KRASH
RUMMBL
KREEOI
BOOMM
DOOMM
KADOOOM

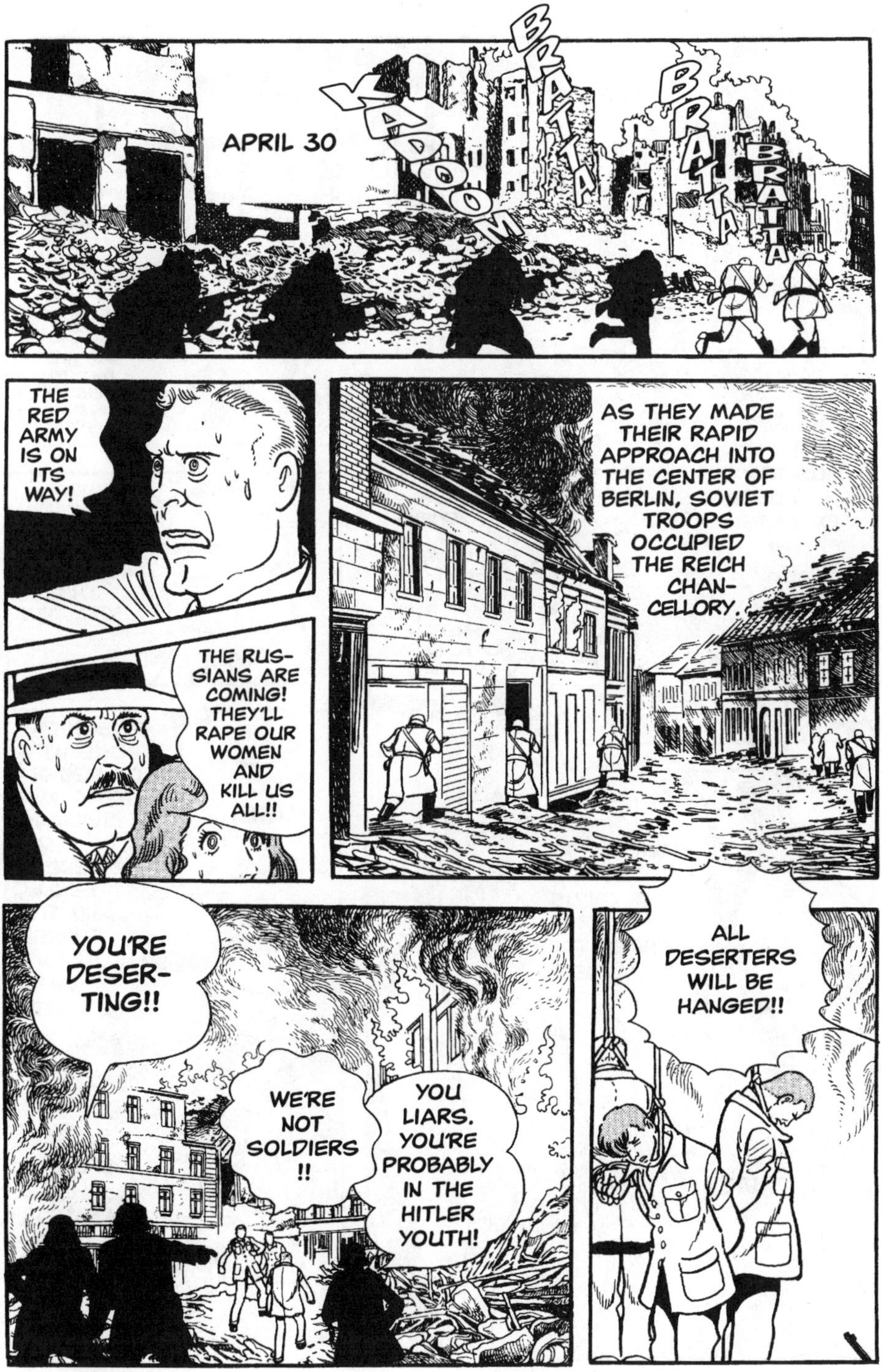
APRIL 30
KADOOM
BRATTA
BRATTA
BRATTA
THE RED ARMY IS ON ITS WAY!
THE RUSSIANS ARE COMING! THEY'LL RAPE OUR WOMEN AND KILL US ALL!!
AS THEY MADE THEIR RAPID APPROACH INTO THE CENTER OF BERLIN, SOVIET TROOPS OCCUPIED THE REICH CHANCELLORY.
YOU'RE DESERTING!!
WE'RE NOT SOLDIERS !!
YOU LIARS. YOU'RE PROBABLY IN THE HITLER YOUTH!
ALL DESERTERS WILL BE HANGED!!

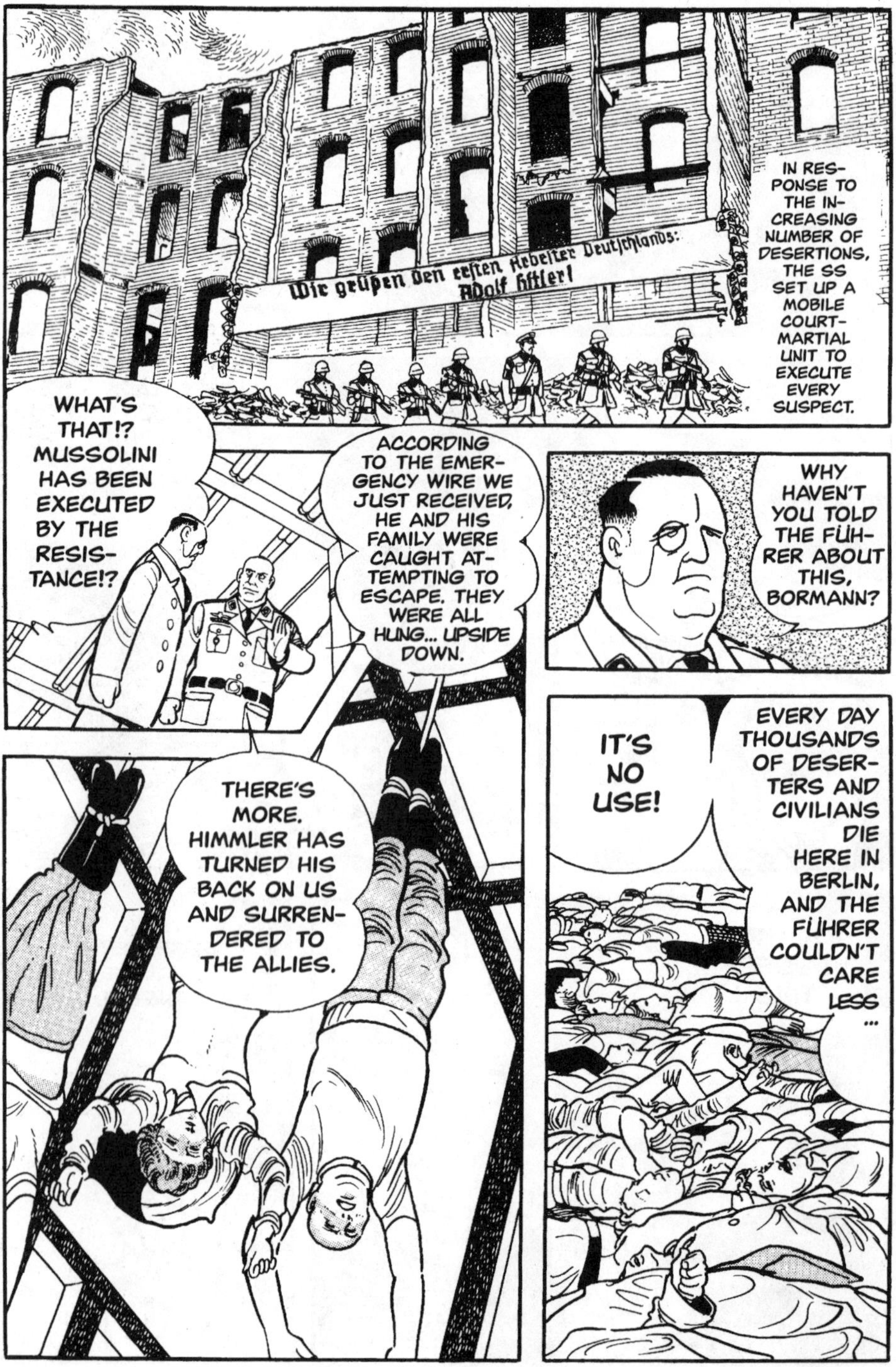
Wir grüßen den ersten Arbeiter Deutschlands: Adolf Hitler!
IN RESPONSE TO THE INCREASING NUMBER OF DESERTIONS, THE SS SET UP A MOBILE COURT-MARTIAL UNIT TO EXECUTE EVERY SUSPECT.
WHAT'S THAT!? MUSSOLINI HAS BEEN EXECUTED BY THE RESISTANCE!?
ACCORDING TO THE EMERGENCY WIRE WE JUST RECEIVED, HE AND HIS FAMILY WERE CAUGHT ATTEMPTING TO ESCAPE. THEY WERE ALL HUNG... UPSIDE DOWN.
WHY HAVEN'T YOU TOLD THE FÜHRER ABOUT THIS, BORMANN?
THERE'S MORE. HIMMLER HAS TURNED HIS BACK ON US AND SURRENDERED TO THE ALLIES.
IT'S NO USE!
EVERY DAY THOUSANDS OF DESERTERS AND CIVILIANS DIE HERE IN BERLIN, AND THE FÜHRER COULDN'T CARE LESS...

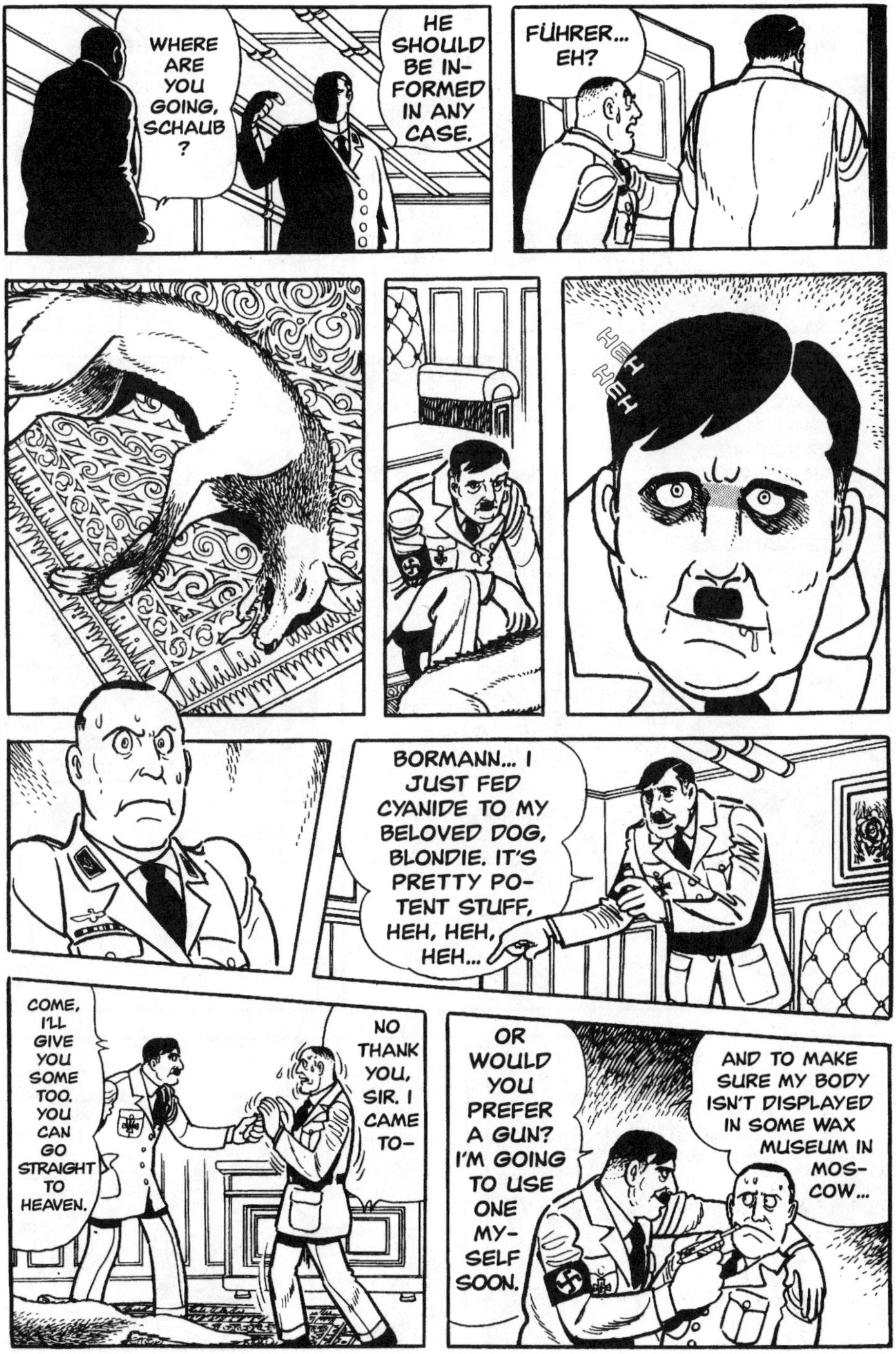
WHERE ARE YOU GOING, SCHAUB ?
HE SHOULD BE INFORMED IN ANY CASE.
FÜHRER... EH?
HEH HEH
BORMANN... I JUST FED CYANIDE TO MY BELOVED DOG, BLONDIE. IT'S PRETTY POTENT STUFF, HEH, HEH, HEH...
COME, I'LL GIVE YOU SOME TOO. YOU CAN GO STRAIGHT TO HEAVEN.
NO THANK YOU, SIR. I CAME TO-
OR WOULD YOU PREFER A GUN? I'M GOING TO USE ONE MYSELF SOON.
AND TO MAKE SURE MY BODY ISN'T DISPLAYED IN SOME WAX MUSEUM IN MOSCOW...

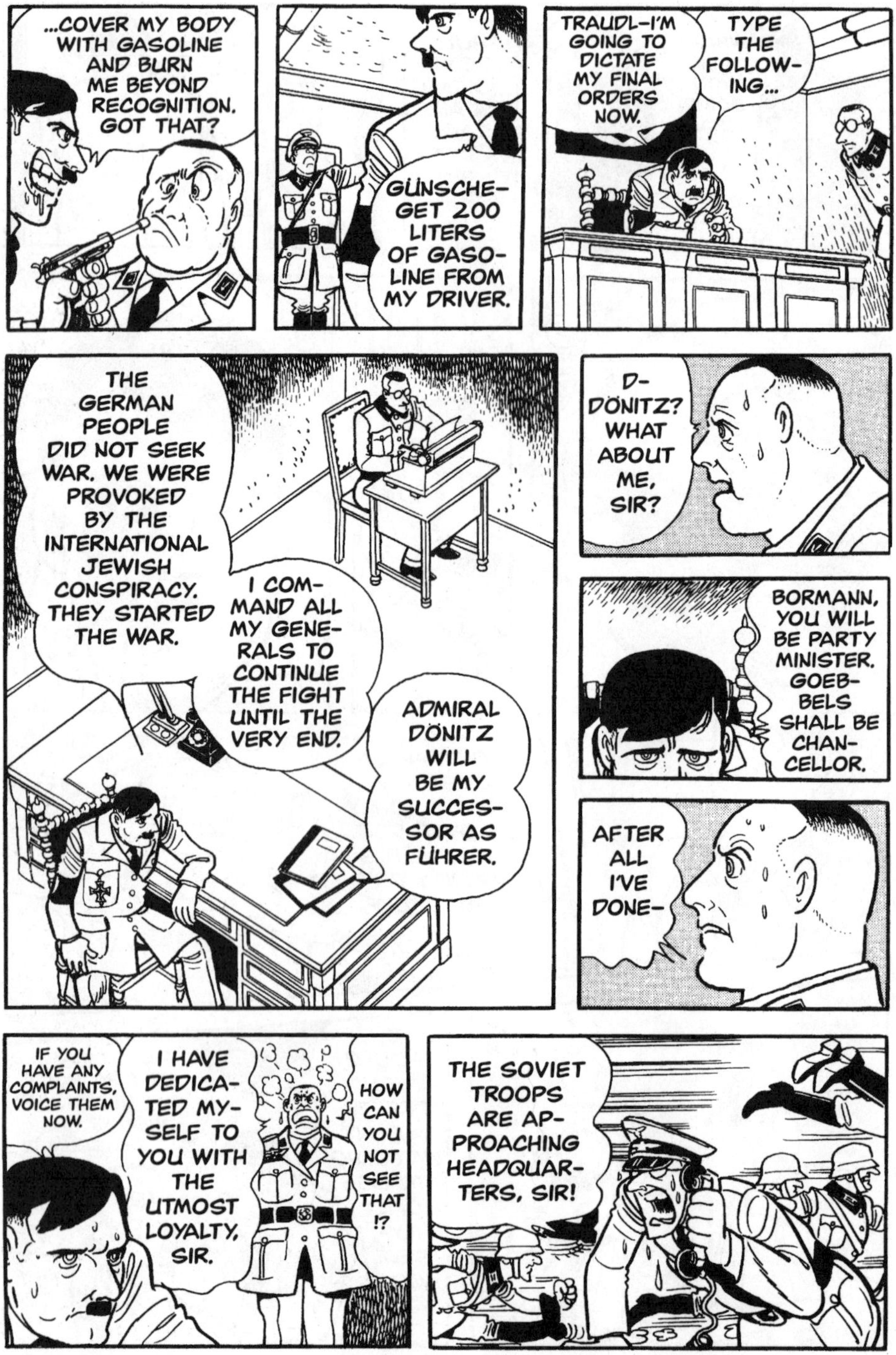
...COVER MY BODY WITH GASOLINE AND BURN ME BEYOND RECOGNITION. GOT THAT?
GÜNSCHE-GET 200 LITERS OF GASOLINE FROM MY DRIVER.
TRAUDL-I'M GOING TO DICTATE MY FINAL ORDERS NOW.
TYPE THE FOLLOWING...
THE GERMAN PEOPLE DID NOT SEEK WAR. WE WERE PROVOKED BY THE INTERNATIONAL JEWISH CONSPIRACY. THEY STARTED THE WAR.
I COMMAND ALL MY GENERALS TO CONTINUE THE FIGHT UNTIL THE VERY END.
ADMIRAL DÖNITZ WILL BE MY SUCCESSOR AS FÜHRER.
D-DÖNITZ? WHAT ABOUT ME, SIR?
BORMANN, YOU WILL BE PARTY MINISTER. GOEBBELS SHALL BE CHANCELLOR.
AFTER ALL I'VE DONE-
IF YOU HAVE ANY COMPLAINTS, VOICE THEM NOW.
I HAVE DEDICATED MYSELF TO YOU WITH THE UTMOST LOYALTY, SIR.
HOW CAN YOU NOT SEE THAT!?
THE SOVIET TROOPS ARE APPROACHING HEADQUARTERS, SIR!

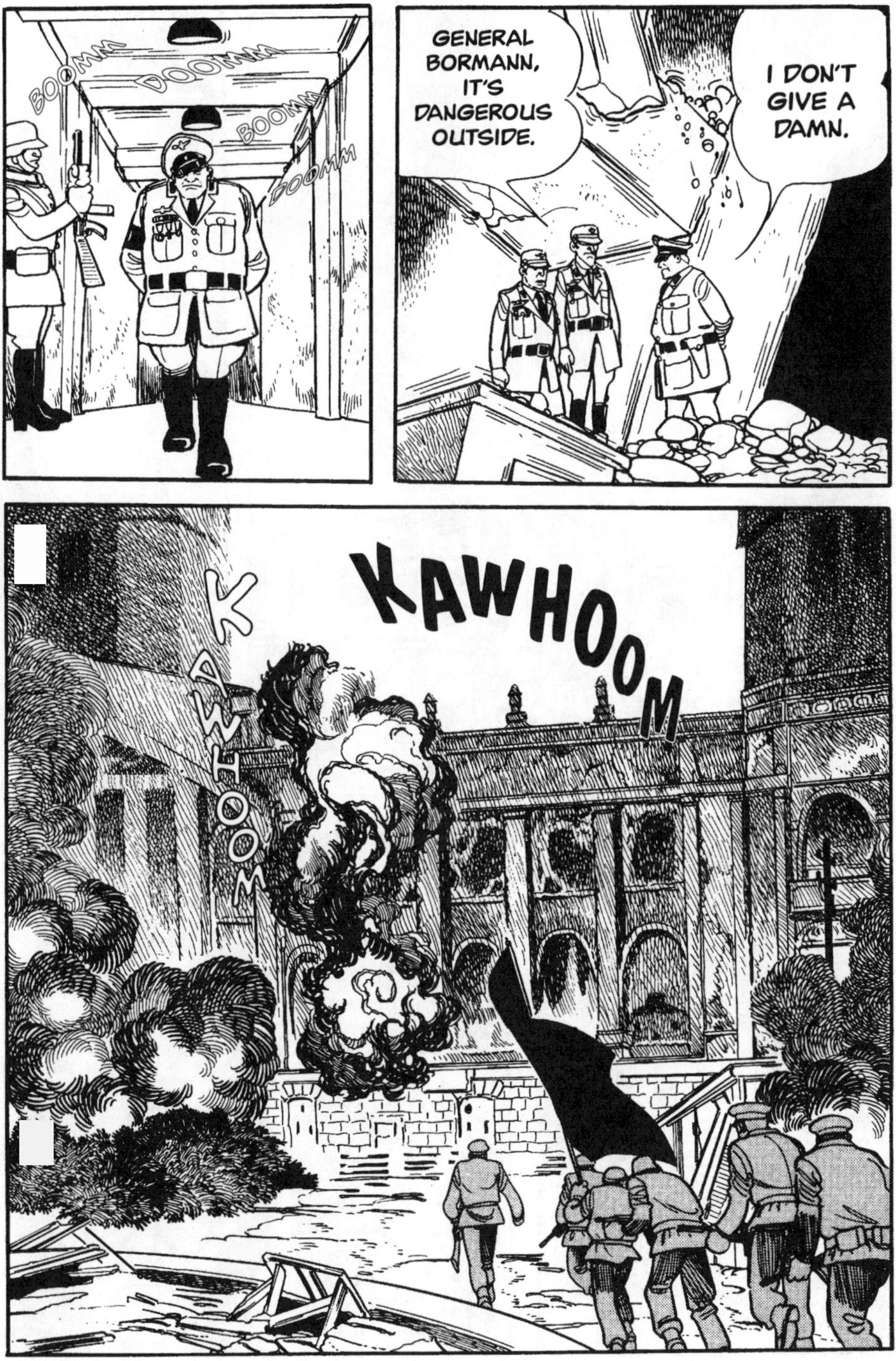
BOOMM
DOOMM
BOOMM
DOOMM
GENERAL BORMANN, IT'S DANGEROUS OUTSIDE.
I DON'T GIVE A DAMN.
KAWHOOOM
KAWHOOOM

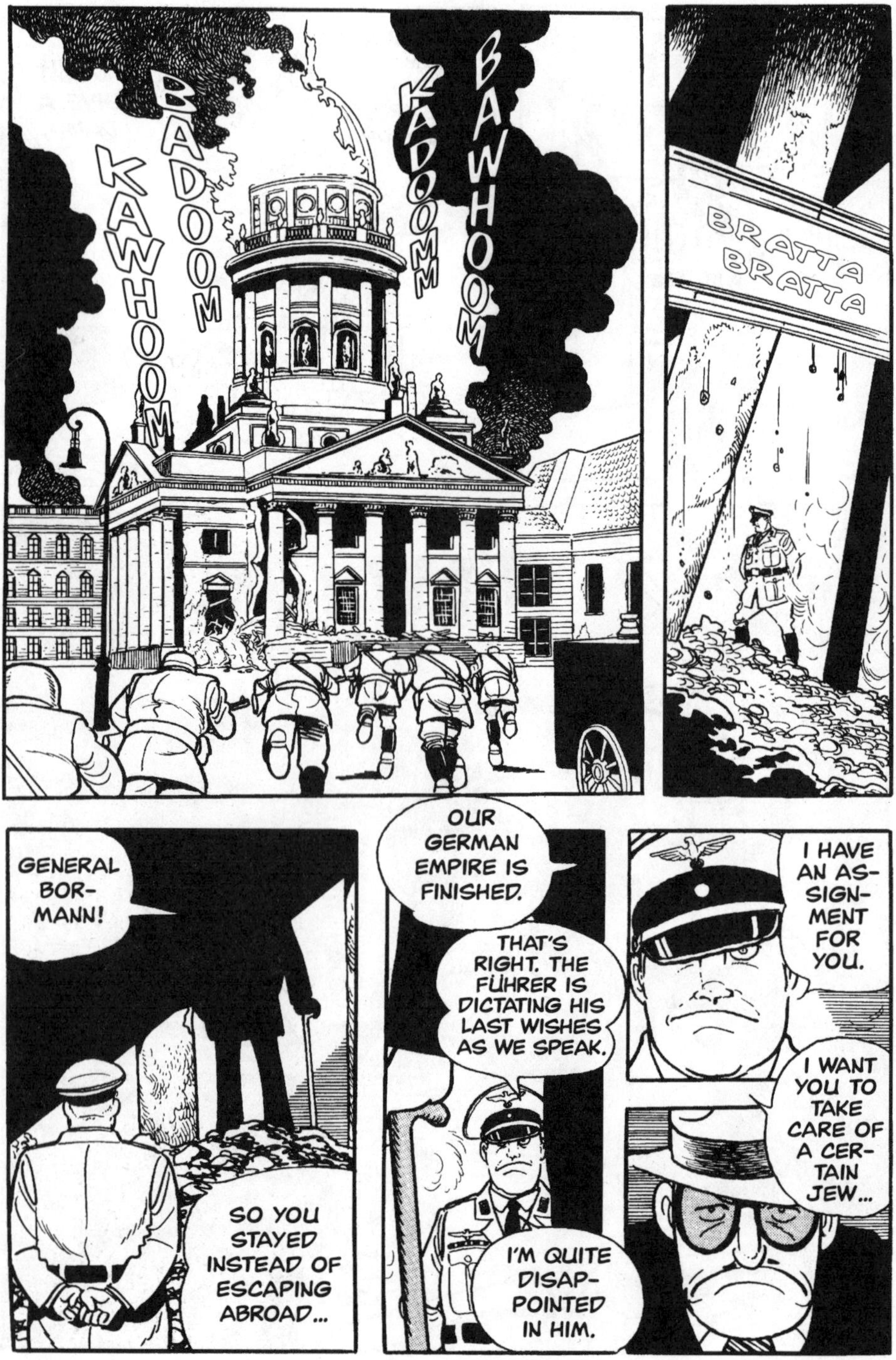
KAWHOOOM
BADOOOM
KADOOOMM
BAWHOOOM
BRATTA BRATTA
GENERAL BORMANN!
SO YOU STAYED INSTEAD OF ESCAPING ABROAD...
OUR GERMAN EMPIRE IS FINISHED.
THAT'S RIGHT. THE FÜHRER IS DICTATING HIS LAST WISHES AS WE SPEAK.
I'M QUITE DISAPPOINTED IN HIM.
I HAVE AN ASSIGNMENT FOR YOU.
I WANT YOU TO TAKE CARE OF A CERTAIN JEW...

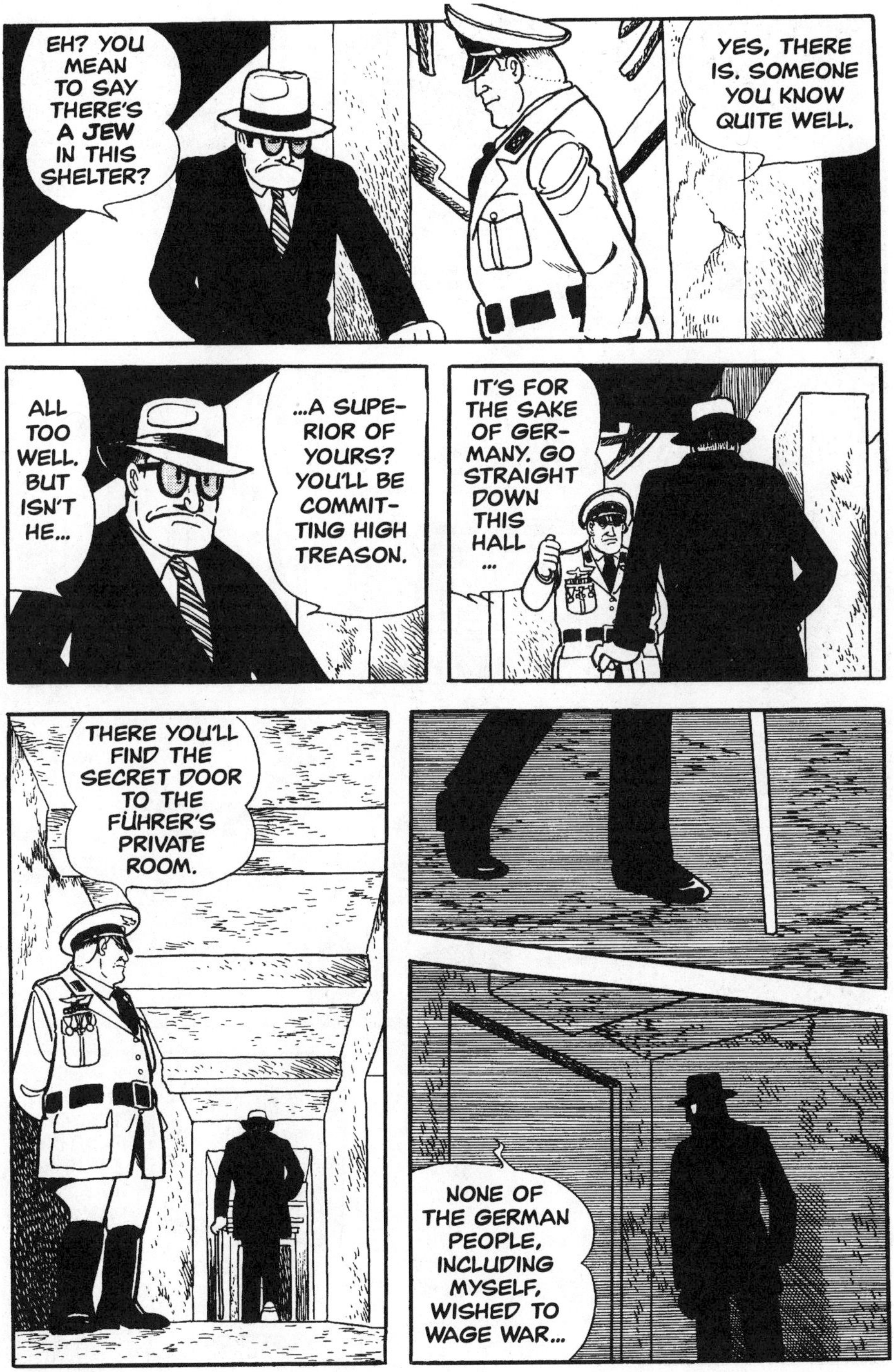
EH? YOU MEAN TO SAY THERE'S A JEW IN THIS SHELTER?
YES, THERE IS. SOMEONE YOU KNOW QUITE WELL.
ALL TOO WELL. BUT ISN'T HE...
...A SUPERIOR OF YOURS? YOU'LL BE COMMITTING HIGH TREASON.
IT'S FOR THE SAKE OF GERMANY. GO STRAIGHT DOWN THIS HALL ...
THERE YOU'LL FIND THE SECRET DOOR TO THE FÜHRER'S PRIVATE ROOM.
NONE OF THE GERMAN PEOPLE, INCLUDING MYSELF, WISHED TO WAGE WAR...

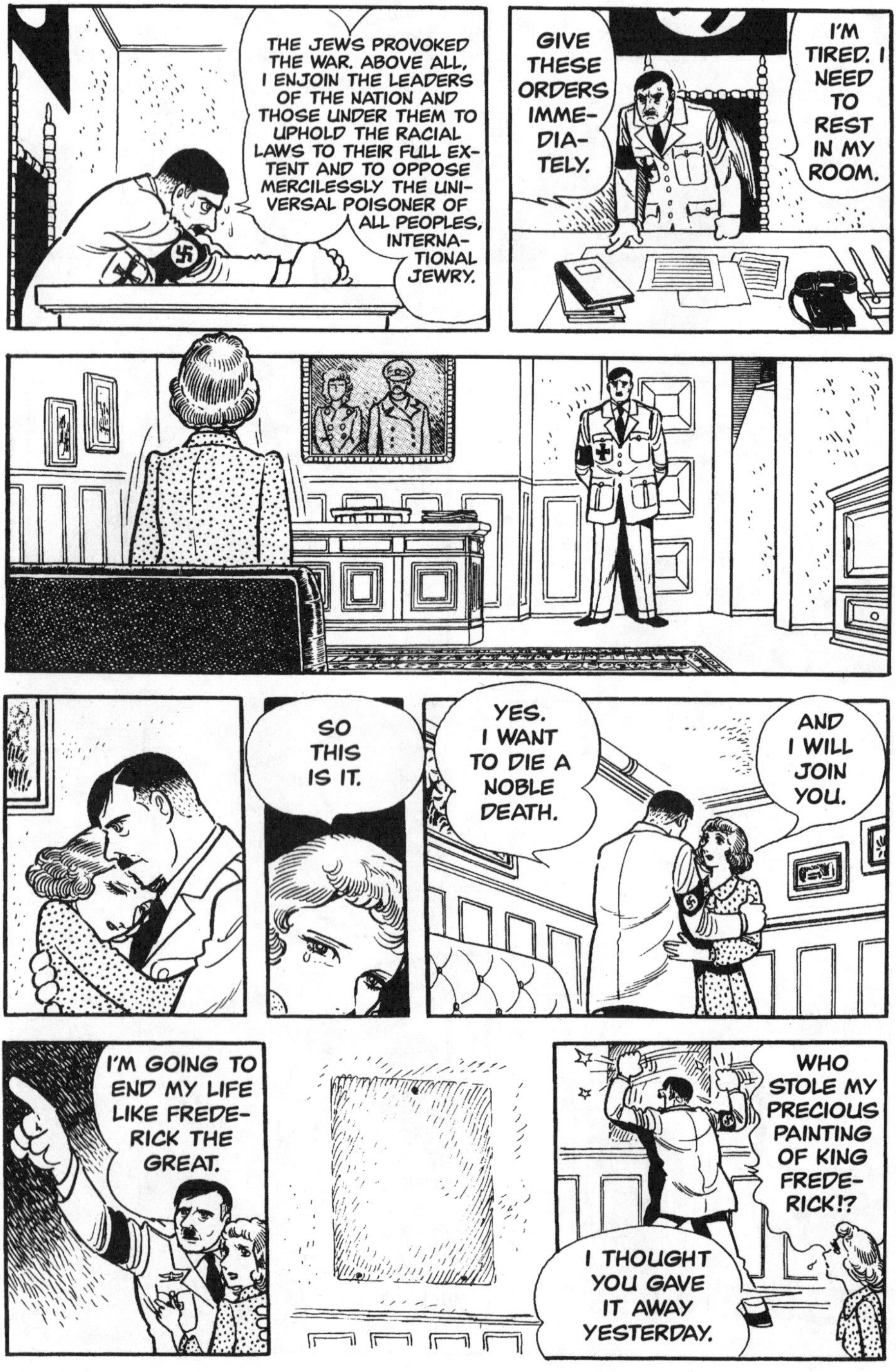
THE JEWS PROVOKED THE WAR. ABOVE ALL, I ENJOIN THE LEADERS OF THE NATION AND THOSE UNDER THEM TO UPHOLD THE RACIAL LAWS TO THEIR FULL EXTENT AND TO OPPOSE MERCILESSLY THE UNIVERSAL POISONER OF ALL PEOPLES, INTERNATIONAL JEWRY.
GIVE THESE ORDERS IMMEDIATELY.
I'M TIRED. I NEED TO REST IN MY ROOM.
SO THIS IS IT.
YES. I WANT TO DIE A NOBLE DEATH.
AND I WILL JOIN YOU.
I'M GOING TO END MY LIFE LIKE FREDERICK THE GREAT.
WHO STOLE MY PRECIOUS PAINTING OF KING FREDERICK!?
I THOUGHT YOU GAVE IT AWAY YESTERDAY.

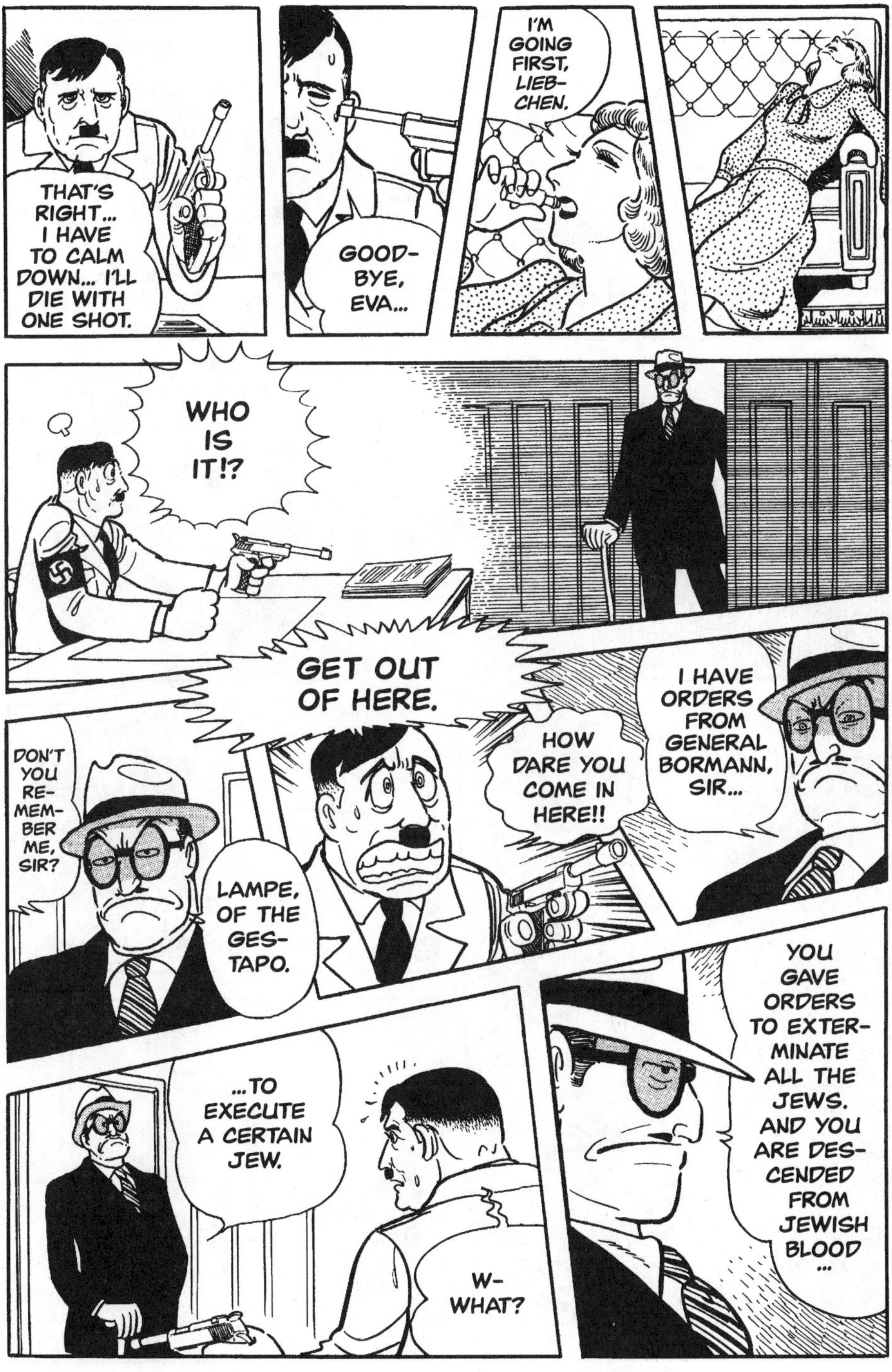
THAT'S RIGHT... I HAVE TO CALM DOWN... I'LL DIE WITH ONE SHOT.
GOOD-BYE, EVA...
I'M GOING FIRST, LIEB-CHEN.
WHO IS IT!?
DON'T YOU RE-MEM-BER ME, SIR?
LAMPE, OF THE GES-TAPO.
GET OUT OF HERE.
HOW DARE YOU COME IN HERE!!
I HAVE ORDERS FROM GENERAL BORMANN, SIR...
...TO EXECUTE A CERTAIN JEW.
W-WHAT?
YOU GAVE ORDERS TO EXTER-MINATE ALL THE JEWS. AND YOU ARE DES-CENDED FROM JEWISH BLOOD ...

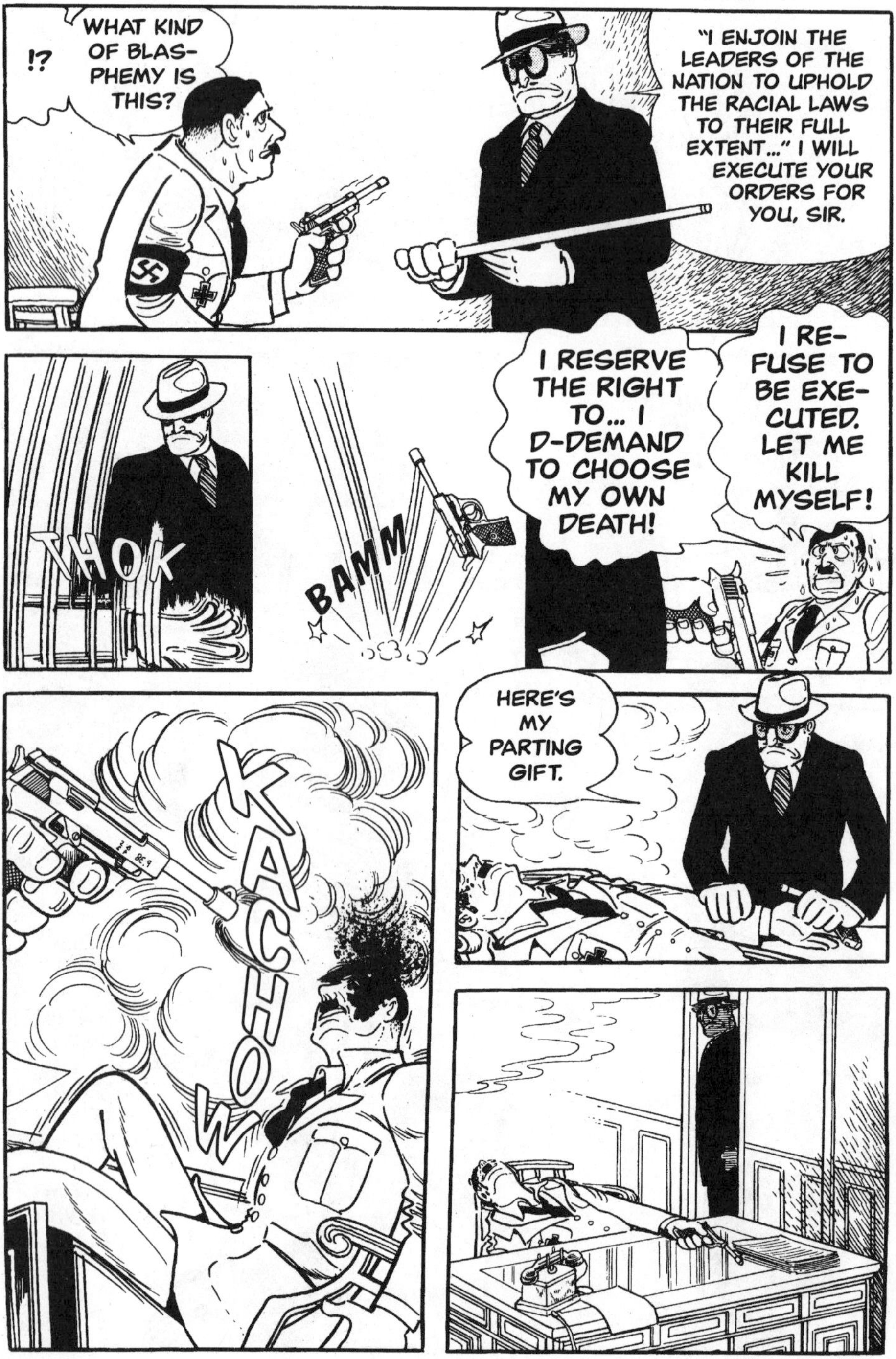
!?
WHAT KIND OF BLAS-PHEMY IS THIS?
"I ENJOIN THE LEADERS OF THE NATION TO UPHOLD THE RACIAL LAWS TO THEIR FULL EXTENT..." I WILL EXECUTE YOUR ORDERS FOR YOU, SIR.
THOK
BAMM
I RESERVE THE RIGHT TO... I D-DEMAND TO CHOOSE MY OWN DEATH!
I RE-FUSE TO BE EXE-CUTED. LET ME KILL MYSELF!
KACHOW
HERE'S MY PARTING GIFT.

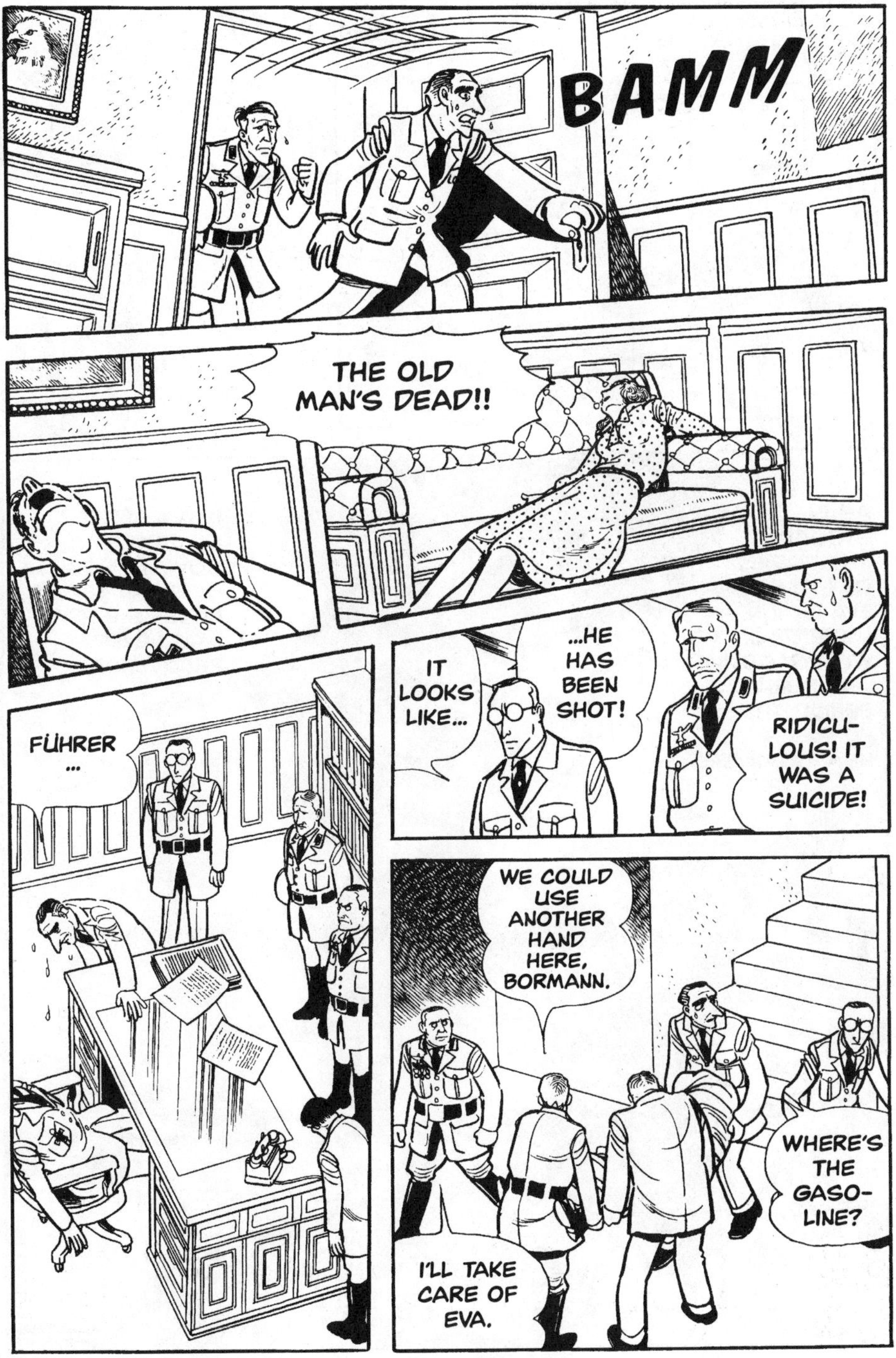
BAMM
THE OLD MAN'S DEAD!!
FÜHRER ...
IT LOOKS LIKE...
...HE HAS BEEN SHOT!
RIDICULOUS! IT WAS A SUICIDE!
WE COULD USE ANOTHER HAND HERE, BORMANN.
WHERE'S THE GASOLINE?
I'LL TAKE CARE OF EVA.

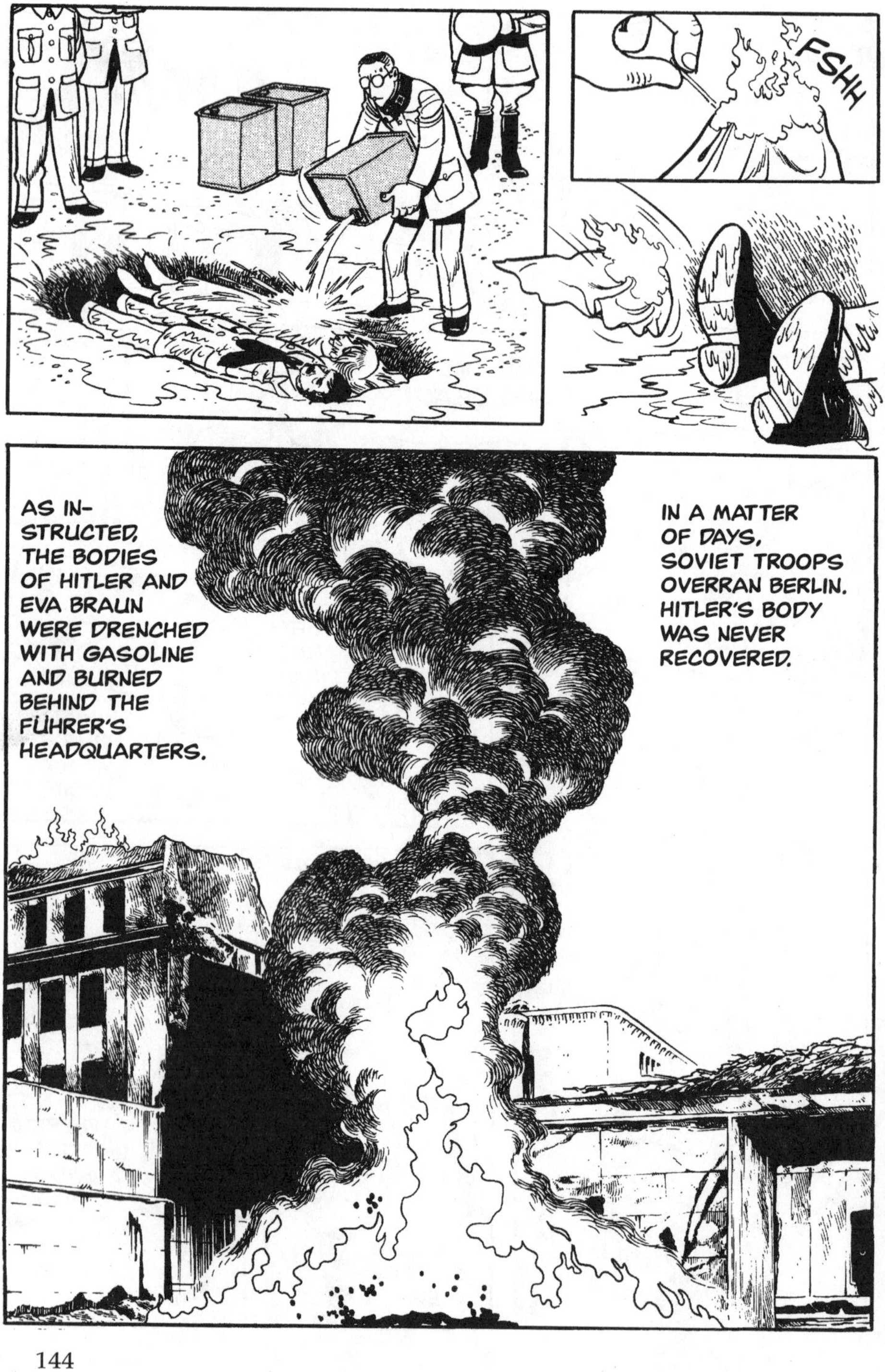
FSHH
AS INSTRUCTED, THE BODIES OF HITLER AND EVA BRAUN WERE DRENCHED WITH GASOLINE AND BURNED BEHIND THE FÜHRER'S HEADQUARTERS.
IN A MATTER OF DAYS, SOVIET TROOPS OVERRAN BERLIN. HITLER'S BODY WAS NEVER RECOVERED.

CHAPTER SIX

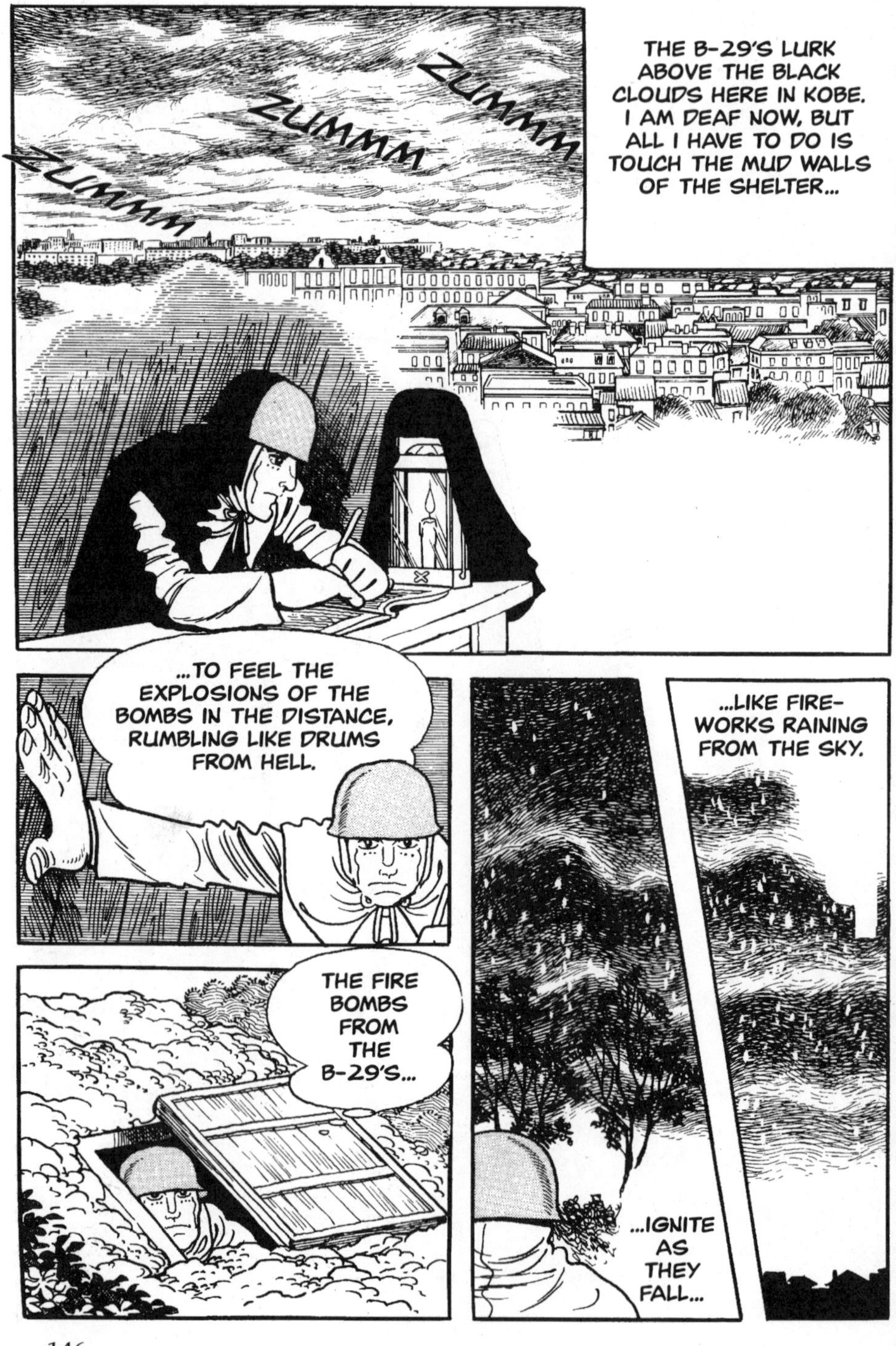
ZUMMM
ZUMMM
ZUMMM
THE B-29'S LURK ABOVE THE BLACK CLOUDS HERE IN KOBE. I AM DEAF NOW, BUT ALL I HAVE TO DO IS TOUCH THE MUD WALLS OF THE SHELTER...
...TO FEEL THE EXPLOSIONS OF THE BOMBS IN THE DISTANCE, RUMBLING LIKE DRUMS FROM HELL.
THE FIRE BOMBS FROM THE B-29'S...
...IGNITE AS THEY FALL...
...LIKE FIRE-WORKS RAINING FROM THE SKY.

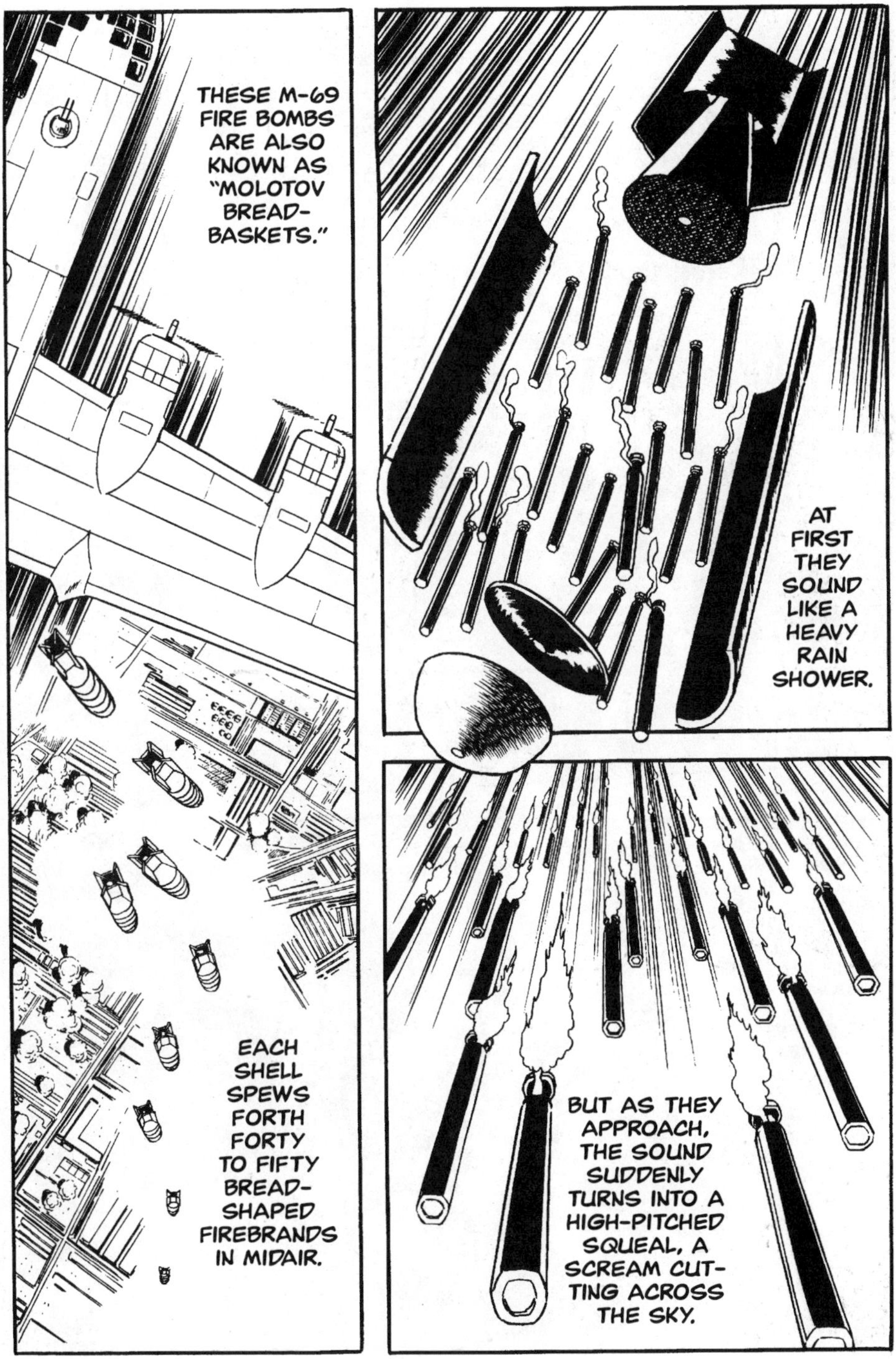
THESE M-69 FIRE BOMBS ARE ALSO KNOWN AS "MOLOTOV BREAD-BASKETS."
EACH SHELL SPEWS FORTH FORTY TO FIFTY BREAD-SHAPED FIREBRANDS IN MIDAIR.
AT FIRST THEY SOUND LIKE A HEAVY RAIN SHOWER.
BUT AS THEY APPROACH, THE SOUND SUDDENLY TURNS INTO A HIGH-PITCHED SQUEAL, A SCREAM CUTTING ACROSS THE SKY.

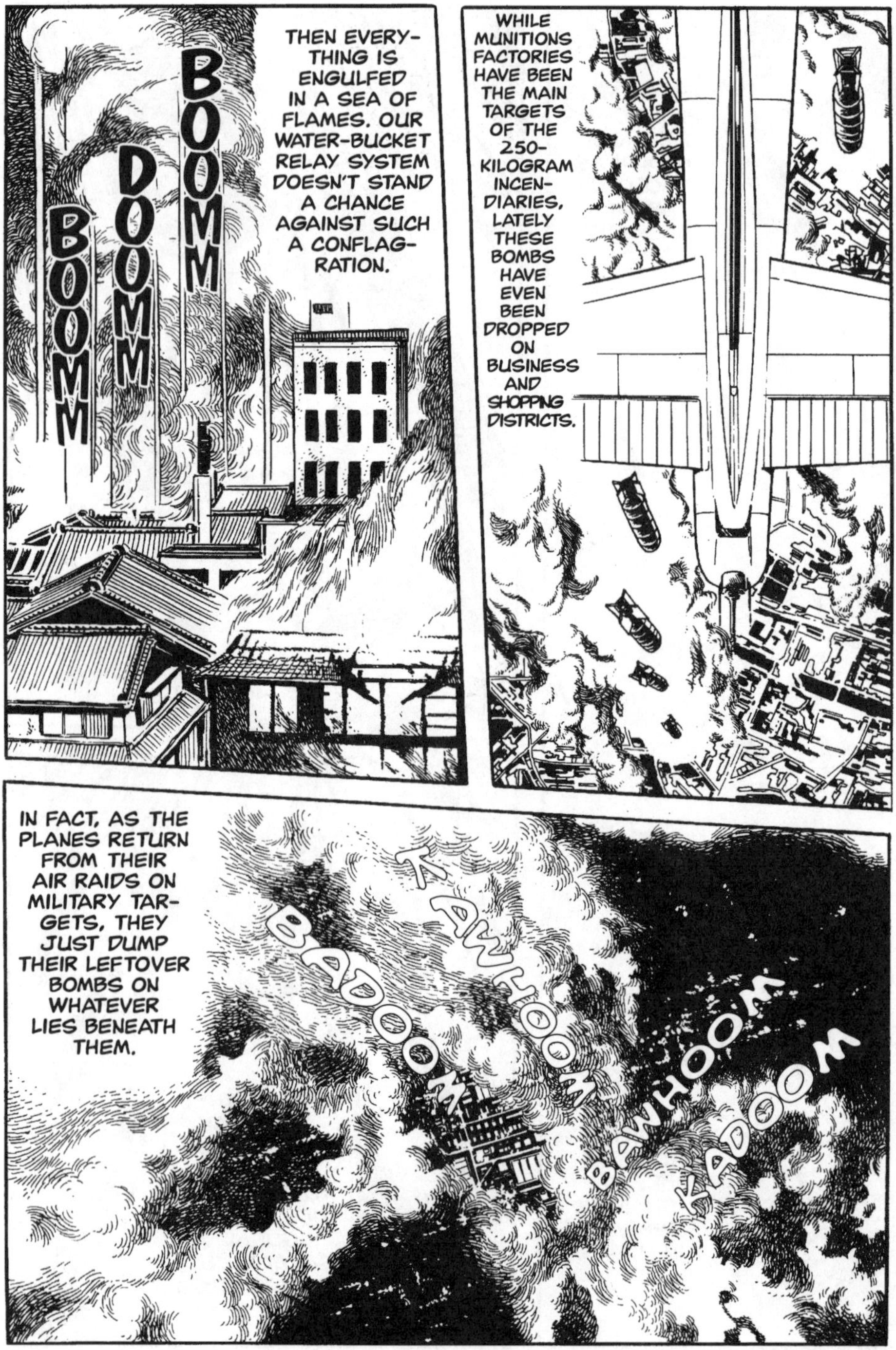
THEN EVERYTHING IS ENGULFED IN A SEA OF FLAMES. OUR WATER-BUCKET RELAY SYSTEM DOESN'T STAND A CHANCE AGAINST SUCH A CONFLAGRATION.
BOOMM
DOOMM
BOOMM
WHILE MUNITIONS FACTORIES HAVE BEEN THE MAIN TARGETS OF THE 250-KILOGRAM INCENDIARIES, LATELY THESE BOMBS HAVE EVEN BEEN DROPPED ON BUSINESS AND SHOPPING DISTRICTS.
IN FACT, AS THE PLANES RETURN FROM THEIR AIR RAIDS ON MILITARY TARGETS, THEY JUST DUMP THEIR LEFTOVER BOMBS ON WHATEVER LIES BENEATH THEM.
KAWHOOM
BADOOOM
BAWHOOM
KADOOM

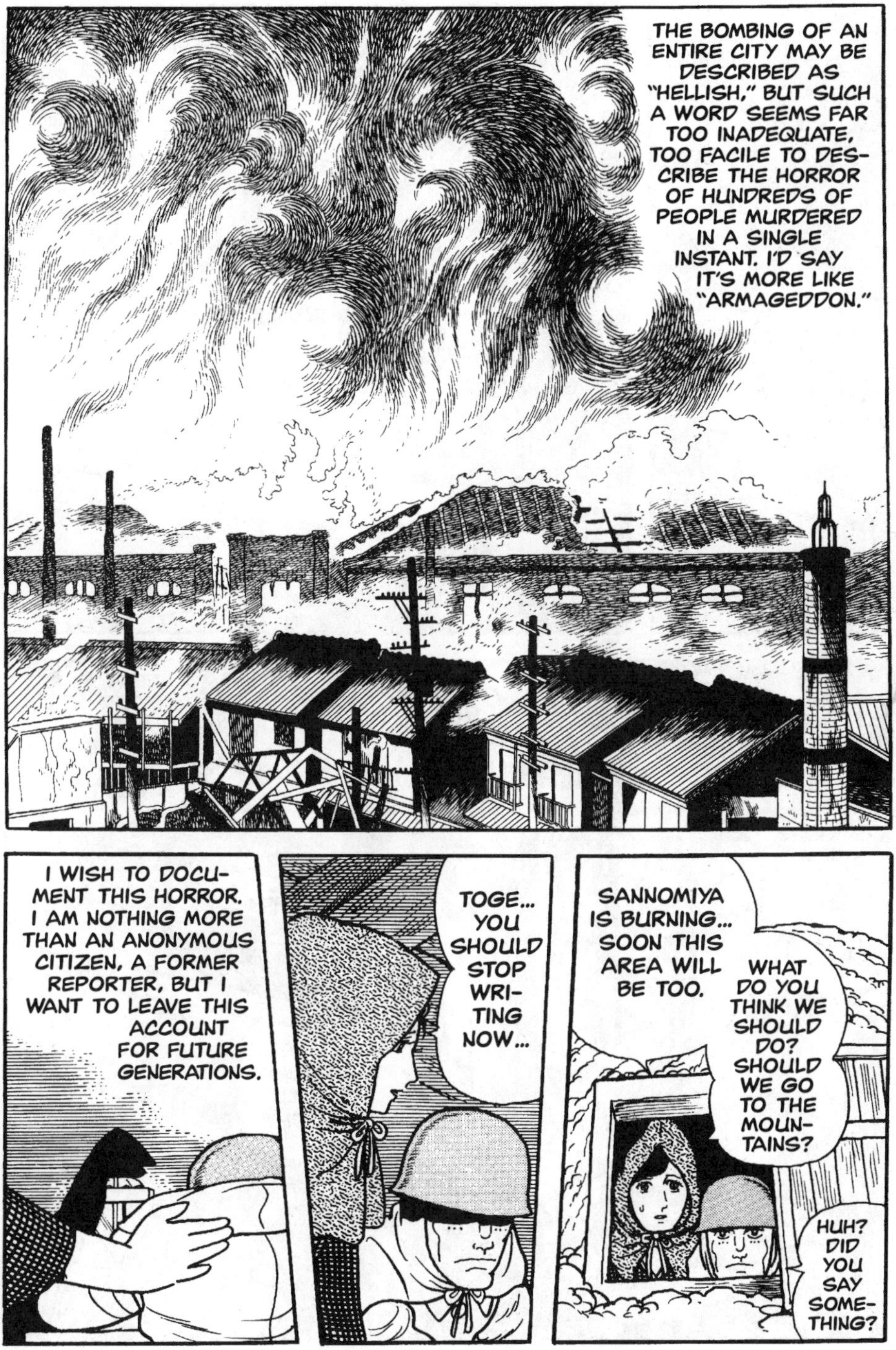
THE BOMBING OF AN ENTIRE CITY MAY BE DESCRIBED AS "HELLISH," BUT SUCH A WORD SEEMS FAR TOO INADEQUATE, TOO FACILE TO DESCRIBE THE HORROR OF HUNDREDS OF PEOPLE MURDERED IN A SINGLE INSTANT. I'D SAY IT'S MORE LIKE "ARMAGEDDON."
I WISH TO DOCUMENT THIS HORROR. I AM NOTHING MORE THAN AN ANONYMOUS CITIZEN, A FORMER REPORTER, BUT I WANT TO LEAVE THIS ACCOUNT FOR FUTURE GENERATIONS.
TOGE... YOU SHOULD STOP WRITING NOW...
SANNOMIYA IS BURNING... SOON THIS AREA WILL BE TOO.
WHAT DO YOU THINK WE SHOULD DO? SHOULD WE GO TO THE MOUNTAINS?
HUH? DID YOU SAY SOMETHING?

Adolf

I... I DON'T WANT TO LEAVE...

I UNDERSTAND HOW YOU FEEL.

BUT THIS PLACE WILL BE UP IN FLAMES SOON.

ZUMMM

I DON'T WANT TO LEAVE MY HOUSE!

YOUR HOUSE MEANS A LOT TO YOU. IT'S FILLED WITH SO MANY MEMORIES...

YOU SHOULD GO, THOUGH. YOU SHOULDN'T HAVE TO PUT UP WITH MY SELFISHNESS.

ARE YOU KIDDING? WE'RE IN THIS TOGETHER!

SHUT THE DOOR! BOMBS!

KRETCH

BADOOM

KADOOM

BADOOM

NEXT DOOR AND ACROSS THE STREET...

WHAT ABOUT OUR HOUSE?

IT LOOKS ALL RIGHT.

WHAT'S THAT?

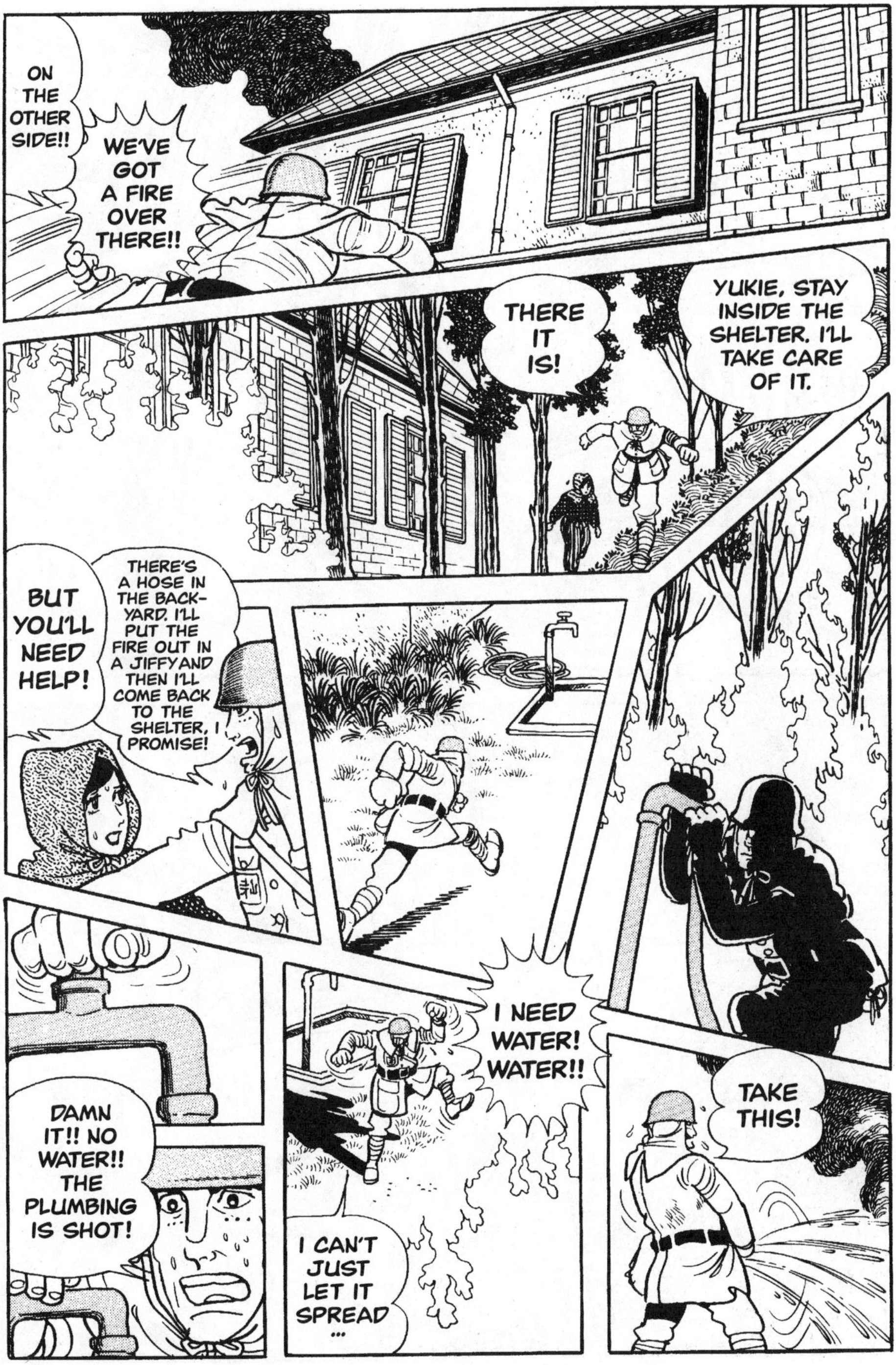
ON THE OTHER SIDE!!
WE'VE GOT A FIRE OVER THERE!!
THERE IT IS!
YUKIE, STAY INSIDE THE SHELTER. I'LL TAKE CARE OF IT.
BUT YOU'LL NEED HELP!
THERE'S A HOSE IN THE BACK-YARD. I'LL PUT THE FIRE OUT IN A JIFFY AND THEN I'LL COME BACK TO THE SHELTER, I PROMISE!
DAMN IT!! NO WATER!! THE PLUMBING IS SHOT!
I NEED WATER! WATER!!
I CAN'T JUST LET IT SPREAD ...
TAKE THIS!

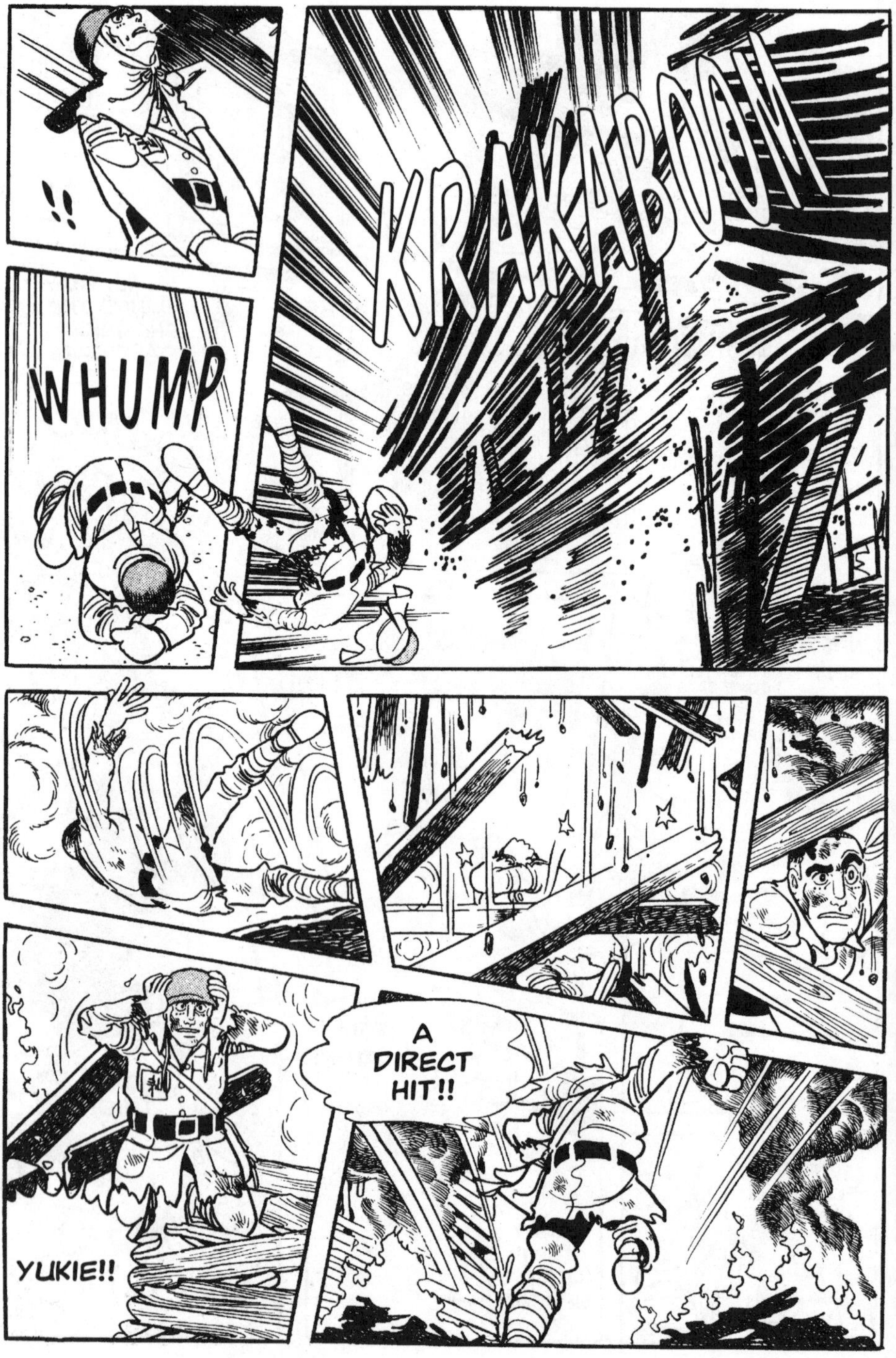
!!
KRAKABOOM
WHUMP
YUKIE!!
A DIRECT HIT!!

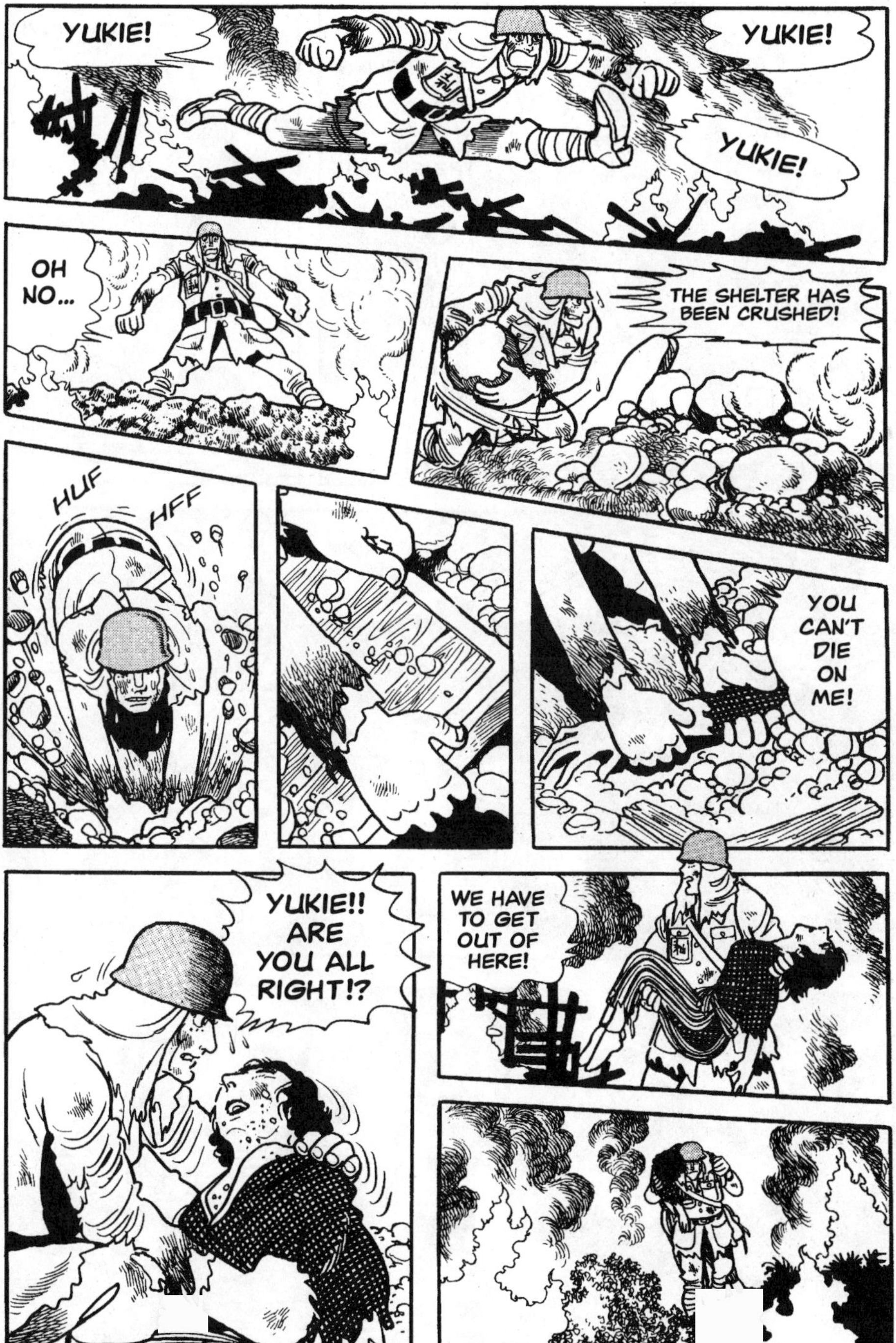
YUKIE!
YUKIE!
YUKIE!
OH NO...
THE SHELTER HAS BEEN CRUSHED!
HUF
HFF
YOU CAN'T DIE ON ME!
YUKIE!! ARE YOU ALL RIGHT!?
WE HAVE TO GET OUT OF HERE!

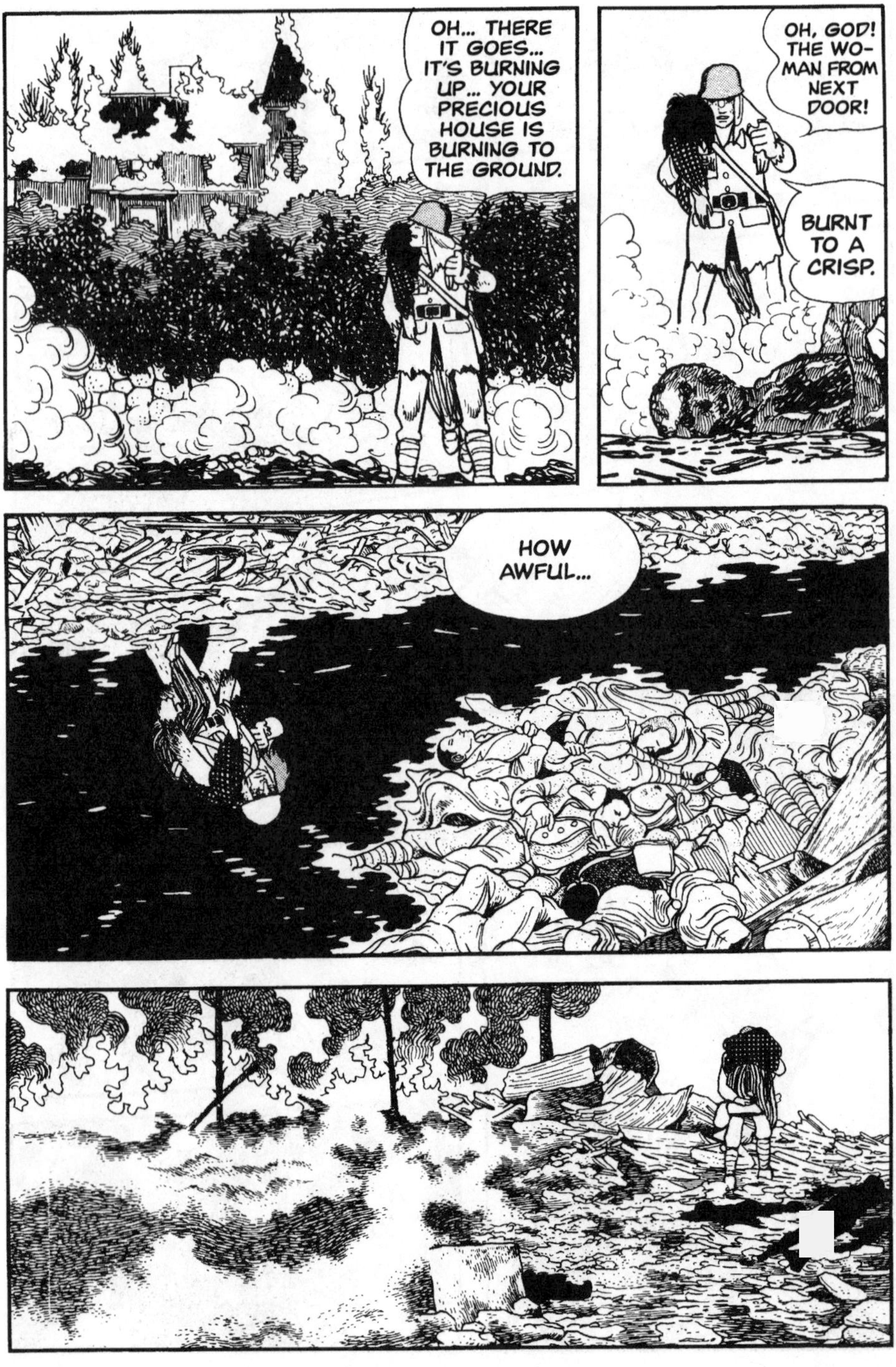
OH... THERE IT GOES... IT'S BURNING UP... YOUR PRECIOUS HOUSE IS BURNING TO THE GROUND.
OH, GOD! THE WO-MAN FROM NEXT DOOR!
BURNT TO A CRISP.
HOW AWFUL...

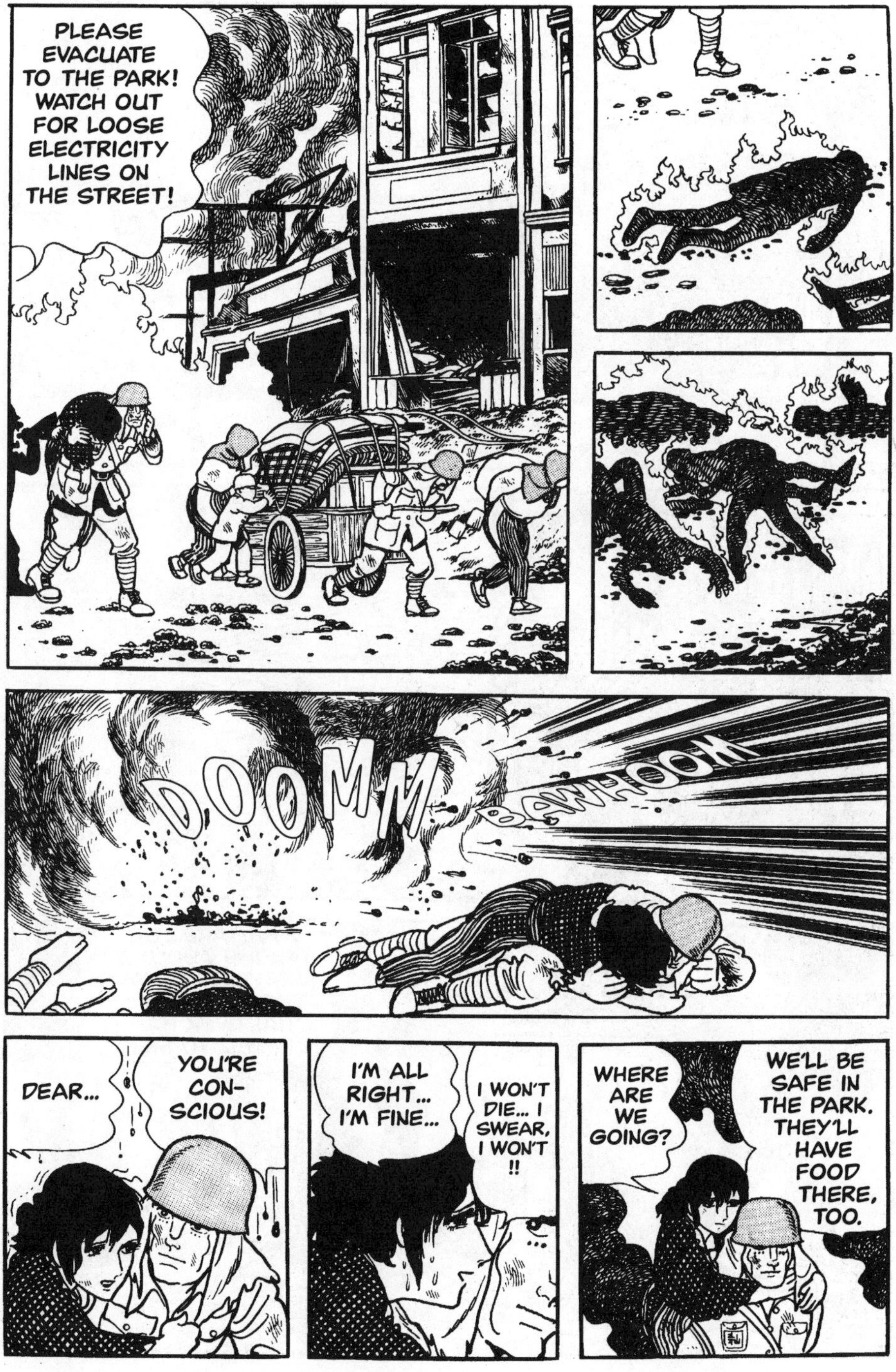
PLEASE EVACUATE TO THE PARK! WATCH OUT FOR LOOSE ELECTRICITY LINES ON THE STREET!
DOOMM
BAWHOOM
DEAR...
YOU'RE CON- SCIOUS!
I'M ALL RIGHT... I'M FINE...
I WON'T DIE... I SWEAR, I WON'T !!
WHERE ARE WE GOING?
WE'LL BE SAFE IN THE PARK. THEY'LL HAVE FOOD THERE, TOO.

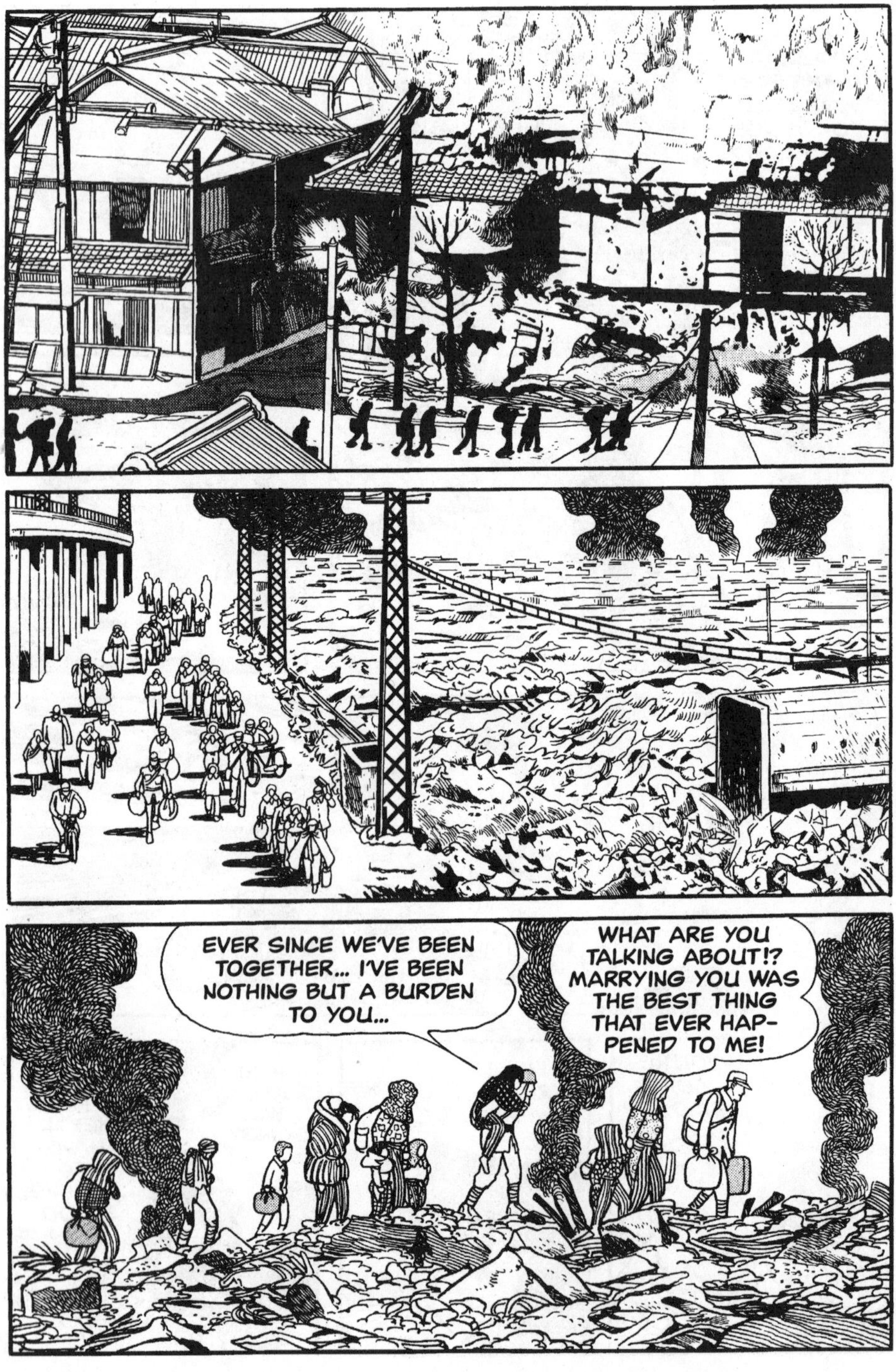
EVER SINCE WE'VE BEEN TOGETHER... I'VE BEEN NOTHING BUT A BURDEN TO YOU...
WHAT ARE YOU TALKING ABOUT!? MARRYING YOU WAS THE BEST THING THAT EVER HAP-PENED TO ME!

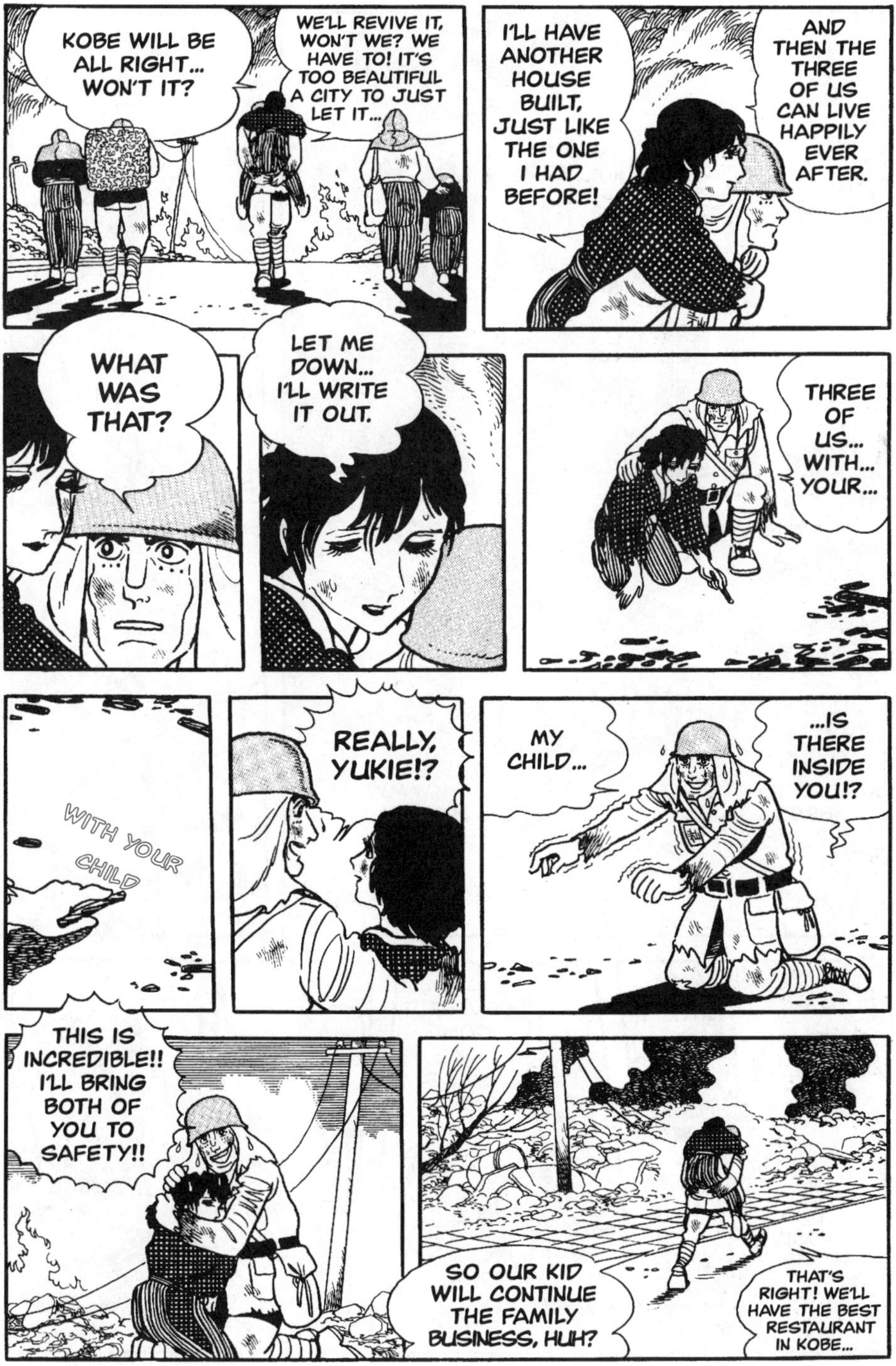
KOBE WILL BE ALL RIGHT... WON'T IT?
WE'LL REVIVE IT, WON'T WE? WE HAVE TO! IT'S TOO BEAUTIFUL A CITY TO JUST LET IT...
I'LL HAVE ANOTHER HOUSE BUILT, JUST LIKE THE ONE I HAD BEFORE!
AND THEN THE THREE OF US CAN LIVE HAPPILY EVER AFTER.
WHAT WAS THAT?
LET ME DOWN... I'LL WRITE IT OUT.
THREE OF US... WITH... YOUR...
WITH YOUR CHILD
REALLY, YUKIE!?
MY CHILD...
...IS THERE INSIDE YOU!?
THIS IS INCREDIBLE!! I'LL BRING BOTH OF YOU TO SAFETY!!
SO OUR KID WILL CONTINUE THE FAMILY BUSINESS, HUH?
THAT'S RIGHT! WE'LL HAVE THE BEST RESTAURANT IN KOBE...

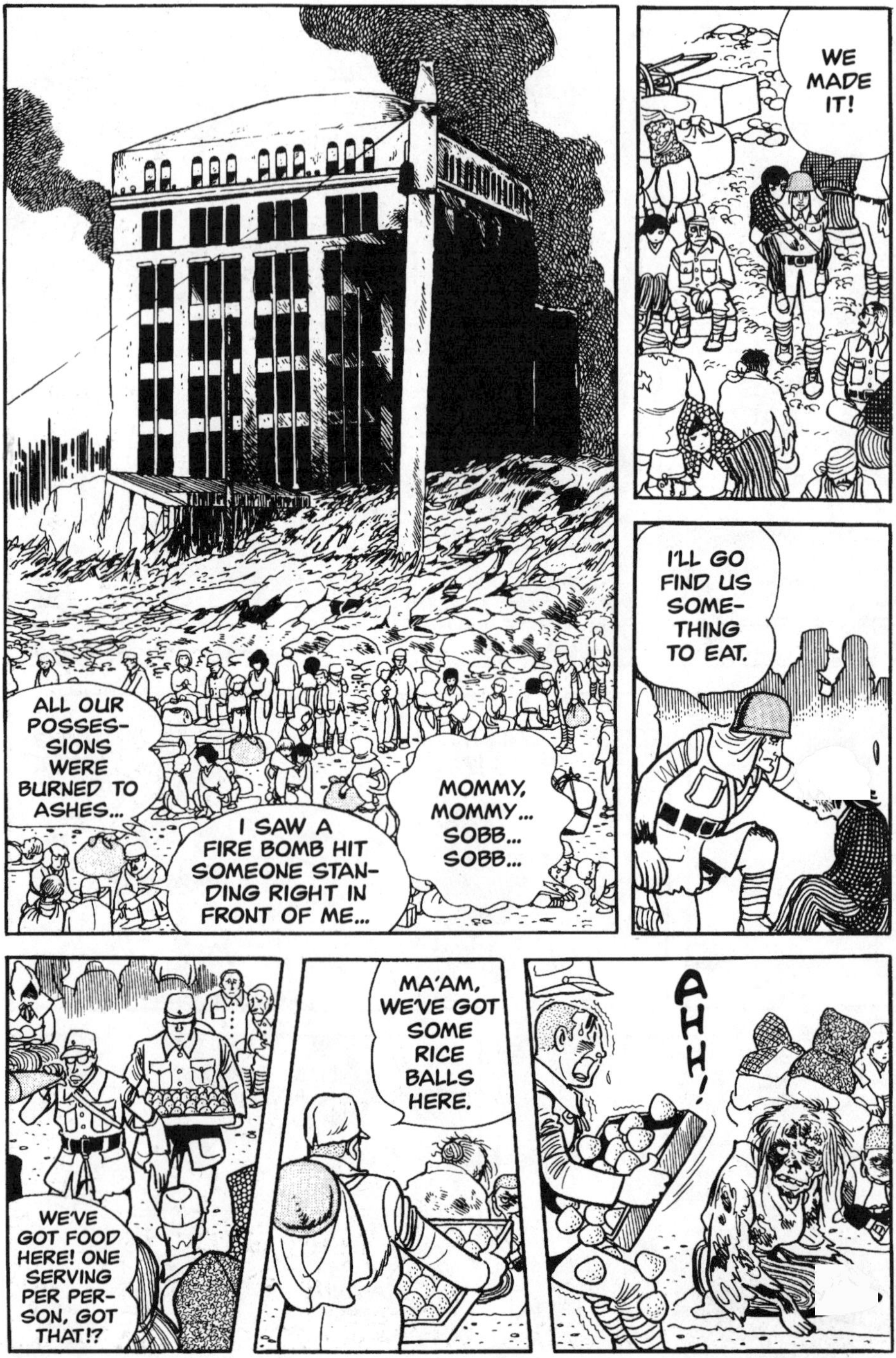
ALL OUR POSSESSIONS WERE BURNED TO ASHES...
I SAW A FIRE BOMB HIT SOMEONE STANDING RIGHT IN FRONT OF ME...
MOMMY, MOMMY... SOBB... SOBB...
WE MADE IT!
I'LL GO FIND US SOMETHING TO EAT.
WE'VE GOT FOOD HERE! ONE SERVING PER PERSON, GOT THAT!?
MA'AM, WE'VE GOT SOME RICE BALLS HERE.
AHH!

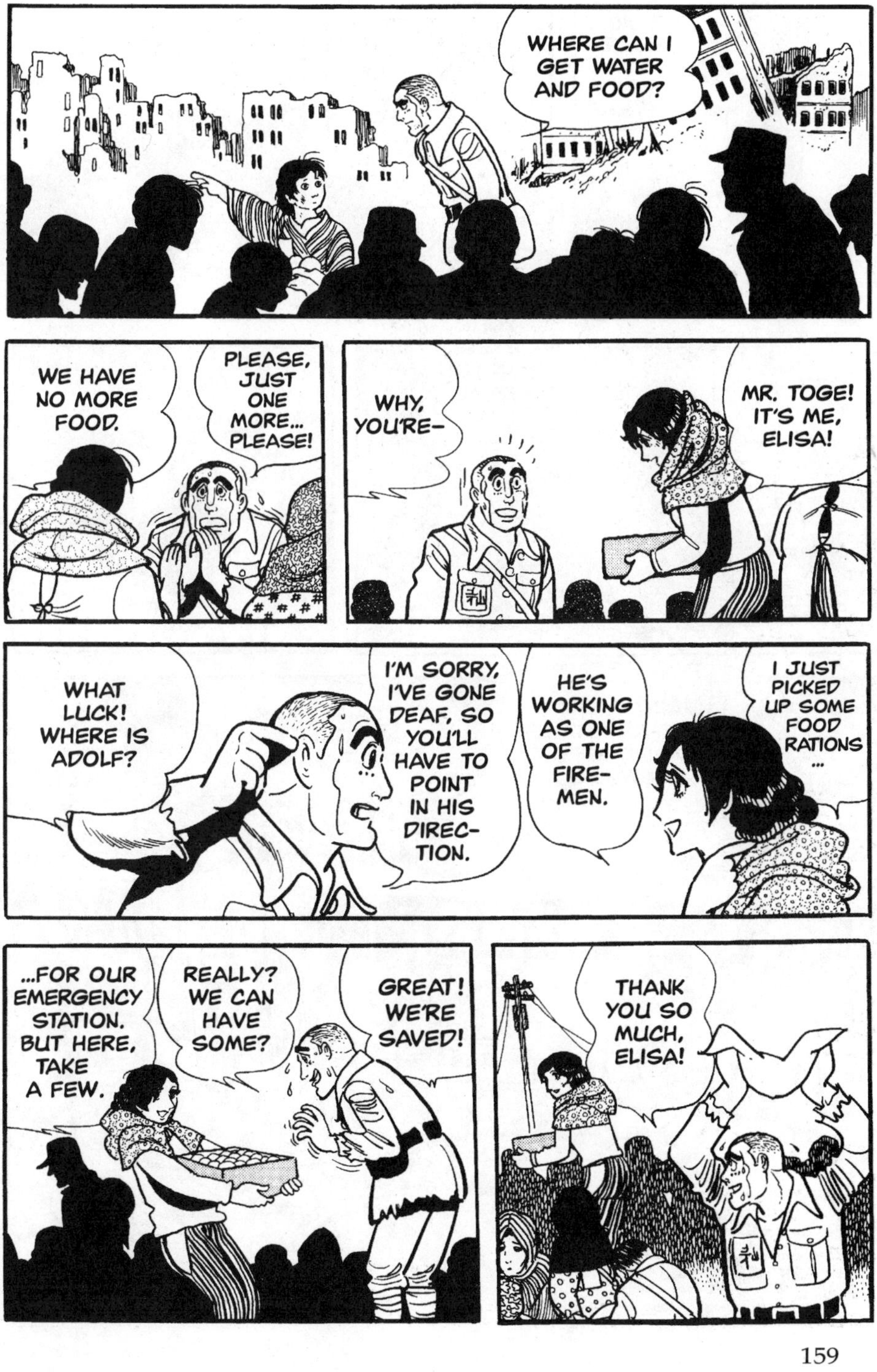
WHERE CAN I GET WATER AND FOOD?
WE HAVE NO MORE FOOD.
PLEASE, JUST ONE MORE... PLEASE!
WHY, YOU'RE–
MR. TOGE! IT'S ME, ELISA!
WHAT LUCK! WHERE IS ADOLF?
I'M SORRY, I'VE GONE DEAF, SO YOU'LL HAVE TO POINT IN HIS DIRECTION.
HE'S WORKING AS ONE OF THE FIRE-MEN.
I JUST PICKED UP SOME FOOD RATIONS ...
...FOR OUR EMERGENCY STATION. BUT HERE, TAKE A FEW.
REALLY? WE CAN HAVE SOME?
GREAT! WE'RE SAVED!
THANK YOU SO MUCH, ELISA!

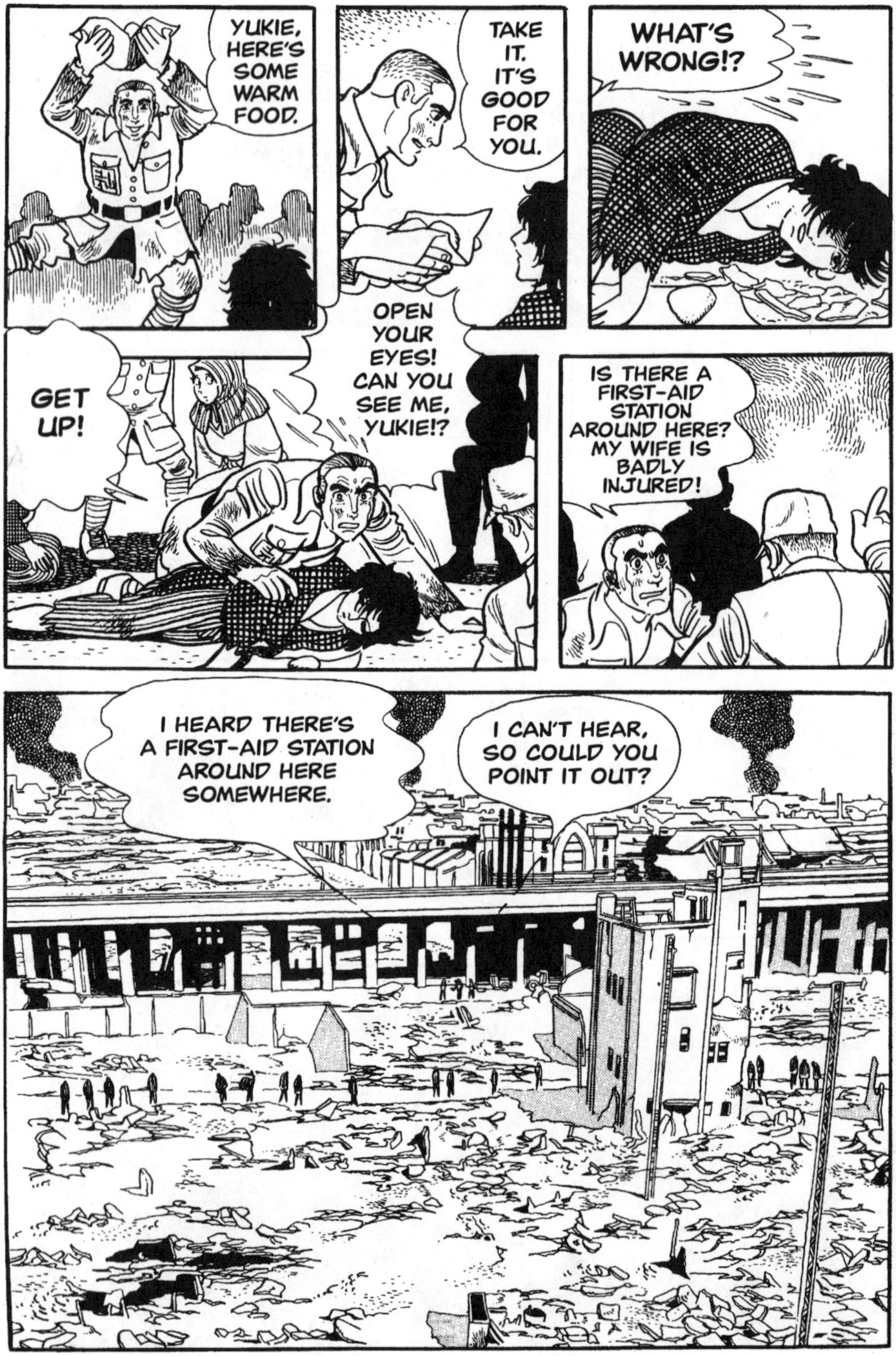
YUKIE, HERE'S SOME WARM FOOD.
TAKE IT. IT'S GOOD FOR YOU.
WHAT'S WRONG!?
GET UP!
OPEN YOUR EYES! CAN YOU SEE ME, YUKIE!?
IS THERE A FIRST-AID STATION AROUND HERE? MY WIFE IS BADLY INJURED!
I HEARD THERE'S A FIRST-AID STATION AROUND HERE SOMEWHERE.
I CAN'T HEAR, SO COULD YOU POINT IT OUT?

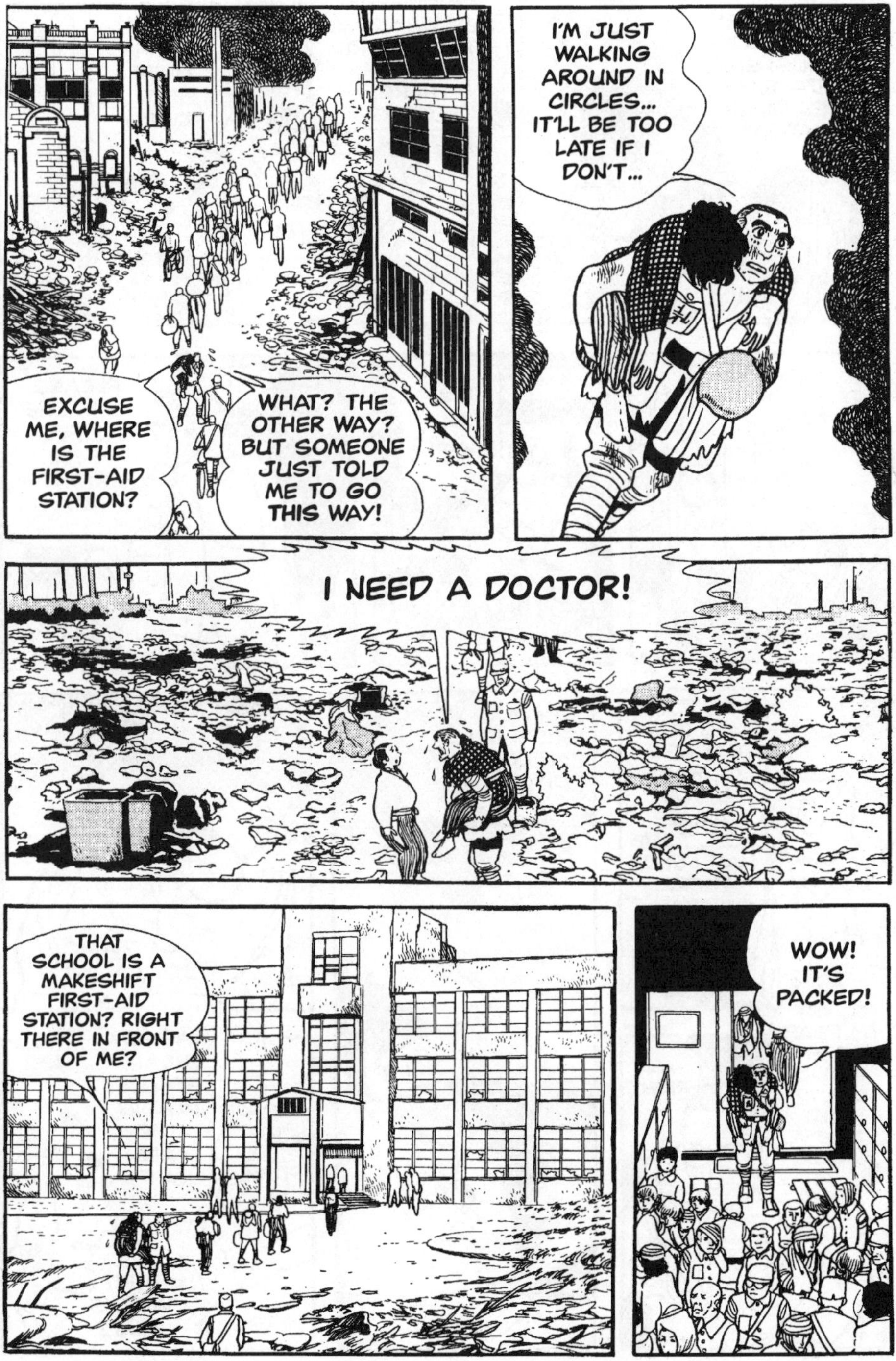
EXCUSE ME, WHERE IS THE FIRST-AID STATION?
WHAT? THE OTHER WAY? BUT SOMEONE JUST TOLD ME TO GO THIS WAY!
I'M JUST WALKING AROUND IN CIRCLES... IT'LL BE TOO LATE IF I DON'T...
I NEED A DOCTOR!
THAT SCHOOL IS A MAKESHIFT FIRST-AID STATION? RIGHT THERE IN FRONT OF ME?
WOW! IT'S PACKED!

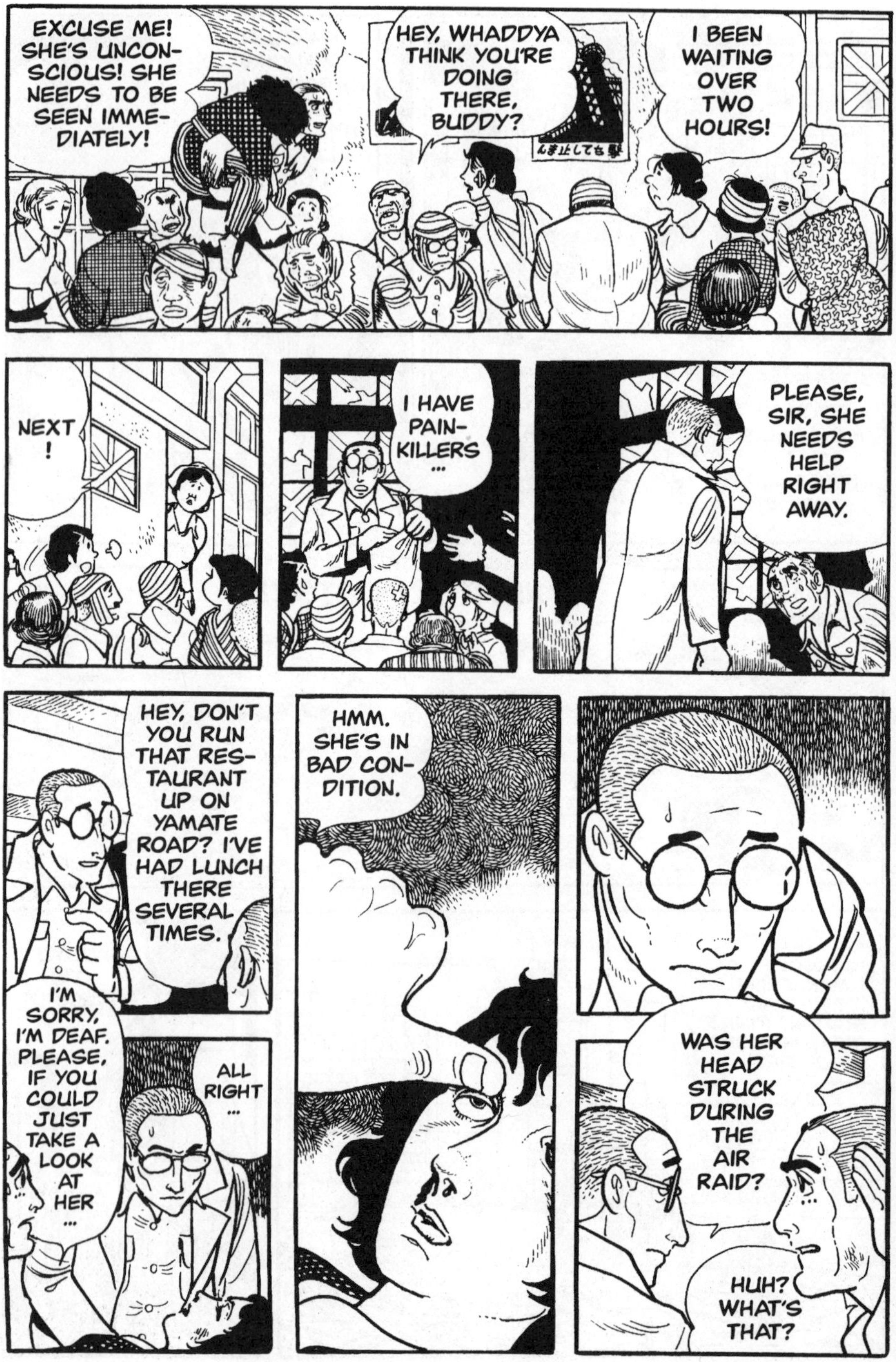
EXCUSE ME! SHE'S UNCONSCIOUS! SHE NEEDS TO BE SEEN IMMEDIATELY!
HEY, WHADDYA THINK YOU'RE DOING THERE, BUDDY?
I BEEN WAITING OVER TWO HOURS!
NEXT!
I HAVE PAIN-KILLERS ...
PLEASE, SIR, SHE NEEDS HELP RIGHT AWAY.
HEY, DON'T YOU RUN THAT RESTAURANT UP ON YAMATE ROAD? I'VE HAD LUNCH THERE SEVERAL TIMES.
I'M SORRY, I'M DEAF. PLEASE, IF YOU COULD JUST TAKE A LOOK AT HER ...
ALL RIGHT ...
HMM. SHE'S IN BAD CONDITION.
WAS HER HEAD STRUCK DURING THE AIR RAID?
HUH? WHAT'S THAT?

THE SHELTER COLLAPSED ON HER. ONE OF THE BEAMS MIGHT HAVE FALLEN ON HER HEAD.

THERE MIGHT BE SOME BRAIN DAMAGE. SHE'S IN CRITICAL CONDITION.

WHAT'S WRONG WITH HER?

I'LL WRITE IT OUT FOR YOU.

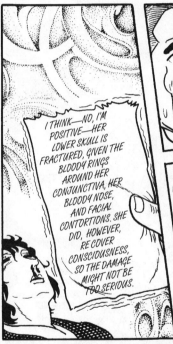

I THINK—NO, I'M POSITIVE—HER LOWER SKULL IS FRACTURED, GIVEN THE BLOODY RINGS AROUND HER CONJUNCTIVA, HER BLOODY NOSE, AND FACIAL CONTORTIONS. SHE DID, HOWEVER, RECOVER CONSCIOUSNESS, SO THE DAMAGE MIGHT NOT BE TOO SERIOUS.

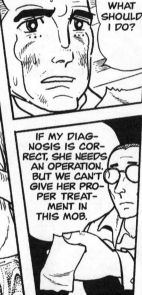

W-WHAT SHOULD I DO?

IF MY DIAGNOSIS IS CORRECT, SHE NEEDS AN OPERATION, BUT WE CAN'T GIVE HER PROPER TREATMENT IN THIS MOB.

HOW CAN YOU SAY THAT!? PLEASE, DOCTOR, TELL ME WHAT TO DO!!

I'LL DO ANYTHING, I PROMISE!!

THE ONLY ADVICE I HAVE IS TO TAKE HER TO KOBE UNIVERSITY HOSPITAL, OR SOME OTHER LARGE HOSPITAL WHERE SHE CAN RECEIVE PROPER TREATMENT.

BUT HOSPITALS LIKE THAT ARE EVEN MORE SWAMPED THAN WE ARE.

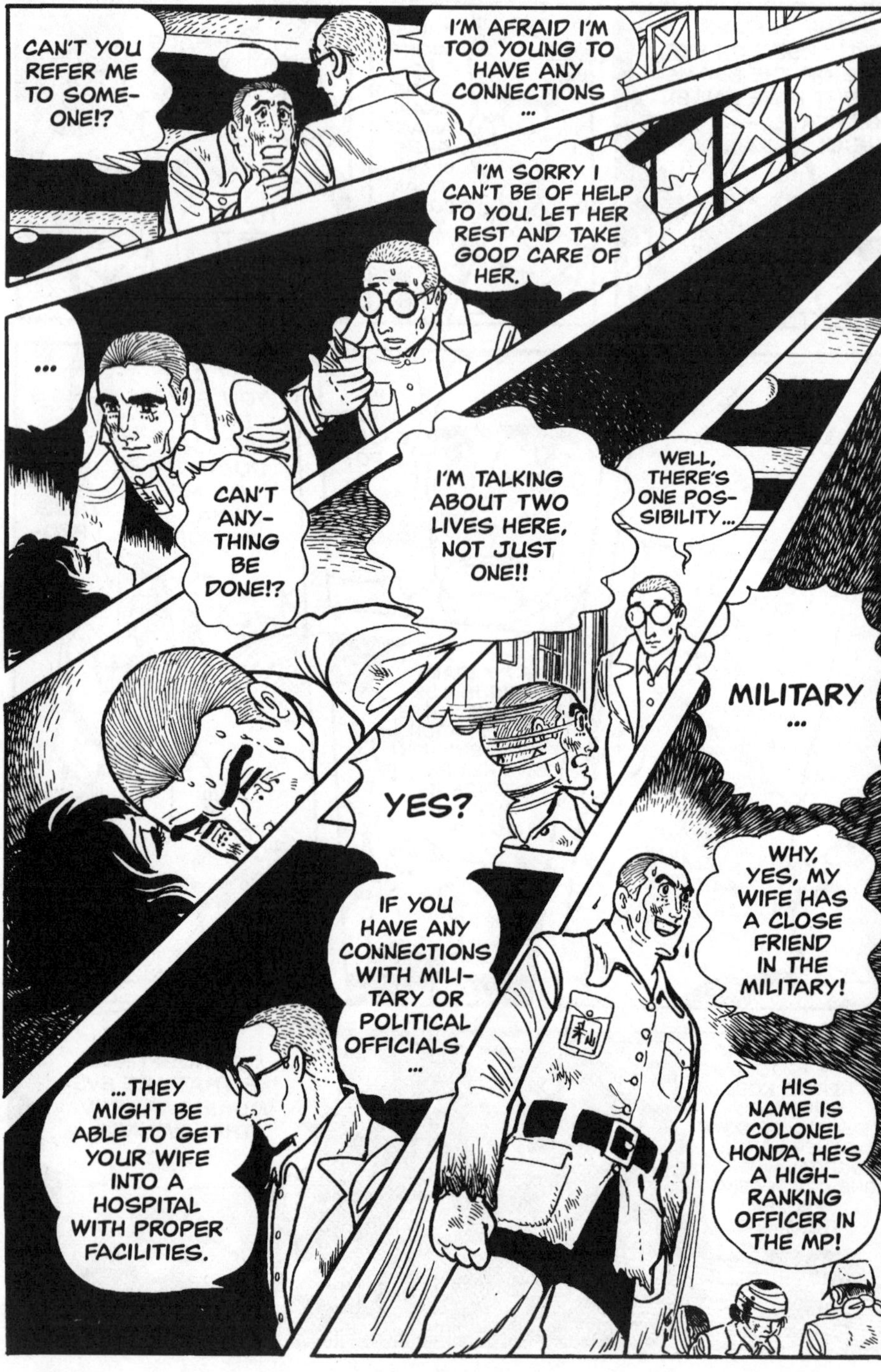
CAN'T YOU REFER ME TO SOME-ONE!?
I'M AFRAID I'M TOO YOUNG TO HAVE ANY CONNECTIONS ...
I'M SORRY I CAN'T BE OF HELP TO YOU. LET HER REST AND TAKE GOOD CARE OF HER.
...
CAN'T ANY-THING BE DONE!?
I'M TALKING ABOUT TWO LIVES HERE, NOT JUST ONE!!
WELL, THERE'S ONE POS-SIBILITY...
MILITARY ...
YES?
IF YOU HAVE ANY CONNECTIONS WITH MILI-TARY OR POLITICAL OFFICIALS ...
...THEY MIGHT BE ABLE TO GET YOUR WIFE INTO A HOSPITAL WITH PROPER FACILITIES.
WHY, YES, MY WIFE HAS A CLOSE FRIEND IN THE MILITARY!
HIS NAME IS COLONEL HONDA. HE'S A HIGH-RANKING OFFICER IN THE MP!

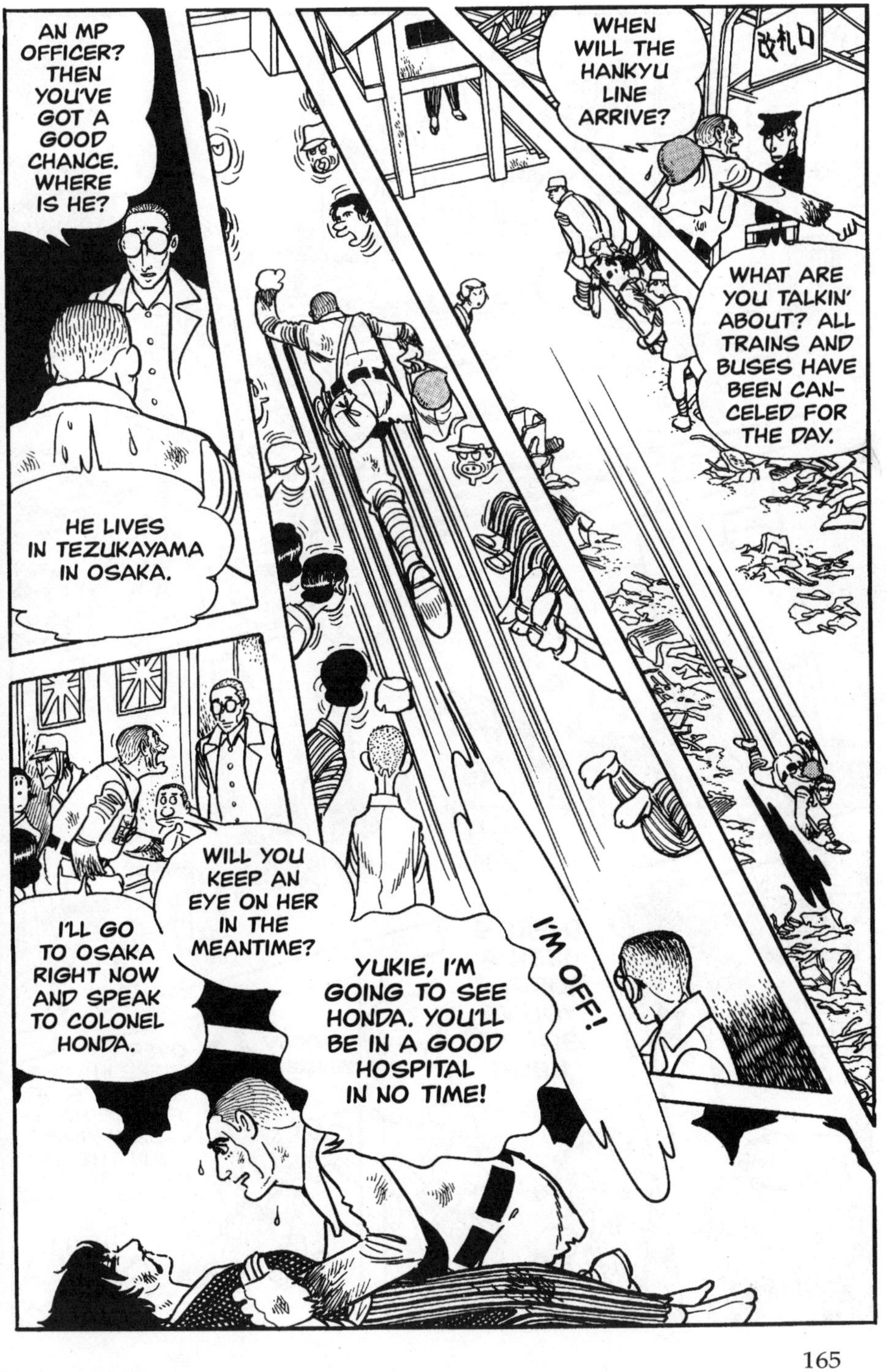
AN MP OFFICER? THEN YOU'VE GOT A GOOD CHANCE. WHERE IS HE?
HE LIVES IN TEZUKAYAMA IN OSAKA.
I'LL GO TO OSAKA RIGHT NOW AND SPEAK TO COLONEL HONDA.
WILL YOU KEEP AN EYE ON HER IN THE MEANTIME?
YUKIE, I'M GOING TO SEE HONDA. YOU'LL BE IN A GOOD HOSPITAL IN NO TIME!
I'M OFF!
改札口
WHEN WILL THE HANKYU LINE ARRIVE?
WHAT ARE YOU TALKIN' ABOUT? ALL TRAINS AND BUSES HAVE BEEN CANCELED FOR THE DAY.

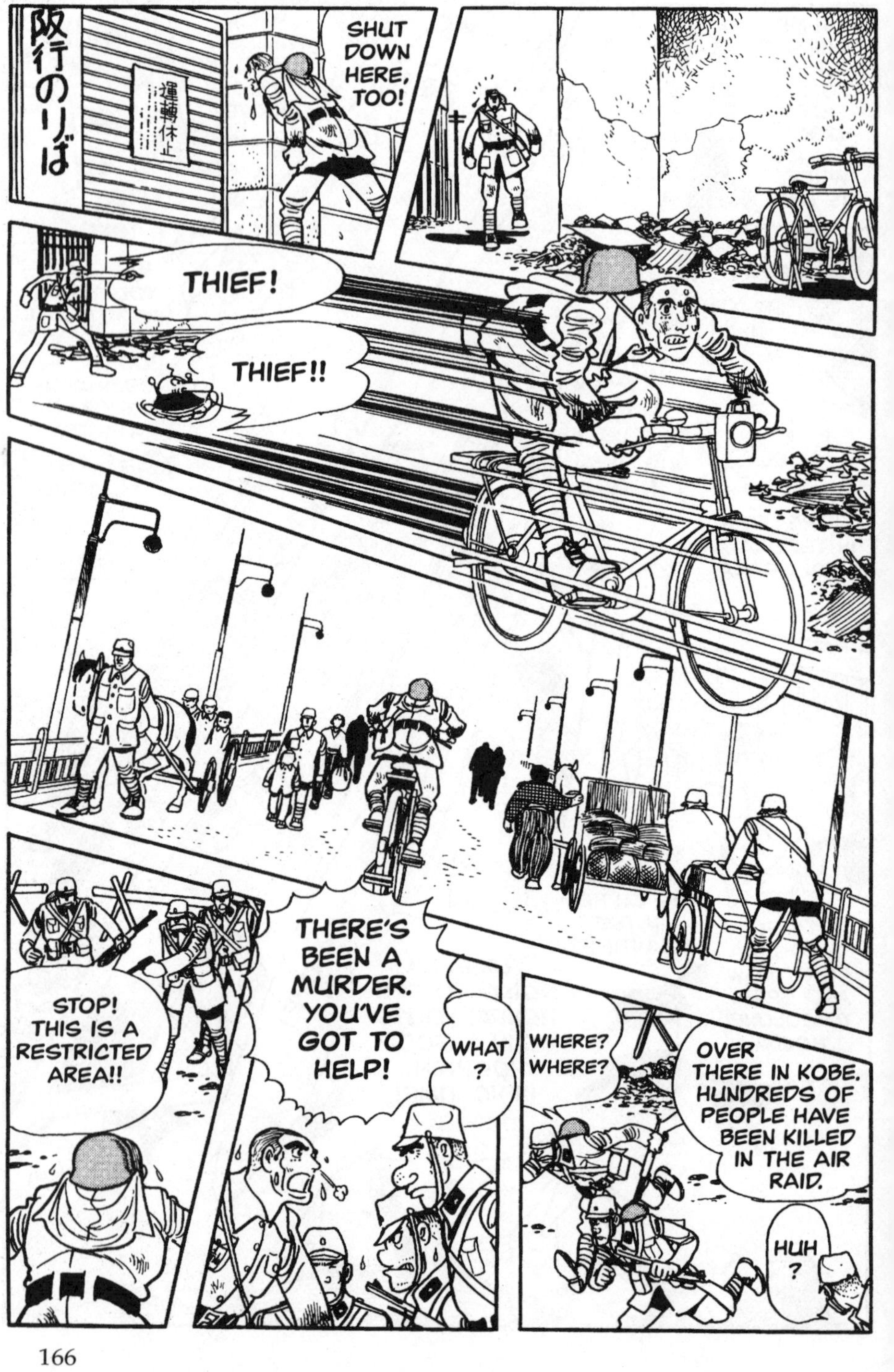
阪行のりば
運轉休止
SHUT DOWN HERE, TOO!
THIEF!
THIEF!!
STOP! THIS IS A RESTRICTED AREA!!
THERE'S BEEN A MURDER. YOU'VE GOT TO HELP!
WHAT?
WHERE? WHERE?
OVER THERE IN KOBE. HUNDREDS OF PEOPLE HAVE BEEN KILLED IN THE AIR RAID.
HUH?

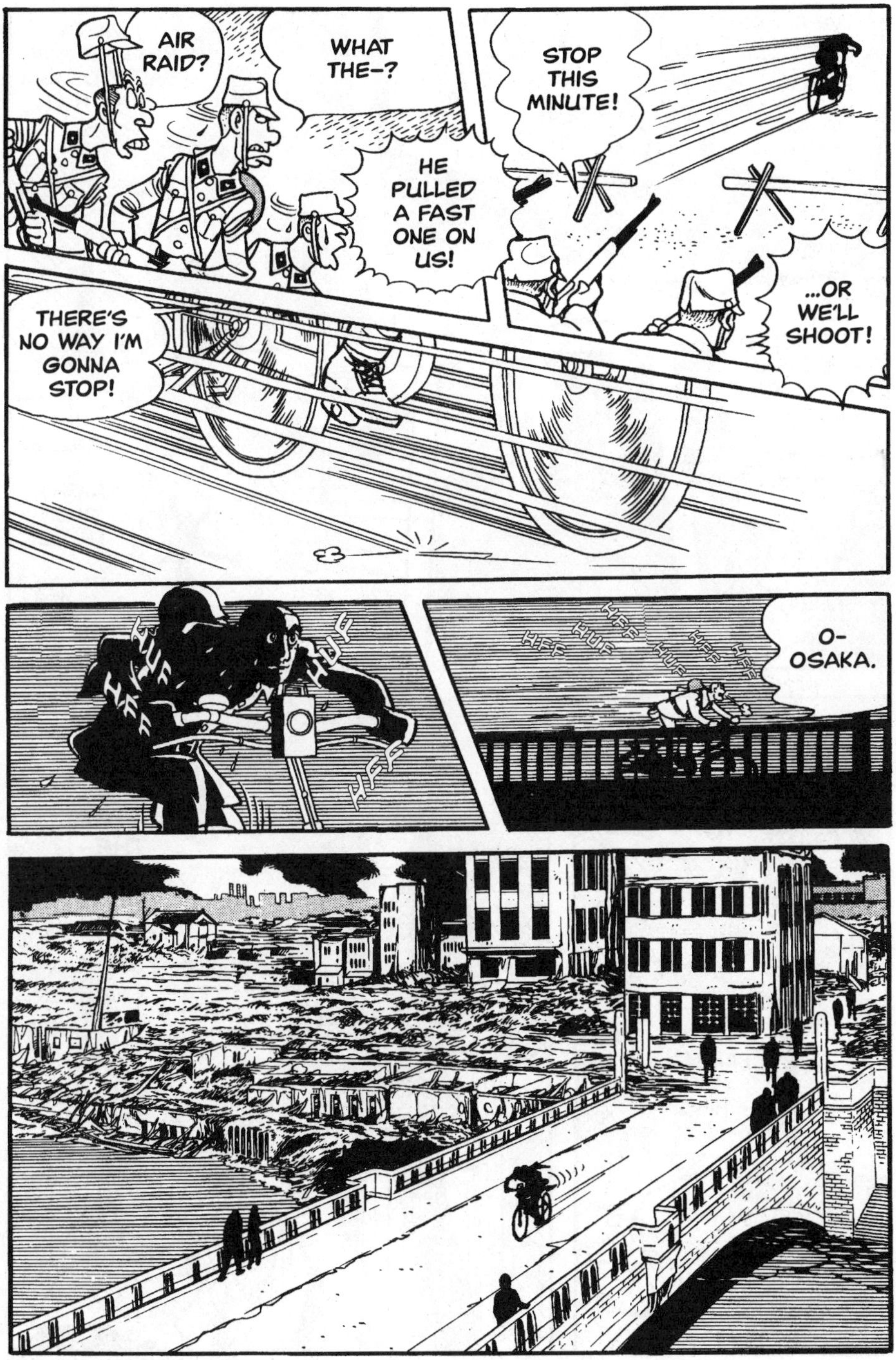
AIR RAID?
WHAT THE–?
HE PULLED A FAST ONE ON US!
STOP THIS MINUTE!
...OR WE'LL SHOOT!
THERE'S NO WAY I'M GONNA STOP!
HUF HFF HUF HFF
HFF HUF HUF HFF HFF
O- OSAKA.

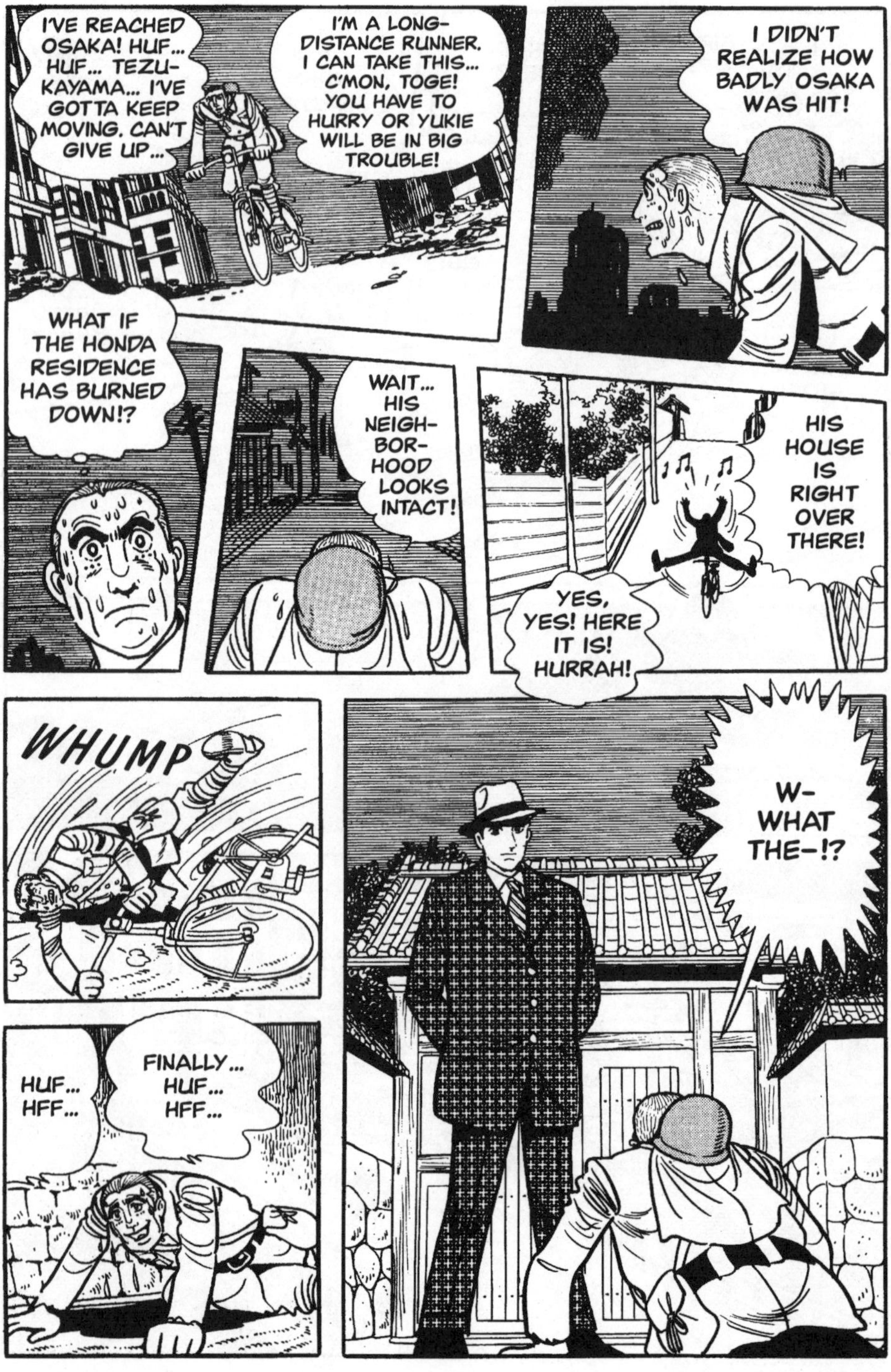
I'VE REACHED OSAKA! HUF... HUF... TEZU-KAYAMA... I'VE GOTTA KEEP MOVING. CAN'T GIVE UP...
I'M A LONG-DISTANCE RUNNER. I CAN TAKE THIS... C'MON, TOGE! YOU HAVE TO HURRY OR YUKIE WILL BE IN BIG TROUBLE!
I DIDN'T REALIZE HOW BADLY OSAKA WAS HIT!
WHAT IF THE HONDA RESIDENCE HAS BURNED DOWN!?
WAIT... HIS NEIGH-BOR-HOOD LOOKS INTACT!
HIS HOUSE IS RIGHT OVER THERE!
YES, YES! HERE IT IS! HURRAH!
WHUMP
HUF... HFF...
FINALLY... HUF... HFF...
W-WHAT THE-!?

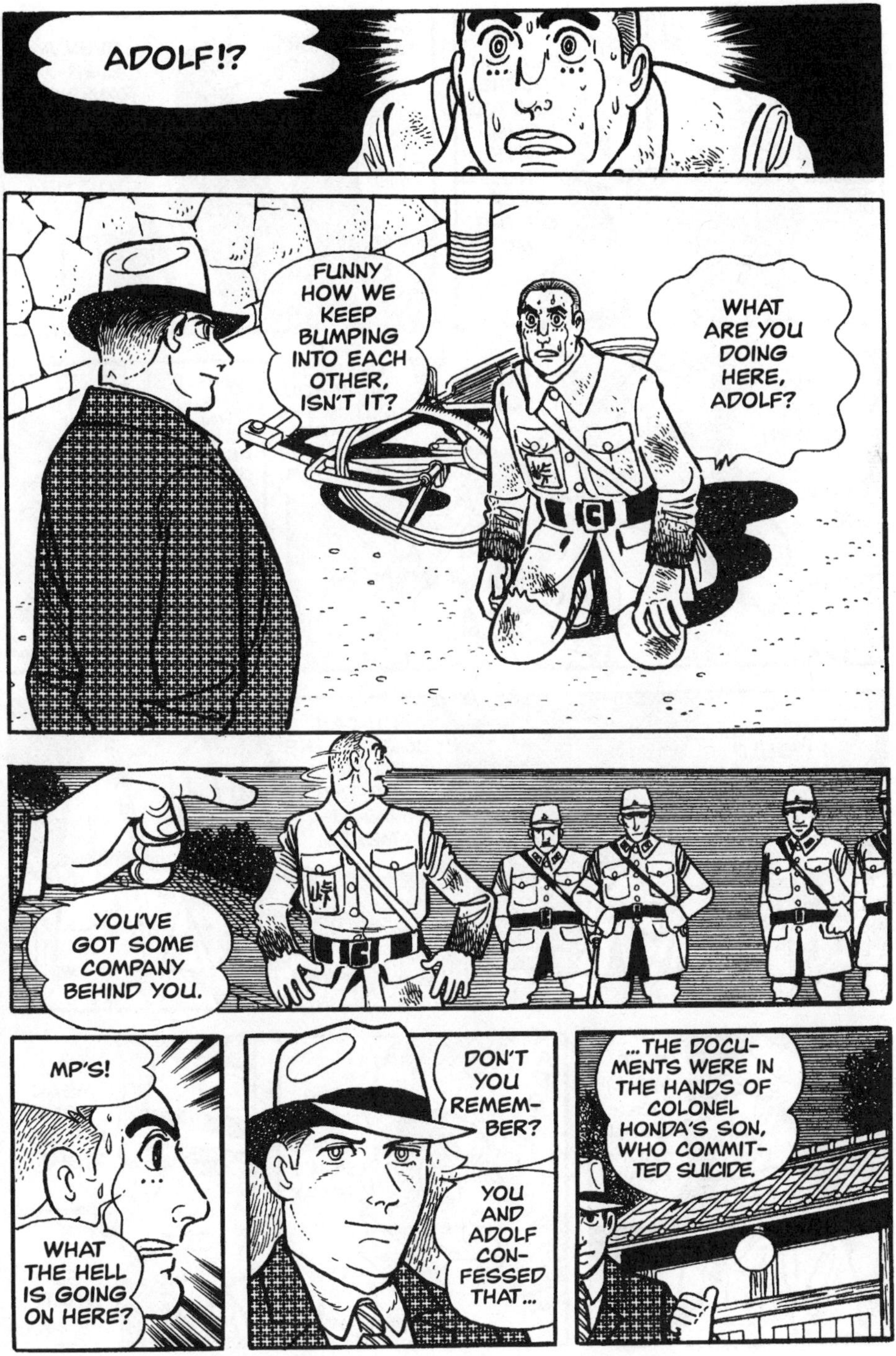
ADOLF!?
FUNNY HOW WE KEEP BUMPING INTO EACH OTHER, ISN'T IT?
WHAT ARE YOU DOING HERE, ADOLF?
YOU'VE GOT SOME COMPANY BEHIND YOU.
MP'S!
WHAT THE HELL IS GOING ON HERE?
DON'T YOU REMEMBER?
YOU AND ADOLF CONFESSED THAT...
...THE DOCUMENTS WERE IN THE HANDS OF COLONEL HONDA'S SON, WHO COMMITTED SUICIDE.

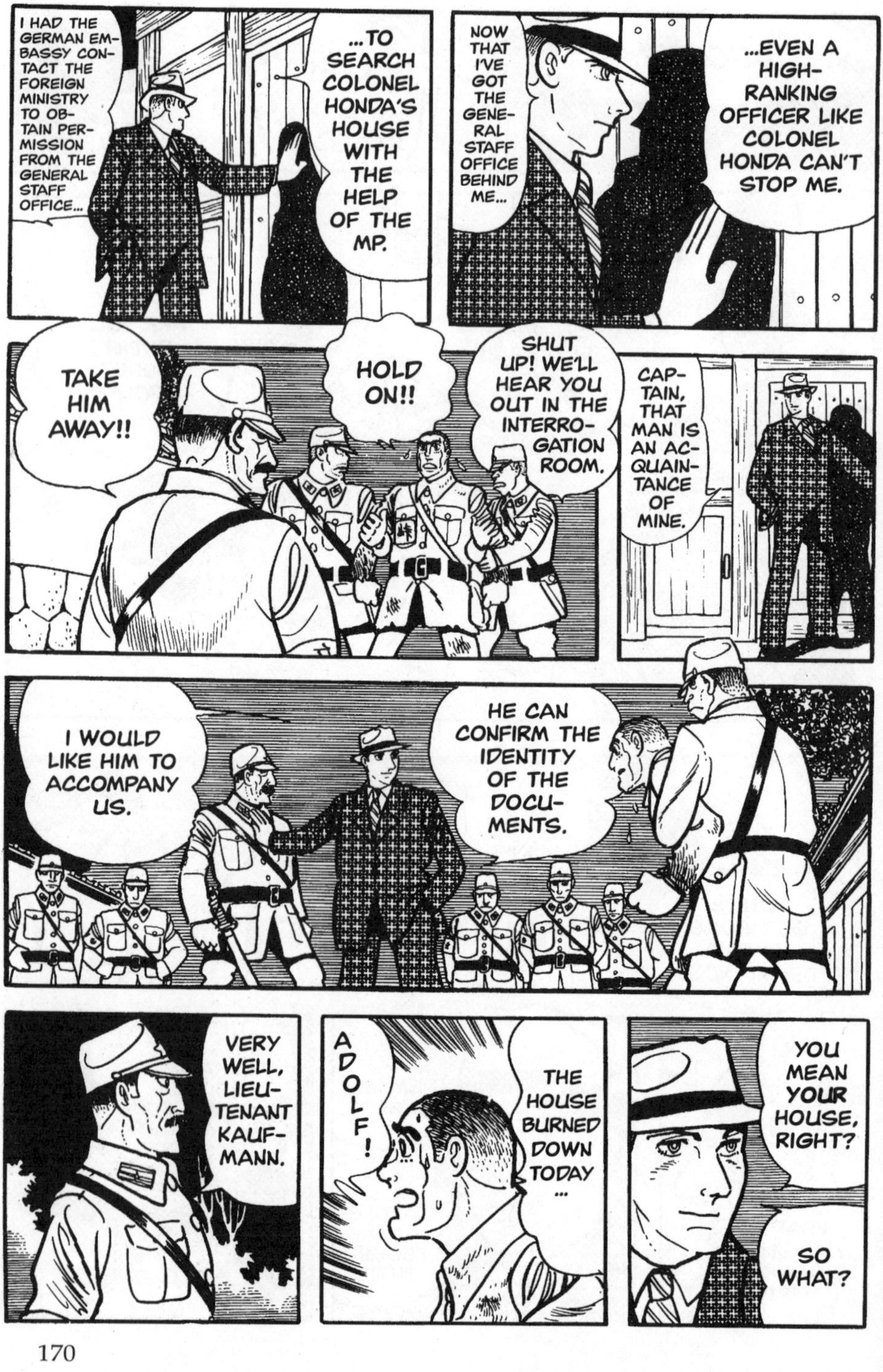
I HAD THE GERMAN EMBASSY CONTACT THE FOREIGN MINISTRY TO OBTAIN PERMISSION FROM THE GENERAL STAFF OFFICE...
...TO SEARCH COLONEL HONDA'S HOUSE WITH THE HELP OF THE MP.
NOW THAT I'VE GOT THE GENERAL STAFF OFFICE BEHIND ME...
...EVEN A HIGH-RANKING OFFICER LIKE COLONEL HONDA CAN'T STOP ME.
TAKE HIM AWAY!!
HOLD ON!!
SHUT UP! WE'LL HEAR YOU OUT IN THE INTERROGATION ROOM.
CAPTAIN, THAT MAN IS AN ACQUAINTANCE OF MINE.
I WOULD LIKE HIM TO ACCOMPANY US.
HE CAN CONFIRM THE IDENTITY OF THE DOCUMENTS.
VERY WELL, LIEUTENANT KAUFMANN.
ADOLF!
THE HOUSE BURNED DOWN TODAY ...
YOU MEAN YOUR HOUSE, RIGHT?
SO WHAT?

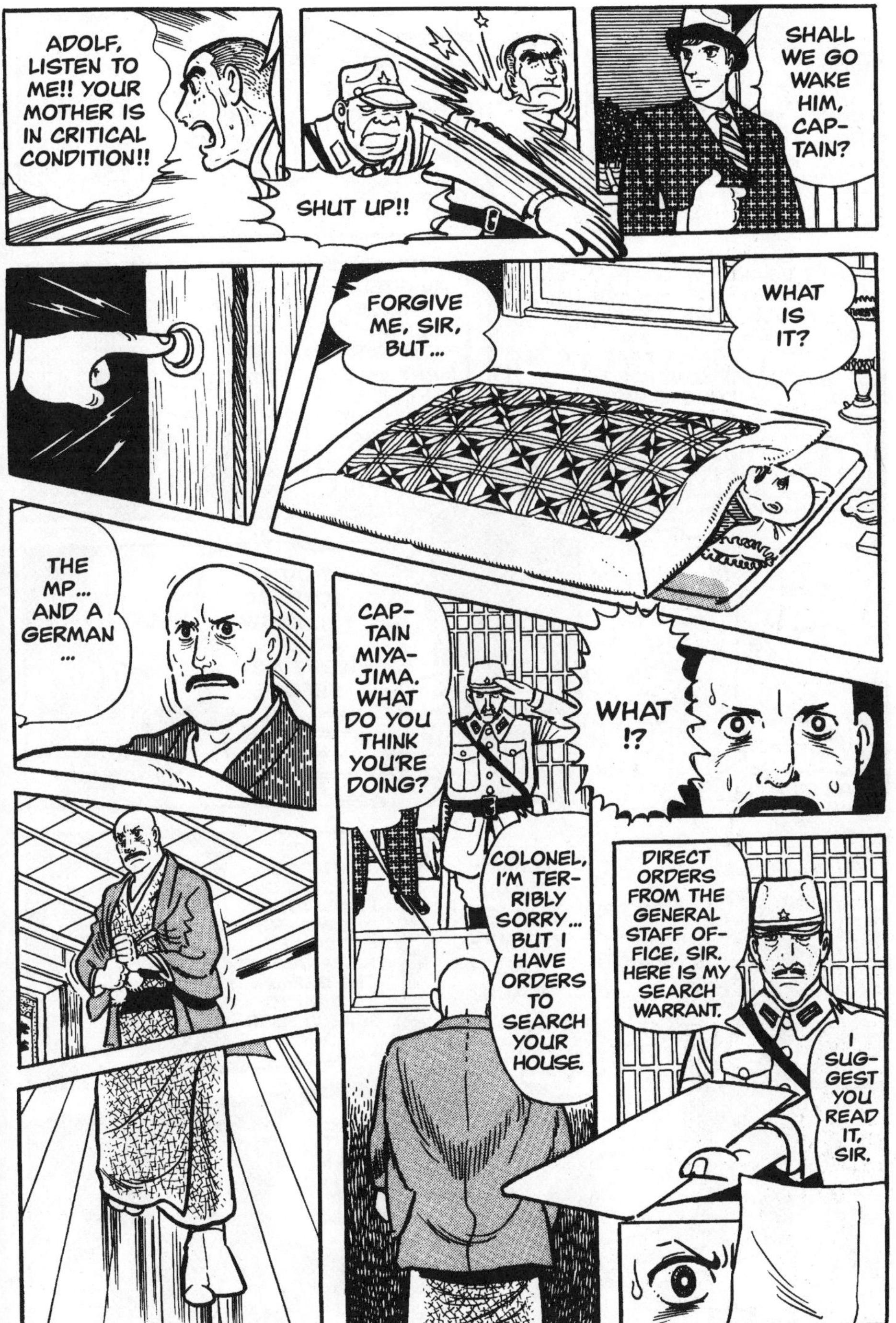
ADOLF, LISTEN TO ME!! YOUR MOTHER IS IN CRITICAL CONDITION!!
SHUT UP!!
SHALL WE GO WAKE HIM, CAP-TAIN?
FORGIVE ME, SIR, BUT...
WHAT IS IT?
THE MP... AND A GERMAN ...
CAP-TAIN MIYA-JIMA. WHAT DO YOU THINK YOU'RE DOING?
WHAT !?
COLONEL, I'M TER-RIBLY SORRY... BUT I HAVE ORDERS TO SEARCH YOUR HOUSE.
DIRECT ORDERS FROM THE GENERAL STAFF OF-FICE, SIR. HERE IS MY SEARCH WARRANT.
I SUG-GEST YOU READ IT, SIR.

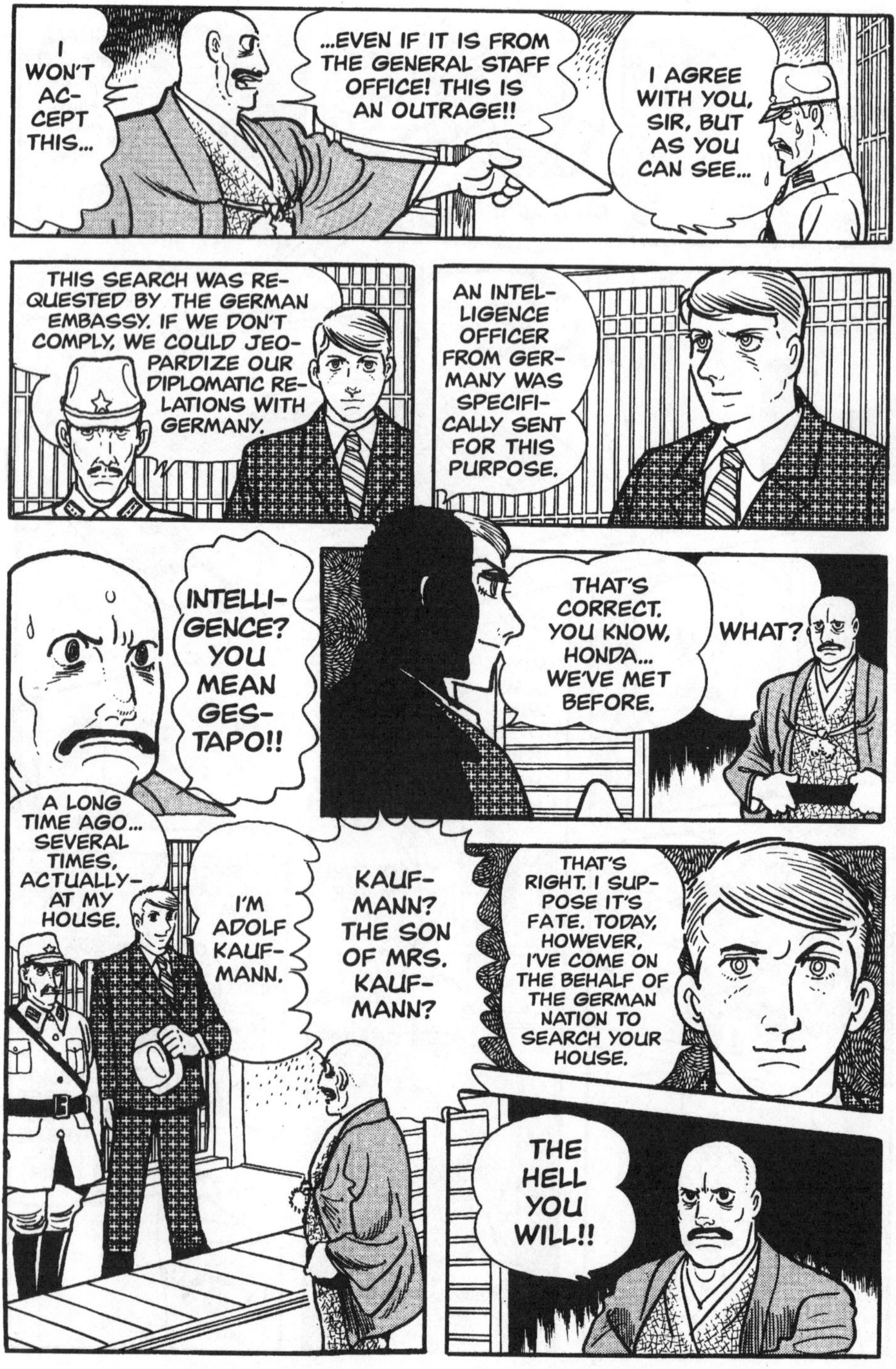
I WON'T ACCEPT THIS...
...EVEN IF IT IS FROM THE GENERAL STAFF OFFICE! THIS IS AN OUTRAGE!!
I AGREE WITH YOU, SIR, BUT AS YOU CAN SEE...
THIS SEARCH WAS REQUESTED BY THE GERMAN EMBASSY. IF WE DON'T COMPLY, WE COULD JEOPARDIZE OUR DIPLOMATIC RELATIONS WITH GERMANY.
AN INTELLIGENCE OFFICER FROM GERMANY WAS SPECIFICALLY SENT FOR THIS PURPOSE.
INTELLIGENCE? YOU MEAN GESTAPO!!
THAT'S CORRECT. YOU KNOW, HONDA... WE'VE MET BEFORE.
WHAT?
A LONG TIME AGO... SEVERAL TIMES, ACTUALLY-AT MY HOUSE.
I'M ADOLF KAUFMANN.
KAUFMANN? THE SON OF MRS. KAUFMANN?
THAT'S RIGHT. I SUPPOSE IT'S FATE. TODAY, HOWEVER, I'VE COME ON THE BEHALF OF THE GERMAN NATION TO SEARCH YOUR HOUSE.
THE HELL YOU WILL!!

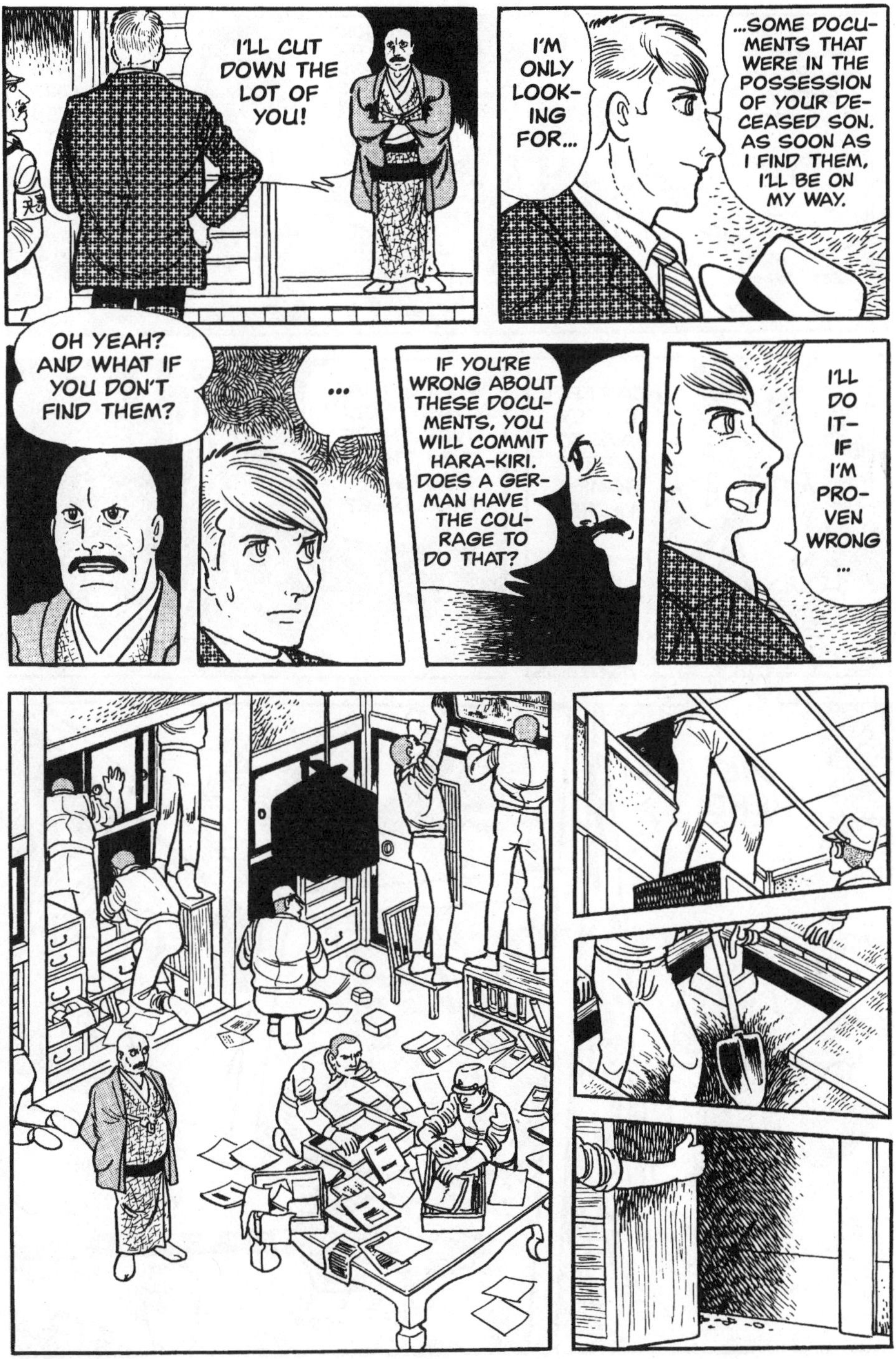
I'LL CUT DOWN THE LOT OF YOU!
I'M ONLY LOOKING FOR...
...SOME DOCUMENTS THAT WERE IN THE POSSESSION OF YOUR DECEASED SON. AS SOON AS I FIND THEM, I'LL BE ON MY WAY.
OH YEAH? AND WHAT IF YOU DON'T FIND THEM?
...
IF YOU'RE WRONG ABOUT THESE DOCUMENTS, YOU WILL COMMIT HARA-KIRI. DOES A GERMAN HAVE THE COURAGE TO DO THAT?
I'LL DO IT— IF I'M PROVEN WRONG ...

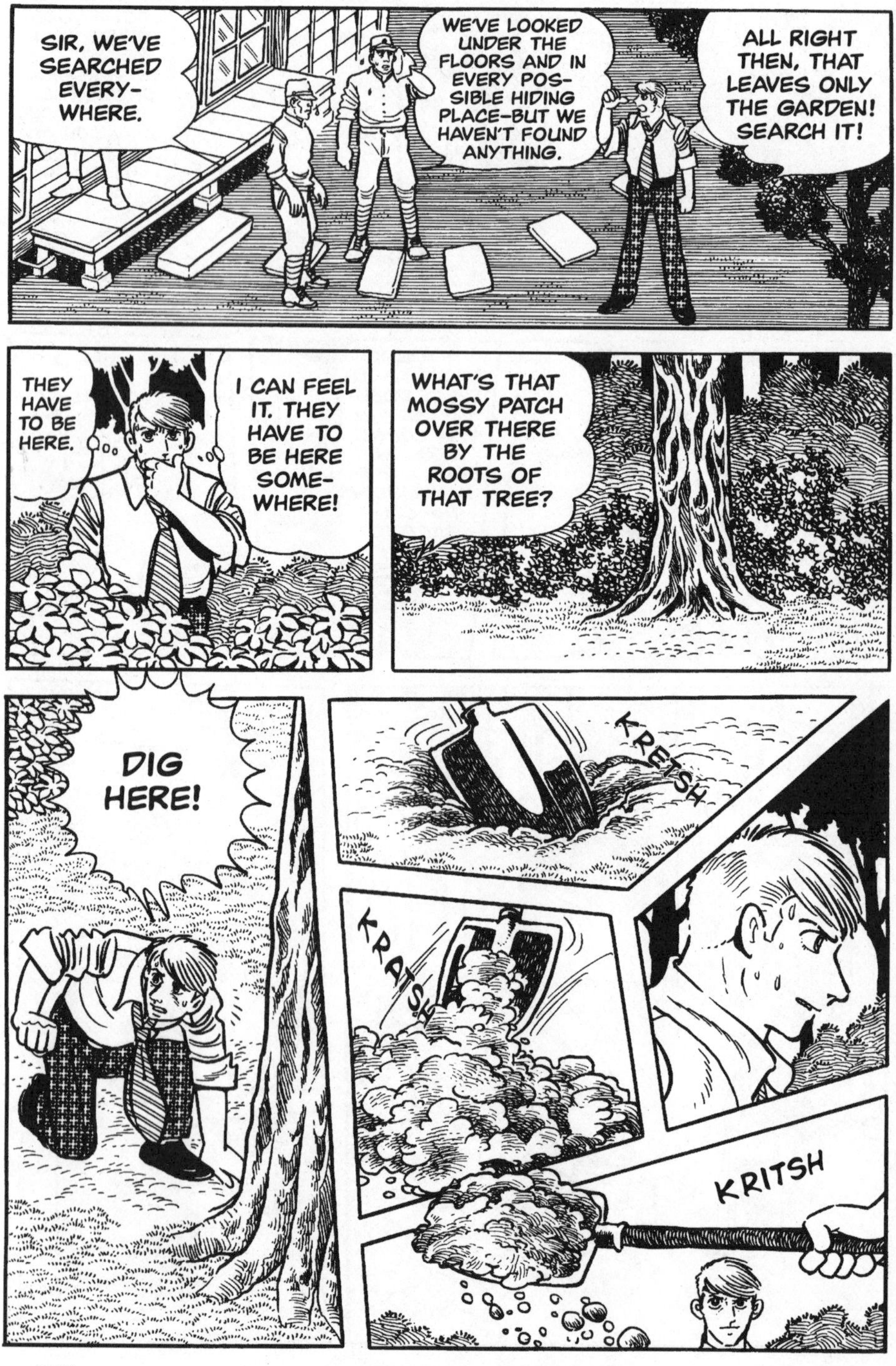
SIR, WE'VE SEARCHED EVERY-WHERE.
WE'VE LOOKED UNDER THE FLOORS AND IN EVERY POS-SIBLE HIDING PLACE—BUT WE HAVEN'T FOUND ANYTHING.
ALL RIGHT THEN, THAT LEAVES ONLY THE GARDEN! SEARCH IT!
THEY HAVE TO BE HERE.
I CAN FEEL IT. THEY HAVE TO BE HERE SOME-WHERE!
WHAT'S THAT MOSSY PATCH OVER THERE BY THE ROOTS OF THAT TREE?
DIG HERE!
KRETSH
KRATSH
KRITSH

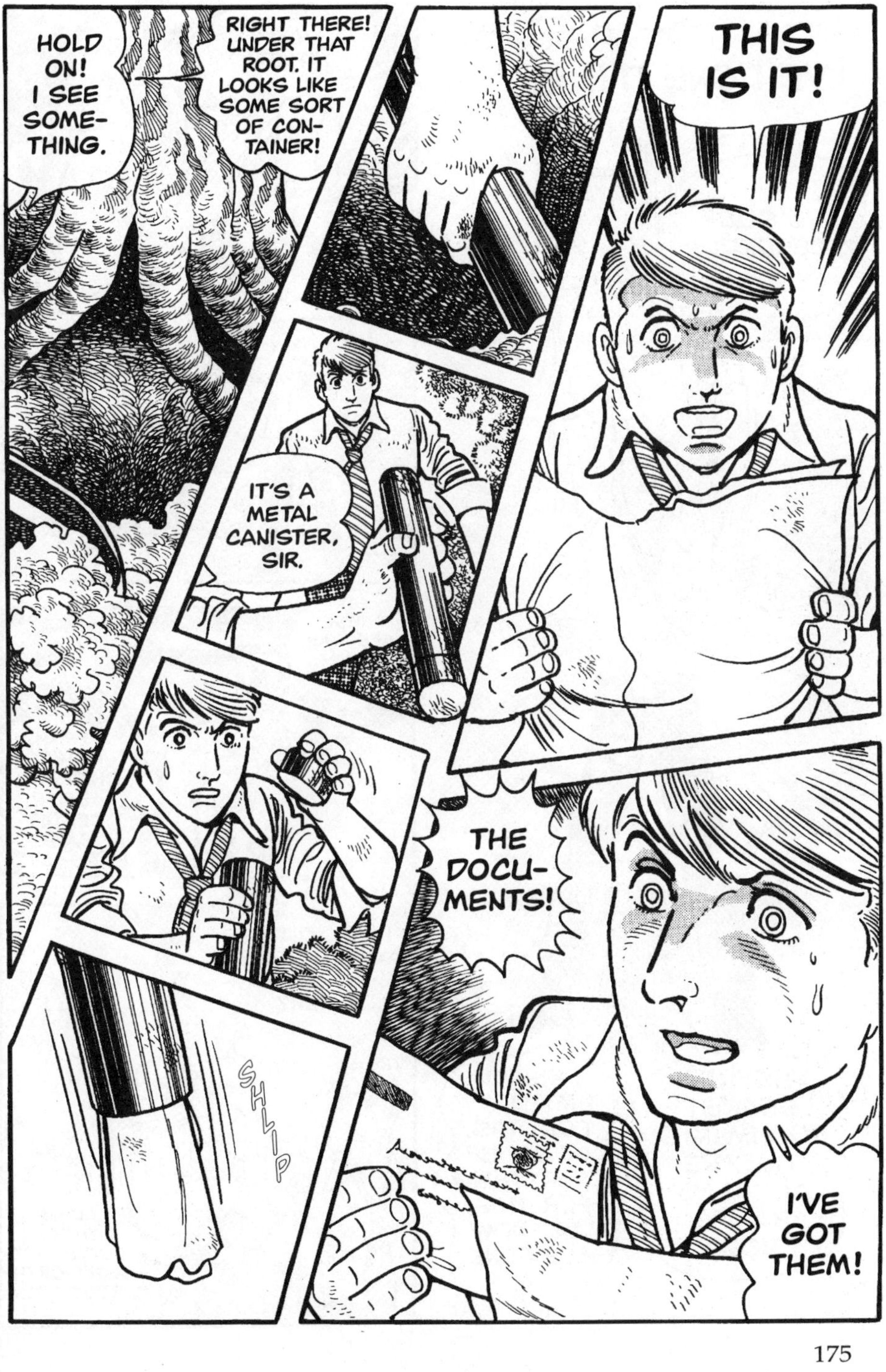
HOLD ON! I SEE SOME-THING.
RIGHT THERE! UNDER THAT ROOT. IT LOOKS LIKE SOME SORT OF CON-TAINER!
IT'S A METAL CANISTER, SIR.
THIS IS IT!
SHLIP
THE DOCU-MENTS!
I'VE GOT THEM!

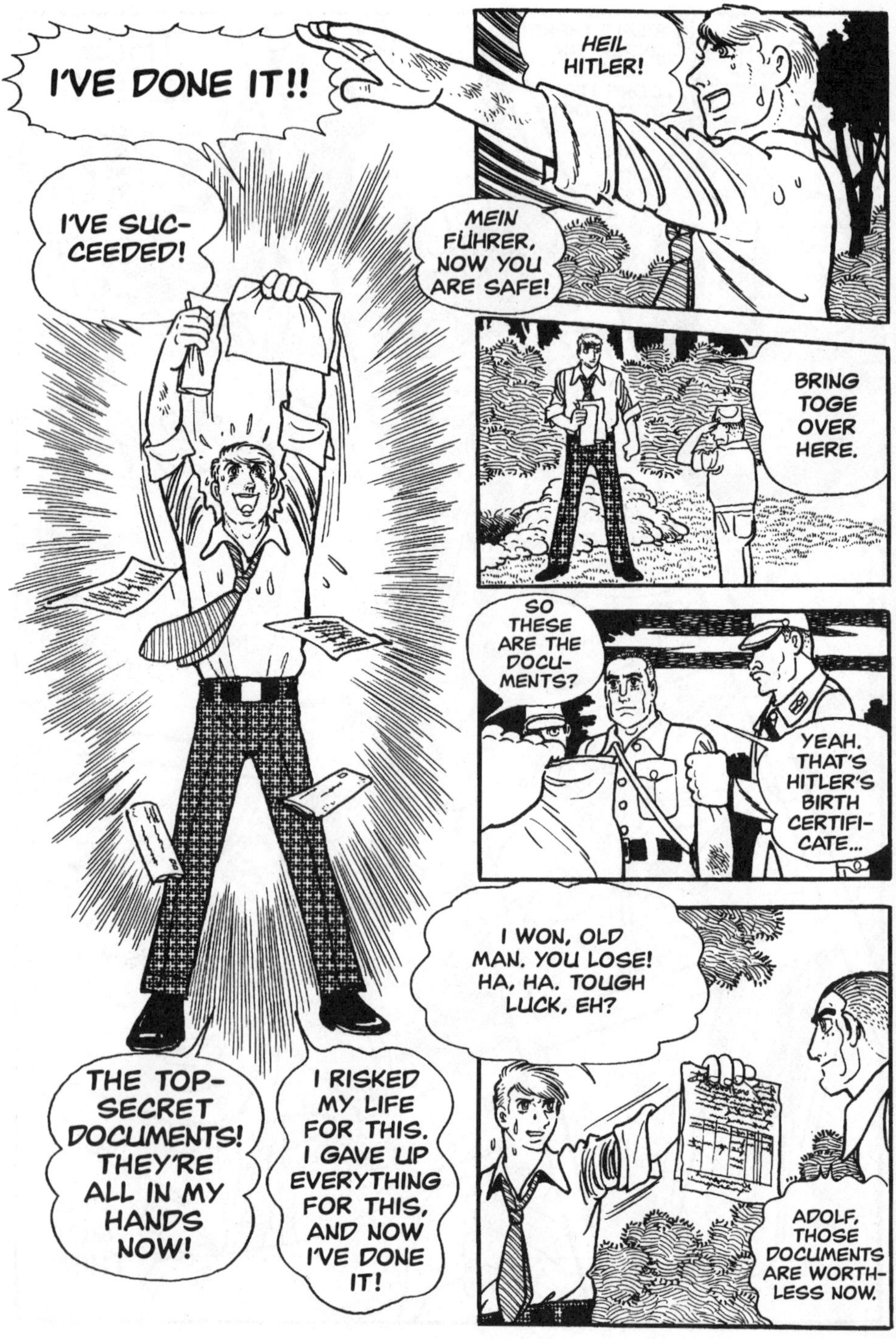
I'VE DONE IT!!
I'VE SUCCEEDED!
THE TOP-SECRET DOCUMENTS! THEY'RE ALL IN MY HANDS NOW!
I RISKED MY LIFE FOR THIS. I GAVE UP EVERYTHING FOR THIS, AND NOW I'VE DONE IT!
HEIL HITLER!
MEIN FÜHRER, NOW YOU ARE SAFE!
BRING TOGE OVER HERE.
SO THESE ARE THE DOCUMENTS?
YEAH. THAT'S HITLER'S BIRTH CERTIFICATE...
I WON, OLD MAN. YOU LOSE! HA, HA. TOUGH LUCK, EH?
ADOLF, THOSE DOCUMENTS ARE WORTHLESS NOW.

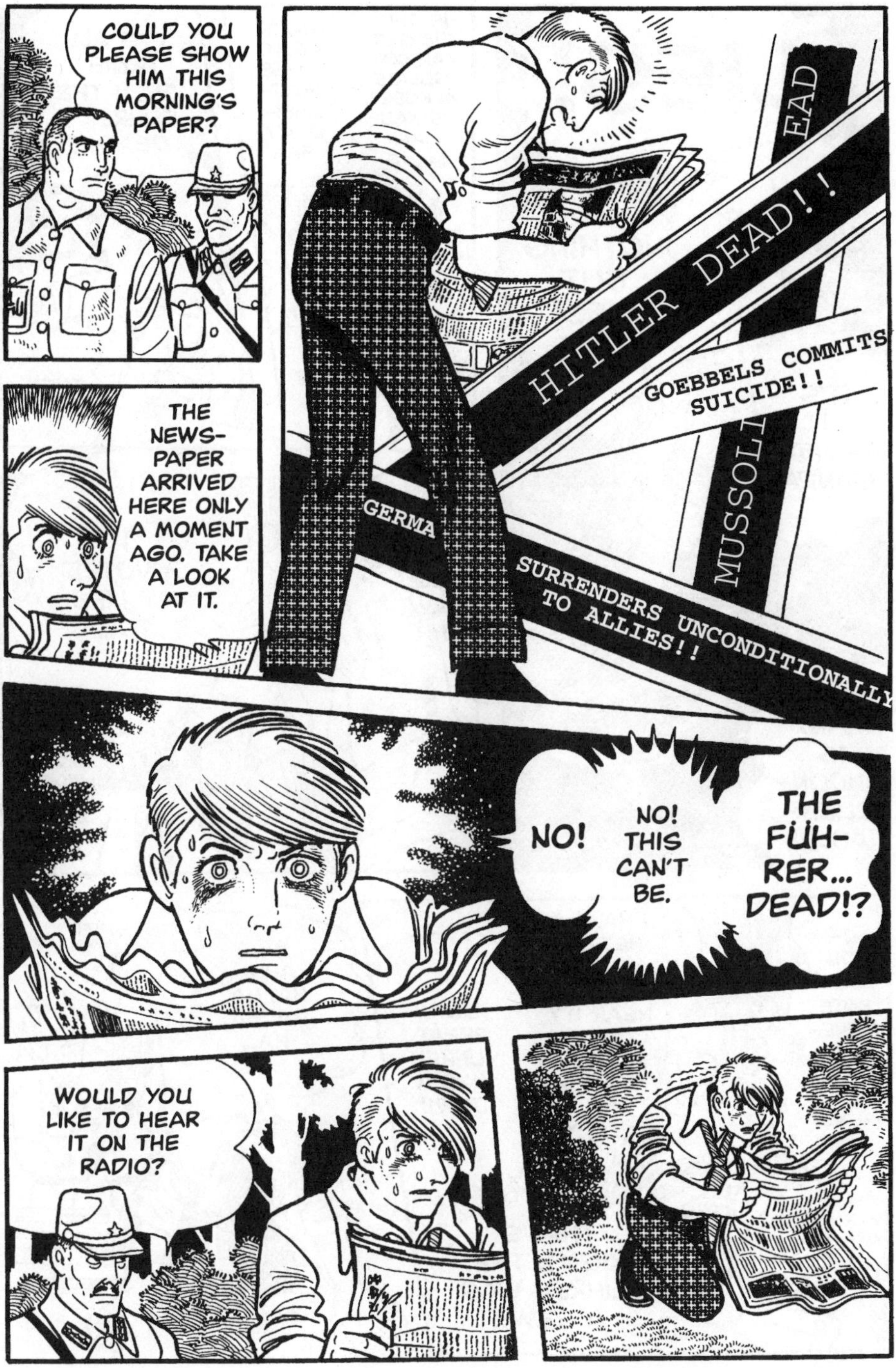
COULD YOU PLEASE SHOW HIM THIS MORNING'S PAPER?
THE NEWS-PAPER ARRIVED HERE ONLY A MOMENT AGO. TAKE A LOOK AT IT.
EAD
HITLER DEAD!!
GOEBBELS COMMITS SUICIDE!!
MUSSOLI
GERMA
SURRENDERS UNCONDITIONALLY TO ALLIES!!
NO!
NO! THIS CAN'T BE.
THE FÜHRER... DEAD!?
WOULD YOU LIKE TO HEAR IT ON THE RADIO?

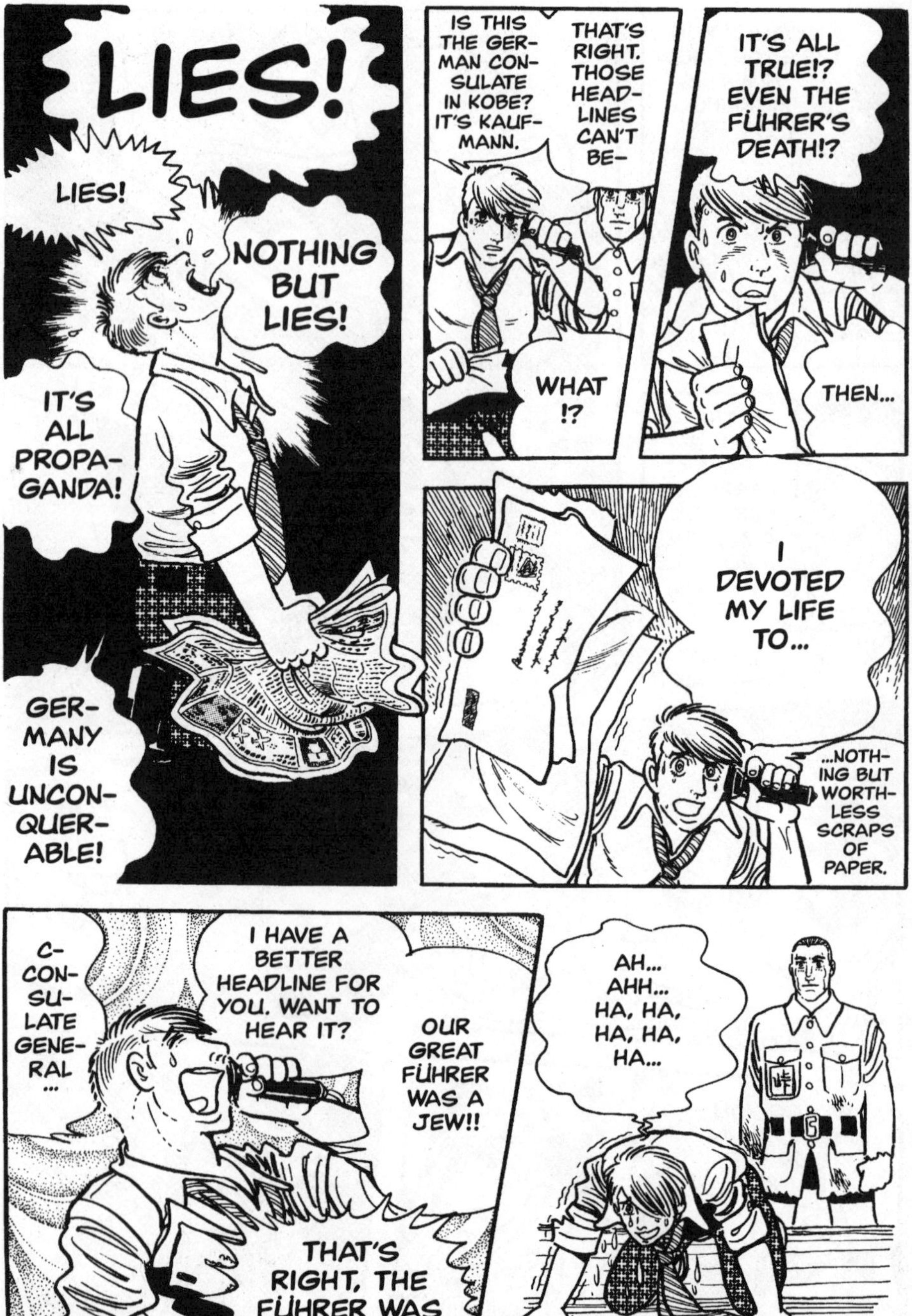
LIES!
LIES!
NOTHING BUT LIES!
IT'S ALL PROPAGANDA!
GERMANY IS UNCONQUERABLE!
IS THIS THE GERMAN CONSULATE IN KOBE? IT'S KAUFMANN.
THAT'S RIGHT. THOSE HEADLINES CAN'T BE-
WHAT!?
IT'S ALL TRUE!? EVEN THE FÜHRER'S DEATH!?
THEN...
I DEVOTED MY LIFE TO...
...NOTHING BUT WORTHLESS SCRAPS OF PAPER.
C-CONSULATE GENERAL...
I HAVE A BETTER HEADLINE FOR YOU. WANT TO HEAR IT?
OUR GREAT FÜHRER WAS A JEW!!
THAT'S RIGHT, THE FÜHRER WAS A JEW!!
AH... AHH... HA, HA, HA, HA, HA...

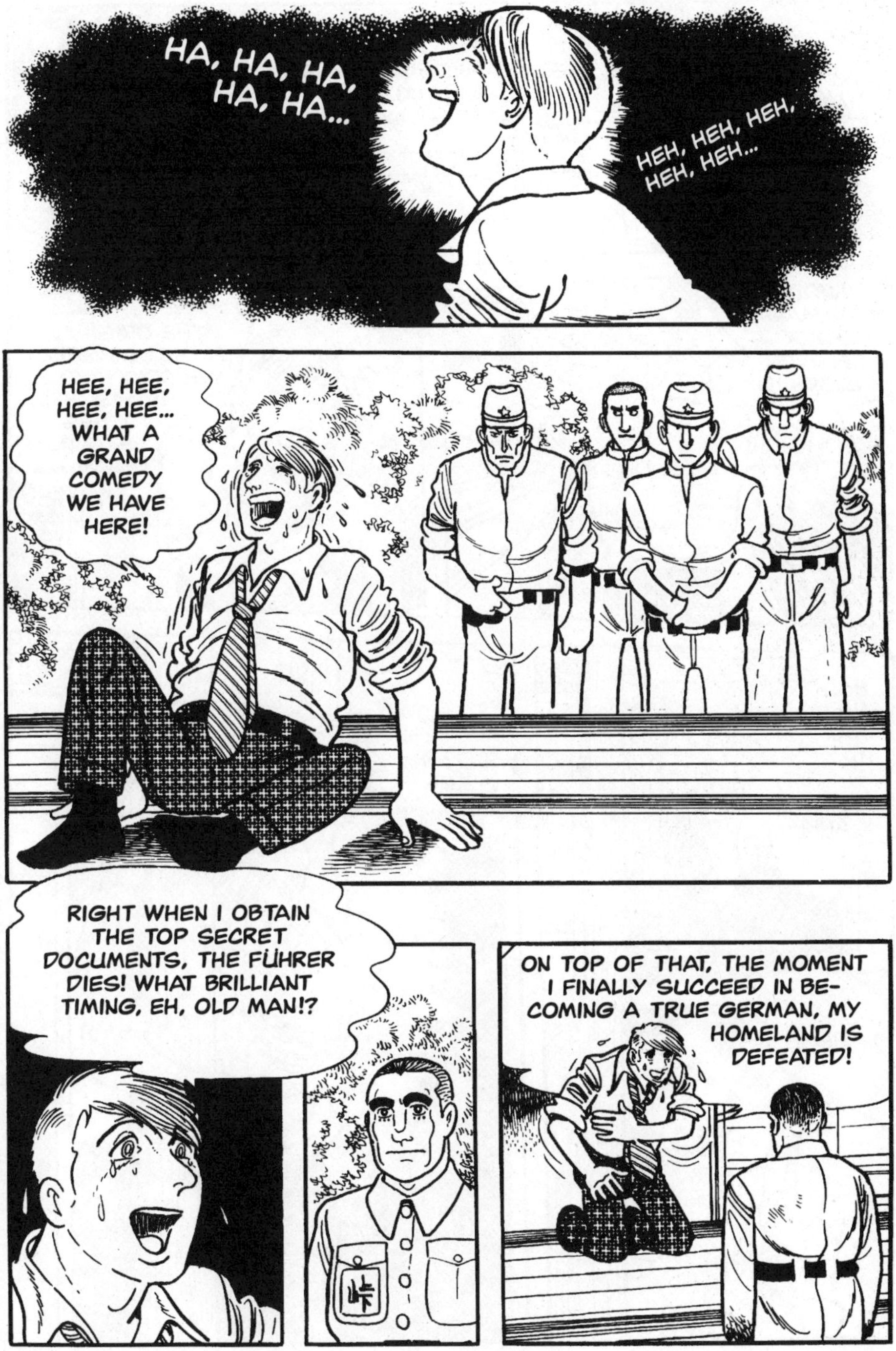
HA, HA, HA,
HA, HA...
HEH, HEH, HEH,
HEH, HEH...
HEE, HEE, HEE, HEE... WHAT A GRAND COMEDY WE HAVE HERE!
RIGHT WHEN I OBTAIN THE TOP SECRET DOCUMENTS, THE FÜHRER DIES! WHAT BRILLIANT TIMING, EH, OLD MAN!?
ON TOP OF THAT, THE MOMENT I FINALLY SUCCEED IN BE-COMING A TRUE GERMAN, MY HOMELAND IS DEFEATED!

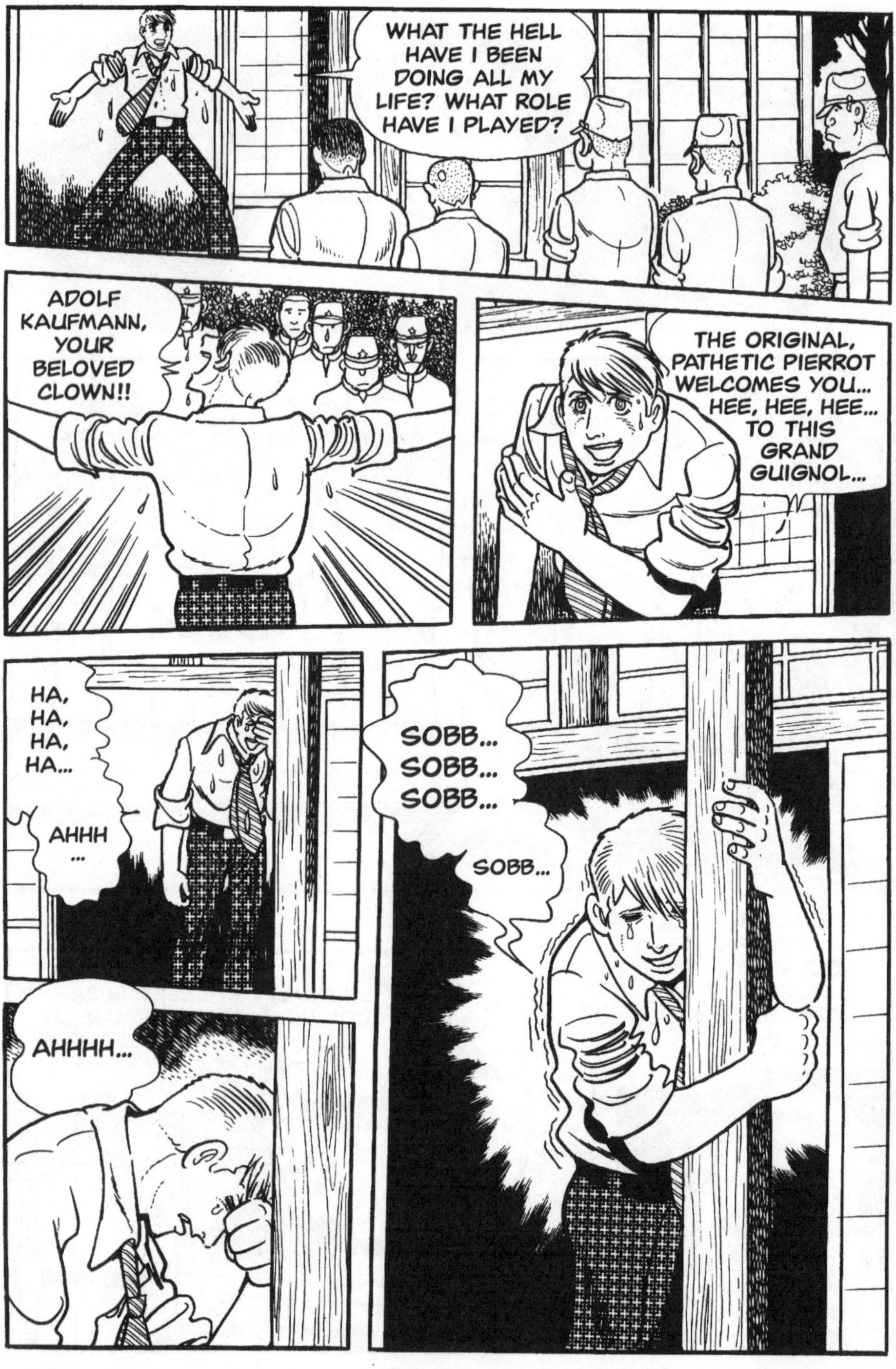
WHAT THE HELL HAVE I BEEN DOING ALL MY LIFE? WHAT ROLE HAVE I PLAYED?
ADOLF KAUFMANN, YOUR BELOVED CLOWN!!
THE ORIGINAL, PATHETIC PIERROT WELCOMES YOU... HEE, HEE, HEE... TO THIS GRAND GUIGNOL...
HA, HA, HA, HA...
AHHH ...
AHHHH...
SOBB... SOBB... SOBB...
SOBB...

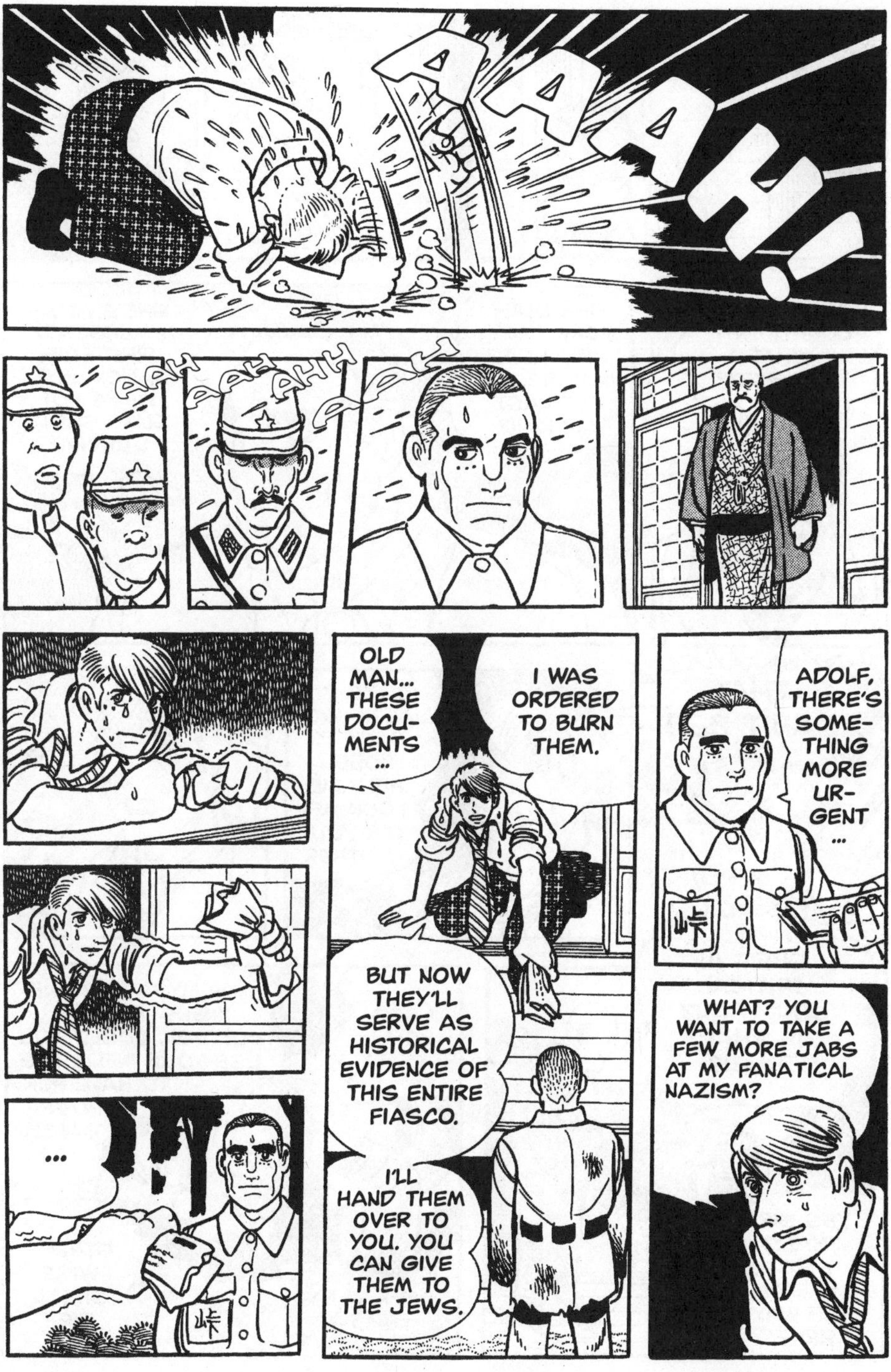
AAAH!!
AAH
AAH
AHH
AAH
OLD MAN... THESE DOCUMENTS...
I WAS ORDERED TO BURN THEM.
BUT NOW THEY'LL SERVE AS HISTORICAL EVIDENCE OF THIS ENTIRE FIASCO.
I'LL HAND THEM OVER TO YOU. YOU CAN GIVE THEM TO THE JEWS.
ADOLF, THERE'S SOMETHING MORE URGENT...
WHAT? YOU WANT TO TAKE A FEW MORE JABS AT MY FANATICAL NAZISM?
...

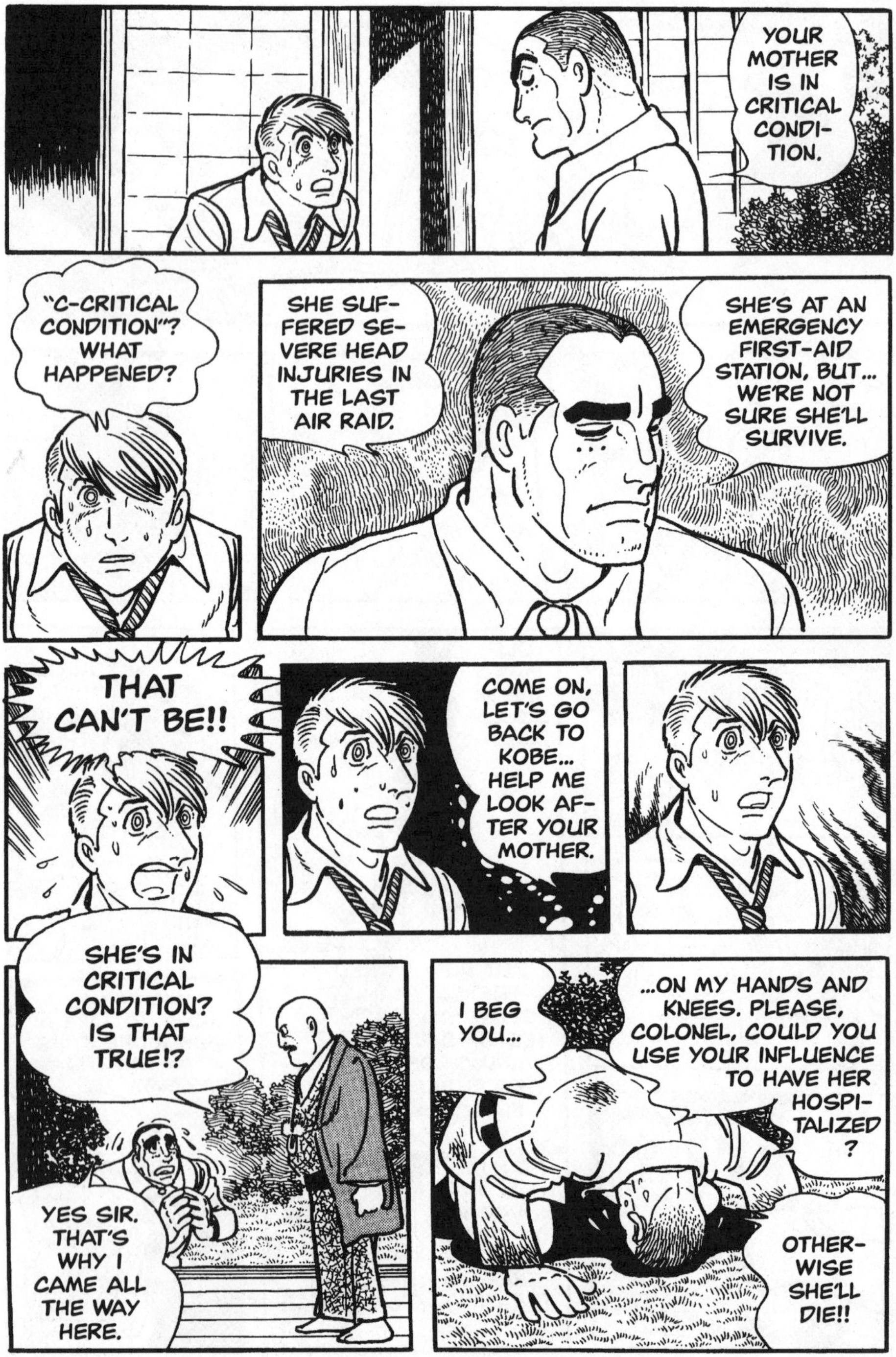
YOUR MOTHER IS IN CRITICAL CONDITION.
"C-CRITICAL CONDITION"? WHAT HAPPENED?
SHE SUFFERED SEVERE HEAD INJURIES IN THE LAST AIR RAID.
SHE'S AT AN EMERGENCY FIRST-AID STATION, BUT... WE'RE NOT SURE SHE'LL SURVIVE.
THAT CAN'T BE!!
COME ON, LET'S GO BACK TO KOBE... HELP ME LOOK AFTER YOUR MOTHER.
SHE'S IN CRITICAL CONDITION? IS THAT TRUE!?
YES SIR. THAT'S WHY I CAME ALL THE WAY HERE.
I BEG YOU...
...ON MY HANDS AND KNEES. PLEASE, COLONEL, COULD YOU USE YOUR INFLUENCE TO HAVE HER HOSPITALIZED?
OTHERWISE SHE'LL DIE!!

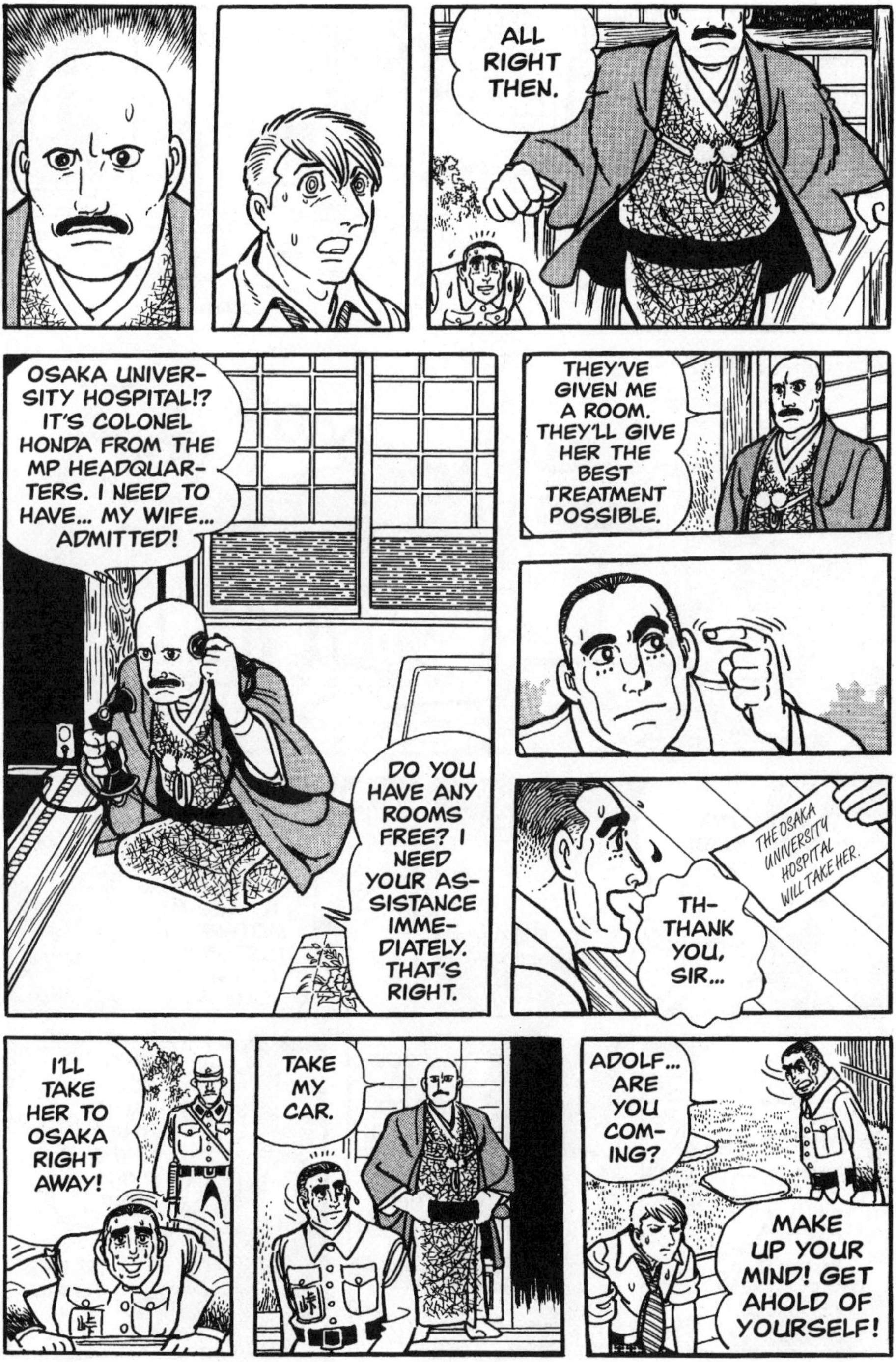
ALL RIGHT THEN.
OSAKA UNIVERSITY HOSPITAL!? IT'S COLONEL HONDA FROM THE MP HEADQUARTERS. I NEED TO HAVE... MY WIFE... ADMITTED!
DO YOU HAVE ANY ROOMS FREE? I NEED YOUR ASSISTANCE IMMEDIATELY. THAT'S RIGHT.
THEY'VE GIVEN ME A ROOM. THEY'LL GIVE HER THE BEST TREATMENT POSSIBLE.
THE OSAKA UNIVERSITY HOSPITAL WILL TAKE HER.
TH-THANK YOU, SIR...
I'LL TAKE HER TO OSAKA RIGHT AWAY!
TAKE MY CAR.
ADOLF... ARE YOU COMING?
MAKE UP YOUR MIND! GET AHOLD OF YOURSELF!

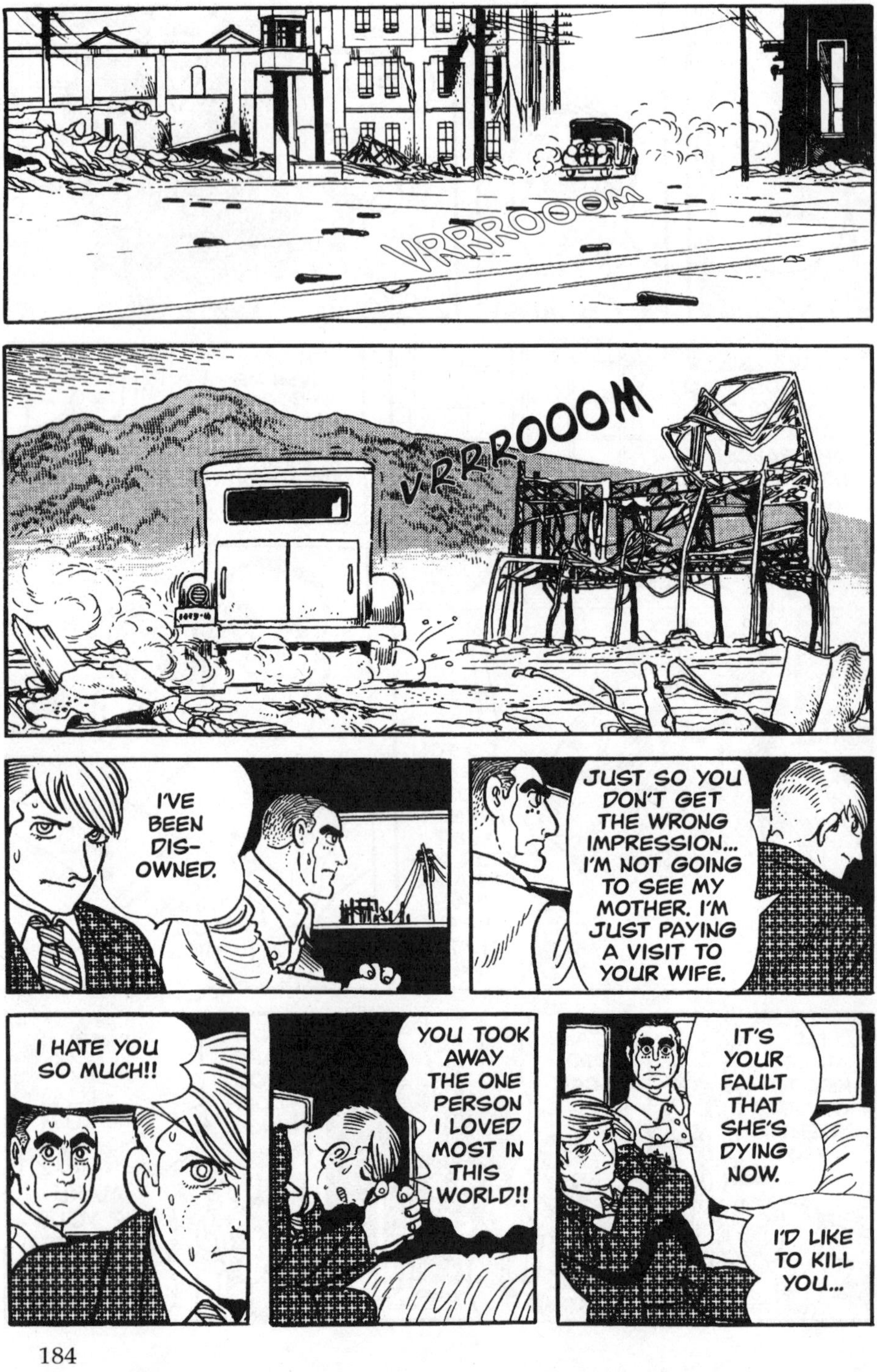
VRRROOOM
VRRROOOM
I'VE BEEN DIS-OWNED.
JUST SO YOU DON'T GET THE WRONG IMPRESSION... I'M NOT GOING TO SEE MY MOTHER. I'M JUST PAYING A VISIT TO YOUR WIFE.
I HATE YOU SO MUCH!!
YOU TOOK AWAY THE ONE PERSON I LOVED MOST IN THIS WORLD!!
IT'S YOUR FAULT THAT SHE'S DYING NOW.
I'D LIKE TO KILL YOU...

WHAT ARE YOU MUMBLING ABOUT? I CAN'T HEAR A THING, REMEMBER?

NOTHING. I'M JUST TALKING TO MYSELF.

GERMANY IS DEFEATED! BUT MY CRUSADE FOR JUSTICE WILL CONTINUE!

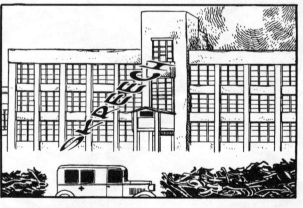

DOCTOR!

TOGE...

WE FOUND A HOSPITAL!

GREAT! SHE'S OVER THERE...

185

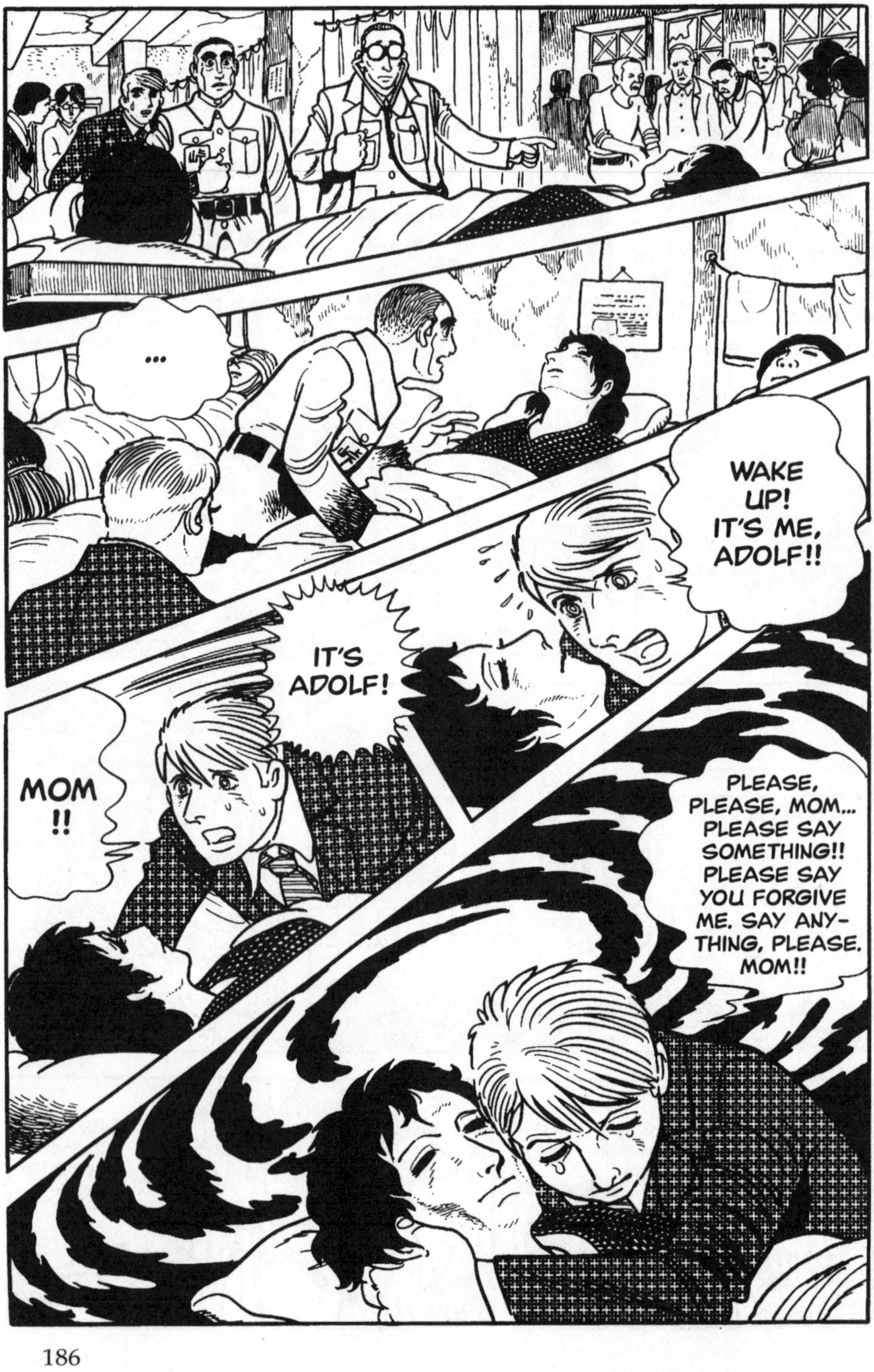
...
WAKE UP! IT'S ME, ADOLF!!
IT'S ADOLF!
MOM !!
PLEASE, PLEASE, MOM... PLEASE SAY SOMETHING!! PLEASE SAY YOU FORGIVE ME. SAY ANY-THING, PLEASE. MOM!!

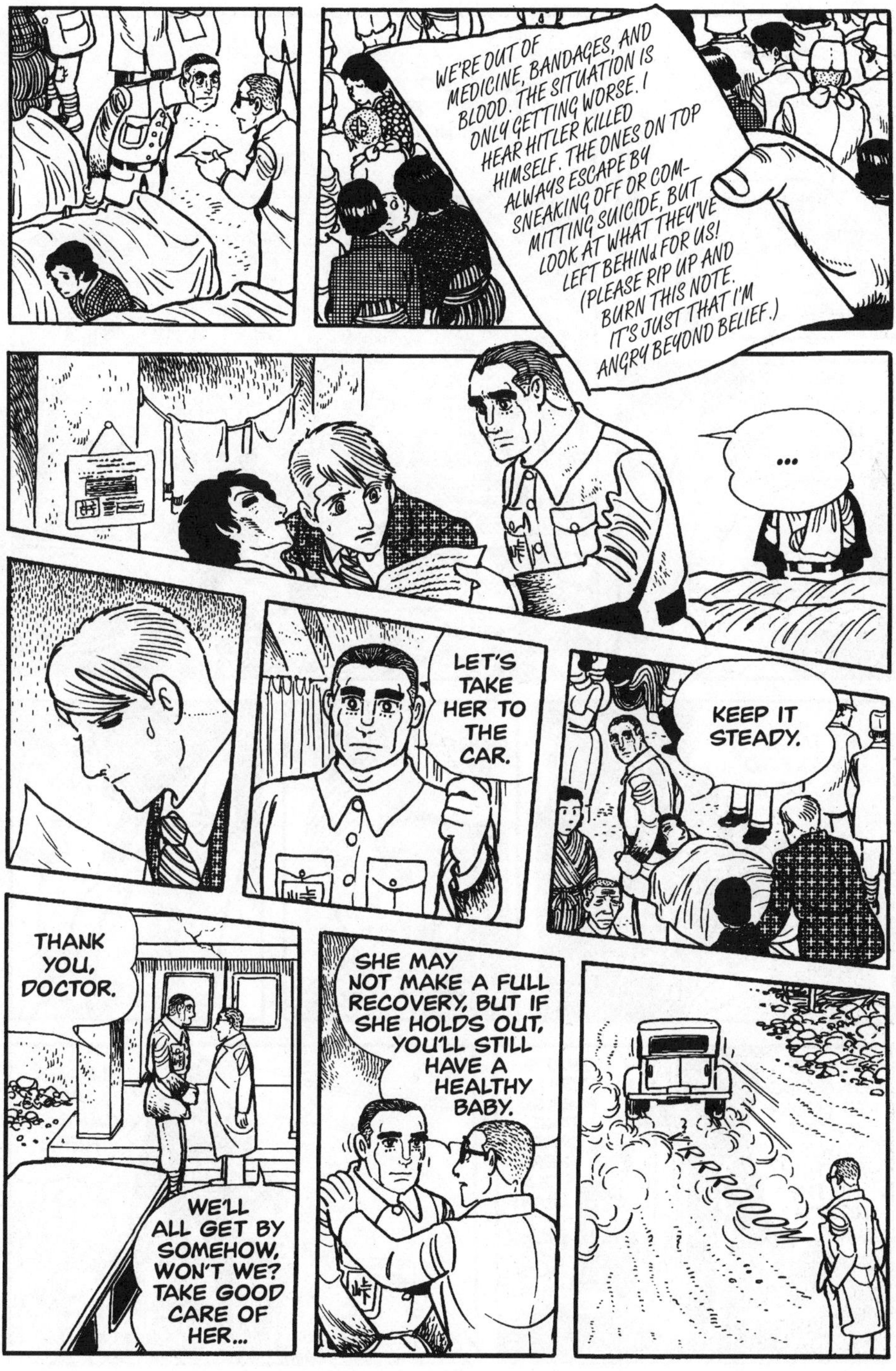
WE'RE OUT OF MEDICINE, BANDAGES, AND BLOOD. THE SITUATION IS ONLY GETTING WORSE. I HEAR HITLER KILLED HIMSELF. THE ONES ON TOP ALWAYS ESCAPE BY SNEAKING OFF OR COM-MITTING SUICIDE, BUT LOOK AT WHAT THEY'VE LEFT BEHIND FOR US! (PLEASE RIP UP AND BURN THIS NOTE. IT'S JUST THAT I'M ANGRY BEYOND BELIEF.)
...
LET'S TAKE HER TO THE CAR.
KEEP IT STEADY.
THANK YOU, DOCTOR.
WE'LL ALL GET BY SOMEHOW, WON'T WE? TAKE GOOD CARE OF HER...
SHE MAY NOT MAKE A FULL RECOVERY, BUT IF SHE HOLDS OUT, YOU'LL STILL HAVE A HEALTHY BABY.
VRRROOOM

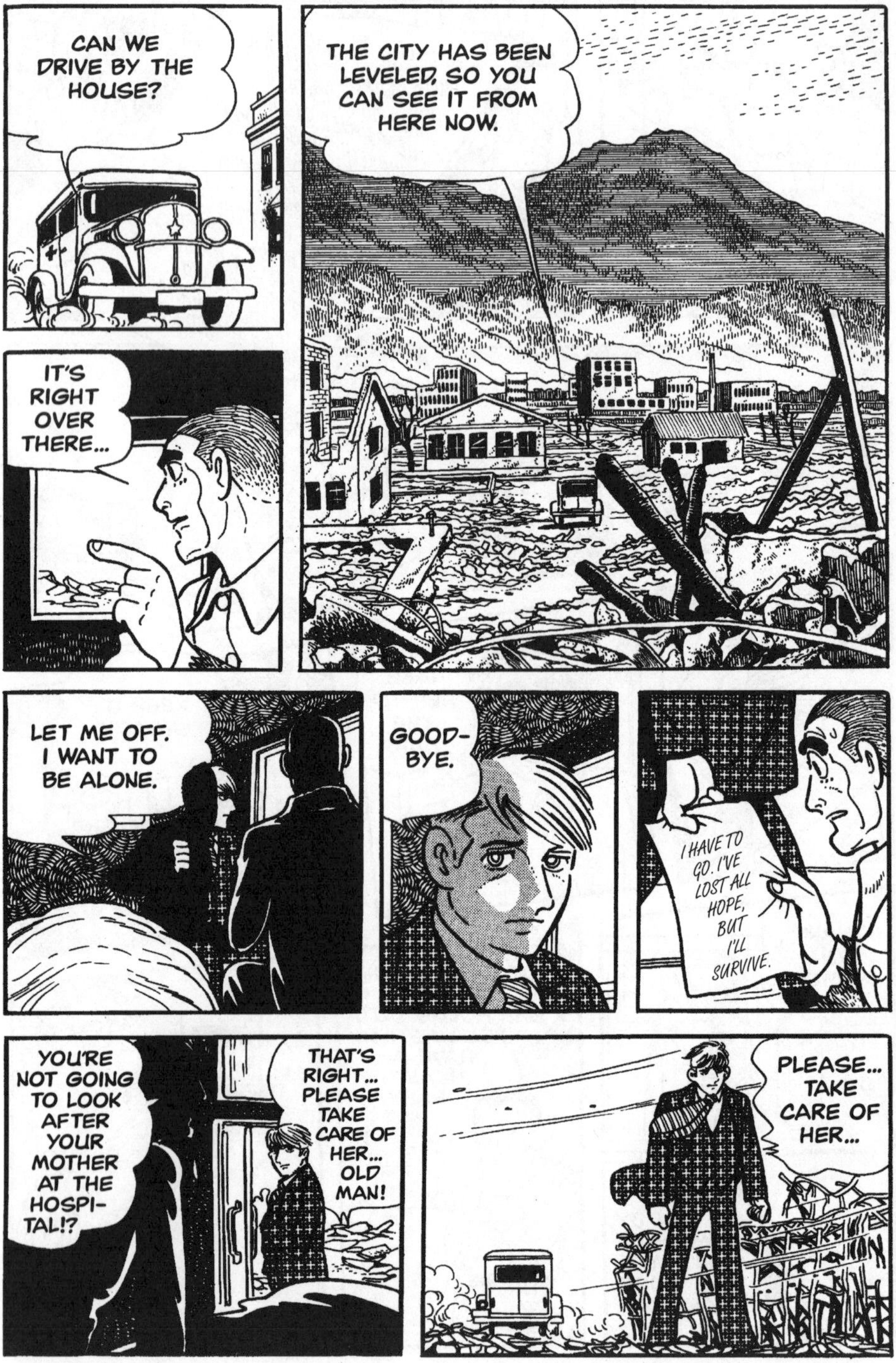
CAN WE DRIVE BY THE HOUSE?
THE CITY HAS BEEN LEVELED, SO YOU CAN SEE IT FROM HERE NOW.
IT'S RIGHT OVER THERE...
LET ME OFF. I WANT TO BE ALONE.
GOOD-BYE.
I HAVE TO GO. I'VE LOST ALL HOPE, BUT I'LL SURVIVE.
YOU'RE NOT GOING TO LOOK AFTER YOUR MOTHER AT THE HOSPITAL!?
THAT'S RIGHT... PLEASE TAKE CARE OF HER... OLD MAN!
PLEASE... TAKE CARE OF HER...

CHAPTER
SEVEN

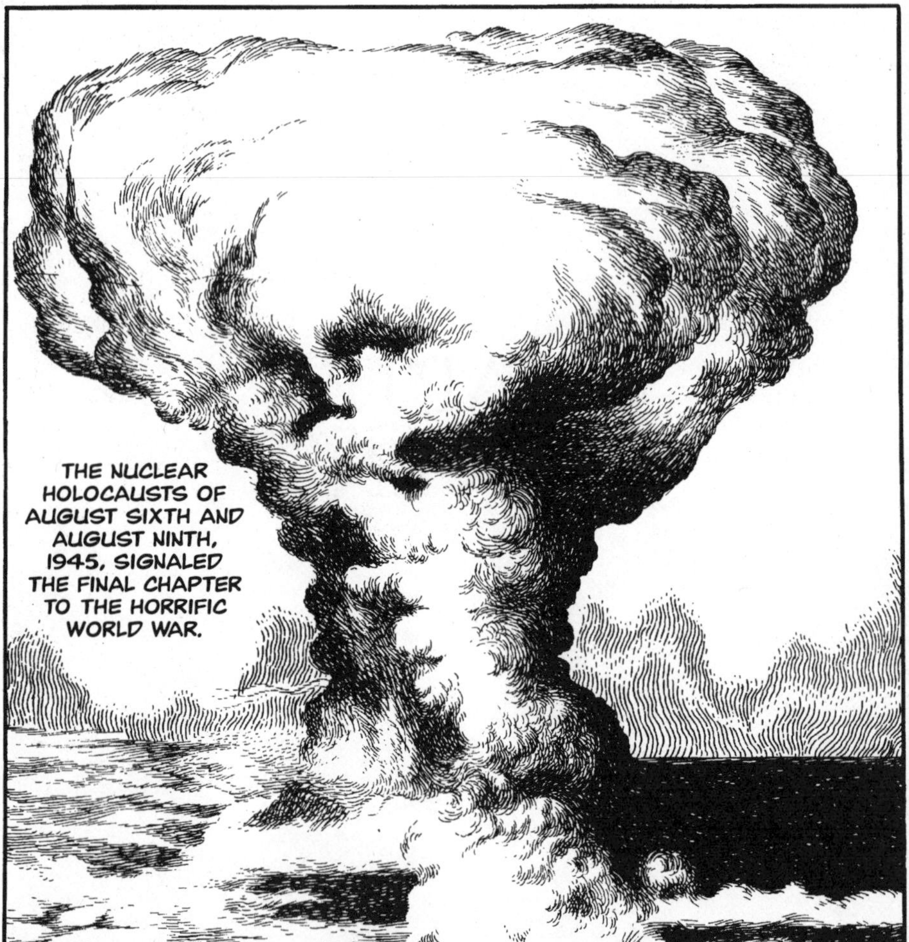
THE NUCLEAR HOLOCAUSTS OF AUGUST SIXTH AND AUGUST NINTH, 1945, SIGNALED THE FINAL CHAPTER TO THE HORRIFIC WORLD WAR.

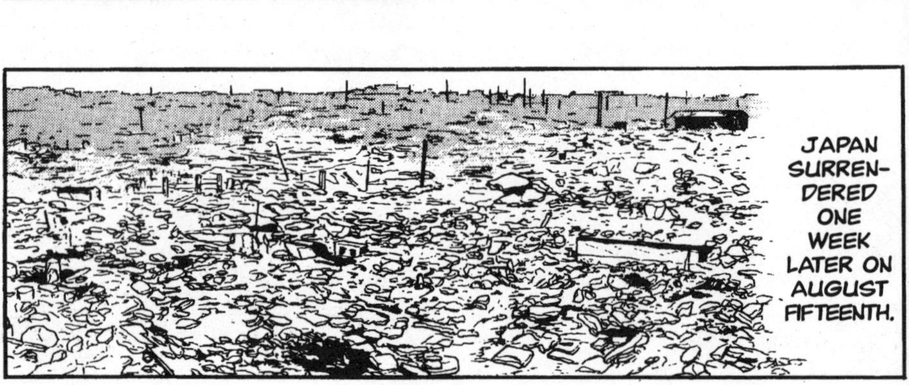
JAPAN SURREN-DERED ONE WEEK LATER ON AUGUST FIFTEENTH.

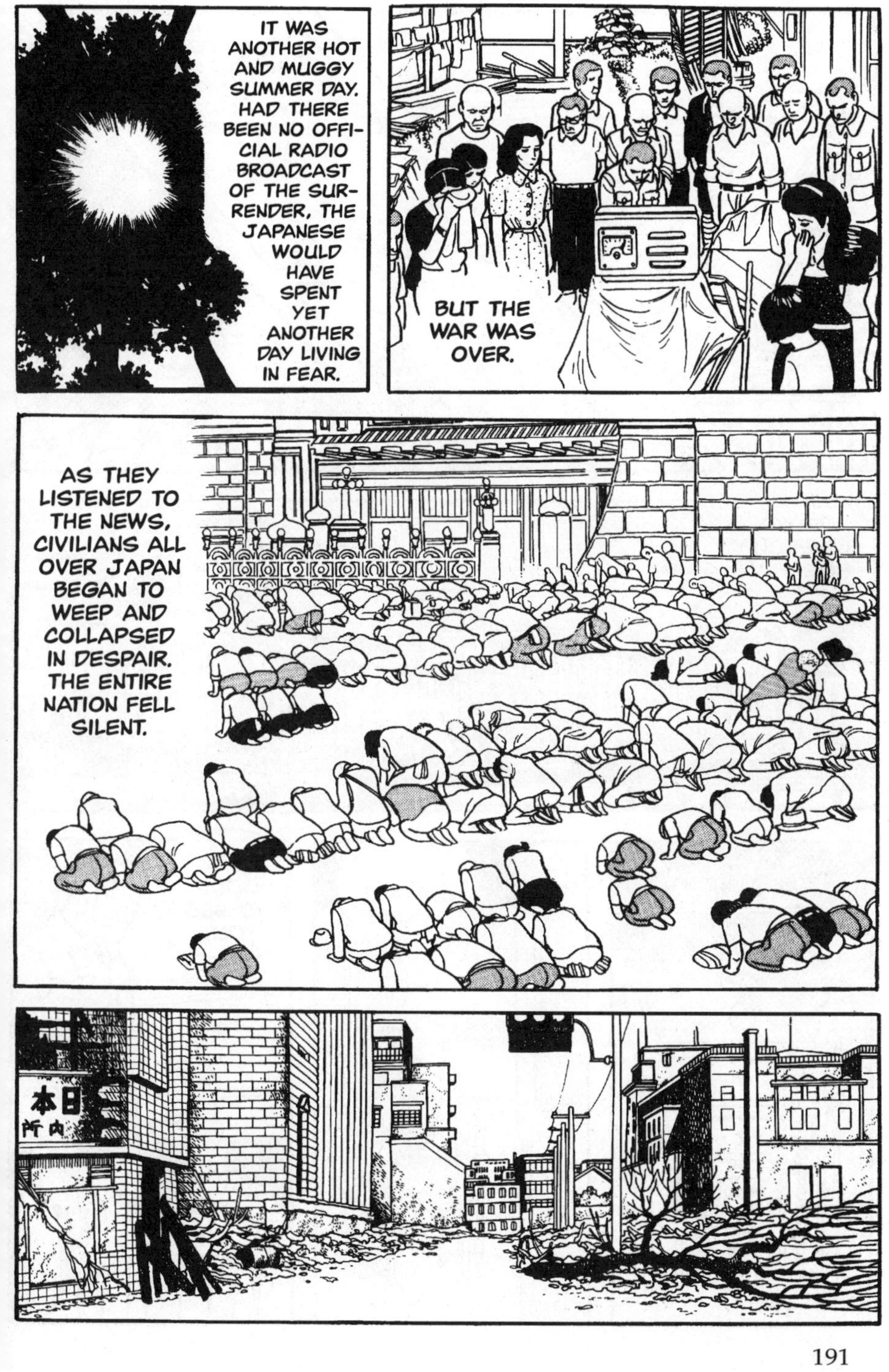
IT WAS ANOTHER HOT AND MUGGY SUMMER DAY. HAD THERE BEEN NO OFFICIAL RADIO BROADCAST OF THE SURRENDER, THE JAPANESE WOULD HAVE SPENT YET ANOTHER DAY LIVING IN FEAR.
BUT THE WAR WAS OVER.
AS THEY LISTENED TO THE NEWS, CIVILIANS ALL OVER JAPAN BEGAN TO WEEP AND COLLAPSED IN DESPAIR. THE ENTIRE NATION FELL SILENT.

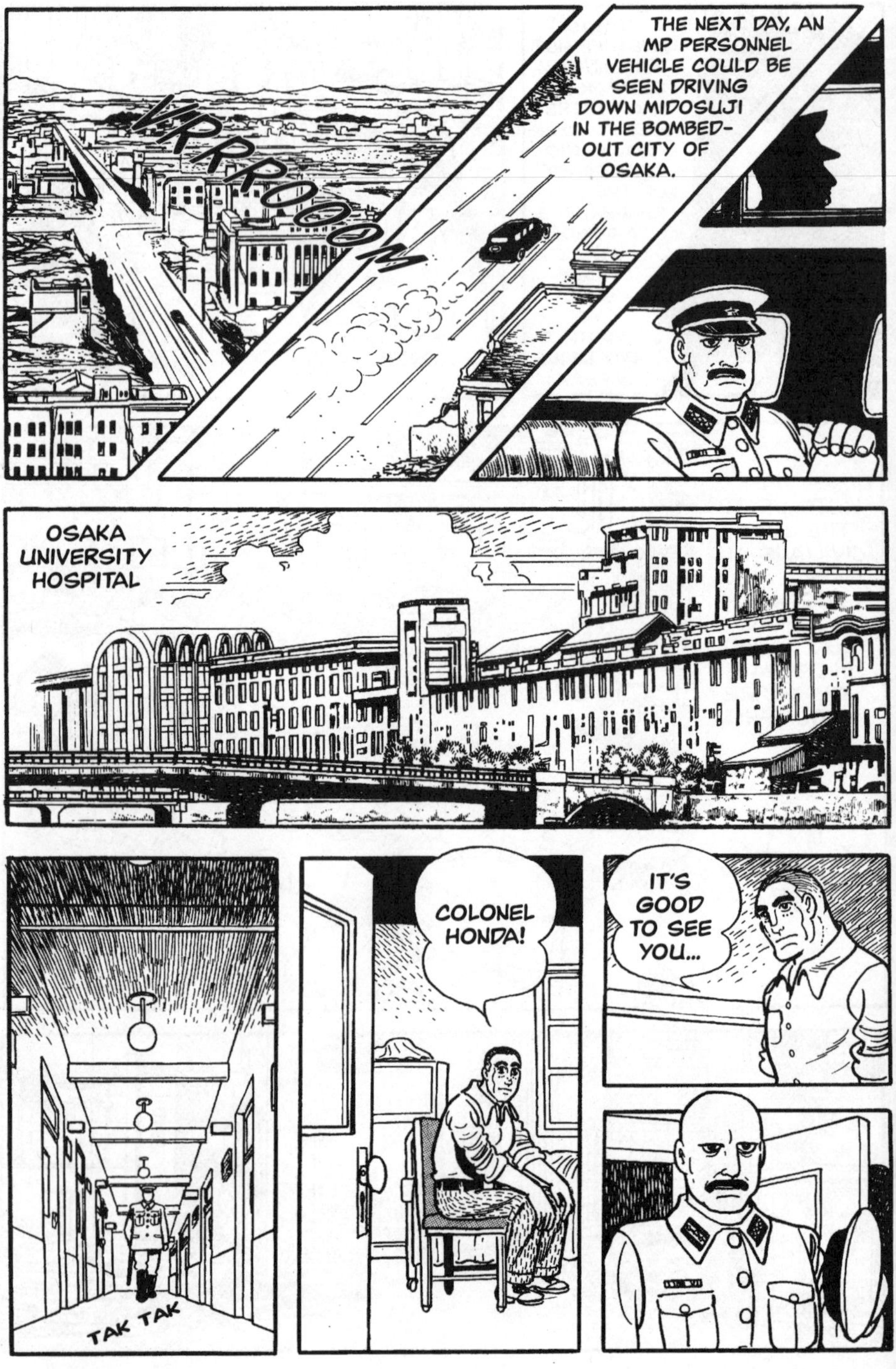
VRRROOOM
THE NEXT DAY, AN MP PERSONNEL VEHICLE COULD BE SEEN DRIVING DOWN MIDOSUJI IN THE BOMBED-OUT CITY OF OSAKA.
OSAKA UNIVERSITY HOSPITAL
TAK TAK
COLONEL HONDA!
IT'S GOOD TO SEE YOU...

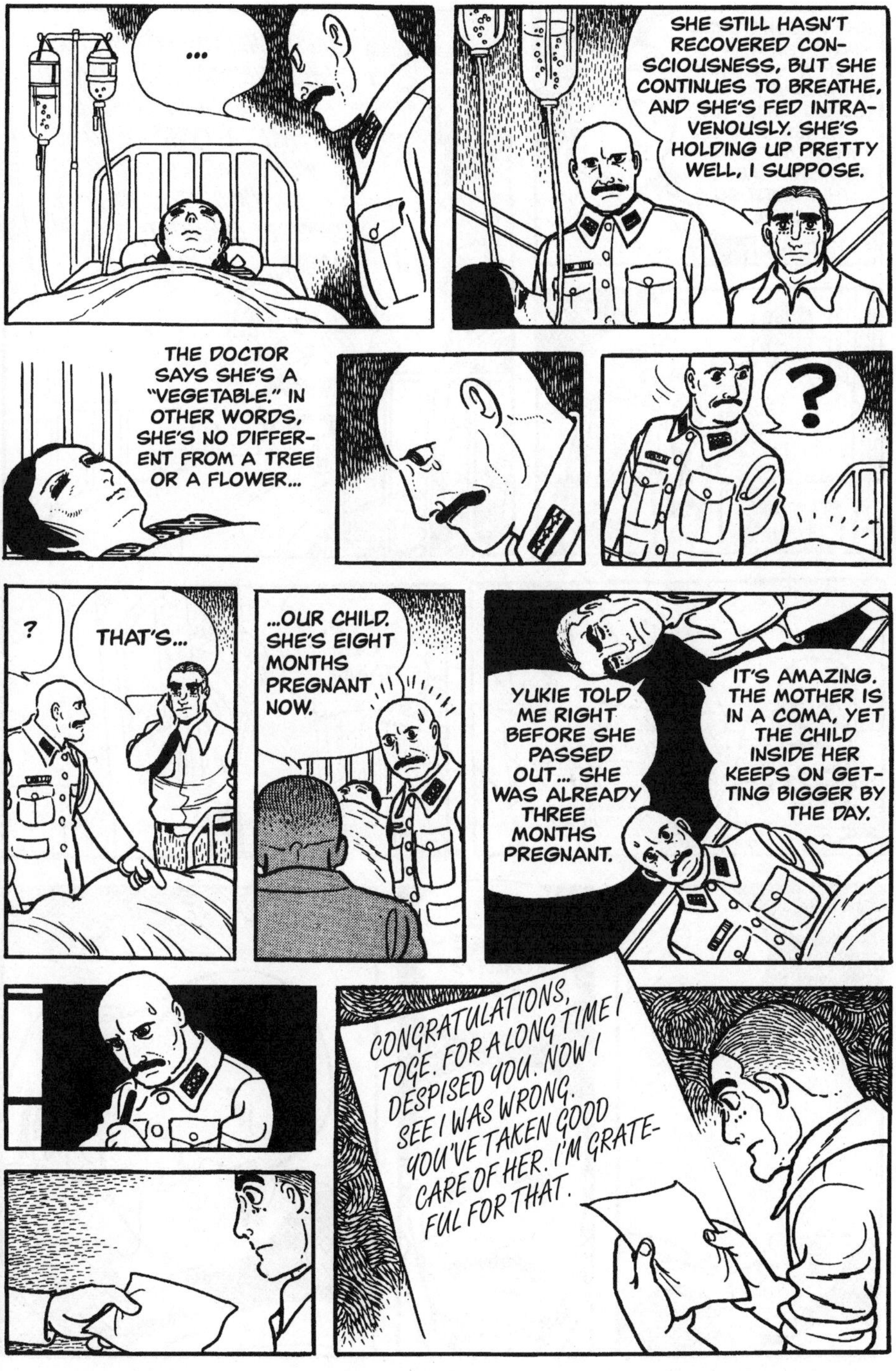
...
SHE STILL HASN'T RECOVERED CONSCIOUSNESS, BUT SHE CONTINUES TO BREATHE, AND SHE'S FED INTRAVENOUSLY. SHE'S HOLDING UP PRETTY WELL, I SUPPOSE.
THE DOCTOR SAYS SHE'S A "VEGETABLE." IN OTHER WORDS, SHE'S NO DIFFERENT FROM A TREE OR A FLOWER...
?
?
THAT'S...
...OUR CHILD. SHE'S EIGHT MONTHS PREGNANT NOW.
YUKIE TOLD ME RIGHT BEFORE SHE PASSED OUT... SHE WAS ALREADY THREE MONTHS PREGNANT.
IT'S AMAZING. THE MOTHER IS IN A COMA, YET THE CHILD INSIDE HER KEEPS ON GETTING BIGGER BY THE DAY.
CONGRATULATIONS, TOGE. FOR A LONG TIME I DESPISED YOU. NOW I SEE I WAS WRONG. YOU'VE TAKEN GOOD CARE OF HER. I'M GRATEFUL FOR THAT.

Adolf

SHE DOESN'T EVEN KNOW THE WAR IS OVER. IF SHE ONLY KNEW, SHE WOULD BE SO RELIEVED! THEN SHE WOULDN'T HAVE TO WORRY ABOUT THIS CHILD SO MUCH.

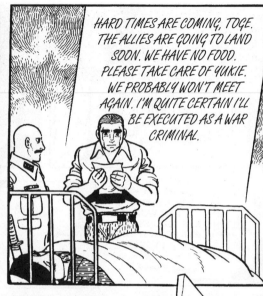

HARD TIMES ARE COMING, TOGE. THE ALLIES ARE GOING TO LAND SOON. WE HAVE NO FOOD. PLEASE TAKE CARE OF YUKIE. WE PROBABLY WON'T MEET AGAIN. I'M QUITE CERTAIN I'LL BE EXECUTED AS A WAR CRIMINAL.

I HAVE ONE REQUEST. COULD YOU PLEASE LET ME HAVE A MOMENT ALONE WITH HER?

YES, CER-TAINLY...

YUKIE, PLEASE FORGIVE ME...

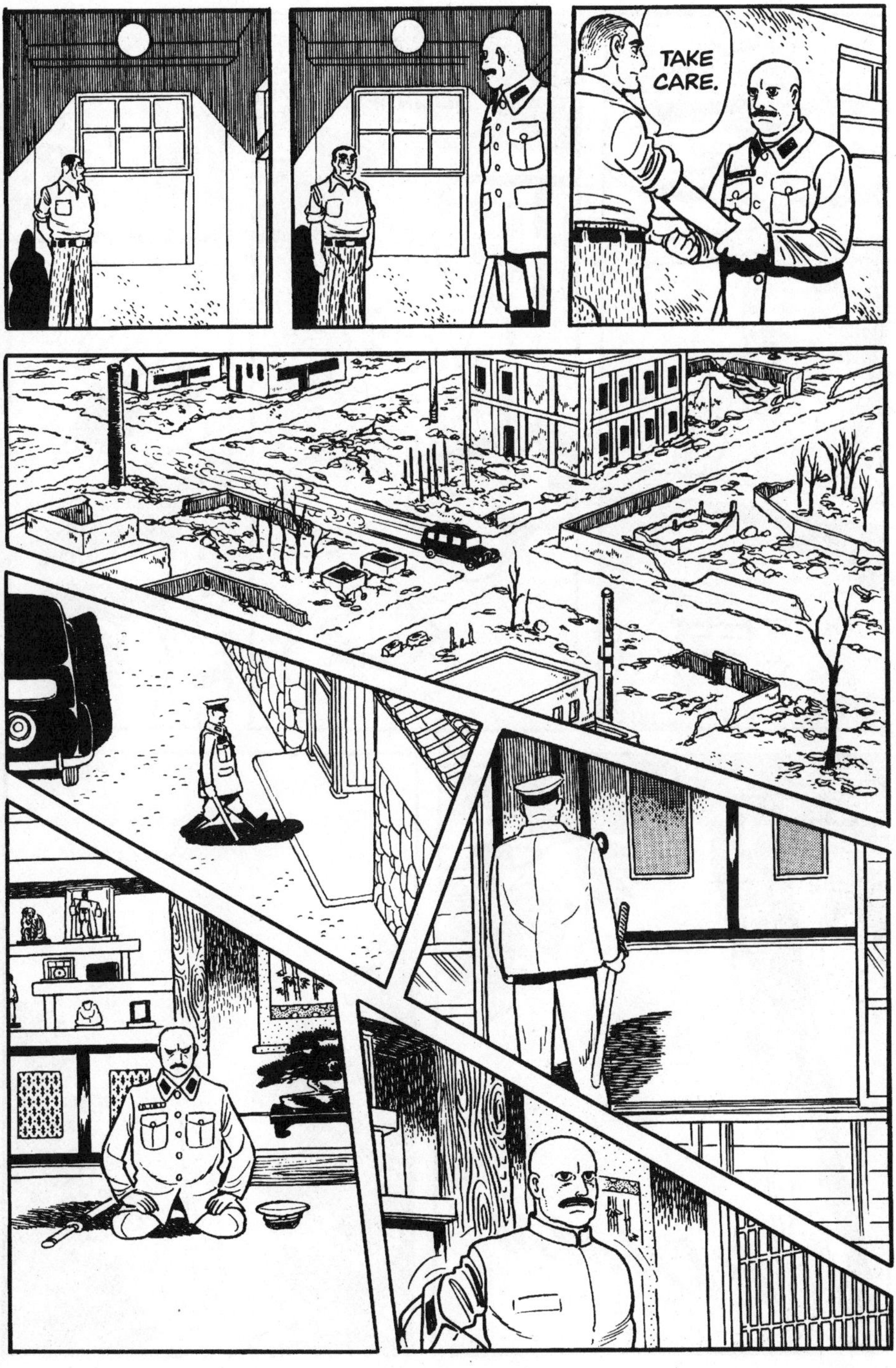
TAKE CARE.

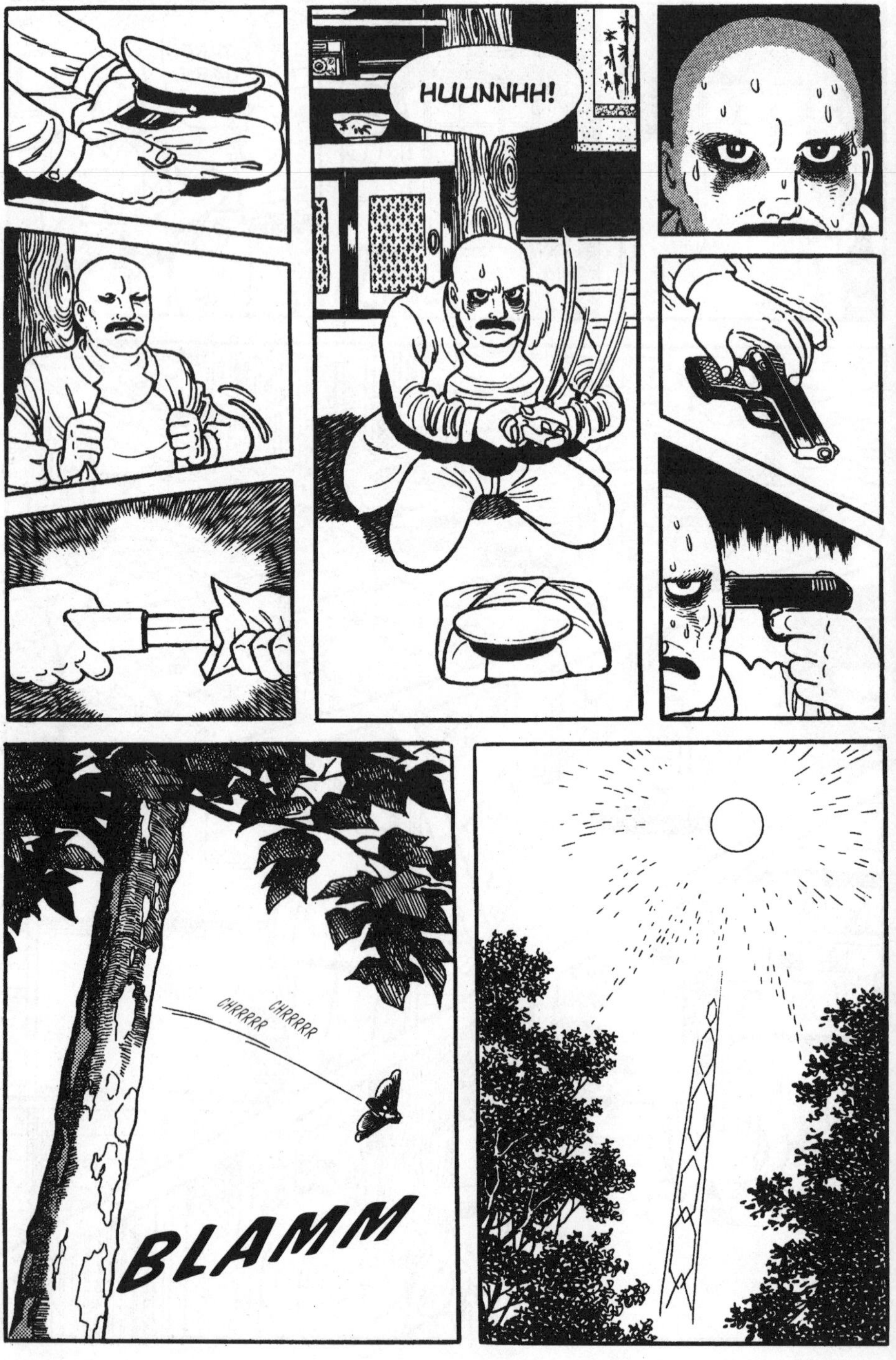
HUUNNHH!
CHRRRRR CHRRRRR
BLAMM

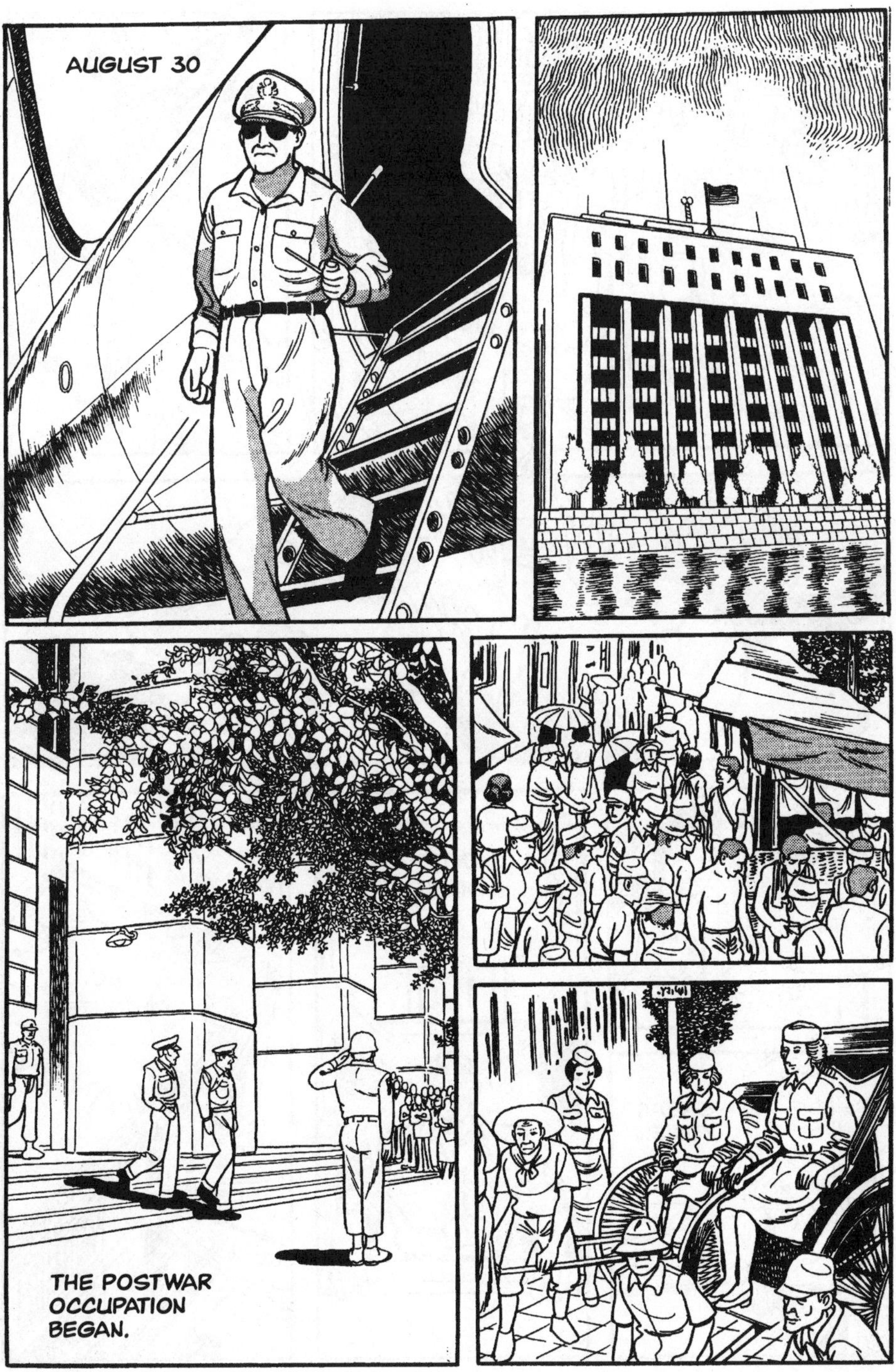
AUGUST 30
THE POSTWAR OCCUPATION BEGAN.

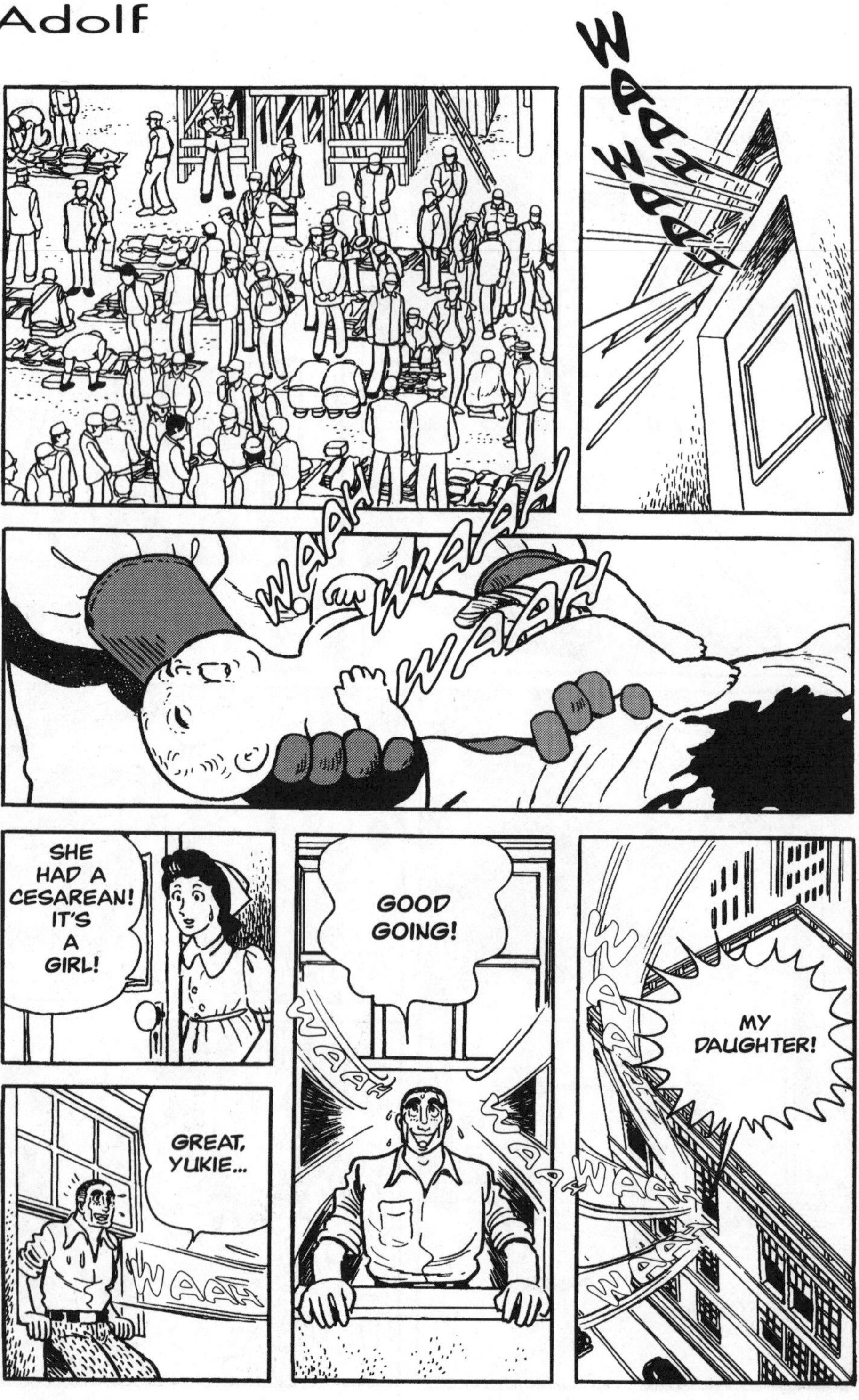
WAAH WAAH WAAH
SHE HAD A CESAREAN! IT'S A GIRL!
GREAT, YUKIE...
WAAH
GOOD GOING!
MY DAUGHTER!

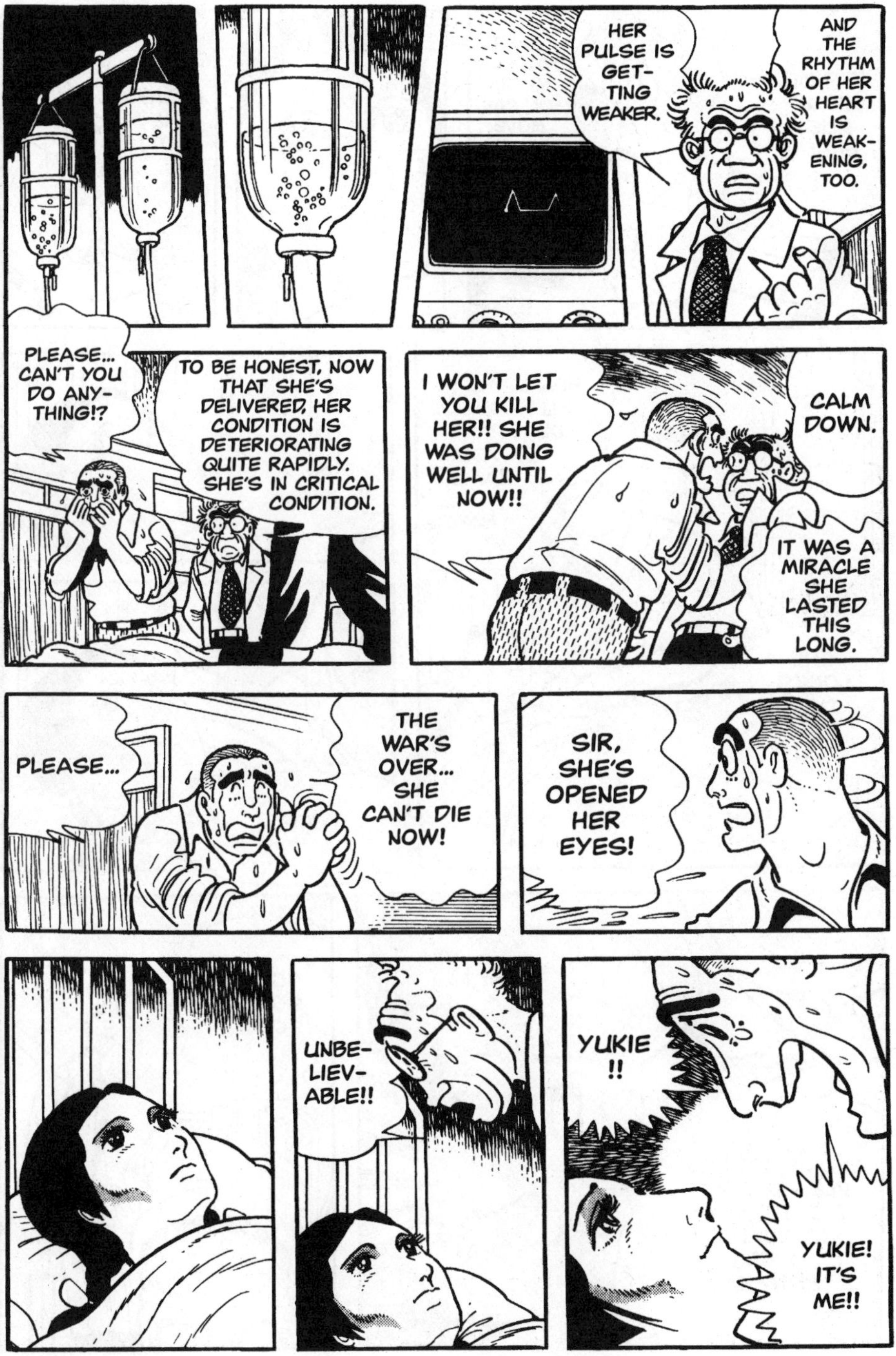
HER PULSE IS GETTING WEAKER.
AND THE RHYTHM OF HER HEART IS WEAKENING, TOO.
PLEASE... CAN'T YOU DO ANYTHING!?
TO BE HONEST, NOW THAT SHE'S DELIVERED, HER CONDITION IS DETERIORATING QUITE RAPIDLY. SHE'S IN CRITICAL CONDITION.
I WON'T LET YOU KILL HER!! SHE WAS DOING WELL UNTIL NOW!!
CALM DOWN.
IT WAS A MIRACLE SHE LASTED THIS LONG.
PLEASE...
THE WAR'S OVER... SHE CAN'T DIE NOW!
SIR, SHE'S OPENED HER EYES!
UNBELIEVABLE!!
YUKIE !!
YUKIE! IT'S ME!!

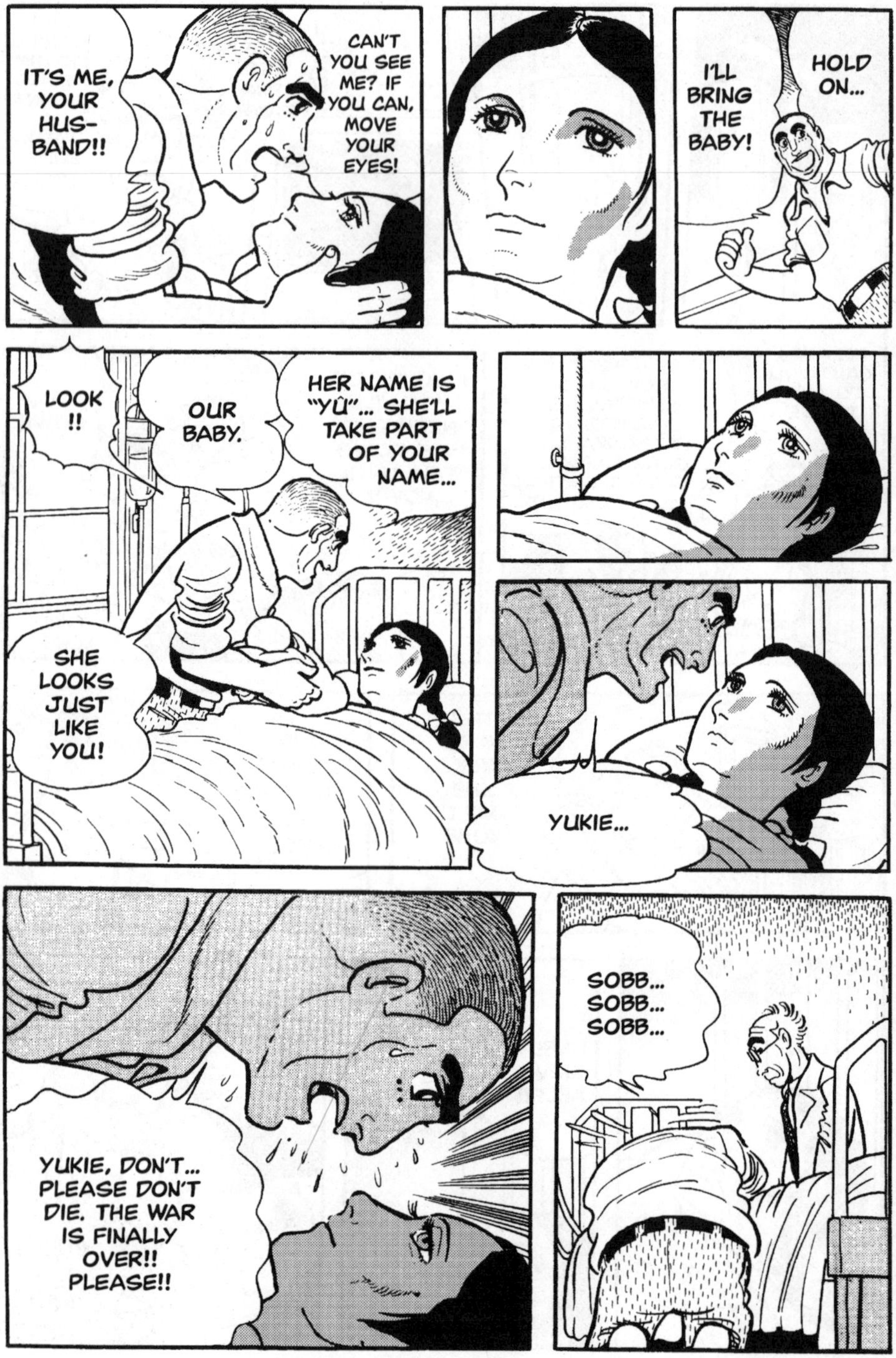
IT'S ME, YOUR HUS-BAND!!
CAN'T YOU SEE ME? IF YOU CAN, MOVE YOUR EYES!
I'LL BRING THE BABY!
HOLD ON...
LOOK !!
OUR BABY.
HER NAME IS "YÛ"... SHE'LL TAKE PART OF YOUR NAME...
SHE LOOKS JUST LIKE YOU!
YUKIE...
YUKIE, DON'T... PLEASE DON'T DIE. THE WAR IS FINALLY OVER!! PLEASE!!
SOBB... SOBB... SOBB...

"THOSE WHO FOUGHT AT SEA BECAME FLOATING CORPSES."

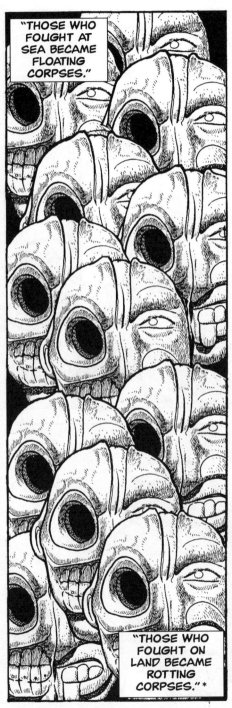

"THOSE WHO FOUGHT ON LAND BECAME ROTTING CORPSES." *

MANY OF THOSE WHO DID NOT EVEN FIGHT DIED, AND THEIR CORPSES DECAYED EVERYWHERE, FROM CITIES TO OPEN FIELDS.

BUT NEW LIVES WERE BEING BORN, NEW LIVES WHO KNEW NOTHING OF THE WAR.

THESE WORDS FROM A POEM BY YAKAMOCHI OTOMO, COLLECTED IN THE CLASSIC EIGHTH-CENTURY ANTHOLOGY MANYOSHU, WERE SUNG AT NAVY FUNERALS DURING WORLD WAR II.

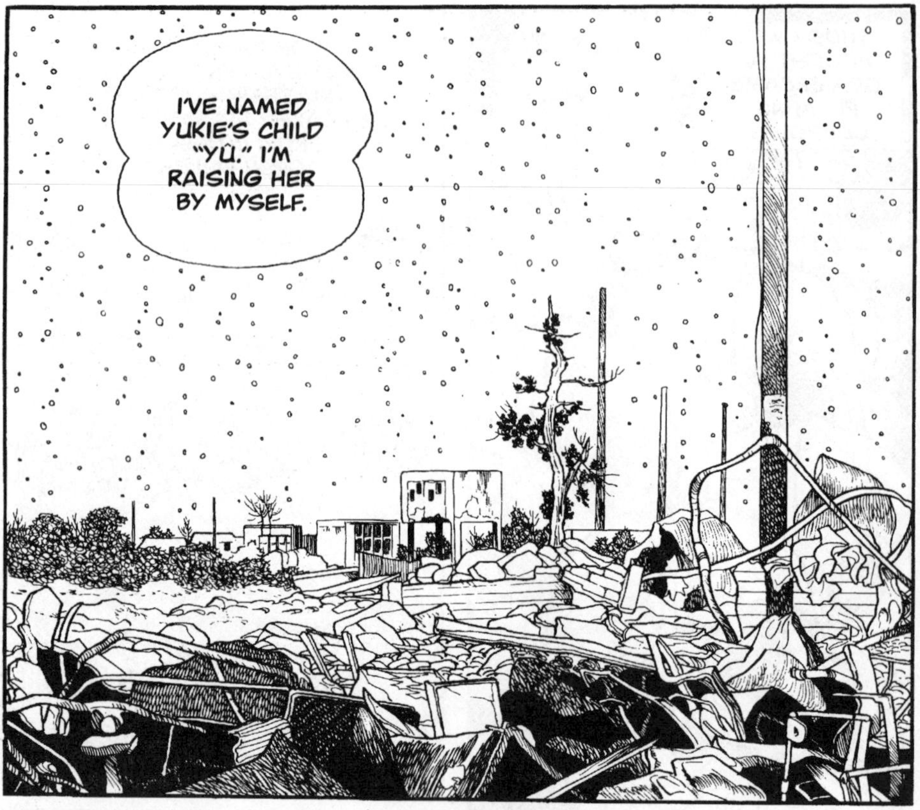
I'VE NAMED YUKIE'S CHILD "YÛ." I'M RAISING HER BY MYSELF.

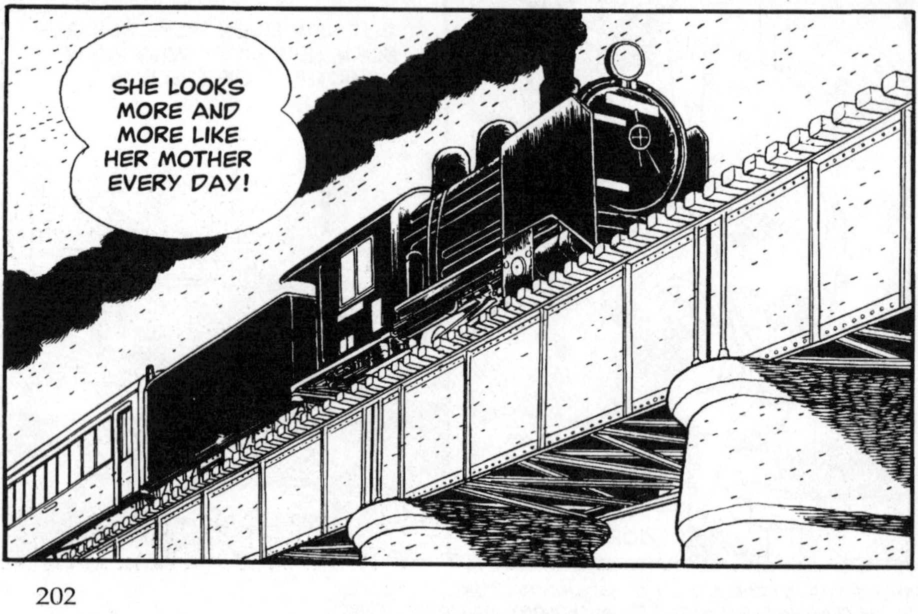
SHE LOOKS MORE AND MORE LIKE HER MOTHER EVERY DAY!

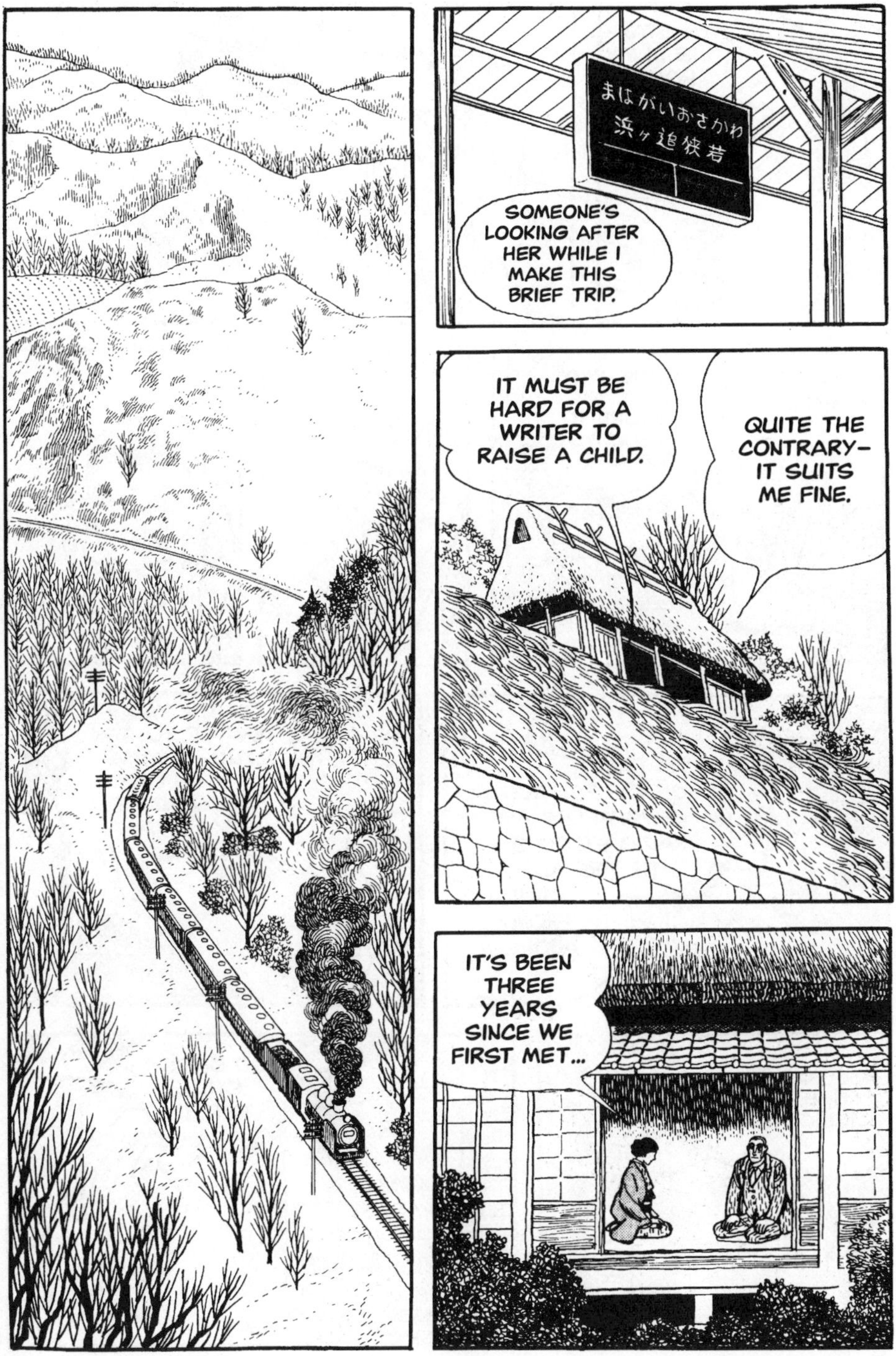
まはがいおさかわ
浜ヶ追狭若
SOMEONE'S LOOKING AFTER HER WHILE I MAKE THIS BRIEF TRIP.
IT MUST BE HARD FOR A WRITER TO RAISE A CHILD.
QUITE THE CONTRARY– IT SUITS ME FINE.
IT'S BEEN THREE YEARS SINCE WE FIRST MET...

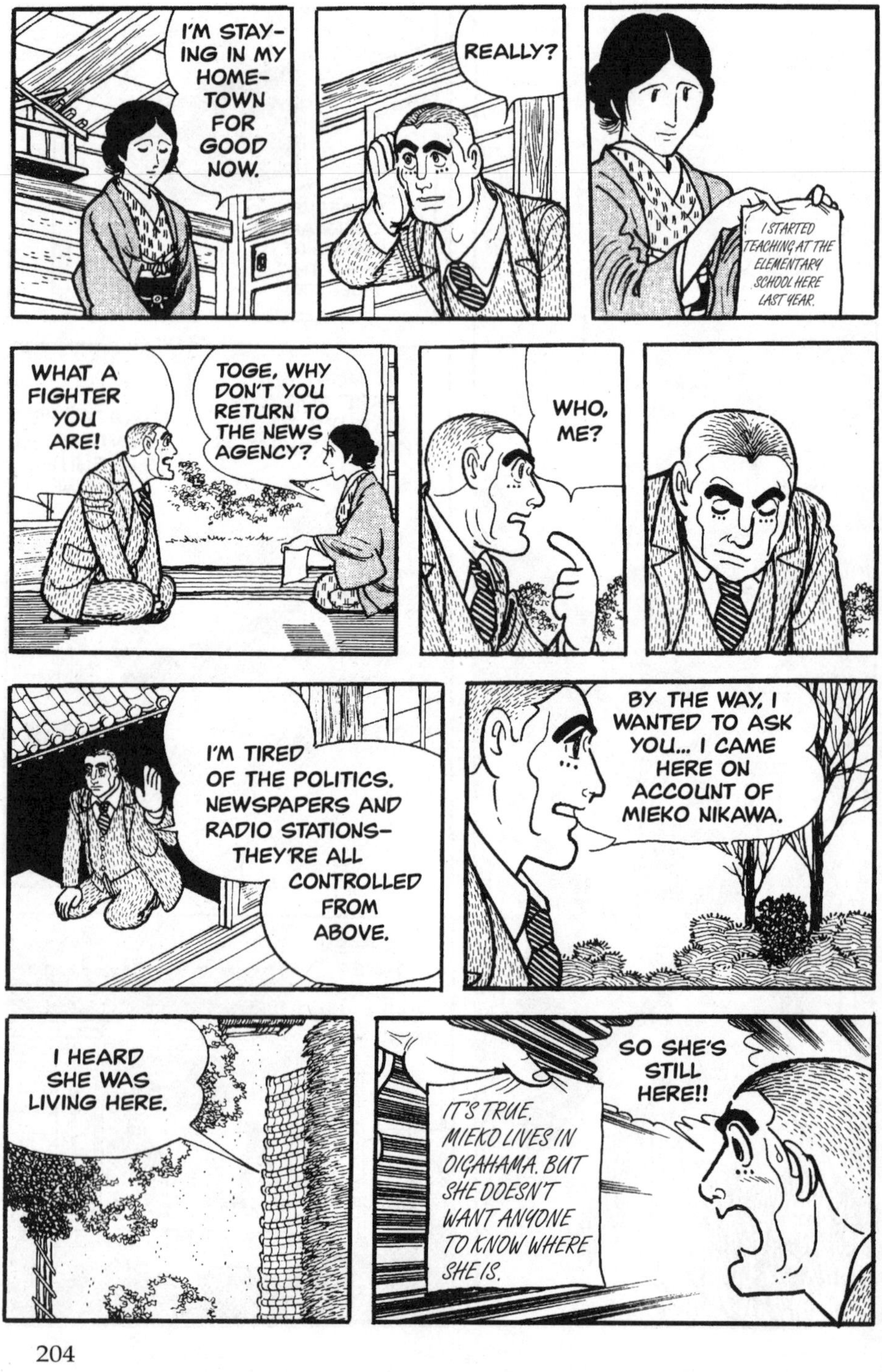
I'M STAYING IN MY HOMETOWN FOR GOOD NOW.
REALLY?
I STARTED TEACHING AT THE ELEMENTARY SCHOOL HERE LAST YEAR.
WHAT A FIGHTER YOU ARE!
TOGE, WHY DON'T YOU RETURN TO THE NEWS AGENCY?
WHO, ME?
I'M TIRED OF THE POLITICS. NEWSPAPERS AND RADIO STATIONS- THEY'RE ALL CONTROLLED FROM ABOVE.
BY THE WAY, I WANTED TO ASK YOU... I CAME HERE ON ACCOUNT OF MIEKO NIKAWA.
I HEARD SHE WAS LIVING HERE.
IT'S TRUE. MIEKO LIVES IN OIGAHAMA. BUT SHE DOESN'T WANT ANYONE TO KNOW WHERE SHE IS.
SO SHE'S STILL HERE!!

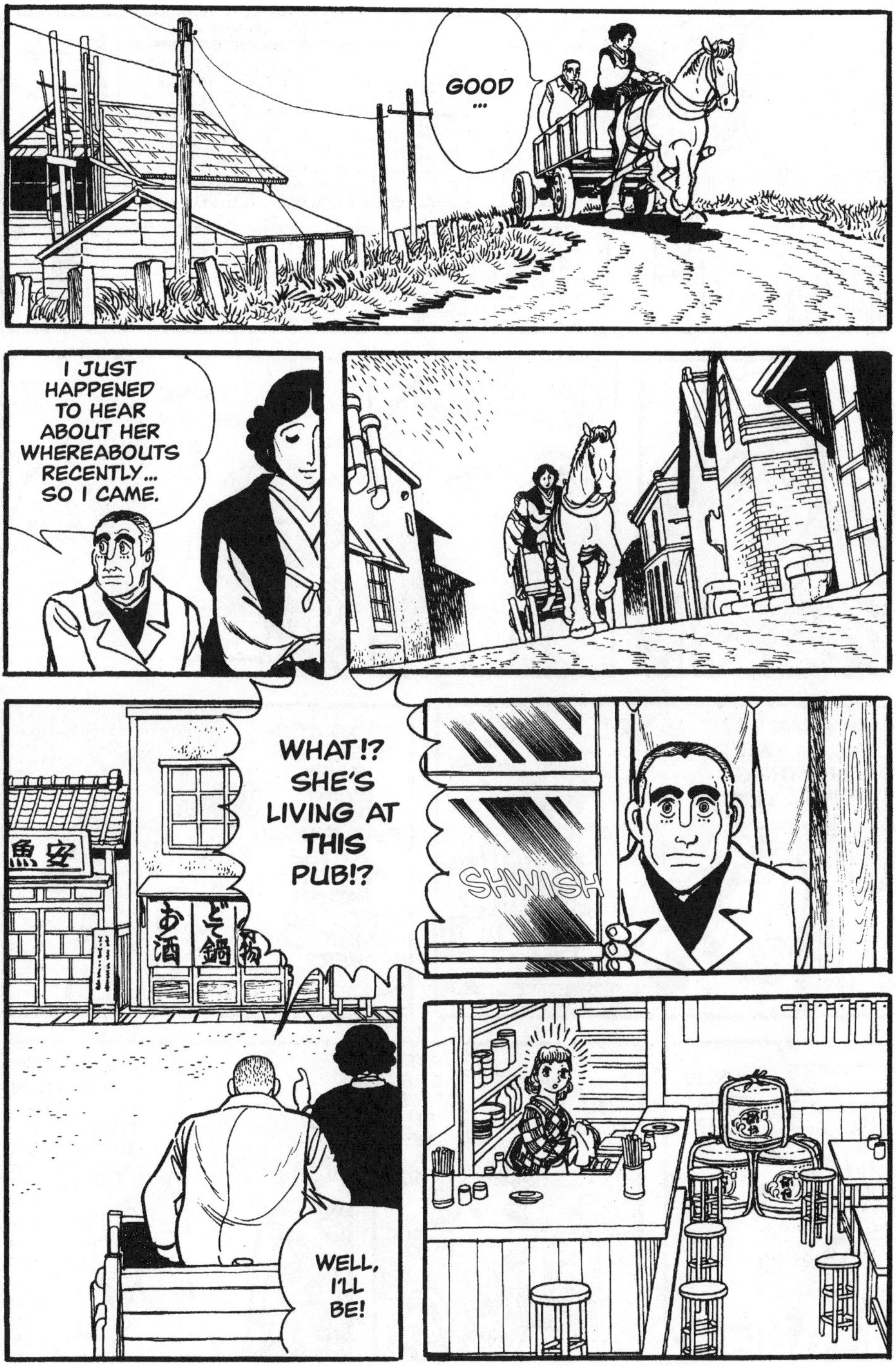
GOOD ...
I JUST HAPPENED TO HEAR ABOUT HER WHEREABOUTS RECENTLY... SO I CAME.
魚安
お酒
どて鍋
WHAT!? SHE'S LIVING AT THIS PUB!?
WELL, I'LL BE!
SHWISH

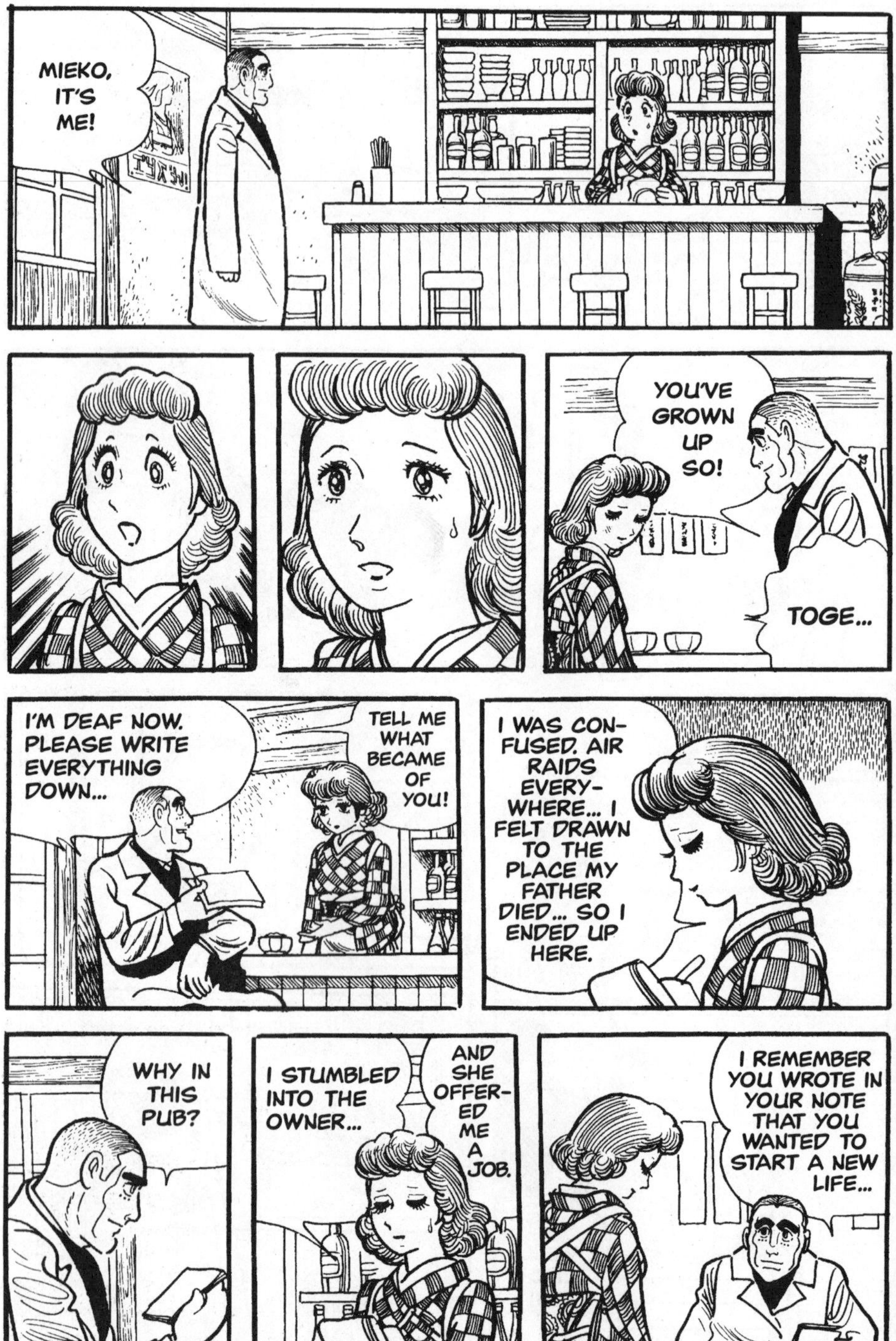
MIEKO, IT'S ME!
YOU'VE GROWN UP SO!
TOGE...
I'M DEAF NOW. PLEASE WRITE EVERYTHING DOWN...
TELL ME WHAT BECAME OF YOU!
I WAS CONFUSED. AIR RAIDS EVERYWHERE... I FELT DRAWN TO THE PLACE MY FATHER DIED... SO I ENDED UP HERE.
WHY IN THIS PUB?
I STUMBLED INTO THE OWNER...
AND SHE OFFERED ME A JOB.
I REMEMBER YOU WROTE IN YOUR NOTE THAT YOU WANTED TO START A NEW LIFE...

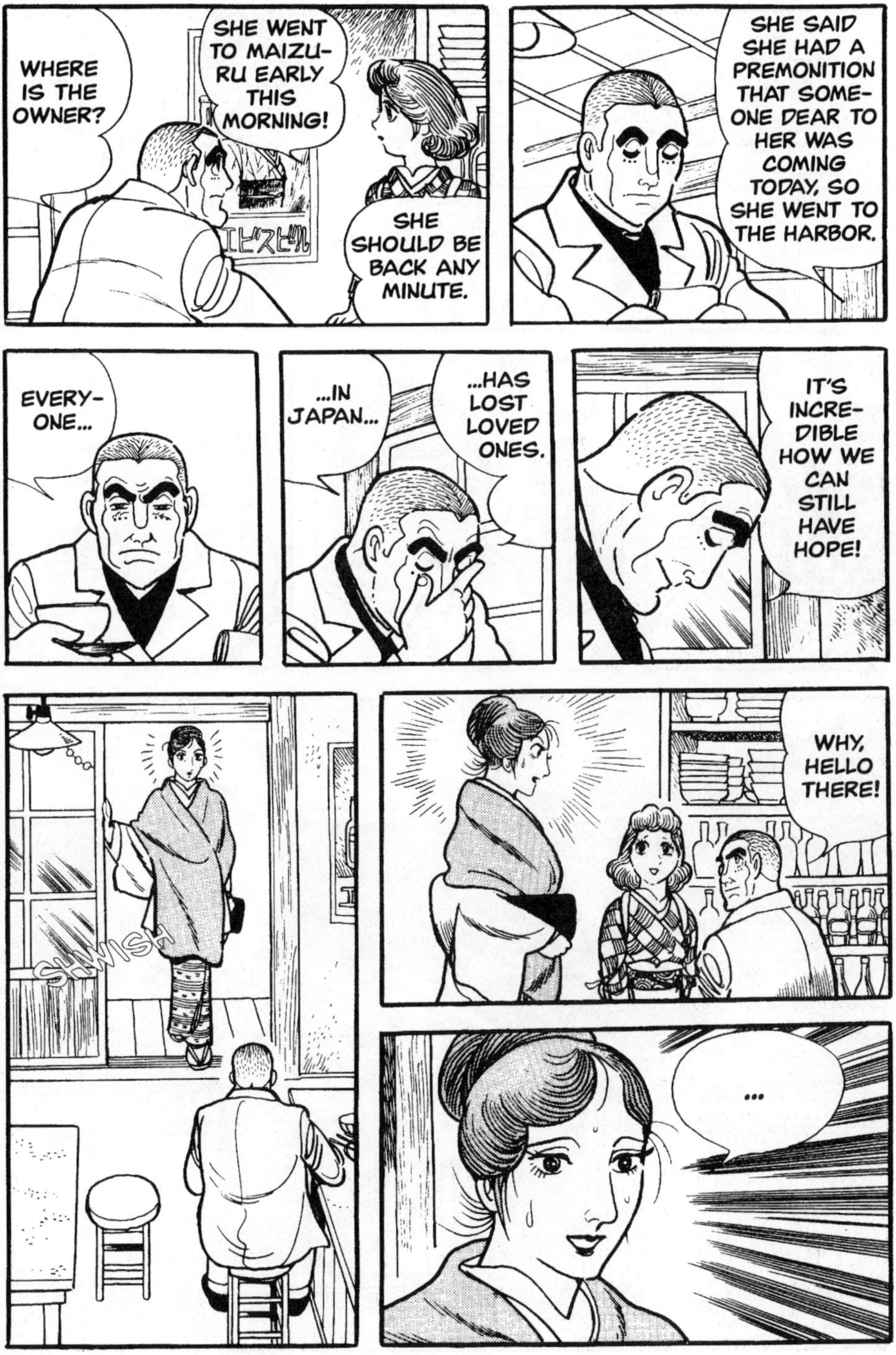
WHERE IS THE OWNER?
SHE WENT TO MAIZURU EARLY THIS MORNING!
エビスビール
SHE SHOULD BE BACK ANY MINUTE.
SHE SAID SHE HAD A PREMONITION THAT SOMEONE DEAR TO HER WAS COMING TODAY, SO SHE WENT TO THE HARBOR.
EVERYONE...
...IN JAPAN...
...HAS LOST LOVED ONES.
IT'S INCREDIBLE HOW WE CAN STILL HAVE HOPE!
SHWISH
WHY, HELLO THERE!
...

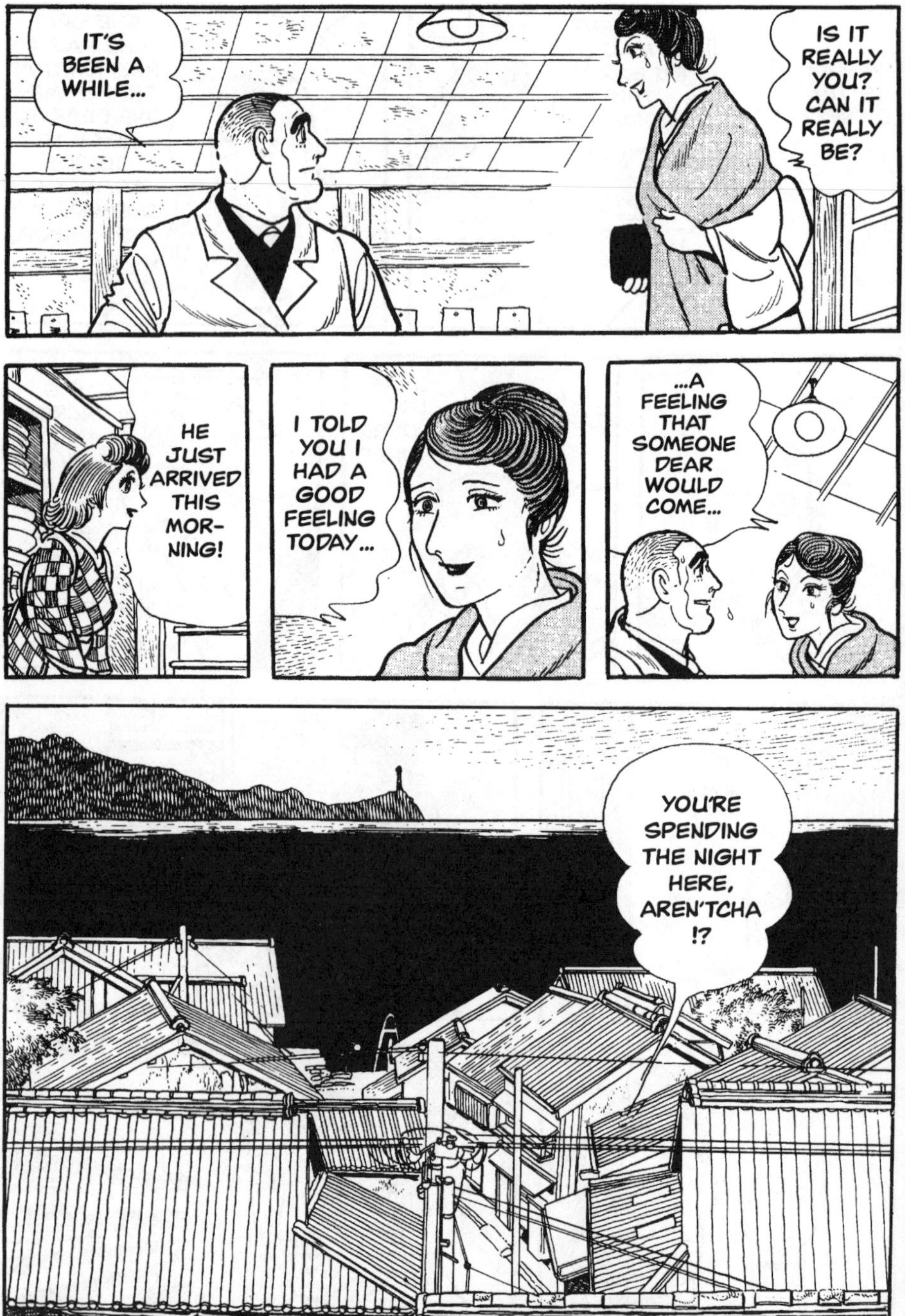
IT'S BEEN A WHILE...
IS IT REALLY YOU? CAN IT REALLY BE?
HE JUST ARRIVED THIS MOR-NING!
I TOLD YOU I HAD A GOOD FEELING TODAY...
...A FEELING THAT SOMEONE DEAR WOULD COME...
YOU'RE SPENDING THE NIGHT HERE, AREN'TCHA !?

CHAPTER
EIGHT

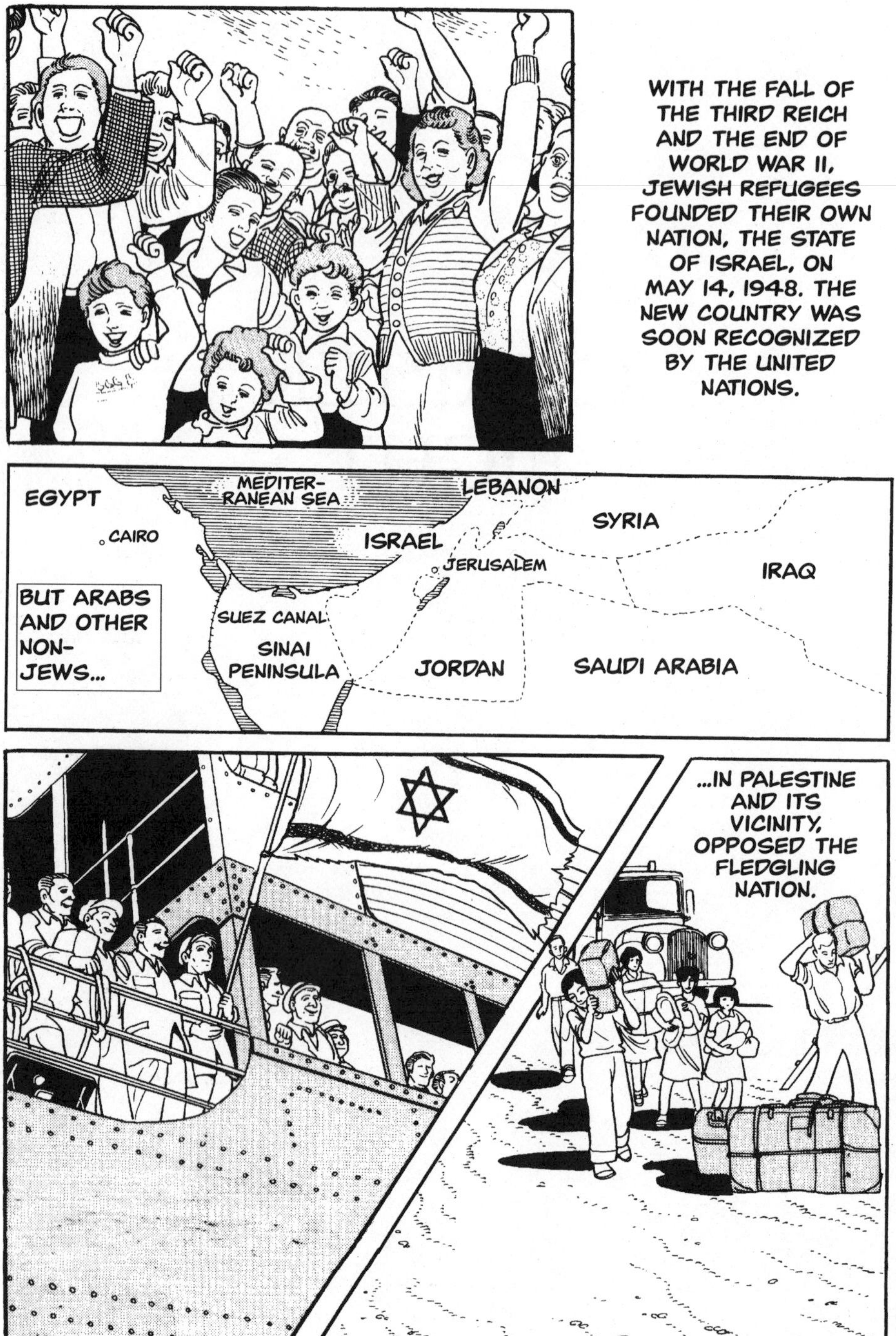
WITH THE FALL OF THE THIRD REICH AND THE END OF WORLD WAR II, JEWISH REFUGEES FOUNDED THEIR OWN NATION, THE STATE OF ISRAEL, ON MAY 14, 1948. THE NEW COUNTRY WAS SOON RECOGNIZED BY THE UNITED NATIONS.
EGYPT
MEDITER-RANEAN SEA
LEBANON
CAIRO
ISRAEL
SYRIA
JERUSALEM
IRAQ
BUT ARABS AND OTHER NON-JEWS...
SUEZ CANAL
SINAI PENINSULA
JORDAN
SAUDI ARABIA
...IN PALESTINE AND ITS VICINITY, OPPOSED THE FLEDGLING NATION.

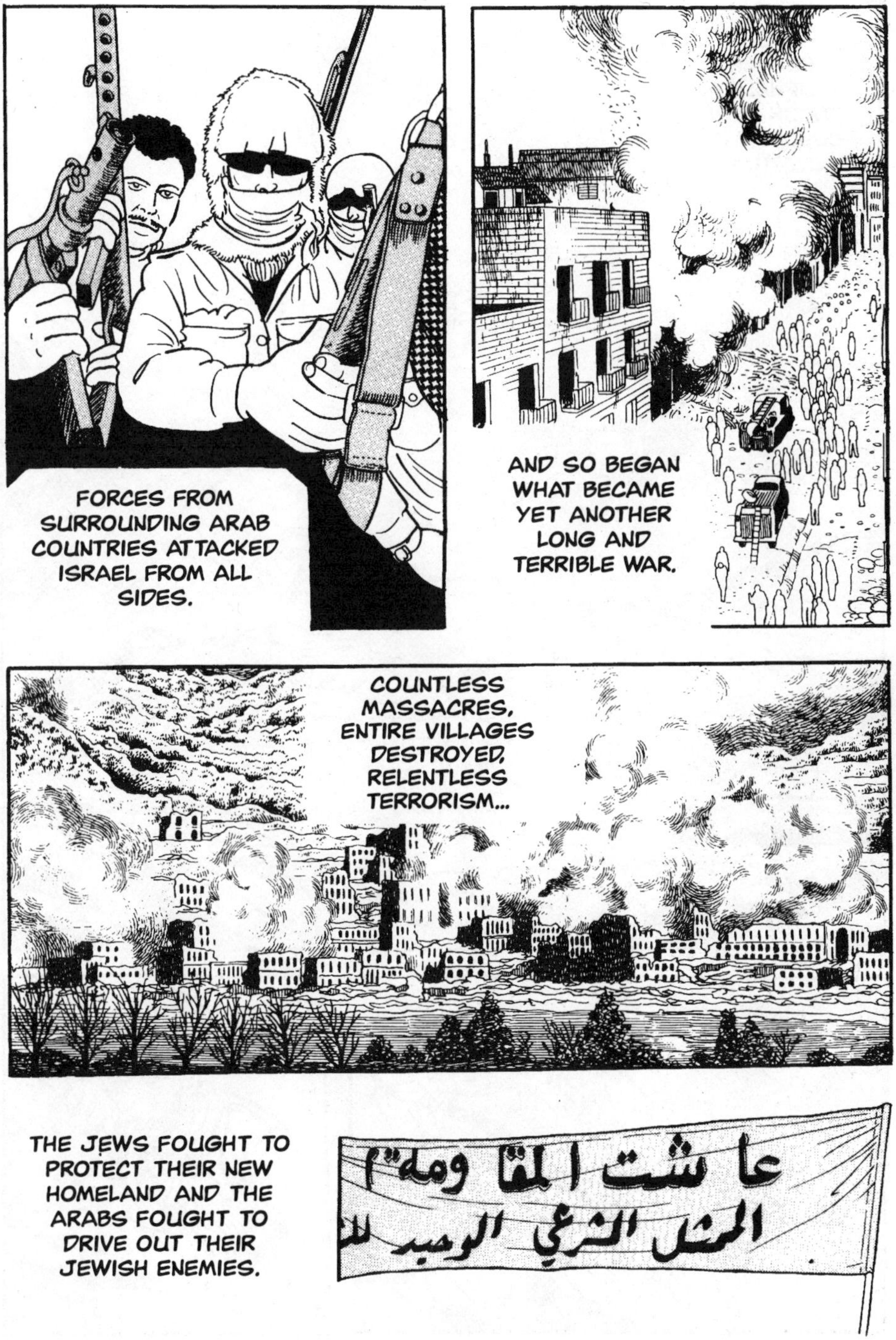
FORCES FROM SURROUNDING ARAB COUNTRIES ATTACKED ISRAEL FROM ALL SIDES.
AND SO BEGAN WHAT BECAME YET ANOTHER LONG AND TERRIBLE WAR.
COUNTLESS MASSACRES, ENTIRE VILLAGES DESTROYED, RELENTLESS TERRORISM...
THE JEWS FOUGHT TO PROTECT THEIR NEW HOMELAND AND THE ARABS FOUGHT TO DRIVE OUT THEIR JEWISH ENEMIES.
عاشت المقاومة
الممثل الشرعي الوحيد لل

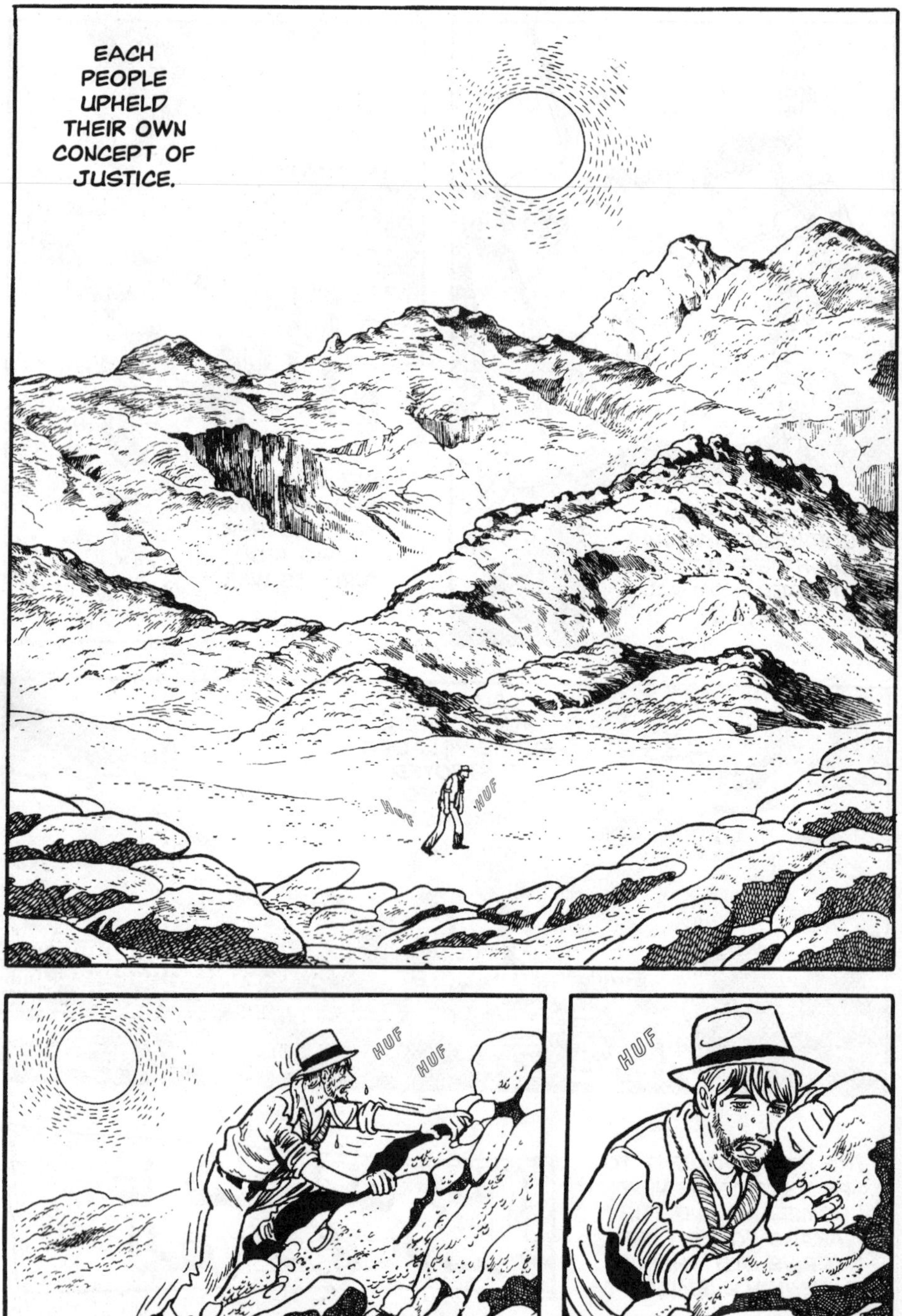
EACH PEOPLE UPHELD THEIR OWN CONCEPT OF JUSTICE.
HUF
HUF
HUF
HUF
HUF

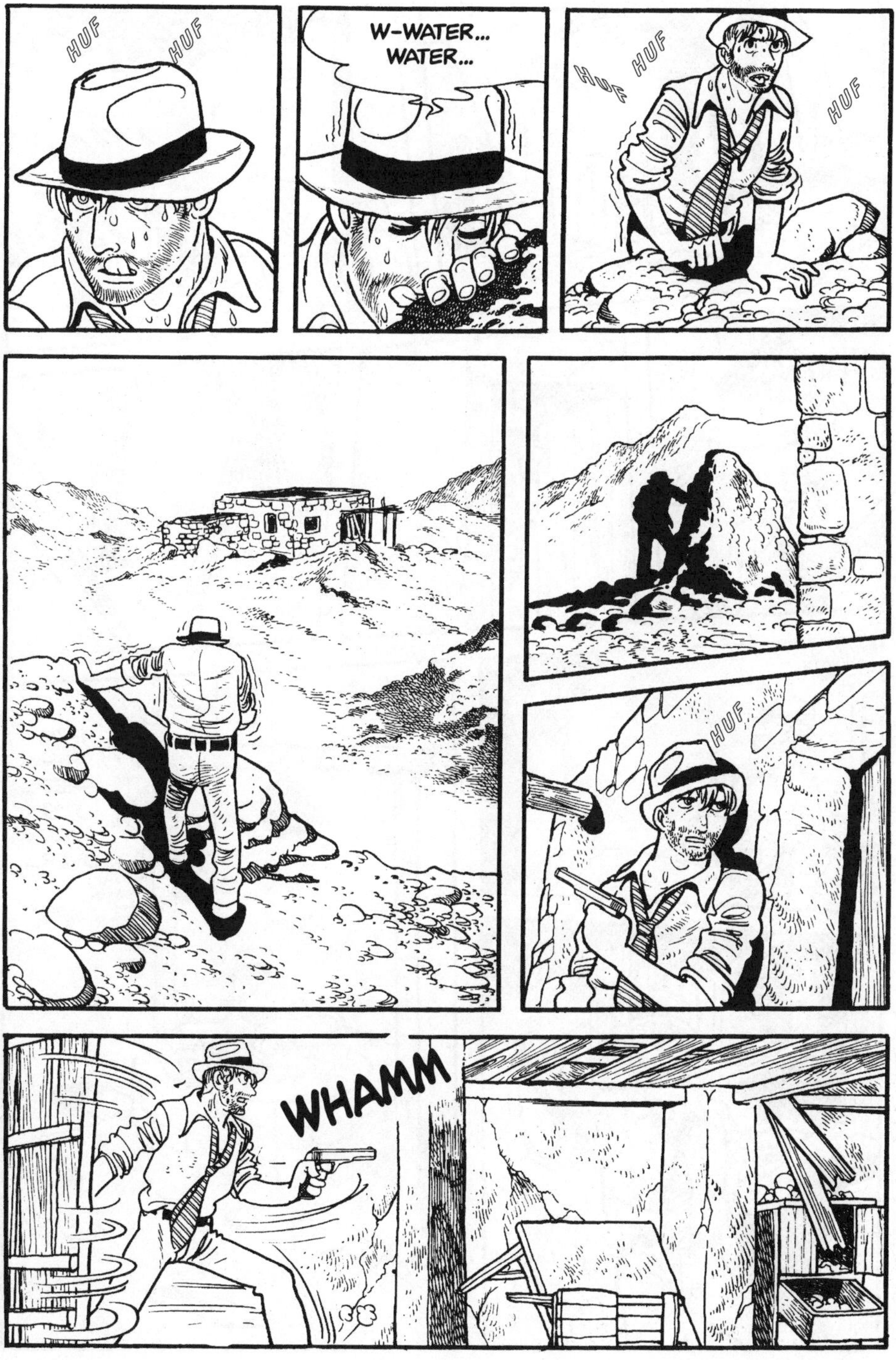
HUF
HUF
W-WATER...
WATER...
HUF
HUF
HUF
HUF
WHAMM

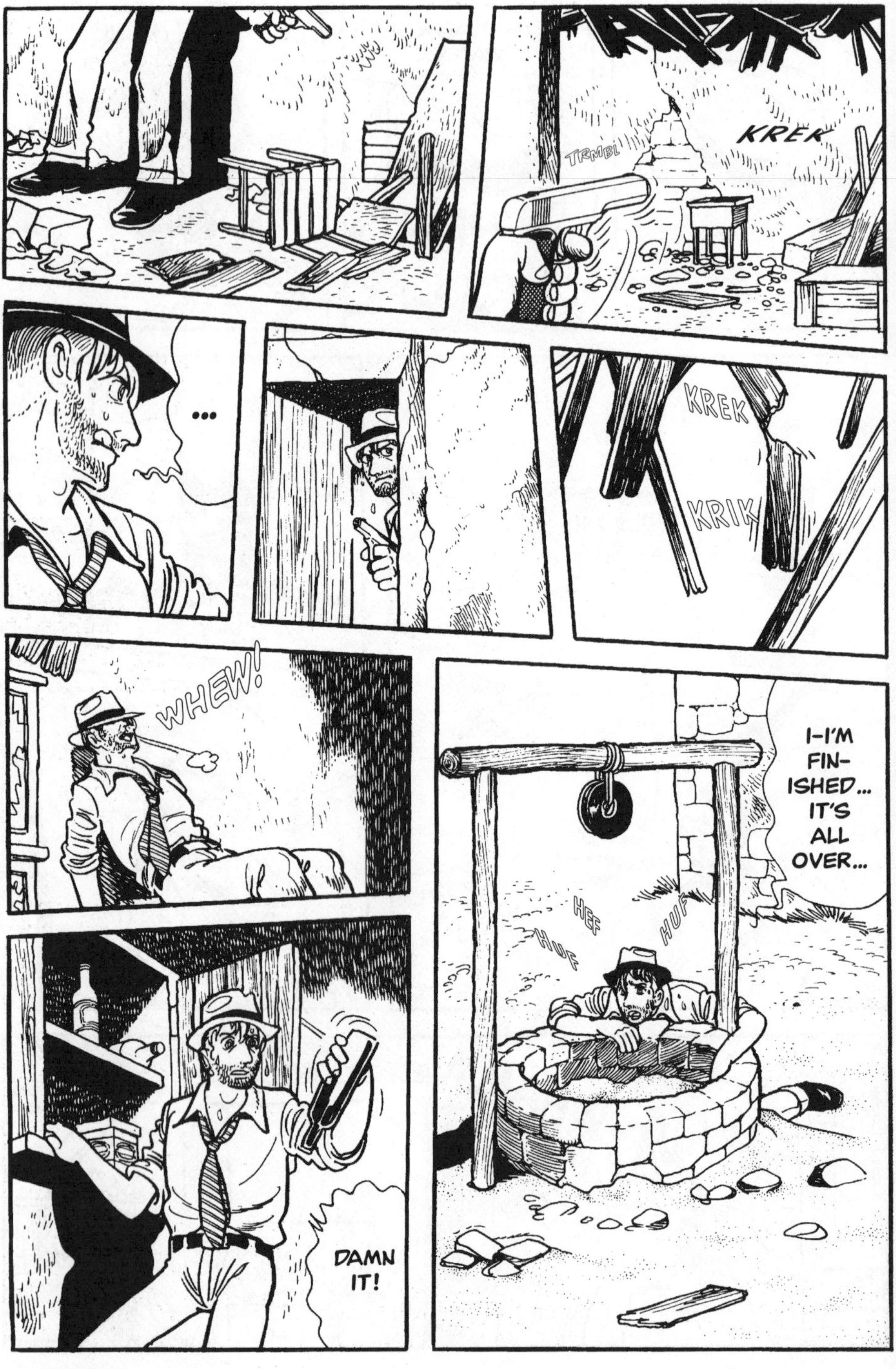
TRMBL
KREK
...
KREK
KRIK
WHEW!
I-I'M FIN-ISHED... IT'S ALL OVER...
HEF
HUF
HUF
DAMN IT!

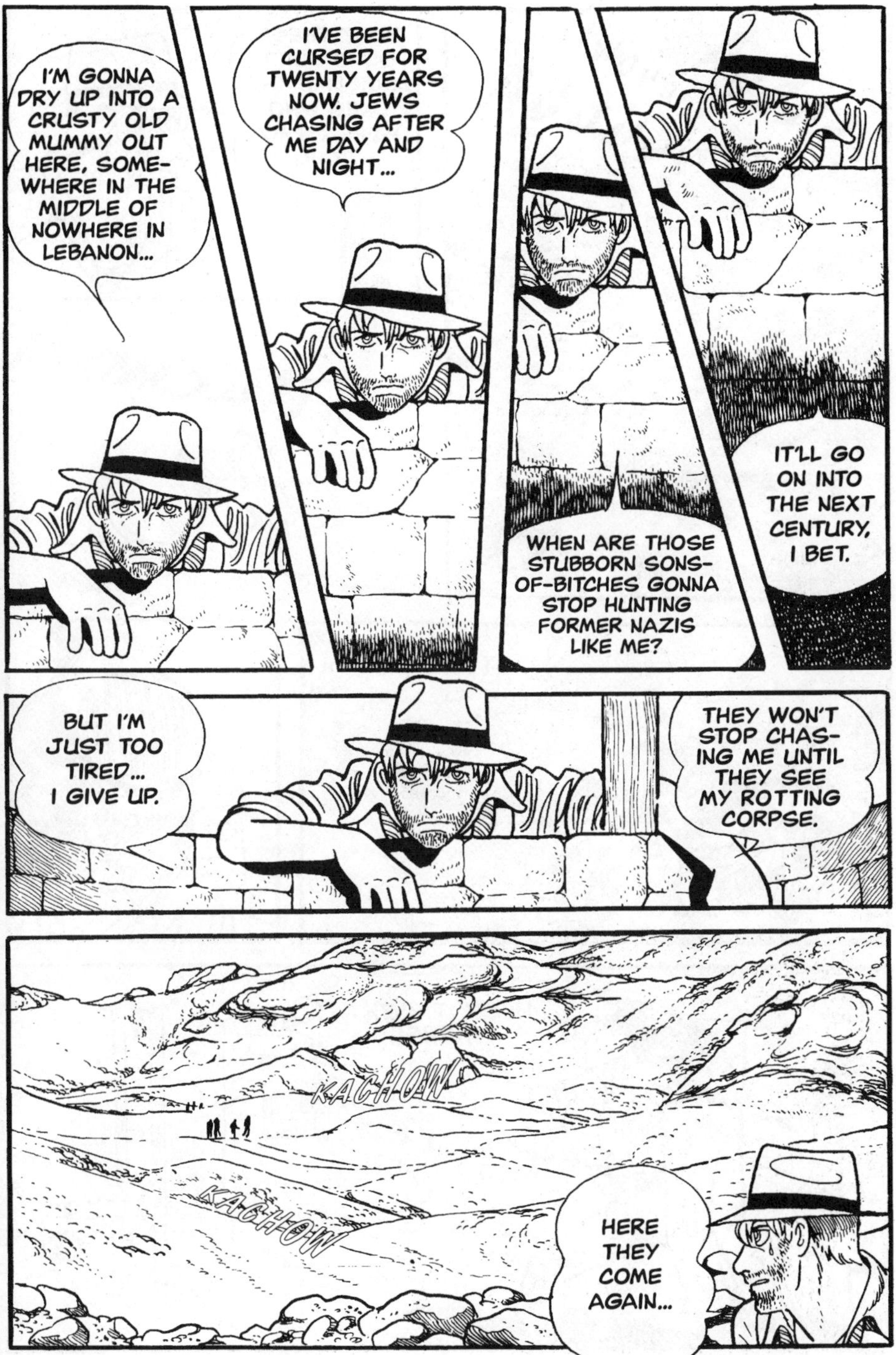
I'M GONNA DRY UP INTO A CRUSTY OLD MUMMY OUT HERE, SOME-WHERE IN THE MIDDLE OF NOWHERE IN LEBANON...
I'VE BEEN CURSED FOR TWENTY YEARS NOW. JEWS CHASING AFTER ME DAY AND NIGHT...
WHEN ARE THOSE STUBBORN SONS-OF-BITCHES GONNA STOP HUNTING FORMER NAZIS LIKE ME?
IT'LL GO ON INTO THE NEXT CENTURY, I BET.
BUT I'M JUST TOO TIRED... I GIVE UP.
THEY WON'T STOP CHAS-ING ME UNTIL THEY SEE MY ROTTING CORPSE.
KACHOW
KACHOW
HERE THEY COME AGAIN...

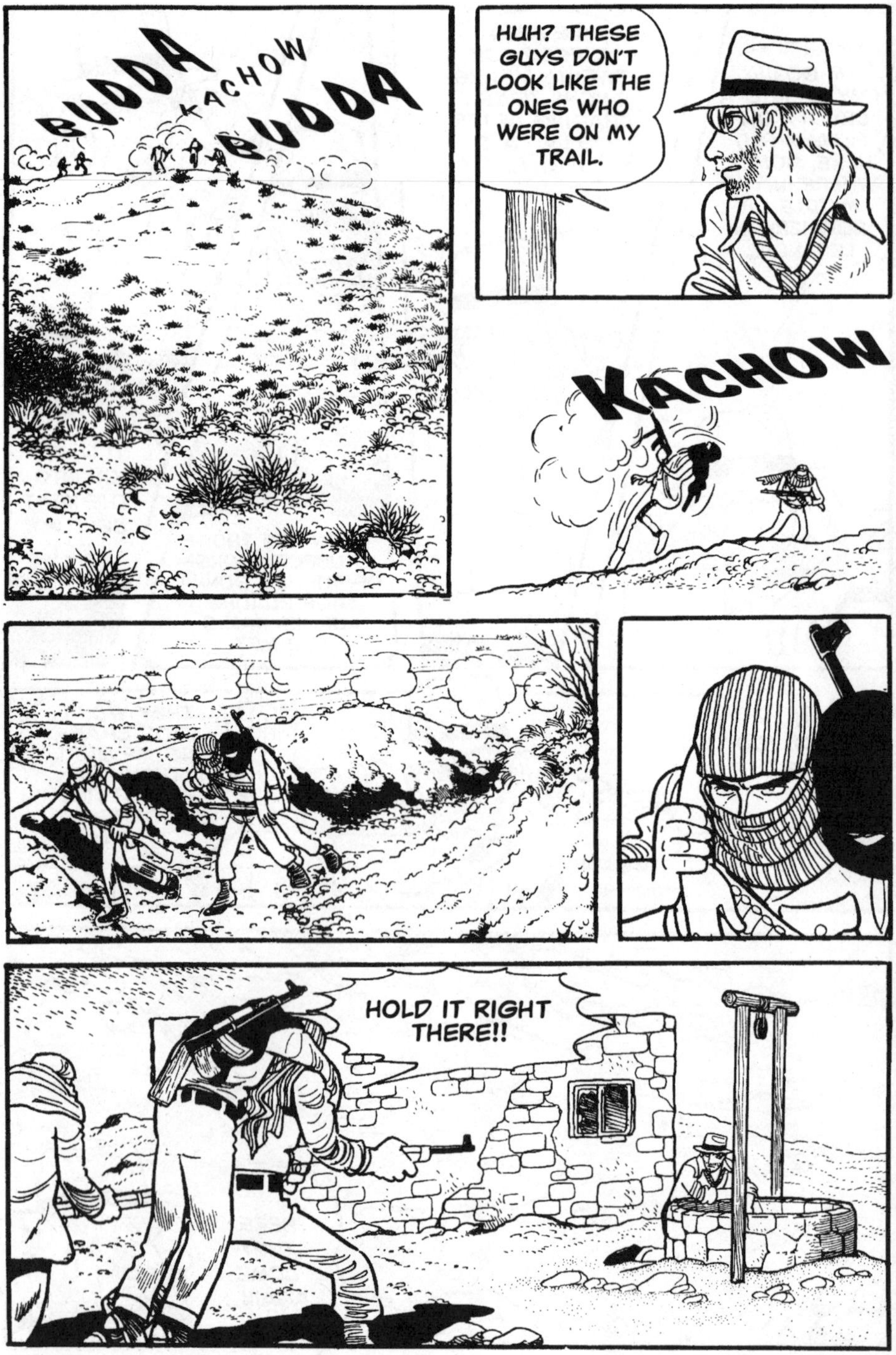
BUDDA
KACHOW
BUDDA
HUH? THESE GUYS DON'T LOOK LIKE THE ONES WHO WERE ON MY TRAIL.
KACHOW
HOLD IT RIGHT THERE!!

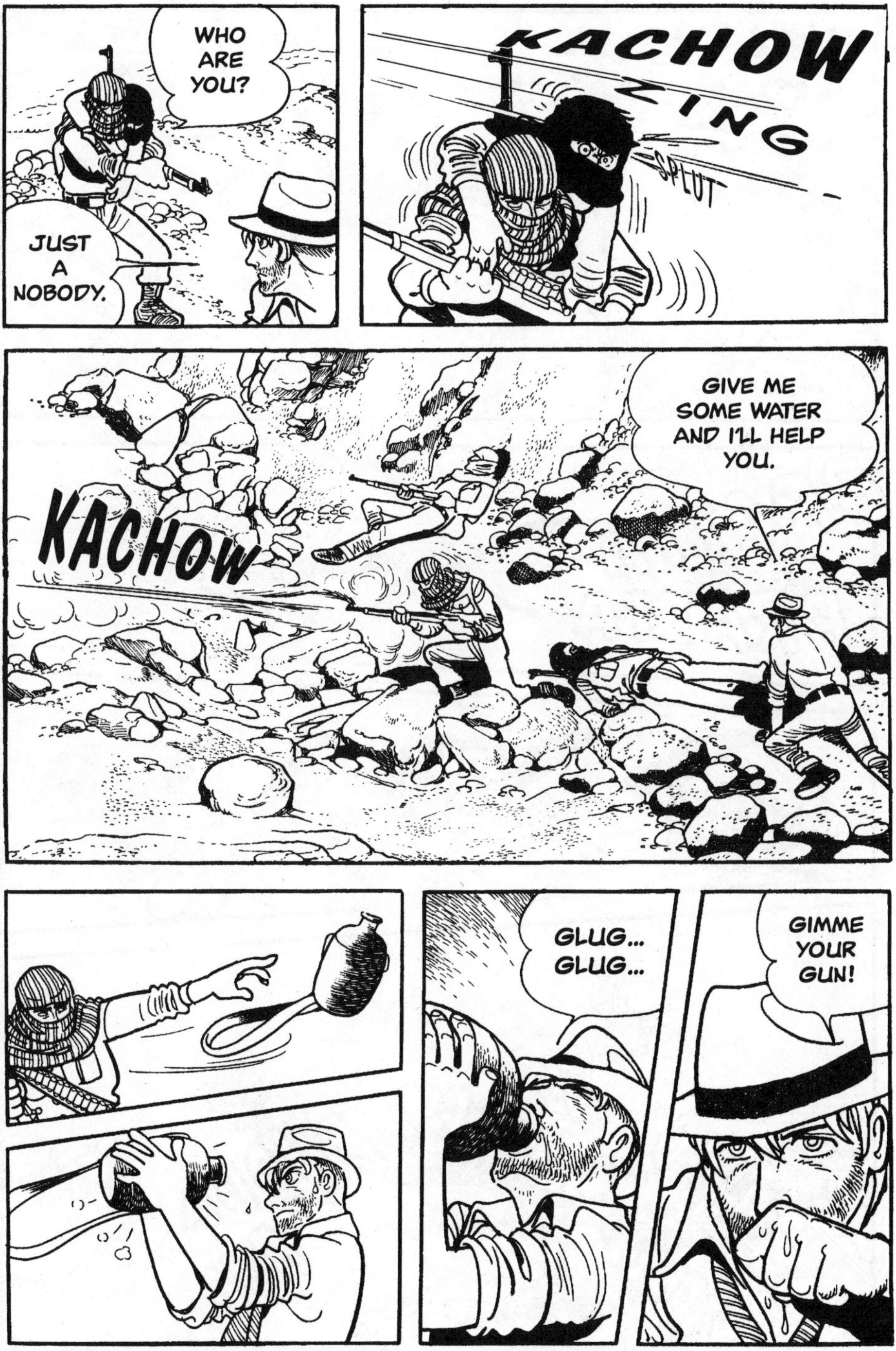
WHO ARE YOU?
JUST A NOBODY.
KACHOW
ZING
SPLUT
KACHOW
GIVE ME SOME WATER AND I'LL HELP YOU.
GLUG... GLUG...
GIMME YOUR GUN!

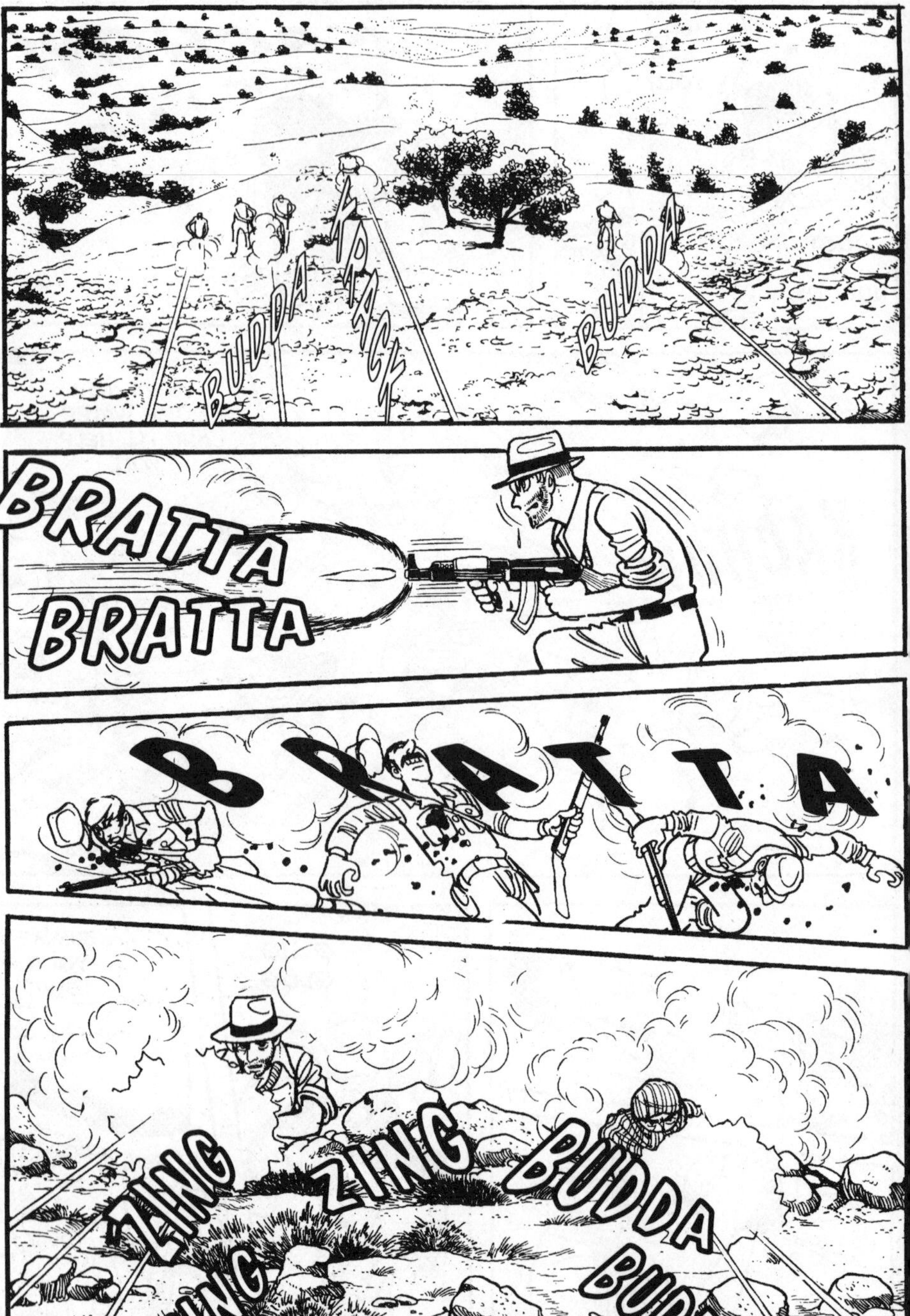
BUDDA
KRACK
BUDDA
BRATTA
BRATTA
BRATTA
ZING
ZING
ZING
BUDDA
BUDDA

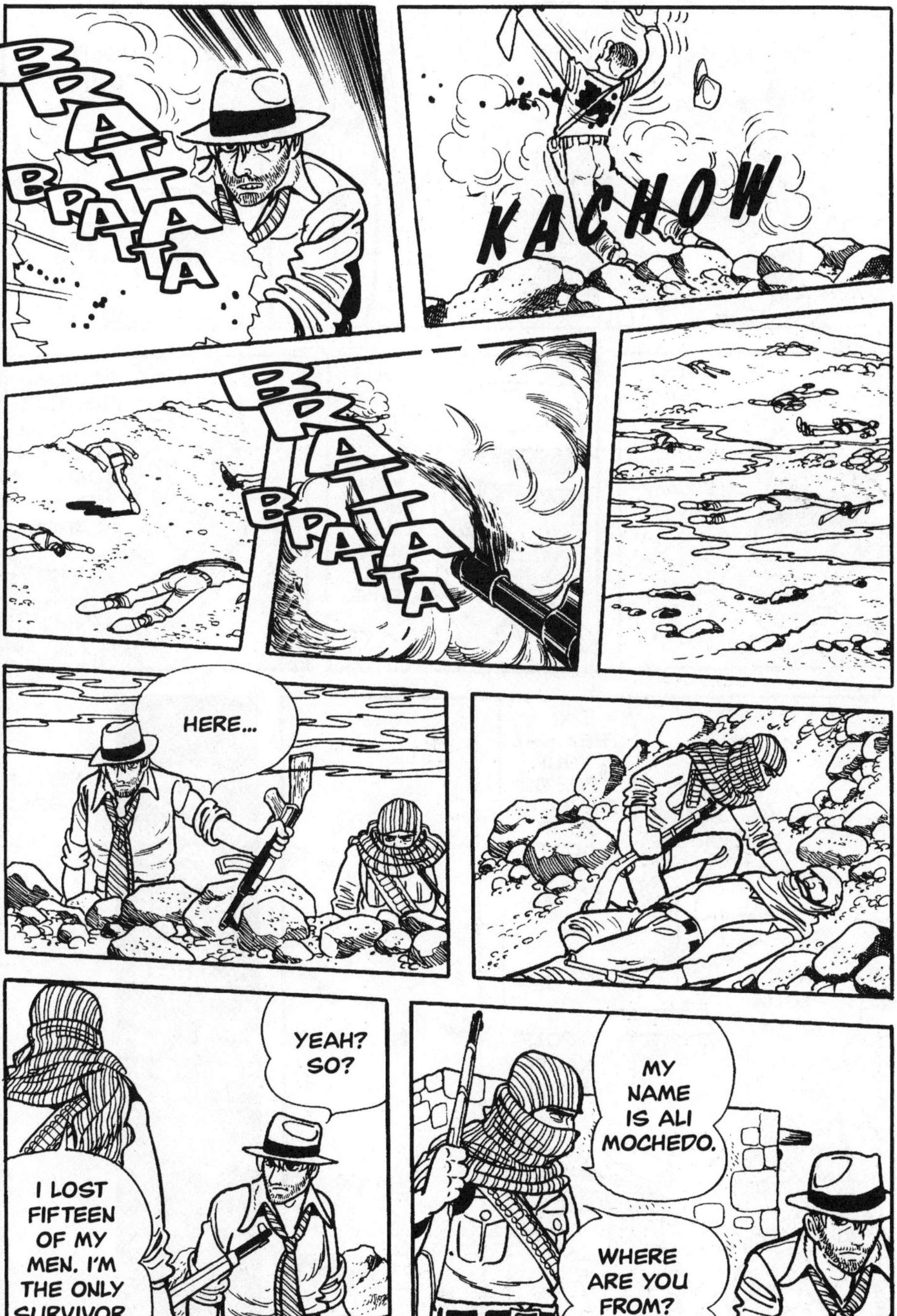
BRATTA
BRATTA
KACHOW
BRATTA
BRATTA
HERE...
YEAH? SO?
I LOST FIFTEEN OF MY MEN. I'M THE ONLY SURVIVOR.
MY NAME IS ALI MOCHEDO.
WHERE ARE YOU FROM?

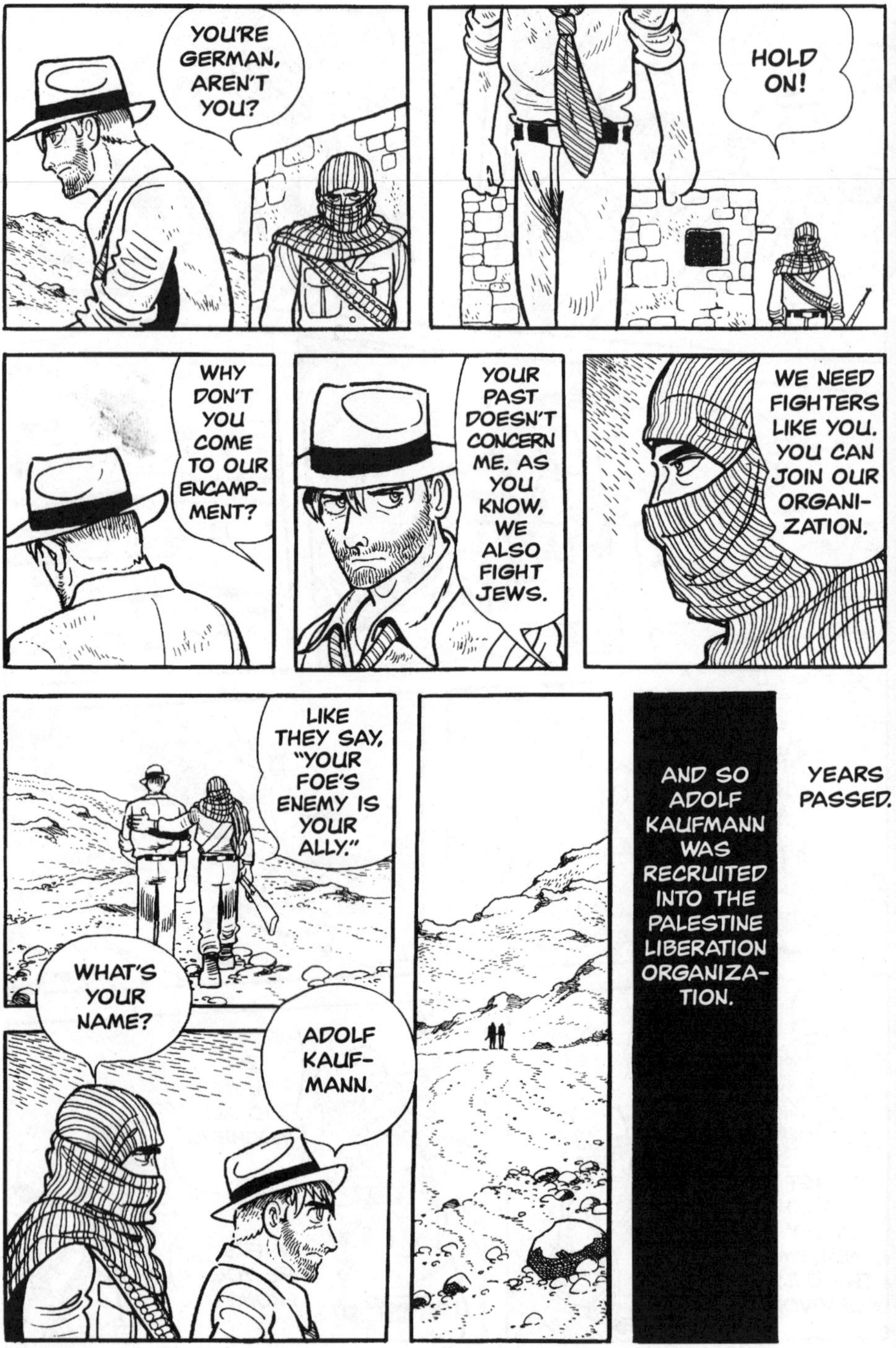
YOU'RE GERMAN, AREN'T YOU?
HOLD ON!
WHY DON'T YOU COME TO OUR ENCAMPMENT?
YOUR PAST DOESN'T CONCERN ME. AS YOU KNOW, WE ALSO FIGHT JEWS.
WE NEED FIGHTERS LIKE YOU. YOU CAN JOIN OUR ORGANIZATION.
LIKE THEY SAY, "YOUR FOE'S ENEMY IS YOUR ALLY."
WHAT'S YOUR NAME?
ADOLF KAUFMANN.
AND SO ADOLF KAUFMANN WAS RECRUITED INTO THE PALESTINE LIBERATION ORGANIZATION.
YEARS PASSED.

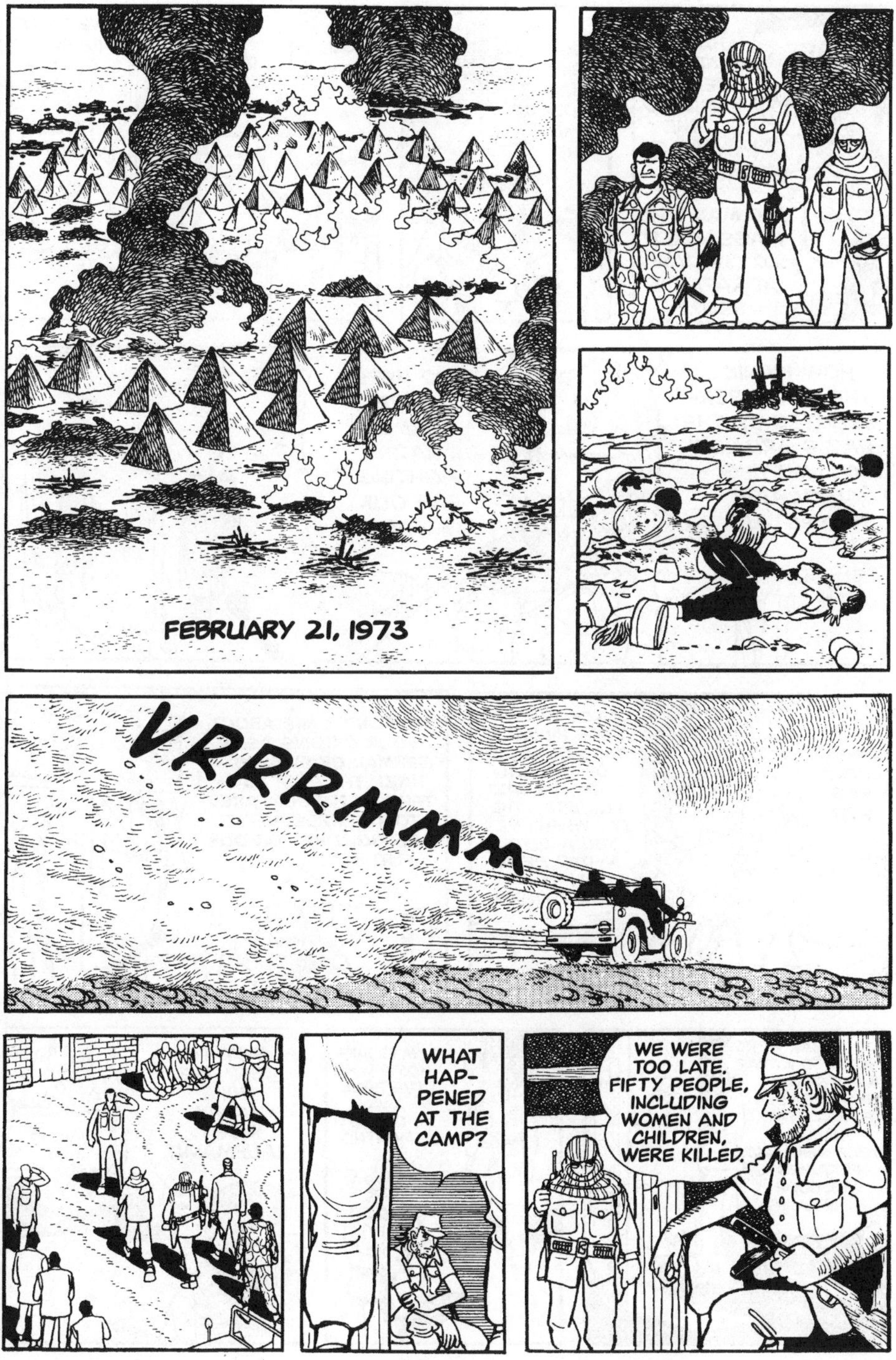
FEBRUARY 21, 1973
VRRRMMMM
WHAT HAP-PENED AT THE CAMP?
WE WERE TOO LATE. FIFTY PEOPLE, INCLUDING WOMEN AND CHILDREN, WERE KILLED.

Adolf

RUMOR HAS IT THAT LIEUTENANT KAMIL LED THE ATTACK.

THE MAN WHO MASSACRED 20 CIVILIANS AT RAFAH IN 1967.

LIEUTENANT ADOLF KAMIL, EH?

YOU KNOW HIM?

WE WERE FRIENDS DURING MY DAYS AS A HITLER YOUTH...

HOW IRONIC... THE JEWS PERSECUTED BY THE NAZIS ARE NOW COMMITTING ATROCITIES AGAINST US.

AND HERE YOU ARE, A FORMER NAZI, FIGHTING FOR OUR LIBERATION.

TEN YEARS HAVE PASSED...

...SINCE THAT DAY I WAS HIDING IN THE MOUNTAINS ON THE RUN FROM THE NAZI HUNTERS... THE DAY WHEN I MET YOU AND YOU INVITED ME TO JOIN "BLACK SEPTEMBER."

WE DON'T CARE ABOUT YOUR ORIGINS AS A GERMAN OR EVEN AS A NAZI. THE PAST MATTERS LITTLE COMPARED TO THE PRESENT. WE ARE FIGHTING FOR OUR FUTURE!

NEXT YEAR WE'RE GOING TO KIDNAP A DUTCH MAN WHO HAS BEEN FUNDING THE ISRAELIS. YOUR GERMANIC FEATURES WILL COME IN HANDY.

I'M GOING HOME NOW. I'VE BEEN AWAY FOR TWO MONTHS.

GOT TO KEEP THE WIFE HAPPY, RIGHT, KAUFMANN?

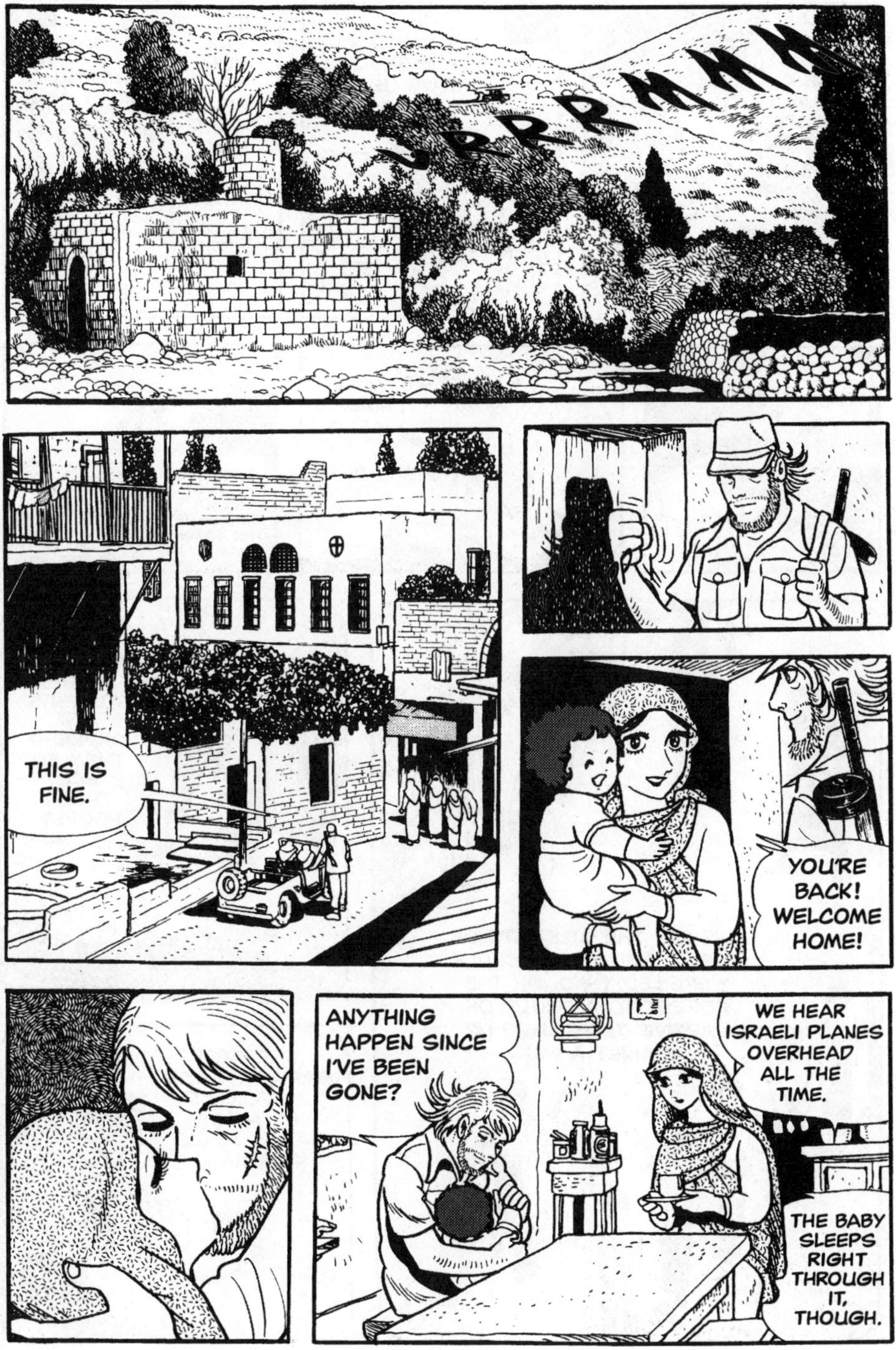
VRRRMMMM
THIS IS FINE.
YOU'RE BACK! WELCOME HOME!
ANYTHING HAPPEN SINCE I'VE BEEN GONE?
WE HEAR ISRAELI PLANES OVERHEAD ALL THE TIME.
THE BABY SLEEPS RIGHT THROUGH IT, THOUGH.

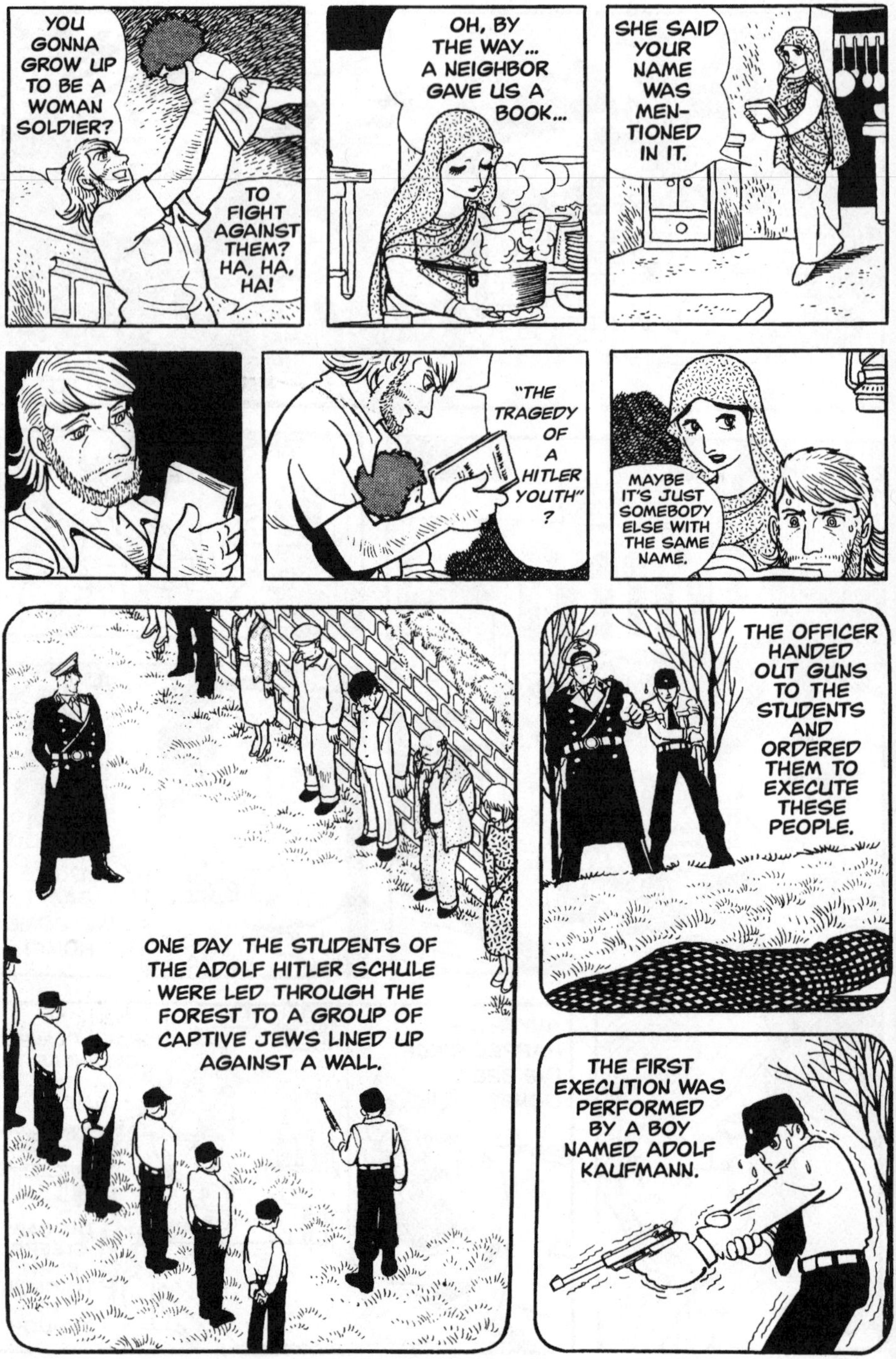
YOU GONNA GROW UP TO BE A WOMAN SOLDIER?
TO FIGHT AGAINST THEM? HA, HA, HA!
OH, BY THE WAY... A NEIGHBOR GAVE US A BOOK...
SHE SAID YOUR NAME WAS MEN-TIONED IN IT.
"THE TRAGEDY OF A HITLER YOUTH"?
MAYBE IT'S JUST SOMEBODY ELSE WITH THE SAME NAME.
ONE DAY THE STUDENTS OF THE ADOLF HITLER SCHULE WERE LED THROUGH THE FOREST TO A GROUP OF CAPTIVE JEWS LINED UP AGAINST A WALL.
THE OFFICER HANDED OUT GUNS TO THE STUDENTS AND ORDERED THEM TO EXECUTE THESE PEOPLE.
THE FIRST EXECUTION WAS PERFORMED BY A BOY NAMED ADOLF KAUFMANN.

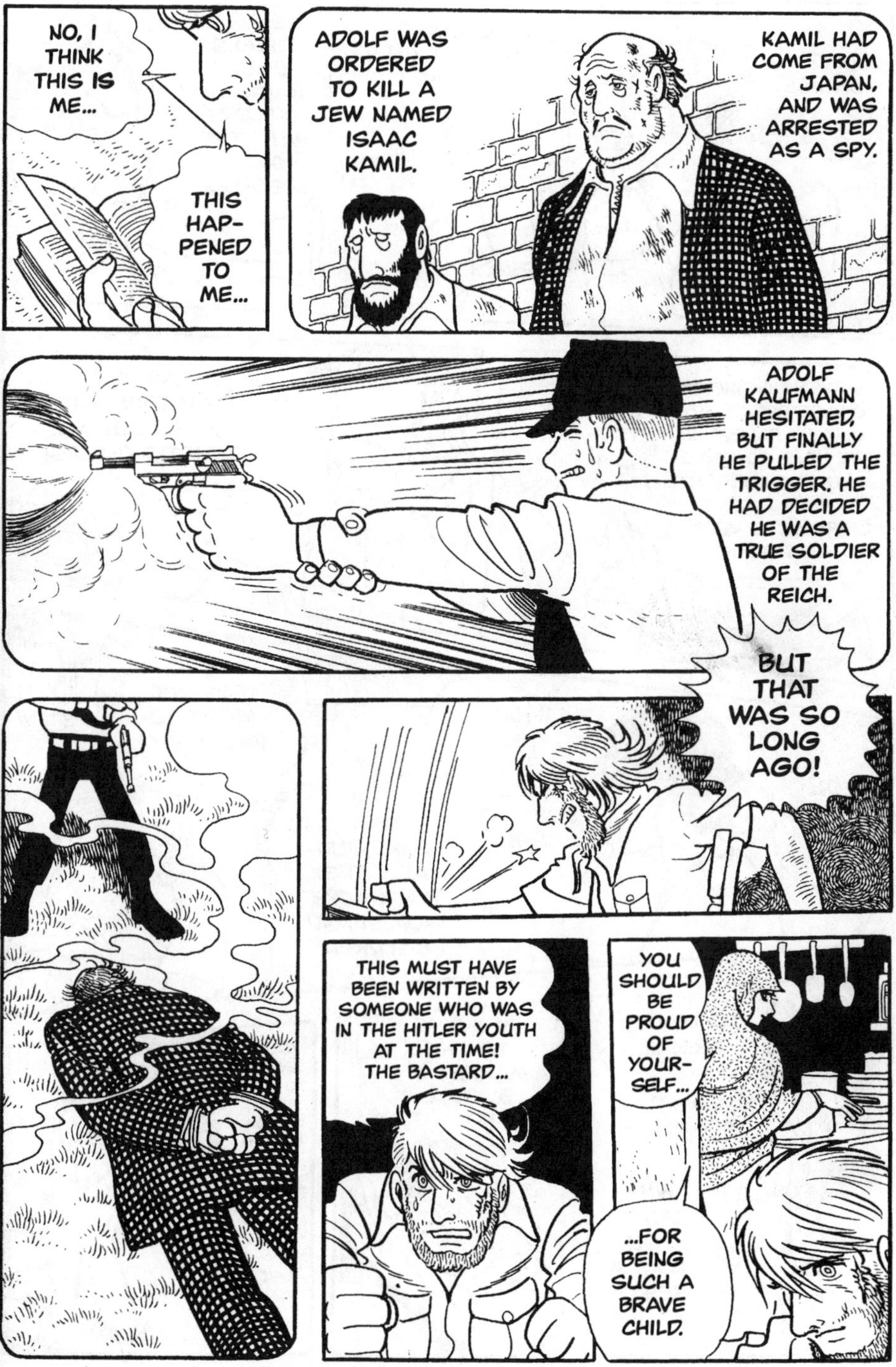
NO, I THINK THIS IS ME...
THIS HAP-PENED TO ME...
ADOLF WAS ORDERED TO KILL A JEW NAMED ISAAC KAMIL.
KAMIL HAD COME FROM JAPAN, AND WAS ARRESTED AS A SPY.
ADOLF KAUFMANN HESITATED, BUT FINALLY HE PULLED THE TRIGGER. HE HAD DECIDED HE WAS A TRUE SOLDIER OF THE REICH.
BUT THAT WAS SO LONG AGO!
THIS MUST HAVE BEEN WRITTEN BY SOMEONE WHO WAS IN THE HITLER YOUTH AT THE TIME! THE BASTARD...
YOU SHOULD BE PROUD OF YOUR-SELF...
...FOR BEING SUCH A BRAVE CHILD.

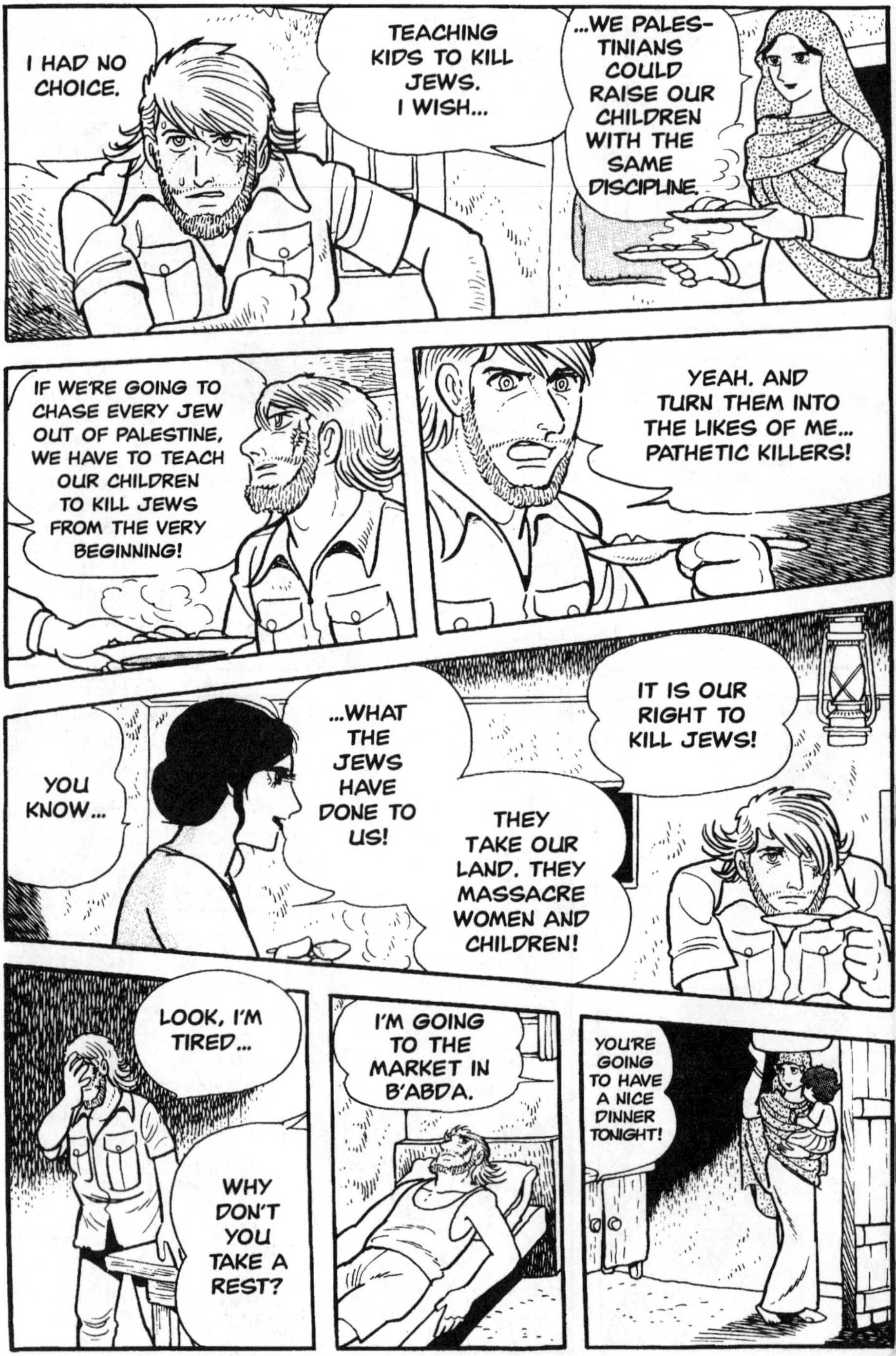
I HAD NO CHOICE.
TEACHING KIDS TO KILL JEWS. I WISH...
...WE PALESTINIANS COULD RAISE OUR CHILDREN WITH THE SAME DISCIPLINE.
IF WE'RE GOING TO CHASE EVERY JEW OUT OF PALESTINE, WE HAVE TO TEACH OUR CHILDREN TO KILL JEWS FROM THE VERY BEGINNING!
YEAH. AND TURN THEM INTO THE LIKES OF ME... PATHETIC KILLERS!
YOU KNOW...
...WHAT THE JEWS HAVE DONE TO US!
IT IS OUR RIGHT TO KILL JEWS!
THEY TAKE OUR LAND. THEY MASSACRE WOMEN AND CHILDREN!
LOOK, I'M TIRED...
WHY DON'T YOU TAKE A REST?
I'M GOING TO THE MARKET IN B'ABDA.
YOU'RE GOING TO HAVE A NICE DINNER TONIGHT!

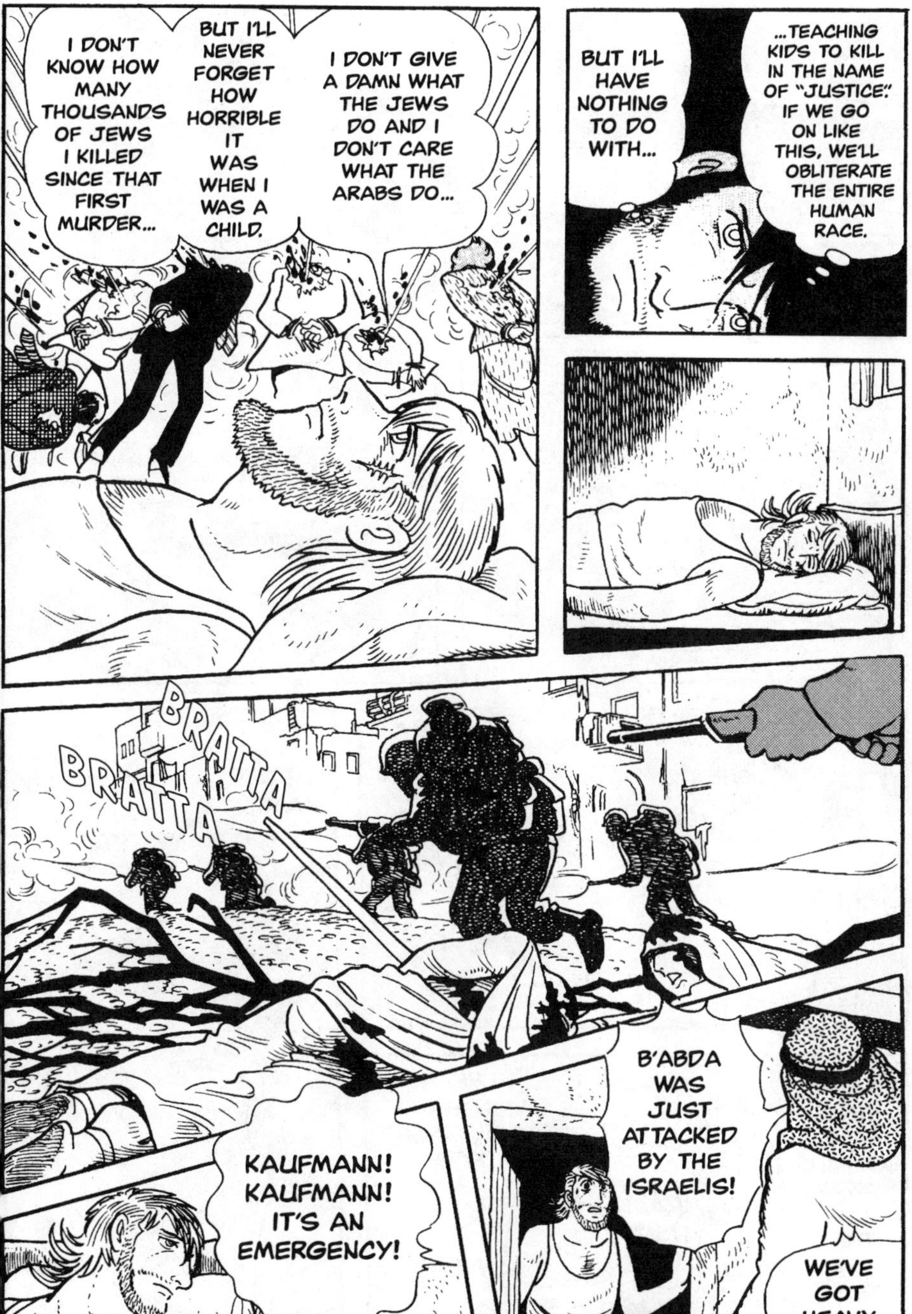
I DON'T KNOW HOW MANY THOUSANDS OF JEWS I KILLED SINCE THAT FIRST MURDER...
BUT I'LL NEVER FORGET HOW HORRIBLE IT WAS WHEN I WAS A CHILD.
I DON'T GIVE A DAMN WHAT THE JEWS DO AND I DON'T CARE WHAT THE ARABS DO...
BUT I'LL HAVE NOTHING TO DO WITH...
...TEACHING KIDS TO KILL IN THE NAME OF "JUSTICE." IF WE GO ON LIKE THIS, WE'LL OBLITERATE THE ENTIRE HUMAN RACE.
BRATTA
BRATTA
BRATTA
KAUFMANN! KAUFMANN! IT'S AN EMERGENCY!
B'ABDA WAS JUST ATTACKED BY THE ISRAELIS!
WE'VE GOT HEAVY CASUAL-TIES!

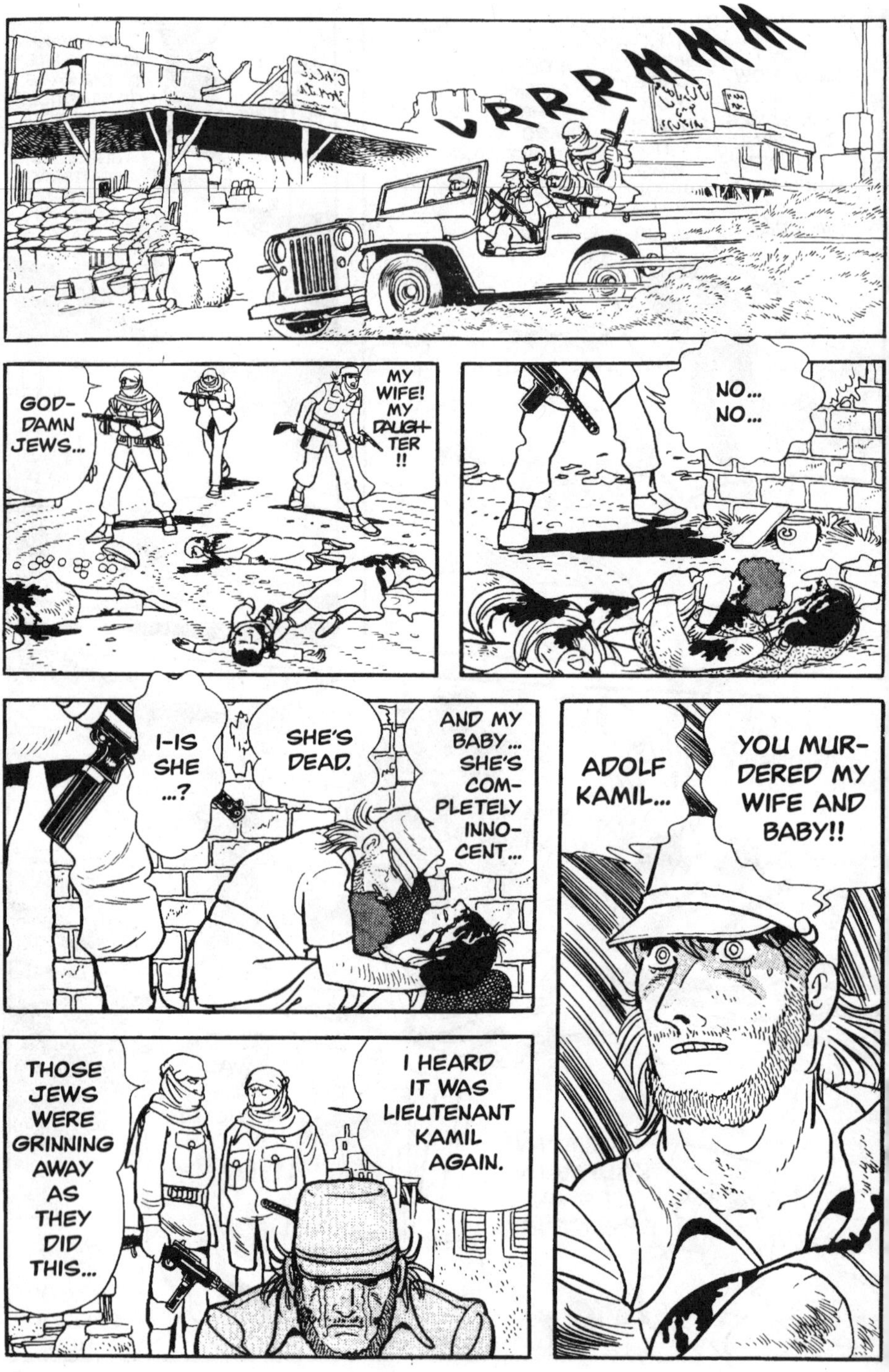
URRRMMMM
GOD-DAMN JEWS...
MY WIFE! MY DAUGHTER!!
NO... NO...
I-IS SHE ...?
SHE'S DEAD.
AND MY BABY... SHE'S COMPLETELY INNOCENT...
THOSE JEWS WERE GRINNING AWAY AS THEY DID THIS...
I HEARD IT WAS LIEUTENANT KAMIL AGAIN.
ADOLF KAMIL...
YOU MURDERED MY WIFE AND BABY!!

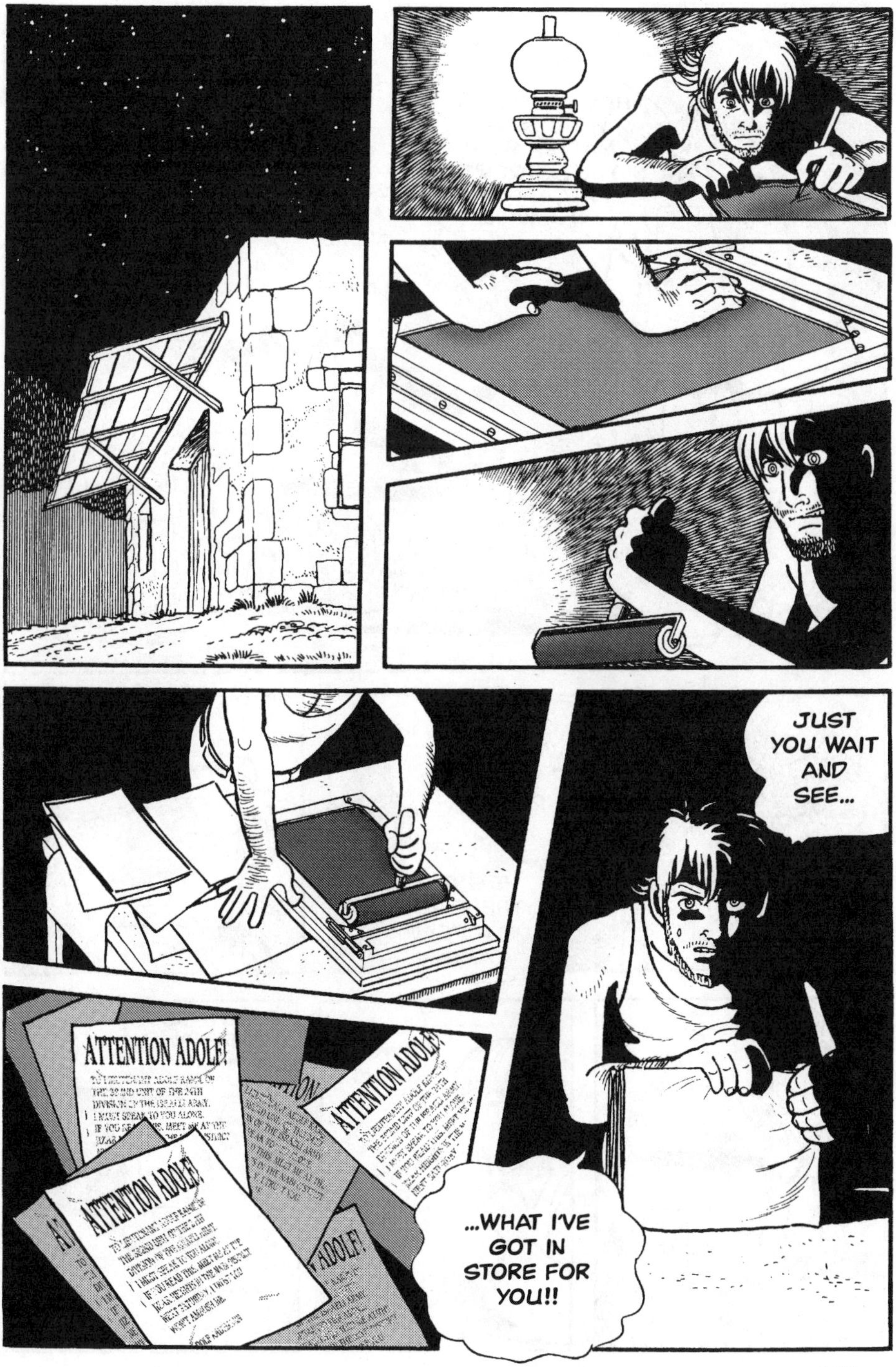
ATTENTION ADOLF!
JUST YOU WAIT AND SEE...
...WHAT I'VE GOT IN STORE FOR YOU!!

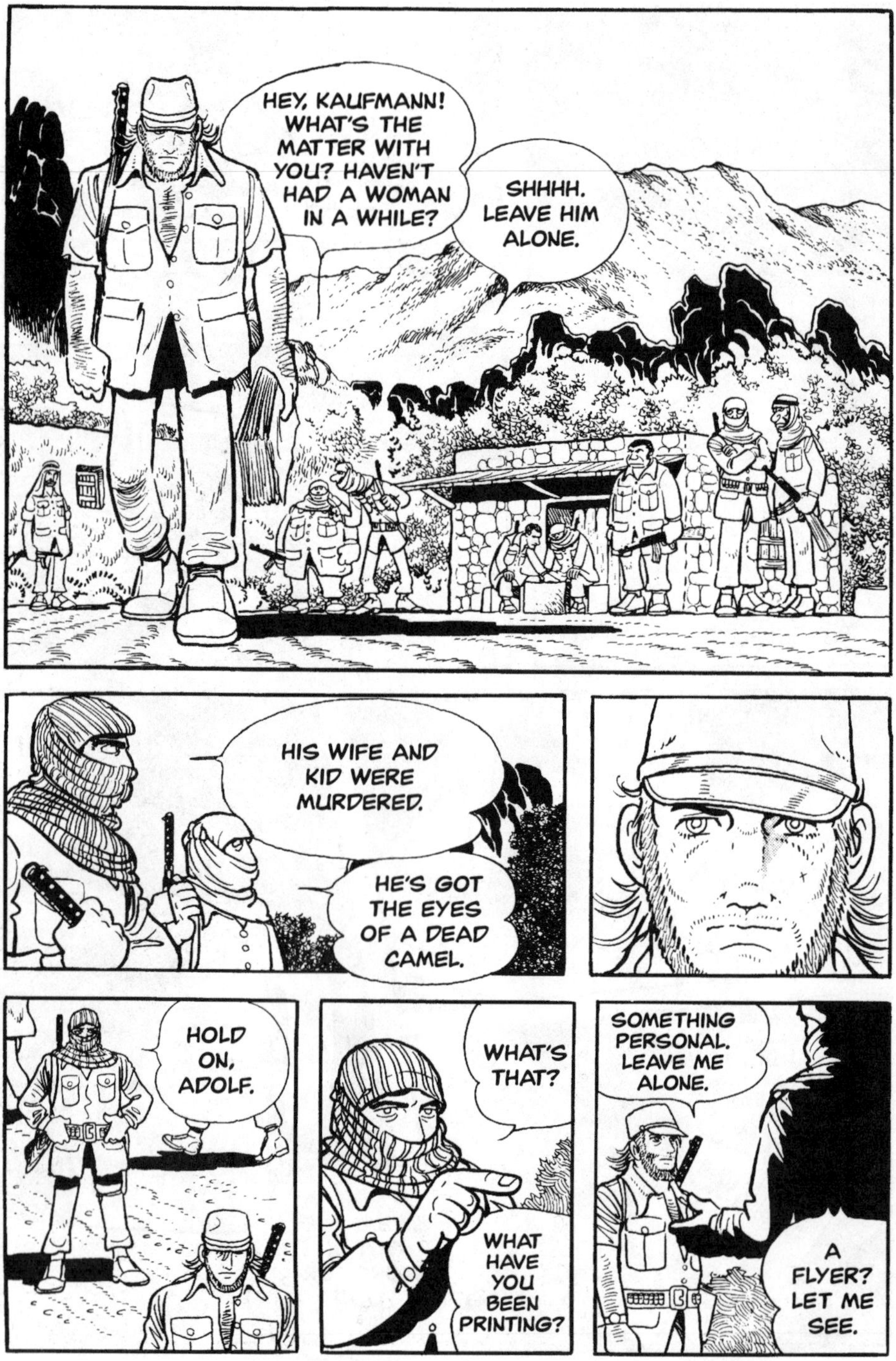
HEY, KAUFMANN! WHAT'S THE MATTER WITH YOU? HAVEN'T HAD A WOMAN IN A WHILE?
SHHHH. LEAVE HIM ALONE.
HIS WIFE AND KID WERE MURDERED.
HE'S GOT THE EYES OF A DEAD CAMEL.
HOLD ON, ADOLF.
WHAT'S THAT?
WHAT HAVE YOU BEEN PRINTING?
SOMETHING PERSONAL. LEAVE ME ALONE.
A FLYER? LET ME SEE.

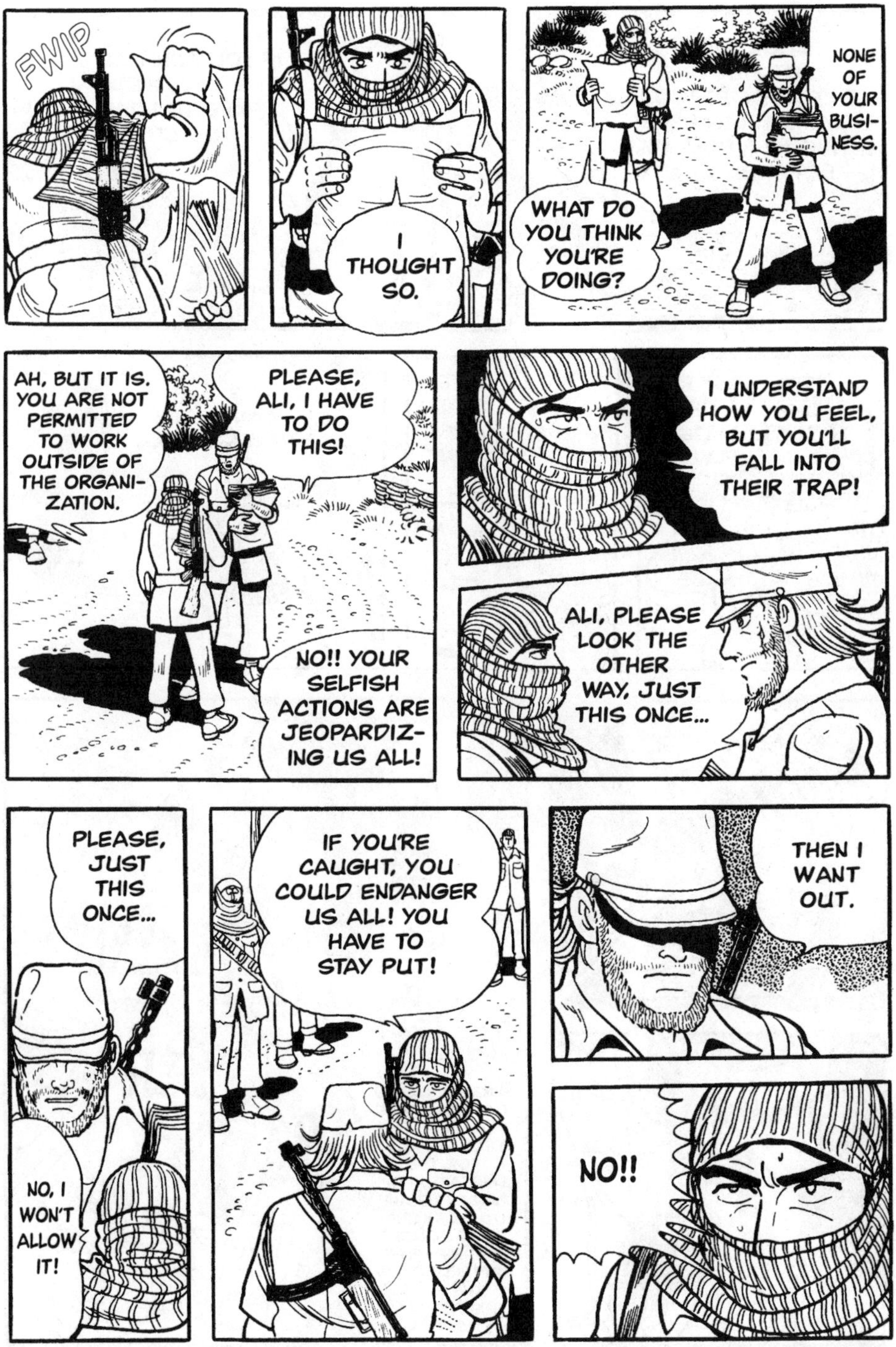
FWIP
I THOUGHT SO.
WHAT DO YOU THINK YOU'RE DOING?
NONE OF YOUR BUSI-NESS.
AH, BUT IT IS. YOU ARE NOT PERMITTED TO WORK OUTSIDE OF THE ORGANI-ZATION.
PLEASE, ALI, I HAVE TO DO THIS!
NO!! YOUR SELFISH ACTIONS ARE JEOPARDIZ-ING US ALL!
I UNDERSTAND HOW YOU FEEL, BUT YOU'LL FALL INTO THEIR TRAP!
ALI, PLEASE LOOK THE OTHER WAY, JUST THIS ONCE...
PLEASE, JUST THIS ONCE...
NO, I WON'T ALLOW IT!
IF YOU'RE CAUGHT, YOU COULD ENDANGER US ALL! YOU HAVE TO STAY PUT!
THEN I WANT OUT.
NO!!

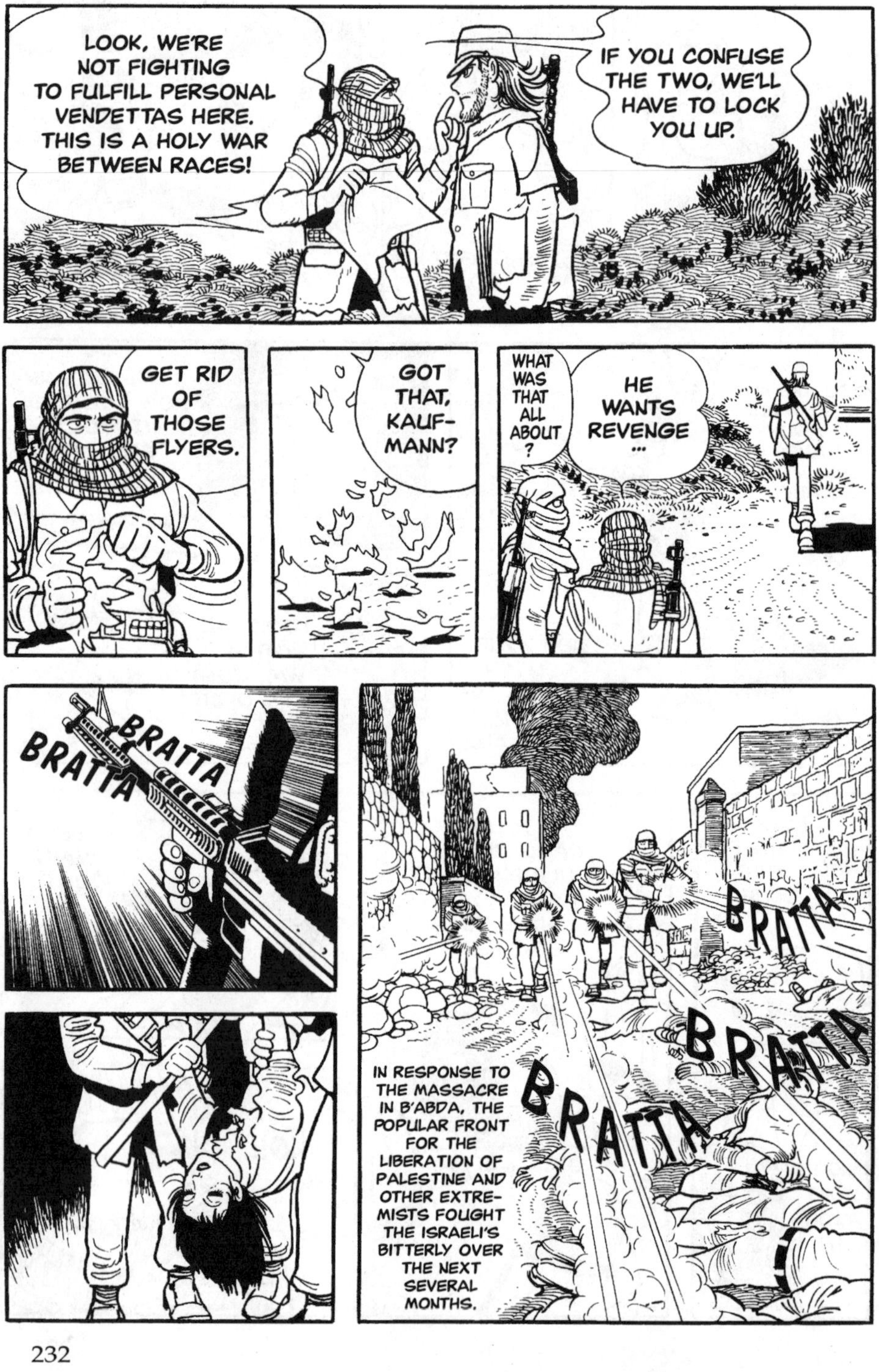
LOOK, WE'RE NOT FIGHTING TO FULFILL PERSONAL VENDETTAS HERE. THIS IS A HOLY WAR BETWEEN RACES!
IF YOU CONFUSE THE TWO, WE'LL HAVE TO LOCK YOU UP.
GET RID OF THOSE FLYERS.
GOT THAT, KAUF-MANN?
WHAT WAS THAT ALL ABOUT?
HE WANTS REVENGE ...
BRATTA
BRATTA
BRATTA
BRATTA
BRATTA
IN RESPONSE TO THE MASSACRE IN B'ABDA, THE POPULAR FRONT FOR THE LIBERATION OF PALESTINE AND OTHER EXTRE-MISTS FOUGHT THE ISRAELI'S BITTERLY OVER THE NEXT SEVERAL MONTHS.

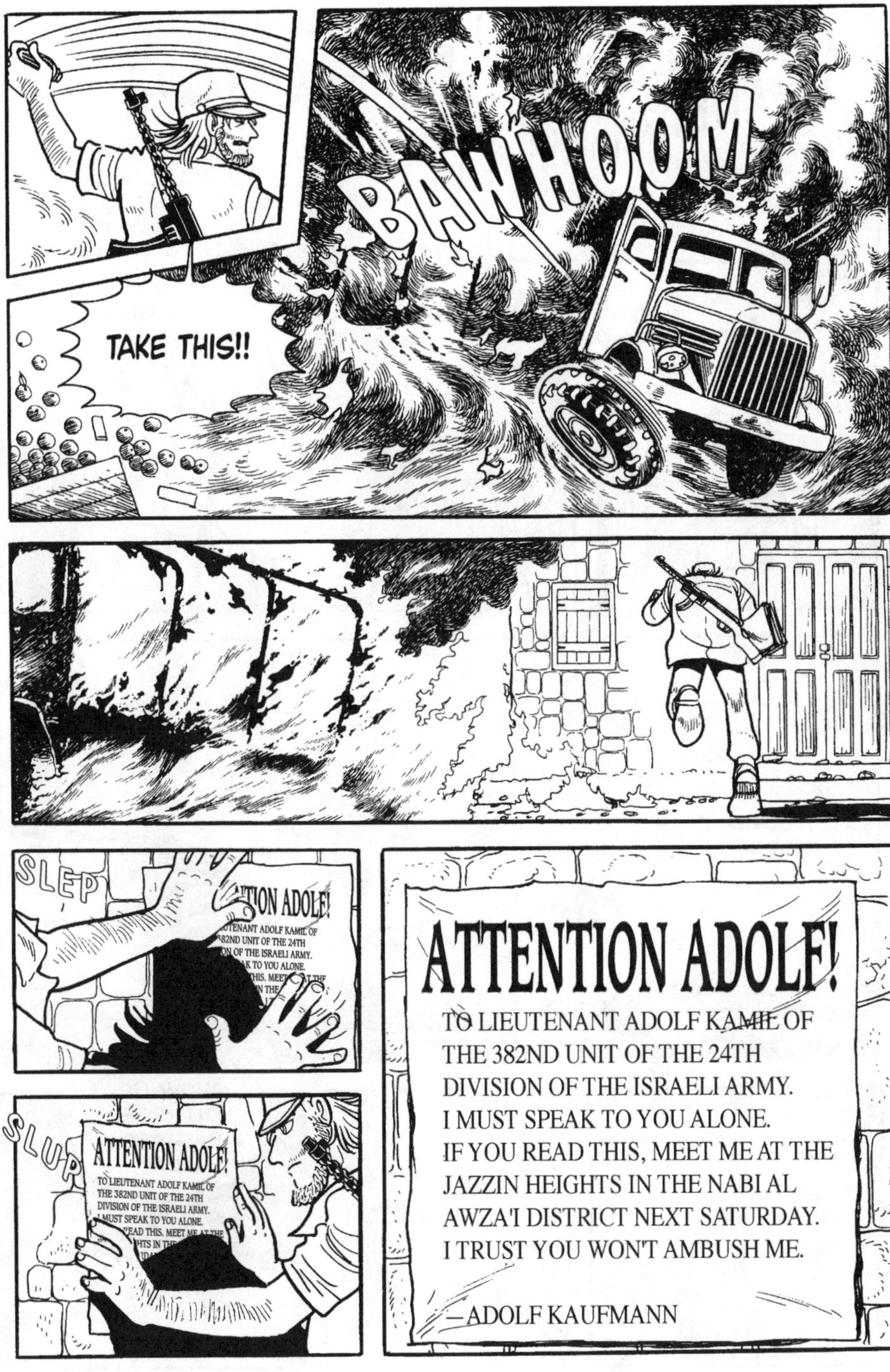
TAKE THIS!!
BAWHOOM
SLEP
SLUP
ATTENTION ADOLF!
TO LIEUTENANT ADOLF KAMIL OF
THE 382ND UNIT OF THE 24TH
DIVISION OF THE ISRAELI ARMY.
I MUST SPEAK TO YOU ALONE.
ATTENTION ADOLF!
TO LIEUTENANT ADOLF KAMIL OF
THE 382ND UNIT OF THE 24TH
DIVISION OF THE ISRAELI ARMY.
I MUST SPEAK TO YOU ALONE.
IF YOU READ THIS, MEET ME AT THE
JAZZIN HEIGHTS IN THE NABI AL
AWZA'I DISTRICT NEXT SATURDAY.
I TRUST YOU WON'T AMBUSH ME.
—ADOLF KAUFMANN

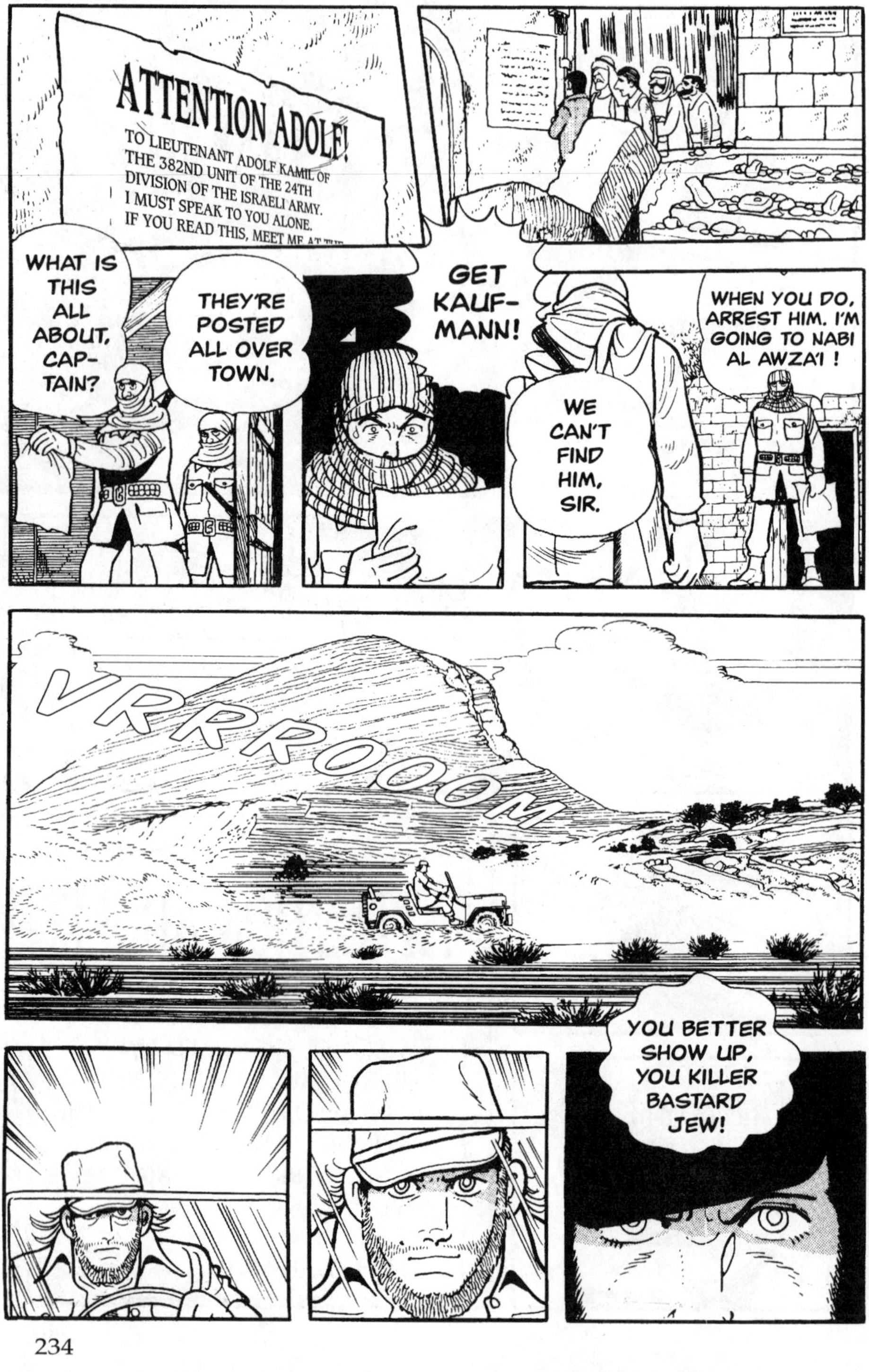
ATTENTION ADOLF!
TO LIEUTENANT ADOLF KAMIL OF THE 382ND UNIT OF THE 24TH DIVISION OF THE ISRAELI ARMY. I MUST SPEAK TO YOU ALONE. IF YOU READ THIS, MEET ME AT
WHAT IS THIS ALL ABOUT, CAP-TAIN?
THEY'RE POSTED ALL OVER TOWN.
GET KAUF-MANN!
WE CAN'T FIND HIM, SIR.
WHEN YOU DO, ARREST HIM. I'M GOING TO NABI AL AWZA'I !
VRRROOOM
YOU BETTER SHOW UP, YOU KILLER BASTARD JEW!

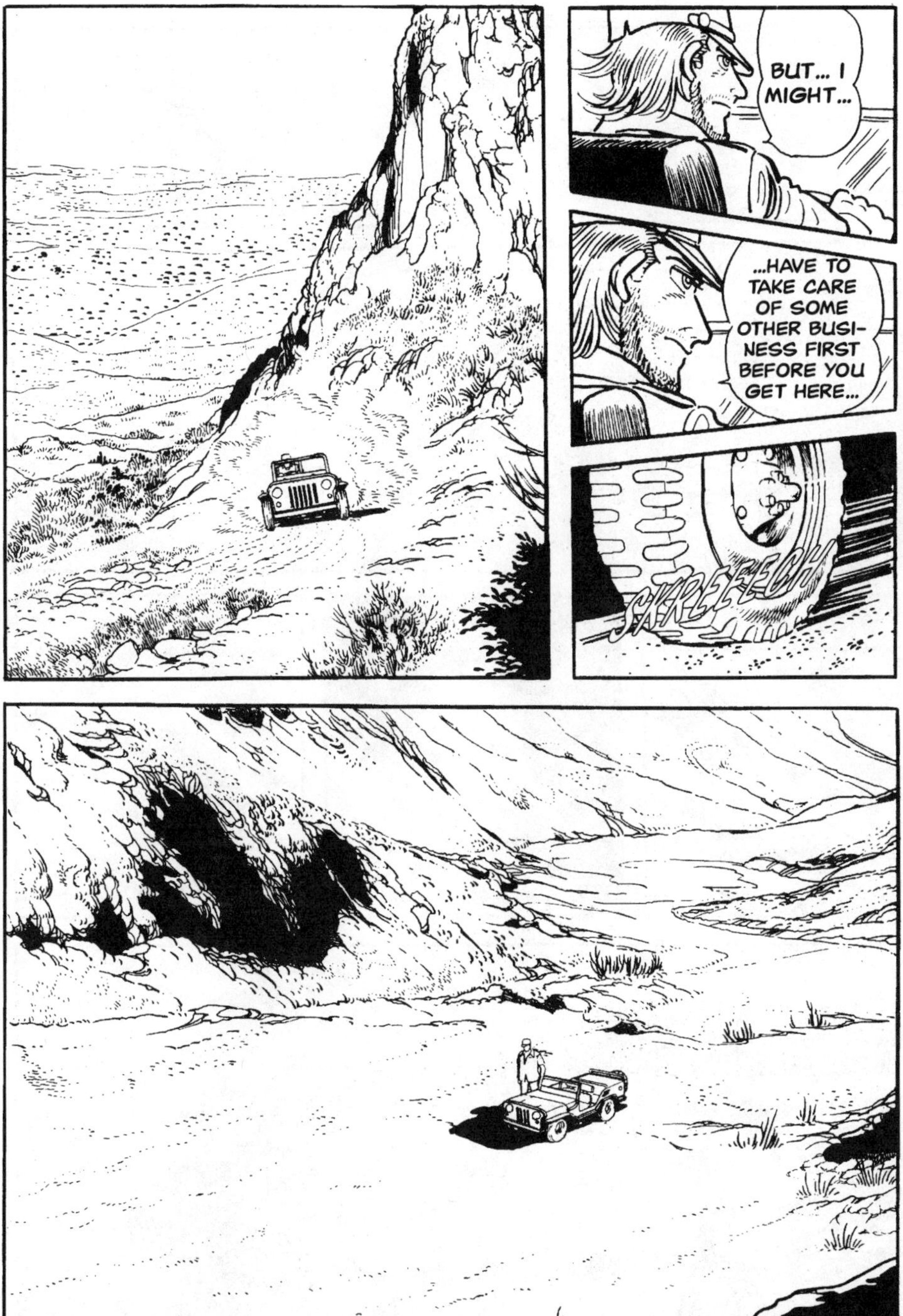
BUT... I MIGHT...
...HAVE TO TAKE CARE OF SOME OTHER BUSINESS FIRST BEFORE YOU GET HERE...
SKREEEECH

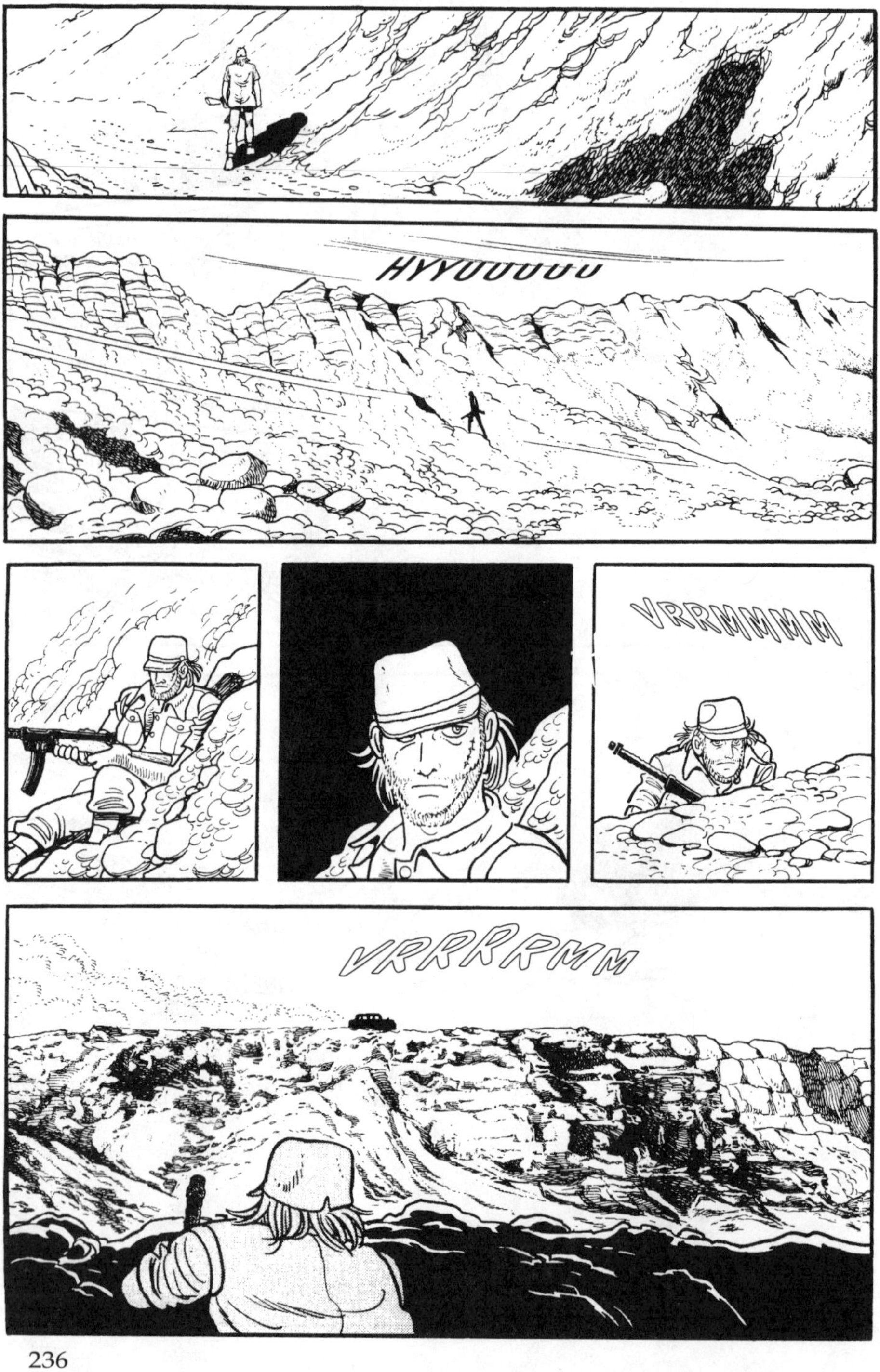
HYYUUUUU
VRRMMMMM
VRRRRRMM

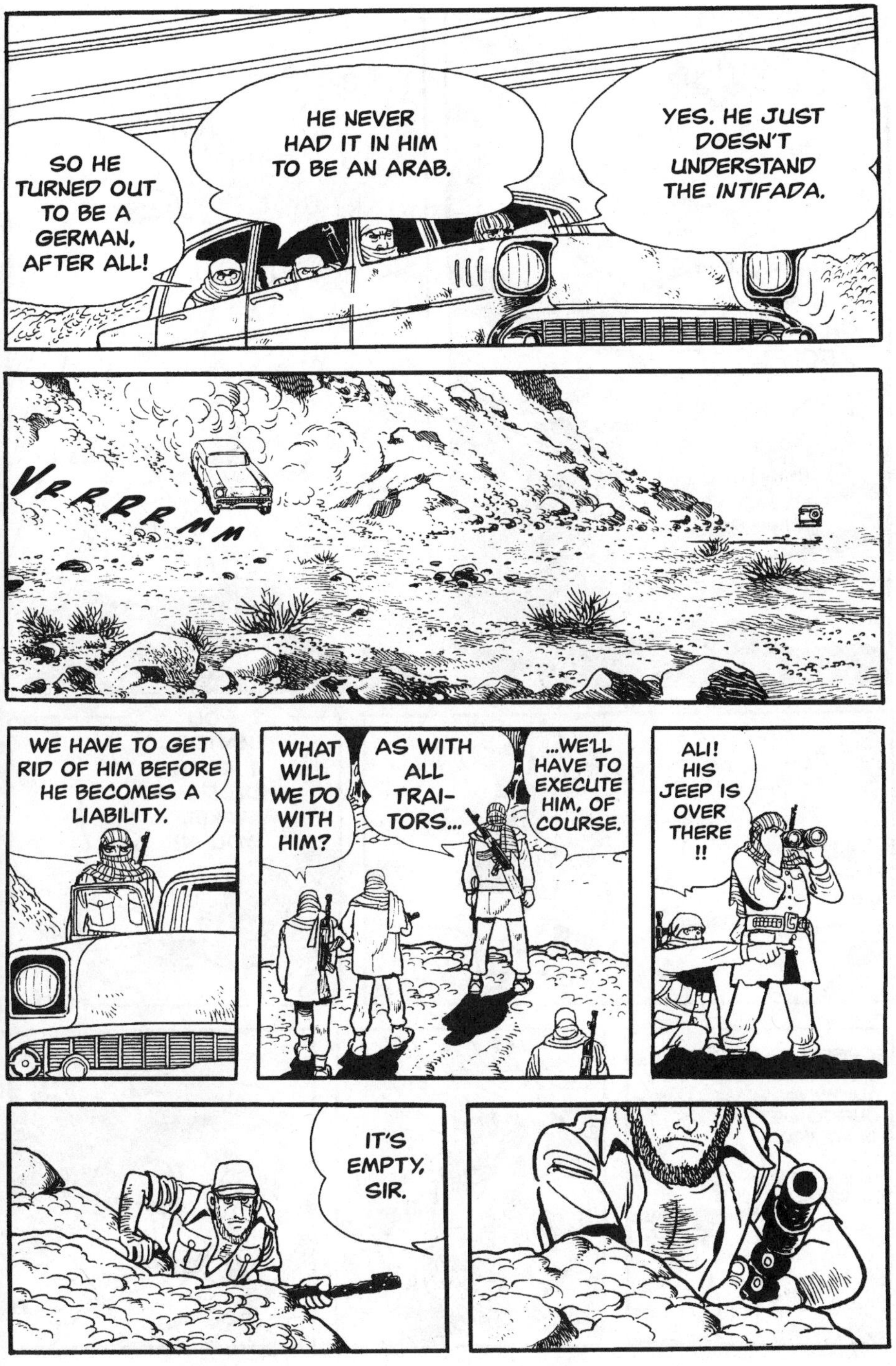
SO HE TURNED OUT TO BE A GERMAN, AFTER ALL!
HE NEVER HAD IT IN HIM TO BE AN ARAB.
YES. HE JUST DOESN'T UNDERSTAND THE INTIFADA.
VRRRRRMMM
WE HAVE TO GET RID OF HIM BEFORE HE BECOMES A LIABILITY.
WHAT WILL WE DO WITH HIM?
AS WITH ALL TRAITORS...
...WE'LL HAVE TO EXECUTE HIM, OF COURSE.
ALI! HIS JEEP IS OVER THERE !!
IT'S EMPTY, SIR.

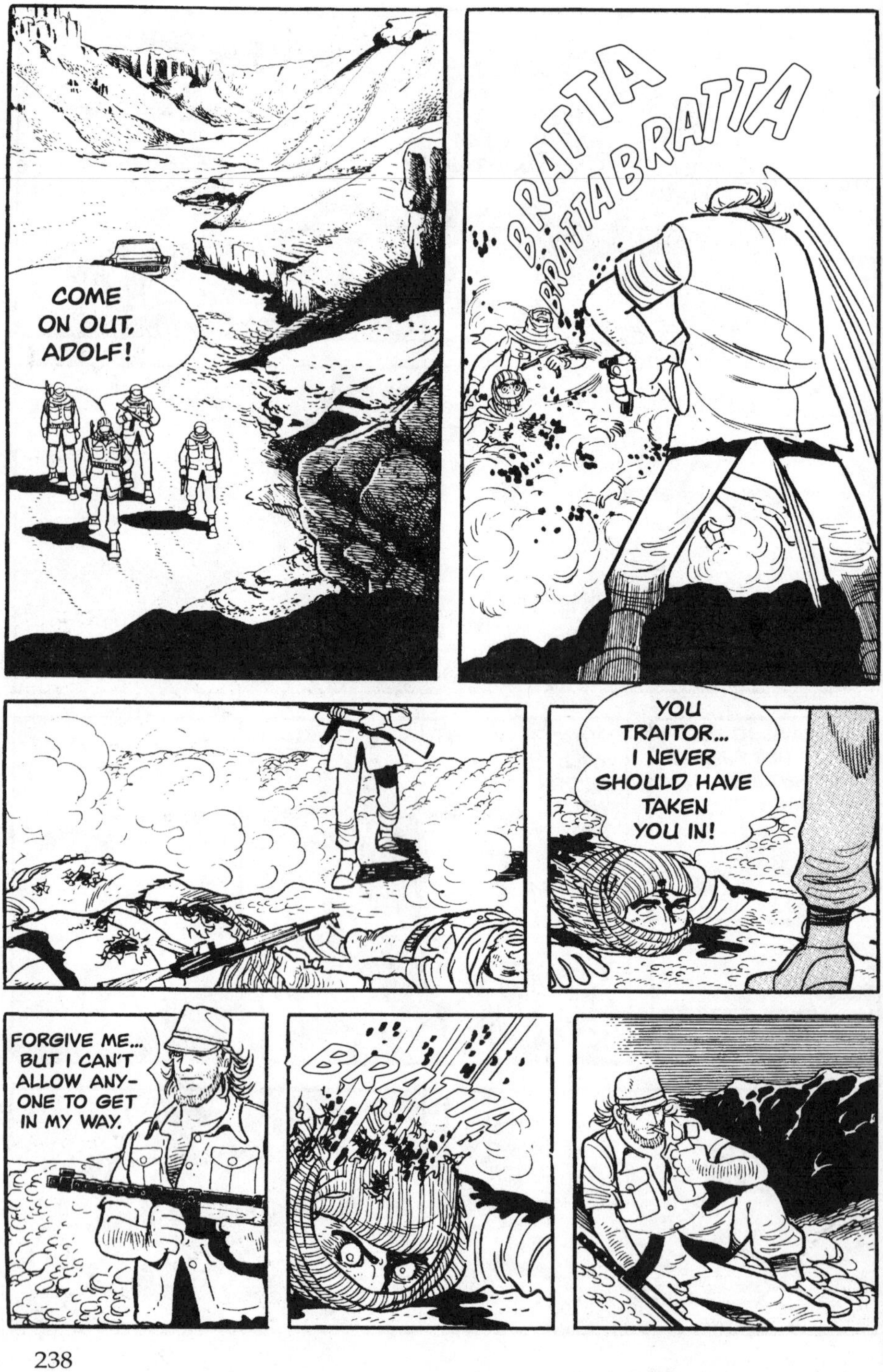
COME ON OUT, ADOLF!
BRATTA BRATTA BRATTABRATTA
YOU TRAITOR... I NEVER SHOULD HAVE TAKEN YOU IN!
FORGIVE ME... BUT I CAN'T ALLOW ANY-ONE TO GET IN MY WAY.
BRATTA

SATURDAY, NOON

KREE

KRAW

KREE

HERE HE COMES.

VRRMMMM

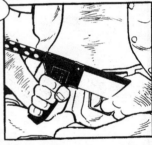

WHAT WAS IT ALL FOR?

I ANSWERED ONE NATION'S CALL AND THEN ANOTHER'S...

AND IN THE PROCESS I LOST EVERYTHING... MY FAMILY... MY FRIENDS... EVEN MYSELF...

I'M NO GOOD. AND IT'S BECAUSE OF NE'ER-DO-WELLS LIKE ME THAT NATIONS CAN BRANDISH THEIR BANNERS OF SO-CALLED RIGHTEOUSNESS...

VRRROOOM

VRRMM

SKREEECH

239

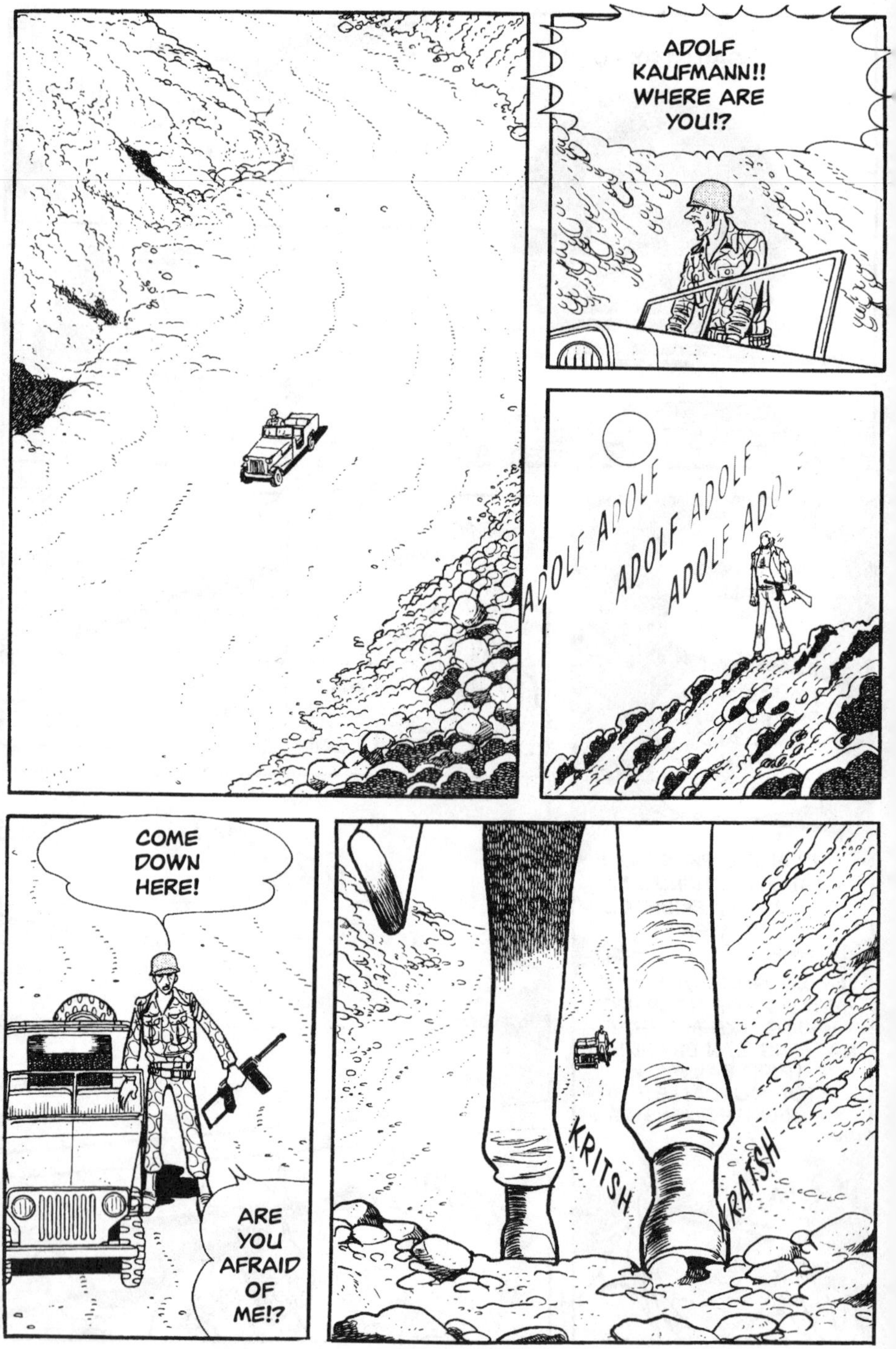
ADOLF KAUFMANN!! WHERE ARE YOU!?
ADOLF ADOLF
ADOLF ADOLF
ADOLF ADO
COME DOWN HERE!
ARE YOU AFRAID OF ME!?
KRITSH
KRATSH

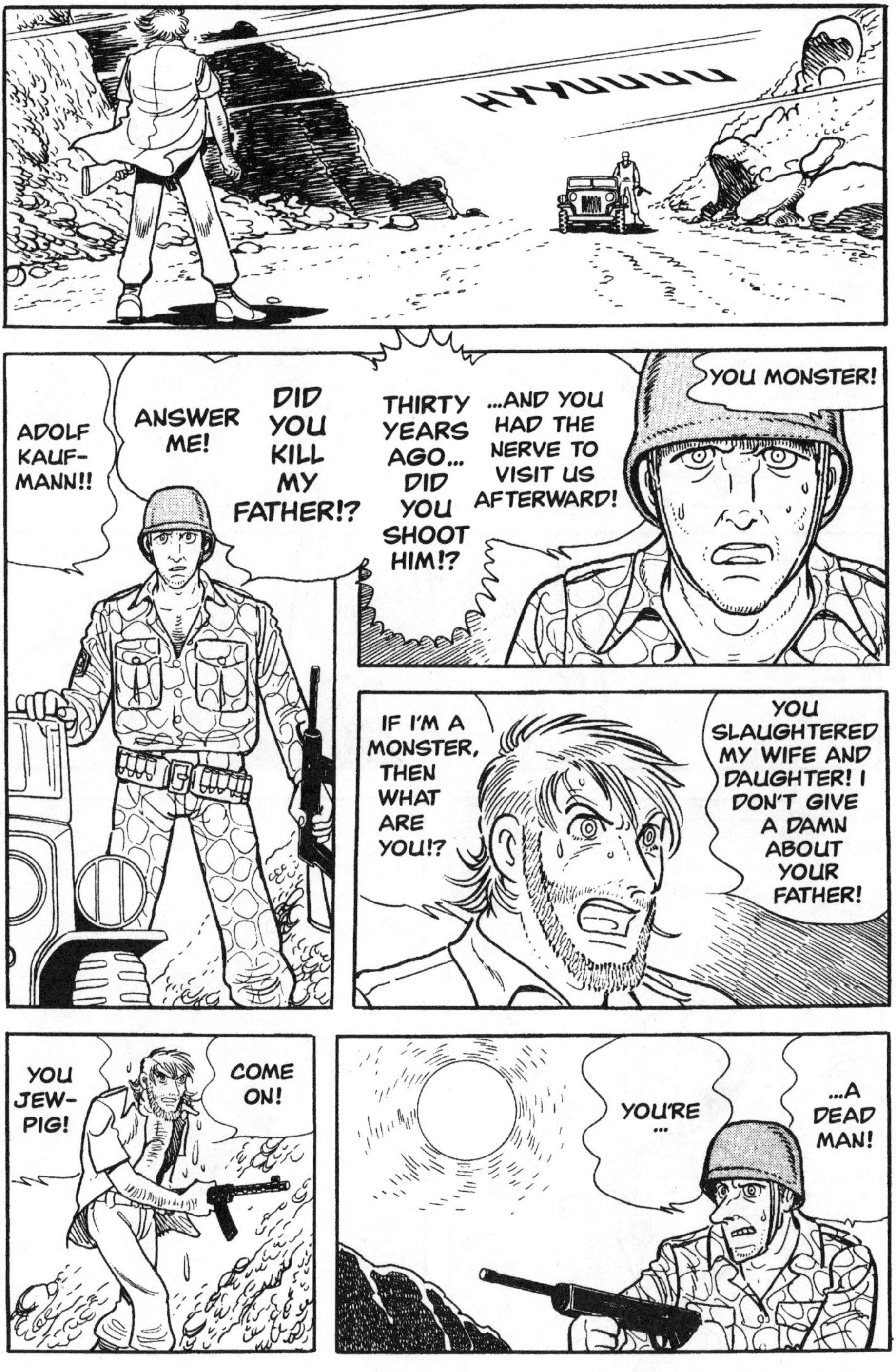
HYYUUUUH
ADOLF KAUF-MANN!!
ANSWER ME!
DID YOU KILL MY FATHER!?
THIRTY YEARS AGO... DID YOU SHOOT HIM!?
...AND YOU HAD THE NERVE TO VISIT US AFTERWARD!
YOU MONSTER!
IF I'M A MONSTER, THEN WHAT ARE YOU!?
YOU SLAUGHTERED MY WIFE AND DAUGHTER! I DON'T GIVE A DAMN ABOUT YOUR FATHER!
YOU JEW-PIG!
COME ON!
YOU'RE ...
...A DEAD MAN!

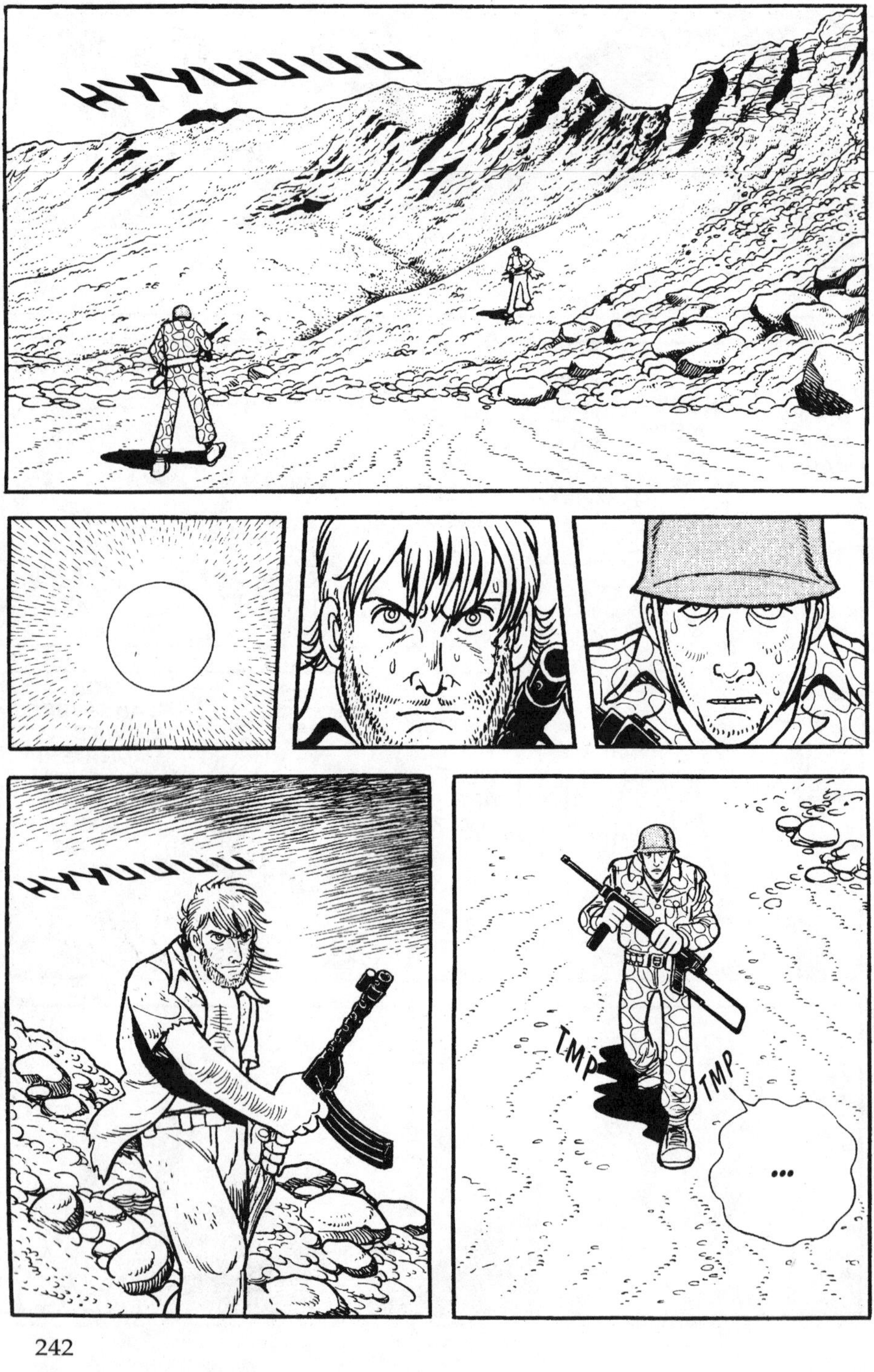
HYYUUUU
HYYUUU
TMP
TMP
...

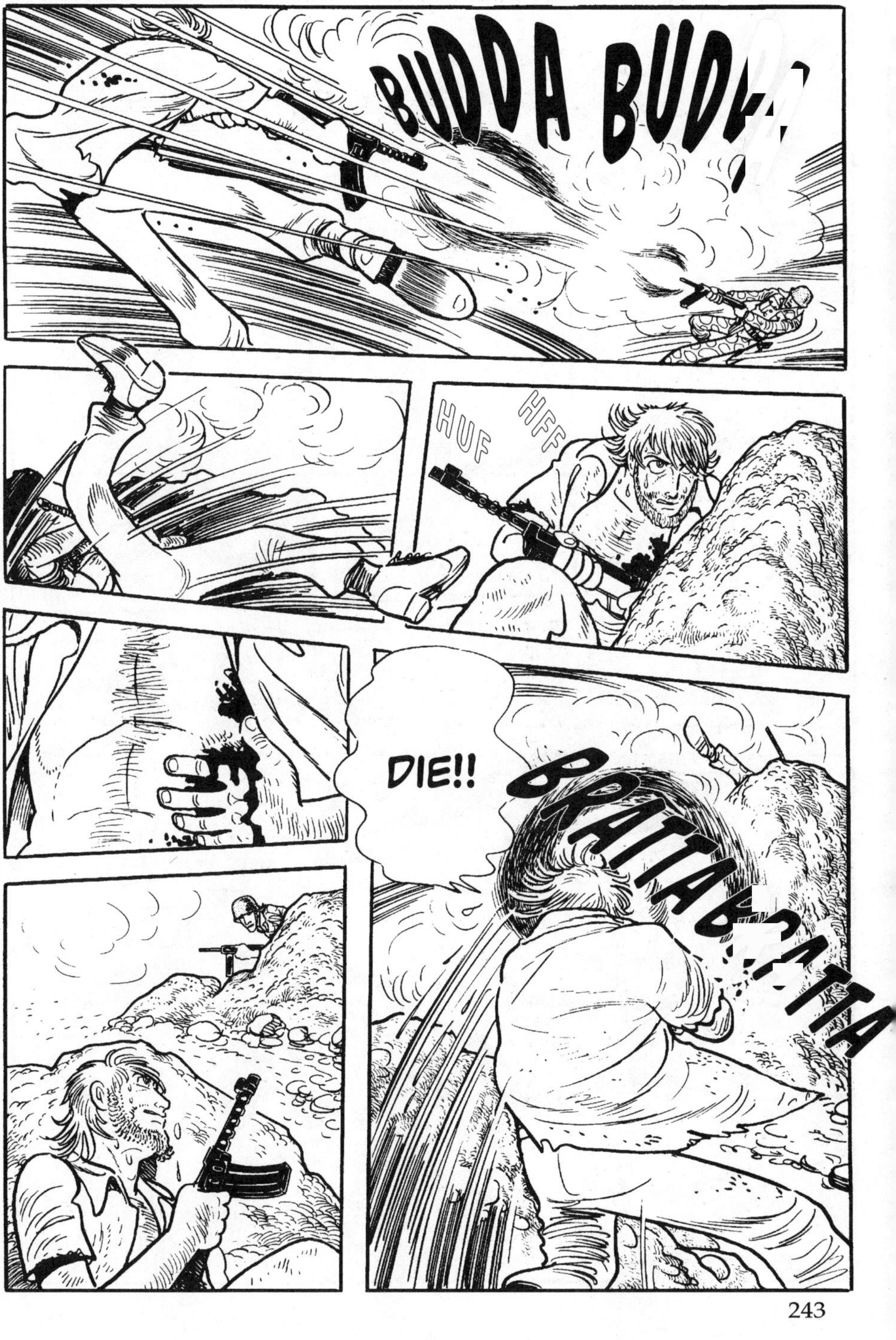
BUDDA BUD
HUF
HFF
DIE!!
BRATTA

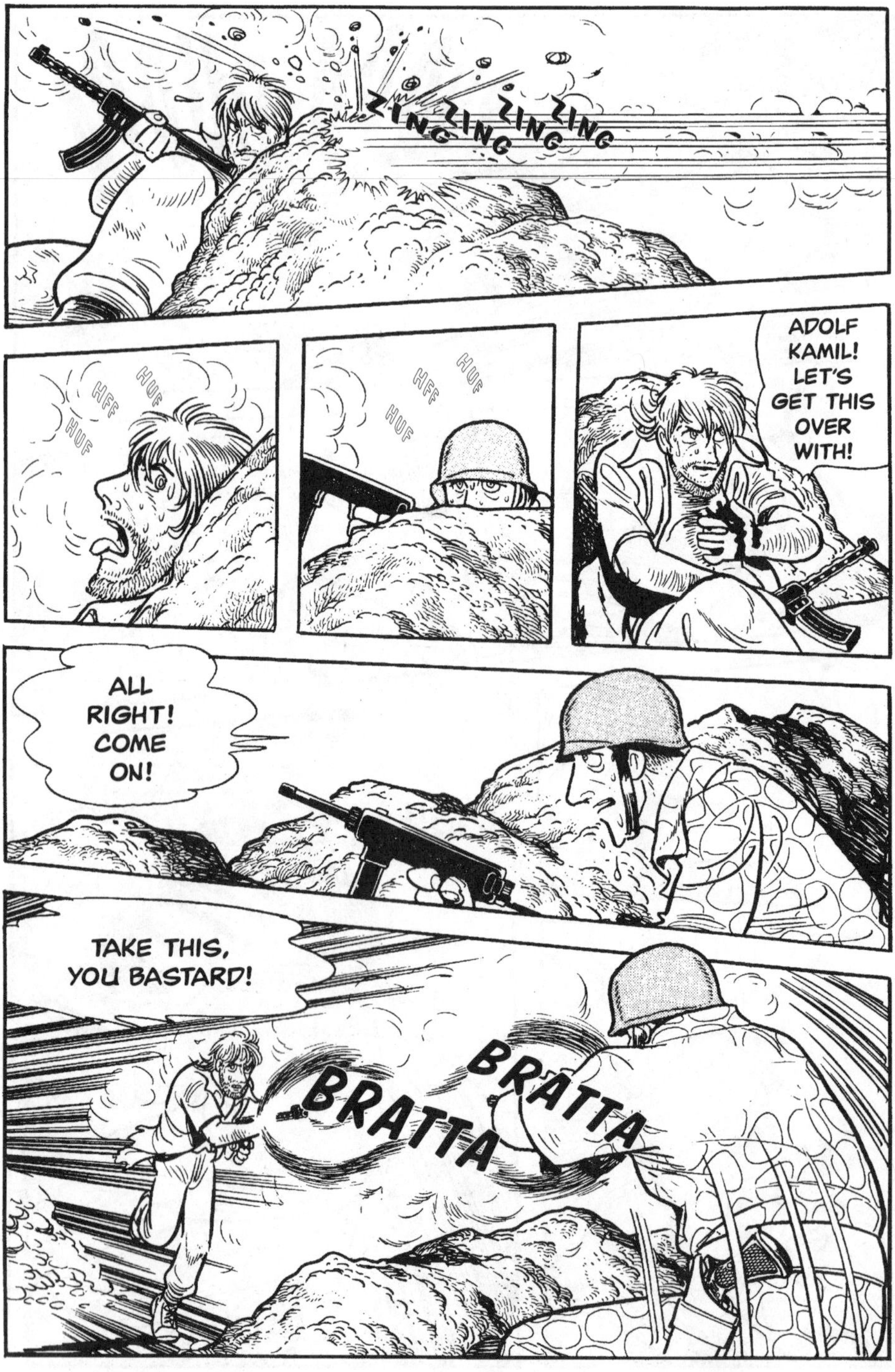
ZING ZING ZING ZING
HFF HUF HUF
HFF HUF HUF
ADOLF KAMIL! LET'S GET THIS OVER WITH!
ALL RIGHT! COME ON!
TAKE THIS, YOU BASTARD!
BRATTA
BRATTA

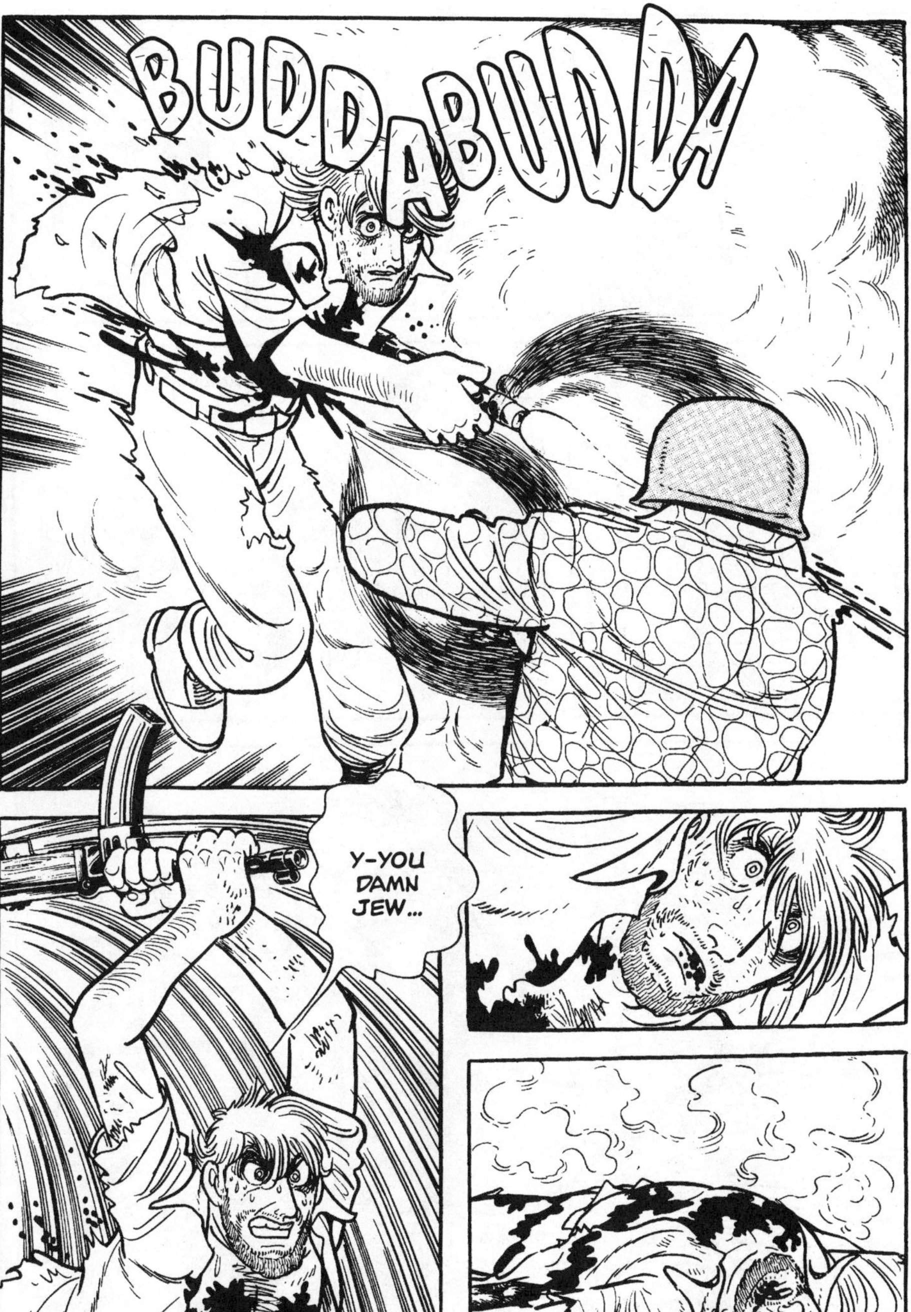
BUDDABUDDA
Y-YOU DAMN JEW...

ADOLF KAUF-MANN...

NOW GO AND ASK FORGIVE-NESS FROM MY FATHER IN THE NEXT WORLD.

WE'LL MEET AGAIN THERE SOMEDAY...

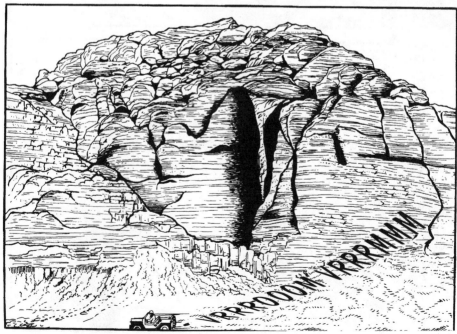

VRRRDDOW VRRRMMM

CHAPTER NINE

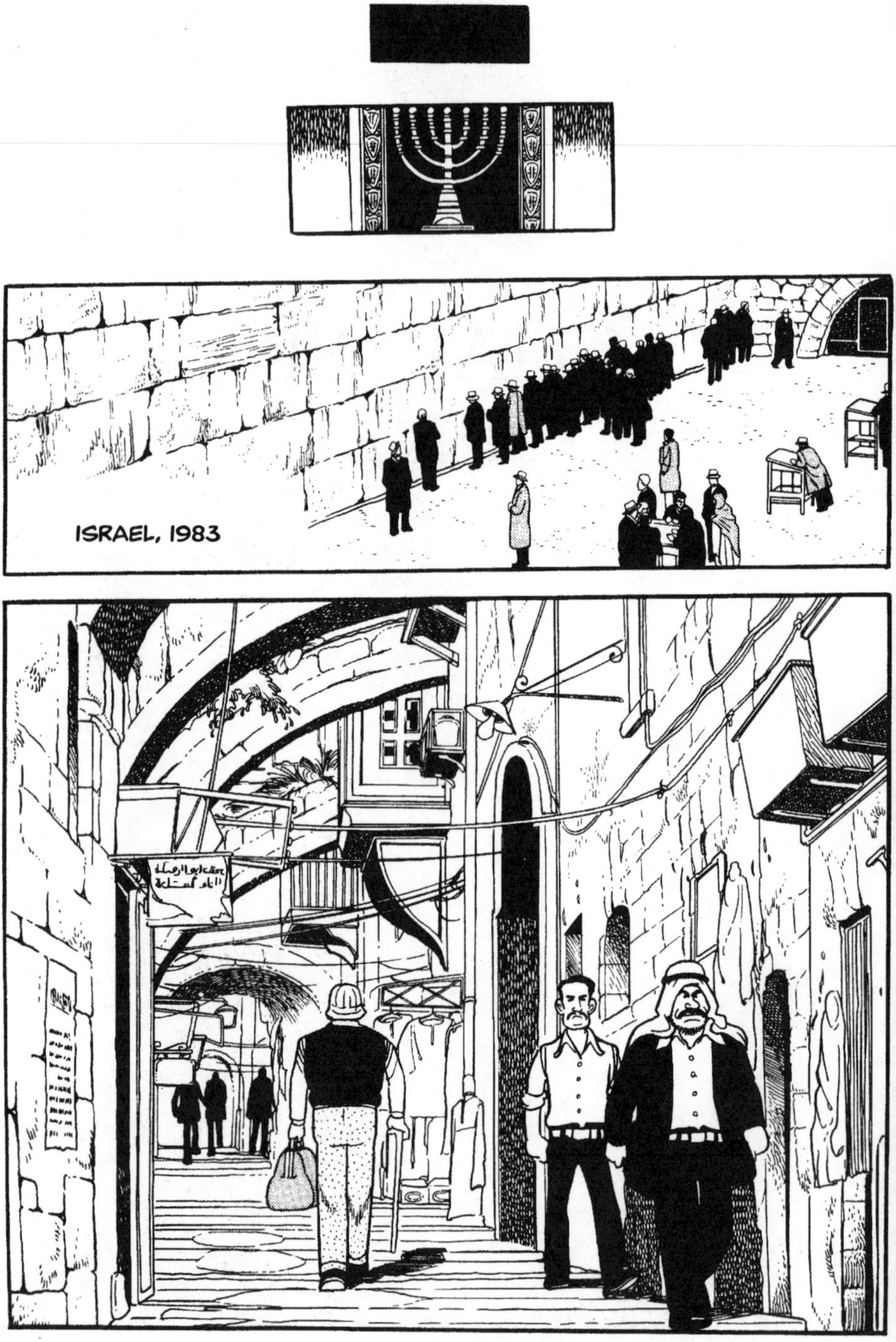
[redacted]
ISRAEL, 1983

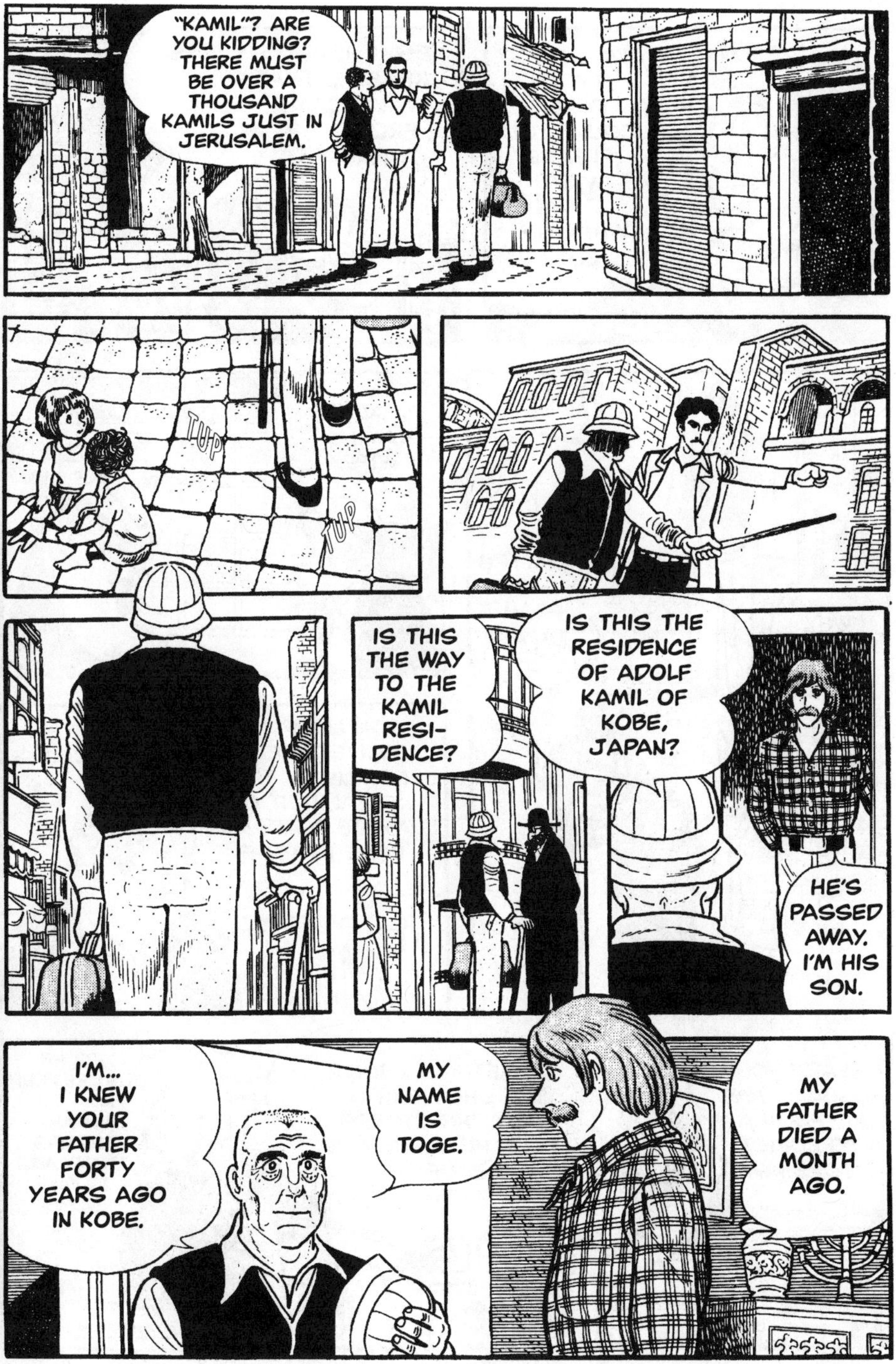
"KAMIL"? ARE YOU KIDDING? THERE MUST BE OVER A THOUSAND KAMILS JUST IN JERUSALEM.
TUP
TUP
IS THIS THE WAY TO THE KAMIL RESI- DENCE?
IS THIS THE RESIDENCE OF ADOLF KAMIL OF KOBE, JAPAN?
HE'S PASSED AWAY. I'M HIS SON.
I'M... I KNEW YOUR FATHER FORTY YEARS AGO IN KOBE.
MY NAME IS TOGE.
MY FATHER DIED A MONTH AGO.

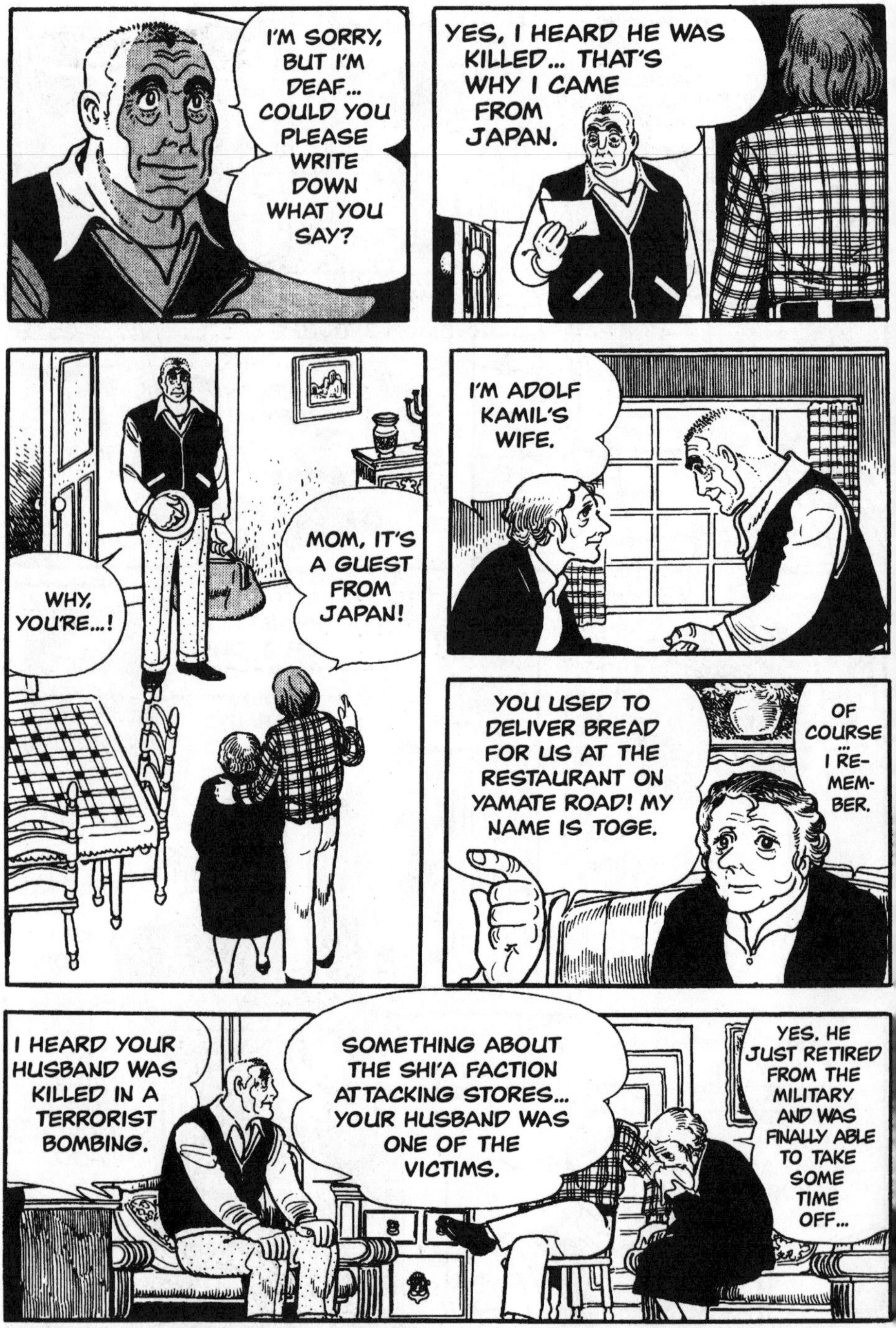
I'M SORRY, BUT I'M DEAF... COULD YOU PLEASE WRITE DOWN WHAT YOU SAY?
YES, I HEARD HE WAS KILLED... THAT'S WHY I CAME FROM JAPAN.
WHY, YOU'RE...!
MOM, IT'S A GUEST FROM JAPAN!
I'M ADOLF KAMIL'S WIFE.
YOU USED TO DELIVER BREAD FOR US AT THE RESTAURANT ON YAMATE ROAD! MY NAME IS TOGE.
OF COURSE ... I RE-MEM-BER.
I HEARD YOUR HUSBAND WAS KILLED IN A TERRORIST BOMBING.
SOMETHING ABOUT THE SHI'A FACTION ATTACKING STORES... YOUR HUSBAND WAS ONE OF THE VICTIMS.
YES. HE JUST RETIRED FROM THE MILITARY AND WAS FINALLY ABLE TO TAKE SOME TIME OFF...

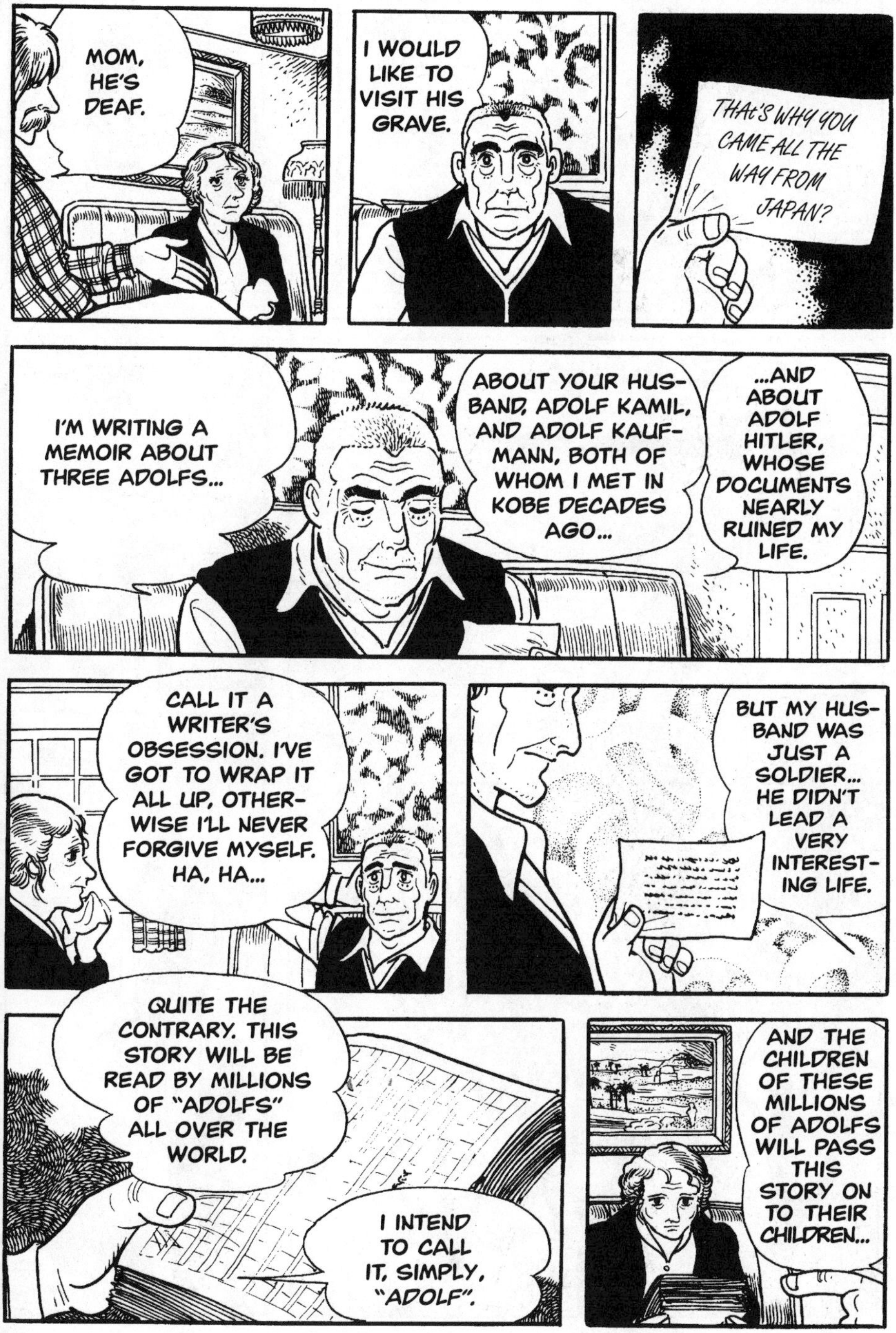
MOM, HE'S DEAF.
I WOULD LIKE TO VISIT HIS GRAVE.
THAt'S WHY YOU CAME ALL THE WAY FROM JAPAN?
I'M WRITING A MEMOIR ABOUT THREE ADOLFS...
ABOUT YOUR HUSBAND, ADOLF KAMIL, AND ADOLF KAUFMANN, BOTH OF WHOM I MET IN KOBE DECADES AGO...
...AND ABOUT ADOLF HITLER, WHOSE DOCUMENTS NEARLY RUINED MY LIFE.
CALL IT A WRITER'S OBSESSION. I'VE GOT TO WRAP IT ALL UP, OTHERWISE I'LL NEVER FORGIVE MYSELF. HA, HA...
BUT MY HUSBAND WAS JUST A SOLDIER... HE DIDN'T LEAD A VERY INTERESTING LIFE.
QUITE THE CONTRARY. THIS STORY WILL BE READ BY MILLIONS OF "ADOLFS" ALL OVER THE WORLD.
I INTEND TO CALL IT, SIMPLY, "ADOLF".
AND THE CHILDREN OF THESE MILLIONS OF ADOLFS WILL PASS THIS STORY ON TO THEIR CHILDREN...

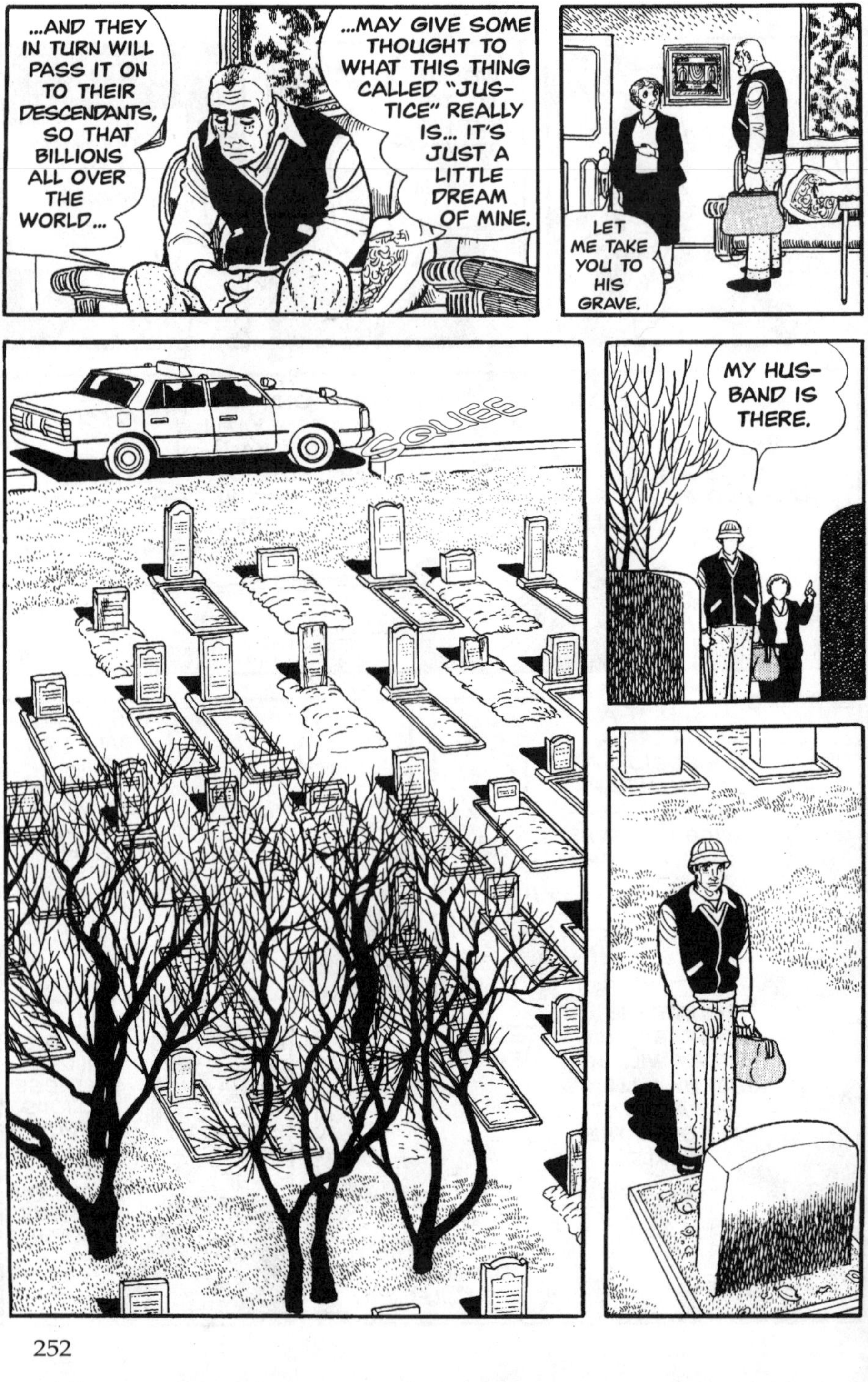
...AND THEY IN TURN WILL PASS IT ON TO THEIR DESCENDANTS, SO THAT BILLIONS ALL OVER THE WORLD...
...MAY GIVE SOME THOUGHT TO WHAT THIS THING CALLED "JUS-TICE" REALLY IS... IT'S JUST A LITTLE DREAM OF MINE.
LET ME TAKE YOU TO HIS GRAVE.
SQUEE
MY HUS-BAND IS THERE.

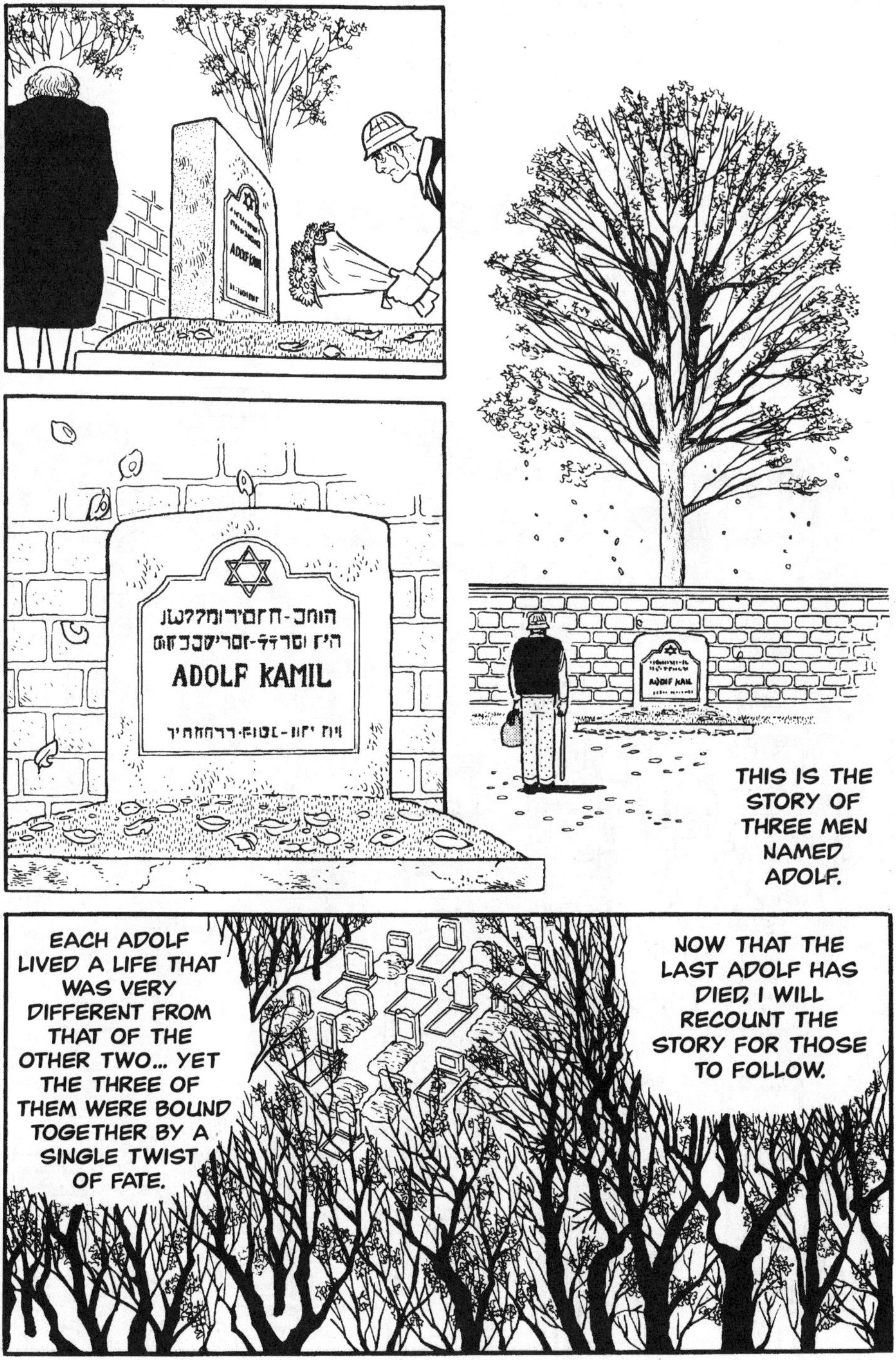
ADOLF KAMIL
THIS IS THE STORY OF THREE MEN NAMED ADOLF.
EACH ADOLF LIVED A LIFE THAT WAS VERY DIFFERENT FROM THAT OF THE OTHER TWO... YET THE THREE OF THEM WERE BOUND TOGETHER BY A SINGLE TWIST OF FATE.
NOW THAT THE LAST ADOLF HAS DIED, I WILL RECOUNT THE STORY FOR THOSE TO FOLLOW.

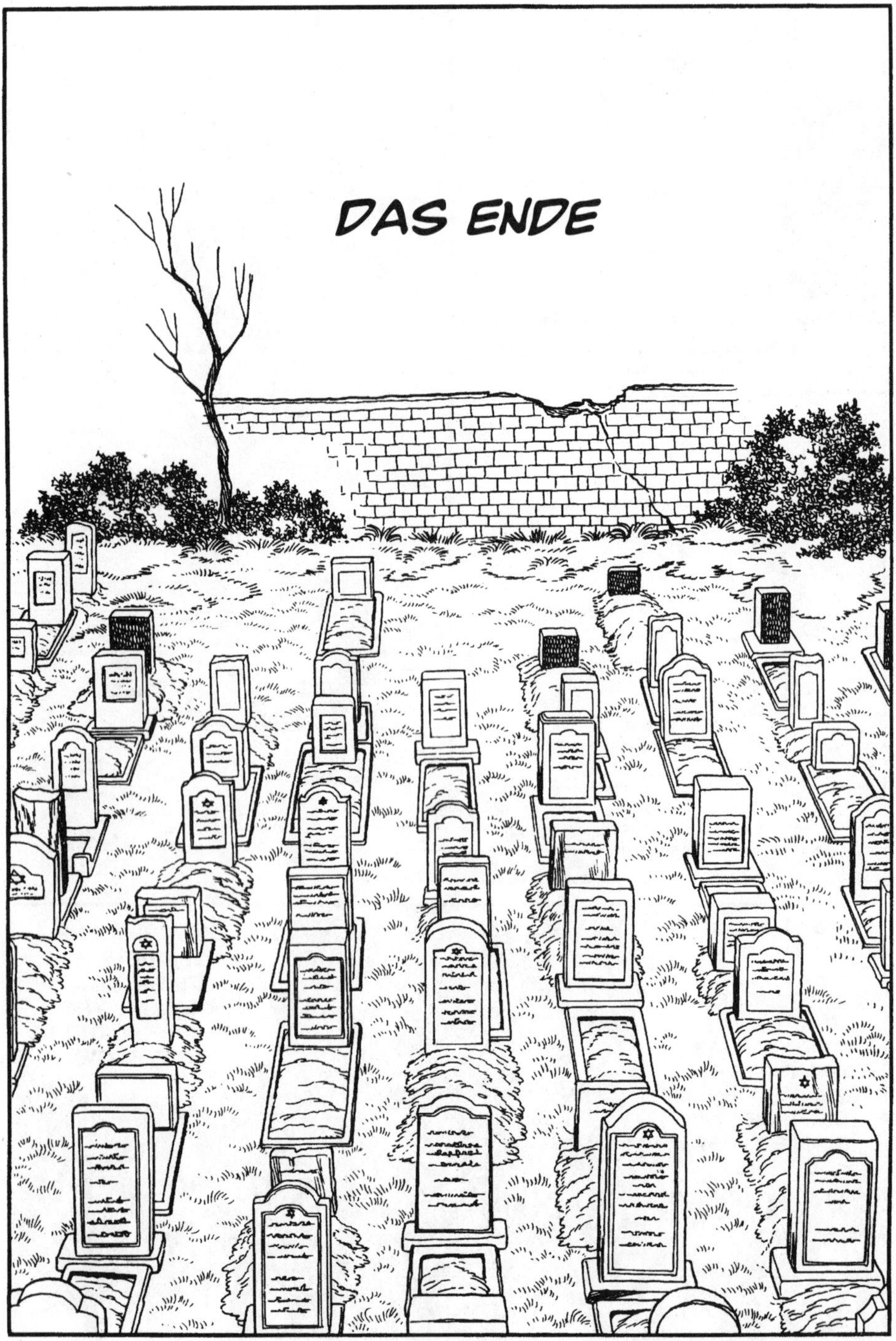
DAS ENDE

VALPEY & CO.

JUN 1 2 2001 DA ✓